Summer Youth Programs
Food Stamps
Rail Strike Settlement
Selective Service
Urban Fellowships
Consular Treaty
Safety At Sea Treaty
Narcotics Treaty

D. C. Visitors Center
FHA-VA Interest Rate Program
Health Manpower
Eisenhower College

...blic Health Reorganization
...pe Lookout Seashore
...ater Research
...uadalupe National Park
...volutionary War Bicentennial
...sh-Wildlife Preservation
...ater for Peace
...ti-Inflation Program
...ientific Knowledge Exchange
...ltural Materials Exchange
...reign Investors Tax
...rcel Post Reform
...vil Service Pay Raise
...ockpile Sales
...rticipation Certificates
...otection for Savings
...exible Interest Rates
...eedom of Information

Anti-Racketeering
Product Safety Commission
Small Business Aid
Inter-American Bank

Gun Controls
Aid-to-Handicapped Children
Redwoods Park
Flaming Gorge Recreation Area
Biscayne Park
Heart, Cancer and Stroke Programs
Hazardous Radiation Protection
Colorado River Reclamation
Scenic Rivers
Scenic Trails
National Water Commission
Federal Magistrates
Vocational Education
Veterans Pension Increases
North Cascades Park
International Coffee Agreement
Intergovernmental Manpower
Dangerous Drugs Control
Military Justice Code

———1968———
Fair Housing
Indian Bill of Rights
Safe Streets
Wholesome Poultry
Food for Peace
Commodity Exchange Rules
U.S. Grain Standards
School Breakfasts
Bank Protection
Defense Production
Corporate Takeovers
Export Program
Gold Cover Removal

———1967———
...ucation Professions
...ucation Act
...r Pollution Control
...rtnership for Health
...cial Security Increases
...ge Discrimination
...holesome Meat
...ammable Fabrics
...ban Research
...blic Broadcasting
...ter Space Treaty
...odern D.C. Government
...etnam Veterans Benefits
...deral Judicial Center
...vilian-Postal Workers Pay
...af-Blind Center
...ollege Work Study

Truth-in-Lending
Aircraft Noise Abatement
Auto Insurance Study
New Narcotics Bureau
Gas Pipeline Safety
Fire Safety
Sea Grant Colleges
D.C. School Board
Tax Surcharge
Better Housing
International Monetary Reform
International Grains Treaty
Oil Revenues for Recreation
Virgin Islands Elections
San Rafael Wilderness
San Gabriel Wilderness
Fair Federal Juries
Candidate Protection

Presented to
The President
With warm respect and good
wishes from his Cabinet.

Hubert H. Humphrey
Dean Rusk
Henry H. Fowler
Ramsey Clark
W. Marvin Watson
Stewart L. Udall
Orville Freeman
C. R. Smith
Willard Wirtz
Wilbur J. Cohen
Robert C. Weaver
Alan S. Boyd
J. R. Wiggins

THE VANTAGE POINT

PERSPECTIVES OF THE PRESIDENCY

1963–1969

THE VANTAGE POINT

Perspectives of the Presidency
1963–1969

LYNDON BAINES JOHNSON

HOLT, RINEHART AND WINSTON
New York   Chicago   San Francisco

To my mother, Rebekah Baines Johnson;
my wife, Lady Bird;
and my two daughters, Lynda and Luci—
whose strength and love and courage
have sustained me throughout my life.

CONTENTS

PREFACE

It has been said that the Presidency is the loneliest office in the world. I did not find it so. Even during the darkest hours of my administration, I always knew that I could draw on the strength, support, and love of my family and my friends.

But if I was seldom lonely, I was often alone. No one can experience with the President of the United States the glory and agony of his office. No one can share the majestic view from his pinnacle of power. No one can share the burden of his decisions or the scope of his duties. A Cabinet officer, no matter how broad his mandate, has a limited responsibility. A Senator, no matter how varied his interests, has a limited constituency. But the President represents all the people and must face up to all the problems. He must be responsible, as he sees it, for the welfare of every citizen and must be sensitive to the will of every group. He cannot pick and choose his issues. They all come with the job. So his experience is unique among his fellow Americans.

For better or worse, then, this is a book that only a President could have written. That is the sole excuse for its existence. I make no pretense of having written a complete and definitive history of my Presidency. I have tried, rather, to review that period from a President's point of view—reflecting a President's personal and political philosophy, a President's experience and knowledge, a President's aspirations, and a President's response to the demands that were made on him.

I have not written these chapters to say, "This is how it was," but to say, "This is how I saw it from my vantage point." Neither have I attempted to cover all the events of my administration. I have selected what I consider to be the most important problems, the most pressing goals, and the most historic accomplishments of my years as President.

Finally, I have tried to avoid engaging in historical pamphleteering. I did not set out to write a propaganda piece in support of my decisions. My purpose has been to state the problems that I faced as President, to record the facts as they came to me, to list the alternatives available, and to review what I did and why I did it. Others will have to judge the results on their merits. The struggle in Vietnam, for example, inspired one of the most passionate and deeply felt debates in our nation's life. That debate will go on, no matter what is written in these pages. History will make its judgments on the decisions made and the actions taken.

In writing this book, I have drawn heavily on the printed record—public papers, memoranda, notes from meetings and from phone calls, diaries, letters, Secret Service logs, and so on. I emphasize this, first, because I know that memory is an unreliable source for any writer and, second, because there are instances when my memory failed me entirely. When I had an important decision to make as President, I tried to focus my powers of concentration on that issue like a laser beam, shutting out all outside thoughts and distractions. Then, when the decision was made, I immediately erased all the facts and figures and arguments from my mind so that I could address myself completely to the next decision that demanded my attention. The result was good for concentration but bad for memory. Recognizing this, I have tried to document every statement made in this book. Only in a few cases have I had to rely entirely on memory. In most instances, I have cut what I could not document.

I have been aided in the preparation, research, writing, and editing of this book by dozens of people. I am particularly indebted to Robert Hardesty, William Jorden, Harry Middleton, Walt Rostow, Tom Johnson, and Doris Kearns—all of whom served on my staff in the White House.

I have had the counsel of dozens of members of my administration and long-time associates who read certain portions of the manuscript and gave me their valued judgments. And, of course, I have had the invaluable assistance of my wife and daughters, who read each word with love for the author.

I am also indebted to a number of very able and scholarly researchers, particularly Dorothy Territo, and to the patient and good-natured ladies who typed this manuscript through its many drafts.

Lyndon B. Johnson

Johnson City, Texas
April 1971

THE VANTAGE POINT

PERSPECTIVES OF THE PRESIDENCY

1963–1969

This nation will keep its commitments
from South Vietnam to West Berlin.

—First Address before Joint Session
of Congress, November 27, 1963

My first job after college was as a teacher in Cotulla, Texas, in a small Mexican-American school. . . . Somehow you never forget what poverty and hatred can do when you see its scars on the hopeful face of a young child. . . . I never thought then, in 1928, that I would be standing here in 1965. It never even occurred to me in my fondest dreams that I might have the chance to help the sons and daughters of those students and to help people like them all over this country.

But now I do have that chance—and I'll let you in on a secret: I mean to use it.

—Address before Joint Session
of Congress, March 15, 1965

I

The Beginning

W E'RE GOING TO CARRY TWO STATES next year if we don't carry any others: Massachusetts and Texas."

The speaker was John F. Kennedy.

The time was Friday morning, November 22, 1963.

I had gone to the President's eighth-floor suite in the Hotel Texas in Fort Worth to introduce my younger sister, Lucia Alexander, to him. The President's spirits were high. He had come to Texas for politics, and the trip so far was successful—much more successful than I had expected. He had been warmly received everywhere he went. The crowds in San Antonio and Houston on the previous day had been large and enthusiastic.

That morning in Fort Worth he had already made two speeches, one to a large gathering in a parking lot across the street from the hotel and another to a chamber of commerce breakfast in the hotel. Money and power were represented at the breakfast, but the parking lot audience— made up of workers, mothers, and children—gave me more assurance about the mood of Texas. Many of them had waited in a steady drizzle for more than an hour to hear him and to see Mrs. Kennedy.

"Where's Jackie?" someone in the crowd shouted.

"Mrs. Kennedy is organizing herself," the President said. "It takes longer, but of course she looks better than we do when she does it." The crowd loved this, and roared its approval.

Now it was time to leave for Dallas. John Kennedy was thinking about the future, about the approaching Presidential campaign and the necessity for carrying Texas. No one, including the President, considered his reelection to be a cinch. In fact, the President's ratings in the polls were as low as they had ever been. But his reception thus far in Texas seemed to disprove the polls, and this fact was very much on President Kennedy's mind.

1

The polls may have given him cause for gloom, but the people certainly did not.

That was obviously what he was thinking about when he remarked to me, cheerfully, that we would at least carry Massachusetts and Texas. They were the last words John Kennedy ever spoke to me.

I was just going out the door when he said this. I turned and smiled at him. "Oh, we are going to do better than that, Mr. President," I replied. He returned the smile and nodded.

On that note I left the room, pulling the door shut behind me, and went to join Lady Bird for the motorcade trip to *Air Force Two,* which would take us to Dallas.

I shared the President's optimism that morning and I shared the sense of implied partnership in the coming campaign. Reports had been circulating in Washington that I was going to be "dumped" from the ticket in 1964. In fact, the November 22 edition of *The Dallas Morning News* quoted Richard Nixon as predicting that under certain circumstances I would be "dumped." I believed these reports to be rumors and nothing more.

When John Kennedy first offered me the Vice Presidential nomination, I asked him to be candid with me. If it was only a courteous gesture, I said, I wanted him to say so. He replied that he needed me to run with him if the ticket was to be successful.

I served John Kennedy for three years—as a candidate and as his Vice President. I served him loyally, as I would have wanted my Vice President to serve me. We did not always see things in the same light. I did not always agree with everything that happened in his administration. But when I did disagree with the President, I did so in private, and man to man.

Never once in those three years did I have any reason to believe that John Kennedy looked upon me as a liability. I had every reason to believe that he intended for us to go forward together, and that Theodore Sorensen, his special assistant, spoke the literal truth when he wrote to me, just a month before I left office, in 1969:

> Contrary to some published reports, Jack Kennedy never regretted his selection of his Vice Presidential running mate. . . .

For me, President Kennedy made his position quite clear in what was to be his next-to-last press conference, on October 31, 1963, only twenty-two days before his death. He was asked: "Now, sir, assuming that you run next year, would you want Lyndon Johnson on the ticket, and do you expect he will be on the ticket?" The President answered without hesitation: "Yes, to both of those questions. That is correct."

What some people did not understand was that our relationship, which dated back to our service together in the House of Representatives, had always been one of mutual respect, admiration, and cooperation. When I was running for Senate Minority Leader in 1953, John Kennedy called me from Massachusetts and said: "I want you to know you can count on my support." It was purely a self-initiated act on his part. I hadn't even contacted him.

Then, in the fall of 1955, Senator Kennedy's father, Ambassador Joseph Kennedy, called me at my ranch. He said that he and John Kennedy wanted to support me for President and would like to work for my nomination at the 1956 Democratic convention if I would run. I thanked him but said that I did not wish to be a candidate. As it later developed, my name *was* placed in nomination, but purely for reasons of local Democratic politics. Remembering that Governor Allan Shivers of Texas had left the party in 1952 to support General Eisenhower, House Speaker Sam Rayburn felt that someone should head the Texas delegation who could be depended on to support the national ticket. Without consultation or my permission, he announced that he would support Lyndon Johnson as a favorite-son candidate and chairman of the Texas delegation to the Democratic convention. As a result, we maintained control of the delegation and I cast the vote of the Texas delegation for John Kennedy for the Vice Presidential nomination at that convention.

A few days later, after I had returned home, I wrote the following letter to Joe Kennedy:

August 25, 1956

Dear Joe:

For a week now I have been taking care of Lyndon Johnson—sunning, swimming and sleeping as much as my folks would let me. But in addition, I have been thinking of a lot of things, one of them being that phone call from you in October of last year.

You said then that you and Jack wanted to support me for President in 1956 but that if I were not interested, you planned to support Adlai Stevenson. I told you I was not interested and it occurs to me that you may be somewhat mystified about my activities in Chicago last week. When I see you I will explain how they involved a local political situation here in Texas and were not inconsistent with what I told you last October.

But this note, Joe, is being sent your way to tell you how proud I am of the Democratic Senator from Massachusetts and how proud I am of the Texas Delegation and other Delegations from the South for their support of him in Chicago last Friday afternoon. In my opinion, that session of the Convention lighted the brightest lamp of hope for a truly great Democratic Party. I hope we can talk about this sometime when you are in Washington.

With all good wishes and warmest regards, I am

Sincerely,
Lyndon B. Johnson

Honorable Joseph Kennedy
Villa Les Fal Eze
Eze s/Mer, A.M. France

Once he became President, John Kennedy was always courteous, thoughtful, and solicitous of me. I think he felt the Vice Presidency was basically a difficult job, and he did everything he could to give it substance. He sent me to twenty-six foreign countries on goodwill or fact-finding missions. He sent me as his representative to West Berlin on a most urgent and important mission shortly after the Berlin Wall was raised. He appointed me Chairman of the President's Committee on Equal Opportunity and asked Congress to pass a bill relieving him of the chairmanship and designating me as Chairman of the National Aeronautics and Space Council.

I do not think that any President ever made a greater effort to make sure that his Vice President was briefed and kept fully informed on all the vital and sensitive issues of the day. In fact, I do not think I missed a single meeting on national security affairs, unless I was sick or out of town.

I considered President Kennedy a great and inspiring national leader and a compassionate man of vision and imagination. I was honored to serve him. My personal feelings toward him were those of admiration, fondness, and respect—and I always believed that those feelings were returned in kind by the President.

I remember that on many occasions, after a tiring meeting was over or when he wanted to shed his cares after a long day in the Oval Office, he would ask me to stay behind and visit with him and a few friends. At those sessions the President was relaxed and companionable, a lively conversationalist, and easy to be with.

Now, in Texas on this November day, Lady Bird and I were going to have a chance to return his hospitality. We were scheduled to fly that afternoon from Dallas to Austin for a fund-raising dinner. That night the Kennedys were going to be our guests at the LBJ Ranch. We were eagerly looking forward to the visit. The President had visited our ranch before, but Mrs. Kennedy had not. I was particularly anxious for her to enjoy herself, and knowing how she liked to ride, we had made special plans for some of our best horses to be available for her.

Mrs. Johnson and I arrived at Dallas' Love Field aboard *Air Force Two* at 11:35 A.M. We were greeted by the local dignitaries and immediately joined the reception line to welcome the First Family when *Air Force One* touched down five minutes later.

There was a large, joyful crowd behind the fence, and when the Kennedys stepped out of the plane a great roar went up from thousands of throats. I remember thinking how radiant Mrs. Kennedy looked. The skies had cleared, the air was warm and the sun bright. Her pink suit and pink hat added to the beauty of the day. Someone in the reception line added the final touch by presenting her with a bouquet of dark red roses.

After the formalities, President and Mrs. Kennedy walked along the fence, shaking hands and stopping to sign autographs. Lady Bird and I followed, shaking hands and exchanging greetings with old friends in the crowd. Ten minutes later we took seats in the automobiles to begin the motorcade through town to the Trade Mart, where the President was scheduled to make a luncheon speech. President and Mrs. Kennedy got into the big Presidential Lincoln. Governor John Connally of Texas and his wife, Nellie, were in the jump seats directly in front of them. On orders of the President, the famous "bubble top" had been removed from the car. It was a beautiful day and the President wanted no barriers between himself and the people.

Dallas Police Chief Jesse Curry led the motorcade in his car. Then came the Presidential limousine, the Secret Service follow-up car, and the Vice Presidential car, a rented Lincoln convertible. Behind us were several cars for members of Congress, press cars, a VIP bus, and finally the press buses. In the front seat of our car were the driver, a Texas highway patrolman named Hurchel Jacks, and the Secret Service agent in charge of my detail, Rufus Youngblood. I was sitting in the right rear seat, Lady Bird was in the center, and Senator Ralph Yarborough of Texas was in the left rear seat, directly behind the driver. It was approximately 11:55 A.M.

As we drove through the less populated areas, the crowds were thin. But I recall that even then the three of us commented on the visible enthusiasm of the people along the route and their obvious good wishes.

Closer to town the crowds grew in size as well as in spirit. In some places they were lined three and four deep along the streets. Children were smiling, waving homemade signs of welcome. People were hanging out of windows, cheering and throwing confetti. The more the crowds grew, the more enthusiastic they became. Dallas was giving the President a genuinely warm welcome.

My thoughts returned to John Kennedy's earlier comment to me in the hotel. We *would* carry Texas. If we could get a turnout like this in Dallas, I thought, we could carry the state.

Dallas has never been exactly a citadel of Democratic politics. And I knew from experience what an angry Dallas crowd could be like to an unwelcome visitor. I remembered the painful incident during the 1960 Presidential campaign when Lady Bird and I were harassed and jeered in a Dallas hotel lobby. It had also been less than a month since UN Ambassador Adlai Stevenson had been shoved, booed, and spat upon by anti-UN demonstrators in Dallas.

But Dallas put on a different face on the afternoon of November 22: a smiling, happy, festive face eager to do honor to its President and his lady and to make them feel welcome.

I think we were all surprised. I know I was.

I had been worried about this visit—worried about the political climate; worried about the problems we might encounter.

A great deal has been written about the purpose of that fateful trip to Texas. Much of what has been written is wrong.

President Kennedy came to Texas to raise money for the Democratic campaign coffers and to pave the way for a Democratic victory in Texas in 1964. We were soon to be involved in a Presidential election. We would need millions of dollars for the campaign, and the Democratic National Committee was still painfully in debt. The President hoped to raise several hundred thousand dollars in Texas.

President Kennedy also came to Texas to try to shore up our slipping popularity there. A Texas poll, taken a few weeks before his trip, showed that only 38 per cent of the people approved of what he was doing as President. The same poll showed Governor Connally with an 81 per cent approval. The fact is that Governor Connally was more in tune with the prevailing political thinking in Texas. Some of the administration's actions —particularly the Bay of Pigs, the fiscal policy, and the civil rights program—had hurt us in Texas and throughout the South.

So President Kennedy had decided to go to the people—to let them see him and get to know him; to appeal to them directly for their support. He also wanted to consolidate the party machinery of the State of Texas behind him—from the Governor on down. He wanted to come to the large Texas cities, where he could gain maximum exposure.

The President had originally wanted to come on my birthday, August 27. He suggested this date to Governor Connally and me in June 1963 at the Cortez Hotel in El Paso, where we met following a visit to the missile range at White Sands, New Mexico. The President had already attended two fund-raising dinners in New York and a dinner in Boston in May 1961. He planned another dinner in Boston for the fall of 1963. He now wanted to come to Texas. The President had reminded me on several occasions that Massachusetts, New York, and Texas were going to have to bear the burden of financing the 1964 Presidential campaign.

He suggested at our El Paso meeting that we hold a series of four fund-raising dinners—in Dallas, Fort Worth, San Antonio, and Houston. John Connally opposed that plan, and I think he shocked President Kennedy by his immediate and frank reaction. He said that, in the first place, the date was impossible; it was too close to Labor Day. The rich people would be in Colorado cooling off, he said, and everyone else would be down at the Gulf of Mexico cooling off. "You won't be able to get a crowd." In the second place, he said, the worst thing the President could do would be to go into four cities and charge people $100 apiece to see their President. "They will think you only came here to take their money."

Connally suggested instead a single fund-raising dinner in Austin and a series of nonpolitical public appearances in the other four cities—"at the proper time." President Kennedy reluctantly agreed to this suggestion and postponed the trip.

The following October President Kennedy met with Governor Connally in Washington and they agreed on the November date. When I heard that John Connally was in town, I naturally asked him to dinner. That evening he said that he assumed the President would tell me about it, but he advised me that they had discussed the Texas trip and had made some definite plans concerning it. The next I heard about the trip was when the President asked Bill Moyers to make advance preparations for it. Bill, a Texan, had worked for me in the Senate and had joined the Kennedy administration as Deputy Director of the Peace Corps.

The idea that President Kennedy came to Texas to settle a political feud between Senator Ralph Yarborough and me is not true. Whatever differences the Senator and I may have had could have been settled in Washington, where neither of us was more than ten minutes away from the White House. There was no need for anyone to travel to Texas to settle our differences. In addition, President Kennedy was too smart to try to intervene in local political controversies. That's a buzz saw that most Presidents seek to avoid.

The difference that Senator Yarborough and I had was over patronage. I had made an agreement with President Kennedy—when he asked me to go on the ticket in Los Angeles—that I would be allowed to pass on all federal appointments in Texas. Senator Yarborough resented this. If I had been in his position, I might have resented it too. He felt that he should have complete control over those appointments. He knew that other Senators could make recommendations that did not have to be approved by the Vice President and he was not pleased to find that his did.

Senator Yarborough did refuse to ride in the car with us on the previous day in San Antonio and Houston. He never told me that, but I was informed that he told members of the Kennedy staff and President Kennedy was very irritated by it. So Senator Yarborough and I had our differences. But they were differences between two rather strong-minded men, and President Kennedy, quite rightly, never tried to intervene. These political differences had nothing to do with his coming to Texas or not coming to Texas. The trip was Presidential politics, pure and simple. It was the opening effort of the 1964 campaign. And it was going beautifully.

As the crowds reached their peak on Main Street, President Kennedy stopped the motorcade several times to shake hands. Whenever he did so, people would surge through the police lines on both sides of the street—

from one side to touch their President and from the other side to get a closer look at Mrs. Kennedy.

Shortly before 12:30 P.M. the motorcade turned right on Houston Street and then a block later made a sharp left turn on Elm Street, which would take us through the underpass and on to Stemmons Freeway, to the Trade Mart. We were traveling about ten or fifteen miles per hour. Just after our car made the left turn at the top of Elm, I was startled by an explosion.

In the reading I have done since that day of horror, it is apparent that there were many reactions to the first shot. Some people thought it was a firecracker. Some thought it was a bomb. Some thought it was a truck backfiring. Some thought it might be a shot. Some were positive it was a shot.

I did not know what it was.

Before the echo had subsided, before the noise had completely registered on my consciousness, Agent Youngblood spun around, shoved me on the shoulder to push me down, and shouted to all of us, "Get down!" Almost in the same movement, he vaulted over the seat, pushed me to the floor, and sat on my right shoulder to keep me down and to protect me. "Get down!" he shouted again to all of us. Agent Youngblood's quick reaction was as brave an act as I have ever seen anyone perform. When a man, without a moment's thought or hesitation, places himself between you and a possible assassin's bullet, you know you have seen courage. And you never forget it.

I still was not clear about what was happening. I was bent down under the weight of Agent Youngblood's body, toward Lady Bird and Senator Yarborough, and I remember turning my head to make sure that they were both down. They were. Agent Youngblood had seen to that.

At some time in this sequence of events, I heard other explosions. It was impossible to tell where they were coming from, and I still was not certain what they were. Then a voice came crackling over the radio system: "Let's get out of here." Suddenly our car accelerated and we wheeled around a corner, careening over the curb—almost, it seemed to me, on two wheels. I was later told that we were traveling between seventy and eighty miles per hour.

There was some frantic conversation coming over Youngblood's radio and I heard him speaking into it several times. But I could not distinguish the words. I asked him what had happened. He released his weight from me but still kept me in a crouching position on the floor. He said that he was not sure but that he had heard that the motorcade was headed for a hospital.

I did not realize it at the time, but we were then speeding past the Trade Mart, where 2,500 persons were waiting to greet the President of the United States. By now we were all aware that someone had been injured. But what had happened? Was it a bomb? A bullet? A firecracker exploding in front of someone's face? And who was hurt? From that first moment Rufus Youngblood had taken charge. He was determined, and there was a tone of authority in his voice to back it up. "When we get to the hospital," he instructed, "you and Mrs. Johnson follow me and the other agents." He said that we were going in fast and we were not to become involved with any other people.

"All right," I replied, and it seemed that as soon as I said it the car was braking and people were jumping out. When Lady Bird and I got out, we were immediately surrounded by agents. Youngblood ordered us to follow them into the building, to stay close to them, and not to stop under any circumstances. We followed, almost in a trot. Our entrance into the hospital, I later learned, had started a rumor, which the press circulated throughout the nation, that I was having a heart attack and was being rushed to the emergency area for treatment. We were taken to a very small room in the hospital, lined with white sheets.

Our first specific information came from Emory Roberts, the agent in charge of the White House detail. He said that President Kennedy had been wounded by gunshot and that his condition was quite serious. He added that Governor Connally had also been injured. I was stunned. My President and leader . . . my confidant and friend . . . both shot; both undergoing emergency treatment just yards from where I stood; both, for all I knew, dying. The day, which had begun so cheerfully, had turned into a nightmare.

The Secret Service now decided that we should leave the hospital and make plans to return to Washington immediately.

Agent Youngblood concurred. He said that no one knew whether the shooting was the work of one man or several men, or was part of a conspiracy to kill the top leadership of the country. "We need to get back to Washington—the White House will be the safest place for you," he said.

I replied that it would be unthinkable for me to leave with President Kennedy's life hanging in the balance. And under any circumstances, the decision should be made by someone on the President's staff.

While the other agents secured the area, Agent Youngblood pulled down the shades on the windows in the small hospital room. We waited— in silence, in confusion, in doubt, and in terrible agony—for news of the President and Governor Connally.

What does a man think about at such a time? Looking back on it now, it is impossible for me to re-create the thoughts and emotions that surged through me during the forty-five terrible, interminable minutes that we spent in Parkland Hospital. Everything had happened so fast, and all of us were completely unprepared for it. I suppose we were all in a state of shock.

A few people came and went silently. There was very little conversation. Lady Bird, of course, was at my side. Cliff Carter, one of my assistants, was also there. Congressmen Homer Thornberry and Jack Brooks of Texas were there for a while. Numerous agents were in and out.

The reports on the President's condition became more discouraging by the minute. Agent Emory Roberts came in and said the President would not make it. Then Kenneth O'Donnell, the President's appointments secretary, came in and said the President was in a "bad way." I knew how those words must have stuck in O'Donnell's throat. He had been at John Kennedy's side through most of his public life, and despite his tough, tight-lipped exterior, I knew how devoted he was to him.

I sent for Secret Service Agent Roy Kellerman for a report on John Connally's condition. He said that the Governor had been taken to surgery but that he was expected to recover.

My thoughts turned to Jacqueline Kennedy and Nellie Connally. They were both going through this heartbreaking experience alone, and I didn't see how they could stand up under the agony. I asked Agent Youngblood if Mrs. Johnson and I could walk down the corridor and try to see them. He shook his head emphatically, insisting that I was not to leave the room. He did say, however, that it would be all right for Mrs. Johnson to go. "You ought to try to see Jackie and Nellie," I told her. She started out to find them immediately, escorted by Congressman Brooks and several Secret Service agents.

About 1:20 P.M. Central Standard Time Ken O'Donnell informed us of the President's death. "He's gone," was all he said. A minute or two later Emory Roberts confirmed the tragic news.

I found it hard to believe that this nightmare had actually happened. The violence of the whole episode was unreal, shocking, and incredible. A few hours earlier I had been having breakfast with John Kennedy—alive, young, strong, and vigorous. I could not believe that he was dead. I was bewildered and distraught. Along with grief I felt anguish, compassion, and a deep concern for Mrs. Kennedy and the children.

But despite our emotions, there were practical matters to attend to— and the most urgent matter, as far as the Secret Service was concerned, was getting me out of that hospital to a place where I could be better protected. Agent Roberts went to find Ken O'Donnell for further instructions. O'Donnell thought that we should depart for Washington immediately.

I asked what Mrs. Kennedy wanted to do. O'Donnell replied that Mrs. Kennedy would not leave the hospital without the President's body. He said that they were waiting for a casket. I could not desert Mrs. Kennedy in that situation and emphatically said so. I told O'Donnell that I would not return to Washington until Mrs. Kennedy was ready to go, and that we would carry the President's body back with us if that was what she wanted. I did agree to go immediately to *Air Force One* and to wait there until Mrs. Kennedy and the President's body were brought aboard the plane.

Just a minute or so before we left—it must have been about 1:30 P.M. —Assistant Press Secretary Malcolm Kilduff came into the room and addressed me as "Mr. President." This was the first time anyone had called me that and I must have looked startled; I certainly felt strange.

"Mr. President," he said, "I have to announce the death of President Kennedy. Is it all right with you if the public announcement is made now?"

I suppose I naturally assumed that the announcement had already been made. On brief reflection I concluded that it would be best to make the announcement after we had left the hospital, purely for security reasons. I told Kilduff, and he and the Secret Service agreed.

Our departure from the hospital was similar to our arrival: swift and tense. The Secret Service agents had obtained three unmarked cars from the Dallas police. The same instructions were grimly conveyed to Mrs. Johnson and me: "We're going to move out fast. Please stick close to us."

We left the room, ushered—or I should say, surrounded—by a cordon of agents. Agent Youngblood insisted that Lady Bird and I travel in different cars. I sat in the rear seat of the lead car, driven by Dallas Police Chief Curry. Congressman Thornberry got in the front seat. Rufus Youngblood followed me into the car and told me to keep my head below window level. Mrs. Johnson was ushered into the second car with Congressman Brooks and several agents. There was a follow-up car with the remaining agents.

As we started away from the hospital, Congressman Albert Thomas of Texas came running up to the car. He saw Congressman Thornberry— I don't think he saw me—and he asked the Congressman to wait for him. We were about to pull out anyway, but when I learned who it was, I told the driver to stop and pick him up. He got into the front seat and Congressman Thornberry climbed into the rear seat with us. I rode to the airfield between him and Rufus Youngblood.

As we were speeding toward Love Field, Kilduff was making the following announcement at Parkland Hospital before the frantic reporters who had been covering the Presidential trip:

President John F. Kennedy died at approximately 1:00 o'clock, Central Standard Time, today, here in Dallas. He died of a gunshot wound in the brain. I have no other details regarding the assassination of the President.

The journey to Love Field took less than ten minutes, but those few minutes were as crucial as any I have ever spent. I knew from the moment President Kennedy died that I must assume the awesome responsibility of uniting the country and moving toward the goals that he had set for us. Like everyone else, I continued to be stunned. My President—the man with whom I had worked and had been proud to serve—had been killed, and killed in my own state. It was almost unbearable.

But in spite of the enormity of the tragedy, in spite of my sense of personal loss and deep shock, I knew I could not allow the tide of grief to overwhelm me. The consequences of all my actions were too great for me to become immobilized now with emotion. I was a man in trouble, in a world that is never more than minutes away from catastrophe.

I had not yet seen Mrs. Kennedy. I wondered with what inadequate words I could try to console her.

I had a staff—and a government—that would be plunged in the depths of despair, and I had to mobilize both for action. I had many decisions to make. No one was certain yet whether a widespread assassination plot might be involved.

Most of all I realized that, ready or not, new and immeasurable duties had been thrust upon me. There were tasks to perform that only I had the authority to perform. A nation stunned, shaken to its very heart, had to be reassured that the government was not in a state of paralysis. I had to convince everyone everywhere that the country would go forward, that the business of the United States would proceed. I knew that not only the nation but the whole world would be anxiously following every move I made—watching, judging, weighing, balancing.

I was catapulted without preparation into the most difficult job any mortal man can hold. My duties would not wait a week, or a day, or even an hour.

On the way to the airport, Agent Youngblood was in communication with *Air Force One,* to make sure it was secured and ready for us. When we arrived, we dashed up the ramp. Secret Service men rushed through the interior ahead of us, pulling down the shades and closing both doors behind us. The air conditioning was off and it was extremely hot inside the plane.

I realized that the staff and Secret Service had been right in insisting that I go to *Air Force One* immediately. That plane is the closest thing to a traveling White House that man can devise. It affords the personnel, the security, and the communications equipment a President must have to do his job.

At first, Mrs. Johnson and I were ushered into the private quarters of the plane, which contained a bedroom and bathroom for the use of the President and his family. I told one of the agents that we preferred that these quarters be held for Mrs. Kennedy's use and we went forward to the crowded stateroom, which serves as the Presidential office and sitting room aboard the plane.

When I walked in, everyone stood up. I still recall the deep emotion I felt. Here were close friends like Homer Thornberry and Jack Brooks; here were aides who were like members of my family; here were Secret Service agents who had covered every movement I had made, twenty-four hours a day, for three years. All of them were on their feet. It was at that moment that I realized nothing would ever be the same again. A wall—high, forbidding, historic—separated us now, a wall that derives from the Office of the Presidency of the United States. No one but my family would ever penetrate it, as long as I held the office. To old friends who had never called me anything but Lyndon, I would now be "Mr. President." It was a frightening, disturbing prospect. I instinctively reached for Lady Bird's hand for reassurance. I believe it was Congressman Thomas who broke the silence. "We are ready to carry out any orders you have, Mr. President," he said.

The television was on. CBS commentator Walter Cronkite was discussing the terrible attack when a Dallas newscaster broke in with the first public announcement of President Kennedy's death. I knew I had to call Attorney General Robert Kennedy immediately. I went back into the bedroom for a few minutes to use the phone because it was the only private place on the plane where I could speak quietly and be able to hear.

I knew how grief-stricken the President's brother must have been and I tried to say something that would comfort him. In spite of his shock and sorrow he discussed the practical problems at hand with dispatch. Perhaps the full impact of his brother's death had not yet reached him. He said that the FBI had no indication as to the extent of the plot—if, indeed, there was a plot—but that it was gathering information as quickly as possible. We discussed the matter of my taking the oath of office. I told him that both the Secret Service and the members of the late President's staff felt that I should return to Washington at once.

Attorney General Kennedy said he would look into the matter and report to me on whether the oath should be administered immediately or after we returned to Washington. He also said that he would provide us with the proper wording of the oath.

I then received a call from the White House from McGeorge Bundy, the President's national security adviser, and from Walter Jenkins of my staff. They both said that my return to Washington should not be delayed. I told them that Mrs. Kennedy had not arrived with the President's body and that I would not leave under any circumstances until she was aboard.

At that point the Attorney General came back on the line. He said that the oath of office should be administered immediately—before taking off for Washington—and that it could be administered by any judicial officer of the United States. The next call came from Deputy Attorney General Nicholas Katzenbach, calling, I presumed, at the Attorney General's direction. He dictated the wording of the oath of office to my personal secretary, Marie Fehmer.

I then called Irving Goldberg, a lawyer friend for many years. We agreed that Judge Sarah Hughes, whom President Kennedy had appointed to the U.S. District Court in Dallas, should be asked to administer the oath. Goldberg telephoned Judge Hughes at her office. She was not there but was expected in momentarily, and a few minutes later she called me. I explained the situation and told her that we would send a car for her immediately. She replied that she could get to the airfield faster on her own and would be there in ten minutes. As soon as I hung up, I asked Agent Youngblood to check on the location of Mrs. Kennedy and to let me know the second she arrived.

In the meantime, a small private plane was approaching Love Field, and its passenger was requesting clearance from the tower to pull up alongside *Air Force One*. The passenger was identified as Bill Moyers, who had been handling the advance preparations for the scheduled dinner in Austin. As soon as Bill learned of the shooting, he had chartered a plane to fly to Dallas. Colonel James Swindal, our pilot, gave the clearance, and a few minutes later Bill joined us aboard the plane.

About 2:15 the moment arrived against which I had been steeling myself—and dreading to the depths of my being. Mrs. Kennedy was coming aboard with the President's body. Lady Bird and I went to the rear of the plane to meet her. I had not seen Mrs. Kennedy since morning, when we had gotten into our cars at the airport to begin the motorcade. I was shocked by the sight that confronted me. There stood that beautiful lady, with her white gloves, her pink suit, and her stockings caked with her husband's blood. There was a dazed look in her eyes.

I do not remember much of the conversation. It was not really a conversation, just clumsy, aching words of condolence and some half-finished, choked sentences in reply. Nothing anybody can say under such circumstances is the right thing to say, because no words can ever ease the pain. Men are not very good at such things. It was Lady Bird who said the most and whose words were the most comforting, and Mrs. Kennedy replied: "Oh, Lady Bird, we've always liked you both so much." She seemed to be trying to offer *us* words of strength.

We saw her to the bedroom and then left her alone. Privacy seemed the only kindness at such a time. The casket was brought up the ramp and placed in the rear of the plane. Special Assistants Larry O'Brien and Ken O'Donnell remained there, as if to stand guard over the fallen leader.

I tried to comfort them as best I could, and I asked them then to stay on to serve another President. "I need you more than John Kennedy did,"

I told them. They were of course in no mood to discuss the future but I wanted them to know that they were on my mind and important to me. I knew that I *did* need them. I needed the experience that they had gained in nearly three years at the seat of power, but more than anything else I wanted to treat President Kennedy's people the way I would have expected him to treat mine.

About that time Agent Youngblood came to me with a query from Mac Kilduff regarding the press coverage of the swearing-in. I sent for Kilduff and asked if it was absolutely necessary for the press to be present. I did not want to make a public spectacle over such a somber occasion. Kilduff did not hesitate in his recommendation. He strongly urged that the press be represented and that a photographer also be present.

"Then," I said, "we should ask everyone on the plane who wants to come to be present."

We were still waiting for Judge Hughes when the press pool entered. The pool consisted of Merriman Smith of the United Press International, Charles Roberts of *Newsweek* magazine, and Sid Davis of Westinghouse Broadcasting Company. At approximately 2:30 Judge Sarah Hughes was escorted into the plane. I thanked her for coming and told her we would be ready to begin in a minute or two.

The crowded stateroom was filling with more people. Members of the Kennedy staff, members of the press, members of Congress, members of my staff, and Secret Service agents squeezed into the small enclosure. The air conditioning still was not on and it was sweltering. Larry O'Brien went to look for a Bible, and he returned with a Catholic missal, unopened in its original box.

I asked Larry O'Brien to find out if Mrs. Kennedy wished to stand with us during the administration of the oath. A moment later she came out to join us—she standing on one side of me and Lady Bird on the other.

At approximately 2:40 P.M. Central Standard Time Malcolm Kilduff held a dictating machine in front of us (a tape recorder was not available) and I repeated the oath of office after Judge Hughes:

> I do solemnly swear that I will faithfully execute the Office of President of the United States and will, to the best of my ability, preserve, protect, and defend the Constitution of the United States, so help me God.

Judge Hughes departed the plane and within five minutes we were airborne, headed back to Washington. While in the air I called President Kennedy's mother, Mrs. Rose Kennedy, in Massachusetts. I told her of our grief and our sorrow for her. And then she, as Jacqueline Kennedy had done a few minutes earlier, had the thoughtfulness to say something to strengthen me. "Thank you very much," she replied. "I know you loved Jack and he loved you."

Next I called my dear friend Nellie Connally in Dallas. We had been close to Nellie and John for many years, sharing moments of sorrow and happiness alike. She reported that the surgeon had just finished operating and that John was going to be all right.

I knew that I would be expected to say something when we touched down at Andrews Air Force Base. The nation would not want to hear a lengthy speech from me, but I felt that the people would want to know there was leadership and purpose and continuity in their government. As far as the rest of the world was concerned, there must be no sign of hesitancy or indecision. I worked on the statement, off and on, as we flew toward Washington.

I also sent for Major General Chester V. Clifton, the military aide to the President, and told him that I would want to meet with three groups as soon as possible after I got to the White House. First, I wanted to hold a Cabinet meeting. I realized then that most of the Cabinet members, including the Secretary of State, were on their way to Japan for a conference. I gave orders for them to return immediately and was told that their plane had turned around as soon as word of the assassination had been received. The plane was refueling in Hawaii at that moment. The Cabinet meeting would have to wait until the following day.

The second meeting I requested was with Secretary of Defense Robert McNamara and McGeorge Bundy. I felt a national security meeting was essential at the earliest possible moment. Finally, I wanted a meeting with the bipartisan leadership of the Congress. I told General Clifton to have Bundy set up both meetings for that same evening.

With this business out of the way, I returned to the rear of the plane and asked the members of the Kennedy staff if they would like to come up and join us. They thanked me, but declined. They wanted to share their grief together and to draw whatever strength they might from each other's company.

If there was friction aboard the plane, I was not aware of it, and neither was my staff. There was confusion and grief and uncertainty, God knows. It was not a pleasant trip for anyone.

We landed at Andrews Air Force Base outside Washington about 6 P.M. Eastern Standard Time. There was a cluster of people waiting and watching as we pulled up to the parking ramp. There were bright glaring lights pouring out of the black night, a sign that television cameras were waiting to record our arrival.

As we pulled to a stop, a ramp was brought up to the front door and a forklift to the rear. Both doors were opened. I instructed my staff to wait, saying that none of us should leave until the casket was off and Mrs. Kennedy had deplaned.

When the time came, Lady Bird and I walked down the ramp, with the blinding lights in our eyes and the cameras following us. I walked slowly up to the microphones and made the following statement:

> This is a sad time for all people. We have suffered a loss that cannot be weighed. For me, it is a deep personal tragedy. I know that the world shares the sorrow that Mrs. Kennedy and her family bear. I will do my best. That is all I can do. I ask for your help—and God's.

As I walked to the helicopter, its long blades whirring with impatience, I recalled that someone had once remarked that the Presidency is the loneliest job in the world. But my thoughts kept going back to Mrs. Kennedy, who at that moment was accompanying the body of her dead husband to Bethesda Naval Hospital, and I knew that my loneliness was only a fraction of the despair weighing so heavily on her heart—that my loneliness could not be compared with hers.

Then the door of the helicopter slammed shut behind me—and so ended a tragic chapter in American history.

2

"I feel like I have already been here a year"

Every President has to establish with the various sectors of the country what I call "the right to govern." Just being elected to the office does not guarantee him that right. Every President has to inspire the confidence of the people. Every President has to become a leader, and to be a leader he must attract people who are willing to follow him. Every President has to develop a moral underpinning to his power, or he soon discovers that he has no power at all.

For me, that presented special problems. In spite of more than three decades of public service, I knew I was an unknown quantity to many of my countrymen and to much of the world when I assumed office. I suffered another handicap, since I had come to the Presidency not through the collective will of the people but in the wake of tragedy. I had no mandate from the voters.

A few people were openly bitter about my becoming President. They found it impossible to transfer their intense loyalties from one President to another. I could understand this, although it complicated my task. Others were apprehensive. This was particularly true within the black community. Just when the blacks had had their hopes for equality and justice raised, after centuries of misery and despair, they awoke one morning to discover that their future was in the hands of a President born in the South.

Yet in spite of these yearnings for a fallen leader, in spite of some bitterness, in spite of apprehensions, I knew it was imperative that I grasp the reins of power and do so without delay. Any hesitation or wavering, any false step, any sign of self-doubt, could have been disastrous. The nation was in a state of shock and grief. The times cried out for leadership.

There was doubt and bewilderment about what had actually happened in Dallas on November 22, 1963, and the uncertainty was compounded two days later when Lee Harvey Oswald was shot to death while in the custody of the Dallas police. A horror-stricken, outraged nation wanted the truth and no one could immediately provide it. The entire world was watching us through a magnifying glass. Any signs of weakness or indecision could have had grave international consequences—in Berlin, in Southeast Asia, in Latin America. Friend and foe alike had to be convinced that the policies of our country were going to be continued and that we were one nation undivided in our resolve to maintain international order.

Months later Washington columnists would be writing that I had accomplished a political masterstroke in convincing most of the Kennedy appointees to continue serving in my administration. I saw it neither as political nor as a masterstroke.

It is true that I asked the top Kennedy-appointed officials to stay on, not just for a while, but for as long as I was President. It is true that by remaining on the job they helped give the government and the nation a sense of continuity during critical times—a sense of continuity which in turn strengthened my hand as Chief Executive. It is also true that I benefited from the experience that these officials had gained during the nearly three years of the Kennedy administration. But in the final analysis, when I asked those appointees to stay on I did so out of a deep-rooted sense of responsibility to John F. Kennedy. Rightly or wrongly, I felt from the very first day in office that I had to carry on for President Kennedy. I considered myself the caretaker of both his people and his policies. He knew when he selected me as his running mate that I would be the man required to carry on if anything happened to him. I did what I believed he would have wanted me to do. I never wavered from that sense of responsibility, even after I was elected in my own right, up to my last day in office.

I eventually developed my own programs and policies, but I never lost sight of the fact that I was the trustee and custodian of the Kennedy administration. Although it was my prerogative to do so, I would no more have considered changing the name of the *Honey Fitz*—the name Jack Kennedy had given one of the Presidential yachts—than I would have thought of changing the name of the Washington Monument. I did everything I could to enhance the memory of John Kennedy, beginning with honoring Mrs. Kennedy's request to rename Cape Canaveral for her late husband. That was a fitting tribute to him. I wrote to Mrs. Kennedy when I sent her a copy of the Executive order:

> I am delighted to see that the reaction at Cape Kennedy and at the Kennedy Space Center has been one of deep gratification. It is clear that once again you have hit with unerring taste on the right thing to do.

Among the top officials I inherited from President Kennedy were some extraordinary men who served me with fidelity, brilliance, and distinction. That list begins with Dean Rusk. Actually, the situation involving Rusk represented one of the first problems I had to face. There had been a persistent rumor that President Kennedy planned to replace the Secretary of State after the 1964 election. That was, I think, nothing more than a rumor—the invention of men who were jealous and critical of Dean Rusk. But rumor or not, it was not making Rusk's job any easier.

I knew Rusk was a loyal, honorable, hard-working, imaginative man of conviction, and I decided to ask him to remain as my Secretary of State. When he returned from the Pacific the day after the assassination, I assured him in the strongest terms that I wanted him to remain. I believe I made a wise decision for the country and for myself. He served me with distinction and great ability. He stood by me and shared the President's load of responsibility and abuse. He never complained. But he was no "yes man." He could be determined, and he was always the most determined when he was telling me I shouldn't do something that I felt needed to be done.

Another source of great strength to me was Secretary of Defense Bob McNamara. When I met with him in the Executive Office Building on the night of November 22, I told him that if he ever tried to quit I would send the White House police after him. Brilliant, intensely energetic, publicly tough but privately sensitive, a man with great love for his country, McNamara carried more information around in his head than the average encyclopedia. He was a loyal Cabinet officer and we had a close working relationship that endured some of the most trying circumstances imaginable. When I nominated him to the presidency of the World Bank late in 1967, the story circulated that I had fired him because of a disagreement over Vietnam.

The fact is that he knew in the summer of 1967 that I was seriously considering retiring from office at the end of the current term. When I informed him of my thoughts, I told him that he was invaluable to me and that he was entitled to receive any consideration my administration could give him. When there were indications that the presidency of the World Bank would eventually be vacant, and the incumbent, George Woods, urged McNamara to consider the job, McNamara came to me. He told me the World Bank presidency was the one job that deeply interested him, so when the time arrived I called in Secretary of the Treasury Henry Fowler and instructed him to "tell the Bank members that our nominee is Bob McNamara."

Naturally, all the Cabinet members were deeply shaken by President Kennedy's death, but apart from the Attorney General few of them had been close to him before 1961. The effect on the White House staff was quite another matter. Many of them had been with Jack Kennedy since his early days in Congress. His loss was the deepest kind of tragedy to them, yet most of them put their country and their government ahead of personal feelings.

Ted Sorensen was a case in point. I knew that the bottom had dropped out of his world when Jack Kennedy died. He had been one of Kennedy's closest aides and confidants for more than a decade. It was obvious to me that he was not going to remain on the White House staff indefinitely, but while he was there—until March 1964—he served with ability, working almost around the clock in an effort to smooth the transition and benefit the country.

McGeorge Bundy became another trusted aide. A former Harvard dean, he had served as President Kennedy's foreign affairs adviser and remained in that capacity for more than two years of my administration. Even after he left government to assume the presidency of the Ford Foundation, he remained available to return when he could be helpful.

Larry O'Brien, President Kennedy's legislative liaison man, also remained and helped to steer many of the Great Society programs through Congress. I thought well of O'Brien and I later named him Postmaster General. In that capacity, he was responsible for the study which recommended turning the Post Office Department into a self-sustaining government corporation. He was described as probably the first Cabinet officer in history to advocate the abolition of his job.

But all these events were in the future, and on November 22, 1963, I had no way of knowing what the future held. All I knew then was that I had inherited a talented staff and a distinguished Cabinet—but I had inherited neither their loyalty nor their enthusiasm. Those I would have to earn. That was the central problem I faced, not just with Kennedy appointees, but with much of the federal bureaucracy, with the Congress, and indeed with the entire nation. I had to prove myself.

Another immediate problem that confronted me was the mammoth task of preparing a $100 billion budget for the federal government in less than two months. Finally, I knew I must break the legislative deadlock which had delayed most of President Kennedy's programs on Capitol Hill. Congressional foot-dragging and refusal to enact vitally needed legislation were developing into a national crisis.

In all these areas time was the enemy. During my first thirty days in office I believe I averaged no more than four or five hours' sleep a night. If I had a single moment when I could go off alone, relax, and forget the pressures of business, I don't recall it.

Fortunately, a period of relative quiet enabled me to buy a little time on the international front, so that I was able to devote most of my energies to domestic concerns. On Saturday morning, November 23, I walked into Mac Bundy's office in the basement of the White House and received an international intelligence briefing from John McCone, Director of the Central Intelligence Agency. Bundy's office was just a few yards away from the Situation Room—a twenty-four-hour-a-day nerve center for all our diplomatic and intelligence activities. I had been in that windowless room before, during the Cuban missile crisis, waiting to learn whether the Russian response to our naval blockade would be reason or international suicide. I was to spend many more anxious hours there in the years ahead. But on that sad November morning in 1963 the international front was about as peaceful as it ever gets in these turbulent times. The world, it seemed, had ceased its turmoil for a moment—caught in the shock of John Kennedy's death.

President Kennedy had kept me well informed on world events, so I was not expecting any major surprises in that first intelligence briefing. Still, I was reassured to learn that there was nothing that required an immediate decision. McCone, a gray-haired, soft-spoken man, led me on a tour of the troubled globe, pointing out areas of unrest, international subversion, and potential crisis. I listened and asked an occasional question.

Only South Vietnam gave me real cause for concern. The next day, November 24, I received my first full-dress briefing from Henry Cabot Lodge, who had just returned to Washington from his post as Ambassador in Saigon. But compared with later periods, even the situation in Vietnam at that point appeared to be relatively free from the pressure of immediate decisions.

The most important foreign policy problem I faced was that of signaling to the world what kind of man I was and what sort of policies I intended to carry out. It was important that there be no hesitancy on my part— nothing to indicate that the U.S. government had faltered. It was equally important for the world to understand that I intended to continue the government's established foreign policies and maintain the alliances of Harry S. Truman, Dwight D. Eisenhower, and John F. Kennedy—policies of firmness on the one hand and an effort to thaw the Cold War on the other.

I used every public occasion available to me to get this point across. On November 26 I invited a number of Latin American representatives to the White House to discuss with them the future of the Alliance for Progress. Mrs. Kennedy sent me word that she would like to be present. With Mrs. Kennedy seated near me, I reaffirmed the pledge of her husband "to improve and strengthen the role of the United States in the Alliance for Progress for Latin America."

On November 27 I went before a Joint Session of Congress and declared:

In this age when there can be no losers in peace and no victors in war, we must recognize the obligation to match national strength with national restraint.

I pledged to the Congress, and to the country on nationwide television, that the United States would keep its commitments "from South Vietnam to West Berlin." On December 17 I addressed the UN General Assembly, stating that it was this nation's policy to help create a world that "can be safe for diversity and free from hostility."

Equally as important as the public forums during that first month in office was the opportunity I had to speak personally and privately with dozens of chiefs of state and heads of government who were in Washington to attend President Kennedy's funeral. On Monday, November 25, I met with President Charles de Gaulle of France. Just a few hours before our conversation, I received a report from Paris of a recent meeting between De Gaulle and an allied Ambassador. They had discussed what the European response would be in the event of a Soviet invasion of Western Europe. President de Gaulle, according to the report, had said that the United States could not be counted on in such an emergency. He mentioned that the United States had been late in arriving in two world wars and that it had required the holocaust of Pearl Harbor to bring us into the latter.

With this account fresh in my mind, I met with the French President. I thanked him for crossing the Atlantic to express the sympathy of France in our hour of sadness. The General spoke of the affection that both he and the French people had felt for John Kennedy. He then went on to say that the difficulties between our two countries had been greatly exaggerated, and that while changing times called for certain adjustments in our respective roles, the important thing was that Frenchmen knew perfectly well they could count on the United States if France were attacked.

I stared hard at the French President, suppressing a smile. In the years that followed, when De Gaulle's criticism of our role in Vietnam became intense, I had many occasions to remember that conversation. The French leader doubted—in private, at least—the will of the United States to live up to its commitments. He did not believe we would honor our NATO obligations, yet he criticized us for honoring a commitment elsewhere in the world. If we had taken his advice to abandon Vietnam, I suspect he might have cited that as "proof" of what he had been saying all along: that the United States could not be counted on in times of trouble.

In spite of all this, I decided after our meeting that the interests of our two nations were too close for me to indulge in petty bickering. I made it a rule for myself and for the U.S. government simply to ignore President de Gaulle's attacks on our policies and the doubts he had raised about the value of our pledges. Nothing he could say would, in my judgment, divert the French people from their friendship with the American people, a friendship firmly rooted in history.

Having met with the leader of France, our oldest ally, I turned to our relations with an adversary: the Soviet Union. On Tuesday morning, November 26, Soviet Deputy Premier Anastas Mikoyan came to my office. I knew that I was dealing with one of the shrewdest men ever to come up through the Communist hierarchy. One of the few surviving Bolsheviks with real power, Mikoyan had been brought to Moscow by Stalin in 1926, had escaped innumerable purges, and had demonstrated an uncanny ability to survive and to associate himself with the right faction at the right time.

We talked for fifty-five minutes and the conversation was not all diplomatic pleasantries. I remembered how Nikita Khrushchev had misjudged President Kennedy's character and underestimated his toughness after their 1961 meeting in Vienna. That misjudgment, many people believe, led Khrushchev to test the United States with a new crisis in Berlin. I considered it essential to let Mikoyan understand that while the United States wanted peace more than anything else in the world, it would not allow its interests, or its friends' and allies' interests, to be trampled by aggression or subversion.

I told Mikoyan that both Chairman Khrushchev and I would fail all humanity if we were unable to find a way in which the Communist and non-Communist worlds could live together peacefully. I noted that Mr. Khrushchev and President Kennedy had been making some progress toward that goal. "Under my administration," I said, "I can assure you that not a day will go by that we will not try in some way to reduce the tensions in the world."

Mikoyan said he was happy to hear those words from the new President of the United States, and he assured me of the Soviet Union's desire to live in peace and friendship. I told him that from the point of view of the United States peace and friendship between our two nations were constantly being strained by the Castro-prompted subversion in Latin America. Mikoyan's black eyes flashed. He said he could not understand how such a small nation as Cuba could subvert anyone, let alone a big power, and he asserted that he knew Cuba did not want to subvert anyone.

It was a cat-and-mouse game. I had seen a large number of reliable intelligence reports on Castro's activities throughout the hemisphere, and Mikoyan obviously knew that. I replied that I was merely trying to point up a major area of potential irritation between the United States and the Soviet Union. I said that the United States had no plans to invade Cuba and that we believed there was no justification for Cuba to invade others "by subversion or otherwise."

I did not expect Mikoyan to admit that Castro was exporting his revolution. But I did want him to get the message that we would not tolerate this. We ended the meeting on a note of hope. We both understood that the future of mankind depended on the actions of our two nations. I handed him a letter to take to Chairman Khrushchev expressing my desire to ease the tensions between our nations. The letter said:

November 26, 1963

Dear Mr. Chairman:

In addition to the public message which I have sent to you, I should like you to know that I have kept in close touch with the development of relations between the United States and the Soviet Union and that I have been in full accord with the policies of President Kennedy. I hope that we can make progress in improving our relations and in resolving the many serious problems that face us.

May I say that I am fully aware of the heavy responsibility which our two countries bear for the maintenance and consolidation of peace. I hope that we can work together for the achievement of that great goal, despite the many and complex issues which divide us. I can assure you that I shall devote myself to this purpose.

Sincerely yours,
Lyndon B. Johnson

Other letters to Khrushchev were to follow in January, extending the hand of peace.

One of the most urgent tasks facing me after I assumed office was to assure the country that everything possible was being done to uncover the truth surrounding the assassination of President Kennedy. John Kennedy had been murdered, and a troubled, puzzled, and outraged nation wanted to know the facts.

Led by the Attorney General who wanted no stone unturned, the FBI was working on the case twenty-four hours a day and Director J. Edgar Hoover was in constant communication with me. Some very disturbing facts about Lee Harvey Oswald were coming to light—notably, that he considered himself a Communist, that he had once given up his citizenship to live in Russia, and that when he finally returned to the United States, with a Russian wife, he immediately hoisted the banner of Fidel Castro.

What did all this mean? Was Oswald the killer? If so, was he carrying out orders from someone else? Did he have accomplices or did he act alone? There was hope, at least, that Oswald would supply the answers. But on Sunday, November 24, with millions of people watching on their television sets, Jack Ruby, a previously anonymous nightclub operator, walked calmly into the garage of the Dallas jail and shot Lee Harvey Oswald to death. The answers were lost, perhaps for all time.

With that single shot the outrage of a nation turned to skepticism and doubt. The atmosphere was poisonous and had to be cleared. I was aware of some of the implications that grew out of that skepticism and doubt. Russia was not immune to them. Neither was Cuba. Neither was the State of Texas. Neither was the new President of the United States.

Lady Bird had told me a story when I finally arrived at our home in northwest Washington on the night of November 22. She and Liz Carpenter had driven home immediately after our arrival at the White House, while I stayed on to work. On their way to our house, Liz had commented: "It's a terrible thing to say, but the salvation of Texas is that the Governor was hit."

And Lady Bird replied: "Don't think I haven't thought of that. I only wish it could have been me."

Now, with Oswald dead, even a wounded Governor could not quell the doubts. In addition, we were aware of stories that Castro, still smarting over the Bay of Pigs and only lately accusing us of sending CIA agents into the country to assassinate him, was the perpetrator of the Oswald assassination plot. These rumors were another compelling reason that a thorough study had to be made of the Dallas tragedy at once. Out of the nation's suspicions, out of the nation's need for facts, the Warren Commission was born.

The idea of a national commission was first mentioned to me by Eugene Rostow of the Yale Law School. He called the White House the day Oswald was shot and suggested that with the prime suspect now dead, a blue-ribbon commission was needed to ascertain the facts. Dean Rusk and columnist Joseph Alsop soon made the same recommendation to me.

While I was considering what sort of investigative body to commission for this task, two facts became abundantly clear. First, this could not be an agency of the Executive branch. The commission had to be composed of men who were known to be beyond pressure and above suspicion. Second, this represented too large an issue for the Texas authorities to handle alone. Several columnists reported that a "Texas commission" would be set up. Waggoner Carr, the Attorney General of Texas, considered setting up a board of inquiry. I urged him to examine every possible aspect and to explore all avenues fully, but I also told him that I hoped he would sit in on the national commission, and that is what he wisely did.

The commission had to be bipartisan, and I felt that we needed a Republican chairman whose judicial ability and fairness were unquestioned. I don't believe I ever considered anyone but Chief Justice Earl Warren for chairman. I was not an intimate of the Chief Justice. We had never spent ten minutes alone together, but to me he was the personification of justice and fairness in this country.

I knew it was not a good precedent to involve the Supreme Court in such an investigation. Chief Justice Warren knew this too and was vigorously opposed to it. I called him in anyway. Before he came, he sent word through a third party that he would not accept the assignment. He opposed serving on constitutional grounds. He said that if asked, he would refuse. He thought the President should be informed of that.

Early in my life I learned that doing the impossible frequently was necessary to get the job done. There was no doubt in my mind that the Chief Justice had to be convinced that it was his duty to accept the chairmanship of the commission. We had to bring the nation through that bloody tragedy, and Warren's personal integrity was a key element in assuring that all the facts would be unearthed and that the conclusions would be credible.

When the Chief Justice came into my office and sat down, I told him that I knew what he was going to say to me but that there was one thing no one else had said to him: In World War I he had put a rifle to his shoulder and offered to give his life, if necessary, to save his country. I said I didn't care who brought me a message about how opposed he was to this assignment. When the country is confronted with threatening divisions and suspicions, I said, and its foundation is being rocked, and the President of the United States says that you are the only man who can handle the matter, you won't say "no," will you?

He swallowed hard and said, "No, sir."

I had always had great respect for Chief Justice Warren. From that moment on I became his great advocate as well.

As for the makeup of the rest of the commission, I appointed the two men Bobby Kennedy asked me to put on it—Allen Dulles and John McCloy—immediately. Then I called each of the prospective members personally and obtained his agreement to serve. The final roster of the commission members included Chief Justice Warren, Senator Richard Russell of Georgia, Senator John Sherman Cooper of Kentucky, Representative Hale Boggs of Louisiana, Representative Gerald Ford of Michigan, former CIA Director Allen W. Dulles of Washington, and former U.S. High Commissioner of Germany John J. McCloy of New York. They all served with great distinction and great sacrifice.

The Warren Commission brought us through a very critical time in our history. I believe it fair to say that the commission was dispassionate and just.

If the days immediately following John Kennedy's death called for leadership, they also underlined the need for a renewed sense of national unity. I saw my primary task as building a consensus throughout the country, so that we could stop bickering and quarreling and get on with the job at hand. Unfortunately, the word "consensus" came to be profoundly misunderstood.

What consensus meant to some people was a search for the lowest common denominator, an effort to discover what programs were acceptable to a majority of the people before trying to obtain their enactment into law. Nothing could be further from the truth. In politics the lowest common denominator almost invariably means inaction, and that was the last thing we could afford.

To me, consensus meant, first, deciding what needed to be done regardless of the political implications and, second, convincing a majority of the Congress and the American people of the necessity for doing those things. I was President of the United States at a crucial point in its history, and if a President does not lead he is abandoning the prime and indispensable obligation of the Presidency. We did build a consensus. I think we did convince the vast majority of Americans that the time for stalling and procrastinating had passed; that the time for positive action had arrived.

I think that an off-the-record talk that I gave to forty of the nation's Governors on the evening of November 25 best summed up what I thought needed doing immediately, and what I believed we should do in the future. I wish now that we had released the full text of those remarks, because I think this would have given the country a better understanding of what I was trying to accomplish.

I believed it was important to make the Governors understand that the federal government was not an alien power that threatened the authority of their states; rather the purpose of the federal establishment was to help the states solve their problems, as a partner. I told the Governors that I had never questioned the capacity or the sincerity or the ability of a man because he belonged to a different political party. No party had an overriding claim to patriotism. The times, I said, demanded that we put away our differences and close ranks in a determined effort to make our system of government function.

"We are going to have plenty of time after the conventions to get out and campaign and talk about ourselves and our merits," I told them. "Let's talk about our country until then and let's not just talk about it, but let's get some action on it and do something."

I said that we were going to honor our commitments abroad but that we were going to try to avoid rash actions that could result in World War III. I told them that we lived under a system of checks and balances and that for the past few years Congress had certainly been exercising its check on the Chief Executive—with the result that little legislation was being passed. Of immediate importance, I said, was the passage of a tax reduction. I pledged that my administration would be prudent, frugal, and thrifty in an effort to justify a tax reduction which I believed was necessary for the health of the economy. Another bill of immediate concern was the civil rights measure, which was also stalled on Capitol Hill. I tried to convince the Governors that the nation could not live with racial tensions much longer.

I talked to them about the mood of the country, about all the hatred and bitterness and uncertainty that we were experiencing in the wake of President Kennedy's assassination. As I spoke, I was really thinking about my program for the years ahead:

> We have hate abroad in the world, hate internationally, hate domestically where a President is assassinated and then they [the haters] take the law into their own hands and kill the assassin. That is not our system. We have to do something about that. We have to do something about the hate and you have to get to the root of hate. The roots of hate are poverty and disease and illiteracy, and they are broad in the land.

That meeting with the Governors foreshadowed the strategy of what came to be known as consensus and the foundation of the Great Society.

Teddy Roosevelt used to call the Presidency a "bully pulpit." During my first thirty days in office I preached many sermons from that pulpit. I knew I had to secure the cooperation of the people who were the natural leaders of the nation. I talked with those leaders, from every walk of life.

I talked with the Cabinet members and impressed on them the fact that even though John Kennedy was dead, it was the responsibility of every one of us to keep the business of the country moving ahead. I asked them to remain in their posts and to speak frankly and candidly with me always. I spoke before a Joint Session of Congress, and in pleading for a continuation of President Kennedy's programs I asked the Congress to pledge its help in enacting these programs into law. I spoke with black groups and with individual leaders of the black community and told them that John Kennedy's dream of equality had not died with him.* I assured them that I was going to press for the civil rights bill with every ounce of energy I possessed.

I talked regularly with the congressional leaders from both sides of the aisle and urged them to start the legislative machinery moving forward. I particularly remember a telephone conversation with Senator Everett Dirksen of Illinois. I asked him to convey to his Republican colleagues, in the Senate and throughout the nation, that it was essential to forget partisan politics, so that we could weather the national crisis in which we were involved and unite our people. There was a long pause on the other end of the line and I could hear him breathing heavily. When he finally

---

* During my first two weeks in office, I met individually with Roy Wilkins, Whitney M. Young, Jr., Martin Luther King, Jr., James L. Farmer, A. Philip Randolph, and Clarence Mitchell.

spoke, he expressed obvious disappointment that I would even raise the question of marshaling his party behind the President.

"Well, Mr. President," he said, "you know I will." And he did.

I spoke with such captains of industry as Roger Blough of U.S. Steel, Frederick Kappel of AT & T, Henry Ford II of the Ford Motor Company, W. B. Murphy of Campbell Soup, Frank Stanton of CBS, George R. Brown of Brown & Root, and Thomas J. Watson, Jr., of IBM. I made it clear that the days of labor-management feuds should end, and that the economic pie was big enough for everyone—and growing much faster than our population. I pointed out that the more people who were employed and working at good wages, the more people there would be to buy their products. I asked them to help me persuade Congress to pass the tax reduction legislation, so that we could infuse new vitality into the economy and put more people to work.

I spoke with the nation's labor leaders, including George Meany of the AFL-CIO, Walter Reuther of the United Auto Workers, Joseph A. Beirne of the Communications Workers, and A. Philip Randolph of the Brotherhood of Sleeping Car Porters. I told them we needed their help in passing such urgently required measures as Medicare, higher minimum wages, and civil rights. I praised them for opening their ranks to black workers, but I told them they would have to do even better in the months and years ahead.

I spoke with government workers and warned them that we must not let the nation falter or hesitate. I told them that even in an hour of tragedy we must move ahead with assurance. I spoke with foreign Ambassadors and emphasized that we coveted no territory and sought to dominate no nation. "We want nothing that anyone else has, but we do want peace in the world."

I brought people together who under ordinary circumstances would have fled at the sight of each other. But these were not ordinary times and most Americans were ready to rise above past differences. I spoke with some of the nation's leading newspeople, including Merriman Smith, James Reston, William S. White, Walter Lippmann, Joseph Alsop, Ben McKelway, Gene Pulliam, Russ Wiggins, Kay Graham, and many others. I spoke to former Presidents, to religious leaders, to old friends, and to old adversaries.

But I didn't just talk; I listened carefully to what my visitors had to say. After I had listened, I always returned to my basic theme: People must put aside their selfish aims in the larger cause of the nation's interest. They must start trusting each other; they must start communicating with each other; and they must start working together.

I pleaded. I reasoned. I argued. I urged. I warned.

There were a few—former high government officials, elder statesmen, and long-time advisers to Presidents—who needed no convincing; who only wanted to offer their services. Among them were three former Presidents, two of whom belonged to another party. Each pledged his loyalty, his support, and his help in any way he could give it. Herbert Hoover, although ailing, sent word to me through our mutual friend Richard Berlin of Hearst newspapers: "I am ready to serve our country in any capacity from office boy up."

President Truman gave me many good suggestions and wise counsel from his own experience of being suddenly thrust into the Presidency. He pledged his support for our efforts in Vietnam. He told me he had faced the same problems of aggression—in Greece and Turkey and Korea. He said that if we didn't stand up to aggression when it occurred, it would multiply the costs many times later. He said that his confrontation of those international challenges—particularly in Korea—had been horrors for him politically, bringing his popularity down from a high of 87 per cent to a low of 23 per cent. But he said they represented his proudest achievements in office. He told me always to bear in mind that I was the voice of *all* the people. A few of the big voices, he said, would try to drown me out from time to time, but the duty of the President was to lead and champion the people's causes.

President Eisenhower drove down to Washington from Gettysburg on November 23, the day after President Kennedy's assassination. After spending the better part of an hour with me in my office in the Executive Office Building, he went to my outer office, picked up a yellow tablet, and began writing in longhand the things he would do if he were in my place. He then asked if General Andrew Goodpaster's former secretary, Alice Boyce, was still working in the White House. He knew her and he trusted her. I told him that she was working for McGeorge Bundy, and he asked if she could come over to work with him. After dictating from his notes to Miss Boyce, he told her to make only two copies of the memorandum—"one for the President and one for me."

CONFIDENTIAL

NOTES FOR THE PRESIDENT

In accordance with your request, I present below for your consideration certain recommendations:

1. Because of your known competence in the judgment and integrity of Robert Anderson, I would suggest that in the near future you send for him to confer on general subjects, and particularly those of a fiscal and financial character.

2. I bring to your attention two men—one an officer without any partisan allegiance, and the other a Democrat. I believe it would be profitable for you to talk to Mr. Gordon Gray, an ex-Secretary of the Army, and General Good-

paster, who is now an assistant to the Chairman of the Joint Chiefs of Staff. Both of these men are highly experienced in many types of organization, and particularly in the kind of organizational machinery that could be valuable to the President in obtaining thoroughly studied analyses of important international factors and in making certain that the decisions of the President are carried out even to minute detail. For the abilities and patriotism of these two men I personally vouch.

3.   I am bold enough to suggest that you call a Joint Session of the Congress to make a speech of not over ten or twelve minutes. I think it might cover the following points:

A.   Point out first that you have come to this office unexpectedly and you accept the decision of the Almighty, who in His inscrutable wisdom has now placed you in the position of highest responsibility of this nation.

B.   You are sworn to defend the Constitution and execute the laws. In doing so you will follow the instincts, principles and convictions that have become a part of you during many years of public service. No revolution in purpose or policy is intended or will occur. Rather it will be your purpose to implement effectively the noble objectives so often and so eloquently stated by your great predecessor.

C.   You realize that if we are to have effective implementing programs, the first necessity is a close cooperation with the Congress. To achieve this cooperation, you will go more than half way.

D.   Equally, it is your purpose to establish and sustain the closest possible relation with every segment of the American economy so as to achieve a healthy climate for economic expansion and reduction of unemployment. Therefore, you will cooperate with management, with labor, and with capital. In such a cooperative effort there must be mutual confidence and good faith; you intend to offer no special favors and you pledge there will be no persecution. One matter of immediate and urgent import is the possibility of a prompt tax cut. On the necessity of such a cut you believe we all agree. In order to make even more firm the basis for such a cut, it will be your purpose to reduce the expenditures of fiscal year 1964—so far as may be profitable but consistent with our nation's security. It will be your further purpose to present the budget for 1965 in connection with any subsequent expenditures so that they will not exceed those of 1964 except in the case of unforeseen emergency. Other important legislation may have to go over until the opening of the next session, but the interval will give you time to present your specific recommendations to the Congress on all those matters of an important character.

E. Conclusion: You hope that people of government and the entire nation may now mobilize their hearts, their hands and their resources for one purpose—to increase the spiritual and material resources of the nation and to advance her prestige and her capacity for leadership in the world for peace.

Dwight D. Eisenhower

I was deeply moved that the former President should go into such specific detail and give me his recommendations and his support. President Eisenhower's concern was a source of solid encouragement and strength to me when both were sorely needed.

Much of the job of building a consensus had to be accomplished before John Kennedy was buried, while the flags hung at half-staff in the gray chill that had settled over the Capitol and before we had paid our final tribute to the fallen President. Like every American, my own spirit was heavy with grief; but the work had to go on. For me and for the top leadership of the government, those days were marked by a strange counterpoint. There was the frenzied pace of meetings and briefings held behind closed doors, then the measured cadence of the funeral march; there was the harsh glare of office lights burning deep into the night, then the somber hush and the dim, soft light in the East Room from the four large candles flanking John Kennedy's coffin.

I remember marching behind the caisson to St. Matthew's Cathedral. The muffled rumble of the drums set up a heartbreaking echo off the buildings along Seventeenth Street and Connecticut Avenue.* I remember the long procession that wound its way to Arlington National Cemetery. We stood in chill and silence for the final firing of salute and the folding of the flag— then made our way back across the river to the waiting appointments, the manifold meetings, the ringing phones, the stacks of reading material, the endless, unavoidable, demanding details.

The most significant advantage I had during the transition period was a genuine desire for national unity on the part of most people. Americans had learned, in the cruelest way possible, where hatred and divisiveness could lead the nation, and I think they were ready to try another route. My task was to show them the way, using the "bully pulpit" of the Presidency. Those were frantic days. I recall holding my first news conference on December 7 and being asked how I felt about the prospect of spending my first night in the White House—that evening.

"I feel like I have already been here a year," I replied.

Under our system of government, with its clearly defined separation of powers, the greatest threat to the Chief Executive's "right to govern" comes

---

* I saw Mrs. Kennedy often and spoke with her regularly on the phone. She wrote me on November 26, thanking me for walking behind President Kennedy's coffin to the church. "You did not have to do that—I am sure many people forbid you to take such a risk—but you did it anyway," she wrote. Once, on the telephone, she insisted that I take a nap every day to conserve my energy. "It changed Jack's whole life after he became President," she said. And in the depth of her mourning, she had the thoughtfulness to call us from the White House on Thanksgiving evening to wish us well.

traditionally from the Congress. Congress is jealous of its prerogatives. All too often that jealousy turns into a stubborn refusal to cooperate in any way with the Chief Executive.

The Congress had been in such a mood from the first day that John Kennedy took office in 1961, and the situation had been getting worse instead of better. On paper, the 1960 election had given the Democrats an 89-vote majority in the House and a 28-vote majority in the Senate, but those majorities were only on paper. An entire program of social legislation proposed by President Kennedy—from aid to education to food stamps to civil rights—remained bottled up in committee, while the Congress defiantly refused to budge or act in any way.

This situation had grown so intolerable that when I assumed office, a month before the end of the year, more than half of the appropriations bills remained unpassed—which meant that the federal government had been operating on billions of dollars' worth of promises since July 1. We had not faced a similar situation in thirty-two years. I remember telling Senator Dirksen that "we're going to be in a hell of a shape if the Congress won't even pay its own bills."

In October 1963, shortly before President Kennedy's assassination, columnist Walter Lippmann surveyed the stalemate and wrote:

> This is one of those moments when there is reason to wonder whether the Congressional system as it now operates is not a grave danger to the Republic. There are two great measures before Congress, and in all probability Senator Goldwater was right when he said the other day that "the President has to make up his mind whether he wants the Civil Rights Bill or a tax cut, because he cannot get them both." . . . This Congress has gone further than any other within memory to replace debate and decision by delay and stultification. The President first announced his plan to seek a reduction of taxes in order to stimulate the economy on August 13, 1962. That was over a year ago. A tax bill passed the House last week. But the Senate has not even begun to hold hearings. . . . I do not see how a modern government can be conducted successfully if on a major issue, such as fiscal policy, the Executive is refused for more than a year a debate and a decision.

Another column put the matter more succinctly a week later: "Congress is beginning to look like a sit-down strike."

We were, in my opinion, facing a real crisis, and it was more than a crisis of unfulfilled needs throughout the nation. There was also a crisis of confidence in our system of government. There was a clear reason for moving forward, and moving with dispatch and energy; for acting while the sobering influence of national tragedy caused men in all walks of life to think of the country's interests rather than their own.

I recognized, as did many others, including some of my advisers and some of my old and trusted counselors from Capitol Hill, that an activist program involved enormous political risks. As a new President with no electoral mandate and with barely a full month of preparation available before it would be necessary to face the reconvening Congress, I knew the effort to break the legislative logjam might be foredoomed. Furthermore, I was acutely aware that if the effort was undertaken and failed to produce results, the consequences might be fatal to all future hopes of passing the legislation that we needed so desperately.

On the other hand, I had learned from Speaker Rayburn in the House— and from my own experience with a Senate majority of one—that narrow majorities in a legislative body can, with leadership, produce results that far outstrip their numbers. "With a big, unwieldy majority on your side," Mr. Rayburn used to say, "half your people are back home campaigning, or off on vacation someplace because they don't think their individual votes are that important. But with a thin majority, you can develop a strong sense of party discipline and be assured that every man will be on the floor for a crucial vote."

The most important factor that influenced my decision to press for congressional action was this: If any sense were to come of the senseless events which had brought me to the Office of the Presidency, it would come only from my using the experience I had gained as a legislator to encourage the legislative process to function as the modern era required. I felt that if we were going to move we would have to move quickly, so that we could establish some semblance of unity before the bigots and the dividers moved in. As I said at the congressional leadership breakfast in the White House on December 3: "I don't anticipate a very long honeymoon —especially with a Presidential election only a few months away."

What I wanted to do more than anything was to try to unify the leaders in the administration, the leaders in the two parties, and the leaders in the Congress—for a while at least, until we could get Congress into action. I wanted to persuade people to begin consulting each other again. Frankly, I was not certain I could get a single bill through Congress. The ultraconservative Democrats and the Republicans in tandem had put a block on everything. Together their numbers had outstripped and outmaneuvered the administration forces. But I knew I had to try.

Two bills headed my list of priorities, not only because of their merits and the national needs they represented but also because of their symbolic importance. If we could get the tax reduction bill and the civil rights bill passed, we would win valuable prestige in reestablishing some degree of Executive leadership in Congress. I knew there was no hope of getting either bill passed before the end of the year, but I decided to begin laying the groundwork.

The key to the tax reduction bill was the budget. The administrative budget recommended to President Kennedy shortly before his death was $102.2 billion. The revenue estimates were $93.1 billion. These figures indicated a deficit of $9 billion. To ask the Congress to reduce taxes in the face of a budget imbalance amounting to $9 billion was the nearest thing to asking it to pass a joint resolution endorsing sin. Harry Byrd of Virginia and other conservatives in the Senate would not go along with it, and it was Byrd's conservative Senate Finance Committee that was in a position to kill the bill or pass it.

I spread the word as quickly and as clearly as I could: Start reviewing the budget, start cutting expenditures; nothing is sacred. My fiscal advisers argued against budget reduction. They reiterated that we needed a tax cut to stimulate the economy; that unless we obtained the tax cut, there would be a marked slowdown in the economy in the last half of 1964. Thus, they argued, the tax bill would *not* further imbalance the budget but would actually produce more revenues in the long run.

I told them they might be able to sell me on the New Economics, but not Harry Byrd.

They argued that the budget had already been cut to the bone. They didn't see how they could get any more out of it. I told them that in my judgment they could have their budget intact or they could have their tax cut, but that Congress would not give them both. Looking at it in that light, they decided to see if they could get some more fat out of the budget.

I worked as hard on that budget as I have ever worked on anything. I was thoroughly familiar with the budget process from my years in Congress, but that experience is a different thing from drawing up your own budget, one that reflects your own political philosophy and your own priorities. To the average citizen, the federal budget is a dry, unfathomable maze of figures and statistics—thicker than a Sears-Roebuck catalog and duller than a telephone directory—which adds up to the huge outlay of his tax dollars. In reality, it is a human document affecting the daily lives of every American. The budget determines how many unemployed men and women are going to be trained; how many hungry children are going to be fed; how many poor people are going to be housed; how many sick people are going to be cared for; how many schoolchildren are going to receive federal aid for books; and how our entire population is going to be protected against a possible enemy attack.

Every cut in the budget affects some segment of our society, so even when cuts are necessary they are never made casually. Day after day I went over that budget with the Cabinet officers, my economic advisers, and the Budget Director. I studied almost every line, nearly every page, until I was dreaming about the budget at night.

At the same time, we began a comprehensive economy drive to cut all excess expenditures throughout the government. We asked each department and agency head to reexamine his programs for possible expenditure cuts, and we made some meaningful reductions. On December 7, for example, we announced that the Defense Department was planning a series of steps to save $1.5 billion in the current fiscal year and $4 billion by fiscal 1967. Such announcements had the added advantage of making newspaper headlines and generating favorable editorials and news stories, which added to the pressure on the Senate Finance Committee. They also helped to reassure the country. A recent Harris poll had indicated that the most unpopular aspect of the Kennedy administration was what the public considered fiscal irresponsibility. I knew that we had to turn that feeling around.

We also worked closely with private nonpartisan groups to distribute information about the economy and the effect that a tax cut would have on it. One group was the Citizens' Committee for Tax Reduction and Revision, composed of forty-five leaders of small business, labor, agriculture, housing, welfare, and education. The Business Committee for Tax Reduction was another strong ally. I met with both of these groups in the White House and explained that every month of delay on the tax measure meant that about $550 million was being withheld in taxes which would otherwise be pumped into the economy.

When I delivered my first State of the Union message to the Congress— on January 8—I tried to impart a sense of urgency by discussing first the tax cut and then the 1965 budget. I announced that the budget I would soon submit would be the smallest since 1951 in proportion to our gross national product. At $97.9 billion, $4 billion less than the previous year's request, this budget allowed us to cut our projected deficit in half.

The civil rights bill—designed to end segregation in public restaurants and hotels—was another matter. Civil rights was both an emotional and a moral issue. As an emotional issue, it contained the seeds of rebellion on Capitol Hill—not just over civil rights, but over my entire legislative program. As a moral issue, however, it could not be avoided regardless of the outcome. John Nance Garner, a great legislative tactician, as well as a good poker player, once told me that there comes a time in every leader's career when he has to put in all his stack. I decided to shove in all my stack on this vital measure.

I did so against the advice of staff members and long-time advisers whose judgment I greatly respected. I remember two particularly heated debates in the first few days of my Presidency: one at my home, The Elms, and another in my office in the Executive Office Building.* Some of those pres-

---

* I had insisted that Mrs. Kennedy take her time in moving from the White House. Mrs. Johnson and I therefore remained in residence at The Elms until December 7. The Attorney General notified me when the Presidential office was vacated, and I worked out of my Vice Presidential office until then, Tuesday morning, November 26.

ent urged me not to push for the civil rights bill. They did not think the bill could be passed.

"Mr. President," one of them said, "you should not lay the prestige of the Presidency on the line."

"What's it for if it's not to be laid on the line?" I asked.

Five days after assuming office I appeared before a Joint Session of Congress and "laid it on the line" as strongly as I knew how. "We have talked long enough in this country about equal rights," I told my former colleagues. "We have talked for one hundred years or more. It is time now to write the next chapter, and to write it in the books of law."

The decision to press for the civil rights bill was not without penalties for me. It was destined to set me apart forever from the South, where I had been born and reared. It seemed likely to alienate me from some of the Southerners in Congress who had been my loyal friends for years.

Sometime after the bill had been passed, I was having lunch at the LBJ Ranch with a judge whom I had known from boyhood. I was reading a speech to him that I was shortly going to deliver to the White House conference "To Fulfill These Rights." I came to the passage announcing my intention to ask Congress to pass a federal jury reform bill to preclude all-white juries when blacks were on trial.

"One clear concern," I read from the speech, "is the jury—the cornerstone of our system of justice in this country. If its composition is a sham, its judgment is a shame. And when that happens, justice itself is a fraud, casting off the blindfold and tipping the scales one way for whites and another way for Negroes."

My friend was very upset at that passage. He thought I ought to omit it.

"Why?" I asked.

"Because I don't think it's pertinent. I haven't seen an all-white jury with a Negro defendant in several years."

"Do you remember old Otto so-and-so?" I asked him, naming a boy we had both grown up with.

"Yes, I remember him."

"Well, when Otto was in high school he drank too much beer one Saturday night and drove to a dance at Albert.* The first thing he did was walk in and announce to the entire dance hall that he could 'lick any Dutch knucklehead in the house.'

"At that, a great big German farm boy with biceps like boulders grabbed Otto by his shirt collar and said, 'Vot you say?'

" 'I can whip any Dutch knucklehead in the house,' Otto repeated. 'Are you a Dutch knucklehead?'

" 'No, no,' the farm boy said.

_____
* A German community near Johnson City.

" 'Well, then,' said Otto, 'I wasn't talking about you.'

"So, I am not talking about *you*," I said to my friend. We laughed and the tension passed.

But to me there is more pain than humor in that story. Just as the judge had reacted to my statement personally, so many people who had stood by me for many years decided I was "talking about them" when I decried injustice and bigotry in America. Some of them believed I had let them down, once I had reached the pinnacle of power.

But the issue could not be avoided. I was not just the President of Southern Americans or white Americans. I was the President of all Americans. I believed that a huge injustice had been perpetrated for hundreds of years on every black man, woman, and child in the United States. I did not think that our nation could endure much longer as a viable democracy if that injustice were allowed to continue.

While we were planning our long-range strategy and laying the groundwork for passage of the tax bill and the civil rights bill, we found ourselves faced with a test of Executive authority that we had not counted on. This grew out of the foreign aid appropriations bill that the Congress had been considering at the time of President Kennedy's assassination.

The administration wanted to sell surplus wheat to Russia and to the Communist nations of Eastern Europe. We wanted to be able to sell the grain on credit if we considered it necessary and in the best interest of the United States. However, Senator Karl Mundt, a Republican from South Dakota, introduced an amendment to the bill which would have prohibited the Export-Import Bank or any other federal agency from guaranteeing loans to finance trade with any Communist country. The vote on the amendment was scheduled for Tuesday, November 26—the day after President Kennedy's funeral.

I called Larry O'Brien as soon as we returned to the White House from the funeral and asked him to take a head count of the Senate. He was still in his formal striped trousers. I knew the emotional strain he was under, but Larry is a professional. He understood the importance and the urgency of the task and he immediately went to work. We could not afford to lose a vote like that, after only four days in office. If those legislators had tasted blood then, they would have run over us like a steamroller when they returned in January, when much more than foreign aid would depend on their actions.

All of us worked far into the night on that amendment. We defeated it by a vote of 57 to 36. But the crisis did not end there. On December 16 the House passed a foreign aid appropriations bill with a credit restriction identical to the Mundt amendment. Again we had to turn our attention to the Senate in an effort to have the amendment deleted when the bill came up there. Again the Senate voted down the restriction.

The two foreign aid bills then went to a Senate-House conference committee to resolve the differences, and we concentrated our efforts on keeping the Mundt amendment out of the final bill. Time was becoming more crucial each day, for the Congressmen were anxious to end the session and return to their homes for Christmas.

After several days of debate, on December 20, the conferees agreed to permit the Export-Import Bank credit guarantees if the President felt it was in the national interest to use them. Just as we were congratulating ourselves, the House, on December 21, refused to accept the conference version of the bill. The House was still demanding restrictions. To complicate matters, many pro-administration Congressmen had already left town for the Christmas holidays.

The bill went back to conference, and upon the advice and with the help of Speaker John McCormack of Massachusetts and Democratic Floor Leader Carl Albert of Oklahoma, I decided to call House members back to town for another vote. This was a rash gamble and many advisers thought I was unwise to take it. Some of them argued that the Congressmen, already tired and testy, would be furious at being called back to Washington. Others said that by calling them back I was really calling their bluff. If I lost the vote, it would be a serious blow to the President's prestige. But I concluded that if I permitted the opposition to tack on that amendment, I would be powerless in January anyway. I called them back.

To soften the blow, Lady Bird and I held a Christmas reception in the White House on December 23, just a few hours before Christmas Eve. Many members of Congress and their wives were present, and I took the opportunity to stand up on a chair in the State Dining Room and plead my case with our guests.

The next morning, the day before Christmas, the House met at an unprecedented 7 A.M. session and accepted a second conference report without the Mundt amendment credit restrictions. At that moment the power of the federal government began flowing back to the White House.

A weary Congress headed for home. An even wearier President boarded *Air Force One* and flew to the LBJ Ranch for the Christmas holidays.

I had just completed one of the most trying and most intensive, sustained efforts of my life. While I knew there would be hard days ahead—and bitterly fought battles—I knew at least that the reins of government were firmly in my hands for a while. And I believe the nation knew it too.

Four days after assuming office we witnessed one of the first evidences that we were gaining the support and confidence of the American people. On November 26—the first day the New York Stock Exchange was open after the assassination—the stock market staged the biggest one-day rally in the history of the Dow Jones Industrial Averages up to that time. The averages were up 32.03 points.

There *was* a consensus—a broad, deep, and genuine consensus among most groups within our diverse society—which would hold together, I hoped and prayed, long enough for the important tasks to be accomplished.

We had finally begun to break up the stubborn legislative barriers behind which so much serious and vital legislation had languished. The major battles lay ahead, but we had won our first big test with the Congress. We had pruned the budget far below the level that anyone had believed possible, and we had put the power and prestige of the Presidency solidly behind the most sweeping civil rights bill since Reconstruction. I felt so confident about having broken the legislative logjam that I thought it was safe to add some proposals—including a comprehensive and unprecedented poverty measure—to the list of "must legislation" for the coming session. I also organized many task forces, made up of new and active people, to develop legislation in my long-time favorite fields: health, education, conservation, environmental control, civil rights, and aid for the aged.

The next ten months saw the passage of the tax bill, the civil rights bill, the food stamp bill, the War on Poverty, the Urban Mass Transit Act, the Housing Act, the Wilderness Areas Act, the Fire Island National Seashore Act, and the Nurse Training Act. The next ten months also saw a new spirit of cooperation among our people, a national recommitment to the cause of civil rights, new initiatives in the field of international disarmament, and a surge of fresh vitality in our economy.

Looking back, I believe that John Kennedy would have approved of the way his successor brought the nation together and mobilized its energies in the wake of tragedy, uncertainty, and doubt. That remains one of the great satisfactions of my Presidency.

3

Steady on Course
[*VIETNAM 1963–1964*]

As *Air Force One* CARRIED US swiftly back to Washington after the tragedy in Dallas, I made a solemn private vow: I would devote every hour of every day during the remainder of John Kennedy's unfulfilled term to achieving the goals he had set. That meant seeing things through in Vietnam as well as coping with the many other international and domestic problems he had faced. I made this promise not out of blind loyalty but because I was convinced that the broad lines of his policy, in Southeast Asia and elsewhere, had been right. They were consistent with the goals the United States had been trying to accomplish in the world since 1945.

President Kennedy believed in our nation's commitment to the security of Southeast Asia, a commitment made in the SEATO Treaty and strengthened by his predecessor, President Eisenhower. President Kennedy had explained on many occasions the reasons he took this position. By late 1963 he had sent approximately 16,000 American troops to South Vietnam to make good our SEATO pledge.

His words, almost his last words in public, were fresh in my mind. That last morning, at breakfast with the Chamber of Commerce of Fort Worth, he had talked almost exclusively of America's international role. He had underlined the critical importance of the United States to the safety and stability of the rest of the world. He had recalled our pledges and our alliances. And he had said:

> So this country, which desires only to be free, which desires to be secure, which desired to live at peace for eighteen years under three different administrations, has borne more than its share of the burden, has stood

watch for more than its number of years. I don't think we are fatigued or tired. We would like to live as we once lived. But history will not permit it. The Communist balance of power is still strong. The balance of power is still on the side of freedom. We are still the keystone in the arch of freedom, and I think we will continue to do as we have done in our past, our duty. . . .

Those final words regarding "our duty" would apply, I resolved, to the Johnson administration as well. Our policy would be "steady on course." At a Joint Session of Congress on November 27, 1963, five days after I was sworn in, I gave my solemn pledge to the Congress and to the people of the United States: "We will keep our commitments from South Vietnam to West Berlin."

My first exposure to details of the problem of Vietnam came forty-eight hours after I had taken the oath of office. Ambassador Henry Cabot Lodge had flown to Washington a few days earlier for scheduled conferences with President Kennedy, Secretary of State Dean Rusk, and other administration officials. I sent for him and asked him to give me a firsthand account of recent events. I wanted his estimate and felt it was important that he go back to Saigon with a clear understanding of my personal views. We met in my office in the Executive Office Building. Secretaries Rusk and Mc-Namara were there, as well as Under Secretary of State George Ball, CIA Director John McCone, and McGeorge Bundy.

Lodge was optimistic. He believed the recent change of government in Saigon was an improvement. He was hopeful and expected the new military leaders to speed up their war efforts. He stated that our government had put pressure on the regime of Ngo Dinh Diem to change its course. Those pressures, he admitted, had encouraged the military leaders who carried out the coup on November 1, 1963. However, if Diem and his brother Nhu had followed his advice, Lodge said, they would still be alive. In his last talk with Diem on the afternoon of November 1, Lodge had offered to help assure the Vietnamese leader's personal safety, but Diem had ignored the offer.

I turned to John McCone and asked what his reports from Saigon in recent days indicated. The CIA Director replied that his estimate was much less encouraging. There had been an increase in Viet Cong activity since the coup, including more VC attacks. He had information that the enemy was preparing to exert even more severe pressure. He said the Vietnamese military leaders who carried out the coup were having difficulties organizing their government and were receiving little help from civilian leaders. Mc-Cone concluded that he could see no basis for an optimistic forecast of the future.

I told Lodge and the others that I had serious misgivings. Many people were criticizing the removal of Diem and were shocked by his murder.

Congressional demands for our withdrawal from Vietnam were becoming louder and more insistent. I thought we had been mistaken in our failure to support Diem. But all that, I said, was behind us. Now we had to concentrate on accomplishing our goals. We had to help the new government get on its feet and perform effectively.

I told Lodge that I had not been happy with what I had read about our Mission's operations in Vietnam earlier in the year. There had been too much internal dissension. I wanted him to develop a strong team; I wanted them to work together; and I wanted the Ambassador to be the sole boss. I assured him of full support in Washington. In the next few months we sent Lodge a new deputy, a new CIA chief, a new director of the U.S. Information Agency (USIA) operations, and replacements for other key posts in the U.S. Embassy. By midyear General William C. Westmoreland had replaced General Paul Harkins as head of our Military Assistance Command.

As our meeting drew to a close, I spoke about our general attitude toward Vietnam and the rest of Southeast Asia. I told my advisers that I thought we had spent too much time and energy trying to shape other countries in our own image. It was too much to expect young and underdeveloped countries to establish peace and order against well-trained and disciplined guerrillas, to create modern democratic political institutions, and to organize strong economies all at the same time. We could assist them with all three jobs, I said, but the main objective at present was to help them resist those using force against them. As for nation-building, I said that I thought the Vietnamese, Thai, and other peoples of Asia knew far better than we did what sort of nations they wanted to build. We should not be too critical if they did not become thriving, modern, twentieth-century democracies in a week.

In addition to my talk with Ambassador Lodge, I discussed the Honolulu meeting, held just before the assassination, with some of the principal participants—especially Rusk and McNamara—and with Mac Bundy and others. The net result of the Honolulu briefings and discussions was a modestly encouraging assessment of prospects in Vietnam, though Secretaries Rusk and McNamara expressed some reservations. Nonetheless, they reaffirmed the estimate that we could begin withdrawing some of our military advisers by the end of the year and a majority of them by the end of 1965. Most of my counselors believed that over the next two years the South Vietnamese should be able to take over the training, supply, and support functions that our forces were performing.

The Honolulu report, originally prepared for President Kennedy, emphasized three problem areas in particular. One was the new and inexperienced government that had taken power in Saigon, and its need for our strong support. Another was the problem of dealing with a predicted $100 million deficit in the South Vietnamese budget in 1964. Unless handled properly, that budget imbalance could undermine everything the Vietnamese were doing militarily and politically. We had to explore what more we could do through our AID and military assistance programs, and what the Vietnamese could do for themselves through additional taxes, austerity measures, and other possible actions. Finally, those at the Honolulu meeting believed it was of the greatest importance that the U.S. Mission in Vietnam be a unified team and that there be the fullest consultation among them, especially between military and civilian elements. My advisers urged that previous divisiveness be eliminated.

While the mid-Pacific conference had not changed their overall assessment on Vietnam, President Kennedy's principal foreign affairs advisers agreed that it was important to underline, especially within government circles, the continuity of policy and direction under the new President. I agreed and on November 26 approved National Security Action Memorandum 273.* It was my first important decision on Vietnam as President, important not because it required any new actions but because it signaled our determination to persevere in the policies and actions in which we were already engaged.

NSAM 273, addressed to the senior officers of the government responsible for foreign affairs and military policy, began:

> It remains the central objective of the United States in South Vietnam to assist the people and Government of that country to win their contest against the externally directed and supported communist conspiracy. The test of all U.S. decisions and actions in this area should be the effectiveness of their contribution to this purpose.

The memorandum restated our goal concerning the withdrawal of U.S. advisory forces as described on October 2 in a White House statement following the McNamara-Taylor report. With reference to past bickering within the official American community, I said I expected that "all senior officers of the government will move energetically to insure the full unity of support for established U.S. policy in South Vietnam." The NSAM also assigned various specific actions to the appropriate department or agency of government. Among other things, it defined the Mekong Delta as the area of greatest potential danger in the coming months.

This was the view of Vietnam I received during those first few tense days in office. It was a view shared by the top levels of our Mission in Saigon and by my principal advisers in Washington. I had one important reservation about this generally hopeful assessment. I believed the assassi-

---

* A National Security Action Memorandum (NSAM) was a formal notification to the head of a department or other government agency informing him of a Presidential decision in the field of national security affairs and generally requiring follow-up action by the department or agency addressed.

nation of President Diem had created more problems for the Vietnamese than it had solved. I saw little evidence that men of experience and ability were available in Vietnam, ready to help lead their country. I was deeply concerned that worse political turmoil might lie ahead in Saigon.

I knew from my conversations with them that this worry was shared increasingly by Secretaries Rusk and McNamara. When McNamara made his estimate early in October, foreseeing the end of our principal job in Vietnam in about two years, he made it clear that his judgment was based on the assumption that political confusion in Vietnam would not affect military operations. The same assumption underlay the Honolulu conclusions. As time passed it became increasingly questionable whether this was a valid assumption.

Still, we remained convinced that the new Vietnamese leaders were determined to win the fight for their country's freedom and independence. Our increasing assistance was having a favorable effect on morale and performance. Unless there were unforeseen setbacks, such as further changes in the government, McNamara felt the United States could begin pulling its military advisers home on schedule, and our major effort, as far as personnel was concerned, could be ended by the close of 1965. We concluded that outlays for military and economic assistance would probably have to increase as the Vietnamese stepped up their campaign against the Viet Cong.

When a President makes a decision, he seeks all the information he can get. At the same time, he cannot separate himself from his own experience and memory. This is especially true when his decisions involve the lives of men and the safety of the nation. It was natural, as I faced critical problems during those first few months in office, that I should recall crises of the past and how we had met them or failed to meet them. No one who had served in the House or Senate during the momentous years of the 1930s, 1940s, and 1950s, as I had, could fail to recall the many highs and lows of our performance as a nation. Like most men and women of my generation, I felt strongly that World War II might have been avoided if the United States in the 1930s had not given such an uncertain signal of its likely response to aggression in Europe and Asia.

I could not forget the refusal of the House of Representatives in 1939 and 1940 to provide $5 million in funds for the strengthening of Guam, for fear of antagonizing the Japanese. I could not forget the long and difficult fight over the Selective Service Act in 1940, when major wars were already being fought in both Europe and China. I remembered the 1-vote margin (203–202) in the House by which the length of service for draftees was extended half a year only four months before Pearl Harbor.

Many Americans were convinced that the League of Nations failed in the 1930s largely because the United States had refused to join and support that organization. This conviction was in our minds when we took the lead in organizing the United Nations. But with the end of fighting in 1945 we almost repeated the errors of the past by dismantling too quickly the huge military force we had developed. Our haste provided an irresistible temptation to Stalin, who moved to consolidate control over Eastern Europe by 1948 and simultaneously exerted increased pressure on Western Europe. We righted the balance barely in time through the Marshall Plan and the North Atlantic Treaty Organization.

In 1947 I was in the heat of the legislative battle over President Truman's proposal to give economic and military aid to Greece and Turkey. It was clear from that debate that the voices of isolationism and appeasement had not been completely stilled, despite the painful lessons of the past. I remember standing on the floor of the House as a young Congressman during the debate and saying:

> We all want to avoid war. If we could clearly foresee the future and know with certainty that defeat of this measure would, in the words of one great appeaser, mean "peace in our time," or that its passage would mean war in this generation, our votes would be unanimous. No one wants war. The tongues of our dead still enforce our attention. We all want peace. The issue, then, is one of calculated risks.
>
> That issue cannot be resolved by an appeal to fear, to sentiment, or to any other prejudice. Each must determine for himself and within his own conscience the path he thinks this country, in dignity and responsibility, must follow to lead the world in the ways of peace. The passage of this bill and the policy it embraces is costly. Once we so act, we are committed to a course we must see through. And none should indulge in the self-deception that it will not be expensive. Peace in this day is not cheap. . . .

I concluded:

> Decisions must be made in times of danger, and I hope your decision will be mine. In terms of dollars, the Truman doctrine will be costly. But I pray that we are still a young and courageous nation; that we have not grown so old and fat and prosperous that all we can think about is to sit back with our arms around our money bags. If we chose to do that, I have no doubt that the smoldering fires will burst into flame and consume us—dollars and all.

The aid that saved Greece and Turkey won approval from the Congress, but over the opposition of more than one hundred Representatives and twenty-three Senators.

Another day stood out sharply in my memory—June 27, 1950, the day President Truman decided that American military force would be used to resist aggression in Korea. The day after that decision was made I sat down and wrote a letter to our Commander in Chief. I told President Truman that I admired and was grateful for his courage. I told him that I thought most Americans shared my feeling that his response to the challenge in Korea had reaffirmed our capacity for world leadership. I promised to do everything I could as a Senator to contribute to the success of the President's policy.*

The spirit that motivated us to give our support to the defense of Western Europe in the 1940s led us in the 1950s to make a similar promise to Southeast Asia. The Southeast Asia Collective Defense Treaty was signed in Manila on September 8, 1954, by representatives of seven countries— Australia, France, New Zealand, Pakistan, the Philippines, Thailand, and the United Kingdom—as well as the United States. The principal American delegates at the Manila meeting were Secretary of State John Foster Dulles, Senator H. Alexander Smith of New Jersey, and the present Senate Majority Leader, Mike Mansfield of Montana.

On the first day of February 1955 Senator Hubert Humphrey of Minnesota rose in the Senate and moved that the SEATO treaty be considered immediately. The Senate agreed. The text of the treaty was read and the separate articles were discussed in detail. The Senate then approved the treaty by a vote of 82 to 1. The only dissenting voice was that of Senator William Langer of North Dakota, a long-time opponent of the United Nations, NATO, and other forms of U.S. involvement in the world. Among my old Senate colleagues who gave their advice and consent to SEATO that day were Aiken and Case, Fulbright and Gore, Mansfield and Morse.

Thirteen Senators were absent the day SEATO was approved. Most were away on personal business; a few were ill. Among the latter was one Senator who within a few years, as President, would honor the promise his nation had made: John F. Kennedy of Massachusetts. I too was absent, recovering from surgery at the Mayo Clinic.

In the key portion of the treaty, Article IV, each party recognized that armed aggression in Southeast Asia against a treaty member or a protocol state protected by the treaty, of which South Vietnam was one, "would endanger its own peace and security." Each pledged that in the event of armed aggression, it would "act to meet the common danger in accordance with its constitutional processes." Any action taken under SEATO would be reported immediately to the UN Security Council. It was further agreed that steps to resist aggression would be taken only "at the invitation or with the consent of the government concerned."

* For the text of my letter to President Truman see Appendix, p. 573.

I believe every Senator understood what his vote for the Southeast Asia treaty meant. We all knew how deeply concerned President Eisenhower was about the danger of Communist aggression in that area. In 1953, soon after taking office, he had said that "aggression in Korea and Southeast Asia are threats to the whole free community to be met by united action." In 1954, as the Indochina situation worsened, he wrote to Winston Churchill. His message to the British Prime Minister stated convictions I had heard him express in private:

> It is no solution simply to urge the French to intensify their efforts. And if they do not see it through and Indochina passes into the hands of the Communists, the ultimate effect on our and your global strategic position with the consequent shift in the power ratios throughout Asia and the Pacific could be disastrous and, I know, unacceptable to you and me. . . . This has led us to the hard conclusion that the situation in Southeast Asia requires us urgently to take serious and far-reaching decisions.

In presenting the Southeast Asia treaty to the Senate, Secretary of State Dulles spelled out its main purposes: to deter Communist aggression and subversion in Southeast Asia, and to help defeat them if they could not be deterred.

Before the Senate Foreign Relations Committee on November 11, 1954, Secretary Dulles spoke in detail about the antisubversion aspect of the treaty, which he described as a "novel feature" of the pact. He said:

> . . . as I pointed out, we deal with that in this treaty more specifically than we have with any other treaty. We recognize the danger more clearly. I must admit that the mere fact of recognizing the danger does not mean that we automatically have found a way to meet the danger. Subversion in that area is a very difficult thing to combat. It is virulent, it is well organized, it is effectively prosecuted by trained persons, and the task of meeting the threat will tax our resources and ingenuity to the utmost. . . . This threat is most acute at the moment in Vietnam, but, as I indicated, there are threats of the same character as to Laos, Cambodia, Thailand, and Malaya; and Burma and Indonesia are not free from that danger.
>
> Therefore, I think it is of the utmost importance that we should have an early meeting of the signatories in which we begin to think of ways and means to meet this subversive threat which is recognized by the treaty as being a particular danger in this area.

In its report to the full Senate, the Foreign Relations Committee spelled out the meaning of the Southeast Asia treaty with great clarity. The committee's report stated:

> The Southeast Asia Treaty is a long step toward a more comprehensive, collective security arrangement, which has been regarded as desirable by the administration and the committee.

The committee is not impervious to the risks which this treaty entails. It fully appreciates that acceptance of these additional obligations commits the United States to a course of action over a vast expanse of the Pacific. Yet these risks are consistent with our own highest interests. There are greater hazards in not advising a potential enemy of what he can expect of us, and in failing to disabuse him of assumptions which might lead to a miscalculation of our intentions.

I respect a Langer, even if I disagree heartily with him, when he argues against our having any involvements in Europe or Asia or the rest of the world—and votes his convictions. I respect far more an Eisenhower or a Kennedy who sees our responsibilities in the world and acts to carry them out. I have little understanding for those who talk and vote one way, and after having given our nation's pledge, act another; for those who stand firm while the sun is shining, but run for cover when a storm breaks. The protection of American interests in a revolutionary, nuclear world is not for men who want to throw in our hand every time we face a challenge.

Under President Eisenhower American economic and military assistance to South Vietnam increased. It helped give the young republic strength and confidence. When the Vietnamese people voted for Ngo Dinh Diem to replace former Emperor Bao Dai as Vietnam's chief of state in late 1955, most Western experts thought the new country would last little more than six months. Long years of war had weakened it. The French had given very few Vietnamese a chance to acquire skills or experience in government and administration. It seemed certain that the highly disciplined Communists would take over. But under Diem's leadership the South Vietnamese moved forward. Non-Communist Vietnam began to heal its wounds and to prosper. The small country absorbed about 900,000 refugees who fled from Ho Chi Minh's rule in the North. Production increased; so did exports; so did the number of schools. Living standards rose. South Vietnam was making progress.

Ho Chi Minh and his colleagues in Hanoi had long dreamed of controlling all of Vietnam and the rest of Indochina. By the end of the 1950s that dream was fading fast. But in the period after the first Sputnik Communists everywhere were in an optimistic, aggressive mood. Khrushchev boasted that the Soviets would surpass the United States in production during the 1960s; Mao Tse-tung claimed the East Wind was prevailing over the West Wind; Castro took control in Cuba; Moscow laid down its ultimatum on Berlin. For Ho Chi Minh, there was unfinished business: to conquer Laos and South Vietnam.

In Laos the Communist-dominated Pathet Lao controlled two northern provinces which had been assigned to it in the Geneva Accords of 1954 to regroup its military forces "pending a political settlement." These the Pathet Lao converted into a base from which to extend Communist power.

In South Vietnam the Communists had many agents and an underground apparatus. They had stockpiled thousands of weapons when the French began to pull out. The Communists had never abandoned terrorism and sabotage in the South, but in the late 1950s the order went out from Hanoi to begin a large-scale campaign of violence. The main target was the Diem government. Ho Chi Minh seemed confident that with Diem out of the way, his followers in the South would have no trouble taking over.

President Eisenhower was reacting to this situation when he spoke at Gettysburg College in Pennsylvania in April 1959. He said:

> Because of the proximity of large Communist military formations in the North, Free Vietnam must maintain substantial numbers of men under arms. Moreover, while the government has shown real progress in cleaning out Communist guerrillas, those remaining continue to be a disruptive influence in the nation's life. . . .
>
> Strategically South Vietnam's capture by the Communists would bring their power several hundred miles into a hitherto free region. The remaining countries in Southeast Asia would be menaced by a great flanking movement. The freedom of twelve million people would be lost immediately and that of one hundred fifty million others in adjacent lands would be seriously endangered. The loss of South Vietnam would set in motion a crumbling process that could, as it progressed, have grave consequences for us and for freedom. . . .
>
> We reach the inescapable conclusion that our own national interests demand some help from us in sustaining in Vietnam the morale, the economic progress, and the military strength necessary to its continued existence in freedom.

By the final months of 1960 the situation in Vietnam had worsened and in Laos it was, if anything, even more critical. President Eisenhower was convinced that further Communist successes could be a disaster for Southeast Asia and for the United States as well. But 1960 was an election year and Eisenhower, as he later told me, felt he should not make a major commitment that another President would have to carry out. He expressed his views strongly, however, in a meeting with President-elect Kennedy the day before the latter's inauguration. I was not at the meeting but I read the reports of three of the participants.

Eisenhower was deeply concerned about the disintegration in Laos. He considered that country vital to the security of neighboring Thailand and South Vietnam. He said it was imperative that Laos not fall under Communist control. The United States would have to help defend it—preferably with its allies if they would act, alone if they would not. That warning of the former President was fresh in the mind of John F. Kennedy at his inauguration on January 20, 1961, when he said:

> Let every nation know, whether it wishes us well or ill, that we shall

pay any price, bear any burden, meet any hardship, support any friend, oppose any foe to assure the survival and the success of liberty.

During the first months of the Kennedy administration the situation in Laos deteriorated. Communist forces, supported and supplied by North Vietnam, were on the march. The Soviet Union organized an airlift that carried large quantities of war supplies from Hanoi to the Laotian Communists. President Kennedy, at a news conference on March 23, 1961, devoted special attention to the threat in Laos. He cited the danger of "the present armed attacks by externally supported Communists" and recalled our special treaty obligations to help oppose aggression in Laos under SEATO. The United States, he said, was not going to be "provoked" into action, but our country was going to honor its obligations.

Soon, however, some of the heat went out of the Laos situation. This was not accidental. President Kennedy passed the word quietly around Washington that he did not rule out sending limited forces into the Mekong Valley. Military units on Okinawa were alerted. A small unit of marines moved into Thailand. These preparations did not go unnoticed, as Khrushchev told the President later in Vienna. In any case, an uneasy ceasefire was arranged in Laos, and before the middle of May representatives of fourteen nations assembled in Geneva to work out a Laos settlement, including conditions for that country's neutralization. Geneva in 1954 had failed to establish peace in Laos; perhaps in 1961 it would produce something better. At least that was our hope. As the possibility of a negotiated settlement in Laos increased, the administration focused its attention more closely on Vietnam.

After the 1960 election, President-elect Kennedy invited me to Palm Beach to discuss working arrrangements for the new administration. He had several specific jobs he wanted me to do, especially to represent him on overseas trips. He mentioned Asia in particular. Early in May President Kennedy invited me to his office. He recalled that we had talked earlier about my going to the Far East and he said he thought the time had come. He wanted me to take a close, hard look at what was happening there. Above all, he wanted me to go to Vietnam and confer with President Diem. He said the Vietnamese were in trouble and we had to help them, but they had to help themselves too. He wanted my views on the situation and recommendations for the future.

He also asked me to visit the Philippines, Taiwan, Thailand, India, and Pakistan. This would be my first trip to the Far Pacific since World War II, and my first visit to Vietnam. I looked forward to going because I was convinced that an important chapter in the future of mankind would be written in Asia. More than half the human race lived there, and the region was rapidly awakening and developing. Pearl Harbor and a long and bloody war had made it clear that we Americans were a Pacific as well as an Atlantic people. Our national interest and our own security dictated that we help establish in Asia the sort of stable and peaceful order among nations that has been the principal goal of our foreign policy since the end of World War II.

There were elements in Asia bent on a very different kind of order. The leaders of North Korea had demonstrated that they were willing to use force to get what they wanted. We had defeated them in the early 1950s, but they were still dangerous. Ho Chi Minh was another leader willing to use force to realize his dreams: Communist control over all of Vietnam as well as Laos and Cambodia. Peking had helped North Korea and was helping Ho Chi Minh. Red China's leaders preached the doctrine of violence and wars of "national liberation." So there was both hope and danger in Asia, and I wanted to see for myself as much of the region as possible.

On May 8, 1961, President Kennedy wrote to Ngo Dinh Diem and asked me to deliver the letter in person. Kennedy told President Diem he was "ready to join with you in an intensified endeavor to win the struggle against communism and to further the social and economic advancement of Vietnam.

"If such an expanded joint effort meets with your approval," he added, "we are prepared to initiate in collaboration with your government a series of joint, mutually supporting actions in the military, political, economic, and other fields. We would propose to extend and build on our existing programs, including the Counterinsurgency Plan, and infuse into our actions a high sense of urgency and dedication."

The President then spelled out ways he thought American assistance could best be used: to support 20,000 additional regular Vietnamese troops under our Military Assistance Program; to enlarge the size and mission of our Military Assistance Advisory Group; to support the 68,000-man Civil Guard; to strengthen the Vietnamese Junk Fleet; and to cooperate in other programs. He also offered to send economic experts to work with the Vietnamese in developing "a financial plan on which our joint efforts can be based." Before departure, I discussed my mission and its purpose in detail with Senators Mansfield and Fulbright and other congressional leaders.

The next day, May 9, Mrs. Johnson and I left Washington aboard a Presidential jet. President Kennedy's sister Jean and her husband, Stephen Smith, went with us. Members of my staff and representatives of the Departments of State and Defense made up the rest of the party. We arrived in Saigon the evening of May 11.

The next morning I rode to Independence Palace for my first meeting with President Diem. Ambassador Fritz Nolting accompanied me. I knew Diem was a hard bargainer and a proud man, and I expected differences on more than one issue. The Vietnamese President received us cordially. After exchanging greetings and gifts, as is customary, we immediately got down to business. I gave Diem the President's letter and sat back while he read it. Then he responded, one by one, to President Kennedy's proposals, and in less than three hours we had agreed on all of them. After I received President Kennedy's approval from Washington, we issued a joint communiqué the following day listing the fundamental elements of our agreement.

One major U.S. newspaper headlined its report on the communiqué as follows: "U.S.-Vietnam Announce Plan to Guard Asia." Several papers forecast that if the steps agreed upon in Saigon proved inadequate, the Kennedy administration was ready to do more. Most press reports emphasized the statement in the communiqué that the steps about to be taken "may be followed by more far-reaching measures if the situation, in the opinion of both governments, warrants."

From Saigon we flew to Manila, then on to Taipei, Bangkok, New Delhi, and Karachi. We returned to Washington on May 24. From Andrews Air Force Base outside the capital I flew by helicopter to the White House to report to President Kennedy on the trip. I spoke in detail about each of the countries we had visited and its main problems and gave my impressions of the various government leaders I had met. In summing up, I told the President that the main conclusion I had brought back from the trip was this:

> The fundamental decision required of the United States—and time is of the greatest importance—is whether we are to attempt to meet the challenge of Communist expansion now in Southeast Asia by a major effort in support of the forces of freedom in the area or throw in the towel. This decision must be made in a full realization of the very heavy and continuing costs involved in terms of money, of effort and of United States prestige. It must be made with the knowledge that at some point we may be faced with the further decision of whether we commit major United States forces to the area or cut our losses and withdraw should our other efforts fail. We must remain master of this decision. What we do in Southeast Asia should be part of a rational program to meet the threat we face in the region as a whole. It should include a clear-cut pattern of specific contributions to be expected by each partner according to his ability and resources. I recommend we proceed with a clear-cut and strong program of action.

President Kennedy shared this estimate. He regarded our commitment to Southeast Asia as a serious expression of our nation's determination to resist aggression. As President, he was determined to keep the promises we had made. He understood what they meant, and what they might mean in the future.

The day before President Kennedy announced my trip to Southeast Asia he had a long talk with Senator Fulbright, Chairman of the Senate Foreign Relations Committee. They discussed Southeast Asia and the possibility that our involvement there might require American forces. After the meeting, Fulbright told reporters about his talk with the President. *The New York Times* began its report of the Senator's comments as follows:

Senator J. W. Fulbright strongly indicated tonight that the Kennedy Administration was considering the possibility of direct military intervention to counteract Communist threats in South Vietnam and Thailand.

The Arkansas Democrat, who is chairman of the Senate Foreign Relations Committee, said he would support the moves in South Vietnam and Thailand if they were considered necessary and if the nations concerned wished them.

The Kennedy-Fulbright discussion pointed up what everyone concerned with Southeast Asia in the administration knew after President Eisenhower's talk with the President-elect just before inauguration—that keeping our word might mean spilling our blood.

Following up on the agreement I had reached with Diem, President Kennedy sent to Vietnam a special economic mission headed by Dr. Eugene Staley of the Stanford Research Institute. The six-man mission hammered out with the Vietnamese specific details of the general agreement we had reached in May. Its report, submitted to the President at the end of July, proposed several programs of increased assistance, including a 15 per cent boost in Vietnam's armed forces and a long-range development program.

During the summer and fall the situation continued on the downgrade in Vietnam. Hanoi sent more men into the South, especially trained political agents, saboteurs, and military technicians. The Viet Cong relied increasingly on terrorism and assassination. Government officials, even technicians and schoolteachers, were singled out as preferred targets. Diem and his government asked for additional help.

President Kennedy realized that more had to be done if South Vietnam was to survive the onslaught. But before acting, he wanted to know several things: Was there real hope that South Vietnam could remain independent with American help? What forms of assistance would be most effective? He asked one of the United States' most distinguished soldiers, former Chief of Staff General Maxwell D. Taylor, to assemble a team of experts to go to Vietnam for a thorough look. The Taylor mission, composed of civilian and military specialists, was asked to study every aspect of the situation and then to recommend actions—military, political, economic, intelligence, and psychological—to help Vietnam resist the aggression that was slowly succeeding in the South. The Taylor mission left Washington on October 15, 1961, and General Taylor submitted his recommendations to the President on November 3.

Following this visit President Diem put into writing the request for additional assistance which he had made through the American Ambassador in Saigon. On December 7, 1961, he wrote to President Kennedy as follows:

> Mr. President, my people and I are mindful of the great assistance which the United States has given us. Your help has not been lightly received, for the Vietnamese are proud people, and we are determined to do our part in the defense of the free world. . . .
>
> But Viet-Nam is not a great power and the forces of international communism now arrayed against us are more than we can meet with the resources at hand. We must have further assistance from the United States if we are to win the war now being waged against us.
>
> We can certainly assure mankind that our action is purely defensive. Much as we regret the subjugation of more than half of our people in North Viet-Nam, we have no intention, and indeed no means, to free them by use of force. . . .
>
> When communism has long ebbed away into the past, my people will still be here, a free united nation growing from the deep roots of our Vietnamese heritage. They will remember your help in our time of need. This struggle will then be a part of our common history. And your help, your friendship, and the strong bonds between our two peoples will be a part of Viet-Nam, then as now.

In his answer to Diem on December 14, 1961, President Kennedy wrote:

> Your letter underlines what our own information has convincingly shown—that the campaign of force and terror now being waged against your people and your Government is supported and directed from the outside by the authorities at Hanoi. They have thus violated the provisions of the Geneva Accords designed to insure peace in Viet-Nam and to which they bound themselves in 1954.
>
> At that time, the United States, although not a party to the Accords, declared that it "would view any renewal of the aggression in violation of the agreements with grave concern and as seriously threatening international peace and security." We continue to maintain that view.
>
> In accordance with that declaration, and in response to your request, we are prepared to help the Republic of Viet-Nam to protect its people and to preserve its independence. We shall promptly increase our assistance to your defense effort. . . .

The President had by that time studied carefully the Taylor report and its recommendations. He had consulted his principal advisers and had decided to adopt most of the proposals Taylor and his colleagues had suggested. This meant expanding the U.S. Military Assistance Advisory Group, assigning our men to work directly with Vietnamese combat units, and increasing our support for the South Vietnamese government and armed forces. The number of American military advisers serving with the Vietnamese was increased about 400 per cent, from about 700 late in 1961 to 3,400 by mid-1962. We sent planes and helicopters to give the Vietnamese army greater mobility. We increased assistance to the Vietnamese navy to enable it to protect the coast against infiltration from the North and to patrol the inland waterways used extensively by the Viet Cong. A new command—the Military Assistance Command, Vietnam—was formed, with General Paul Harkins in charge, to direct all aspects of the expanding U.S. effort.

President Kennedy also decided to give the Diem government additional specialists in administration and in such fields as agriculture, health, education, information, and finance. This effort failed, however, to bring about urgently needed administrative reform at the top level of the government in Saigon. I do not know whether such an effort could have succeeded, but I do know that it was not tried in any intensive or effective way, and we paid a heavy price for that failure later.

General Taylor and his group recommended sending to South Vietnam a military task force composed largely of combat engineers. General Taylor proposed that this force work with the Vietnamese initially to repair the effects of a devastating flood which had recently swept over many of the Mekong Delta provinces. Such a force would have provided an emergency reserve to back up the Vietnamese army in case of a serious military crisis. Many of our officers feared that the Viet Cong were preparing a major offensive in the Central Highlands. President Kennedy did not accept this proposal, nor did he reject it. He deferred action. We had mobile forces assigned to the Seventh Fleet and additional troops were on Okinawa and elsewhere in the area. I believe he planned to depend on those forces, which could have been moved quickly in an emergency.

In his report to the President, General Taylor not only analyzed the existing situation in Vietnam and suggested what needed to be done about it but also looked ahead to what might come and told the President what he considered the most critical problem we faced. Taylor reported:

> While we feel that the program recommended represents those measures which should be taken in our present knowledge of the situation in Southeast Asia, I would not suggest that it is the final word. Future needs beyond this program will depend upon the kind of settlement we obtain in Laos and the manner in which Hanoi decides to adjust its conduct to that settlement. If the Hanoi decision is to continue the irregular war declared on South Vietnam in 1959 with continued infiltration and covert support of guerrilla bands in the territory of our ally, we will then have to decide whether to accept as legitimate the continued guidance, training, and support of a guerrilla war across an international boundary,

while the attacked react only inside their borders. Can we admit the establishment of the common law that the party attacked and his friends are denied the right to strike the source of aggression, after the fact of external aggression is clearly established? It is our view that our government should undertake with the Vietnamese the measures outlined herein, but should then consider and face the broader question beyond.

General Taylor added:

It is my judgment and that of my colleagues that the United States must decide how it will cope with Khrushchev's "wars of liberation" which are really para-wars of guerrilla aggression. This is a new and dangerous communist technique which bypasses our traditional political and military responses. While the final answer lies beyond the scope of this report, it is clear to me that the time may come in our relations with Southeast Asia when we must declare our intention to attack the source of guerrilla aggression in North Vietnam and impose on the Hanoi Government a price for participating in the current war which is commensurate with the damage being inflicted on its neighbors to the South.

This warning from one of his most trusted military advisers had considerable impact on the President. Discussions at the time made it clear that President Kennedy did not consider the conflict in Vietnam as an internal matter or a civil war. It was a carefully planned campaign of naked aggression controlled from and by Hanoi. Two months later, in his January 1962 message to Congress on the State of the Union, President Kennedy said of Vietnam:

The systematic aggression now bleeding that country is not a "war of liberation"—for Vietnam is already free. It is a war of attempted subjugation—and it will be resisted.

The following month the President sent his brother, Attorney General Robert Kennedy, to Vietnam following a visit to Indonesia. At a news conference in Saigon on February 18, 1962, Robert Kennedy told the assembled correspondents: * "We are going to win in Vietnam. We will remain here until we do win." He said that "Vietnam's struggle to preserve its independence against Communist aggression is a grave one which affects free countries everywhere.

"This is a new kind of war," the Attorney General continued, "but war it is in a very real sense of the word. It is war fought not by massive divisions but secretly by terror, assassination, ambush and infiltration.

"Hanoi may deny its responsibility," he added, "but the guilt is clear. In a flagrant violation of its signed pledge at Geneva in 1954, the North

---

* Quotations from Attorney General Kennedy's news conference in Saigon are from the account in *The New York Times* of February 19, 1962.

Vietnamese regime has launched on a course to destroy the Republic of Vietnam."

He concluded: "The American people will see Vietnam through these times of trouble to a period when the Vietnamese people will find a long-sought opportunity to develop their country in peace, dignity and freedom."

That was the mood in Washington, the mood of the President and his top advisers, as the administration expanded its participation in the defense of Vietnam and Southeast Asia in 1962. By autumn of that year the tide of battle was moving in favor of the South. The influx of American military advisers and trainers, for both ground and air forces, was a great boost for the South Vietnamese. Helicopters and transports gave their armed forces a mobility they had never known, and they began to take the fight to the Viet Cong. Though the turnaround was not 180 degrees, the trend was in the right direction. South Vietnamese military men and politicians, who had been sunk in gloom in 1961, began to realize that their country had a chance to survive.

The optimism did not last long, for several reasons. First, it quickly became obvious that the North Vietnamese had no intention of living up to the solemn promises they had made at Geneva on July 23, 1962, in the Declaration on the Neutrality of Laos. In that declaration the North Vietnamese, together with all other participants, gave their word that

> they will not introduce into the Kingdom of Laos foreign troops or military personnel in any form whatsoever . . .;
>
> they will not establish nor will they in any way facilitate or connive at the establishment in the Kingdom of Laos of any foreign military base, foreign strong point or other foreign military installation of any kind;
>
> they will not use the territory of the Kingdom of Laos for interference in the internal affairs of other countries;
>
> they will not use the territory of any country, including their own, for interference in the internal affairs of the Kingdom of Laos.

In addition, they agreed that

> all foreign regular and irregular troops, foreign para-military formations and foreign military personnel shall be withdrawn from Laos in the shortest time possible. . . .

The North Vietnamese never pulled their forces out of Laos as they had promised to do. They never stopped sending men and war supplies to assist the Pathet Lao. More important for South Vietnam, Hanoi continued using the jungle trails and roads of eastern Laos and the panhandle to move fighting forces and war matériel into the South in support of its aggression there. The North Vietnamese did not even permit the coalition government of Laos or the International Control Commission to exercise their functions in the Communist-held areas of Laos. The Russians had given their word at Geneva that the North Vietnamese would honor the agreement. Moscow's negotiator, Georgi Pushkin, assured Assistant Secretary of State Averell Harriman that the Soviets could "guarantee" North Vietnam's adherence to the treaty. Despite periodic reminders of their pledge, the Russians failed to force Hanoi to live up to its word. The Ho Chi Minh Trail remained open for business. The failure to obtain North Vietnamese compliance with the Laos Accords of 1962 was a bitter disappointment to President Kennedy.

There was another reason the modest successes of late 1962 were not enlarged and multiplied in 1963. This was internal disruption inside South Vietnam in opposition to the Diem government and, especially, in fearful reaction to Diem's brother Nhu, who was quietly taking the levers of power into his own hands. Trouble had been brewing for some time, and it burst into the open in the ancient capital city of Hué on May 8, 1963. On that day 8,000 to 10,000 Buddhists marched in protest against a government order banning parades and the display of Buddhist flags on Buddha's birthday. Army troops fired into the crowds, killing nine persons. The disorder soon spread to Saigon and other cities. A long, tense summer of protest had begun. A number of monks committed suicide, dying in flames on the streets. The government responded by sending police and special-forces units into Buddhist pagodas across the country, arresting Buddhist leaders. The protest spread to students in the universities, then the high schools. There were more arrests. A large number of those jailed were related to government officials, army officers, and businessmen. Bitterness against the regime, especially against Nhu, reached fever pitch.

Opinion was sharply divided in the U.S. Mission about the course we should pursue. Similar differences divided the official family in Washington. Some experts argued that there was no way to "win with Diem." Others thought that if Nhu left Vietnam, unity could be restored. Others believed that whatever his weaknesses and mistakes, Diem was the only qualified leader on the scene. They favored encouraging him to settle his differences with his opponents and get on with fighting the Viet Cong and building his country.

This controversy led to a crucial decision that never received the serious study and detached thought it deserved. Too much emotionalism was involved. After the attacks on the Buddhist pagodas, a message prepared in the State Department was sent to Saigon on August 24. In effect, it told Ambassador Lodge to advise Diem that immediate steps had to be taken to correct the situation and to meet the outstanding Buddhist demands. If Diem did not act promptly, the Ambassador was instructed to advise key Vietnamese military leaders that the United States would not continue to support the Saigon government militarily or economically. This ultimatum meant the removal of Nhu and his politically active wife from any continued influence or responsibility in the government. If Diem refused, the United States could no longer support him. If the military leaders then took over, we would support them.

This hasty and ill-advised message was a green light to those who wanted Diem's downfall. Once the Ambassador acted on his instructions, preparations for a coup were stimulated. In my judgment, this decision was a serious blunder which launched a period of deep political confusion in Saigon that lasted almost two years. In the weeks that followed President Kennedy urged the Diem government to change its attitude and method of operation. He had not revised his assessment of our role there or of the importance of South Vietnam to Southeast Asia and our own security. He opposed a U.S. withdrawal, which some people were beginning to urge. He continued to believe that the conquest of South Vietnam would have the most serious impact on Asia and on us.

In an interview with CBS early in September 1963, President Kennedy was asked about Diem's prospects. He said:

> Our best judgment is that he can't be successful on this basis. We hope that he comes to see that; but in the final analysis it is the people and the government itself who have to win or lose this struggle. All we can do is help, and we are making it very clear, but I don't agree with those who say we should withdraw. That would be a great mistake. That would be a great mistake. . . .

A week later, in a similar interview with NBC, the President was asked if he had any reason to doubt "this so-called 'domino theory.' " He answered:

> No, I believe it. I believe it. I think that the struggle is close enough. China is so large, looms so high just beyond the frontiers, that if South Vietnam went, it would not only give them an improved geographic position for the guerrilla assault on Malaya but would also give the impression that the wave of the future in Southeast Asia was China and the Communists. So I believe it.

Late in September President Kennedy asked Secretary McNamara and General Taylor, then Chairman of the Joint Chiefs of Staff, to go to Vietnam for another firsthand look. Events there beginning in May had raised questions in the President's mind about prospects for success against the Viet Cong in the short run, as well as about the long-range effectiveness of our effort.

They returned on October 2 and reported immediately to President Kennedy that "the military campaign has made great progress and continues to progress." They concluded that while the unpopularity of the

Diem government was growing, political strife had not yet affected military operations. If that continued to be true, they believed we could bring home some of our military advisers by the end of 1963. Vietnamese forces could begin taking over most or all of the functions then being performed by Americans, and most of our men could be withdrawn by the end of 1965. They warned that continued political disruption could affect the military situation as well as their estimate for the future. The chief findings of the McNamara-Taylor mission were made public in a White House statement that same day.*

The coup against the South Vietnamese regime finally took place on November 1, only twenty-one days before President Kennedy's death. Diem called Ambassador Lodge on the phone and our envoy offered assistance to assure the President's personal safety, but Diem did not respond. Diem and Nhu tried to locate military forces willing to come to their defense. They failed. The two brothers then escaped from the palace, but they were discovered hiding in a church in the Chinese sector of Saigon the next morning and were captured. They were killed in the rear of an armored personnel carrier en route to Vietnamese military headquarters.

There were profound regrets in Washington, as there should have been. Those regrets deepened as political confusion swept in waves over Saigon in the following months. But then it was too late to reconsider. President Kennedy was deeply concerned about the effects of the overthrow of Diem. One of his final acts concerning Vietnam was to order his principal advisers and the top echelon of our Mission in Saigon to conduct a full-scale review of all aspects of the situation. More than forty senior U.S. officials, including Secretary of State Rusk and Secretary of Defense McNamara, Chairman of the Joint Chiefs Taylor, Director of CIA McCone, Ambassador Lodge from Vietnam, and top military commanders in the Pacific and Vietnam, gathered in Honolulu on November 20. Fate decreed that their report would come to me and not to the man who had requested it. Vietnam and the consequences of Diem's murder became mine to deal with.

As I dug deeper into the Vietnam situation over the following weeks, I became convinced that the problem was considerably more serious than earlier reports had indicated. Rusk, McNamara, McCone, Bundy, and others shared my growing concern. At the beginning of December I read a review of the military situation developed by the State Department's intelligence analysts. This report concluded that the military effort had been deteriorating in important ways for several months. Early in December Ambassador Lodge sent in a detailed study of a key province prepared by

---

* For the text of the White House statement see Appendix, page 574.

one of his field representatives. The document reported that in that northern delta province "the past thirty days have produced . . . a day-by-day increase in Viet Cong influence, military operations, physical control of the countryside, and Communist-controlled combat hamlets."

I believe two things were wrong with the reporting in 1963: an excess of wishful thinking on the part of some official observers and too much uncritical reliance on Vietnamese statistics and information. Many Vietnamese officials and officers in the field apparently reported as fact what they thought their own government wanted to hear. Some of our officials in turn accepted many of those reports at face value.

Secretary McNamara was preparing to go to Europe for a NATO meeting early in December. I asked him to return by way of Saigon. While in Vietnam, I wanted him to investigate all facets of the conflict and produce the most accurate estimate possible of the real situation. He agreed wholeheartedly. I think we all felt we had been misled into over-optimism.

The Defense Secretary spent December 18–20, 1963, in Vietnam. He reported to me on the 21st in the White House, less than thirty days after I had assumed the Presidency. Rusk, McCone, and other advisers were present. McNamara's appraisal was gloomy indeed. "The situation is very disturbing," he said. "Current trends, unless reversed in the next two or three months, will lead to neutralization at best and more likely to a Communist-controlled state."

"Neutralization" of Vietnam was in many people's minds at that time, and it had a particular meaning. In August 1963 French President Charles de Gaulle had suggested that North and South Vietnam be unified and neutralized, and that all foreign forces be withdrawn. Most thinking people, I believe, recognized that the De Gaulle formula for "neutralization" would have meant the swift communization of all Vietnam, and probably of Laos and Cambodia as well. President Kennedy had been asked his opinion of the French proposal during the CBS interview on September 2, 1963, and he had brushed it aside as irrelevant. He said:

> What, of course, makes Americans somewhat impatient is that after carrying this load for eighteen years, we are glad to get counsel but we would like a little more assistance, real assistance. But we are going to meet our responsibility anyway.
>
> It doesn't do us any good to say: "Well, why don't we all just go home and leave the world to those who are our enemies."

McNamara told me he had found the new South Vietnamese government "indecisive and drifting." He was deeply concerned about the "grave reporting weakness" on the part of U.S. personnel. He said:

> Viet Cong progress has been great during the period since the coup

[November 1], with my best guess being that the situation has in fact been deteriorating in the countryside since July to a far greater extent than we realize because of our undue dependence on distorted Vietnamese reporting.

He granted that his estimate might be "overly pessimistic." He pointed out that Ambassador Lodge, General Harkins, and South Vietnamese chief of state General Duong Van Minh all felt that improvements would come in the next month or so, and they were not discouraged. I had confidence in McNamara's perception and I concluded that his judgment was closer to the hard truth.

McNamara did not recommend any immediate increase in U.S. personnel to meet the worsening situation. He did think that we should send more of our men into the field to obtain reliable and independent U.S. appraisals of all operations. CIA Director McCone also made recommendations for checking and improving the quality of intelligence reporting. I promptly accepted the suggestions of these two key advisers.

We expanded our advisory effort, setting up a separate channel for our own military evaluations and reports. The CIA improved its reporting methods. The U.S. Embassy refined and expanded province reporting. At my request, I began receiving detailed weekly reports from Ambassador Lodge which pulled no punches in describing problems as well as progress. From that time until I left office, I received a steady flow of comprehensive reports on all aspects of the Vietnam problem through both civilian and military channels. In addition, individuals from outside as well as from inside the government gave me their personal observations after trips to Southeast Asia. These included Congressmen, Senators, specialists from business and labor, technicians, doctors, and countless reporters and editors, including many who disagreed with American policy there. I was, of course, reading the daily papers and listening to television reports. There was no shortage of information at any time. The information I received was more complete and balanced than anyone outside the mainstream of official reporting could possibly realize.

As we moved into 1964 events confirmed the gloomy forecast Secretary McNamara had made in December. Late in January a group of officers headed by General Nguyen Khanh replaced the military junta that had overthrown Diem. More political turmoil followed. Six months later religious rivalries, which had been pushed into the background, broke out again. From then until well into 1965 governmental changes seemed to take place every few months. There was military rule, then civilian, then military again. First one man was in charge. Then there was a triumvirate. Then a council. General Khanh was in, and out, then in again.

The South Vietnamese often seemed to have a strong impulse toward political suicide. They hated the Communists and wanted to be able to run their own lives. But they had great trouble trying to get together to govern themselves. The busy critics of South Vietnam had a field day. When there were demonstrations or protests, the South Vietnamese were described as lacking in patriotism. When the government moved to limit protests, the leadership was called dictatorial. The South Vietnamese were attacked from both sides, and we were in no position to do much about it.

I had moments of deep discouragement, times when I felt the South Vietnamese were their own worst enemies. But I felt even more impatience with those who were always ready only to criticize. Building a new nation is never easy under the best of circumstances—with unlimited time, solid political traditions, a healthy economy, and peace. The South Vietnamese had none of these things, yet they were trying desperately to find their way to nationhood. I thought they needed and deserved understanding and patience, not constant vilification. But then a patient understanding of others is a great human deficiency, whether in personal relationships or in international affairs. Criticism is much easier, even if it is destructive and invariably makes matters worse for those criticized.

While political confusion dominated the scene in Saigon, the Viet Cong naturally took advantage of every shakeup and bloodless coup in the South Vietnamese capital. A sizable portion of the military leadership became involved in politics in both Saigon and the provinces, and the effectiveness of units in the field dropped accordingly. Morale sagged. Leadership declined. The Communists pushed recruitment in the countryside and began to build up their battalions. Then they created regiments. By the end of the year the Viet Cong had organized a division and put it into action.

In March 1964 I asked McNamara and Taylor to go to Vietnam once again for a firsthand assessment. I wanted a report on the situation in all its dimensions and requested recommendations on measures to improve the situation. They made the journey and reported to me on March 16 in my office, and the next day at a session of the National Security Council.*

They said that conditions had "unquestionably been growing worse." They cited specific weaknesses in security, morale, and political effectiveness. They said that Hanoi's involvement in the insurgency, "always significant, has been increasing." The Defense Secretary once again described the disastrous consequences likely to follow should South Vietnam fall to the Communists. His first recommendation, regarding our posture, was:

---

* Statutory members of the NSC are the President, Vice President, Secretary of State, Secretary of Defense, and Director of the Office of Emergency Planning. The Director of the CIA and the Chairman of the Joint Chiefs of Staff are designated advisers to the NSC. The President can, and usually does, invite others at his discretion. For example, from the time I became President until a new Vice President had been elected in November 1964, I invited Speaker of the House McCormack, who would have been my legal successor, to attend NSC meetings. Attendance at NSC meetings varied from twelve to thirty or more persons, depending on the number and importance of the problems to be discussed, the availability of experts, and other factors.

The U.S. at all levels must continue to make it emphatically clear that we are prepared to furnish assistance and support for as long as it takes to bring the insurgency under control.

McNamara listed a number of specific actions he believed we should take promptly. These included meeting a South Vietnamese request for assistance in increasing their armed forces by 50,000 men, raising both the quantity and quality of military supplies going to those forces, and providing several forms of budgetary support to help the Vietnamese bear the costs of an expanding war.

McNamara concluded his report as follows:

> If the Khanh Government can stay in power and the above actions can be carried out rapidly, it is my judgment that the situation in South Vietnam can be significantly improved in the next four to six months. The present deterioration may continue for a part of this period, but I believe it can be levelled out and some improvement will become visible during the period. I therefore believe that this course of action should be urgently pursued while we prepare such additional actions as may be necessary for success.

His final recommendation was that we be ready to carry out, on three days' notice, certain border control actions as well as retaliation against North Vietnam. We should also be in a position, the Secretary said, to conduct a program of graduated military pressure against the North on a month's notice. The Defense Secretary specified that he was not in favor of either of these actions "at this time" but was recommending that we be prepared if they should prove necessary in the future.

Secretary McNamara's recommendations on expanding the Vietnamese effort grew out of his talks with the leadership in Saigon and reflected their desire to do more for themselves. He reported that Ambassador Lodge and the members of the U.S. Country Team * in Saigon favored his proposals. So did all concerned departments and agencies in Washington. At the NSC meeting no one opposed any of the military recommendations.

The Joint Chiefs of Staff thought the proposed actions might not be sufficient and favored taking immediate measures against the North. When this possibility was raised, then and later in the year, my key advisers voiced two principal objections, which I shared. First, we were concerned that the political and military base in the South was too fragile to invite increased action from the enemy. Second, we feared that striking the North

---

* The Country Team is a formal organization used by an Ambassador to keep informed of the activities of other government agencies represented in his mission and to maintain control over them. The team is generally composed of the top officials of AID, CIA, Defense, and USIA. The Ambassador acts as chairman. In practice, Ambassadors often expand the membership to include the Deputy Chief of Mission, the chief political officer, the U.S. Embassy's administrative officer, the commander of a major military command that may be present, and others.

might lead to involvement by the Chinese or the Soviets, or both. We did not know what secret military arrangements or agreements Hanoi might have worked out with Peking and Moscow. I approved the twelve actions on the McNamara list on March 17 and instructed the Executive departments to carry them out, but rejected proposals to do more than that.

The leaders in Hanoi obviously liked what they saw happening in the South at that time. In the summer of 1964 they decided the time was ripe to move from guerrilla warfare to a more conventional general offensive. They developed large unit formations in the South and by the end of the year were sending regular units of the North Vietnamese army into South Vietnam to join the battle. Their goal was clear: smash the South Vietnamese army, bring on a political collapse in Saigon, and take over. Hanoi was pushing the war throttle.

Meanwhile, we were trying to put on the brake. On June 17 Blair Seaborn, the new Canadian member of the International Control Commission for Vietnam, would be going to Hanoi in connection with his assignment. We outlined my first peace suggestion, along with some of our hopes and expectations, and asked him to sound out the authorities in North Vietnam regarding the chances for peace. We told him he could assure Ho Chi Minh and his colleagues that the United States had no intention of trying to overthrow their regime. We had no wish to retain military bases or a military position in the South. We were, of course, aware of Hanoi's control of the Viet Cong. We asked only that the leaders in Hanoi abide by the agreements reached with the French at Geneva in 1954 and in the Laos settlement in 1962: keep their men inside their own territory and stop sending military supplies into the South. If our peace proposal was accepted, we would assist all the countries of the area in their economic development. North Vietnam could benefit from that improvement along with her neighbors.

Seaborn, an experienced diplomat, presented our views not as an advocate but as a dispassionate intermediary. He listened to the North Vietnamese views in the same spirit. All he heard from Hanoi's leaders was propaganda repeated many times since: The United States should withdraw totally from the South; a "neutral" regime should be set up in accordance with the National Liberation Front's program; the Front would have to take a leading role in determining the future of the country.

Obviously, the Communist leaders believed they were winning in the South. With things presumably going their way, they had no interest in a peaceful settlement or compromise of any description. They slammed the door shut on our peace offer. In August, when Seaborn tried again to discuss the idea of a peaceful settlement with them, they slammed the door even harder. We could only conclude from his experience that the North Vietnamese had no desire to limit their actions or to negotiate; they were interested in only one thing, victory on the battlefield. This experience of trying to open an avenue to peace negotiations and coming up against a roadblock was repeated dozens of times over the next several years.

In the United States that summer we were in the midst of a Presidential election campaign. I tried as far as possible to keep the war out of the political race, but the issue was too important to be ignored. I stated and restated our goals and explained why we were involved in Southeast Asia.* On several occasions I insisted that American boys should not do the fighting that Asian boys should do for themselves. I was answering those who proposed, or implied, that we should take charge of the war or carry out actions that would risk a war with Communist China. I did not mean that we were not going to do any fighting, for we had already lost many good men in Vietnam. I made it clear that those who were ready to fight for their own freedom would find us at their side if they wanted and needed us. We were not going to rush in and take over, but we were going to live up to the commitments we had made. Any thinking American knew there were already many thousands of Americans in Asia, not just in Vietnam but in Korea, Japan, Okinawa, Taiwan, the Philippines, and Thailand. They were there for a purpose: to defend what four American Presidents and the Congress of the United States had said were vital American and world interests.

A good many people compared my position in 1964 with that of the Republican nominee, Senator Barry Goldwater of Arizona, and decided that I was the "peace" candidate and he was the "war" candidate. They were not willing to hear anything they did not want to hear. Certainly I wanted peace. I wanted it every day of every month I was in the White House. All through 1964 and after, I hoped and prayed the men in Hanoi would agree to sit down and negotiate. But I made it clear from the day I took office that I was not a "peace at any price" man. We would remain strong, prepared at all times to defend ourselves and our friends. But we would also be ready always to work for a just peace. This is the way I described my views from one end of the country to the other.

The American people knew what they were voting for in 1964. They knew Lyndon Johnson was not going to pull up stakes and run. They knew I was not going to go back on my country's word. They knew I would not repudiate the pledges of my predecessors in the Presidency. They knew too that I was not going to wipe out Hanoi or use atom bombs to defoliate the Vietnamese jungles. I was going to do what had to be done to protect our interests and to keep our promises. And that is what I did.

---

* For example, see excerpts from my talk before the American Bar Association in New York City on August 12, 1964, in the Appendix, page 575.

4

War on Poverty

THE FIRST FULL DAY of my Presidency was loaded with the urgencies of government in crisis. When I recall that day, I think of people: people entering my office, people leaving my office, people meeting in my office, people waiting in my reception room, a steady stream of people. They included former Presidents, Cabinet officers, leaders of Congress, and staff members.

Among the latter was Walter Heller, Chairman of the Council of Economic Advisers, who came to see me at 7:40 in the evening. He wanted to tell me about the research recently conducted on the problem of poverty. Although most citizens were still unaware of how extensive poverty was in the United States, a few writers and government experts were beginning to understand its real impact by the early 1960s.

Heller told me that early in November he had asked the departments and agencies of the federal government for ideas that could be used in developing a program to alleviate poverty. He said that he had discussed the subject with John Kennedy three days before his assassination. At that time, Heller told me, President Kennedy had approved his going ahead with plans for a program but had given no guidance as to the specific content. Now Heller had come to ask me an urgent question: Did I want the Council of Economic Advisers to develop a program to attack poverty?

I swung around in my chair and looked out the window. Lights were burning in the West Wing of the White House, across West Executive Avenue, in the offices of grief-stricken men who were struggling to carry on the business of government. I turned back and looked into Heller's eyes as he waited for my reply. This dedicated and brilliant professor of economics, whom President Kennedy had brought to Washington from the

University of Minnesota, was stunned, like most other officials of government. And yet, like the rest of those charged with making the machinery of government run, he was submerging himself in work that looked toward the future.

Before me now was a call for action, a call for a revolutionary new program to attack one of the most stubbornly entrenched social ills in America. Like most social change, such a revolution would not come without a struggle. My perceptions of America persuaded me that three separate conditions were required before social change could take root and flourish in our national life—a recognition of need, a willingness to act, and someone to lead the effort. In 1963 I saw those three conditions coming together in historic harmony.

The problems confronting us were hardly new. The lack of specific training, the denial of civil rights to black Americans, the neglect of the educational needs of our young, the inadequacy of health care, the invisible barriers around our ghettos—all these had been with us for generations. But little had been done to ameliorate the problems and they were growing to overwhelming and unmanageable size. So the *need* for action was there. The need was more apparent every day.

The second condition was the willingness to act. Traditionally, legislation that helps the American people keep abreast of changing times has come only after the problems reach crisis proportion. The pattern of social reform in America has been like a vast pendulum, swinging over the years from creative activity to almost total inaction, and then back to action again. Despite Theodore Roosevelt's impressive legislative record, many troubles grew untended in the early years of the century. Then a burst of activity brought the reforms of Woodrow Wilson's day—the Federal Reserve Act, the Clayton Antitrust Act, the Federal Trade Commission Act, among others.

By the end of World War I the nation wanted to return to "normalcy" and rest for a while. We rested while the disasters of the late 1920s accumulated and brought about new demands for urgent change—demands met by Franklin Roosevelt's dynamic New Deal. After the upheaval of World War II, the desire to relax grew strong once more. President Truman, who perceived the need for social change in the United States as clearly as any leader in our history, had to fight this apathy throughout his administration. Again, in the 1950s, the nation obtained the breathing space it clamored for and the problems festered unchecked. Then two traumatic events shook the nation and created a new climate for action.

Russia's Sputnik, which orbited the earth in 1957, was the first. That small man-made sphere jolted us into developing our own program to explore the new frontiers of space, and forced us to examine the weaknesses in our educational system. The second event was John Kennedy's assassination. This act of violence shocked the nation deeply and created the impetus to send the country surging forward. His death touched all our hearts and made us, for a while at least, a more compassionate people, more sensitive to the troubles of our fellow men.

So the second condition was met—the people were ready for action. And when I looked inside myself, I believed that I could provide the third ingredient—the disposition to lead.

My entire life, from boyhood on, had helped me recognize the work that needed to be done in America. My view of leadership had always been an activist one. I had first run for public office in 1937 under the slogan "He gets things done." I built my record in the House and Senate on the same philosophy. Now, as President, watching the pendulum move, I believed that I could—for a while, at least—really get things done.

The poverty program Heller described was my kind of undertaking.

"I'm interested," I responded. "I'm sympathetic. Go ahead. Give it the highest priority. Push ahead full tilt."

Work on the program continued through December. I announced at a news conference that poverty legislation would be "high on the agenda of priority" in our requests to Congress in 1964. We continued our search for ways to reduce spending, mainly in Defense but in other departments as well, so that money could be used to launch the poverty program. A poverty bill that would increase the budget at the outset would have little chance of success.

We were moving into uncharted territory. Powerful forces of opposition would be stirred. Many people warned me not to get caught in the snare of a program directed entirely toward helping the poor. One of my staff aides, Horace Busby, set out in a long memorandum the adverse political effect which such a program could eventually have on "the American in the middle—the man who earns $3,000 to $9,000."

"America's real majority," he wrote, "is suffering a minority complex of neglect. They have become the real foes of Negro rights, foreign aid, etc., because, as much as anything, they feel forgotten, at the second table behind the tightly organized, smaller groups at either end of the U.S. spectrum."

We foresaw clearly the problems and dangers. But the powerful conviction that an attack on poverty was right and necessary blotted out any fears that this program was a political landmine. Harry Truman used to say that 13 or 14 million Americans had their interests represented in Washington, but that the rest of the people had to depend on the President of the United States. That is how I felt about the 35 million American poor. They had no voice and no champion. Whatever the cost, I was determined to represent them. Through me they would have an advocate and, I believed, new hope.

When economist John Kenneth Galbraith wrote of our "affluent society" at the end of the 1950s, he said that "the arithmetic of modern politics makes it tempting to overlook the very poor"—that because the poor were an "inarticulate minority," the "modern liberal politician" did not align himself with them. I did not suffer the disadvantage of being considered a "modern liberal politician." The closest I came to that description was being called a "Populist," which is the term some liberals reserve for progressives who come from the Southern and Western parts of the nation. So I determined that this Populist politician would be the one who finally gave poor Americans some representation and helped them find their voice and improve their lot.

I told Douglass Cater of the *Reporter* magazine—who later came to work for me at the White House—that I did not know whether we would pass a single law or appropriate a single dollar. But one thing I did know: When I got through, no one in this country would be able to ignore the poverty in our midst.

I did not look upon a program to combat poverty as one for the benefit of the poor alone, to the detriment of the middle class or any other group. I believed a program that eliminated poverty—or even reduced it—would strengthen the moral and economic fiber of the entire country. It was on that basis that I prepared to move forward and commit the resources and prestige of the new administration.

Walter Heller and Kermit Gordon, Director of the Bureau of the Budget, worked together as the government's "poverty team" in those early days. They came to the LBJ Ranch over the Christmas week at the end of 1963. I spent many long hours with them, discussing, planning, and evolving the outlines of a poverty program. Occasionally, staff members sat in on those sessions and made valuable contributions. I sought the wise counsel of Jesse Kellam, who had been my deputy when I served as Texas Director of the National Youth Administration in the 1930s and succeeded me when I left to go to Congress. I asked Jesse to come out from Austin to join in our ranch discussions, because my thoughts kept going back to those NYA days when Aubrey Williams, Mary Bethune, Elizabeth Wickenden, and many others had worked so hard on Depression problems.

The problem of poverty in the 1960s was not the same as that of the hard times in the 1930s. During the Depression we had been concerned mainly with educated and trained people who had been temporarily dislocated by the sickness of the economy. The poverty of the 1960s, the paradoxical poverty in the midst of plenty, was of another breed. The economy was booming. Jobs were plentiful, but the unemployed were incapable of filling them. The most significant aspects of this new poverty, once the spotlight of attention was thrown on it, were the dismaying nature of its stubborn entrenchment and the total entrapment of its victims from one generation to the next. A man was poor if he did not have enough money to live on, but that was only part of it. If he was poor, the consequences were that he had little education, that he received inadequate medical care and substandard nutrition, that he lived in crowded and unsanitary conditions. He had no real chance to train for a decent job.

Moreover, he had been poor all his life and was destined to die poor. His children could look forward to the same hopeless cycle, from a deprived youth to a bleak and despairing old age. The poor man was trapped; no escape was possible; hope was beyond his understanding. To defeat poverty meant breaking this cruel pattern.

In spite of the differences in the times and the poverty structure, those NYA experiences were valuable to me, suggesting some of the solutions we were searching for in the present. For one thing, I was convinced that a successful program would have to provide not only special services but, more important, the opportunities for people to lift themselves out of the treadmill of poverty. For another, I wanted to place heavy emphasis on efforts to help children and youth. They offered the best hope of breaking the poverty cycle.

There was something both amusing and fitting about the beginning work on the poverty program. One evening during those Christmas holidays in 1963 I walked from the main ranch house to a little green frame house we call the "guest house," a distance of about two hundred yards. Inside, seated around a small kitchen table, were Walter Heller, Budget Director Kermit Gordon, Bill Moyers, and Jack Valenti. The table was littered with papers, coffee cups, and one ashtray brimming over with cigarettes and torn strips of paper. Just a few feet from the window several of my whitefaced Herefords were grazing placidly and a little noisily. It was an incongruous setting for Gordon and Heller, those two urbane scholars. I sat down at the table to talk about the program they were preparing.

I joked with Kermit Gordon about the half-hearted attempt he was making to blend in with his Southwestern surroundings. He was wearing a pair of fashionable slacks—what we Texans would call "city-bought trousers"—and a khaki Western shirt I had lent him. He told me with a smile that he was blending urban and cattle country. It struck me that the poverty program itself was a blend of the same: of the needs and desperate desires of the poor in the city ghettos and the poor in obscure rural hollows. Perhaps the setting, with scholars and government officials sitting around a kitchen table on a ranch far from an urban center, was not inappropriate for the drafting of a new program that would touch the lives of city and country dwellers alike.

Gordon and Heller had been thinking in terms of a pilot venture to be carried out in a limited number of "demonstration project" cities. But I urged them to broaden their scope. I was certain that we could not start small and hope to propel a program through the Congress. It had to be big and bold and hit the whole nation with real impact.

We managed to earmark $500 million in the budget to launch the anti-poverty drive, much of it derived from Defense Department economies. In addition, the budget contained another $500 million for federal agency efforts—such as manpower training—which would also strike at poverty in one way or another. I instructed Gordon to incorporate those funds in the poverty program so that we could launch the campaign at a $1 billion level.

The challenge I presented to my advisers was the development of a new concept. I didn't want to paste together a lot of existing approaches. I wanted original, inspiring ideas.

The title War on Poverty was decided on during those days at the Ranch. It had disadvantages. The military image carried with it connotations of victories and defeats that could prove misleading. But I wanted to rally the nation, to sound a call to arms which would stir people in the government, in private industry, and on the campuses to lend their talents to a massive effort to eliminate the evil. One of the titles suggested was Point One, patterned after Harry Truman's Point Four program. But neither Point One nor any of the other titles proposed conveyed the sense of drama and importance required. So in the end, we came back to the War on Poverty.

Two of the men on the Bureau of the Budget staff, Bill Cannon and Sam Hughes, came up with an idea which was passed on to Heller with the kind of endorsement not often found in a bureaucracy. "I am very enthusiastic," read the covering memo from one of Heller's assistants. "This may be the way to really make something of this poverty program." Basically, the idea was this: Local organizations would be formed in the neighborhoods and communities where the poor people themselves lived, and programs to help the poor would be channeled through organizations on the scene. This plan had the sound of something brand new and even faintly radical. Actually, it was based on one of the oldest ideas of our democracy, as old as the New England town meeting—self-determination at the local level.

A similar approach had been tried on a small and experimental scale by a committee formed by President Kennedy to combat juvenile delinquency. The Ford Foundation had also granted funds to a few cities to test a concept of this nature, but I remembered experiments even earlier than those. When I taught school at Cotulla, Texas, in the 1930s, I worked with Leonides V. Lopez, one of the leading Mexican-American merchants in town, to persuade the poor parents of my pupils to join a parent-teacher association. Such involvement was a new experience for them, but they started coming to meetings. When they came, I was able to encourage them to consider more productive ways for the students to spend their afterschool hours. I had expected to propose using afterschool time to train the children for jobs. But the parents were more interested in providing them with recreation and hobbies. I found that they had about the same hopes for their children that bankers do. So we organized a choir, a base-ball team for the boys, and a volleyball team for the girls. The point is that those parents became actively involved in the life of their school, once they realized they had a voice in it.

I took that knowledge with me into the NYA, and I soon found that when the people affected had a hand in shaping a project, it was much more successful than any program passed down by decree from a govern-ment office.

Gordon and Heller jointly recommended that we give the local organiza-tion idea a try, although they warned me of the risks—particularly the political risks—that might make the outcome uncertain. I was willing to take the chance. Community participation would give focus to our efforts. I realized that a program as massive as the one we were contemplating might shake up many existing institutions, but I decided that some shaking up might be needed to get a bold new program moving. I thought that local governments had to be challenged to be awakened. The concept of com-munity action became the first building block in our program to attack poverty.

On January 8, 1964, in my first State of the Union address to the Con-gress, I announced: "This administration today, here and now, declares unconditional war on poverty in America." I warned that "it will not be a short or easy struggle" but that it was a war "we cannot afford to lose." It was a war not only on economic deprivation but on the tragic waste of human resources. The effort was not only morally justified but economically sound.

"One thousand dollars invested in salvaging an unemployable youth today," I pointed out, "can return forty thousand dollars in his lifetime."

Once the poverty "war" was declared, I faced the task of submitting a full-scale program to Congress as quickly as possible. The time had come to move the planning out of the Council of Economic Advisers and the Budget Bureau orbit. They had done a good job in getting the project started. But I thought the people destined to run the program should now take over development of the plans.

Some of my advisers and Cabinet officers, particularly Secretary Willard Wirtz of the Department of Labor, recommended that the administration of the program be handled through one of the Cabinet departments or some other existing agency. Only by operating through already established channels, they argued, could we launch our efforts with speed and efficiency.

Attorney General Bobby Kennedy also favored this approach. He noted that "the need for a coordinated effort can best be met at this time directly by a Cabinet-level committee, with one of its members as chairman."

Others, including Kermit Gordon and Walter Heller, argued for a new and independent agency which, they maintained, would be far more likely to move along new paths of innovation and experimentation. John Kenneth Galbraith was another who subscribed to this view. He sent me a memorandum on January 31, 1964, which urged: "Do not bury the program in the departments. Put it in the Executive offices, where people will know what you are doing, where it can have a new staff and a fresh man as director."

I agreed. I concluded that the program should be handled by an independent agency in the Executive branch, reporting directly to the President. I wanted a strong man at its head. A number of names were proposed. I decided on Sargent Shriver. He had demonstrated ability as Director of the Peace Corps. In planning that organization, he had personally visited and briefed many Senators and Congressmen, obtaining a measure of congressional respect not always given to a bureaucrat. He had shown that he could get along with diverse groups.

Shriver took over the directorship of the poverty program on February 1, 1964. I told him he would have to work fast. Not only did I want to propel a program through the Congress immediately but I wanted the plan to produce visible results, so that there would be no question about Congress' continuing the effort with adequate funding in the years ahead.

Shriver attacked this new job with vitality and enthusiasm. Within a few days of our meeting he held an all-day session with experts and advisers from both inside and outside the government to examine ways to eliminate poverty. Some of those who met that day served as the nucleus of a task force that began final formulation of the poverty program.

Members of Shriver's organization started working in the Peace Corps Building. When they needed more room, they moved over to the old Federal Court of Claims. When it was discovered that this ancient building was literally falling apart, they were ordered out on two hours' notice and they evacuated the premises, carrying their files and papers with them. They set up office in what had been the morgue in the basement of an abandoned emergency hospital.

Their excitement was contagious. Hundreds of people—high school and college students, returning Peace Corpsmen, housewives, and even congressional wives—volunteered to work thousands of hours in every kind of capacity. Many wrote and phoned in to offer their services. Others simply walked in off the street to give assistance.

I followed closely the work of those men over the next few weeks. They went at it with a fervor and created a ferment unknown since the days of the New Deal, when lights had burned through the night as men worked to restructure society. The task force solicited ideas from more than 150 leaders in every section of the nation's life: businessmen and teachers, mayors and social workers, officials in private organizations and officers of state governments.

Soon other ideas began to take their place beside community action in the emerging legislative proposal: programs to give a special educational head start to children from deprived backgrounds; plans to train school dropouts for productive jobs; a blueprint to draw on the volunteer spirit of American youth; new ways to help small businessmen in the slums get started and to help impoverished farmers keep going; programs to enable students from low-income families to work while they pursued an education.

Only six weeks after the task force had first assembled, the program was ready to go. On March 16 I approved it and sent it to the Congress. In a special message I told the Congress that poverty was "a domestic enemy which threatens the strength of our nation and the welfare of our people." That language was in keeping with the fact that I was calling for a war, one which would strike "at the causes and not just the consequences of poverty, one which would treat not just poor individuals but poor communities as well." The strategy for that war was best described in the title of the bill itself. It was called the Economic Opportunity Act.

Hearings before a subcommittee of the House Education and Labor Committee began the day after the bill was received, March 17.

We had known from the outset that our legislation would have a hard time making it through the House of Representatives. Many Republicans would oppose the bill out of habit, as they opposed all progressive social legislation. Their opposition could be expected to be particularly strong in an election year. It was also clear that Republican opponents of the bill would try to enlist the aid of Southern Democrats by stirring the Southerners' fears that certain provisions would enforce integration. Many uninformed people believed that the poverty program was entirely Negro-oriented, despite the fact that about four out of every five families then living in poverty in the United States were white.

I discussed these problems with Larry O'Brien and other members of my staff who concentrated on congressional matters. We all agreed that we were going to have to pull, as O'Brien expressed it, "a magnificent rabbit out of a hat." We did. We induced Representative Phil Landrum of Georgia to sponsor the bill. Landrum, whom I admired, was generally known as a conservative Congressman. But both Larry and I knew he was a thoughtful legislator, amenable to change.

When O'Brien and I first talked about asking Landrum to sponsor the poverty bill, the possibility of his accepting the challenge seemed remote.

But the more we discussed it, the more the idea seemed worth trying. Landrum would be a strong and effective leader, and certainly his sponsorship would render the bill considerably more palatable to the Southerners. I talked to Phil about it and found him receptive to the program, because he basically was dedicated to the people.

But there remained a serious hurdle. Because of his cosponsorship of the 1959 Landrum-Griffin bill, which put certain restrictions on union powers, he was regarded as an enemy of labor. Labor support was absolutely fundamental to the success of any poverty bill. I suggested to O'Brien that he and Shriver have a talk with George Meany of the AFL-CIO. Meany and his subordinates were at first incredulous. For years, O'Brien reported to me, the AFL-CIO had been using "Landrum" as a dirty word. And now Phil Landrum was going to father the *poverty bill*?

I got in touch with George Meany myself soon after that. In my experience with Meany I knew he could always be counted on to put the interests of his country first. That is precisely what he did this time. My message to him was simple. "After all, it's the result we're after," I told him. Before the poverty bill passed, Landrum and Meany were sitting down together for quiet and friendly talks.

The attacks on the bill began as soon as the hearings started. The ranking Republican on the House Education and Labor Committee, wealthy Peter Frelinghuysen of New Jersey, set the tone for the opposition by contending that there was nothing new in the program. "This country has been engaged in fighting poverty since it was founded," he said.

Clearly Frelinghuysen had fallen victim in his thinking to the old Republican "trickle down" theory of economics. This theory argues that if there is prosperity within the business community, money will eventually find its way down to the people at the bottom of the economic pyramid. This philosophy works just as it sounds. By the time the money filters down to the bottom it is no more than a trickle, even when the country is prosperous. When the nation experiences a recession, the money stops altogether. Clearly a strong, growing economy is essential to the well-being of all Americans, but the War on Poverty recognized that the inveterate poor need something more—they need specific attention.

Shriver understood this. In his opening remarks before the House Education and Labor Committee on March 17, he emphasized the genuine essence of the poverty program: its spirit. He cited a headline he had seen in a newspaper the night before: "Johnson Unveils Program to Aid the Poor." "I wonder," he said, "how many times in American history the poor ever got up to the headlines, just the poor people."

We did everything we could to keep the poor people in the headlines while the bill was in committee. Many Cabinet officers and other high-ranking government officials took up the poor people's cause in their speeches across the country, and they received good press coverage. Lady Bird and I made a special trip to the Middle West and through the scarred mountains of Appalachia to focus the nation's attention on the problem of poverty. It was a full and long day that I still vividly recall.

At a schoolhouse in South Bend . . . at a meeting of the League of Women Voters in a Pittsburgh ballroom . . . at a convocation in a Steelworkers' Union hall on the other side of town . . . in the courthouse square at Paintsville, Kentucky . . . and finally at the moonlit airport in Huntington, West Virginia, I delivered my message to the nation: The War on Poverty was not a partisan effort. It was a moral obligation and its success rested on every one of us. Wherever we went, along every mile of the road of our travels, the people sounded their approval.

I saw the poor that day in Appalachia with my own eyes. And I believe that through my eyes, and through the eyes of reporters and photographers who traveled with me, all America saw them too: the gaunt, defeated men whom the land had abandoned; their tired, despairing wives; their pale, undernourished children—all holding up homemade signs of welcome as we visited their hills.

I will not forget them.

I will not forget the man whose home I visited on the banks of Rock Castle Creek on a mountainside in eastern Kentucky. His name was Tom Fletcher. His house was a tar-papered, three-room shack which he shared with his wife and their eight children. I sat on the porch with him while he described the struggle he had to support them all on $400 a year. He regretted more than anything else that his two oldest children had already dropped out of school, and he was worried that the same fate would overtake the others. So was I. The tragic inevitability of the endless cycle of poverty was summed up in that man's fear: poverty forcing children out of school and destroying their best chance to escape the poverty of their fathers.

"I want you to keep those kids in school," I said to Mr. Fletcher when I left him. But I knew he couldn't do it alone. He had to have help, and I resolved to see that he got it. My determination was reinforced that day to use the powers of the Presidency to the fullest extent I could, to persuade America to help all its Tom Fletchers. They lived in the hollows of Appalachia and the hill country of central Texas, in swamp and desert, in cane brake and forest, and in the crumbling slums of every American city and every state. They were black and they were white, of every religion and background and national origin. And they were 35 million strong.

Back in Washington, I continued to seek support for the War on Poverty from every sector of American life. A few days later I spoke to a chamber of commerce delegation and, on the same day, to a group of labor editors. My words to them were the same:

People are just not going to stand and see their children starve and be driven out of school and be eaten up with disease in the twentieth century. They will forego stealing and they will forego fighting, and they will forego doing a lot of violent things and improper things as long as they possibly can, but they are going to eat, and they are going to learn, and they are going to grow. The quicker you find it out, the better.

I asked both groups for their help.

"Mr. President," one of the labor editors asked, "what specifically can we do?"

You can help, I answered, by writing editorials, by writing news articles, by helping to mold public opinion. Ask people to write their Congressmen and Senators; tell folks about the need for united action. Let them know that everybody is not eating three meals a day the way they are, that there are conditions in this country that are insupportable, and except for the grace of God they could find themselves in the same spot.

After the bill was reported out of the Education and Labor Committee, it went to the House Rules Committee, where the octogenarian chairman, Howard Smith of Virginia, made no secret of his fear that such an act would be used as a tool to force integration. He demanded of Landrum whether Job Corps camps would be racially integrated. Landrum said they would. But racial integration, he observed, was "a matter of law over which neither you nor I can prevail."

"White boys in your state or mine," Smith said in a warning tone, "have a very deep feeling about living with Negroes."

Landrum made the only sensible reply possible. Enrollment in the Job Corps, he pointed out, was entirely voluntary.

Chairman Smith held hearings for three days and then held up the bill for six weeks. His excuse was that he wanted to wait until the Republicans had held their national convention. At the time, I regretted the Rules Committee's action, and I appealed to the committee not to block the legislative process. As it happened, we decided to work for a Senate vote first. The House division appeared dangerously close. If the bill passed the Senate, that might influence some of the waverers.

The bill was approved by the Senate on July 23 by a vote of 61 to 34. Then we prepared for the final vote in the House. We had no assurance of victory, and as late as July 31 Larry O'Brien told me that his head count showed the House deadlocked, with thirty Southerners undecided.

The bill came in for the stormy attack we expected on the House floor. Phil Landrum did a masterful job of defending it. He called it "the most conservative bill I've ever seen," because it aimed at taking people off the welfare rolls and making them into "taxpayers instead of tax-eaters."

While this struggle was taking place on the floor of Congress, the fight was being waged on another front—in congressional offices and cloak-rooms. Conservationists, who at first had been ignored, were approached by Shriver with the assurance that at least 40 per cent of the Job Corps workers would be used on conservation projects, drawing on the practice of the Civilian Conservation Corps of Roosevelt's day. Rallying quickly, the conservationists swayed as many as twenty key votes.

When the final vote in the House came, on August 8, the result reflected the strong effort we had all made. The tally was 226 to 185, a margin of victory much wider than we had expected. Within minutes after the final vote I received a phone call from Congressman Carl Albert, the Democratic Floor Leader, and Congressman Hale Boggs, the Democratic Whip. They told me they were sitting alone, toasting our victory.

"I really can't figure out, Mr. President," Carl Albert said, "how in the world we ever got this through. I honestly don't know." I told them how proud I was of them and of the entire Congress. It just couldn't have been a more encouraging or rewarding week.

When I signed the Economic Opportunity Act on August 20, I tried to set it in historical perspective. "Today," I said, "for the first time in all the history of the human race, a great nation is able to make and is willing to make a commitment to eradicate poverty among its people."

Because poverty itself is a complex problem composed of many inter-locking facets, our assault on it had to be an integrated attack launched on many fronts. No single poverty program could reverse centuries of dis-crimination and deprivation. That reversal would come only with the long, hard work of dozens of campaigns fought on hundreds of battlegrounds, and it would take time.

There was no magic formula. We had to try a wide variety of ap-proaches. Some worked better than others. Some failed completely. I heard bitter complaints from the mayors of several cities. Some funds were used to finance questionable activities. Some were badly mismanaged. That was all part of the risk. We created new bureaus and consolidated old ones. We altered priorities. We learned from mistakes. But as I used to tell our critics: "We have to pull the drowning man out of the water and talk about it later."

Our manpower training programs focused on preparing unskilled men and women for jobs. Aid to schools was designed to prevent poverty from crippling young minds. The poor started receiving proper medical attention, many for the first time, through our new health programs. Increased social security payments benefited the elderly poor. New housing programs provided decent homes and neighborhoods for many poor families. Civil rights laws bettered the conditions of life for all black

Americans, particularly for those who were poor. All these programs were an important part of the broad strategy to fight poverty, and they all needed public funds. The Economic Opportunity Act opened the door and made these funds available, followed by the Elementary and Secondary Education Act, Medicare, the Rent Supplements Act, and further extensions to the War on Poverty.

A certain amount of discouragement was inevitable. Failures are never easy to take. These failures offered fodder to diehard opponents who had resisted the program from the start. Our work was just beginning, but there were those who felt that even this beginning was too much. They did everything they could to set us back. When the poverty bill came up for extension in 1967, they mounted an all-out effort to defeat it.

I tried to anticipate the criticisms of this faction in my State of the Union address in 1967. I promised that my administration would "intensify our efforts to give the poor a chance to enjoy and to join in this nation's progress." At the same time, I said that I would propose "certain administrative changes [in the War on Poverty] suggested by the Congress as well as some that we have learned from our own trial and error."

But the Republicans were on another track altogether. Arguing that "the War on Poverty is a political tool which seeks to decrease and abolish poverty by government fiat," the House Republicans proposed a replacement: an Opportunity Crusade. The Opportunity Crusade aimed at nothing short of abolishing the Office of Economic Opportunity and transferring its major programs to other agencies where "the extravagant costs, mismanagement, abuse, kickbacks, and political profiteering now characterizing OEO could be brought under tight control."

One House Democrat, Joe Resnick of New York, accused the Republicans of trying to "dismantle the entire poverty program" and commented wryly on the Opportunity Crusade:

> In a nutshell, the creators of this radical new idea would enlarge the war against poverty and at the same time reduce its cost, by beheading the organization and then scattering its arms, legs, and vital organs all over Washington. The Office of Economic Opportunity itself would literally be wiped out of existence.

To put it mildly, I reacted negatively to this Republican "alternative," not only because of the trumped-up charges but even more because I strongly believed that the poor needed their own advocate, a solid, authoritative voice to speak on their behalf. The Republican proposal would have silenced that voice and dissipated our strength at a critical juncture.

The first hurdle was the Senate. We marshalled wide-ranging support for OEO. Thousands of people—Republicans and Democrats, blacks and whites, rich and poor—from local communities all over the country came to Washington, sent petitions, or wrote letters in support of OEO. One such petition was delivered personally to Shriver by three hundred residents of Westchester County, one of the richest counties in America.

"It's the first time three hundred people in Westchester County have gone anywhere together for any reason," Shriver told me, "except perhaps the annual Harvard-Yale game."

All this work paid off. The Senate vote produced the best margin yet (60 to 21), with nineteen Republicans in support. But the House continued to be our major worry. All summer long anti-OEO sentiment had been building in the House, and early in the fall the House accepted an amendment to the pending federal pay raise that prohibited increases for all employees of OEO, the only agency singled out for such discriminatory action.

Open hearings on the OEO bill began in the House in June. Normally, after this "public" phase committees go into closed sessions to draft the final bill. But this time House Education and Labor Committee Chairman Carl Perkins of Kentucky decided to keep the hearings open from beginning to end. "If they [the Republicans] want to kill this bill," he said, "then they're going to have to do it on the floor, out in the open and for the record. We're not going to let them do it behind closed doors."

This "markup" stage was a critical time for us to solidify support within the committee in order to produce a compromise bill that could withstand the assault of amendments from the floor. The most important compromise centered on the amendment of Representative Edith Green of Oregon requiring local government participation in neighborhood community action programs. We recognized the problems inherent in this amendment in certain areas. We knew that our tacit acceptance of it would be considered a sellout by the ultraliberals. But we knew for a fact that in many cases locally elected officials were already participating and, where they were, community action got the best results. More important, we knew that with this amendment we could win the support of several Southern Democrats and solidify the support of Democrats from big cities who were under pressure for tighter local control.

Meanwhile, poverty program supporters throughout the country were prompting editorials, citizens' petitions, and letters. There was an outpouring of spontaneous support for this domestic program, and the response proved that where it counted, in the local neighborhoods, the poverty program was indeed working. On November 15, 1967, the poverty bill passed the House almost entirely intact. Not one of the spinoff proposals was accepted. OEO would live to see another day and to fight other and even more difficult battles.

July 20, 1967, was another day when conservatives mounted an attack, this time a day of shame and defeat. On that day a simple, uncomplicated bill came before the House of Representatives which proposed to provide federal grants to local neighborhoods for developing and carrying out rat control and extermination efforts. I had recommended this important project in my message that year on urban and rural poverty, and I had deliberately separated it from the rest of my program in the hope of making more fortunate American people aware of the terrible problem of rats in our urban ghettos.

Every year thousands of people, especially those living in the slums of our cities, are bitten by rats in their homes and tenements. The overwhelming majority of victims are babies lying in their cribs. Some of them die of their wounds. Many are disfigured for life. Rats carry a living cargo of death. Directly and indirectly, more human beings have been killed by rats than have been killed in all the wars since the beginning of time. In their travels from sewers to trash heaps to kitchens, rats carry the germs of fatal epidemic jaundice and typhus.

But the greatest damage cannot be measured in objective terms. You cannot measure the demoralizing effect that the plague of rats has on human beings—a mother awakened by a cry in the middle of the night to find her child bleeding with rat bites on his nose, lips, or ears . . . a father reluctant to repair his damaged property, knowing that rats will only destroy it again . . . the disgust, fear, and hatred intrinsic to rodent-infested warrens of substandard living.

It was midafternoon when House Resolution 749 reached the floor. The resolution was a rule to consider the Rat Extermination and Control Act of 1967. Everything seemed in order for quick and easy passage of the bill. But something happened in the House that afternoon, something shameful and sad. A handful of Republicans joined together not merely to defeat the bill but to try to make low comedy of the entire program. Congressman Joel Broyhill, a Republican from Virginia, helped set the tone: "Mr. Speaker, I think the 'rat smart thing' for us to do is to vote down this rat bill 'rat now.' "

The floodgates opened. The House, as it is prone to do on occasion, had a field day—laughing about high commissioners of rats, hordes of rat bureaucrats, and enormous demands for rat patronage; jesting about the new civil "rats" bill, "throwing money down a rathole," and "discriminating between city and country rats." At the end of this burlesque the rat bill was defeated by a vote of 207 to 176. The old Republican-conservative-Democratic coalition had won again.

When I heard the description of this sorry spectacle, I felt outraged and ashamed. I was ashamed of myself for not having prepared the House of Representatives and the nation to approach this issue more intelligently and with a proper sense of urgency. I thought I had done

THE BEGINNING. The trip was Presidential politics, pure and simple. It was the opening effort of the 1964 campaign. And it was going beautifully . . .

Fort Worth, Texas, November 22, 1963: President Kennedy with Vice President Johnson, Senator Ralph Yarborough, Governor John Connally.

Dallas, November 22: Taking the oath of office from Judge Hughes aboard *Air Force One,* with Mrs. Kennedy and Mrs. Johnson. Washington, November 24: President Johnson lays wreath at foot of casket.

Funeral cortege moves toward the Capitol

Johnson meets with former U.S. Presidents and foreign leaders during first days. LEFT: With Dwight D. Eisenhower. BELOW, L.: Soviet Deputy Premier Anastas Mikoyan; R.: President Charles de Gaulle; BOTTOM: Harry S. Truman.

Early Days. LEFT: With Senate leaders Mansfield and Dirksen. RIGHT: With Chief Justice Earl Warren (TOP) and FBI Director J. Edgar Hoover "to assure the country that everything possible was being done to uncover the truth surrounding the assassination." BOTTOM: Old and new White House aides— Pierre Salinger, Bill Moyers, Ted Sorensen, Jack Valenti.

Addressing UN General Assembly, December 17, Johnson called for the creation of a world "safe for diversity and free from hostility."

I pledged to the Congress, and to the country on nationwide television, that the United States would keep its commitments "from South Vietnam to West Berlin."

Address before Joint Session of Congress (INSET, with House Speaker John McCormack, *c.*, and Carl Hayden, President Pro Tem of Senate).

STEADY ON COURSE: Vietnam 1963–1964. CIA Director John McCone reports at first meeting of National Security Council, December 5. BOTTOM, L.: Secretary of State Dean Rusk (*r.*) and Secretary of Defense Robert McNamara. Johnson receives first briefing on Vietnam from Ambassador Henry Cabot Lodge, November 24 (*clockwise,* Lodge, Rusk, McNamara, George Ball).

Top military and
civilian advisers meet
at LBJ Ranch.

During my first thirty days in office I believe I averaged no more than four or five hours' sleep a night. If I had a single moment when I could go off alone, relax, and forget the pressures of business, I don't recall it.

President Johnson keeps busy in the Oval Office.

everything I could; I thought the logic of exterminating rats was self-evident. But I was wrong. This was a case where I left undone something that I should have done.

I tried to remedy the situation by issuing a statement immediately: "The effect of today's House action in denying a rule to the Rat Extermination Act is a cruel blow to the children of America." I kept at it on succeeding days. The bill became a personal challenge. I was determined not to compound my error by failing to help build public sentiment.

I spoke about rats in every public forum I could find—in press conferences, in bill-signing ceremonies, in labor conventions, in meetings with Jaycees, in visits to scientific institutes. I recorded dozens of spot announcements for use on radio and television: "If we can spend literally millions to protect our cows from the screwworms, why can't we spend a little money to protect our children from the rats?" I asked my staff to encourage civil rights groups, social service groups, and urban and religious organizations to issue statements condemning the House action.

I argued economics with the conservatives: "If rats cost us about nine hundred million dollars a year, does it make economic sense to argue against a forty million dollar program of control?" I stressed morality with the moderates: "Have you ever lived in a broken-down tenement where you could hear rats scurrying inside the walls at night? Have you ever awakened in terror to the screams of your child being bitten by rats? . . . I know I haven't in my house. . . . As a child, with the help of some cheese, a few house cats, and traps, we got rid of most of them in the barns on the farm. We've been lucky . . . but can we ignore those who are less fortunate than we?" I talked politics with the Republicans: "I thought you'd like to know about an article in the current issue of *The Democrat:* its title is something like 'Republicans Laugh as Slum Dwellers Battle Rats'; now you can't afford to have us saying things like that, can you?"

On September 20 the House reconsidered its action. With the heat of public indignation upon them, the Republicans had stopped laughing. By a 44-vote margin the House voted to add a rat control amendment to our Partnership for Health bill.

June 29, 1967, was one of the memorable days, a day of hope and progress. This was the day I visited Reverend Leon Sullivan's antipoverty project in Philadelphia. Sullivan's operation, the Opportunities Industrialization Center, was concerned primarily with training the unemployed. Reverend Sullivan had started it himself in 1964. The center was located in four large buildings in various parts of the city and had an enrollment of 1,500, with a waiting list of 10,000. More than 80 per cent of its graduates were placed in skilled jobs, ranging from cooking to draftsmanship to machine operation.

I had heard about the center for many months. One of my young assistants had visited Philadelphia as part of a program I inaugurated in 1967 to send seven members of my personal staff to fourteen cities. Each of these young staffers lived incognito for several days in some of the worst ghetto areas. They talked with the residents, walked the streets, visited programs, listened to complaints, and reported their findings to me. My staffer described Sullivan's operation as the pride of Philadelphia's poverty program.

I stopped first at the converted jail where Sullivan's OIC had begun. I saw the ancient cell blocks, a remnant of the old mixed with the new. Reverend Sullivan told me why he had chosen that old building in 1964: "It is the most dank, most dismal place in town, a symbol of tragedy. If I could transform that building, I could transform men."

There was no question about the physical transformation of the building. A clean, sparkling welding shop filled the basement. On the first floor were a kitchen and dining room, where men and women were learning the art and craft of cooking. On the second floor was an electronics lab, where men and women were taught the skills of assembling radio and TV receiving sets. Across the hall was a machine shop—at one end men were learning draftsmanship; at the other end women were being taught to use industrial sewing machines.

The physical change was extraordinary, but the more important transformation was less tangible. I glimpsed it in the trainees who came forward to shake my hand. I saw men and women with pride in their eyes instead of defeat. I saw men and women whose shoulders were held straight and high, whose chins were up, and whose faces reflected courage and hope. I saw men and women whose self-respect was beginning to burn inside them like a flame, like a furnace that would fire them all their lives.

I knew what had built that center. The federal government had not built it . . . nor the city . . . nor the state. Yes, we had helped, but our part was small. What had built that center was the spirit in the breast of every human being who was a part of it—the spirit that wants to say "yes" to life itself, that wants to affirm the dignity of man, whatever his race, color, or creed.

As I left the center, a good-natured crowd of spectators gathered around me. Women held their children up to me with outstretched arms. People strained forward to shake my hand or touch my body. I tried as best I could to express my feelings.

"What Reverend Sullivan has shown me this morning opens my eyes and I hope will open the eyes of all the nation to the opportunity that lies here," I said. "Now, when you really talk about what is right, you don't appear to be nearly as interesting as you are when you talk about what is wrong. But I have seen so many things that are right here this morning that I wish everyone in America could not only see them but emulate them—and follow them.

"If somebody falls down the steps—that will get a lot of attention. But the poor lady that lifts him up goes unnoticed.

"If I had to sum up my feelings in a single phrase this morning, I would say to all of you: 'I believe we are going to make it.' "

When I left office, government reports showed that of the 35 million Americans who had been trapped in poverty in 1964, 12.5 million had been lifted out—a reduction of almost 36 per cent in just over four years. Not only because of the War on Poverty but also because of the expanding economy, people were coming out of poverty during those years at a rate two and a half times faster than at any time in our history.

We started something in motion with the attack on poverty. Its effects were felt in education, law, medicine, and social welfare, in business and industry, in civil and philanthropic life, in the labor movement, and in religion. Poverty became one of the compelling issues of our time. Finally and firmly, it was brought to the conscience of the nation. The poor had finally found their spokesman.

Of course, we had not lifted everyone out of poverty. There would be setbacks and frustrations and disappointments ahead. But no one would ever again be able to ignore the poverty in our midst, and I believe that is enough to assure the final outcome and to change the way of life for millions of our fellow human beings.

5

The 1964 Campaign

IN THE EARLY MONTHS of 1964, whenever I was asked about my intentions to campaign for a full term in the White House, I replied that I had not yet made firm plans. Many members of the press found this hard to understand, especially from a President who was very active. Actually, my activity was directed toward getting the country moving on the programs John F. Kennedy had pleaded for, which had been stalled in the Congress when he died. But it was widely interpreted in press reports to mean that I was racing hard to capture the Democratic nomination.

While I had not ruled out the possibility of running for the Presidency, I was beset with many doubts and reservations about the wisdom of doing so—doubts I had long felt; doubts that were not dispelled by holding the office.

The first serious mention I remember of my being a possible Presidential candidate appeared in a *Time* magazine cover story on June 22, 1953, when I was Minority Leader of the Senate. Part of that story is worth quoting:

> Occasionally a Democrat will speculate on whether Lyndon Johnson, the party's key man of 1953, may himself be the party's presidential candidate in 1956. Johnson's thoughts do not run that way. . . . When asked about the Presidency, Johnson says: "I'm not smart enough to make a President. I come from the wrong part of the country. I like the Senate job; it's the best job I've ever had. I want to stay here."

I repeated that sentiment often in the years that followed. Most of the time it went unnoticed.

Newspaper stories coming out of the Southern Governors' Conference in the fall of 1954 again speculated on my being a Presidential candidate.

I was asked about this in an interview by an Associated Press reporter on New Year's Day, 1955. I answered: "I have no interest, no ambitions in that direction." The interview was reported in *The New York Times* the following day.

I also received a large number of letters on the subject during the mid-1950s. The following answer, which I wrote to a constituent in Raymond-ville, Texas, was typical of all the responses I made: "Frankly," I said, "I am not a candidate for the Presidency or for any job other than the one I now hold. I have gone further in life than anyone, except my mother, ever thought I would, and I have found my present responsibilities so very heavy that I could not possibly think of reaching for more."

The job of Senate Democratic leadership gave me a unique opportunity to make a useful contribution to the nation's life. But it was a big job. And I knew, as no one else did, how hard I had to work to fill it. Later in 1955 I suffered a serious heart attack. I recovered, but the experience left me deeply aware of my physical limitations. There was also the problem of geography. I frankly did not think anyone from the South would be nominated, much less elected, in my lifetime.*

After the Democratic defeat of 1956, interest naturally began to focus on the 1960 race, and speculation again began to surround the names of all the party leaders. I stated my own position in the fall of 1957 in a release to the press: "I have made it absolutely clear both in public and private that I do not seek the nomination. There are absolutely no reservations in my mind on this question."

That took care of the matter—for a while. But anyone who has ever held a position of political leadership in America, or stood even briefly in the spotlight of Presidential speculation, learns one lesson quickly. Any expression of noninterest he makes will sooner or later be measured against William Tecumseh Sherman's famous disclaimer of 1884: "If nominated I will not accept; if elected I will not serve."'

Eventually I had to assess my own position against Sherman's unequivocal standard. In a radio report to my constituents on November 15, 1959, I once again made it clear that I did not want to be a Presidential candidate. I made this observation, however: "General Sherman, as a military man, had a number of considerations in mind when he made [his] statement, but I think that anyone who loves his country has to be careful about saying that he would refuse to serve his country."

Throughout the period between the 1956 convention and the 1960 convention, when my name was placed in nomination, I was aware, and gratefully so, of the growing interest in me expressed by people who ap-

---

* These are some of the doubts I related to former Ambassador Joseph Kennedy in October 1955, when he and Senator Jack Kennedy asked me to seek the 1956 nomination. See Chapter 1.

proved of the way I was handling my job in the Senate. But I never encouraged any effort to promote me as a Presidential candidate.

My position had not changed when the political campaign season of 1960 came around. I still had no enthusiasm for running. Once again Sam Rayburn tried to force me into the race. He asked John Connally, then practicing law in Fort Worth, Texas, to come to Washington. In May, along with some other backers, they opened a "Johnson for President" office without my approval. As soon as I found out about it, I had the sign taken down and the office closed.

But Mr. Rayburn kept pressuring me, and my response was always a flat "no." My objections were consistently the same: I was satisfied with my job, and a Southerner could not, and probably should not, be elected.

Finally, the Speaker presented his argument this way: Even if I did not win, he thought I could run a better race against John Kennedy for the nomination than any of the other candidates, none of whom could command substantial Southern support. If a strong contest were not made, he said, it would look as if the Catholic bosses behind Kennedy were running the Democratic party. He went down the list—Carmine De Sapio in New York, David Lawrence in Pennsylvania, Michael DiSalle in Ohio, Richard Daley in Chicago, Pat Brown in California. For the Democratic party to win, he said, we would have to show great diversified strength.

Mr. Rayburn was very much afraid of Richard Nixon's being elected. He believed Nixon had called him and President Truman traitors. Nixon always denied this. (Later Nixon showed me the words he had said that led to what he considered Mr. Rayburn's misunderstanding, and it seemed to me that he was being open and honest about it.) But the Speaker went to his grave believing that Nixon had impugned his patriotism, and he did not want Nixon to be President.

Shortly after that, on June 23, Philip Graham, publisher of *The Washington Post,* privately and personally made much the same argument for my candidacy. Graham strongly believed that a contest would be good for the party and, incidentally, for my leadership in the Senate. He offered to make a contribution to launch the race and to help me prepare the statement announcing that I would try for the nomination.

So only six days before the convention opened on July 11, in the auditorium of the new Senate Office Building in an open press conference, I reluctantly announced my candidacy for the Democratic nomination for the Presidency with a statement Graham helped me prepare. Once I was committed, I fought with all the energy I possessed.

The night John Kennedy won the nomination, I sent him a telegram of congratulations and issued the following statement to the press:

> The delegates have made their decision and I accept it with all my heart.

Senator Kennedy has my sincere congratulations, and my solemn assurance that in the coming months of this campaign, no one will be more dedicated than I—no one will work harder than I to make doubly sure of what all Democrats here and throughout the country know must come about for the good of the nation and the free world—that John F. Kennedy will be elected the next President of the United States.

We have a winner—he has proved it here.

Now, let our party unite behind our candidate—let us sweep the country this November, so that in January Democratic leadership may be restored to America in what promise to be the most challenging and difficult days in our history.

Then I went to bed.

The phone woke me about an hour after midnight. The caller was Speaker Rayburn. He told me he had heard that I was to be offered the Vice Presidential nomination, and he hoped that under no circumstances would I accept it. I thought it was most unlikely that I would be offered the nomination, but I assured him that I had no intention of accepting it if it were offered. I had not wanted the top spot on the ticket; the second spot appealed to me considerably less.

I went back to sleep. A few hours later the phone awakened me again. This time it was Jack Kennedy. He said he would like to come by and talk to me. I suggested that I come to see him instead, but he insisted that he would come to my room. He arrived about midmorning. He said he had given a lot of thought to putting together a ticket that could win the election. Adlai Stevenson's two defeats, he said, were very much on his mind. He had thought it over carefully and had concluded that he wanted me on the ticket with him. He told me frankly that he had also considered Senators Stuart Symington and Henry Jackson and Governor Orville Freeman of Minnesota, but that he did not believe any of them could assure support in the Southern states, which he thought was crucial. He was sure I would attract such support, so he was asking me to be his Vice Presidential running mate.

I thanked him for his frankness and his consideration of me, but I told him that I was interested only in being the party's Majority Leader in the Senate and in helping him to get a strong program enacted when he was elected. Anyway, I said, I had assured Speaker Rayburn that I would not take the second spot. Kennedy asked if I had any objection to his talking to Mr. Rayburn.

"No, of course not," I said.

He left then and went to Mr. Rayburn's room. Soon afterward the Speaker came to see me. He had a recommendation which astonished me. He said he thought that I should go on the ticket with Kennedy. I pointed out to him that only a few hours earlier he had told me under no circumstances should I do that. Now he was asking just the opposite. Why?

I remember his words very clearly. "Because," he said, "I'm a damn sight wiser man this morning than I was last night." Kennedy had persuaded him that without me on the ticket he could not carry the South, perhaps not even one Southern state. That would guarantee the election to the Republicans.

Bobby Kennedy came to my room later that morning. He said he thought I ought to know that Walter Reuther and Governor G. Mennen Williams of Michigan were both very upset that John Kennedy had decided to put a Southerner on the ticket. I told Bobby that I appreciated his concern, but that his information did not greatly surprise me. Later Bobby talked to Mr. Rayburn and John Connally and told them he thought I should be made Democratic National Chairman. Mr. Rayburn—as he later reported it to me—asked him: "Who speaks for the Kennedys?" When Bobby replied that it was Jack Kennedy, Rayburn made it clear that Jack Kennedy was the only one he would listen to.

Phil Graham also urged me to take the Vice Presidential nomination. So did Jim Rowe, a friend of mine of long standing, who was knowledgeable about politics and the Washington scene. A graduate of Harvard Law School, Rowe had been one of Justice Oliver Wendell Holmes's last Supreme Court clerks, and later an administrative assistant to President Franklin D. Roosevelt. Graham and Rowe visited my room together, where they learned of the exchange between Speaker Rayburn and Bobby Kennedy. Graham got in touch with Jack Kennedy. Following Graham's visit, Senator Kennedy called me on the phone and told me he was going to make a statement to the press that I was to be on the ticket with him. He asked me to make a similar announcement.

We both made our statements and that settled the matter—until that night. Then Mr. Rayburn informed me that Walker Stone, a newspaperman and a personal friend of both the Speaker and myself, had just told him that a wild story was making the rounds to the effect that Mr. Rayburn and I had threatened John Kennedy with defeat if he did not put me on the ticket. A number of people were convinced that Bobby had leaked the story to satisfy those to whom he had given assurance that I would not be selected.

Mr. Rayburn told me he was going to nail this lie right away. He apparently did so with a single telephone call to the candidate. The newspapers the next morning carried Senator Kennedy's forceful denial that there was any truth to the story. Kennedy and I went on from that day to join forces, and campaign, and win.

Four years later I was in the White House. But I had decidedly mixed feelings about whether I wanted to seek a four-year term there in my own right. On the one hand, I had a zest for the job, some very clear ideas about what should be accomplished, and confidence in my ability to work with the Congress in getting it done. On the other hand, I experienced a reluctance which must be viewed in the perspective of those days.

I had come to the White House in the cruelest way possible, as the result of a murderer's bullet. I had taken my oath of office in a climate of national anguish. I knew clearly enough, in those early months in the White House, that the Presidency of the United States was a prize with a heavy price. Scathing attacks had begun almost immediately, not only on me but on members of my family. I knew that unfounded rumors, crass speculations, remorseless criticism, and even insult would intensify in a political campaign.

There was, in addition, the constant uncertainty as to whether my health would stand up through a full four-year term. The strain of my work in the Senate had helped to bring on my severe heart attack when I was only forty-six. Now I was nine years older. All these considerations made retirement look exceedingly welcome. I felt a strong inclination to go back to Texas while there still was time—time to enjoy life with my wife and my daughters, to work in earnest at being a rancher on the land I loved, to slow down, to reflect, to live. I had spent three decades of my life in public service, and I had given the best I had to every position of public trust I ever held, including the Presidency itself for the brief time I occupied it. I believed I could retire in good conscience.

I discussed this matter with several people—Senator Dick Russell of Georgia, Walter Jenkins of my staff, friends from home like Jesse Kellam and Judge A. W. Moursund, and of course Lady Bird. She and I went over it many times, from every viewpoint. That spring of 1964 I asked her to summarize and put down on paper the pros and cons and her own conclusions. This was the memo she gave me on May 14, written by hand on several sheets torn from a stenographer's notebook:

I. If you do get out

We will most probably return to the ranch to live.

1. In the course of the next few months—or until we are forgotten—we will be criticized and our motives questioned—"What skeletons in the closet"—what fear of what disclosures—caused you to make this decision? etc. etc.

That will be painful.

2. There will be a wave of feeling, national this time and not largely statewide of—"You let us down"—keen, even bitter disappointment—similar to the wave of feeling after you accepted the Vice Presidency job with Kennedy.

This will be more painful.

3. You may live longer, and certainly you will have more time for

the hill country you love, and for me and Lynda and Luci. And that we'll all love.

But Lynda and Luci will in a year or so cease to be permanent residents of our life—only available for occasional companionship.

4.   You will have various ranch lands, small banking interests, and presumably the TV to use up your talents and your hours.

They are chicken-feed compared to what you are used to.

That may be relaxing for a while. I think it is not enough for you at 56. And I dread seeing you semi-idle, frustrated, looking back at what you left. I dread seeing you look at Mr. X running the country and thinking you could have done it better.

You may look around for a scape-goat. I do not want to be it.

You may drink too much—for lack of a higher calling.

II.   If you do *not* get out

You will most probably be elected President.

1.   In the course of the campaign and in the ensuing years, you— and I—and the children—will certainly get criticized and cut up, for things we have done, or maybe partly-in-a-way have done—and for others that we never did at all.

That will be painful.

2.   You are bound to make *some* bad decisions, be unable to achieve some high-vaulting ambitions, be disappointed at the inadequacies of some helpers—or perhaps of your own.

That will be painful even more.

3.   You may die earlier than you would otherwise. Nobody can tell that—as the last six months show. . . .

My Conclusions

Stay in.

Realize it's going to be rough—but remember we worry much in advance about troubles that never happen!

Pace yourself, within the limits of your personality.

If you lose in November—it's all settled anyway!

If you win, let's do the best we can for 3 years and 3 or 4 months— and then, the Lord letting us live that long, announce in February or March 1968 that you are not a candidate for re-election.

You'll then be 59, and by the end of that term a mellow 60, and I believe the juices of life will be stilled enough to let you come home in relative peace and acceptance. (We may even have grandchildren.)

Your loving
Wife

Through our years together I have come to value Lady Bird's opinion of me, my virtues and flaws. I have found her judgment generally excellent. But in this instance although I respected her logic, I was not convinced. As spring of 1964 turned to summer and then summer began to pass, I remained uncertain.

This period was, to be sure, a time of many great achievements. Our efforts to get a solid program through Congress were bearing fruit. The tax bill, the civil rights bill, the farm bill, and the antipoverty bill were all put on the books during these active and exciting months. But with all the triumphs there were troubles too. In July, scarcely two weeks after the landmark Civil Rights Act of 1964 was passed, Negro rioters went on the rampage in Harlem and Brooklyn. In the days that followed other black riots broke out in Rochester, New York, and in Jersey City, Elizabeth, and Paterson, New Jersey. And early in August U.S. Navy ships were attacked in the Gulf of Tonkin.

No one could then predict the scope of the problems that the riots or the Tonkin Gulf incident represented, but it was clear, from the viewpoint of the Presidency at least, that both events foreshadowed dark days of trial ahead. I believed that the nation could successfully weather the ordeals it faced only if the people were united. I deeply feared that I would not be able to keep the country consolidated and bound together. True, we had survived a time of crushing national sorrow, but I felt this was due partly to the shock of tragedy and partly because of a twenty-hour-a-day effort on my part to unite all sections and groups. I seriously doubted that I could continue such a pace indefinitely.

The burden of national unity rests heaviest on one man, the President. And I did not believe, any more than I ever had, that the nation would unite indefinitely behind any Southerner. One reason the country could not rally behind a Southern President, I was convinced, was that the metropolitan press of the Eastern seaboard would never permit it. My experience in office had confirmed this reaction. I was not thinking just of the derisive articles about my style, my clothes, my manner, my accent, and my family—although I admit I received enough of that kind of treatment in my first few months as President to last a lifetime. I was also thinking of a more deep-seated and far-reaching attitude—a disdain for the South that seems to be woven into the fabric of Northern experience. This is a subject that deserves a more profound exploration than I can give it here—a subject that has never been sufficiently examined. Perhaps it all stems from the deep-rooted bitterness engendered by civil strife over a hundred years ago, for emotional clichés outlast all others and the Southern cliché is perhaps the most emotional of all. Perhaps someday new understanding will cause this bias to disappear from our national life. I hope so, but it is with us still. To my mind, these attitudes represent an automatic reflex, unconscious or deliberate, on the part of opinion molders of the North and East in the press and television.

I expressed this feeling to James Reston of *The New York Times* in the spring of 1964. Scotty Reston disagreed with me, and a few days later he asked James Rowe to persuade me I was wrong. Jim wrote to me expressing his belief that as long as Reston and Walter Lippmann supported me, I would "get a good press" from the rest of the Washington news corps, who represent newspapers all over the country. But it was not long before those two reporters ceased to support me and began their tireless assaults on me and my administration. When that happened, I could not help noting that it was hard to find many words of support anywhere in the Washington press corps or television media.

So throughout the spring and summer months of 1964, while it was widely and positively and authoritatively assumed that I would be the Democratic nominee, I privately wrestled with grave doubts. There were days, of course, when the road seemed clear and I accepted the inevitability of my running. But there were other days when the outcome of the debate going on in my mind was, to me, exceedingly questionable.

My press secretaries used to tell the reporters that I liked to keep all my "options open." Many reporters disliked that, for they felt it denied them advance notice of my actions and decisions. I'm sure this approach caused them inconvenience at times, but that is the way I have always worked. I prefer to maintain as much flexibility as a man can until the moment a decision becomes final. Thus during that period, while I considered the question of whether or not to run for President, I foreclosed nothing. I took no action that would automatically trap me into a decision. I *did* keep all my options open.

I did not decide, fully and finally, until three o'clock on the afternoon of August 25, the day after the Democratic convention opened in Atlantic City. All the doubts that had been plaguing me for so long came to a head that morning. I knew all too well that time was running out and that an irrevocable decision would soon have to be made. I sat at my desk in the Oval Office and wrote out the following statement on a yellow pad:

> 44 months ago I was selected to be the Democratic Vice President. Because I felt I could best serve my country and my party, I left the Majority Leadership of the Senate to seek the Vice Presidential post, believing I could help unify the country and thus better serve it.
>
> In the time given me, I did my best. On that fateful day last year I accepted the responsibilities of the Presidency, asking God's guidance and the help of all of the people. For nine months I've carried on as effectively as I could.
>
> Our country faces grave dangers. These dangers must be faced and met by a united people under a leader they do not doubt.
>
> After 33 years in political life most men acquire enemies, as ships accumulate barnacles. The times require leadership about which there is no doubt and a voice that men of all parties, sections and color can follow.

I have learned after trying very hard that I am not that voice or that leader.

Therefore, I shall carry forward with your help until the new President is sworn in next January and then go back home as I've wanted to since the day I took this job.*

As soon as I had finished writing, I read the statement over the phone to George Reedy, my press secretary. His reaction was swift. Reedy said my decision had come too late and that my refusal to run would "just give the country to Goldwater." I replied that I would trust the democratic processes under which the country had been operating for two hundred years. I told him I would decide by three o'clock that afternoon about the statement—if, how, and when it should be released.

During the next hour, before and after a meeting with the National Security Council, I sought the counsel of two other close friends. The first was Walter Jenkins of my staff. I told him that I imagined the convention would nominate either Bobby Kennedy or Hubert Humphrey. Whoever was chosen, I thought he would have more hope of success as President than I would. "I just don't think a white Southerner is a man to unite this nation in this hour," I said.

"Mr. President," Walter said, "you just cannot do it. Maybe you could have three or four months ago, but it's too late now. The convention is upon us."

At noon I talked to Judge A. W. Moursund, a principal contact with the Texas delegation, then meeting in Atlantic City. I read my statement to him. He listened in silence. Then he said: "I don't ever want to be in the position of telling you what you ought to do. But I just don't know where the party will go if you don't run."

Later that day I received a note from my wife responding to my request for her reaction to the proposed statement I had written out. Her answer read:

Beloved—
You are as brave a man as Harry Truman—or FDR—or Lincoln. You can go on to find some peace, some achievement amidst all the pain. You have been strong, patient, determined beyond any words of mine to express. I honor you for it. So does most of the country.

* When Juanita Roberts, who had been by my side for many years, sent the statement to the files later that day, she appended this note to it:

The President came in alone. Sat without making phone calls or seeing anyone for a long time (10:40 to 11:06 a.m.) writing at his signing table.

He buzzed me to come in twice—asking "when was I sworn in?"—and again "when did I become leader?"

The attached is what he wrote. He apparently talked with Mrs. J. about his thinking—perhaps Senator Russell also. He mentioned it in conversations with Walter Jenkins and George Reedy on this date.

To step out now would be *wrong* for your country, and I can see nothing but a lonely wasteland for your future. Your friends would be frozen in embarrassed silence and your enemies jeering.

I am not afraid of *Time* * or lies or losing money or defeat.

In the final analysis I can't carry any of the burdens you talked of— so I know it's only *your* choice. But I know you are as brave as any of the thirty-five.

I love you always.

Bird

In a few words she hit me on two most sensitive and compelling points, telling me that what I planned to do would be wrong for my country and that it would show a lack of courage on my part. The message I read most clearly in her note to me was that my announcement to the 1964 convention that I would not run would be taking the easy way out. I decided finally that afternoon, after reversing my position of the morning and with a reluctance known to very few people, that I would accept my party's nomination.

Throughout this period, because I was keeping all my options open, I had to consider the question of the Vice Presidential candidate. Speculating on the Democratic ticket for 1964, the press was not dogmatic about its choice of the Vice Presidential nominee. Fully a dozen candidates were freely discussed every day. I told reporters at one news conference that I was gratified to see so much renewed interest in the Vice Presidency and the qualifications of the man who might occupy the office. Only a short time ago, I observed, so many people were asking, "Whatever happened to Lyndon Johnson?"

Among the most prominent names most widely and frequently mentioned were leading members of the administration. They included Bob McNamara, Dean Rusk, Adlai Stevenson, Sargent Shriver, Bobby Kennedy, and Secretary of Agriculture Orville Freeman. Any one of these men could have made a good campaign for Vice President, some better than others. To my mind, however, the speculation centering on them as a group was unfortunate. Whether I was to be the Presidential candidate or not, and none of these men was aware of my own doubts, I was still going to be the President for the remainder of the year. I wanted the Cabinet members to do their jobs, without consideration—in their minds or anyone else's—of how their performances would affect their political fortunes. If they wanted to campaign for office, I thought they should resign from the Cabinet.

---

* *Time* magazine, which just that week had run a highly critical article about Lady Bird.

A group was drumming up support for Dean Rusk; others were pushing Orville Freeman; there was some sentiment for McNamara. There were groups meeting and urging the nomination of Bobby Kennedy. I told Jim Rowe and Bob McNamara in July that I had decided to stop all the speculation, so that people wouldn't feel that everyone in the Cabinet was running for Vice President and that the business of government had come to a halt. I therefore announced that it would be "inadvisable for me to recommend to the convention [for Vice President] any member of the Cabinet or any of those who meet regularly with the Cabinet. . . ."

Before releasing this statement, I personally notified each of the gentlemen concerned. My conversation with the Attorney General was the only one to receive substantial attention. My relationship with Bobby Kennedy from the earliest hours of my Presidency—and before that, as far back as the 1960 campaign—had usually been cordial, though never overly warm. John Kennedy and I had achieved real friendship. I doubt his younger brother and I would have arrived at genuine friendship if we had worked together for a lifetime. Too much separated us—too much history, too many differences in temperament. But we had, I believe, a regard for each other's abilities. I remember hearing early in 1964 that there were some anti-Bobby stories going around the Democratic National Committee. I called Cliff Carter at the committee headquarters and told him: "Don't ever participate in anything that is anti-Kennedy. If anyone else does, fire him."

I also knew the strength Bobby had given to his brother. I appreciated the offer he voluntarily and surprisingly made early in my Presidency to become Ambassador to Vietnam. In a letter that he wrote to me on June 11, 1964, Attorney General Kennedy said: "I just wanted to make sure you understood that if you wished me to go to Vietnam in any capacity I would be glad to do so." He said that the Vietnam situation was "obviously the most important problem facing the United States" and he wanted me to know that if I felt he could help, he was at my service.

Bobby said he had discussed this matter with both Secretary McNamara and General Taylor and that they both understood his feelings. He recognized that there were complications in his taking this delicate overseas post, but he said he felt sure they could be worked out.

"In any case," he concluded, "I wished you to know my feelings on this matter."

I did not accept his offer because I feared, as did Secretaries Rusk and McNamara, that the potential danger to the late President's brother was too great. But it was a courageous offer for him to make.

On July 29 I asked Bobby to come to my office. I told him I felt that no member of the President's Cabinet should be considered for the Vice

Presidential nomination. In addition, I said, in my judgment he would not be the Democrats' strongest Vice Presidential candidate in 1964. In fairness to him, I wanted to tell him why I felt as I did. I explained that the Democratic ticket should have as much appeal as possible in the Middle West and the Border States and stir as little adverse reaction as possible in the South. The reason this was necessary, I thought, was that Senator Barry Goldwater, whom the Republicans had just nominated as their standard bearer, would find his greatest strength in the South, the Southwest, the Border States, and possibly the Middle West.

I told the Attorney General that I was sure he would understand my decision and the factors that entered into it, because President Kennedy had had to make a similar decision in 1960. I told Bobby that I foresaw an excellent career of public service for him in the future and that I would do what I could to further his career. There were reports that Adlai Stevenson was thinking of stepping down from the United Nations, and I suggested to Bobby that he might want to consider representing our country in that post should a vacancy occur.

These points and others were contained in a memorandum of talking points which I had had Clark Clifford prepare for the meeting after consulting leading Democrats, members of the Cabinet, and members of my staff. The memorandum was on my desk during our conversation, and I literally read it to him.*

The meeting between Bobby and me was later described in the press as a bitter occasion. It was not. We had a frank discussion, but there was no unpleasantness. When the conversation ended, I walked to the door with him. He looked at me and smiled and said words to this effect: "Well, I'm sorry that you've reached this conclusion, because I think I could have been of help to you."

I said: "Well, I think you *will* be of help to us—and to yourself too."

Shortly after this conversation took place, Bobby decided to run for the Senate in New York against Kenneth Keating. He asked me to help him. I willingly did to the best of my ability. I campaigned for him in New York City and throughout the state, first and foremost because I wanted him to win. I thought he would make a good Senator. But there was another important reason—the loyalty I felt to the memory of his brother. I had to disappoint a friend—Adlai Stevenson, who at that point had decided to seek the New York senatorial nomination himself. He abandoned the idea when I told him that I felt I must support Bobby. Stevenson was hurt, and my inability to encourage him constituted one of my deepest regrets about the New York campaign.

---

* For the full text of the memorandum for my meeting with Bobby Kennedy see Appendix, pp. 576–77.

With the Cabinet officers eliminated from consideration, the list of Vice Presidential possibilities narrowed considerably. I had said that I would make my recommendation if and when I became the Presidential nominee. I gave the matter extremely careful thought. Two men whom I looked upon as prospects were the Senators from Minnesota, Eugene McCarthy and Hubert Humphrey. Humphrey had always been a strong contender, in my opinion, but I liked McCarthy and believed he should be considered. I was still reviewing various possibilities when I heard that Senator McCarthy intended to remove himself from consideration to support Humphrey. From the White House I placed a telephone call to McCarthy in Atlantic City. When I reached him, I asked him not to announce that he was taking himself out of the running immediately. But McCarthy said it was too late; he had already given the press the text of his telegram to me, announcing his decision. In the end, I concluded that Hubert Humphrey was the best choice in the light of all the circumstances. I asked him to come to the White House for a conference.

There was a brief flurry of press speculation when Senator Thomas J. Dodd of Connecticut accompanied Humphrey to this meeting. There was sentiment within the Democratic party that favored Dodd as the Vice Presidential nominee because his conservative tendencies would counter Goldwater's. I felt that his selection was not indicated, but I had told Dodd earlier that I would advise him of my decision before I announced it publicly. Consequently, I asked him to come to the White House with Humphrey. We then went to Atlantic City, and I presented my recommendation in person to an enthusiastic convention.

Atlantic City in August 1964 was a place of happy, surging crowds and thundering cheers. To a man as troubled as I was by party and national divisions, this display of unity was welcome indeed. But ovations, however deafening, can be short-lived. As I stood there warmed by the waves of applause that rolled in on us, touched to the heart by the display of affection, I could only hope that this harmonious spirit would endure times of trouble and discouragement as well.

Whenever John Kennedy had looked ahead to the election of 1964, he always viewed Senator Barry Goldwater of Arizona as the Republican nominee. So had I. Goldwater was solidly entrenched with the delegates to the Republican convention, but his strength had a much wider base than that. He had built an attractive image in many parts of the country with various segments of the population. Many people have forgotten it, but in the early 1960s Senator Goldwater was a popular figure on many college campuses. He had a stalwart following among members of the business community, and he appealed to Southerners as well as Westerners.

Barry Goldwater and I, both coming from the Southwest, had been friends in the Senate. After I had accepted the Vice Presidential nomination on the Democratic ticket in 1960, I received a letter from Goldwater confessing to a "numb feeling of despair." He wrote that he found it "incredible to try to understand how you are going to try to embrace the socialist platform of your party. . . . You were intended for great things, but I don't think you are going to achieve them now. . . ."

I replied that "all of us have to decide for ourselves what represents a 'socialist platform.' . . ." It was unlikely that Goldwater and I would ever agree on social issues. Our separate experiences had shaped political philosophies in substantial opposition to each other. This was the nature of the political difference—Goldwater was entirely correct when he called his candidacy a "choice," not just an "echo"—that the campaign of 1964 offered to the voters of America. Our differences came to light most clearly on the two overriding questions of peace and domestic reform.

Goldwater brought the peace issue into focus early in the campaign with a series of statements implying that he would more than willingly threaten to use, or even use, nuclear weapons to gain American ends. Statements such as "I want to lob one into the men's room of the Kremlin and make sure I hit it" created the image of an impulsive man who shoots from the hip, who talks and acts first and thinks afterward.

From a political point of view, I did not believe that Goldwater's rash statements needed any comment from me. He was clearly isolating himself from the majority of voters. I decided that the most important thing I could do to hold the country together was not to attack political foes but to build programs. I thought the best answer to Goldwater's repeated suggestions that we consider using "tactical" nuclear weapons on the battlefield was my relentless search for a detente with the Soviet Union and my insistence on restraint in Vietnam.

The debate on domestic issues got off to an equally dramatic start when Goldwater went to Knoxville, Tennessee, the home of TVA, and attacked public power; then he proceeded to the heart of Appalachia and criticized the poverty program; and then he traveled to Florida, the retirement home of millions of Americans, and denigrated Medicare.

With this unusual beginning, it was clear that the Goldwater effort was not going to be a traditional centrist campaign. The political theory underlying the Goldwater strategy assumed that a "hidden majority" of frustrated, conservative Americans had for decades stayed away from the polls in protest against the moderating influence of the two-party system. These people, according to the theory, would emerge as a decisive force in Presidential politics if only the Republican party would turn its back on "me-tooism" and offer them a genuine choice.

The genius of our two parties is that they pull to the center, where the vast majority of the votes traditionally are in this country. But Goldwater moved out of that middle ground and left it to us.

I decided early in the campaign to separate the Goldwater challenge from the traditional Republican party. This separation was at the heart of our "frontlash" strategy, an attempt to practice a politics of consensus that would make it as easy as possible for lifelong Republicans to switch their votes in November to the Democratic column. Moreover, I deeply believed that the conservative leadership that triumphed in San Francisco in 1964 was in the best interests of the Republican party. I expressed these views to a group of young people in a television program on October 24, 1964:

> A great strength of the two-party system is that basically we have been in general agreement on many things and neither party has been the party of extremes or radicals, but temporarily some extreme elements have come into one of the parties and have driven out or locked out or booed out or heckled out the moderates. . . . I think an overwhelming defeat for them will be the best thing that could happen to the Republican party in this country in the eyes of all the people. Because then you would restore moderation to that once great party of Abraham Lincoln and the leadership then could unite and present a solid front to the world.

Beyond this base of consensus politics lay a critical choice: whether to play it safe by staying in the center or to shape the mandate by placing my views and programs squarely before the voters. As any campaign wears on, a candidate feels increasing pressure to talk only in platitudes, to alienate no one, and to keep the maximum number of people with him. But I knew that the Republican party's swing to the right gave me a rare opportunity to further the cause of social reform. Having inherited the entire political center, if only for the time being, I decided to seek a new mandate from the people. If Goldwater wants to give the voters a choice, I concluded, then we'll give them a *real* choice—a choice not between conservatism and "stand-patism" but between programs of social retreat and programs of social progress.

Goldwater asked the voters to give him a mandate to abolish social security; I asked them for a mandate to expand it with Medicare. Goldwater called for a return to a sink-or-swim policy toward the poor; I called for an expanded government program to eradicate poverty. Goldwater called for a strengthening of states' rights; I called for more federal protection for civil rights. Goldwater favored what amounted to an unregulated economy; I favored imaginative fiscal and monetary policies that would eliminate the old cycles of boom and bust.

Suddenly all the old nit-picking arguments that separated our parties had been swept aside. We were now engaged in a colossal debate over the very principles of our system of government. Would we cast aside thirty years of progress and reform and return to the days of Harding,

Coolidge, and Hoover, or would we strengthen and build on the programs of Franklin Roosevelt, Harry Truman, and John Kennedy? Goldwater allowed no middle ground, and I accepted that challenge.

I had no doubt as to how the vast majority of voters would respond. I was convinced that given such a clear-cut choice, the American people would elect to move forward with a program of social progress. Before I left Atlantic City after my nomination, I met with the members of the Democratic National Committee, who were primed for political battle. I told them: "We are going to finish the work that Jack Kennedy left us, but we have a mandate to begin a new program of our own." We built the campaign strategy around a progressive program, the program that formed the framework of the Great Society. The Great Society was never, in my mind, just a visionary utopian ideal. I considered it a realistic outline of what this nation could achieve in a limited period of time if we marshaled our will and committed our resources.

A man's vision reflects his memories. As I looked out on the nation from the President's Oval Office, my reflections included images burned deep in my mind for over a half a century. I remembered my father's concern for the tenant farmer and for the workers' need for collective bargaining. I remembered my mother's deep faith in the value of education. I remembered the pinched and hopeless look of poverty I saw on the faces of the Mexican-American children I had taught. I remembered the army of jobless and ragged men who rode grimy boxcars across our country during the Depression. These and a hundred other separate recollections of struggle and hope were all part of my heritage. They formed a portion of the background against which I developed the programs I felt America wanted and needed.

At the heart of it, I thought of the Great Society as an extension of the Bill of Rights. When our fundamental American rights were set forth by the Founding Fathers, they reflected the concerns of a people who sought freedom in their time. But in our time a broadened concept of freedom requires that every American have the right to a healthy body, a full education, a decent home, and the opportunity to develop to the best of his talents.

The Great Society was described with different words at different times. In substance, I saw it as a program of action to clear up an agenda of social reform almost as old as this century and to begin the urgent work of preparing the agenda for tomorrow. The program we submitted to the voters during the 1964 campaign would commit the nation to press on with the War on Poverty, to provide greater educational opportunities for all American children, to offer medical care to the elderly, to conserve our water and air and natural resources, and to tackle the country's long-standing housing shortage. The people responded to that program with an enthusiasm that made its mark on American history. Not only did the

voters give the Democratic ticket the most extensive plurality in history *
but they also sent to the Congress the largest Democratic majority since
1936.

A political campaign is a blur, a whirlwind, an excitement—frustrating,
exhilarating, exhausting, and necessary. While a campaign is in progress,
the participants are so close to the fire and the fury that they often find
it difficult to judge how the race is going. Here instinct, a sensitivity for
events and people, is the only gauge. But in 1964 one day near the beginning of the campaign offered a revealing and prophetic glimpse of what
was to come. This was the day we all began to sense that something big
was in the wind, what a landslide was in the making.

The day was Monday, September 28. I left the south lawn of the White
House by helicopter at 8:05 A.M. for a trip through New England. This
trip was to provide the first large testing of public response, and we had
planned an exhausting schedule with six stops in six states: Providence,
Rhode Island; Hartford, Connecticut; Burlington, Vermont; Portland,
Maine; Manchester, New Hampshire; and a final stop in Boston, Massachusetts, not so much to campaign as to visit Senator Edward Kennedy—
seriously injured from a plane crash—in New England Baptist Hospital.

At 8:15 A.M. we were airborne from National Airport, headed for
Providence, our first stop. An hour and twenty minutes later we came in at
Theodore Green Airport, named for an old and valued friend, the late
Senator Green of Rhode Island. As we landed, I had no inkling of what
was in store. No pollster or political guide, no seer or wise adviser, had
any notion of what this incredible day was to produce in the way of
surprises and political portents. When we alighted from the plane, the
airport was jammed with people. They were everywhere, packed together
and cheering wildly. Banners were waving, and bands were playing. It
was a tumultuous beginning and Senators John Pastore and Claiborne
Pell were plainly pleased—perhaps jubilant would be a better description.
Pastore had been my personal choice for keynote speaker at the convention, and I considered him one of my dearest friends. This enthusiastic
display made me very happy, for him as well as for myself.

The motorcade crept toward the city. It was heavy going. The crowds
thickened. Along the sidewalks, spilling over into the street, people stood
five and six deep. I asked the driver of the car to stop frequently, so that I
could touch their hands and speak to them. As we moved through a pre-
dominantly black section of Providence, children, teenagers, and adults
pressed around the car—laughing, cheering, and calling out to me. One tall
black man, I remember especially, grabbed my hand, held on to it, and

* A plurality of nearly 16 million votes, 61 per cent of the votes cast.

shouted, "Thank you, Mr. President. Thank you. God love you." I felt his sincere warmth, and even as the car moved on he was still shouting, "Thank you!"

By the time we reached the downtown area, every political veteran in that motorcade grasped the significance of the moment. The newspapers estimated the crowds to be about half a million, totally unprecedented. The drive from the airport to Meehan Auditorium at Brown University, where I made my principal speech of the day, took one hour and fifty minutes. The distance was only eight miles.

At 12:37 P.M. we were airborne from Green Airport on our way to Hartford. The airport reception there was a duplicate of the Providence turnout. We received an overwhelming welcome from thousands of people. With Governor John Dempsey, Senators Abraham Ribicoff and Tom Dodd and Congressman Emilio Daddario by my side, we made our way to the motorcade. As we moved slowly toward the city, again the crowds began to swell, and the warmth of their greeting increased. We paused in Constitution Plaza, where I made a short speech and led a brief pep rally. I called out, "Are you going to vote Democratic in November?" and the responding "yes" rocked the street.

It was almost impossible for our cars to move forward, so heavy were the crowds. At the Hartford Times Square, where I was to speak, there was literally no open space. The square was a sea of laughing, friendly faces. The police estimate of the total crowd in Hartford was more than a quarter of a million. I am generally skeptical of crowd estimates, but I was quite willing to believe those figures, after what I had seen.

We left Hartford at 3:50 P.M. headed for an airport rally in Burlington, Vermont, whose population according to the 1960 census was 35,531. Governor Philip Hoff had joined us in Hartford to accompany us to his home state. When we landed at Burlington, I think even Governor Hoff was surprised at the throng that had gathered, an estimated 15,000 people, almost half the population of the city. It was a happy multitude. The people were enthusiastic and quickly made known their friendly feelings toward me. One pretty little girl in the front line held up a large sign which read: "You can pull my ears anytime, Mr. President." Mrs. Johnson laughed at that and so did I.

At 6:30 P.M. we landed in Portland, Maine, once more to a rousing airport welcome. Senator Edmund Muskie accompanied me in the motorcade. There were so many people filling the streets that we could only inch ahead. When we finally reached downtown Portland dusk had fallen, and the throngs were so thick that Ed Muskie could only exclaim, "Unbelievable!" We were two hours behind schedule by that time, but the people waited patiently. Some of my staff considered the Portland, Maine, reception the most unusual of the day. *The Washington Post* reported that "almost the entire population of 70,000 jammed the streets." At one point the motorcade moved less than a block in five minutes. By the time we reached City Hall Plaza it was almost 8 P.M. Since my arrival in Boston was certain to be late, I instructed a member of my staff to call Senator Kennedy and ask if I should still visit him. The Senator, though in pain, insisted that he would be expecting me and wanted to see me.

We arrived in Manchester, New Hampshire, at 9:30 P.M., hours behind schedule, but the people were still waiting, at the airport and in the streets, with undimmed excitement. Bands were playing and signs and placards were waving in the dark night, streaked with the lights of our motorcade. Our destination was the Carpenter Motor Inn, where I made a short speech. Governor John King and Senator Tom McIntyre were with me. At 11:45 P.M. our plane was airborne once again, headed for our last stop, Boston, Massachusetts. Governor Endicott Peabody had arrived in Manchester to fly with me to his home state.

We landed in Boston at 12:25 A.M. I immediately motored to New England Baptist Hospital. A large gathering of people was still congregated in front of the hospital, though it was long after midnight. I went inside and met with Senator Kennedy and his beautiful wife, Joan. I described the exciting day, and he told me how pleased he was with the reception New England had accorded me. I wished him a speedy recovery, and at 2.05 A.M. our plane was at last on its way home to Washington. We landed at National Airport twenty hours after we had taken off for what had turned out to be the most fascinating and surprising day of the campaign.*

As my staff and I assessed that day, it was clear to us that our message was getting through to the people. Though the advance polls had been satisfactory, this trip through New England early in the campaign not only verified the polls but also pointed to a possible victory of massive proportions. I have been in politics too long ever to be overoptimistic or overconfident. I knew, though, that what we had accomplished in the previous year and our announced goals for the years ahead were clearly in accord with the hopes and needs of the people.

I set off on another campaign trip a week later. Before my departure, I took my wife across the Potomac to the Alexandria, Virginia, railroad station, where a special train—the "Lady Bird Special"—stood waiting to

---

* Reporters who covered that hectic day of campaigning evidently assessed it the same way. Douglas Kiker, writing in the *New York Herald Tribune,* said: "Massive, surging, uncontrollable crowds, by far the largest and the most enthusiastic to greet him since he assumed office cheered President Johnson through New England yesterday. . . . They were wild, they were happy, and they were with him all the way." Jack Steele, reporting for Scripps-Howard newspapers, wrote: "Most of New England seems to have given its heart to Lyndon Johnson and to be ready to vote for him on November 3. . . . Even Democratic Chairman John M. Bailey was wide-eyed with wonder as he watched the swelling crowds, whose enthusiasm matched their numbers. . . . For Mr. Johnson belted the political ball over the fence yesterday."

carry her on a whistle-stop campaign through the South. I spoke briefly to the thousands who had assembled there. But it was Lady Bird's gentle words that moved the listeners and set the tone for the entire remarkable trip she was about to undertake. "I wanted to tell you," she said, "that to this President and his wife the South is a respected and valued and beloved part of this country."

I returned to Washington, and the next day, October 7, I flew to the heartland of the nation, the Middle West. It was New England all over again.

We landed in Des Moines, Iowa, and the airport was crowded. With Governor Harold Hughes beside me in the car, we crept the six miles into town through cheering crowds. At one point we passed a group of young people holding up a sign which read: "Please, Mr. President, shake our hands." I stopped the car and happily complied, as they gathered round. The turnout in Des Moines was described by both Governor Hughes and the police chief as the largest in Iowa's history. Every moment I was part of it I was caught up in its generous and eager spirit.

We left Des Moines that afternoon and flew to Illinois—first to Springfield and then to Peoria. Though Illinois is normally Republican territory, great waves of people greeted us in both places. Senator Paul Douglas, an old campaigner, said there had never been such turnouts in central Illinois for either political party. The next day, through industrial sections of Indiana, along the streets of Indianapolis, and in Cleveland, Ohio, the same experience was repeated: the vast crowds, the warm welcomes, the rousing cheers.

The following day we witnessed it all again in Louisville, Kentucky, and Nashville, Tennessee, as we headed south. I remember a grinning letter carrier in Louisville. I called out to him, "You all right?" His smile grew even broader, and he shouted back, "Everybody's all right."

From Nashville we flew to New Orleans, Louisiana. In the evening I went to the railroad station to wait for the Lady Bird Special to arrive, ending its four-day, 1,700-mile trip. By every standard the whistle-stop tour had been a spectacular success. Lady Bird had described the trip as a "journey of the heart," and everywhere she stopped, hearts seemed to respond. The people who gathered around her railroad car platform, who turned out to hear her speak, or who just stood and waved as her train passed by reciprocated her affection for them. Politicians and reporters alike praised her grace and warmth and poise. She had endured hecklers with dignity; she had conquered thousands with love. I was terribly proud of her as I welcomed her that evening in New Orleans. We went together to the Jung Hotel, where I was scheduled to make a speech. That speech was one of my major civil rights addresses of the campaign.

Politically, the issue of civil rights was unpredictable. Public opinion expert Sam Lubell made this observation: "The racial issue is the only one that can elect Goldwater." A member of my staff repeated to me a statement made to him by the mayor of a major city. "Young man," the mayor had said, "I am scared. I am sixty-seven years old. I have been in politics a long time. I have never seen what we are seeing among the voters today. The backlash is only part of it. The antivote—the 'against' vote—is big and is going to get bigger." Under the circumstances, many people advised me to avoid the racial issue. I disagreed. I was concerned that the riots foreshadowed trouble and divisiveness in the country, but I knew this issue could not and should not be avoided. I made it clear that I considered civil rights in all its aspects an important campaign issue.

When the black militants inaugurated their protests in the North, I stated my belief that there could be no compromise with the preservation of law and order in any section of the country. "American citizens," I said then, "have a right to protection of life and limb—whether driving along a highway in Georgia, a road in Mississippi, or a street in New York City."

I had confidence that given the proper leadership, the American people would repair the injustice so long borne by the Negro. I did not think the majority of Americans would retreat from justice because of the destructive work of a lawless few, black or white. I wanted to make this point absolutely clear. I chose to make it, not in New York or Chicago or Los Angeles, but in New Orleans—near home, in my own backyard.

Those who were preparing my trip had recommended in a memorandum: "The less said about civil rights the better." The speech I had with me contained only one rather mild reference: "If we are to heal our history and make this nation whole, prosperity must know no Mason-Dixon line and opportunity must know no color line."

But when I stood up to speak that night and looked out over the crowd of people who had been in my camp so long, knowing how sorely our unity was going to be strained and how often the racial issue had been used to divide us before, I knew I could only say what I deeply believed. I spoke off the cuff and from the heart.

"Whatever your views are," I told the 2,500 people gathered there, "we have a Constitution and we have a Bill of Rights, and we have the law of the land, and two-thirds of the Democrats in the Senate voted for it and three-fourths of the Republicans. I signed it, I am going to enforce it, and I am going to observe it, and I think that any man that is worthy of the high office of President is going to do the same thing."

The applause was less than overwhelming. But I was in it, and I had to continue. I wanted the whole nation to know how profoundly animosity and hatred waste the common effort and dissipate the national energy. So many more important considerations are ignored, to the detriment of the people, when passions are spent in prejudice.

I told the New Orleans assembly a story about Senator Joe Bailey, who was reared and educated in Mississippi and elected to the House and then the Senate from Texas. Bailey had been talking to Congressman Sam Rayburn about the economic problems of the South and had mentioned the great future the South could enjoy if it could develop its resources.

"I wish I felt a little better, Sammy," Joe Bailey said to Mr. Rayburn. "I would like to go back to old Mississippi and make them one more Democratic speech. I feel like I have at least one more left in me."

I looked over the members of the audience, then gave them the old Senator's final words to Mr. Rayburn on that occasion: "Poor old Mississippi, they haven't heard a Democratic speech in thirty years. All they ever hear at election time is 'Nigger, Nigger, Nigger.' "

After New Orleans I stopped at the Ranch for a brief rest, and then I hit the road again. In every part of the country, from the Gulf Coast to New England and across the mountains to the West Coast, I took my message to crowds as enthusiastic, as enormous, as vibrant as I have ever seen anywhere at any time. I can summon from memory now the sight and sound of those huge crowds of men, women, and children, and I don't think I will ever forget them. We had, they and I, an historic adventure that will stir pride in me as long as I live.

On the night of November 3, 1964, I watched the election results in the company of my family and old friends at the Driskill Hotel in Austin. That was a memorable evening. I had said during the campaign that history was being made on the main streets of America. As the returns came in, it was clear that history *had* been made. I spoke late that night to the American people, amid the happy debris of victory in the Municipal Auditorium in Austin, the city that had first sent me to Congress more than a quarter of a century before. I voiced the deepest wish of my heart when I called our overwhelming vote "a mandate for unity"—the goal that had been so consistently in my heart and mind for so long. Our victory was, in any event, a mandate for action, and I meant to use it that way.

Thousands of words have been written and spoken about the size and nature of that victory in 1964 and what it portended. The words I liked best—for they were nearer to what I believe is the truth than any others—are these:

> In 1964 [President Johnson] won the greatest popular victory in modern times. . . . He has gained huge popularity, but he has never failed to spend it in the pursuit of his beliefs or in the interest of his country. He has led us to build schools and clinics and homes and hospitals, to clean the water and to clear the air, to rebuild the city and to recapture

the beauty of the countryside, to educate children and to heal the sick and comfort the oppressed on a scale unmatched in our history.

Those words describe how I felt victory should be used. They are from a speech made by Senator Robert F. Kennedy to New York State Democrats on June 3, 1967, almost three years after the 1964 Democratic landslide victory and only a year before his death.

6

Challenge and Response
[*VIETNAM 1964–1965*]

I N AUGUST 1964 an unexpected crisis developed, one that threatened for a time to change the nature of the war in Vietnam. During the early hours of Sunday morning, August 2, a high-priority message came in reporting that North Vietnamese torpedo boats had attacked the destroyer USS *Maddox* in the Gulf of Tonkin. The duty officer in the White House Situation Room gathered all the available data, prepared a summary, and sent it to my bedroom. The report began:

Mr. President:
Early this morning the USS Maddox was attacked by three DRV *
PT boats while on patrol approximately 30 miles off the North Vietnamese coast in the Gulf of Tonkin.
The Captain of the Maddox returned the fire with 5-inch guns and requested air support from the carrier Ticonderoga on station nearby in connection with reconnaissance flights in that area.
Ticonderoga jets arrived shortly and made strafing attacks on the PT boats resulting in one enemy boat dead in the water, two others damaged and turned tail for home.
The Maddox reports no personnel or material damages.

The *Maddox* was on what we called the De Soto patrol. One purpose was to spot evidence of Hanoi's continuing infiltration of men and war supplies into South Vietnam by sea. Another was to gather electronic intelligence. The actions and objectives of the patrol were similar to those of Soviet trawlers off our coasts and to the intelligence activities of many nations throughout the world. In an important way our De Soto patrol

---

* Democratic Republic of (North) Vietnam.

was far more justified, for Hanoi was sending troops south to kill Americans.

I called a meeting of key advisers later that morning in the White House. Attending were Secretary Rusk and Under Secretary Ball from State, Deputy Secretary of Defense Vance, General Wheeler of the Joint Chiefs of Staff, and several experts in technical intelligence. We studied the latest reports and discussed what we should do about this attack on the high seas. We concluded that an overeager North Vietnamese boat commander might have been at fault or that a shore station had miscalculated. So we decided against retaliation, but I ordered the Navy to continue the patrol, add another destroyer, and provide air cover. We were determined not to be provocative, nor were we going to run away. We would give Hanoi the benefit of the doubt—this time—and assume the unprovoked attack had been a mistake.

Another form of naval activity, not connected with our patrol, was going on in the area. During 1964 the South Vietnamese navy made small-scale strikes against installations along the North Vietnamese coast. The purpose was to interfere with Hanoi's continuing program of sending men and supplies into the South by sea. Senators and Representatives designated to oversee our intelligence operations were fully briefed on these South Vietnamese activities, and on our supporting role, in January 1964, again in May, twice in June, and again in early August. Secretary McNamara described the operations, codenamed 34-A, in a closed session with members of the Senate Foreign Relations Committee on August 3, 1964.

One 34-A attack occurred on July 30. At the time, the destroyer *Maddox* had not started its patrol and was 120 miles away. A second South Vietnamese attack took place the night of August 3 when the De Soto patrol was at least 70 miles away. It was later alleged that our destroyers were supporting the South Vietnamese naval action. The fact is our De Soto commanders did not even know where or when the 34-A attacks would occur. Nonetheless, we decided, after the first attack on the *Maddox,* to move its cruising track farther north so there would be even wider separation between the De Soto patrol and any possible South Vietnamese activity along the coast.

Though we had decided to treat the first North Vietnamese strike against our destroyer as a possible error, we drafted a stiff note to the Hanoi regime. We said that our ships had always operated freely on the high seas, and added: "They will continue to do so." We advised the North Vietnamese to be "under no misapprehension as to the grave consequences which would inevitably result from any further unprovoked offensive military action against United States forces." When prompt delivery to Hanoi proved impossible, we broadcast the note on Voice of America radio and released it to the world press.

Two days later the North Vietnamese struck again at our destroyers, this time at night (midmorning Washington time) on August 4. A few minutes after nine o'clock I had a call from McNamara. He informed me that our intelligence people had intercepted a message that strongly indicated the North Vietnamese were preparing another attack on our ships in the Tonkin Gulf. Soon we received messages from the destroyer *Maddox* that its radar and that of the USS *C. Turner Joy* had spotted vessels they believed to be hostile. The enemy ships appeared to be preparing an ambush. The *Maddox* and *C. Turner Joy* had changed course to avoid contact, but they then sent word that the enemy vessels were closing in at high speed. Within an hour the destroyers advised that they were being attacked by torpedoes and were firing on the enemy PT boats. As messages flowed in from Pacific Command Headquarters, McNamara passed along the key facts to me.

We had scheduled a noon meeting of the National Security Council to discuss the situation in Cyprus, and several key advisers had assembled for that session. They included Secretary of the Treasury Douglas Dillon, Attorney General Robert Kennedy, Under Secretary Ball, CIA Director John McCone, USIA Director Carl Rowan, and Edward A. McDermott, Director of Emergency Planning. I was delayed in my office by phone calls, and the discussion proceeded without me. At 12:30 P.M. Rusk, McNamara, General Curtis LeMay of the Joint Chiefs, and Mac Bundy arrived at the White House from their meetings at the Pentagon. Bundy reported their arrival to me and we walked together into the Cabinet Room. Deputy Secretary of Defense Vance arrived from the Pentagon a few minutes later. We immediately took up the crisis in the Tonkin Gulf. McNamara gave us the latest available information. Rusk said that he and McNamara were developing a set of options for response but that the proposals were not yet ready for presentation. I closed the NSC meeting and asked Rusk, McNamara, Vance, McCone, and Bundy to join me for lunch. The unanimous view of these advisers was that we could not ignore this second provocation and that the attack required retaliation. I agreed. We decided on air strikes against North Vietnamese PT boats and their bases plus a strike on one oil depot.

During the afternoon additional intelligence reports flowed in. We intercepted a message from one of the attacking North Vietnamese boats in which it boasted of having fired at two "enemy airplanes" and claimed to have damaged one. The North Vietnamese skipper reported that his unit had "sacrificed two comrades." Our experts said this meant either two enemy boats or two men in the attack group. Another message to North Vietnamese PT boat headquarters boasted: "Enemy vessel perhaps wounded." Clearly the North Vietnamese knew they were attacking us.

Action reports continued to arrive from our destroyers, and from the Pacific Command. A few were ambiguous. One from the destroyer *Maddox* questioned whether the many reports of enemy torpedo firings were all valid.

I instructed McNamara to investigate these reports and obtain clarification. He immediately got in touch with Admiral U. S. G. Sharp, Jr., the Commander in Chief, Pacific, and the Admiral in turn made contact with the De Soto patrol. McNamara and his civilian and military specialists went over all the evidence in specific detail. We wanted to be absolutely certain that our ships had actually been attacked before we retaliated.

Admiral Sharp called McNamara to report that after checking all the reports and evidence, he had no doubt whatsoever that an attack had taken place. McNamara and his associates reached the same firm conclusion. Detailed studies made after the incident confirmed this judgment.

I summoned the National Security Council for another meeting at 6:15 P.M. to discuss in detail the incident and our plans for a sharp but limited response. About seven o'clock I met with the congressional leadership in the White House for the same purpose. I told them that I believed a congressional resolution of support for our entire position in Southeast Asia was necessary and would strengthen our hand. I said that we might be forced into further action, and that I did not "want to go in unless Congress goes in with me." I reminded them that I had given this advice to President Eisenhower and he had followed it in the Middle East and Formosan crises. In both instances Congress had backed him with resolutions.

I was determined, from the time I became President, to seek the fullest support of Congress for any major action that I took, whether in foreign affairs or in the domestic field. I believed that President Truman's one mistake in courageously going to the defense of South Korea in 1950 had been his failure to ask Congress for an expression of its backing. He could have had it easily, and it would have strengthened his hand. I had made up my mind not to repeat that error, but always to follow the advice I myself had given President Eisenhower. Concerning Vietnam, I repeatedly told Secretaries Rusk and McNamara that I never wanted to receive any recommendation for actions we might have to take unless it was accompanied by a proposal for assuring the backing of Congress.

Because of this, it became routine for all contingency plans to include suggestions for informing Congress and winning its support. As we considered the possibility of having to expand our efforts in Vietnam, proposals for seeking a congressional resolution became part of the normal contingency planning effort. But I never adopted these proposals, for I continued to hope that we could keep our role in Vietnam limited.

With the attack on our ships in the Tonkin Gulf, the picture changed. We could not be sure how Hanoi would react to our reprisal strike. We thought it was possible they might overreact and launch an all-out invasion of South Vietnam. They might ask the Chinese Communists to join them in the battle.

Any one of a dozen things could have happened, and I wanted us to be ready for the worst. Part of being ready, to me, was having the advance support of Congress for anything that might prove to be necessary. It was better to have a firm congressional resolution, and not need it, than some day to need it and not have it. This was the thinking behind my decision to ask Congress for its backing.

My first major decision on Vietnam had been to reaffirm President Kennedy's policies. This was my second major decision: to order retaliation against the Tonkin Gulf attacks and to seek a congressional resolution in support of our Southeast Asia policy.

Nine Senators and seven Congressmen * joined me in the Cabinet Room for that meeting. McNamara described in detail what had happened in the Gulf of Tonkin and what we proposed to do. I then read a statement that I planned to deliver to the American people later in the evening.

Senator Leverett Saltonstall noted that in the short statement I had used the word "limited" three times. "Why not use the word 'determined' and let the limitation speak for itself?" he asked.

"We want them [the North Vietnamese] to know we are not going to take it lying down," I said, "but we are not going to destroy their cities and we hope we can prepare them for the course we will follow."

Rusk said he thought there was an advantage "in not leaving in doubt that we are *not* doing this as a pretext for a larger war."

We discussed the advantages and disadvantages of a congressional resolution. Rusk described the nature of the resolution we had in mind, one that applied not just to Vietnam but to our interests in all of Southeast Asia.

Senator Bourke Hickenlooper then observed: "It seems to me there should be no doubt as to whether the President should have the right to order the armed forces into action. It is my own personal feeling that it is up to the President to prepare the kind and type of resolution he believes would be proper. It is up to Congress to see whether they will pass it or not. I have no doubt in my mind that concrete action would be taken."

"I had that feeling," I said, "but I felt I wanted the advice of each of you and wanted to consult with you."

* The Senators were Mike Mansfield (Mont.), Democratic Majority Leader; Everett Dirksen (Ill.), Republican Minority Leader; Hubert Humphrey (Minn.), Democratic Whip; Thomas Kuchel (Calif.), Republican Whip; J. William Fulbright (Dem. of Ark.), Chairman of the Foreign Relations Committee; Bourke Hickenlooper (Iowa), ranking Republican on the Foreign Relations Committee; George Aiken (Rep. of Vt.) of the Foreign Relations Committee; Richard Russell (Dem. of Ga.), Chairman of the Armed Services Committee; and Leverett Saltonstall (Mass.), ranking Republican on the Armed Services Committee. The Representatives were Speaker of the House John McCormack (Mass.); Carl Albert (Dem. of Okla.), Majority Leader; Charles Halleck (Rep. of Ind.), Minority Leader; Thomas Morgan (Dem. of Penn.), Chairman of the Foreign Affairs Committee; Frances Bolton (Ohio), ranking Republican on the Foreign Affairs Committee; Carl Vinson (Dem. of Ga.), Chairman of the House Armed Services Committee; and Leslie Arends (Ill.), ranking Republican on the Armed Services Committee.

I went around the table asking each Senator and Representative for his frank opinion. Each expressed his wholehearted endorsement of our course of action and of the proposed resolution.

"I think it will be passed overwhelmingly," said Congressman Charles Halleck.

"I will support it," said Senator Fulbright.

At the close of the meeting I felt encouraged by this show of solidarity and support. As Speaker McCormack said near the end of our discussion, we were presenting "a united front to the world."

I then tried to reach Republican Presidential candidate Barry Goldwater on the phone, but he was sailing off the California coast and we could not make contact until after 10 P.M. I told him what had happened and what we planned to do. Goldwater agreed completely.

I had expected to go on television and radio at 9 P.M. to inform the American people of our decision, but we had to delay for about two and a half hours until the American attack planes were airborne. The timing was important. We did not want to provide the North Vietnamese with enough advance warning to permit them to take precautions. On the other hand, it was important that the first word of the attack come from an official statement by our government and not from a garbled and misleading version by Hanoi. Another thought was in my mind. We knew that once our planes were in the air, they would be picked up by Red China's radar as well as by Hanoi's. I did not want the leaders in Peking to misunderstand the reason our planes were over the Tonkin Gulf. They had to understand that the retaliation was aimed only at North Vietnam, not Red China, and that the objective was limited.

The retaliatory air strikes damaged or destroyed twenty-five enemy boats and 90 per cent of the oil storage tanks at Vinh. We lost two planes.

The next morning I flew to Syracuse, New York, to dedicate the New-house Journalism Building at Syracuse University. I used this occasion to explain in even greater detail the meaning of the events in the Gulf of Tonkin and the basis for our policy in Vietnam.

In the course of that speech I summarized my basic view in a few sentences:

> The challenge that we face in Southeast Asia today is the same challenge that we have faced with courage and that we have met with strength in Greece and Turkey, in Berlin and Korea, in Lebanon and in Cuba. And to any who may be tempted to support or to widen the present aggression I say this: There is no threat to any peaceful power from the United States of America. But there can be no peace by aggression and no immunity from reply. That is what is meant by the actions that we took yesterday.

When I returned to Washington, Rusk brought me a draft of the Southeast Asia Resolution (often miscalled the "Gulf of Tonkin Resolution"), which he and George Ball, in consultation with the congressional leaders of both parties, had worked out in my absence. I approved it and prepared a written message to the Congress to accompany it. In that message I made it clear that I was asking the support of the Congress not merely to reply to attacks on our own forces, or simply to carry out our obligations in South Vietnam, but to be in a position to do what had to be done to fulfill our responsibilities in all of Southeast Asia.

The resolution as finally approved gave congressional support for the President to "take all necessary measures to repel any armed attack against the forces of the United States and to prevent further aggression." The resolution also stated that the United States was "prepared, as the President determines, to take all necessary steps, including the use of armed force, to assist any member or protocol state of the Southeast Asia Collective Defense Treaty requesting assistance in defense of its freedom."

The resolution reaffirmed our obligations under SEATO and asserted that the maintenance of peace and security in Southeast Asia was vital to our own national interests and to world peace.

I urged full joint hearings of the Committees on Foreign Relations and Armed Services in the Senate and the Committees on Foreign Affairs and Armed Services in the House. I also asked the congressional leadership to insist on roll calls both in committee and on the floor of both houses, so that the record would be complete and indisputable.

The vote in the Senate was 88 to 2, with the negative votes cast by Senators Ernest Gruening of Alaska and Wayne Morse of Oregon. In the House the vote was unanimous, 416 to 0.

Four Senators, Fulbright and Hickenlooper of the Foreign Relations Committee and Russell and Saltonstall of the Armed Services Committee, introduced the resolution in the Senate and answered questions raised by their fellow Senators. The sponsors had attended a long White House discussion on the subject. During the debate on the Senate floor the following exchange took place between Senator Fulbright and Senator John Sherman Cooper of Kentucky.

SENATOR COOPER: . . . Does the Senator consider that in enacting this resolution we are satisfying that requirement of Article IV of the Southeast Asia Collective Defense Treaty? In other words, are we now giving the President advance authority to take whatever action he may deem necessary respecting South Vietnam and its defense, or with respect to the defense of any other country included in the treaty?

SENATOR FULBRIGHT: I think that is correct.

SENATOR COOPER: Then, looking ahead, if the President decided that it was necessary to use such force as could lead into war, we will give that authority by this resolution?

SENATOR FULBRIGHT: That is the way I would interpret it. If a situation later developed in which we thought the approval should be withdrawn, it could be withdrawn by concurrent resolution. That is the reason for the third section.

SENATOR COOPER: I ask these questions . . .

SENATOR FULBRIGHT: The Senator is properly asking these questions.

SENATOR COOPER: I ask these questions because it is well for the country and all of us to know what is being undertaken. . . .

The record is clear. I wanted the Congress and the country to know what was being, or might have to be, undertaken. The resolution served that purpose. I also hoped this strong congressional endorsement would help influence North Vietnam to refrain from accelerating aggression.

The idea of hitting North Vietnam with air power, either on a reprisal basis or in a sustained campaign, had been discussed inside the government, in Saigon, and in the American press for a long time. When McNamara returned from Vietnam with his recommendations for further military action in March 1964, the Joint Chiefs argued that the proposed steps might not be strong enough. They indicated that we should consider attacking military targets in the North immediately. I recall CIA Director McCone describing the Defense Secretary's suggestions at that time as "too little, too late." McCone felt strongly that increased action in the South should be accompanied by intensive air and naval action against the North.

However, during my first year in the White House no formal proposal for an air campaign against North Vietnam ever came to me as the agreed suggestion of my principal advisers. Whenever the subject came up, one or another of them usually mentioned the risk of giving Communist China an excuse for massive intervention in Vietnam. Rusk was concerned that putting direct pressure on North Vietnam might encourage the Soviets to raise the level of tension around Berlin, in the Middle East, or elsewhere. I fully concurred. Our goals in Vietnam were limited, and so were our actions. I wanted to keep them that way.

Many advisers in my administration, in both State and Defense, were concerned that heavy air strikes against the North might cause Hanoi to launch a massive, outright invasion of the South or at least to step up significantly the level of the guerrilla war. American officials in Washington and in Saigon agreed that the political and military machinery in South Vietnam was then much too fragile to survive that kind of hammer blow.

In July 1964 Maxwell Taylor had replaced Henry Cabot Lodge as our Ambassador to Vietnam. Early in September I asked Taylor to return to Washington for a thorough review of the situation in Vietnam. I wanted to hear in detail his estimate of internal political weakness. I also wanted to talk with him and with my senior advisers about any further steps we should be taking, or encouraging the Vietnamese to take. Finally, I thought those in Washington who were urging military action against the North should hear from our man on the scene just how uncertain the base we were operating from would be if their advice was taken.

On September 9 I met in the Cabinet Room with Ambassador Taylor and some of my advisers.* The principal item of business was a recommendation for several specific actions developed by the Departments of State and Defense after consulting with Taylor. They proposed, among other things, that we resume our naval patrols in the Tonkin Gulf, which had been suspended after the August incident, and that we be prepared to retaliate against North Vietnam in case of an attack on U.S. units or of any "special" North Vietnamese–Viet Cong action against South Vietnam.

McNamara reported that the proposals had the support of the Joint Chiefs of Staff. However, he said, I should know that the Air Force and Marine Corps chiefs † thought it would also be necessary to carry out extensive air strikes against the North. General Wheeler said that he and his Navy and Army colleagues had been persuaded by Ambassador Taylor that any drastic action might produce such a strong reaction from the Communists that the still-weak government in Saigon, and its armed forces, might not be able to meet the challenge successfully.

As one gloomy opinion followed another, I suddenly asked whether anyone at the table doubted that Vietnam was "worth all this effort." Ambassador Taylor answered quickly that "we could not afford to let Hanoi win in the interests of our overall position in Asia and in the world." General Wheeler strongly supported the Ambassador's view. It was the unanimous view of the Chiefs of Staff, he said, that if we lost South Vietnam we would lose Southeast Asia—not all at once, and not overnight, but eventually. One country after another on the periphery would give way and look to Communist China as the rising power of the area, he said. John McCone agreed. So did Secretary Rusk, with considerable emphasis.

I returned to the military recommendation and asked if anyone had a different view. Everyone present said he agreed. The proposed actions were limited, but my advisers were convinced that they would keep Hanoi on notice that we were serious and committed, would reassure the South Vietnamese, and might possibly inhibit any increase in North Vietnam's activities. After serious consideration and a great deal of discussion, I finally approved the recommendations. But I told Taylor and the others that our first objective was to strengthen the South Vietnamese in every possible way.

---

* Those present were Secretaries Rusk and McNamara, General Earle Wheeler, CIA Director McCone, Assistant Secretaries of State William P. Bundy and Robert J. Manning, and Assistant Secretary of Defense John T. McNaughton.

† General John P. McConnell, Chief of Staff of the Air Force, and General Wallace M. Greene, Jr., Commandant of the Marine Corps.

Acting on the September 1964 order, the military forces made plans to retaliate by air against the North if the North Vietnamese or Viet Cong hit U.S. forces or carried out some kind of "spectacular" attack in South Vietnam. Twice before the year was out I was asked to put those contingency plans into effect.

The first occasion was on November 1, following a Viet Cong attack on our air base at Bien Hoa, north of Saigon. Communist mortar crews shelled the base, then saboteurs cut through the perimeter wire and destroyed five of our planes and damaged others. The Joint Chiefs of Staff and Ambassador Taylor immediately urged a strike against the North. My civilian advisers, especially Rusk and McNamara, disagreed. Most of us were very much aware of the continuing unsteadiness of the South Vietnamese government and its military weakness. We judged the concerns of September still valid. I was worried too about possible Viet Cong retaliation against U.S. dependents in Saigon. With all these considerations in mind, I decided against a retaliatory strike.

The second test came on Christmas Eve with the bombing of a U.S. officers' billet in downtown Saigon, which killed a number of Americans and Vietnamese. Taylor was angered, and rightly so. He urged strongly that we bomb the North, preferably a military barracks, in retaliation. I knew how he felt, and in his position I would have felt the same. But as President I had to look beyond a single incident.

I knew that attacking the North could bring on a major reaction from Hanoi and its friends. My advisers still argued that the political base in the South was shaky, probably too shaky to withstand a major assault by the Communists. Also there were still many American women and children in Saigon and I feared that they might become targets of Viet Cong retaliation.

Therefore I again regretfully told the Ambassador that I could not approve his recommendation. I did so because I thought prudence and the national interest required it. But I was persuaded increasingly that our forces deserved the support that air strikes against the source of aggression would represent. I also believed the enemy was getting onto very dangerous ground.

As we moved into 1965 my own concern grew steadily. The same was true of those around me who were trying to deal with the problem. For four years we had consistently shown restraint, always carefully limiting all our actions. We asked only that Hanoi stop sending armed men and terrorists and weapons into the South to kill the South Vietnamese and to kill Americans at the same time. But Hanoi's answer was to continue to pour in more men and supplies.

Most important of all, by the end of 1964 we were picking up North Vietnamese army troops wearing regulation uniforms and carrying full field equipment. We soon learned that these regulars were not just replacements for Viet Cong units, as they had been in the past, but members of organized North Vietnamese battalion formations. Ho Chi Minh and his collaborators were sitting in their quiet and peaceful capital giving orders that resulted in the killing of Americans and South Vietnamese every day. In doing so, they were flagrantly violating the Geneva Accords, not only of 1954 but also of 1962, for the bulk of their forces were moving into the South through Laos.

Late in January 1965 General Westmoreland asked for and was given permission to use U.S. jets against the Viet Cong in support of Vietnamese troops when he considered it absolutely necessary. He used that authority for the first time late in February when two companies of Vietnamese and a U.S. Special Forces team were trapped in an enemy ambush in the Highlands. While air power struck the ambushers, troop-carrying helicopters rescued the Vietnamese and Americans without the loss of a man.

The combination of increasing military pressure from the Viet Cong and North Vietnamese and of continuing political confusion and instability in Saigon was slowly tiring the South Vietnamese. Morale had lifted when we attacked the North in August, but the effect was short-lived.

Pessimistic reports continued to come to me from my advisers and from the field. Early in January 1965 Taylor sent in a report concluding that "we are presently on a losing track and must risk a change. . . . To take no positive action now is to accept defeat in the fairly near future." That was the view of every responsible military adviser in Vietnam and in Washington. Painfully and reluctantly, my civilian advisers were driven to the same conclusion by the hard facts.

On January 27, 1965, Mac Bundy sent me a memo saying that he and Bob McNamara were "pretty well convinced that our current policy can lead only to disastrous defeat." They had reached a critical moment in their thinking and wanted me to know how they felt. They argued that the time had come to use more power than we had thus far employed.

As Bundy put it:

> The Vietnamese know just as we do that the Viet Cong are gaining in the countryside. Meanwhile, they see the enormous power of the United States withheld, and they get little sense of firm and active U.S. policy. They feel that we are unwilling to take serious risks. In one sense, all of this is outrageous, in the light of all that we have done and all that we are ready to do if they will only pull up their socks. But it is a fact—or at least so McNamara and I now think.

Bundy and McNamara saw two alternatives: either to "use our military power in the Far East and to force a change of Communist policy" or to "deploy all our resources along a track of negotiation, aimed at salvaging what little can be preserved with no major addition to our present military risks." They said that they were inclined to favor the first alternative—use of more military power—but they believed that both courses should be studied carefully and that alternative programs should be developed and argued out in my presence.

"Both of us understand the very grave questions presented by any decision of this sort," the memo continued. "We both recognize that the ultimate responsibility is not ours. Both of us have fully supported your unwillingness, in earlier months, to move out of the middle course. We both agree that every effort should still be made to improve our operations on the ground and to prop up the authorities in South Vietnam as best we can. But we are both convinced that none of this is enough, and that the time has come for harder choices."

The January 27 memo concluded by pointing out that Dean Rusk did not agree with the McNamara-Bundy assessment. Rusk knew things were going badly, and he did not claim that the deterioration could be stopped. "What he [Rusk] does say," the memo stated, "is that the consequences of both escalation and withdrawal are so bad that we simply must find a way of making our present policy work. This would be good if it was possible. Bob and I do not think it is."

As a result of this memo and the discussions that followed, I asked Rusk to instruct his experts once again to consider all possible ways for finding a peaceful solution. I also asked Bundy to go out to Saigon immediately with a team of military and civilian experts for a hard look at the situation on the ground. He did so and returned to report to me on February 7.

Four days before I received Mac Bundy's report, I had a long talk with CIA Director John McCone. He was deeply worried about the situation in South Vietnam. He expected a serious and immediate political crisis in Saigon. General Nguyen Khanh, head of the South Vietnamese government, was having trouble with his fellow generals as well as with the Buddhists, and it appeared that he might be toppled at any time.

Moreover, McCone pointed out, Soviet Chairman Aleksei Kosygin would soon be visiting Hanoi and that promised only more trouble. Having removed Khrushchev from power, the new Soviet leaders were reversing his policy of relative inaction in Southeast Asia. Early in 1965 the Soviet leaders may have concluded that Hanoi was about to win and that, having removed Khrushchev, they should move in to share credit for the anticipated victory.

Members of the Kosygin mission to Hanoi included the chief of the Soviet air force, Moscow's top specialist on economic aid, and the Soviet Minister of Aviation. McCone and his analysts correctly predicted that Moscow would give Hanoi greatly increased economic and military aid, including anti-aircraft missiles. They also believed that Kosygin would encourage Hanoi to step up its subversion and military and guerrilla warfare activity in South Vietnam. When I asked McCone what he would recommend he made several positive suggestions, including bombing selected targets in North Vietnam, starting at the 17th parallel and working north on a progressively intensive basis.

This was the atmosphere and the trend of thinking in official Washington when word came on the afternoon of February 6 that the Communists had carried out major attacks on the U.S. Army advisers' barracks at Pleiku and on a U.S. Army helicopter base about four miles away, as well as on several Vietnamese targets. Eight Americans had been killed outright in the attacks, one died later, and more than a hundred had been wounded. Five U.S. aircraft had been destroyed and fifteen damaged. When I received word of the attacks that Saturday afternoon, I immediately called a meeting of the National Security Council in the Cabinet Room at 7:45 P.M.*

My advisers strongly urged that we answer the attacks by striking four targets in North Vietnam immediately. United States planes would handle three; the South Vietnamese air force would strike the fourth. The targets were army barracks associated with North Vietnam's infiltration system into the South.

Cy Vance had been in the Situation Room talking on a special security phone with Mac Bundy in Saigon. Vance told me it was the recommendation of Bundy that we go ahead with air strikes at once. Ambassador Taylor, General Westmoreland, and the other top officials in Saigon agreed with this recommendation, he reported.

As we talked, there was an electric tension in the air. Everyone in the room was deadly serious as he considered the possible consequences of this decision. Each man around that table knew how crucial such action could be. How would Hanoi react? Would the Chinese Communists use it as a pretext for involving themselves? What about Kosygin and the Russians in Hanoi?

Someone suggested that Ho Chi Minh had mousetrapped the Soviet leader by attacking us during his visit. If we failed to respond, we were "paper tigers"; if we hit back, Soviet prestige might be further involved. Hanoi would benefit either way. I asked George Ball, as the senior State Department man present, what he thought.

"We are all in accord that action must be taken," Ball replied. "We do need to decide how we shall handle the air strikes publicly. We must make it clear that the North Vietnamese and the Viet Cong are the same. We are retaliating against North Vietnam because Hanoi directs the Viet Cong, supplies arms, and infiltrates men."

I raised again the question of American dependents in Saigon and elsewhere in South Vietnam. Ball wondered whether they should be withdrawn

---

* McNamara and his deputy, Cy Vance, were there, as was General Wheeler. Dean Rusk was out of town, but George Ball, Ambassador Llewellyn Thompson, and Bill Bundy came from the State Department. Others present included Treasury Secretary Douglas Dillon, Carl Rowan from the USIA, and Marshall Carter from the CIA. I had also asked House Speaker McCormack and Senator Mansfield to attend.

immediately or only later if North Vietnam responded to the air strikes. Wheeler and McNamara spoke at one time: "Get them out now."

"I just cannot think about losing American women and children in an attack by the North Vietnamese or Viet Cong in Saigon or elsewhere," I said. I reminded them that I had been urging the evacuation of all dependents for a long time. I was told they could probably be moved in a few days and I said we should begin the evacuation at once.

I went around the table, asking each person if he agreed with the decision. Everyone present expressed his concurrence with one exception. Senator Mike Mansfield was opposed. We should be cautious, he warned. We might be getting into a war with China. We might be healing the split between Moscow and Peking. He strongly opposed the idea of retaliation, but he proposed no alternative.

"We have kept our gun over the mantel and our shells in the cupboard for a long time now," I said. "And what was the result? They are killing our men while they sleep in the night. I can't ask our American soldiers out there to continue to fight with one hand tied behind their backs."

I thought that perhaps a sudden and effective air strike would convince the leaders in Hanoi that we were serious in our purpose and also that the North could not count on continued immunity if they persisted in aggression in the South. I realized the risks of involving the Soviets or the Chinese, as Senator Mansfield feared, I said, but neither of them was trying to bring peace or even urging restraint. I doubted that they wanted direct involvement themselves. I pointed out that our intelligence analysts believed Red China would not enter the war unless there was an invasion in the northern part of North Vietnam or unless the Hanoi regime was in danger of being toppled.

After long discussion I authorized the strikes, provided the South Vietnamese government agreed. There was little doubt about the latter, since Saigon had been urging retaliation against the North for some time. I also ordered the prompt evacuation of our dependents from Vietnam.

We met again the next morning at eight o'clock to review the situation. Three of the four authorized targets had been fogged in; only one had been struck. Should we go back after the other three? The consensus was "no," and I agreed. We all felt that a second-day strike by U.S. planes might give Hanoi and Moscow the impression that we had begun a sustained air offensive. That decision had not been made. However, we all agreed that the South Vietnamese air force should go back after its target. The Vietnamese concurred emphatically.

Following the meeting, we released a statement which said that "as the U.S. Government has frequently stated, we seek no wider war. Whether or not this course can be maintained lies with the North Vietnamese aggressors."

Later in the day we announced the withdrawal of American dependents from South Vietnam. In that statement we said:

> It has become clear that Hanoi has undertaken a more aggressive course of action against both South Vietnamese and American installations, and against Americans who are in South Vietnam assisting the people of that country to defend their freedom. We have no choice now but to clear the decks and make absolutely clear our continued determination to back South Vietnam and its fight to maintain its independence.

We hoped that the leaders in Hanoi would read our messages carefully and understand their meaning. We were issuing no ultimatums they might find impossible to accept, but it was important that they realize they would pay a price if they continued to push their aggression in the South. There were limits to our long-demonstrated restraint and to self-imposed restrictions.

That night Mac Bundy and his specialists * returned to Washington from Saigon. About 11 P.M. Bundy came to the White House to see me. He left with me the report he and his group had developed on their tour of Vietnam. It was the result of long talks they had had with Vietnamese leaders as well as lengthy consultations with Ambassador Taylor, General Westmoreland, and the principal members of our Mission in Saigon. I asked Bundy to send copies at once to the Secretaries of State and Defense so that we could consider his recommendations in detail the following morning.

I read the eight-page report and its five-page annex before going to sleep. Bundy's group of experts had found the situation in Vietnam going downhill, and among other things they recommended major action against the North to reverse the trend.

"The situation in Vietnam is deteriorating," the report began, "and without new U.S. action defeat appears inevitable—probably not in a matter of weeks or perhaps even months, but within the next year or so. There is still time to turn around, but not much."

Bundy assessed our position as follows:

> The stakes in Vietnam are extremely high. The American investment is very large, and American responsibility is a fact of life which is palpable in the atmosphere of Asia, and even elsewhere. The international prestige of the United States, and a substantial part of our influence are directly at risk in Vietnam. There is no way of unloading the burden on the Vietnamese themselves, and there is no way of negotiating ourselves out of Vietnam which offers any serious promise at present. . . .

---

* Members of the party included John McNaughton, Assistant Secretary of Defense; Leonard Unger, Deputy Assistant Secretary of State; General Andrew J. Goodpaster, assistant to the Chairman of the Joint Chiefs; and Chester Cooper of the National Security Council staff.

He believed a negotiated withdrawal of the United States at that time would mean "surrender on the installment plan." Bundy said that a policy of "graduated and continuing reprisal," as outlined in the annex to his report, was "the most promising course available." He added: "That judgment is shared by all who accompanied me from Washington, and I think by all members of the Country Team."

After listing several things that needed to be done—such as helping to strengthen the Vietnamese political structure and improving pacification—Bundy concluded his report as follows:

> There are a host of things the Vietnamese need to do better and areas in which we need to help them. The place where we can help most is in the clarity and firmness of our own commitment to what is in fact as well as in rhetoric a common cause. There is one grave weakness in our posture in Vietnam which is within our own power to fix—and that is widespread belief that we do not have the will and force and patience and determination to take the necessary action and stay the course.
>
> This is the overriding reason for our present recommendation of a policy of sustained reprisal. Once such a policy is put in force, we shall be able to speak in Vietnam on many topics and in many ways, with growing force and effectiveness.
>
> One final word. At its very best the struggle in Vietnam will be long. It seems to us important that this fundamental fact be made clear and our understanding of it be made clear to our own people and to the people of Vietnam. Too often in the past we have conveyed the impression that we expect an early solution when those who live with this war know that no early solution is possible. It is our own belief that the people of the United States have the necessary will to accept and to execute a policy that rests upon the reality that there is no short cut to success in South Vietnam.

The annex to the Bundy report, prepared mainly by Assistant Secretary of Defense John McNaughton, stated at the outset:

> We believe that the best available way of increasing our chance of success in Vietnam is the development and execution of a policy of *sustained reprisal* against North Vietnam—a policy in which air and naval action against the North is justified by and related to the whole Viet Cong campaign of violence and terror in the South.
>
> While we believe that the risks of such a policy are acceptable, we emphasize that its costs are real. It implies significant U.S. air losses even if no full air war is joined, and it seems likely that it would eventually require an extensive and costly effort against the whole air defense system of North Vietnam. U.S. casualties would be higher—and more visible to American feelings—than those sustained in the struggle in South Vietnam.
>
> Yet measured against the costs of defeat in Vietnam, this program

seems cheap. And even if it fails to turn the tide—as it may—the value of the effort seems to us to exceed its cost.

The idea of attacking North Vietnam with air power had been a feature of several planning exercises and position papers in 1964. One such plan, developed at Pacific Command Headquarters, suggested air action against the enemy in three phases, the third of which would be a sustained aerial offensive against the North. The plan included a list of ninety-four possible targets. It had not come to me as a formal proposal, but I was aware of its existence.

The essentials of this plan were revived in August by the Joint Chiefs, but the proposal was strongly opposed by my civilian advisers, especially McNamara and Rusk. It was raised and rejected again as part of our overall review in September. The same thing happened in December.

But now, I knew, we were at a turning point. Though the Bundy report proposed a course of action we had considered and turned down only three months before, I was impressed by its logic and persuaded strongly by its arguments. I knew that the situation had changed and that our actions would have to change too. I looked forward to hearing how my other advisers had reacted in light of altered circumstances and the Bundy report.

The next morning, February 8, 1965, a little before ten o'clock, I met in the Cabinet Room with most of the members of the National Security Council and some of their principal aides.*

Those present either had read the Bundy report or knew its main elements. There was unanimous support for its principal recommendation: a program of sustained reprisal against the North. There were, however, differences of opinion on the pace. Some advisers, especially the Joint Chiefs, favored an intensive program of attacks from the outset. Others favored a more gradual approach. About 10:30 A.M. we were joined by several legislative leaders I had invited—Speaker McCormack and the Republican leader in the House, Gerald Ford, and Senators Mansfield and Dirksen.

McNamara briefed the congressional leaders on the results of the air strikes of the previous two days. George Ball dealt with the diplomatic side. He pointed out that we had explained our case in full to the Secretary General of the United Nations. We had also advised the Russians of the reasons for our retaliation and had assured them that Kosygin's visit to the Far East had no connection with our timing. The North Vietnamese had chosen the time by attacking our men and installations.

* Those present included Under Secretary of State Ball, Ambassador Thompson, Bill Bundy, and Leonard Unger from State; Secretary McNamara, Deputy Secretary Vance, and McNaughton from Defense; Treasury Secretary Dillon; General Wheeler, Chairman of the Joint Chiefs of Staff, and General Goodpaster; CIA Director McCone; USIA Director Rowan; David Bell and William Gaud from AID; and Mac Bundy and a few members of my staff. Secretary Rusk was still away recovering from influenza.

I summarized our position. I explained that we had considered stronger actions against the North several months before but had held off, hoping the South Vietnamese would build a more solid political base. Also I had been concerned that any move against the North might bring retaliation against American women and children in Vietnam. Now we had decided to go forward with the kind of program we had earlier studied and postponed. We were evacuating all dependents.

The North Vietnamese had deliberately and flagrantly struck at our men and installations, and we felt it necessary to respond. However, I said, we were reacting not to isolated incidents but to the whole pattern of aggression and terrorism which Hanoi had been carrying out and recently had accelerated. I assured the congressional leaders that our actions would be temperate and careful, but we would act. Our goal was to "deter and diminish the strength of the North Vietnamese aggressors and try to convince them to leave South Vietnam alone."

Later in the day I cabled Taylor in Saigon. I told him I wanted him to know that I had decided to carry out a plan for "continuing action" against North Vietnam "with modifications up and down in tempo and scale in the light of your recommendations . . . and our own continuing review of the situation." This new approach would take time to prepare, I knew, but I asked the Ambassador to explain our thinking to key South Vietnamese leaders and to express our hope that we could work out our plans and actions with a "unified and going government."

Two days after this decision was made we had a clear signal that the Communists were determined to raise the level of violence. On that day Viet Cong agents blew up an enlisted men's barracks in Qui Nhon, killing twenty-three Americans and seven Vietnamese, and wounding twenty-one American soldiers.

When news of the attack came in, I summoned the National Security Council into session once again.* We met on the afternoon of February 10. McNamara described the Qui Nhon attack. He said that he, the Defense Department, the Joint Chiefs, and Taylor all recommended a prompt response. They proposed a joint U.S.–South Vietnamese air strike against two barracks in the North and one key bridge. Mac Bundy outlined the discussion that had taken place before I joined the meeting. All present had agreed to a response in some form, he reported, but there were differences regarding the kind of response and the timing.

Kosygin was then in North Korea and was due to stop in Peking on his way back to Moscow. George Ball and Ambassador Llewellyn Thompson suggested that the reprisal strike be delayed until the Soviet leader had left

---

* Attendance was virtually the same as at the meeting two days before, except that Vice President Humphrey was present and Admiral D. L. McDonald represented General Wheeler and the Joint Chiefs.

the Far East area. Vice President Humphrey also had doubts as to whether we should strike that day or wait until Kosygin had returned home. Treasury Secretary Douglas Dillon said that he did not believe the Soviets made major policy decisions "based on the whereabouts of Kosygin." Bundy argued that we should not put ourselves in the position of giving Moscow control over our actions by moving their officials or diplomats from one place to another.

After long discussion, we decided to try to satisfy objections raised in the group by deleting the bridge target, which was about seventy-five miles south of Hanoi. The two barracks targets were just north of the 17th parallel. Thompson said he still thought a delay of a few days was desirable, and the Vice President said he had mixed emotions. All the others present agreed with McNamara and the Joint Chiefs that we should proceed. I authorized the strike, provided the South Vietnamese agreed. They concurred, and the combined attack was accomplished the next day.

Two days later, on February 13, we notified Taylor and the Military Command in Saigon that I had approved a three-point program of immediate actions. First, we would intensify the pacification program by all available means. Second, we would carry out "measured and limited air action jointly with the GVN" * against military targets in the North below the 19th parallel. Finally, we would go to the UN Security Council and detail the case against Hanoi's aggression.

In his reply Taylor reported that our decision had been received in Saigon with "deep enthusiasm." The Vietnamese leadership, civilian and military, strongly favored imposing a price on the North for the war it was directing and supplying in the South.

A few days later, on February 17, former President Eisenhower was in Washington, and I asked him to come to the White House for a talk. I had tremendous respect for the opinions of this wise and experienced man who knew so well the problems and the burdens of the Presidency. We talked for about four hours, first in the Cabinet Room and later over lunch.

In discussing Vietnam, Eisenhower stressed the importance of morale among the South Vietnamese as well as our own forces. In his judgment, our air strikes against the North could not prevent the North Vietnamese from infiltrating men and supplies into the South if they wished to bear the cost of that effort. But the strikes could discourage the North Vietnamese and make them pay a price for continuing their aggression. He said that in his opinion our retaliatory strikes had helped the situation greatly, especially in terms of raising morale in the South, but that he felt the time had now come to shift from retaliation to a "campaign of pressure."

Eisenhower was aware of the political confusion that prevailed in the South. Looking back, he said, he thought that Diem had been a capable

* Government of (South) Vietnam.

man despite the difficulties his actions had created. He felt, as I did, that the assassination of Diem had resulted in a great setback for South Vietnam and for us. It was important, he thought, for the Vietnamese to find a leader of courage and ability whom we could support.

I asked him about the possibility of Chinese Communist or Soviet intervention in Vietnam, the two fears expressed to me so often by members of Congress. Eisenhower said that if they threatened to intervene we should pass the word to them, quietly but firmly, that they should take care "lest dire results occur." He recalled how the armistice had been achieved finally in Korea. Talks had been going on inconclusively for a long time. When he became President, he passed three messages through secret channels to the Koreans and the Chinese. The gist of the messages was that if a satisfactory armistice was not signed promptly, he was going to remove the "limits we were observing as to the area of combat and the weapons employed." He thought we should do the same if there were a threat of Chinese Communist intervention in Vietnam.

Eisenhower saw merit in the idea suggested by General Wheeler of putting an American division into Vietnam just south of the demilitarized zone to help protect the South, but he did not favor any large deployment at that time. Later in our talk he said that we could not let the Indochina peninsula fall. He hoped that it would not be necessary to use the six or eight divisions mentioned in some speculation. But if it should prove necessary, he said, "so be it."

He assured me of his full and complete support for any course of action I decided was necessary. He said that he had no intention of complicating the job of the President by commenting from the sidelines, but that he would always be available for consultation.

I told him how grateful I was for his counsel and his support. Throughout my years in the White House I always kept the former President fully informed of all major developments and consulted him on major decisions. I asked General Wheeler to make sure that President Eisenhower knew everything of military significance and that no information was withheld from him. His advice was an unfailing source of strength to me and I look back on our friendship as one of the high points of my years in public life. That relationship was based on many things, but above all on one strongly shared belief: that in our nation's relations with the outside world partisanship should be left behind.

During the week before my meeting with President Eisenhower, and for two weeks thereafter, there were no air strikes against North Vietnam. But the Viet Cong continued their terrorism, sabotage, and attacks. As a result, we went north again on March 2 to attack an ammunition depot and a naval base. We then stopped bombing again for a period of eleven days. After that, our attacks became more frequent.

The policy of gradual but steady reprisal against North Vietnam for its continuing aggression in the South had been put into action. This was my third major Vietnam decision. The decision was made because it had become clear, gradually but unmistakably, that Hanoi was moving in for the kill. Its leaders had sent in regular North Vietnamese army units. They had directly attacked not only our ships but our barracks, our airfields, and our men. They had asked for and received increased aid from Moscow. They were exerting maximum pressure on the military and political situation in South Vietnam. The best advice available to me indicated that if we did not act against the North Vietnamese, they soon might achieve their objectives in the South. Also our forces in the South were increasing and I felt strongly that our men deserved all the support and protection we could give them. If air strikes could destroy enemy supplies and impede the flow of men and weapons coming south, our action would help save American and South Vietnamese lives.

My advisers had long argued that a weak government in Saigon would have difficulty surviving the pressures that might be exerted against the South if we bombed the North. I now concluded that political life in the South would soon collapse unless the people there knew that the North was paying a price in its own territory for its aggression. There were strong military reasons for our action, as the Joint Chiefs had long argued. Now the weight of the political argument as well had shifted to support intensified action.

From the time our planes hit the first military target in North Vietnam early in February, we were subjected to an increasingly heavy propaganda barrage from Hanoi, Peking, and Moscow. Every other Communist capital joined in. The propaganda message was short and sharp: Stop the Bombing. Soon voices in non-Communist countries joined the chorus—Indian, French, Swedish, and others. Before long, some American public figures began to repeat the theme. They all ignored the vital fact that we were bombing the North because Hanoi was stepping up its war in the South.

I decided it was time to make another major statement on Vietnam to the American people. For this purpose I accepted a long-standing invitation from President Milton Eisenhower of Johns Hopkins University in Baltimore to speak there on April 7, 1965. I planned to do three things: to explain our policy as clearly as possible, to urge Hanoi once more to join us in trying to reach a peaceful settlement, and to describe what peace and cooperative effort could do for the economic development of all of Southeast Asia.

As the speech took shape late in March and early in April, it was influenced by an outside development. Government leaders from seventeen nonaligned nations * had met in Belgrade, Yugoslavia, in mid-March to discuss Vietnam among other matters. In an effort to get peace talks started, they sent an appeal to the United States, North and South Vietnam, and other interested parties and governments, as well as to the Secretary General of the United Nations.

Ambassadors of four of the nonaligned nations delivered the appeal to Secretary Rusk in Washington on April 1. The heart of the proposal was a call for negotiations among interested parties "as soon as possible, without posing any preconditions."

Ambassador Taylor was home from Vietnam at that time and we had scheduled a National Security Council meeting on April 2 to hear his report on Vietnamese developments. Rusk opened the NSC meeting by describing the appeal of the seventeen nonaligned nations. He urged that our reply be "serious, restrained, and positive." I agreed and decided to incorporate the main elements of our reply in the Johns Hopkins speech.

At 9 P.M. on the night of April 7 I stepped to the podium of an auditorium on the Johns Hopkins campus and into the glare of television lights, for the speech was being broadcast live. I listed the essential elements of a just peace: an independent South Vietnam that was "securely guaranteed and able to shape its own relationships to all others—free from outside interference—tied to no alliance—a military base for no other country."

"There may be many ways to this kind of peace: in discussion or negotiation with the governments concerned; in large groups or in small ones; in the reaffirmation of old agreements or their strengthening with new ones," I said. "We have stated this position over and over again, fifty times and more, to friend and foe alike. And we remain ready, with this purpose, for *unconditional discussions."*

I then looked forward, beyond war and the coming of peace, to what could happen in that troubled and underdeveloped region of the world.

"These countries of Southeast Asia are homes for millions of impoverished people," I said. "Each day these people rise at dawn and struggle through until the night to wrest existence from the soil. They are often wracked by disease, plagued by hunger, and death comes at the early age of forty." I said there should be "a much more massive effort to improve the life of man in that conflict-torn corner of our world." The first step, I said, was for the countries of Southeast Asia to "associate themselves in a greatly expanded cooperative effort for development."

"We would hope that North Vietnam would take its place in the common effort just as soon as peaceful cooperation is possible," I said. I urged that

---

* The countries represented at the Belgrade conference were Afghanistan, Algeria, Cyprus, Ceylon, Ethiopia, Ghana, Guinea, India, Iraq, Kenya, Nepal, Syria, Tunisia, Uganda, the United Arab Republic, Yugoslavia, and Zambia.

the Secretary General of the United Nations use the prestige of his office to launch a plan for cooperation in economic development.

"For our part," I said, "I will ask the Congress to join in a billion dollar American investment in this effort as soon as it is under way. And I would hope that all other industrialized countries, including the Soviet Union, will join in this effort to replace despair with hope, and terror with progress."

The next day we delivered our formal reply to the proposal made by the seventeen nations at the Belgrade conference. Our answer incorporated the main thoughts, and many of the same words, of the Johns Hopkins speech. The United States would negotiate without preconditions. This was my fourth major Vietnam decision.

The Communists' answer came quickly. On April 9 Radio Peking said my offer was "full of lies and deceptions." The following day Moscow called the proposal "noisy propaganda." Two days after that Hanoi's Communist party newspaper described the Johns Hopkins offer as "bait." On April 20 North Vietnam declared that the seventeen nations that had signed the proposal for unconditional talks "were not accurately informed."

The door to peace remained closed. As for economic cooperation and regional improvement, Hanoi's spokesmen described our proposal as an attempt to "bribe" them. They had no interest in cooperating with their neighbors in a peaceful way; they preferred to take them over by force.

Hanoi was not alone in its policy of aggression. It is important to recall the shape of Asia late in 1964 and 1965. It was the backdrop against which a complicated drama was taking place, of which the war in Vietnam was only one portion. We had to be concerned not only about Vietnam but about the entire region. Our pledge of support, in the SEATO Treaty and in the congressional resolution on Southeast Asia, was not to Vietnam alone but to the security and well-being of its Asian neighbors as well. As we faced these crucial decisions on Vietnam, my advisers and I were acutely aware of what was happening in the rest of Asia. It became increasingly clear that Ho Chi Minh's military campaign against South Vietnam was part of a larger, much more ambitious strategy being conducted by the Communists.

Peking was in a bellicose and boastful mood. In October 1964 the Chinese Communists had set off their first nuclear explosion. Peking was promising Hanoi full support and was urging "wars of national liberation" as the solution to all the problems of non-Communist underdeveloped nations. The Chinese were training Thai guerrillas, and a "liberation front" for Thailand was created with Chinese backing. There were reports that Red China's Foreign Minister, Chen Yi, had boasted at a New Year's Day diplomatic reception in 1965 that "Thailand is next."

Next to China, the most threatening developments were occurring in Indonesia. There President-for-life Achmed Sukarno had turned increasingly to the Indonesian Communist party as the main pillar of support for his regime. Sukarno went to Communist China in November 1964 for conferences with its leaders. Within a month Chen Yi was visiting Sukarno and the Indonesian Communists in Djakarta. The foundations for a Peking-Djakarta axis were laid. In January 1965 Sukarno pulled his country out of the United Nations and threatened to set up a rival organization made up of what he called the "new emerging forces."

Meanwhile, Sukarno was conducting a campaign to destroy the new Malaysian Federation. His troops and agents were regularly probing into the Malay peninsula and Malayan Borneo. In December 1964 Indonesian and Australian gunboats fought off Singapore. The British organized a war fleet of some eighty ships to assist in the defense of Singapore and Malaysia. Early in 1965 the Malayan National Liberation League emerged along the same pattern as its Vietnamese and Thai predecessors, and undoubtedly with the same backing.

Before he died, but after he had been removed from effective power, Sukarno disclosed the grand strategy he had in mind. *The New York Times* on September 7, 1966, quoted him as saying the previous day in Djakarta:

> The strategy for defeating imperialism . . . is for Communist China to strike a blow against the American troops in Vietnam from the North while Indonesia strikes from the South.

Both Sukarno and the Chinese were busily wooing Cambodia's Prince Norodom Sihanouk. He was warmly welcomed in both Peking and Djakarta. This effort bore fruit when, beginning early in 1966, Sihanouk became an active participant in the Chinese Communists' program to supply Communist forces in southern South Vietnam. By the end of 1966 Cambodia's main port, Sihanoukville, had become a principal supply point for Chinese military equipment going to the Viet Cong and North Vietnamese. Other supplies moving down through Laos were also fed into Cambodia for transshipment to the Communist forces in Vietnam.

In Laos Chinese influence was dominant in the country's two northernmost provinces. The North Vietnamese had made eastern Laos and the panhandle their principal supply line, the so-called Ho Chi Minh Trail, into northern South Vietnam. And the Indonesians got into the act as well by training troops to help Laotian General Kong Le in his opposition to the legal government of neutralist Premier Souvanna Phouma.

Far to the north another Communist partner was waiting in the wings—North Korea. The regime in Pyongyang was helping the North Vietnamese in every available way, including fighter pilot training. In the meantime, I have no doubt, the North Koreans were only waiting for us to be thrown out of Vietnam before launching their own offensive against South Korea.

Thus what we saw taking shape rapidly was a Djakarta-Hanoi-Peking-Pyongyang axis, with Cambodia probably to be brought in as a junior partner and Laos to be merely absorbed by the North Vietnamese and Chinese.

The members of this new axis were undoubtedly counting on South Vietnam's collapse and an ignominious American withdrawal. Under such circumstances Britain, already facing financial troubles and moving toward a reduction in its involvement in Asia, would undoubtedly have been even less eager to support Malaysia and Singapore. The entire region would then have been ripe for the plucking.

That was the prospect we faced as we debated what to do in Vietnam and Southeast Asia in the critical months of 1965. Clearly the decisions we were making would determine not merely the fate of Vietnam but also the shape of Asia for many years to come.

Although the bombing of the North remained at a fairly low level during the first few months of what was called the Rolling Thunder campaign, the level of criticism was high. We heard what we had expected to hear from Hanoi, Peking, and Moscow. They insisted that the bombing stop immediately, unconditionally, and with no promises on their part. Others, at home and abroad, argued that only by stopping the bombing or reducing it drastically could we hope to persuade Hanoi to talk about peace.

I had discussed halting the bombing with various advisers. An inter-agency working group was developing a plan for such a pause. Late in April Bobby Kennedy came to see me in the White House. The newly elected Senator from New York had several things on his mind, and one of them was a possible bombing pause. We sat in the small private study next to the Oval Office. I told him that we had been considering a pause for some time and were giving the matter careful study. He suggested that we try it for a few days, even one or two. A brief pause would do no harm, he said, and maybe something useful would come of it. I repeated that we had been discussing such a move and he could rest assured it was receiving very serious consideration.

One concern I had was that a bombing pause might give North Vietnam's leaders the impression we were so eager for a settlement we would do anything. I was also worried that a pause might afford Hanoi a military advantage, making it easier to send more troops and supplies into the South. I consulted General Wheeler and other military advisers, and they assured me that a pause, if it were reasonably short, would cause no serious military harm. I doubted, as did most of my advisers, that stopping the bombing would produce any results at that time. But we decided it was worth the risk on the remote chance Hanoi might respond. If our effort failed, it might at least correct some wishful thinking at home and abroad.

On May 10 I decided to end the bombing for a limited period. We informed the Russians of our position and asked them to pass the information along to the North Vietnamese. But the Soviets refused to act as intermediaries. We delivered a message to the North Vietnamese Embassy in Moscow for their Ambassador. The note was returned to our Embassy the next day in a plain envelope. We later arranged for direct delivery to Hanoi through another government, but that message was also returned.

Our message said that

there would be no air attacks on North Vietnam beginning at noon Washington time, Wednesday, May 12, and running into the next week;

the United States was acting in response to "suggestions from various quarters, including public statements by Hanoi representatives," that there could be no progress toward peace while air attacks continued;

the United States was convinced that the basic trouble in Southeast Asia was armed action against the people and government of South Vietnam;

we would be watching during the pause for signs of "significant reductions in such armed actions";

we hoped that there would be no misunderstanding of our action and that the pause "may meet with a response which will permit further and more extended suspension of this form of military action in the expectation of equally constructive actions by the other side in the future."

Hanoi never answered directly but infiltration into the South continued, as did Viet Cong attacks. Then Hanoi denounced the pause, and Peking even alleged there was no pause. Once again we had tried to open the door; once again Hanoi had slammed it shut. In the face of Hanoi's continued hostility, we resumed bombing on May 18.

My fifth, and by far the hardest, Vietnam decision lay ahead. Throughout the 1950s and especially after 1958 the regime in Hanoi had totally ignored the provisions of the Geneva Accords of 1954. In the face of this situation, President Kennedy had decided in 1961, in answer to an appeal from the Vietnamese government, that our self-imposed restrictions on military equipment and personnel were both dangerous and legally meaningless. After the basic decisions of December 1961 to step up aid to the South Vietnamese, President Kennedy had increased our military advisory force from about 700 to more than 16,000 by the time I took office. We had also improved both the quality and quantity of weapons and other supplies going to the South Vietnamese armed forces.

In answer to further requests from the South Vietnamese and on the recommendation of our Embassy and the Military Command in Saigon, the number of advisers had been increased to nearly 23,000 by the end of 1964. But as we entered the year 1965, the situation in Vietnam was as different from 1963 as 1961 had been from 1959.

Early in 1965 it became clear that northern troops were entering the South not only as replacements for losses by Viet Cong military groups but as fighting units. General Westmoreland had intelligence reports that three North Vietnamese regiments, a total of between 6,000 and 8,000 men, had been sent to the South. By April at least one full regiment of the North Vietnamese 325th Division was in Kontum province in the Central Highlands, and we had information that two more enemy regiments were there. Hanoi was deploying major forces, trying for a military victory.

One reason for Hanoi's actions was undoubtedly the estimate that Ho Chi Minh and his colleagues had made of the political situation in the South. I have mentioned the great difficulties the South Vietnamese were having in cooperating with each other and developing their own political institutions. Encouraging that political weakness was a prime goal of Hanoi's agents and terrorists in the South. In 1964 alone they assassinated more than 400 government officials and kidnaped approximately 1,100 others. Between 1962 and 1965 there were more than 6,000 assassinations among South Vietnam's civilian population. It is obvious what that kind of slaughter means to a small, young nation and its people. A man thinks twice about becoming chief of his village or a district official if two or three of his predecessors have been murdered in their beds or disemboweled in the village square. Even in Saigon it was easier, and safer, to remain in private life rather than work for the government.

Once sustained bombing of the North began, my advisers and I were convinced that the Communists would make the air base near Danang a high-priority target, since many air strikes were launched there. The Vietnamese authorities shared our conviction. In March I agreed to General Westmoreland's request that we land two Marine battalions to provide security for the Danang air base. This released for offensive action against the Viet Cong some of the Vietnamese troops who had been protecting the base. This move, like all previous and subsequent assignments of foreign forces, was approved by Vietnam's civilian and military leaders.

Except for the attack east of Pleiku, most of February and March of 1965 was fairly quiet on the military front. But there were ominous signs that it was only a lull before another storm. Increasing numbers of regular North Vietnamese units were moving into or toward the northern provinces and the Highlands of South Vietnam. In March our estimate of Communist troop strength rose to 37,000 in main-force units and 100,000 in regional forces and local guerrillas. That represented a 33 per cent increase over 1964. In a few months the overall estimate was raised to 153,000.

The total strength of the South Vietnamese military at that time, including regular as well as regional and popular forces, was about 570,000. Many were occupied with static defense, logistics, transportation, and other noncombat assignments. In real combat strength the South Vietnamese had at best about 133 maneuver battalions, and their enemy had 72. That was a ratio of less than 2 to 1, and specialists in guerrilla warfare had long maintained that success against a determined guerrilla enemy called for a ratio of about 10 to 1 in favor of the defense forces. The South Vietnamese had eleven new battalions in training, but these forces would not be ready for combat until much later in the year.

General Harold K. Johnson, Army Chief of Staff, visited Vietnam early in March and went over the worsening military situation in detail with General Westmoreland and his staff and with the Vietnamese Joint General Staff. Soon after, on March 17, General Westmoreland asked permission to land a Marine battalion in the Hué area. Ambassador Taylor concurred in that request, but in doing so he pointed out:

> We will soon have to decide whether to try to get by with indigenous forces or to supplement them with Third Country troops, largely if not exclusively U.S.

He then analyzed the pros and cons of a suggestion made by General Johnson—the introduction of one U.S. division into Vietnam. Ambassador Taylor advised against a quick decision. He said that "considerable additional study is required before we are prepared to make a recommendation either for the introduction of a division or for the assignment of its mission."

"In the meantime," Taylor concluded, "we should be giving much thought both in South Vietnam and in Washington as to the right course of action if and when this issue becomes pressing—as it shortly will."

Late in March Taylor returned to Washington for consultation. Soon after he left Saigon, Viet Cong terrorists detonated several hundred pounds of explosives outside the American Embassy. The explosion killed two Americans and fifteen Vietnamese, and wounded scores, including Deputy Ambassador U. Alexis Johnson. The Communists were continuing their campaign of terror and indiscriminate slaughter.

On April 1 and 2 I met in the White House with Taylor and my principal advisers to consider carefully various recommendations that had been made. The proposals that came to me were a compromise among the views of three groups: those (especially in the armed forces) who wanted to move fast and in strength; my civilian advisers and Ambassador Taylor, who thought we should proceed, but more deliberately; and a few who opposed any significant involvement in the ground war.

With these various considerations before us, we carefully evaluated all suggestions and decided on a number of actions, the most important of which were:

a detailed program of nonmilitary actions submitted by Taylor;

programs in the information and psychological warfare field;

an elaborate military program submitted by General Johnson, with special emphasis on aircraft and helicopter reinforcements.

As for the air campaign, I considered many different points of view. The military chiefs urged that we increase the level of our air attacks. One of the most persuasive arguments for stronger air action at that time came from John McCone, who was preparing to leave his post as CIA Director. In a memo to me early in April McCone wrote:

> I remain concerned, as I have said before, . . . over the limited scale of air action against North Vietnam which we envision for the next few months.
> Specifically I feel that we must conduct our bombing attacks in a manner that will begin to hurt North Vietnam badly enough to cause the Hanoi regime to seek a political way out through negotiation rather than expose their economy to increasingly serious levels of destruction. By limiting our attacks to targets like bridges, military installations and lines of communication, in effect we signal to the Communists that our determination to win is significantly modified by our fear of widening the war. . . .
> I therefore urge that as we deploy additional troops, which I believe necessary, we concurrently hit the North harder and inflict greater damage. . . . We should make it hard for the Viet Cong to win in the South and simultaneously hard for Hanoi to endure our attacks in the North.

But most of my advisers felt that the risks of a sharply increased air war, including the possibility of deeper Chinese and Soviet involvement, outweighed the possible advantages. I accepted that judgment and decided that we should continue the "slowly ascending tempo," adding strikes if Viet Cong operations increased. We would also be ready to "slow the pace" if the Communist forces reduced their actions for more than a "temporary operational lull."

Among the specific military actions I approved were:

an 18,000- to 20,000-man increase in U.S. logistic and support forces;

deployment of two additional Marine battalions (for a total of four) and one Marine air squadron to the Danang-Hué area, with one of the battalions to go to Phu Bai, near Hué, to protect communications facilities and an airfield in that area;

a change in mission for the Marines to permit "their more active use" under rules to be approved by the Secretaries of State and Defense.

This did not mean, as has been frequently interpreted, that the Marines were to have an unlimited combat role. It did mean more aggressive patrolling and limited counterinsurgency combat operations in the vicinity of the Marine bases. I took seriously the reservations that Max Taylor had cited concerning the difficulties American troops might have operating in jungles against a guerrilla enemy. I wanted to be sure that our men could do the job and that they would not be fighting at a disadvantage.

As it turned out, they performed incredibly well. In a short time American forces demonstrated that with their superior conditioning, better logistic support, higher mobility, and greater firepower, they could meet and beat the best the North Vietnamese and Viet Cong could throw at them. The conditions confronting American troops in Vietnam were among the most difficult any large American force has ever faced. But I have no doubt that the forces in that struggle were the best we have ever sent into combat.

At that point, mid-April 1965, the approved level of U.S. forces in Vietnam was slightly over 40,000, and 33,500 were actually in-country. I decided the time had come for a new assessment. I asked Secretary McNamara to go to Honolulu to chair a meeting of Washington officials, leading members of our Mission in Saigon, and representatives of the Pacific Command. McNamara reported to me on April 21 with the results of the conference.

The agreed view, McNamara said, was that a settlement in Vietnam would come as much or more from Communist failure in the South as from "pain" in North Vietnam. The conferees estimated that it would take "perhaps a year or two" to demonstrate that the Communists could not achieve military victory in the South. None of them foresaw any "dramatic improvement in the South in the immediate future."

Of the Honolulu conferees, McNamara reported:

> Their strategy for "victory" over time is to break the will of the DRV/VC * by denying them victory. Ambassador Taylor put it in terms of a demonstration of Communist impotence, which will lead eventually to a political solution. They see slow improvement in the South, but all emphasized the critical importance of holding on and avoiding—for psychological and morale reasons—a spectacular defeat of the GVN † or U.S. forces. And they all suspect that the recent VC lull is but the quiet before the storm.

* DRV = Democratic Republic of (North) Vietnam; VC = Viet Cong.
† Government of (South) Vietnam.

To bolster South Vietnamese forces while they were building up, McNamara and his colleagues recommended further deployments in addition to the 33,500 Americans and 2,000 South Koreans then in Vietnam. These additions, including two U.S. Army brigades, three Marine battalions and three Marine air squadrons, plus logistic troops, would have raised the approved level to 82,000. McNamara also recommended that we encourage the South Vietnamese to ask South Korea and Australia for additional troops.

I approved some but not all of these recommendations during the next ten days—deployment of the 173rd Airborne Brigade, which went in early in May to provide security for the air base at Bien Hoa, and of the 3rd Marine Amphibious Brigade, which landed at Chu Lai a few days later to protect the site of a new airfield. By the end of that month U.S. forces in Vietnam passed the 50,000 mark.

On May 4 I asked Congress to approve a supplemental appropriation of $700 million to meet increasing costs in Vietnam. Three days later I was able to sign the bill in the East Room of the White House. At the signing I said:

> Let the meaning of this action be clear. To the brave people of South Vietnam, who are fighting and who are dying for the right to choose their own way of life, this resolution says: "America keeps her promises. And we will back up those promises with all the resources that we need."
>
> To our own boys who are fighting and dying beside the people of South Vietnam, this resolution says to them: "We are going to give you the tools to finish the job."
>
> To the aggressors, to those who by assassination and terror seek conquest and plunder, and to those who encourage and guide their aggression from afar, this resolution says: "We will not be defeated. We will not grow tired."

Later I said:

> I wish it were possible to convince others with words of what we now find necessary to say with guns and planes—that armed hostility is futile. Because once this is clear, it should also be clear that the only path for reasonable men is the path of peaceful settlement. . . .

The basic mission of the U.S. forces in Vietnam up to mid-May had been to secure the base areas to which they were assigned. This mission had been broadened somewhat to permit active and aggressive patrolling near those bases. In May General Westmoreland asked permission to use his forces in combat support if it became necessary to assist a Vietnamese unit in serious trouble. I granted that permission and announced it in a White House press statement on June 9:

> If help is requested by the appropriate Vietnamese commander, General Westmoreland also has authority within the assigned mission to employ

these troops in support of Vietnamese forces faced with aggressive attack when other effective reserves are not available and when, in his judgment, the general military situation urgently requires it.

Later in June General Westmoreland requested and received additional authority. This permitted him to commit U.S. troops to combat "independently of or in conjunction with" Vietnamese forces if asked by the Vietnamese and if Westmoreland himself judged that their use was "necessary to strengthen the relative position of GVN forces."

The first major ground combat operation by U.S. forces in Vietnam occurred from June 27 to June 30, 1965, when troops of the 173rd Airborne Brigade went into War Zone D, northwest of Saigon. Also in action there were the Vietnamese 48th Regiment, two battalions of Vietnamese airborne troops, and an Australian battalion that had arrived early in June.

During May and June the South Vietnamese army suffered several defeats at the hands of the North Vietnamese and Viet Cong. Early in June General Westmoreland reported on the situation. He said that major, if not all, elements of the North Vietnamese 325th Division were in the Highlands. Another division (the 304th) was in the Laos panhandle and could move into the South quickly. The South Vietnamese had suffered heavy losses. Four battalions had been put out of action in the northern provinces in recent weeks. Morale was sagging. In order to cope with the situation, Westmoreland could see no alternative except to "reinforce our efforts" in South Vietnam with additional U.S. or Third Country forces "as rapidly as is practical during the critical weeks ahead." This was not a recommendation to me, but I was informed of it by the Secretary of Defense and the Joint Chiefs.

Meanwhile, another political crisis was boiling up in Saigon. Prime Minister Phan Huy Quat was feuding with Vietnam's Catholics and was also at odds with the Vietnamese chief of state, Phan Khac Suu. On June 12 Quat resigned, announcing that he was turning power back to the military. The generals set up a National Leadership Committee chaired by General Nguyen Van Thieu, thus making him chief of state. They also selected an Executive Council, which they called their "war cabinet," and picked Marshal Nguyen Cao Ky, chief of the Vietnamese air force, to head it with the powers of Prime Minister.

The military leaders recognized the deteriorating war situation far better than the former civilian ministers. On June 28 Taylor reported on one of his first talks with Prime Minister Ky and the other responsible figures in the new government. "Ky went straight to his principal point— the need for additional U.S. ground combat forces," Taylor reported. "He is sensing for the first time the difficulty which we have anticipated for some time of fielding sufficient combat-ready South Vietnamese units to cope with growing numbers of Viet Cong units during the next few months. He is impressed with the need for injection of additional U.S. (or other Third Country) forces to tide over the monsoon offensive period, and to take off Viet Cong pressure while mobilization measures are being taken. . . ."

The new Vietnamese leaders and Ambassador Taylor agreed that General Westmoreland and Vietnam's newly appointed Minister of Defense, General Nguyen Huu Co, should confer immediately to determine outstanding needs and the best way to use any additional forces that might be introduced.

At the same time, in Washington, the staff of the Joint Chiefs and Defense Department specialists were studying the problem. I was not ready to send additional men without the most detailed analysis. As part of this survey, I asked Secretary McNamara to go to Vietnam again in July to confer with the Vietnamese leaders and with our own military and civilian officials.

I knew we faced a crucial question, one that was at the heart of our treaty commitment in Southeast Asia: If necessary, would we use substantial U.S. forces on the ground to prevent the loss of that region to aggressive forces moving illegally across international frontiers? I wanted to know many things firsthand from the Secretary of Defense: While asking for American combat forces, was the new Vietnamese government pushing its own efforts as hard as possible? Did the Vietnamese and our own people on the scene believe that American fighting forces could be effective against the Viet Cong in the mountains and jungles? Would non-Vietnamese fighting men revive memories of the French colonial years and arouse antiforeign sentiments? If American forces went into combat, how would responsibilities be divided between them and the Vietnamese army? These and dozens of other questions were on Secretary McNamara's list as he took off for Saigon in the middle of July.

One of the first things General Thieu and Prime Minister Ky told McNamara was that they were convinced that American and perhaps other foreign forces would be needed to hold back the Communist attackers. When McNamara asked for their estimate of how many might be needed, the Vietnamese leaders said they thought that in addition to the forty-four battalions they had already requested, there should be another combat division. Their total estimate called for about 200,000 American men in all categories. Thieu and Ky were convinced that American soldiers could fight effectively against the Viet Cong. They were also confident that the presence of non-Vietnamese troops would not create vast problems. They assured McNamara that their government would be making a major effort to explain to the South Vietnamese people that the Americans were there to help them remain free and not to take control as the French had done.

McNamara returned to Washington on July 20 and reported to me immediately. He summarized his outlook as follows:

> The situation in South Vietnam is worse than a year ago (when it was worse than a year before that). After a few months of stalemate, the tempo of the war has quickened. A hard VC push is now on to dismember the nation and to maul the army. The VC main and local forces, reinforced by militia and guerrillas, have the initiative and, with large attacks (some in regimental strength), are hurting ARVN * forces badly. . . . Cities and towns are being isolated as fewer and fewer roads and railroads are usable and power and communciations lines are cut.

The economy was "deteriorating," McNamara said. The odds were "less than even" that the current government would last out the year. The pacification program was making little progress. As for the Communists, they "seem to believe that South Vietnam is on the run and near collapse." They seemed determined to try for nothing less than "a complete takeover." McNamara concluded:

> We must choose among three courses of action with respect to Vietnam all of which involve different probabilities, outcomes and costs:
>
> (a) Cut our losses and withdraw under the best conditions that can be arranged—almost certainly conditions humiliating the United States and very damaging to our future effectiveness on the world scene.
>
> (b) Continue at about the present level, with the U.S. forces limited to say 75,000, holding on and playing for the breaks—a course of action which, because our position would grow weaker, almost certainly would confront us later with a choice between withdrawal and an emergency expansion of forces, perhaps too late to do any good.
>
> (c) Expand promptly and substantially the U.S. military pressure against the Viet Cong in the South and maintain the military pressure against the North Vietnamese in the North while launching a vigorous effort on the political side to lay the groundwork for a favorable outcome by clarifying our objectives and establishing channels of communication. This alternative would stave off defeat in the short run and offer a good chance of producing a favorable settlement in the longer run; at the same time, it would imply a commitment to see a fighting war clear through at considerable cost in casualties and matériel and would make any later decision to withdraw even more difficult and even more costly than would be the case today.

Secretary McNamara recommended the third alternative as "the course involving the best odds of the best outcome with the most acceptable cost to the United States." The Secretary believed that after the recommended ground forces had been deployed and certain actions had been taken in the

* Army of the Republic of (South) Vietnam.

bombing program in the North, we should consider a diplomatic initiative toward peace, including a bombing pause of perhaps six to eight weeks.

There were then fifteen American combat battalions either in Vietnam or en route, and a total force level of 75,000. These forces included Army brigades from the 101st Airborne Division and the 1st Infantry Division, which had landed in July to protect the bases at Cam Ranh Bay and Bien Hoa. McNamara recommended that the number of battalions be increased to thirty-four. The Koreans had promised to send nine battalions; if they failed to do so, we should make up the difference—a total in that case of forty-three battalions. That would raise the level of our forces to 175,000 men, or 200,000 if the Koreans failed to come through as promised.

"It should be understood," McNamara said, "that the deployment of more men (perhaps 100,000) may be necessary early in 1966, and that the deployment of additional forces thereafter is possible but will depend on developments."

He suggested that we ask Congress for the authority to call up 235,000 men in the reserves and the National Guard. He also proposed increasing the size of the regular armed forces by 375,000 men through increased recruitment and draft calls and extensions of tours of duty. The total increase in the military forces would then be 600,000 men by the middle of 1966. We would also have to ask Congress for an additional supplemental appropriation.

McNamara reported that Ambassador Taylor, Deputy Ambassador Alex Johnson, Ambassador-designate Henry Cabot Lodge,* General Wheeler, General Westmoreland, and Admiral Sharp all concurred in the military elements of his recommendation, although some of them did not fully support his proposal to try to inaugurate negotiations.

With the force that he and the others were proposing, McNamara was convinced that the South Vietnamese and allied armies could reverse the downward trend and move to the offensive. He said that the military commanders planned to locate, engage, and destroy the North Vietnamese and Viet Cong main-force units. At the same time, they believed we should press our anti-infiltration campaign by hitting enemy supply lines by air and on the sea. We would also carry the air war more intensively into Viet Cong base areas in the South. Finally, McNamara considered it important that we not give the impression by our increased military build-up and actions that we were thinking of invading North Vietnam.

I wanted to go over this proposal with the greatest care. I realized what a major undertaking it would be. The call-up of large numbers of reserves was part of the package. This would require a great deal of

---

* Lodge had agreed in July 1965 to accept another tour as Ambassador in Saigon, replacing General Taylor, who had taken the post for one year.

money and a huge sacrifice for the American people. I summoned my top advisers to the White House on July 21, the day after McNamara returned.

"What has happened in the recent past that requires this decision on my part?" I asked. "What are the alternatives? Also I want a lot more discussion on what we expect to flow from this decision. I want to discuss it in detail. Let's go over what other countries are doing, and who can do more. Are we the sole defenders of freedom in the world?"

"We must make no snap judgments," I added. "We must consider carefully all our options."

We went into the proposal line by line, argument by argument. We considered many alternatives. Under Secretary of State George Ball had been less than enthusiastic about some aspects of our involvement in Southeast Asia. Often in our meetings he spoke in opposition to one proposal or another. Especially from 1965 onward he played the role of devil's advocate frequently. This meeting was no exception.

"I can foresee a perilous voyage," he said. "I have great apprehensions that we can't win under these conditions."

"But let me be clear," he added. "If the decision is to go ahead, I'm committed."

After more searching discussion, we adjourned for lunch. It was then one o'clock. I asked my advisers to meet with me again at 2:30 P.M. I urged Ball to formulate his ideas into an alternate course of action so that we could consider it.

At the afternoon session I asked Ball to outline his views. His basic thesis was that we could not win a protracted war against local guerrillas in Asian jungles. He thought there was great danger of intrusion by the Chinese Communists. In his opinion, we were losing friends and influence in Europe and elsewhere because of our commitment in Asia. The best thing to do, he thought, was to cut our losses and pull away. He foresaw many problems in that course, but he believed they were outweighed by the advantages of the action he proposed.

We discussed Ball's approach for a long time and in great detail. I think all of us felt the same concerns and anxieties that Ball had expressed, but most of these men in the Cabinet Room were more worried about the results, in our country and throughout the world, of our pulling out and coming home. I felt the Under Secretary had not produced a sufficiently convincing case or a viable alternative.

Dean Rusk expressed one worry that was much on my mind. It lay at the heart of our Vietnam policy. "If the Communist world finds out that we will not pursue our commitments to the end," he said, "I don't know where they will stay their hand."

I felt sure they would *not* stay their hand. If we ran out on Southeast Asia, I could see trouble ahead in every part of the globe—not just in Asia but in the Middle East and in Europe, in Africa and in Latin America. I was convinced that our retreat from this challenge would open the path to World War III.

Our consultations had only begun. I met the next day with the Joint Chiefs of Staff and the Secretaries of the military services. In the afternoon I met again for nearly an hour and a half with Rusk, McNamara, Ball, General Wheeler, Bundy, and several civilian advisers, including Clark Clifford, John McCloy, and Arthur Dean. Later that day I went up to Camp David to reflect. I invited several advisers to join me there for further long discussions on Sunday, July 25.

Secretary McNamara, Ambassador to the United Nations Arthur Goldberg, and Clark Clifford, then Chairman of the President's Foreign Intelligence Advisory Board, joined me in the Aspen Lodge at Camp David in the afternoon. One of the things we wanted to discuss was whether we should take any action in the United Nations in connection with Vietnam. The weight of opinion was against a major effort to persuade the United Nations to act at that time. Most of my advisers felt that the leaders in Hanoi would turn down any UN proposal, because they had consistently declared that Vietnam was not a proper matter for UN involvement. Moreover, it was virtually certain that the Soviet Union would veto any proposal Hanoi might have trouble accepting.

At this session my old friend Clark Clifford was in a reflective and pessimistic mood. "I don't believe we can win in South Vietnam," he said. "If we send in 100,000 more men, the North Vietnamese will meet us. If North Vietnam runs out of men, the Chinese will send in volunteers. Russia and China don't intend for us to win the war."

He urged that in the coming months we quietly probe possibilities with other countries for some way to get out honorably. "I can't see anything but catastrophe for my country," he said.

I told Clifford that he was expressing worries that many Americans, including the President, were experiencing. No one was more concerned than I was, but we could not simply walk out. Nor was I prepared to accept just any settlement as a cover-up for surrender. What we needed was a way to start real negotiations and I intended to keep pressing our offer to talk peace.

We continued our review of the military situation and the requirement for additional forces. Our military commanders had refined their estimates and indicated they could meet the immediate demand with 50,000 men. I called a meeting of the National Security Council two days later, on July 27.*

---

* Those present at this crucial meeting of the NSC, its advisers, and other invitees were Rusk, Ball, Ambassador Thompson, Bill Bundy, and Ambassador Lodge from State; McNamara and McNaughton from Defense; Chairman of the Joint Chiefs General Wheeler; Admiral William F. Raborn, Jr., and Richard Helms from the CIA; Treasury Secretary Henry

I asked McNamara at that time to summarize again the current need as he saw it.

McNamara noted that the Viet Cong had increased in size through local recruitment and replacements from the North. Regular North Vietnamese army units had increased in number and strength. Communist control of the countryside was growing. A dozen provincial capitals were virtually isolated from surrounding rural areas. The South Vietnamese army was growing, but not nearly fast enough to keep pace with the expanding enemy forces. Without additional armed strength, South Vietnam would inevitably fall to Hanoi. I told the NSC there were five possible choices available to us.

"We can bring the enemy to his knees by using our Strategic Air Command," I said, describing our first option. "Another group thinks we ought to pack up and go home.

"Third, we could stay there as we are—and suffer the consequences, continue to lose territory and take casualties. You wouldn't want your own boy to be out there crying for help and not get it.

"Then, we could go to Congress and ask for great sums of money; we could call up the reserves and increase the draft; go on a war footing; declare a state of emergency. There is a good deal of feeling that ought to be done. We have considered this. But if we go into that kind of land war, then North Vietnam would go to its friends, China and Russia, and ask them to give help. They would be forced into increasing aid. For that reason I don't want to be overly dramatic and cause tensions. I think we can get our people to support us without having to be too provocative and warlike.

"Finally, we can give our commanders in the field the men and supplies they say they need."

I had concluded that the last course was the right one. I had listened to and weighed all the arguments and counterarguments for each of the possible lines of action. I believed that we should do what was necessary to resist aggression but that we should not be provoked into a major war. We would get the required appropriation in the new budget, and we would not boast about what we were doing. We would not make threatening noises to the Chinese or the Russians by calling up reserves in large numbers. At the same time, we would press hard on the diplomatic front to try to find some path to a peaceful settlement.

I asked if anyone objected to the course of action I had spelled out. I questioned each man in turn. Did he agree? Each nodded his approval or said "yes."

Fowler; Carl Rowan and Leonard Marks from the USIA; Attorney General Nicholas Katzenbach; and Mac Bundy, Horace Busby, Douglass Cater, Richard Goodwin, Bill Moyers, Bromley Smith, and Jack Valenti from the White House staff; and Clark Clifford.

Before making the decision final and moving ahead, I wanted the opinions and the advice of the leaders in Congress. I invited Senators Mansfield, Dirksen, Hickenlooper, Kuchel, Long, and Smathers and Representatives McCormack, Albert, Arends, Boggs, and Ford to meet with me at the White House that same evening, July 27, 1965.

I described for them the same five alternatives I believed were available to us. I said that in my opinion the real choice lay between alternatives four and five—"to go the full congressional route now" or "to give the congressional leadership the story now and the bill later." I said that declaring a state of emergency at this time had a good deal of appeal to me but that there was a strong argument against it based on the possible reaction of Hanoi and its Communist supporters, China and the Soviet Union. I did not want our action to provoke the Chinese and Russians to increase their assistance to North Vietnam. If we could turn back the enemy forces on the ground and avoid direct Soviet and Chinese involvement, we might then hope to move toward negotiations that Hanoi would accept.

"Frankly," I said, "I don't think there is much chance of an early settlement, but others keep saying we have got to try, even though we have tried many times."

Rusk then reviewed the diplomatic ground and discussed the possibilities of getting into negotiations. McNamara described the military elements of the proposed program and its likely costs. Henry Cabot Lodge, who was returning to Saigon, was present at the meeting. He made a strong and convincing case against the first three alternatives.

We discussed at length the pros and cons of alternatives four and five. Carl Albert said he agreed that alternative five made the most sense. George Smathers asked if any change in policy was involved. I said that the enemy was increasing its efforts to take over South Vietnam and that we were stepping up our measures to prevent such an outcome. Our fundamental policy was unchanged.

Russell Long said it seemed to him that the choice was "put in more men or take a whipping." He said we had better increase our forces.

"I don't think we have any alternative," Speaker McCormack said. "Our military men tell us we need more men and we should send them. The lesson of Hitler and Mussolini is clear. I can see, five years from now, a chain of events far more dangerous to our country if we don't."

Bourke Hickenlooper said he would support the decision even though he was not sure which of the choices, four or five, was the better way. Hale Boggs said that alternative five was "the logical way out."

"My object," I said, "is to get our government together, to get the allies together, and to get the country together." I explained that we were thinking of increasing our forces in three phases and that I thought our total force would be doubled by November 1.

In the entire group the only expression of serious doubt and opposition to the proposed course again came from Mike Mansfield. As always, he expressed his opinion candidly. He spoke of the deepening discontent in the country. He thought the best hope was "a quick stalemate and negotiations." But he concluded by saying that as a Senator and Majority Leader he would support the President's position.

Speaker McCormack closed the meeting by assuring me that I would have united support. "This was an historic meeting," he said. "The President will have the support of all true Americans."

I have described the changing situations and estimates that caused me to consider the hard alternatives of July 1965. I have indicated why among these possible choices, all of them painful, I decided on the one I did.

There was more to it than listening to the arguments and dissents, the explanations and justifications of my wisest advisers in and out of government. When a President faces a decision involving war or peace, he draws back and thinks of the past and of the future in the widest possible terms. On his sworn oath, a President pledges he will protect the nation. The security of the whole country is the foremost responsibility of the Chief Executive. The most important question I had to face was: How will the decisions we make in Vietnam or elsewhere affect the security and the future of our nation?

A President searches his mind and his heart for the answers, so that when he decides on a course of action it is in the long-range best interests of the country, its people, and its security.

That is what I did—when I was alone and sleepless at night in the Executive Mansion, away from official cables and advisers; when I sat alone in the Aspen Lodge at Camp David; when I walked along the banks of the Pedernales River or looked out over the Texas hill country. In those lonely vigils I tried to think through what would happen to our nation and to the world if we did not act with courage and stamina—if we let South Vietnam fall to Hanoi.

This is what I could foresee: First, from all the evidence available to me it seemed likely that all of Southeast Asia would pass under Communist control, slowly or quickly, but inevitably, at least down to Singapore but almost certainly to Djakarta. I realize that some Americans believe they have, through talking with one another, repealed the domino theory. In 1965 there was no indication in Asia, or from Asians, that this was so. On both sides of the line between Communist and non-Communist Asia the struggle for Vietnam and Laos was regarded as a struggle for the fate of Southeast Asia. The evidence before me as President confirmed the previous assessments of President Eisenhower and of President Kennedy.

Second, I knew our people well enough to realize that if we walked away from Vietnam and let Southeast Asia fall, there would follow a divisive and destructive debate in our country. This had happened when the Communists took power in China. But that was very different from the Vietnam conflict. We had a solemn treaty commitment to Southeast Asia. We had an international agreement on Laos made as late as 1962 that was being violated flagrantly. We had the word of three Presidents that the United States would not permit this aggression to succeed. A divisive debate about "who lost Vietnam" would be, in my judgment, even more destructive to our national life than the argument over China had been. It would inevitably increase isolationist pressures from the right and the left and cause a pulling back from our commitments in Europe and the Middle East as well as in Asia.

Third, our allies not just in Asia but throughout the world would conclude that our word was worth little or nothing. Those who had counted so long for their security on American commitments would be deeply shaken and vulnerable.

Fourth, knowing what I did of the policies and actions of Moscow and Peking, I was as sure as a man could be that if we did not live up to our commitment in Southeast Asia and elsewhere, they would move to exploit the disarray in the United States and in the alliances of the Free World. They might move independently or they might move together. But move they would—whether through nuclear blackmail, through subversion, with regular armed forces, or in some other manner. As nearly as one can be certain of anything, I knew they could not resist the opportunity to expand their control into the vacuum of power we would leave behind us.

Finally, as we faced the implications of what we had done as a nation, I was sure the United States would not then passively submit to the consequences. With Moscow and Peking and perhaps others moving forward, we would return to a world role to prevent their full takeover of Europe, Asia, and the Middle East—*after* they had committed themselves.

I was too young at the time to be aware of the change in American mood and policy between the election of Woodrow Wilson in November 1916 ("He kept us out of war") and our reaction to unrestricted German submarine warfare in the Atlantic in April 1917. But I knew the story well. My generation had lived through the change from American isolationism to collective security in 1940–1941. I had watched firsthand in Congress as we swerved in 1946–1947 from the unilateral dismantling of our armed forces to President Truman's effort to protect Western Europe. I could never forget the withdrawal of our forces from South Korea and then our immediate reaction to the Communist aggression of June 1950.

As I looked ahead, I could see us repeating the same sharp reversal once again in Asia, or elsewhere—but this time in a nuclear world with all the dangers and possible horrors that go with it. Above all else, I did not want to lead this nation and the world into nuclear war or even the risk of such a war.

This was the private estimate that brought me to the hard decision of July 1965. None of the very few who opposed the decision gave me facts or arguments that broke or even weakened this chain of conclusions. These were the thoughts, and the profound concerns, that were in my mind when I went to meet the White House press corps on July 28, 1965, and opened the press conference by saying:

> I have asked the commanding general, General Westmoreland, what more he needs to meet this mounting aggression. He has told me. We will meet his needs. I have today ordered to Vietnam the Air Mobile Division and certain other forces which will raise our fighting strength from 75,000 to 125,000 men almost immediately. Additional forces will be needed later, and they will be sent as requested. . . .

Now we were committed to major combat in Vietnam. We had determined not to let that country fall under Communist rule as long as we could prevent it and as long as the Vietnamese continued to fight for themselves. At the same time, I was resolved to do everything possible to keep this a limited war, to prevent it from expanding into a nuclear conflict.

I could not announce that Americans were going into combat without adding a personal note, one that I felt in every fiber of my being:

> I do not find it easy to send the flower of our youth, our finest young men, into battle. I have spoken to you today of the divisions and the forces and battalions and the units, but I know them all, every one. I have seen them in a thousand streets, of a hundred towns, in every state in this Union—working and laughing and building, and filled with hope and life. I think I know too how their mothers weep and how their families sorrow.
>
> This is the most agonizing and the most painful duty of your President.

7

The Struggle for Justice

WHEN I WAS IN THE SENATE, we had an extra car to take back to Texas at the close of each congressional session. Usually my Negro employees—Zephyr Wright, our cook; Helen Williams, our maid; and Helen's husband, Gene—drove the car to the Ranch for us. At that time, nearly twenty years ago, it was an ordeal to get an automobile from Washington to Texas—three full days of hard driving.

On one of those trips I asked Gene if he would take my beagle dog with them in the car. I didn't think they would mind. Little Beagle was a friendly, gentle dog.

But Gene hesitated. "Senator, do we have to take Beagle?"

"Well," I explained, "there's no other way to get him to Texas. He shouldn't give you any trouble, Gene. You know Beagle loves you."

But Gene still hesitated. I didn't understand. I looked directly at him. "Tell me what's the matter. Why don't you want to take Beagle? What aren't you telling me?"

Gene began slowly. Here is the gist of what he had to say: "Well, Senator, it's tough enough to get all the way from Washington to Texas. We drive for hours and hours. We get hungry. But there's no place on the road we can stop and go in and eat. We drive some more. It gets pretty hot. We want to wash up. But the only bathroom we're allowed in is usually miles off the main highway. We keep going 'til night comes—'til we get so tired we can't stay awake any more. We're ready to pull in. But it takes us another hour or so to find a place to sleep. You see, what I'm saying is that a colored man's got enough trouble getting across the South on his own, without having a dog along."

Of course, I knew that such discrimination existed throughout the South. We all knew it. But somehow we had deluded ourselves into believing that the black people around us were happy and satisfied; into thinking that the bad and ugly things were going on somewhere else, happening to other people.

There were no "darkies" or plantations in the arid hill country where I grew up. I never sat on my parents' or grandparents' knees listening to nostalgic tales of the antebellum South. In Stonewall and Johnson City I never was a part of the Old Confederacy. But I was part of Texas. My roots were in its soil. I felt a special identification with its history and its people. And Texas is a part of the South—in the sense that Texas shares a common heritage and outlook that differs from the Northeast or Middle West or Far West.

That Southern heritage meant a great deal to me. It gave me a feeling of belonging and a sense of continuity. But it also created—sadly, but perhaps inevitably—certain parochial feelings that flared up defensively whenever Northerners described the South as "a blot on our national conscience" or "a stain on our country's democracy."

These were emotions I took with me to the Congress when I voted against six civil rights bills that came up on the House and Senate floor. At that time I simply did not believe that the legislation, as written, was the right way to handle the problem. Much of it seemed designed more to humiliate the South than to help the black man.

Beyond this, I did not think there was much I could do as a lone Congressman from Texas. I represented a conservative constituency. One heroic stand and I'd be back home, defeated, unable to do any good for anyone, much less the blacks and the underprivileged. As a Representative and a Senator, before I became Majority Leader, I did not have the power. That is a plain and simple fact.

But what stands out the most when I think of those days is not my Texas background or my Southern heritage but the recognition that I was part of America growing up. This was an America that accepted distinctions between blacks and whites as part and parcel of life, whether those distinctions were the clear-cut, blatant ones of the South or the more subtle, invidious ones practiced in the North. This was an America misled by a mask of submissiveness and good nature that hid the deep despair inside the hearts of millions of black Americans.

So there was nothing I could say to Gene. His problem was also mine: as a Texan, a Southerner, and an American.

All these attitudes began to change in the mid-1950s and early 1960s. The Supreme Court's epic 1954 decision in *Brown v. Board of Education* cast permanent doubt on the conventional wisdom of "separate but equal." This decision gave the civil rights movement a new burst of hope and faith.

Ignited by the promise of freedom, boycotts and marches began to spread from city to city.

At the same time, my own responsibilities were growing. With the Democratic victory in the 1954 congressional election, I was promoted from Minority Leader to Majority Leader of the Senate. My national responsibilities, as well as my ability to get things done, increased. I was aware of the need for change inside myself.

I felt the need for change as Majority Leader when I led the Senate fight for the Civil Rights Act of 1957. We obtained only half a loaf in that fight, but it was an essential half-loaf, the first civil rights legislation in eighty-two years. In order to prevent a Senate filibuster, the sponsors of the bill had to yield on a critical provision that would have given the Attorney General the right to seek court injunctions against deprivation of a wide variety of civil rights. There was no way we could have persuaded a majority of Senators to agree to that provision. To have pressed for the impossible would have been to destroy all hope of the possible, a legislative guarantee to protect voting rights. Once this first guarantee was on the books, the path was opened for later legislation extending federal protection into every area of civil rights.

I felt the need for change as Vice President when, as Chairman of the President's Committee on Equal Employment Opportunity, I came face to face with the deep-seated discrimination that afflicts our entire economic system, North and South. I tried to describe this learning process to a conference on equal employment opportunity on May 19, 1962:

> We have learned in the course of our work that the problem of equal opportunity is not confined solely to availability of jobs. This question cannot be solved until we have not only equal opportunity in employment but equal opportunity in access to the training and the education that qualifies men and women for the job.

I felt the need for change in the spring of 1963 when events in Birmingham, Alabama, showed the world the glaring contrast between the restraint of the black demonstrators and the brutality of the white policemen. I reflected these feelings at Gettysburg on May 30, 1963, when I spoke at Memorial Day services commemorating the one hundredth anniversary of the Battle of Gettysburg:

> One hundred years ago, the slave was freed. One hundred years later, the Negro remains in bondage to the color of his skin. The Negro today asks justice. We do not answer him—we do not answer those who lie beneath this soil—when we reply to the Negro by asking, "Patience."
>
> Until justice is blind to color, until education is unaware of race, until opportunity is unconcerned with the color of men's skins, emancipation will be a proclamation but not a fact. To the extent that the proclamation

of emancipation is not fulfilled in fact, to that extent we shall have fallen short of assuring freedom to the free.

But nothing makes a man come to grips more directly with his conscience than the Presidency. Sitting in that chair involves making decisions that draw out a man's fundamental commitments. The burden of his responsibility literally opens up his soul. No longer can he accept matters as given; no longer can he write off hopes and needs as impossible.

In that house of decision, the White House, a man becomes his commitments. He understands who he really is. He learns what he genuinely wants to be.

So it was for me. When I sat in the Oval Office after President Kennedy died and reflected on civil rights, there was no question in my mind as to what I would do. I knew that, as President and as a man, I would use every ounce of strength I possessed to gain justice for the black American. My strength as President was then tenuous—I had no strong mandate from the people; I had not been elected to that office. But I recognized that the moral force of the Presidency is often stronger than the political force. I knew that a President can appeal to the best in our people or the worst; he can call for action or live with inaction.

Even the strongest supporters of President Kennedy's civil rights bill in 1963 expected parts of it to be watered down in order to avert a Senate filibuster. The most vulnerable sections were those guaranteeing equal access to public accommodations and equal employment opportunity. I had seen this "moderating" process at work for many years. I had seen it happen in 1957. I had seen it happen in 1960. I did not want to see it happen again.

I made my position unmistakably clear: We were not prepared to compromise in any way. "So far as this administration is concerned," I told a press conference, "its position is firm." I wanted absolutely no room for bargaining. And I wanted everyone to know this, from the lowliest bureaucrat to the members of my Cabinet, from the poorest black man in the slums to the richest white man in the suburbs, from the staunchest Baptist in the South to the most devout Catholic in the North.

I spoke out on every suitable occasion—in press conferences, in Cabinet meetings, in private conversations, in messages to Congress. I even managed to create some occasions of my own—a Joint Session before the Congress, a trip to the New York World's Fair, a session with the Plans for Progress group, a memorial to Abraham Lincoln. I knew that the slightest wavering on my part would give hope to the opposition's strategy of amending the bill to death.

Another important consideration was that my old friend, the Southern legislative leader Senator Richard Russell of Georgia, understand my unyielding position, even though it would force him and the other opponents of the bill to go for all or nothing. One could not persuade Senator Russell by sweet talk, hard talk, or any kind of talk. He respected action, not words. It was important that he be informed of my efforts to build the fire of a discharge petition under the House Rules Committee in order to get the bill to the Senate as quickly as possible. He had to realize that I meant to obtain a meaningful civil rights bill.

One of the wisest and ablest men in the Senate, Russell understood the critical nature of the stakes involved. As a friend who knew me well, he recognized that I would not accept a watered-down, ineffective bill.

On January 24, 1964, Senator Russell publicly acknowledged that fact:

> I have no doubt but that [the President] intends to throw the full weight of his powerful office and the full force of his personality—both of which are considerable— . . . to secure passage of this program. . . .
>
> Some of us who have not yet abandoned our faith in constitutional government intend to fight these discriminatory proposals to the last ditch.
>
> Although I differ—and differ vigorously—with President Johnson on this so-called civil rights question . . . I expect to support the President just as strongly when I think he is right as I intend to oppose him when I think he is wrong.

These few words shaped the entire struggle. It would be a fight to total victory or total defeat without appeasement or attrition. The battle would be fought with dignity and perhaps with sorrow, but not with anger or bitterness. We would win, by securing cloture,* or we would lose.

One man held the key to obtaining cloture: the Minority Leader of the Senate, Everett Dirksen. Without his cooperation, we could not enlist the support of the moderate Republicans, and without Republican support we could not obtain the two-thirds vote necessary for cloture. From the outset Senator Dirksen had taken a firm stand against the use of federal injunctions to guarantee equal accommodations or fair employment practices. While he supported several of the bill's titles, particularly the need for increased federal protection of voting rights, he argued that authorizing injunctions would be an open invitation to the Attorney General's staff to roam all over the country as a legal aid society, picking and choosing cases at will.

Dirksen could play politics as well as any man. But I knew something else about him. When the nation's interest was at stake, he could climb the heights and take the long view without regard to party. I based a great deal of my strategy on this understanding of Dirksen's deep-rooted patriotism.

A President cannot ask the Congress to take a risk he will not take him-

---

* The device which sets a time limit on debate, thereby precluding a filibuster.

self. He must be the combat general in the front lines, constantly exposing his flanks. I tried to be that combat general. I gave to this fight everything I had in prestige, power, and commitment. At the same time, I deliberately tried to tone down my personal involvement in the daily struggle so that my colleagues on the Hill could take tactical responsibility—and credit; so that a hero's niche could be carved out for Senator Dirksen, not me.

The liberals were organized as never before. Senator Humphrey did a good job as floor manager. The key to his approach, with my encouragement, was restraint—the restraint of nonpartisan politics, stressing the integrity of the Senate as an institution and the heritage of Lincoln's party. Humphrey constantly emphasized the need for bipartisan cooperation. He never questioned the motives of Republicans or Southern Democrats. The debate at all times was dignified.

A critical factor in holding the campaign together was the pressure applied by the major citizens' groups behind the bill—the religious groups, the unions, the troubled and concerned Southerners, and the civil rights organizations. The potential strength of public opinion had first been evident in the march on Washington late in the summer of 1963. By the spring of 1964 this climate of opinion could be felt by every Senator and Congressman.

As the debate continued through March, April, and May, a new and disturbing element of public opinion came into play. Governor George Wallace of Alabama had declared himself a candidate for President and had entered the Democratic primaries in Indiana, Maryland, and Wisconsin with an emotional campaign of opposition to civil rights and a thinly veiled racist call for law and order. Most analysts predicted that he would receive 10 per cent of the vote; his actual totals more than tripled that prediction.

The strength of the Wallace showing brought the term "white backlash" into our vocabulary, a shorthand phrase for growing white resentment against the pace and tone of Negro demands. The Wallace showing stiffened the Southerners' will to keep on fighting the civil rights measure until the liberal ranks began to crumble.

But the civil rights troops on the Hill did not fall apart. Quite the opposite—the Wallace show of strength served to emphasize more than ever the essential need for national unity through a peaceful and progressive resolution of the racial issue. In this critical hour Senator Dirksen came through, as I had hoped he would. He knew his country's future was at stake. He knew what he could do to help. He knew what he had to do as a leader. On June 10 he took the floor of the Senate to say:

> The time has come for equality of opportunity in sharing in government, in education, and in employment. It will not be stayed or denied. It is here. . . . America grows. America changes. And on the civil rights

issue we must rise with the occasion. That calls for cloture and for the enactment of a civil rights bill.

With this speech, Dirksen sounded the death knell for the Southern strategy of filibuster. For the first time in history the Senate voted cloture on a civil rights bill. With all one hundred Senators present and voting, we needed 67 votes for the two-thirds rule to obtain cloture. We got four more than that. The final tally was 71 to 29.

With cloture, the battle was over. The bill was assured of passage.

In the wake of defeat the Southerners' proposed amendments became gestures only, overwhelmingly voted down one by one on the Senate floor. Three weeks later the Congress passed the Civil Rights Act of 1964, the most sweeping civil rights measure enacted in the twentieth century.

I signed the bill in the East Room of the White House. My thoughts went back to the afternoon a decade before when there was absolutely nothing I could say to Gene Williams, or to any black man, or to myself. That had been the day I first realized the sad truth: that to the extent Negroes were imprisoned, so was I. On this day, July 2, 1964, I knew the positive side of that same truth: that to the extent Negroes were free, really free, so was I. And so was my country.

Many people felt we should rest after the victory of the 1964 Civil Rights Act, take it easy on Congress, and leave some breathing space for the bureaucracy and the nation. But there was no time to rest. Tensions in the South were still running high. That same summer three civil rights workers were brutally murdered in Mississippi. Churches were bombed and lives were threatened. In the North a different set of tensions exploded—the tensions of poverty, squalor, unemployment, and inadequate health care. Riots broke out and continued for four days in Harlem late in July, followed by similar disturbances in four other Northern cities.

The first of several long, hot summers had begun.

The theme of "law and order" became a major thrust of Senator Goldwater's campaign for the Presidency in 1964. I shared the growing concern about violence, but I believed the real danger, far more profound than violence and far more perilous, was the increasing alienation of the black citizens from American society. Our representative system was based on the joint premise that all citizens would be responsible under the law and that the law would be responsive to the needs of all citizens. But in the field of human rights a significant number of citizens had not been fully served by our system. I feared that as long as these citizens were alienated from the *rights* of the American system, they would continue to consider themselves outside the *obligations* of that system. I tried to state this position as fully as I could in the Presidential campaign. I wanted a mandate to move forward, not simply a sanction for the status quo.

On November 3, 1964, the American voters gave me that mandate. I moved to use it quickly. I directed Attorney General Nicholas Katzenbach * to begin the complicated task of drafting the next civil rights bill—legislation to secure, once and for all, equal voting rights. In many ways I believed this act would be even more critical than the previous one. Once the black man's voice could be translated into ballots, many other breakthroughs would follow, and they would follow as a consequence of the black man's own legitimate power as an American citizen, not as a gift from the white man.

I discussed this legislation several times early in 1965 with Roy Wilkins, Executive Director of the NAACP; Martin Luther King, Jr., leader of the Southern Christian Leadership Conference; Whitney Young, Jr., Executive Director of the National Urban League; Clarence Mitchell, Director of the Washington Bureau of the NAACP; A. Philip Randolph, and others. We all knew that the prospects for congressional passage were unpromising, but we decided to go ahead. I would work within the federal government; the black leadership would take their cause directly to the people.

The capstone of their campaign was a fifty-four-mile march through Alabama from Selma to Montgomery. Two abreast, blacks and whites together, the marchers walked, singing the words of an old Baptist hymn:

> We shall stand together, we shall stand together,
> We shall stand together—now.
> Oh, deep in my heart I do believe
> We shall overcome someday.

The singing came to an abrupt end early in the evening of March 7, when the marchers reached the Edmund Pettus Bridge at the southern edge of Selma and were confronted by Sheriff Jim Clark and a mounted posse. The sheriff ordered the marchers to turn around. They knew their rights and refused. The Alabama state troopers took matters into their own hands. With nightsticks, bullwhips, and billy clubs, they scattered the ranks of the marchers. More than fifty men and women were severely injured. The march was over.

But the struggle had just begun. Several nights later Lady Bird and I were hosting a congressional reception in the East Room of the White House. The reception was several hours old when one of my aides brought me an urgent note. James Reeb, a white Unitarian minister from Boston, had been clubbed to death in Selma by a band of four white men, to the shouts of "Hey, nigger lover."

We excused ourselves and went upstairs to call Mrs. Reeb. No matter what I could find to say to her, I had no answer to the one question that

---

* Katzenbach, who succeeded Robert Kennedy, became Acting Attorney General on September 3, 1964, and Attorney General on February 13, 1965.

kept turning over and over in my mind: How many Jim Reebs will die before our country is truly free?

As I watched the reruns of the Selma confrontation on television, I felt a deep outrage. I believed that my feelings were shared by millions of Americans throughout the country, North and South, but I knew that it would probably not take long for these aroused emotions to melt away. It was important to move at once if we were to achieve anything permanent from this transitory mood. It was equally important that we move in the right direction.

The most obvious step, and the one most passionately desired by citizens in the North who supported equal rights for the Negro, was to send federal troops to Alabama. I understood this desire and the deep concern that motivated it. But I knew that a hasty display of federal force at this time could destroy whatever possibilities existed for the passage of voting rights legislation. Such action would play into the hands of those looking for a states' rights martyr in Governor Wallace. Sending federal troops would turn the growing compassion of the Southern moderates into defensive resistance, and would resurrect the bitterness between North and South. We had to have a real victory for the black people, not a psychological victory for the North. I directed Justice Department officials to work night and day to loosen the tangled cords of constitutional and legal questions that were still knotted from the early days of our proposed voting rights bill.

Meanwhile, there was a storm of public protest to contend with. In front of the White House scores of demonstrators marched up and down with placards: "LBJ, just you wait . . . see what happens in '68" . . . "LBJ, open your eyes, see the sickness of the South, see the horrors of your home-land." Inside the East Wing a group of demonstrators who had joined a regular White House tour conducted a sit-in. Everywhere I looked I was being denounced for my "unbelievable lack of action." Across the nation hundreds of sympathy marches and sit-ins were mobilized.

Once again my Southern heritage was thrown in my face. I was hurt, deeply hurt. But I was determined not to be shoved into hasty action. If only there were some way to assure protection for the marchers without the drama of using federal troops; if only the State of Alabama would exercise its state's right and assume its constitutional obligation.

My hopes were answered on Friday, March 12, when Governor Wallace wired me requesting a special meeting to discuss the situation in Selma. I replied immediately that I would be "available at any time." An appointment was set for twelve noon the next day. We sat together in the Oval Office. I kept my eyes directly on the Governor's face the entire time. I saw a nervous, aggressive man; a rough, shrewd politician who had managed to touch the deepest chords of pride as well as prejudice among his people.

It was to his pride as an Alabama patriot that I appealed when I asked the Governor to assure me that he would let the marchers proceed in peace and would provide adequate troops to insure the right of peaceful assembly. The Governor's first response was an automatic one. He said the only problems in Alabama were the troublesome demonstrators themselves. They were the ones who were threatening the lives and safety of the people; they were the ones who were defying law and order.

I told him that I believed the only useful way to handle the demonstrators was to respond to their grievances. "The Negro citizens of Alabama who have been systematically denied the right to register and vote have to be given the opportunity to direct national attention to their plight," I said.

The Governor turned then to the question of troops. In his view, the state held the responsibility to maintain law and order. I agreed with him at once and told him that was precisely my point. But I made it clear that I intended no such misunderstanding to occur as that which arose between Governor Orval Faubus of Arkansas and President Eisenhower during the 1957 Little Rock episode, when the Governor actually used the National Guard to prevent integration. I told him I had seven hundred troops on alert. If the state and local authorities were unwilling or unable to function, I would not hesitate one moment to send in federal troops.

The Governor said he understood, and we parted in a mood of cordiality. In fact, the Governor was later reported to have said: "If I hadn't left when I did, he'd have had me coming out *for* civil rights."

The meeting with Wallace proved to be the critical turning point in the voting rights struggle. Several days later I received word from the Governor that the State of Alabama was unable to bear the financial burdens of mobilizing the National Guard. The state could not protect the marchers on its own. It needed federal assistance. I gave such assistance immediately. I signed an Executive order federalizing the Alabama National Guard.

So the troops went in after all. They went in by order of the President, because the Governor said Alabama couldn't afford them financially. But they were not intruders forcing their way in; they were citizens of Alabama. That made all the difference in the world.

By Sunday morning, March 14, the Justice Department had completed most of its work on the draft of the voting rights bill. The thorny questions of federal power had been resolved. We had decided that federal registrars and trigger provisions * would be absolutely essential to secure the black man's voting rights. But one question remained: What was the best way to transmit the message to the Congress—in person or in writing?

I asked the bipartisan leadership of the Congress to meet with me that

* Specific criteria under which the federal government would send in registrars.

Sunday evening at 5 P.M. The members present included Senators Mansfield, Dirksen, and Kuchel and Representatives McCormack, Albert, Boggs, and William McCulloch of Ohio. I went over the main provisions of the voting rights bill as it was then drafted and asked for their best judgment in approaching the Congress.

Senator Mansfield spoke first. He suggested that I send the bill up Tuesday afternoon. He did not think that I should make a public presentation. Senator Dirksen agreed. He stressed the need to avoid panic. "This is a deliberate government. Don't let these people say we scared him into it. Don't circumvent the Congress."

I understood their hesitation. It is sometimes risky for the President to "go to the people" in support of a bill. If Congress does not support the public appeal, the move can completely backfire. Yet in this case I felt I had to reassure the people that we were moving as far and as fast as we could. I knew this reassurance would not be provided by the cold words of a written message. But if my congressional leaders were against it, I certainly had to weigh their counsel.

At that point Speaker McCormack said: "I disagree. I strongly recommend that the President go to the Congress and present the bill to a Joint Session. I suggest that he tell the Congress and the entire nation about the bill. Such a speech would show bipartisanship . . . it would show the world that action is being taken."

He spoke with intense conviction. His words, and the decades of experience behind them, had an immediate impact on the rest of the leadership. I could see the tide beginning to shift. Majority Leader Albert supported the Speaker. "I agree," he said. "I don't think your coming before the Congress would be a sign of panic. I think it would help."

By the end of the meeting the leadership was unanimous in recommending that I address the Congress before a Joint Session at 9 P.M. the next evening, March 15. The meeting adjourned at 6:30 P.M. Later that evening I assembled some of my key staff men to help prepare the message. A Presidential speech is rarely a private product. The pressures of the office do not afford the luxury of such personal handicraft. But this time, as much as humanly possible, I wanted to reach the American people in my own words.

I sat with my staff for several hours. I described the general outline of what I wanted to say. I wanted to use every ounce of moral persuasion the Presidency held. I wanted no hedging, no equivocation. And I wanted to talk from my own heart, from my own experience.

Between midnight and dawn these loose thoughts were translated into sentences for the first draft of the speech. I received that draft shortly after awakening. I penciled in changes and rewrote sections. The draft went back to the speechwriters. Several hours later a new draft came back. I made additional changes. And so it went, back and forth, right up to the final moments.

I had to be at the podium in the House Chamber at 9 P.M., but at 8 P.M. I was still writing about my experiences in a Cotulla, Texas, schoolroom. The speech still had to be typed and put on the teleprompter. We never made it with the teleprompter. I had to deliver most of the speech from a rough copy lying on the rostrum.

As I stood before the assembled Chamber, the lights were blinding. I began slowly:

> I speak tonight for the dignity of man and the destiny of democracy. . . . At times history and fate meet at a single time in a single place to shape a turning point in man's unending search for freedom. So it was at Lexington and Concord. So it was a century ago at Appomattox. So it was last week in Selma, Alabama.

I could feel the tension in the Chamber. I could hear the emotion in the echoes of my own words. I tried to speed up a little.

> There is no constitutional issue here. The command of the Constitution is plain. There is no moral issue. It is wrong—deadly wrong—to deny any of your fellow Americans the right to vote in this country. There is no issue of states' rights or national rights. There is only the struggle for human rights. . . . This time, on this issue, there must be no delay, no hesitation, and no compromise with our purpose.

I looked up to the Presidential box. I could barely distinguish the faces of Lady Bird and our daughter Lynda. But I felt them with me. Then I looked straight ahead in the Chamber at my Southern friends. I knew that most of them were not with me. I went on:

> But even if we pass this bill, the battle will not be over. What happened in Selma is part of a far larger movement which reaches into every section and state of America. It is the effort of American Negroes to secure for themselves the full blessings of American life.

I paused for breath. In that fleeting moment my thoughts turned to the picket lines in Birmingham, the sit-ins in North Carolina, the marches in Selma. A picture rose before my eyes—a picture of blacks and whites marching together, side by side, chanting and singing the anthem of the civil rights movement.

I raised my arms.

> Their cause must be our cause too. Because it is not just Negroes, but really it is all of us who must overcome the crippling legacy of bigotry and injustice. And . . . we . . . shall . . . overcome.

For a few seconds the entire Chamber was quiet. Then the applause started and kept coming. One by one the Representatives and Senators stood up. They were joined by the Cabinet, the Justices, and the Ambassadors. Soon most of the Chamber was on its feet with a shouting ovation that I shall never forget as long as I live.

I remember the ride home from the Capitol that night. As we circled the reflecting pool, I looked toward the Lincoln Memorial. There had always been something haunting for me in that statue of Lincoln—so life-like and so clear-cut a reminder of the persistent gap between our promises and our deeds. Somehow that night Lincoln's hopes for America seemed much closer.

Four months later our immediate goal was realized. On August 6 I returned to the Capitol to sign the Voting Rights Act of 1965. I remembered the words Reverend King had spoken when his marchers finally reached Montgomery: "We are on the move now. . . . Selma has become a shining monument in the conscience of man."

And I said in return: "So we will move step by step—often painfully, but I think with clear vision—along the path toward American freedom." I spoke these words in the rotunda of the Capitol, directly in front of another statue of Abraham Lincoln.*

With the passage of the Civil Rights Acts of 1964 and 1965 the barriers of freedom began tumbling down. At long last the legal rights of American citizens—the right to vote, to hold a job, to enter a public place, to go to school—were given concrete protection.

But these legislative victories served to illuminate the full dimensions of the American dilemma. No matter how hard we tried to make up for the deprivation of the past and no matter how well we thought we knew the black man, the time would come when we would be forced to realize the measure of his bitterness. And the time would come when we would realize that legislative guarantees were not enough. I talked about this in a commencement speech at Howard University on June 4, 1965:

> You do not wipe away the scars of centuries by saying: Now you are free to go where you want and do as you desire and choose the leaders you please. You do not take a person who, for years, has been hobbled by chains and liberate him, bring him to the starting line of a race, and then say you are free to compete with all the others, and still just believe that you have been completely fair. Thus it is not enough just to open the gates of opportunity. All our citizens must have the ability to walk through those gates. This is the next and the more profound stage of the battle for civil rights. We seek not just freedom but opportunity. We seek not just legal equity but human ability, not just equality as a right and a theory but equality as a fact and equality as a result.

---

* It had once been traditional for Presidents to sign legislation at the Capitol. To dramatize the importance we attached to this bill—and to give full measure to the Congress—I revived the custom on this occasion, the first President to do so in more than a quarter of a century.

Change, real change, was on the horizon—close enough to ignite hope but far enough away to increase frustration. For all the successes of the 1960s, Negroes still were excluded from real equality. Jim Crow was on his way out in the South, but in many ways the Northern style of discrimination—subtle, unpublicized, and deep-rooted—was even tougher to break. All too often the same Northern whites who were perfectly willing to grant the Negro his formal rights as a citizen were unwilling or unable to grant the social acceptance and compassion that would make the formal rights meaningful.

The long history of Negro-white relations had entered a new and more bewildering stage. New problems of racial discrimination came to the forefront: the problems of poverty, slums, inadequate schooling, unemployment, delinquency, and substandard housing. These problems could not be solved entirely by laws, crusades, or marches.

No longer could the struggle for justice be regarded as a peculiarly Southern problem. Nor could it be regarded as a problem to be solved entirely by improved attitudes in the white community. The effect on the black man of centuries of discrimination had become all too visible in the form of apathy, hatred, anger, and violence. The problems at this stage could not be solved by goodwill and compassion; they required large expenditures of public funds.

We were beset by contradictions—movement and progress alongside stalemate and retrogression. Nowhere were these contradictions experienced more deeply than in the black community, where hopes aroused by the early victories were bright but hostilities caused by the persistent gap between promise and fulfillment were deep. It was a volatile mixture.

A new mood began to develop in the black community, symbolized by the "black power" slogan. When asked about black power in 1966, I responded: "I am not interested in black power or white power. What I am concerned with is democratic power, with a small *d*." As I look back now, that answer seems totally insufficient. It is easy for a white man to say he is "not interested in black power or white power." Black power had a different meaning to the black man, who until recently had had to seek the white world's approval and for whom success had come largely on white people's terms. To such a man, black power meant a great deal in areas that mattered the most—dignity, pride, and self-awareness.

As the mask of black submission began to fall, the countless years of suppressed anger exploded outward. The withering of hope, the failure to change the dismal conditions of life, and the complex tangle of attitudes, issues, beliefs, and circumstances all led to the tragic phenomena known as "the riots"—"the long, hot summers."

Rioting in Detroit provided one of the worst instances—so bad, in fact, that the events of July 24–28, 1967, will remain forever etched in my memory. The phone rang at 3 A.M. on the morning of July 24. Attorney General Ramsey Clark * was on the wire.

"Mr. President," he said, "Governor Romney has just called me at home. The situation in Detroit looks bad. There are almost eighty fires unattended. There is extensive looting. The Governor thinks he might need federal assistance. I suggest we put the Army on alert just in case the troops are needed."

I promptly agreed and authorized the Attorney General to tell Army Secretary Stanley Resor to notify his men at Fort Bragg, North Carolina.

"Anything more?" I asked.

"No, sir. Not now," the Attorney General replied. "I'll be leaving for my office shortly and will keep in touch with you from there."

The Attorney General talked with Governor Romney four times more during the night, but no decision was reached on the question of federal troops. Finally, at 8:55 A.M., Governor Romney called him to read a statement "recommending" the use of federal troops. Clark carefully explained that under the Constitution and under federal statutes it would be necessary for the Governor to "request" the use of federal troops, to specify that the city was in a state of insurrection or serious domestic violence, and to certify that such violence could not be brought under control by combined state and local resources. The Governor said he understood and would have the proper statement drafted as soon as possible.

The reasons for such elaborate certification are deeply embedded in our constitutional history. Our forefathers wanted to prevent the abuse of federal authority. In the course of nearly two hundred years, Presidents have followed that counsel of restraint. Federal troops have been used only fifteen times in our history to settle domestic crises.

The Governor's telegram reached the White House at 10:56 A.M. He requested troops but failed to certify that the disturbances amounted to a state of insurrection or a condition of domestic violence that could not be suppressed locally. His request, in short, did not meet constitutional requirements. Later that morning Governor Romney said he was not yet prepared to state that there was a condition of insurrection or domestic violence, because he had been told that such a statement might result in the voiding of insurance policies within the state.

Without this certification, a President cannot properly deploy troops to a specified city or state. He can, however, order troops from one military base to another. I used this authority to airlift troops from Fort Bragg, North Carolina, and Fort Campbell, Kentucky, to Selfridge Air Force Base in Michigan. Since the movement of federal troops is a time-consuming process, I wanted to be in a position to use the forces promptly should conditions of insurrection or domestic violence be established.

* Clark succeeded Nicholas Katzenbach as Attorney General on March 10, 1967.

With troops on their way to Selfridge, I decided to send a trusted observer to Detroit to confer with Governor Romney. In the emotional heat of a crisis incidents are sometimes exaggerated. Rumors spread wildly. In such a situation a President needs the most objective assessment of the disturbance he can obtain.

I thought immediately of Cy Vance. He was a veteran of every major civil disturbance from Oxford, Mississippi, on. At the time of the Detroit riots Vance was suffering from an extremely painful back condition. He could not even tie his shoelaces. And he had just returned from West Virginia, where he had buried his mother. A lesser man would have felt that he had every reason to say "no," and I would have understood completely. But Vance is one of that rare breed who puts service to his country above concern for himself. Within two hours he was on a plane headed for Detroit.

I immediately called Governor Romney to tell him that Vance would be my representative in Detroit, that he was on the way, and that I would await their joint assessment of the situation. Vance met with Governor Romney shortly after he arrived. At 5 P.M. they left together for a personal tour of the riot area. Vance reported his findings directly to me:

> A few fires are still burning but they are now under control. There are large areas of the city with only an occasional broken window. There is no lawlessness in the downtown business area. The situation is much quieter than the preceding day. The incident rate is down one-third, the number of National Guard on the street is up three times, and the full local contingent is not yet deployed. There are still a substantial number of troops waiting for instructions. There is a sharp division among community leaders over the question of federal troops. Representative Diggs favors deployment; Representative Conyers * does not, fearing that it might inflame rather than quell the situation. I have reviewed the evidence with General [John] Throckmorton, Commander of Task Force, Detroit, and the entire staff and we have concluded unanimously that there is an insufficient basis at this time to justify deployment of federal troops.

One hour later Governor Romney held a press conference which seemed to confirm Vance's report. The Governor reported to the press:

> The situation is hopeful. The community is better organized. There are three times the number of National Guard tonight as last night. Last night we were scrambling. There is a rising desire of the people to see this thing ended. I am very hopeful we'll be able to lift the bans and let the people go back to work. There is reason to hope.

But as darkness settled in, our hopes were shattered. The incident rate of violence was rising sharply. Vance's reports sounded increasingly grim.

---

* Charles C. Diggs, Jr., and John Conyers, Jr., Negro Congressmen from Detroit.

I went to my office to meet with Bob McNamara, General Harold K. Johnson, FBI Director J. Edgar Hoover, Secretary of the Army Stanley Resor, and Attorney General Ramsey Clark. New and discouraging reports came in by the minute. We took turns reading the ticker tapes. The atmosphere was heavy with tension and concern. We discussed the problems of the coming summer, aware that we did not know where violence might strike next. Director Hoover was concerned: "They have lost all control in Detroit. Harlem may break loose within thirty minutes. They plan to tear it to pieces."

My thoughts were sharply interrupted by Cy Vance's voice on the White House speaker phone from Detroit: "The situation is continuing to deteriorate. There are twelve hundred persons now being detained in felony court. Reports of incidents are increasing throughout the area. Conditions are worse than ever; I am ready now to recommend the deployment of federal troops. I believe that you should sign the Executive order to federalize the Michigan National Guard. I urge this action."

"Is there any doubt in anyone's mind, including the Governor's, that the National Guard should be federalized and the United States forces sent in?" I asked.

"No, sir, there is no doubt in the Governor's mind or anyone else's."

"What is the legal situation?"

"At this time, the Governor has already declared a state of emergency. All the available police and National Guard have been committed and I have determined that the local law enforcement agencies cannot control the situation. All of this is on its way in writing."

The final moment of decision had come. I knew what I had to do, but I could not erase from my mind the awful prospect of American soldiers possibly having to shoot American citizens. The thought of blood being spilled in the streets of Detroit was like a nightmare. I could imagine the inflammatory photographs appearing within hours on television and on the front pages of newspapers around the world.

I turned my attention back to Cy Vance. "We will follow your recommendations on this matter," I said. "I will sign the Executive order and proclamation at once."

In those final moments I wanted to guarantee that every precaution would be taken to prevent unnecessary use of firepower. I talked with Lieutenant General John Throckmorton, Commander of the 18th Airborne Corps, about the ground rules of engagement. He assured me that his men would be ordered to use minimum force and that individuals or private property would be searched only if deemed necessary to the accomplishment of the mission.

I asked Vance to set up loudspeakers throughout the area to make a last-minute appeal to the people on the streets before the troops arrived.

"I want you to tell them that federal troops are committed to come if necessary . . . ask them to cease and desist . . . ask them to obey the law."

I looked at the tired faces of my advisers. The hour was growing late. I felt exhaustion setting in, but I wanted to talk with the American people and endeavor to reassure them. I knew many were frightened, bewildered, and confused. I knew they too had been listening to the alarming reports from the streets of Detroit. I asked my staff to arrange for a television statement, because I wanted the American people to understand why the federal troops were needed. I spoke to the nation from the White House at 11:58 P.M.:

> I am sure the American people will realize that I take this action with the greatest regret and only because of the clear, unmistakable, and indisputed evidence that Governor Romney of Michigan and local officials in Detroit have been unable to bring the situation under control. . . . Law enforcement is a local matter. . . . The federal government should not intervene—except in the most extraordinary circumstances. . . . I call upon the people of the ravaged areas to return to their homes, to leave the streets, and to permit the authorities to restore quiet and order without further loss of life or property damage.

I finished the statement in ten minutes and returned to the Executive Mansion with several of my assistants. We watched the latest network reports of the riot conditions. "Well," I said finally, "I guess that is all for tonight. I guess we had better get some sleep. Thank you all . . . thank you very much."

At 2:30 A.M. the main body of paratroopers reached the riot area. As General Throckmorton later described it,* the federal troops entered a city saturated with fear. The National Guardsmen were afraid, the citizens were afraid, and the police were afraid. In the confusion of the darkened streets bullets seemed to be flying from every direction. Without lights it was almost impossible to pinpoint the exact location of the snipers. Residents huddled together on the floors of their darkened apartments. Dozens of innocent persons were injured.

That was the atmosphere into which our paratroopers were thrust. Under these circumstances, General Throckmorton set one primary goal for the paratroopers—to reduce fear and restore a semblance of normalcy. Strict orders were given not to fire unless it was certain that the person to be fired upon was a sniper out to kill. Within hours the areas patrolled by the paratroopers were the quietest in the city. But the preceding hours had taken a heavy toll: 43 persons had been killed, 324 injured, and 7,231 arrested.

As I read the reports, several questions haunted me: What if the federal

* See the *Report of the National Advisory Commission on Civil Disorders* (Washington, D.C.: U.S. Government Printing Office, 1968), p. 56.

troops had arrived earlier? What if they had been on the scene before dark? Could some of this bloodshed have been avoided? If I had acted without Governor Romney's and Cy Vance's certification and full concurrence, a dangerous precedent would have been set. Such an action would have gone against the best judgment of all my advisers, and I was bound by the constitutional requirement of certification. But there are always the haunting questions.

The black and stifling smoke had scarcely lifted from the streets of Detroit when an even thicker smoke descended upon the Capitol, the smoke of partisan politics. In this dense atmosphere my concern for constitutional requirements was interpreted by critics as "playing politics," and throughout the country the deep-seated, demanding problems of the ghettos were overshadowed by oversimplified talk of a black conspiracy.

I believed then and believe now that we can never achieve a free society until we suppress the fires of hatred and turn aside from violence, whether that violence comes from the nightriders of the Ku Klux Klan or the snipers and looters in Detroit. Neither old wrongs nor new fears justify arson or murder. A rioter with a Molotov cocktail in his hands is not fighting for civil rights any more than a Klansman wearing a sheet and a mask.

When violence breaks out, my instinct is to ask: What caused it? What can I do about it? It is necessary to search for the deeper causes from which anger and tension grow, the privations and indignities and evidence of past oppression or neglect. In the 1960s that evidence was all too plentiful.

This was the context in which I created the National Advisory Commission on Civil Disorders, headed by Governor Otto Kerner of Illinois and Mayor John Lindsay of New York. I knew we had to dig below the surface and lay bare the roots of the problem. I asked the commission to find out "What happened, why did it happen, and what can be done to prevent it from happening again and again?" I asked the members to make their search completely free. "Let it be untrammeled by what has been called the conventional wisdom. As best you can, find the truth, the whole truth; express it in your report."

The commission completed its report late in February 1968. As soon as I received it, I asked each member of my Cabinet to study it and analyze every recommendation to determine (1) which proposals were already being carried out, (2) which would be covered by our 1968 legislative program, and (3) which had not yet been adopted. The Bureau of the Budget pulled together the individual agency responses.

This analysis reflected extremely close agreement between the commission's proposals and the administration's program. The major difference lay in the scale of effort recommended. The commission called for a substantially increased outlay of resources, doubling or tripling each ongoing program. The Bureau of the Budget estimated that the recommendations would cost in the vicinity of $30 billion, in addition to the $30 billion plus already in the budget for the poor.

That was the problem—money. At the moment I received the report I was having one of the toughest fights of my life, trying to persuade Congress to pass the 10 per cent tax surcharge without imposing deep cuts in our most critical Great Society programs.* I will never understand how the commission expected me to get this same Congress to turn 180 degrees overnight and appropriate an additional $30 billion for the same programs that it was demanding I cut by $6 billion. This would have required a miracle.

With the chance of congressional action so extremely limited, I believed that the key to the report lay in its assertion that "the major need is to generate new will—the will to tax ourselves to the extent necessary to meet the vital needs of the nation." The Kerner report went partway in helping to create this "public will." Its finding that the riots were not caused or carried out by organized plan was useful in unlocking the public's mind on the whole issue of riots. Until people realized that all the riots and demonstrations were not the product of conspiracy, there was little hope of persuading them to focus on fundamental causes—on poverty, discrimination, inadequate schooling, substandard housing, slums, and unemployment.

I would have been delighted to have had an appropriation of an additional $30 billion to solve the problems of our cities, but I knew that was unrealistic. Setting such an unattainable goal could easily have produced a negative reaction that in turn might have endangered funds for the many invaluable programs we had fought so long to establish and were trying so hard to strengthen and expand.

A President cannot appropriate public funds by fiat. Nor can he be, as President Theodore Roosevelt once wished, both "President and Congress too."

A President's limitations are never more evident than when he hears of the death of another man. In that ultimate situation a President is only a man and can do little or nothing to help. I rarely have felt that sense of powerlessness more acutely than the day Martin Luther King, Jr., was killed.

I awakened in the morning feeling optimistic. Something very good had happened the day before, April 3, 1968. The government of North Vietnam had indicated readiness to contact U.S. representatives so that peace talks might begin. "Perhaps," I thought, "a real breakthrough has arrived at last."

At noon the next day I flew to New York City for the investiture of

* See Chapter 19.

the new Catholic Archbishop of New York, Terence James Cooke. Our helicopter touched down in Central Park and we drove to St. Patrick's Cathedral by car. It was a bright, spring day. Hundreds of people lined the streets. They cheered as we drove by. When we entered the church, the congregation broke into spontaneous applause. The church escort said that this had happened on only one other occasion—the visit of His Holiness Pope Paul VI in 1965.

After the ceremony, I stopped at the United Nations to talk with Ambassador Goldberg and Secretary General U Thant. We had a good talk; Hanoi's agreement had given all of us a great lift.

We returned to Washington at dusk. I went back to my office. I remember how quiet the West Wing seemed. Several members of the White House staff—advisers, secretaries, and typists—had already gone to Andrews Air Force Base and boarded *Air Force One.* That night I had planned to go to Hawaii for a strategy meeting with our representatives from South Vietnam. The conference had been scheduled for several weeks. The important development of the preceding day had given the meeting a special significance.

The world that day seemed to me a pretty good place.

But at 7:30 P.M. that mood was completely shattered by a message on a plain white piece of paper brought to me by my aide Tom Johnson: "Mr. President: Martin Luther King has been shot."

A jumble of anxious thoughts ran through my mind. What does it mean? Was it the act of one man or a group? Was the assassin black or was he white? Would the shooting bring more violence, more catastrophe, and more extremism?

A second message arrived at 8:20, from my press secretary, George Christian: "Mr. President: Justice has just advised that Dr. King is dead."

My thoughts turned at once to Mrs. King and her children. I remembered a picture I had seen only a week before of the entire lively family. I called Mrs. King and tried to comfort her as best I could.

Shortly after 9 P.M. I went before the television cameras to make a statement to the American public. I spoke from the West Lobby, the same spot from which, twenty-four hours earlier, I had announced Hanoi's agreement. I said:

> I ask every citizen to reject the blind violence that has struck Dr. King, who lived by nonviolence. . . . We can achieve nothing by law-lessness and divisiveness among the American people. It is only by joining together and only by working together that we can continue to move toward equality and fulfillment for all our people.

I finished my statement and returned to my office and canceled my trip to Hawaii. The strain of the day and this new tragedy were having their effect, but there was no letting up.

The trouble in Washington, D.C., was just beginning. Crowds had started forming at 14th and U Streets, Northwest, at the first word of the King shooting. The atmosphere was hushed. Men, women, and children stood together awaiting further news. At 8:30 P.M. the news media reported Dr. King's death. The crowds started moving north on 14th Street, asking proprietors to close their stores out of respect for Dr. King. Most of the storeowners complied at once. The predominant mood was one of nonviolence, sorrow, and mourning. But one hour later that mood shifted. Inflammatory speeches filled the air; anger and bitterness fanned out. Wild rumors spread. A few windows were smashed. A few items were stolen. I began to fear that once again the dangerous cycle had begun, and my fears came true.

By the next day entire blocks of buildings were going up in smoke. Helmeted troops were patrolling the littered streets. Before the holocaust was over, forty other cities had experienced similar tragic outbreaks— Chicago, Baltimore, Pittsburgh, Kansas City, Trenton, Youngstown, Jacksonville, and on and on and on, from coast to coast.

Perhaps the most disturbing thing about the April riots was the fact that so many of us almost instinctively expected them to happen as soon as the news of Dr. King's death was made known. Were we becoming conditioned to the violence? That prospect disturbed me far more than the initial shock of Watts or Detroit.

The death of a public figure produces a strong interplay of private and public emotions. In the chaos and confusion I reached out instinctively to the Negro leaders with whom I had worked over the years—among them Roy Wilkins; Whitney Young, Jr.; Clarence Mitchell; Walter Washington, Mayor of Washington, D.C.; Bayard Rustin, Executive Director of the A. Philip Randolph Institute; Leon Sullivan, Director of the Opportunities Industrialization Center in Philadelphia; Judge Leon Higginbottham of Philadelphia; Richard Hatcher, Mayor of Gary, Indiana; Walter Fauntroy of the Southern Christian Leadership Conference; and Bishop George Baber of Philadelphia.

I asked these men to meet with me at the White House on the morning after Dr. King's death. I thought it important for the country to see us all working together in an effort to make some sense out of this senseless tragedy. And I needed their advice.

I also invited King's father, Martin Luther King, Sr., to join us. I knew that he would want to be part of anything positive we could possibly bring out of the sacrifice of his son's life. My message reached him at 2 A.M. through one of my staff members: "The President wants you to know his prayers are with you." "Oh, no," he said, "*my* prayers are with the Presi-

dent. And I want so badly to be there tomorrow to do whatever I can."
At that point a nurse got on the line to say that Dr. King was not well
and should not make the trip; he had to preserve his strength for the funeral.
I understood completely and I admired his ability to think of his country
at a time of such private grief.

I wanted Dr. King to know how much his concern meant to me. I thought
there would be a chance to thank him at the funeral. But once again the
strange mixture of public and private capacities inherent in the Presidency
prevented free action. As a private citizen I could have gone to the
funeral in Atlanta. But as President of the United States I had to heed
the unanimous judgment of the Secret Service and the FBI. The situation
in Atlanta was tense and dangerous; they recommended in the strongest
terms that I not attend the funeral.

I met with the civil rights leaders in the Cabinet Room at 11 A.M. on
Friday morning, less than seventeen hours after the fatal shooting. "I have
asked you here today—you leaders of government, the Court, the Congress,
the executive community, the Negro community, the white community,
the religious community—to demonstrate America's unity and commitment,
to demonstrate to the people of the United States that those who served
the cause of justice in the past, along with King, are determined to save
that cause now."

We talked together about the perils of the situation. We knew that none
of us had found an effective way to reach the militant youths on the
streets. Try as we might, we had not been able to bridge the gap in
leadership style, mood, and language. But in spite of this we *had* to keep
moving onward.

Bayard Rustin and Reverend Sullivan captured the essence of our discussion: The large majorities of the Negroes are not in favor of violence,
they said, but we need something to fight back with; we need something
positive to carry to the people. Otherwise we'll be caught with nothing.
And the people just won't behave in a vacuum.

I decided that we should seize the opportunity and press for an open
housing law. For two years we had struggled unsuccessfully for legislation
to prohibit discrimination in the sale and rental of housing. We had lost
our first battle in 1966. The Senate had killed our bill with a month-long
filibuster. We lost again in 1967, when the committee system buried the
bill. In January 1968 observers overwhelmingly predicted a third defeat.
The pressures for compromise grew stronger and stronger. Most of my
advisers, black and white, argued for abandoning the legislative struggle in
favor of an Executive order.

I went against my advisers on this one. But one man stuck with me—
Clarence Mitchell. He knew the depth of opposition at the grassroots level.
In his tireless months of lobbying on this issue he had witnessed the

impact of the backlash slogans: "Open housing is forced housing" . . . "A man's home is his castle" . . . "A man's got a constitutional right to sell to whomever he wants."

He knew how difficult it would be, even with legislation, to induce the people in the heartlands and the suburbs, the cities and the countryside, to change their deep-seated sense of individualism in buying and selling their homes. Mitchell believed, as I did, that without the moral force of congressional approval behind us, the struggle for open housing would be lost before it had even begun. A new Executive order might put more words in the books but it would not put more Negroes into decent houses.

I decided to go all the way. In January 1968 I had proposed legislation for the third time. Now, in the wake of tragedy, that housing legislation seemed more essential than ever before. Continued delay and failure would be a victory for the forces of stalemate and repression. It would feed extremist charges that the "system" was no longer working. On the other hand, passage of the bill would demonstrate America's faith in its Negro citizens and prove the continued strength of moderate leadership, both black and white. It could be a new beginning.

There was reason to hope. In the earlier open housing battles Senator Dirksen had led the opposition. Without his support, it was impossible to stop a filibuster. The Senator knew how strongly I felt about ending this unfair discrimination. But until he felt the urgency on his own, there was little we could do.

Late in February Senator Dirksen shifted his position: "One would be a strange creature indeed," he said, "in this world of mutation if, in the face of reality, he did not change his mind." In the early months of 1968 that reality was clearly changing. On every cloture vote our forces in the Senate were growing stronger. Clarence Mitchell's endless hours of work were beginning to show results. Dirksen could sense the shifting tide. He chose to master that tide. With his support, we once again broke the back of the filibuster. The bill reached the floor on March 11, and surprisingly it passed the Senate that same afternoon.

Speculation immediately centered on the motive behind Dirksen's switch. The rumor mill explained his shift as based on a supposed promise from Washington to "force" the Democratic party in Illinois to deliberately put up a weak candidate to assure Dirksen's victory in his forthcoming campaign for reelection.

I never once discussed supporting Dirksen's 1968 Illinois election with him. No President could "force" a strong local party, headed by as forceful a person as Mayor Richard Daley of Chicago, to commit political hara-kiri—especially over a bill that most of his constituents did not want anyway.

With Senate passage, the fate of the bill rested with the House and, more particularly, with that graveyard of so much progressive legislation, the Rules Committee. The first test vote in the committee came on March 19. We used all the arguments and moral forces we could muster but we lost again, by one vote.

Partisan politics proved our undoing. By that time the open housing issue had become a Democratic liability. More and more Republicans tried to base their 1968 campaigns on promises to protect the individual from "LBJ's bureaucrats," who, they said, would be "swarming over every neighborhood setting up Negro-white quotas, forcing homeowners to sell their property, and encouraging vicious gangs of rioters and looters to destroy neighborhoods which dare to resist."

Things looked bleak. But on March 31, 1968, a new factor entered the equation. I was no longer a candidate of the Democratic party; I was simply the President. That made a tremendous difference, as I had hoped it would when I made my announcement. So there was reason for hope in that first week of April after Martin Luther King's death, but we had to move quickly. Riots were spreading from one city to another, and we knew how swiftly those riots could turn normal compassion into bitterness, anger, and retaliation.

The morning after Dr. King's death I sent letters to both Speaker McCormack and Minority Leader Ford, stressing that "the time for action has come." The second vote in the Rules Committee was scheduled for April 9, the day after Dr. King's funeral. We worked on it the entire weekend, night and day. This time our efforts paid off. The Rules Committee voted to keep the Senate bill intact and to send it to the House floor. Within twenty-four hours the full House gave its approval to the omnibus Civil Rights Act of 1968.

I signed the bill on April 11, 1968, in the presence of many of the Negro leaders with whom I had met the week before. They had all helped produce this victory. As I returned to my office, I thought to myself how different the mood of this day was from that just one week earlier.

So it went . . . some days bright with promise, others shadowed by tragedy; hours of grief, hours of joy; moments of doubt, moments of hope. Spring turned to summer and summer to fall. My term as President was drawing to a close. It was a time for farewells.

I remembered in particular a blustery evening late in autumn. The Urban League had invited me to a dinner in New York City. The room was filled to capacity with more than 2,000 guests. My thoughts that night were with old friends like Whitney Young, Roy Wilkins, Clarence Mitchell, Bayard Rustin, and A. Philip Randolph.

For five long years we had worked side by side, in sadness, joy, anger, and triumph. We had reached together the peaks of victory—the Civil Rights Act of 1964, the Voting Rights Act of 1965, the Fair Housing Act of 1968, the Federal Jury Reform Act of 1968. We had stayed together in the valleys of failure—the summer riots, the burnings, the killings, and the assassinations.

Some of us tried to express our feelings that night. We talked about old times. We relived the struggles. It was a warm, sentimental evening. But nothing meant more to me than the presentation made by Whitney Young. The Urban League, he announced, was pledging $100,000 to establish a scholarship fund in my name at the Lyndon Baines Johnson School of Public Affairs at the University of Texas to provide annual fellowships for deserving black students.

In that fleeting moment the past merged with the future. A picture of idealistic young men starting out on the road of public service, not knowing what great achievements they might come to know, contrasted sharply with the picture of Gene Williams starting out on the uncertain road to Texas only a few years before, not knowing where he could eat or where he could sleep at night.

We had come a long way. In five short years we had put into law our promises of equality—at the ballot box, the employment center, the jury, the public inn, the public school, and the private housing market.

Distinguished black men and women had assumed their rightful places in the highest offices of the land—the Supreme Court, the Cabinet, the foreign service, the Federal Reserve Board, the mayorship of Washington, D.C., the chairmanship of the Equal Employment Opportunity Commission. I had chosen these people—Thurgood Marshall, Robert Weaver, Andrew Brimmer, Patricia Harris, Walter Washington, Clifford Alexander—and many others for their competence, wisdom, and courage, not for the color of their skin. But I also deeply believed that with these appointments Negro mothers could look at their children and hope with good reason that someday their sons and daughters might reach the highest offices their government could offer.

I looked around the room once more. Most of those present were men and women of my generation. We had given everything we had to the struggle, and we had seen many of our towering dreams come true. We could look back at landmarks we had established on the trail. But we were not yet in sight of the plateau we had to gain before our country could rest. Turbulence was still in the air; restlessness was rampant. The reins of leadership were passing from one generation to another and the American struggle for justice was just beginning.

8

A Time of Testing: Crises in the Caribbean

THE FIRST FOREIGN CRISIS of my administration began only six weeks after I had taken office. On January 7, 1964, a group of American students at Balboa High School in the Panama Canal Zone set into motion events that soon threatened our relations with Panama and endangered operation of the Panama Canal. It was, on the surface, an inoffensive act: The students raised the American flag in front of the school.

The flag-raising violated an agreement President Kennedy had made in 1962 with Panamanian President Roberto Chiari. Our two governments had been trying to reach an understanding regarding changes in the sixty-year-old treaty governing U.S. control over the canal and the surrounding zone. No breakthrough had been made in those talks, but the Presidents had agreed that the flags of their two countries would fly side by side at designated sites in the zone.

When I heard about the students' action, I was certain we were in for trouble. Since the summer of 1963 the Central Intelligence Agency had been warning us that we should expect difficulties in Panama late in 1963 or early in 1964. Fidel Castro, working closely with the Panamanian Communist party, had been sending guns, money, and agents into Panama. Demonstrations were likely. An attempted coup against the legal government was possible. If that happened, we expected the canal and the zone to become special targets.

A handful of young students bent on showing their patriotism had stirred up more trouble than they possibly could have imagined. Castro and his Panamanian allies must have yearned for just such a provocation. It provided them automatically with a popular cause that would appeal to Panamanian nationalism.

The reaction came quickly. On June 9, two days after the incident,

Studying a congressional head count

WAR ON POVERTY. With House Majority Leader Carl Albert, BELOW. Strategy session with Sargent Shriver. RIGHT: Appalachia; with Leon Sullivan at job opportunity center in Philadelphia; ". . . youth offered the best hope of breaking the poverty cycle."

STRUGGLE FOR JUSTICE. Until justice is blind to color, until education is unaware of race, until opportunity is unconcerned with the color of men's skins, emancipation will be a proclamation but not a fact.

With Senate Minority Leader Everett Dirksen who held key to civil rights legislation. BOTTOM, L.: Negro leaders meet with Johnson (*l.-r.*, James Farmer, Roy Wilkins, Whitney Young, Jr., and Martin Luther King, Jr.). BOTTOM, R.: With Nicholas Katzenbach, who worked on voting rights bill, and Secretary of Commerce John Connor (*l.*).

Signing Civil Rights Act of 1964

Voting rights campaign ended in fifty-four-mile march from Selma to
Montgomery, Ala.; Alabama state troopers scatter ranks of marchers (R.).
Governor George Wallace (BOTTOM, L.) met with Johnson—it "proved to be
the critical turning point in the voting rights struggle."

August 6, 1965: Voting Rights bill becomes law (with Ralph Abernathy, Martin Luther King, Jr., Clarence Mitchell), BOTTOM.

BREAKTHROUGHS IN SCHOOLROOM AND SICKROOM. John Gardner, the advocate of excellence in education. Stonewall, Texas, April 11, 1965— Johnson signs Elementary & Secondary Education Act (with his first teacher, Mrs. Katherine Deadrich Loney). BOTTOM, L.: HEW Secretary Wilbur Cohen, administration expert on Medicare; R., with grateful beneficiary.

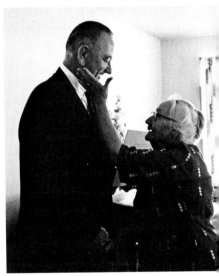

Weekly breakfast strategy session with congressional leaders.
BOTTOM: Great Society measure becomes law of the land.

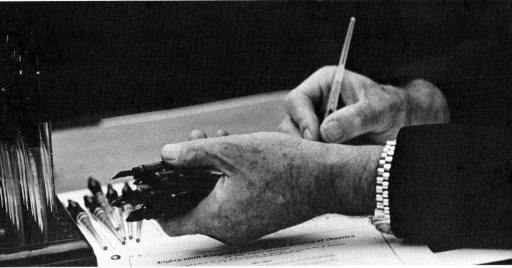

July 30, 1965: Johnson signs Medicare bill in Independence, Missouri.
Former President Truman, who "started it all," is present,
with Mrs. Truman, Humphrey, Mrs. Johnson.

Panamanian students organized a protest march. They entered the Canal Zone and went to Balboa High School. A scuffle with Canal Zone police followed. As they marched out of the zone, the students broke windows, burned automobiles, and caused extensive property damage. Several students and policemen were injured.

More serious trouble followed. Large crowds of Panamanians gathered along the Canal Zone boundary, shouting, jeering, and throwing rocks and anything else that came to hand. Rioting broke out and continued for several days in Panama City and Colón, the major cities at each end of the canal. Panamanian students and civilians threw Molotov cocktails at buildings and automobiles. Cars with Canal Zone license plates were attacked and their occupants were pulled out and savagely beaten.

Panamanian authorities made little effort to maintain law and order. The Panamanian police stood aside, and the National Guard stayed in its barracks to ride out the storm. The Canal Zone police force, consisting of about eighty men, was too small to control the rioters and was in danger of being overwhelmed. The only remaining instruments of security were the U.S. Army troops stationed in the Canal Zone, and they were called out.

At first, we ordered our troops to hold their fire, even though they were being shot at. Finally, with our troops suffering casualties, we had no choice but to order our men to return the fire of rooftop snipers. When the rioting finally ended on January 12, four American soldiers had been killed and dozens wounded. Twenty Panamanian rioters were also dead.

Despite the restraint we used from the outset of the crisis, President Chiari's government decided very quickly—on January 9—to break diplomatic relations with the United States. We were advised formally of this move the next afternoon. The Panamanian government accused our country of aggression, though we were only defending our nationals and protecting territory legally under our control.

Reports from the scene made it clear that the question was not whether the government of Panama could control the rebels and restore order but whether it was willing to do so. Every indication was that the answer was "no." On the evening of January 9 American officials reported that they had made eight separate appeals to the Panamanian National Guard to act. Promises were made by the guard, but never kept. They stayed in their barracks and let the destruction go on.

On the morning of January 10 I met in the Cabinet Room with a group of my advisers * to consider what we should do next. We reviewed

* The principal officers present were Rusk, Ball, and Tom Mann from State; McNamara and Vance from Defense; McCone and Helms from the CIA; Donald Wilson from the USIA; and Mac Bundy, Ralph Dungan, Pierre Salinger, and Bill Moyers from the White House staff.

the reports of the previous twenty-four hours. CIA Director McCone pointed out that trouble had been brewing in Panama for at least six months. Panama's irritation over the unfortunate flag incident was understandable, but the Panamanian students' reaction had served as a trigger to obviously well-planned anti-American demonstrations.

My advisers recommended that I talk directly with President Chiari. I agreed and asked Pierre Salinger to phone Panama and find out if the President was available to talk to me. Salinger went to check.

We made several other decisions. First, we planned to send a top-level delegation to Panama at once. Thomas C. Mann, Assistant Secretary of State for Inter-American Affairs and our highest-ranking Latin American specialist, would head the group. Next, I instructed Rusk to urge the Inter-American Peace Committee of the Organization of American States (OAS) to investigate the situation immediately. Finally, I asked George Ball to contact the congressional leadership and tell them what was happening and what we planned to do.

Salinger returned and told me that President Chiari was waiting for my call. I went to my office and picked up the phone.

"Hello, Mr. President," I said, and he returned the greeting.

"Mr. President," I continued, "I wanted to say to you that we deeply regret the situation of violence that has developed there. We appreciate very much your call to the Panamanian people to remain calm. We recognize that you and I should do everything we can to restore quiet, and I hope that you'll do everything possible to quieten the situation, and I will do the same. You and I should be aware of the possibility, and the likelihood, that there are elements unfriendly to both of us who will exploit this situation."

I told him that I was sending Tom Mann to Panama immediately as my personal representative. Mann and his group would do everything they could to find a solution to the current problems, I said.

Chiari ignored what I said about restoring order and calm. He seemed to want to take advantage of the situation to win larger objectives. "I feel, Mr. President," he said, "that what we need is a complete revision of all treaties which affect Panama-U.S. relations because that which we have at the present time is nothing but a source of dissatisfaction which has recently, or just now, exploded into violence which we are witnessing."

Chiari remarked that he had come to Washington in 1961 and had talked with President Kennedy about treaty revisions, but that since those conversations "not a thing has been done to alleviate the situation." I told the Panamanian President that we had to look forward, not backward, and that violence was no way to settle grievances. First, I said, let us end the violence; then we can begin to talk over our differences and find solutions.

Chiari claimed the United States had shown "indifference" to Panama's problems. I promised that our delegation would be on a plane "in thirty minutes" and would be in Panama in five hours. I could not act much faster than that. Chiari said he was grateful for this cooperation. He said he was glad I was "a man of action and of few words." He expressed confidence that the difficulties could be ironed out.

Apparently, Chiari hoped to use the disturbances to force the United State into a new round of treaty talks. I doubted that he would halt the attacks in the Canal Zone or restore diplomatic relations until he had done everything possible to achieve his goal. Having failed through diplomacy with President Kennedy, Chiari was going to try to exact a new treaty from me by force.

Tom Mann's first report from Panama confirmed my suspicions. Mann later described his group's reception in Panama as "pure theater." When they landed in the Canal Zone, Panamanian authorities said they could not drive directly to the nearby palace where President Chiari was waiting. The route was too dangerous, they said. No one could guarantee their safety. They had to fly to a Panamanian airport and drive to the palace "the back way."

Once at the palace, Chiari welcomed them and seated them in front of a large window. Outside a crowd of approximately six hundred Panamanians suddenly materialized. They began throwing rocks and screaming, "Gringos go home." Chiari implied that he could not control the mobs and hinted that only major U.S. concessions would restore calm.

My personal opinion was that it was indeed time for the United States and Panama to take a fresh look at our treaties. We also had to look ahead and consider the future of interocean traffic across the isthmus. We had known for some time that the canal could not handle the volume of traffic that future trade would require. But I was determined to work this out in an orderly way. Decisions had to be reached on the merits of the case, not in response to rioting in Panama or to attempts by the Panamanian government to gain popular support by putting pressure on us. We insisted that the government of Panama first restore order, resume diplomatic relations, and agree to a sensible procedure of cooperation in studying the whole problem—with no advance commitments by either side.

That, in essence, was what Tom Mann told President Chiari. The United States was not going to give away its treaty rights as the price of being allowed to negotiate with the Panamanians. It took several days to convince the Panamanians that we would not back down under pressure. In the meantime, we took additional steps to protect our troops in the Canal Zone.

President Chiari eventually decided that nothing was to be gained by continued rioting. Once he reached that conclusion, he merely called the Panamanian National Guard out of its barracks, and order was restored within a short time. Even then, Chiari was not quite ready to abandon his demands. Almost three months passed before Panama resumed diplomatic relations with us and we found a formula to discuss our problems. In January 1964 the Inter-American Peace Committee of the OAS tried to negotiate the matter and failed. In March Panama took the problem to the OAS Council. Some progress was made, but in the end the Council also failed. I rejected several proposals which, in an effort to paper over the gap, would have involved substantial U.S. commitments before the negotiators even met.

At last, on April 3, President Chiari agreed to proceed in the spirit of partnership and good faith which the interests of the United States and Panama required. It was a good day for both countries when, in a telephone conversation that same day, I could tell President Chiari that I had appointed Robert Anderson, Secretary of the Treasury during the Eisenhower administration, as special Ambassador to handle the negotiations. I also told Chiari that I was naming Jack Hood Vaughn as our new Ambassador to Panama. Vaughn had spent much of his adult life in Latin America, particularly in Panama, and was then Latin American Director of the Peace Corps. Chiari welcomed both appointments and said he would appoint his Ambassador immediately.

"Now," I said, "[our] two countries can sit down together without limitations or preconditions of any kind, and as friends try to find the proper and fair answer."

"That is the right way to do it," Chiari answered, "and I hope we can get together on that."

I had no idea then, as I talked with Chiari, how long it would take to work out our differences. The negotiations were still going on when I left the White House. But as of April 3, 1964, a new mood had developed, the immediate crisis had been overcome, and reasonable discussion was possible. We had passed our first test in Latin America, but I knew it would not be the last. Castro certainly had not abandoned his plans for testing the United States and its new President.

Our second Latin American crisis broke before the first was settled. This time the confrontation was with Castro himself. The trouble began on a quiet Sunday afternoon, February 2, 1964. The locale was one familiar to deep-sea fishermen and students of piracy—the Dry Tortugas, a small group of islands in the Florida Keys. Just after noon that Sunday a U.S. Coast Guard cutter spotted four Cuban fishing boats trolling near East Key in the Tortugas. They were well within our territorial waters, less than two miles off the coast.

The cutter *Cape Knox* approached the Cuban boats and ordered their captains to drop anchor. Early the next day the Coast Guard escorted the intruders to Key West, Florida. Thirty-six fishermen were turned over to Florida authorities for investigation and legal disposition; two others asked for and received political asylum.

Two of the Cuban captains admitted that they knew they were fishing inside U.S. waters. We also learned that before they left Cuba the crews were told they had been selected for an "historic venture." Their assignment was to "test U.S. reactions." In other words, the incursion of the Cuban boats was a deliberate provocation.

The propaganda overtones surrounding the incident were immediate and noisy. The day after the boats were seized Cuban Foreign Minister Raúl Roa called in Swiss Ambassador Emil Stadelhofer * and registered a strong complaint. He denied that the Cuban fishing vessels had been in U.S. territorial waters and said his government regarded the incident as a violation of international law. We in turn had given the Swiss an account of the incident and had asked them to protest the illegal intrusion. The next day, February 4, the Cuban government complained to the press about American "piracy" and "vandalism." The Embassy of Czechoslovakia, which represented Cuba in Washington, filed a protest with the State Department. Cuba's mission at the United Nations complained to the Security Council.

I went to New York City on Wednesday, February 5, for a series of engagements I had accepted earlier, but I remained in close touch by phone with Secretary Rusk and my other advisers. At midday on Thursday the Cubans revealed their next tactical step. Minister Roa called in the Swiss Ambassador at 11:15 A.M. and informed him that Cuba was cutting off the water supply to our naval base at Guantanamo † at noon and was threatening to continue the water stoppage until the fishermen were released. As the Swiss were informing us of this threat, Radio Havana broadcast Roa's protest. Pierre Salinger, who was with me in New York, handed me the first bulletin a little before one o'clock in my suite at the Carlyle Hotel. I immediately called Mac Bundy at the White House to find out if anything more was known. The official message was essentially the same as the news bulletins. I called McNamara at the Pentagon. We had realized for a long time that the water supply at Guantanamo was precarious, because it was controlled by the Cuban government. The Navy had already developed contingency plans to supply water by tankers in case of emergency. I instructed McNamara to put those plans into effect at once. A message was sent promptly to the Commander of the Caribbean Sea Frontier: "Execute Plan Charlie ‡ immediately." The Commander imposed

---

* Switzerland was representing U.S. interests in Cuba in the absence of diplomatic relations between Washington and Havana.

† The naval base at Guantanamo Bay on Cuba's southeast coast was established in 1903 under a treaty giving the United States rights to the area with a ninety-nine-year lease.

‡ A plan for water conservation.

water-rationing at Guantanamo at once. The Navy estimated that the base had a seven-day supply of water on hand, and that it could last twelve days or more with austerity measures. Sailors at Guantanamo began showering in salt water, and Navy wives served dinner on paper plates. Meanwhile, a tanker began loading fresh water at Port Everglades, Florida, to start the water shuttle to our base in Cuba.

By coincidence, I planned to talk that evening at a Weizmann Institute dinner about water in the Middle East. In the middle of that speech I turned to a water problem closer to home. I told the dinner guests about our troubles with Castro and the background of the shutdown of the water supply to Guantanamo. Then I said:

> The United States has known since Mr. Castro took over and allied himself with a foreign power that he would someday cut off the water to our Guantanamo base. We have made plans for such an eventuality.

I assured my listeners that our Navy men and their families at Guantanamo "will have the water they need."

The next morning, February 7, I met for an hour in the Cabinet Room with Rusk, McNamara, and other advisers to discuss the Cuban situation. We met again late in the afternoon. At the second meeting I made a basic decision to reduce and then eliminate all dependence on Castro's Cuba for successful operation of the base at Guantanamo. This course involved two major steps. First, we would provide the base with a self-sufficient water supply. Second, we would cut back and then end the employment of all Cubans on the base.

Early the following morning a special Navy task force arrived at Guantanamo to begin working out details of the reduction of the Cuban labor force at the base, and the Navy sent an order to the base commander which said: "Action will be taken to insure that even if water is turned on again, it will not be used."

Castro's reaction to our decision was uncharacteristically mild. His tone became less and less aggressive. On February 13 he informed us through diplomatic channels that he would turn the water back on as soon as his fishing boats were released. On February 21 the Florida court that had been hearing the case of the Cuban fishermen dropped charges against the crews, fined the four captains $500 each, and released all the men. They sailed at once for home. That same day Castro ordered the water to Guantanamo turned back on, but we told the Cubans we no longer needed it.

We had already begun reducing the Cuban work force on the base and in one year all 2,000 employees had been released. On April 1, 1964, construction began on a desalination plant at Guantanamo. It was completed in record time, by early in December. Within a year after the crisis started the Guantanamo naval base was operating without reliance on Cuba for water or manpower or anything else.

As we moved into and then out of the Guantanamo crisis, I had no doubt about Castro's purpose. He had decided, perhaps with Soviet encouragement,* to take the measure of the new President of the United States, to push me a little and see what my response would be.

He got his answer. Throughout the Guantanamo affair we acted with restraint, refusing to be provoked into any but necessary actions. What could have developed into a military confrontation, or even worse, was avoided.

Many days in the White House began with frustrating problems and ended with relief, as we succeeded in finding solutions. But other days were the reverse; they began calmly and ended with new crises. Saturday, April 24, 1965, was one of these. Lady Bird and I had been looking forward to the day with great anticipation. We were going to the seaport city of Norfolk, Virginia, for the annual Azalea Festival. Our daughter Luci had been chosen queen of the festival. Then we planned to fly to Camp David to spend a quiet weekend at that peaceful mountaintop retreat.

The festival was a colorful and happy affair. I had the pleasure of placing Luci's crown on her head and I told the press that she had been my queen for a long time. Everyone was in a holiday mood, and so were we as we flew back to Washington and transferred to a helicopter for the short ride to Camp David in the Catoctin Mountains of Maryland. In less than an hour my hopes for a relaxed weekend with family and friends were shattered. Tom Mann, recently promoted to Under Secretary of State for Economic Affairs, had been trying to reach me, and I returned his call. He told me trouble was brewing in the Dominican Republic and he wanted to alert me. A cable had just come in from our Embassy in Santo Domingo, and he read me the first few sentences:

> Santo Domingo is rife with rumors of a coup, promoted by announcement over two radio stations that a number of army officers, including Army Chief of Staff Rivera Cuesta, had been arrested. Word of the overthrow of the government spread like wildfire and brought crowds into the street, much horn-blowing, and a concentration of some 1,000 persons at the palace who were dispersed by a water truck.

There were reports that three demonstrators had been wounded by police gunfire. A second cable advised that the principal station in the country, Radio Santo Domingo, had been retaken by the government, but reports continued to circulate of an attempted coup by a group of military

---

* Castro had been in Moscow shortly before the crisis.

officers. I asked Mann if he thought there was anything we should be doing. He said that there was nothing at the moment, but that he would follow developments closely. I asked him to keep me informed of any changes or deterioration in the situation.

We had been hearing rumors of an impending coup in the Dominican Republic for some time. The most recent information had suggested that it might occur in May or June. To assess those reports and to prepare for what might happen, the State Department had asked our Ambassador in Santo Domingo, W. Tapley Bennett, Jr., to return to Washington on April 23 for consultation. He had stopped in Georgia to see his mother, who was ill, but he was due in Washington the next day.

I had been concerned about the Dominican Republic from the day I took office, and indeed well before that time. The Dominicans had lived for thirty years under the iron-fisted rule of dictator Leonidas Trujillo. During those years, which ended with Trujillo's assassination in 1961, those who opposed Trujillo had three choices: to go into exile, to go underground, or to remain quiet. Most Dominicans had chosen the third course.

The three decades of Trujillo's rule had left the Dominican people in poverty. Worse, it had left them with no progressive political or social leadership. A few Dominicans had made careers of political opposition and criticism from abroad, but they had little constructive to offer their people in the way of practical plans or programs. There were many who still regarded the gun and the knife as legitimate tools of politics. The spirit of freedom and the habit of political cooperation, on which economic and social progress is so dependent, were almost totally lacking on the Dominican scene. This weakness, unless rapidly corrected, promised chronic instability in the Dominican Republic.

Just beyond the horizon lay Cuba and Castro. The Communist leader in Havana was always alert to any exploitable weakness among his neighbors. He was promoting subversion in many countries in the Western Hemisphere, and we knew he had his eye on the Dominican Republic. He had already backed one attempted guerrilla invasion of that country during the Trujillo years, and he was likely to try again if he thought he could succeed. Some Dominicans were undergoing guerrilla and sabotage training in Cuba.

We were encouraged in 1962 when the Dominican people held their first free elections in recent times. I carried the best wishes of the American people to Santo Domingo that year when I attended the inauguration of the newly elected President, Juan Bosch, as President Kennedy's personal representative. However, conversations with Bosch had raised new concerns in my mind. He was an intelligent, pleasant man with an attractive personality, and he was full of ideals, but it was my impression that he had no solid plans for overcoming the profound problems his country faced. Nor did I think he had the experience, the imagination, or the strength needed to put whatever plans he might have into effect.

Nevertheless, we wished Bosch well and did everything in our power to help him and his duly elected government succeed. With John Bartlow Martin in Santo Domingo as American Ambassador, Bosch had as sympathetic a representative of the United States as a new leader in a difficult position could have. We continued to hope that Bosch would be able to do for his people what President Rómulo Betancourt had done for Venezuela after dictatorship had been overthrown there.

But Bosch was no Betancourt. While his aspirations were admirable, his performance was weak. He could inspire men with his words, but actions rarely followed the rhetoric. He lacked the capacity to unite under his leadership the various elements that wanted progress and constitutional government—elements of the non-Communist left and center. Nor was he able to control or satisfy the rightists, including powerful elements in the military, who looked on him with suspicion.

A military junta overthrew Bosch in September 1963. This was a major setback for our common hopes. The U.S. government immediately cut off economic aid and withheld recognition of the new leadership in Santo Domingo until a civilian provisional government was formed and pledged itself to hold free elections within two years.

The temporary regime was headed by former Foreign Minister Donald Reid y Cabral, a moderate who had been abroad when the coup was carried out. Reid was fairly popular and was regarded as an honest man, but he faced difficult problems. One of the most pressing problems was a stagnant economy. Reid had the misfortune to head his government at a time when the cost of producing sugar had steadily risen while the world market price for sugar had fallen drastically. The Dominican Republic depended excessively on sugar for foreign exchange.

Reid's attempts to reform the military ran into strong opposition from high-ranking officers. They had enjoyed unusual privileges under Trujillo (such as bringing goods into their country free of duty and selling them at tremendous profits), and they strongly resisted surrendering those benefits. On the other hand, many junior officers were discontented with the slow pace of reform. In addition, Reid was deeply resented by pro-Bosch forces, who were bitter about the overthrow of their leader. Bosch himself had pledged to work for the collapse of the Reid regime. As often happens in this kind of situation, the left and the right found common cause in harassing the moderate man in the middle.

Reid suspected, with good reason, that a number of Dominican army officers were plotting his overthrow in the spring of 1965. He decided to move against them before their plans were completed. On April 24, 1965, he sent Army Chief of Staff Rivera Cuesta to a military camp northwest of

Santo Domingo to cancel the commissions of four officers accused of con-spiring against the government. Instead of surrendering themselves, the officers made Cuesta a prisoner and seized control of the camp. Another uprising against the government had started.

The situation was confused, and so were the first reports that came in from our Embassy. Rebel elements had seized several radio stations in Santo Domingo and called on the people to go into the streets to celebrate the "overthrow" of the Reid government. They responded by the thousands, some of them shouting support for Juan Bosch, others calling for the return of former President Joaquin Balaguer. The Embassy reported one particu-larly ominous development. Trucks loaded with weapons, manned by junior officers and noncommissioned officers, were moving into the capital from the nearby rebel-held camps. The soldiers were passing out weapons to civilians, especially to those shouting antigovernment slogans.

From Camp David I remained in close touch by phone with Secretaries Rusk and McNamara and with McGeorge Bundy, who had gone to the White House Situation Room to follow developments. I decided that we must take precautions in case we had to evacuate American citizens from the Dominican Republic. At midmorning on Sunday, April 25, we ordered the Atlantic Fleet to move ships toward Santo Domingo. The ships were to remain out of sight of land but to stand by in case of need.

A few hours later we instructed our Embassy to contact authorities on both sides of the conflict and tell them we planned to evacuate Americans and others who wished to leave the country. We requested a ceasefire and the cooperation of the "loyalists" and the "rebels" to help us carry out this movement peacefully. We also hoped that such a ceasefire would permit the warring parties to get together and begin negotiating a settle-ment. But there was too much confusion and passions were running too high to get this kind of agreement quickly.

I had invited my advisers to Camp David for a meeting at 1:30 P.M. on Sunday to discuss Vietnam and other matters. I proposed also to consider the Dominican disturbance at this meeting. But thick fog had settled around the mountaintop and helicopters could not fly in. Instead I drove to Thurmont, at the base of the mountain, and flew from there to Wash-ington. At 5:41 P.M. I entered the Cabinet Room, where Rusk, McNamara, Bundy, and others were already gathered.

Conditions in Santo Domingo had deteriorated. Leaders of the armed forces had failed to come to Reid's support and he had resigned. Pro-Bosch rebels had seized the Presidential palace and installed a Bosch supporter, José Rafael Molina y Ureña, as Provisional President pending Bosch's return. Many Dominican military officers opposed Bosch's return. They considered him "soft" on communism, if not actually pro-Communist. They had decided to oppose the rebel forces. That Sunday afternoon Dominican air force planes attacked the Presidential palace with rockets and machine guns.

The situation in the streets of the Dominican capital was alarming. Our Embassy reported that guns had been passed out at random—many to Communist organizers, who were putting them into the hands of their followers; others to thugs and criminals, the so-called Tigres. Young boys of twelve and thirteen were swaggering around the streets with machine guns over their shoulders. Stores and houses were being looted.

The Tigres were making a specialty of killing policemen, and this had prompted most police officers to shed their uniforms and go into hiding. Law and order had broken down. Seizure of police stations put more weapons into the hands of the rebels. There was no discipline, no control over many of those who had guns, grenades, and other weapons. The mob's answer to the air strikes was to attack and loot the homes of air force officers. Wives and children of the airmen were forced to go to likely target areas in order to discourage the air attacks or to be killed by their own husbands and fathers.

On Monday, April 26, reports continued to pour into Washington from our Embassy in Santo Domingo. The Embassy switchboard there was clogged with calls from Americans—residents and tourists—begging to be taken out of the country. The Embassy began putting evacuation plans into effect. Americans were advised to assemble the next morning at the Embajador Hotel in Santo Domingo for processing and evacuation. Both the rebels and the loyalists had promised not to interfere with the movement of civilians and had agreed that a ceasefire would be put into effect during the evacuation operation. In Washington we were bombarded with requests from other governments to help their nationals leave the Dominican Republic.

Processing of evacuees continued through the night and the early hours of April 27 at the Embajador Hotel. All seemed quiet and orderly, or as orderly as the movement of frightened people can be. Then a disturbance broke out. An anti-Communist radio and television commentator named Bonilla went to the Embajador and tried to join the evacuees who were leaving the country. Though he was accompanied by armed guards, our Embassy officers refused his request and he departed. Apparently, he had been seen and recognized, for the rebel radio called on its supporters to go to the hotel and capture him. Soon a mob armed with rifles and machine guns appeared at the Embajador.

Some rioters entered the hotel and ran around the lobby and through the corridors brandishing their weapons and terrifying the women and children gathered there. Other rebels remained outside and began shooting their guns into the air and into the upper floors of the hotel, where a number of American families were staying. We were dealing not with an army but with a trigger-happy mob with little experience and no discipline. It was a miracle that no one was killed in this incident.

A lieutenant colonel from the rebel forces finally arrived at the hotel and managed to restore order. The evacuation of Americans began just before noon. Buses, trucks, and cars carried approximately 1,000 persons to the port of Haina, west of the capital city. I was relieved when I received the report that the evacuation had begun, but I was disturbed that the cease-fire pledge had been broken and that lives had been endangered.

I realized then that we might have to use our own forces to protect American lives in this situation. I discussed this with McNamara, and he assured me that marines were available from the task force sent to carry out the evacuation. Additional forces had been alerted in case of need.

That same day, Tuesday, April 27, produced a critical juncture in the Dominican revolt. Regular army forces with tanks and infantry under General Wessin * started to move across the Duarte Bridge over the Ozama River to the east of Santo Domingo. Another force of about 1,000 men began entering the capital from the west. The two forces were converging on the rebel stronghold in the southeast part of the city. Dominican air force planes continued to strafe rebel positions.

Provisional President Molina and his closest followers apparently decided that their cause was lost, and that it was time to salvage what they could from the rubble. They went to the American Embassy that afternoon to talk with Ambassador Bennett, who had just returned from Washington. After insisting that they check their guns at the entrance, he invited them into his office.

Bennett reported that Molina appeared "nervous and dejected." He and his backers said they were ready to negotiate. They asked the Ambassador to assume a direct role in the settlement. Bennett told them he had no authority to negotiate an agreement and urged Molina and his backers to deal directly with the regular military forces. Bennett told them that it was time an accord was reached "by Dominicans talking to Dominicans."

Molina rejected this advice. Instead he went to the Colombian Embassy and asked for asylum. Apparently, he assumed that Wessin's men were going to move forward and liquidate the rebel stronghold. Other rebel leaders, both political and military, followed his example and either went into hiding or took refuge in foreign embassies. From that point on Bosch's civilian followers had no effective control over the rebel movement. For the most part, power rested with the Communists and their armed followers and with the dissident military officers and enlisted men. There was no real government of any kind.

As it turned out, Molina had misjudged the strength of the forces moving

* General Elias Wessin y Wessin, a strongly anti-Communist military leader.

on Santo Domingo. When our Embassy officers went out at dawn the next day to survey the situation, they found that Wessin's men had stopped moving. There had been a breakdown in leadership, and the regular forces were almost as dejected as the rebel leaders had been the day before. Our observers reported that control of the rebel movement was increasingly in the hands of the rebel officers and the three major Communist parties in the Dominican Republic—one oriented toward Moscow, another linked to Castro, and a third loyal to Peking. None of these parties was extremely large but all were well armed, tightly organized, and highly disciplined. Perhaps more important, they included dedicated professional revolutionaries trained to exploit the kind of situation in which they then found themselves.

It has been argued with hindsight that Ambassador Bennett should have tried to negotiate a settlement on the afternoon of April 27. It was a decision the Ambassador had to make on his own, since there was no time for consultation with Washington. He decided, in line with our general guidance to him and with our policy of nonintervention, that he should encourage the two sides to settle their differences but should not involve his government directly.

Recalling the atmosphere of violence and the passionate feelings of both sides, I question whether a settlement could have been worked out as easily as a few critics later claimed. Even when the fighting had died down and tempers had begun to cool, it took months of patient and often frustrating effort to find an agreement. All things considered, I believe Ambassador Bennett made the right decision. It is true that the rebels misjudged the military situation at that moment, but that error would have been corrected in hours or a day at the most. If they had really wanted an accommodation, they had ample means for getting in touch with the military junta rather than going into hiding.

Meanwhile, the shooting and the killing continued. In downtown Santo Domingo the crack of rifles and the rattle of machine guns were constant reminders that Dominicans were killing Dominicans. Nor were foreigners immune from the disturbances. The Embassy of El Salvador had been sacked and many other embassies were hit by bullets. On the night of April 27, Ambassador Bennett noted that his house had been struck by rifle fire on several occasions during the day. He concluded his report with the comment: "Our garden is growing bullets this spring."

Later, when the Red Cross made a careful study of the tragic events of April 1965, investigators estimated that at least 1,300 Dominicans were killed in combat or in cold blood between the 24th and 29th of that month. At least another seven hundred were to be killed before peace was finally restored to the republic.

Some of the killing was particularly savage. People were lined up against walls and shot without a trial or even a hearing. Rumors of torture and savagery were widespread. An air force colonel reported that a close friend—a high ranking police officer—had been beheaded by a mob. The log of a Panamanian ship in port at Santo Domingo contained an eyewitness account of another savage incident. The crewman had watched from the deck on April 25 as a mob cornered a policeman on the dock, beheaded him, and carried the head on a pole around the area to arouse the people to action. An OAS study mentioned a headless corpse among those seen by its observers. Dominicans reported seeing many bodies floating down the river, some without heads. Ambassador Bennett received a photograph of another headless victim of the slaughter. I was later criticized in press comments for referring to beheadings. There is no doubt in my mind that these incidents took place. It is an unpleasant subject, but it was part of the background against which we followed developments and made decisions during this time of crisis.

At midmorning on Wednesday, April 28, Radio Santo Domingo, controlled by the regular armed forces, announced that a new governing junta had been formed, headed by Colonel Pedro Benoit of the Dominican Air Force.* The junta's announced goals were to restore peace and to prepare the country for free elections. The junta was self-proclaimed, but after the collapse of the Molina group, more than any other organization it represented authority in the Dominican Republic. Together with the police, the armed forces controlled most of the country, except for the rebel-held areas of downtown Santo Domingo.

One of the new junta's first acts was to contact Ambassador Bennett and ask that the United States land 1,200 marines "to help restore peace to the country." Bennett gave the junta no encouragement. In his cabled report to Washington the Ambassador said: "I do not believe [the] situation justifies such action at this time." He did advise, however, that we make plans "in case [the] situation should break apart and deteriorate rapidly to [the] extent we should need [the] Marines in a hurry to protect American citizens."

Within two hours, however, the Ambassador and his staff had made a new assessment. A high-priority cable—a "critic," as it is called—arrived from Santo Domingo. The Ambassador reported that the situation was "deteriorating rapidly." He warned: "American lives are in danger." He and the Country Team, composed of the top U.S. political, economic, and information officers as well as the military attachés, had unanimously concluded that "the time has come to land the Marines." Evacuation of Americans and other foreigners was continuing and protection was needed. The chief of the Dominican national police had told Ambassador Bennett

---

* Army Colonel Casado Saladin and Navy Captain Manuel Santana Carrasco completed the triumvirate.

that he could no longer protect the road over which the evacuees were moving to Haina.

That afternoon, April 28, I met in the small lounge off the big Oval Office with Rusk, McNamara, Ball, Mac Bundy, and Bill Moyers. We were discussing Vietnam and Southeast Asia. We had already seen Bennett's first message advising that we hold off sending troops. As we talked, I was handed a second urgent cable from Santo Domingo saying that "the time has come." I told my advisers that I was not going to sit by and see American lives lost in this situation. If local authorities could not provide protection, we had no choice but to provide the necessary protection ourselves. They all agreed that we had to act.

I turned to Rusk.

"Mr. Secretary," I said, "I want you to get all the Latin American Ambassadors on the phone. Get your people to touch all bases. Get in touch with the OAS. Tell them the decision I am making and urge them to have an immediate meeting."

I asked McNamara to alert the military forces. He said they were in position to move quickly. Moyers was to call the congressional leaders and invite them to come to the White House as soon as possible. We broke up then and each man went off to carry out his instructions. My decision had been made: The Marines would protect Americans and move them safely out of the Dominican Republic.

I realized the importance of the decision. I knew it would attract a good deal of criticism—from Latin Americans as well as from segments of our own press. We had tried so hard, ever since the days of Franklin Roosevelt, to overcome the distrust of our neighbors in the Western Hemisphere. I did not want those days of suspicion to return, the days when "Yankee imperialism" and "the Colossus of the North" were the catchphrases of anti-American propagandists. But I could not risk the slaughter of American citizens. As their President, it was my duty to protect them with every resource available to me. I would do it again to protect American lives.

At 7:30 P.M. that evening I went into the Cabinet Room to meet with leaders of Congress, the Vice President, and other top officials of the Executive branch.*

Rusk reviewed developments in the Dominican Republic over the previous days. Dominican authorities had told us that Americans could no longer be protected, he said, and Ambassador Bennett had urged that we use our own forces for that purpose. McNamara described the contingency plans we had made for this emergency. I told the congressional leaders I

* In addition to the Vice President, those at the meeting were Rusk, McNamara, Ball, Admiral Raborn (who had been sworn in that day as Director of the CIA), Ambassador Stevenson, and McGeorge Bundy; Senators Mansfield, Dirksen, Fulbright, Hickenlooper, Kuchel, Long, Saltonstall, and Smathers; Speaker McCormack and Representatives Albert, Arends, Boggs, Bolton, Ford, and Morgan; and several members of the White House staff.

planned to announce immediately that our forces were going in to protect U.S. citizens. The order had gone out and several hundred marines would soon be landing. I learned later that as we spoke the first helicopters with marines aboard were landing near the Embajador Hotel. The contingency plans had been well developed and the marines were able to respond to their orders in minutes.

The congressional leaders supported my decision. The only substantial point raised was whether we could do more to get the Organization of American States to help in this crisis. Rusk assured the Senators and Congressmen that we were in close touch with the OAS and would continue to urge it to take positive action. He pointed out that many member states had asked us to help remove their citizens from the Dominican Republic.

Later that evening I went on television to report to the American people. I described the situation that had led to our action. Then I said:

> I have ordered the Secretary of Defense to put the necessary American troops ashore in order to give protection to hundreds of Americans who are still in the Dominican Republic and to escort them safely back to this country. This same assistance will be available to the nationals of other countries, some of whom have already asked for our help.

I reported that four hundred marines had already landed and that no incidents had yet occurred. Once again I urged that both sides in the fighting agree to a ceasefire and an end to the bloodshed. I added:

> I repeat this urgent appeal again tonight. The Council of the OAS has been advised of the situation by the Dominican Ambassador and the Council will be kept fully informed.

Minutes after I finished speaking, the State Department asked the OAS to hold a special meeting the next day, April 29. Our proposal was accepted.

The State Department was in contact with our Embassy in Santo Domingo by phone and Tom Mann relayed the report to me. The Embassy informed us that "the Marines have landed and in good time, since the evacuation area is already under fire from irregular forces." The Marine forces, who were being shot at, asked authority to defend themselves against snipers and that authority was given. A Marine platoon was sent to the Embassy office building that had been under sniper fire since the previous morning. A few marines were also sent to the Ambassador's residence, where the families of several Embassy officers were being housed. The residence too had come under fire, and several windows had been shattered by bullets. Other embassies were begging us to provide marines for their protection. There were not enough men available, but we promised to protect all diplomats and members of their families who went to the Embajador Hotel.

With the road to Haina under sporadic attack, Marine forces used helicopters to move hundreds of people awaiting evacuation. They flew from the hotel to the ships waiting to take them to the United States. All reports indicated that the movement was going smoothly. I regretted that we had found it necessary to send in troops to accomplish this task, but I was thankful we had been able to do it quickly and effectively when it became necessary. Then and later I was grateful for the foresight of President Kennedy, who had laid the groundwork for this readiness.

In October 1963 President Kennedy had been deeply concerned about possible developments in the Caribbean and Central America. He had sent a memorandum to the Secretary of Defense noting that events in the Dominican Republic and other countries in the area might "require active United States military intervention." Kennedy was not sure we were adequately prepared for this. He asked, for example, how many troops we could get into the Dominican Republic in twelve hours, in twenty-four, thirty-six, or forty-eight hours? He asked the same question about several other countries that seemed headed for a crisis.

President Kennedy told McNamara that he thought this matter deserved "the highest priority." He asked for an early report. In little more than a week, on October 12, 1963, the month before I became President, McNamara and the Joint Chiefs produced their report. They also informed President Kennedy that they planned to heighten our readiness by holding mobility exercises in 1964. The result of all this was that U.S. forces were ready to respond quickly when they were urgently needed.

After my television talk on the evening of April 28, I studied carefully two more urgent messages just in from Santo Domingo. Ambassador Bennett reported that the situation was continuing to deteriorate. Some American citizens had warned him that they had no protection in the residential areas. They expected to be the next targets of the mobs, who were sacking Dominican homes and stores. Bennett reported that demonstrators had broken into our AID office and ransacked it. He foresaw a complete breakdown in all government authority. In light of all the circumstances, he recommended that "serious thought be given in Washington to armed intervention which would go beyond the mere protection of Americans and seek to establish order in this strife-ridden country."

He added:

All indications point to the fact that if present efforts of forces loyal to the government fail, power will be assumed by groups clearly identified with the Communist party. If the situation described above comes to pass, my own recommendation and that of the Country Team is that we should intervene to prevent another Cuba from arising out of the ashes of this uncontrollable situation.

The last thing I wanted—and the last thing the American people wanted—was another Cuba on our doorstep. At the same time, the action suggested by the Ambassador would be a grave step. I wanted to know much more than I did then before taking such drastic action. First, I wanted a reading of Latin American opinion on the subject, and I thought we might get that from the OAS meeting scheduled for the next morning. Second, I wanted to know whether the Dominicans could possibly settle their differences without outside interference. Finally, I wanted to be sure there was no alternative to sending military forces to prevent another Cuba. In any case, the Ambassador had asked not that we send in more troops but only that we give the possibility "serious thought." For the time being, I decided to do that and no more.

During the night an urgent call for medicines came from Ambassador Bennett. The Dominican Red Cross estimated that at least 1,200 people had already been wounded. Dominican doctors lacked blood plasma and were operating without anesthesia. We sent the needed supplies immediately. From then until the end of the crisis we continued to supply the Dominican people with badly needed medical supplies and large quantities of food.

The next morning, Thursday, April 29, the OAS Council met in Washington. Ambassador Ellsworth Bunker explained the situation as we saw it and advised the Council of the landing of the Marines to protect lives and to evacuate our citizens and other nationals. A long and often emotional debate followed. The interchange underlined the difficulty of persuading representatives of twenty governments to agree on a course of action or to act quickly in a crisis, especially when they are far removed from the scene and depend largely on news accounts for information. There were many expressions of regret but few proposals for effective reaction to Dominican developments. The OAS Ambassadors would not commit their governments to anything without thorough consultation. That meant sending messages all over the Western Hemisphere and waiting for answers.

I could not help noticing that the OAS representative of one country spent much time in the OAS debate lamenting the loss to democracy entailed by the Dominican developments, although the Ambassador in Santo Domingo from the same country had reported that without forceful intervention the Dominican Republic would fall under Castro-dominated rule. Another OAS Ambassador expressed regret at the intervention of the U.S. Marines. His fellow Ambassador in the Dominican capital reported that the Marines were the only protection he and his people could depend on for their safety. Obviously, things looked very different to diplomats in Santo Domingo than they did to colleagues who were 1,500 miles away in Washington. The only concrete action resulting from the OAS meeting was a decision to ask the Papal Nuncio, the dean of the diplomatic corps in the Dominican capital, to try to arrange a ceasefire between the opposing forces. The idea was raised of holding a meeting of the Foreign Ministers of the hemisphere to discuss the crisis, but no decision was reached immediately.

While the OAS was meeting, we received another situation report from Ambassador Bennett. He reported that the loyalist forces were tired and discouraged and that their morale was low. The police force had been decimated and was largely ineffective. The rebel forces had not broken out of their redoubt in the center of town, he said, but there were indications they might try. Three rebel tanks were reported to be moving westward through a residential section of the city.

I met with McNamara and Mann at noon to go over the latest reports. I decided that the five-hundred-man Marine force already ashore might be too small for the many tasks we were giving it. I instructed McNamara to order the remaining 1,500 men of the Marine Ready Force aboard ship to join the original task force at the Embajador evacuation zone. We informed the Embassy immediately. A few minutes later the State Department sent another message to Bennett asking him to provide an estimate of the situation and a considered judgment as to whether direct intervention of U.S. forces was absolutely necessary. "We cannot afford to permit the situation to deteriorate to the point where a Communist takeover occurs," the message read.

I called a meeting of my principal advisers for 7:30 P.M. that evening. Just before the meeting Rusk, McNamara, Ball, and General Wheeler had a conference call with Ambassador Bennett and his key staff members. They asked him whether a rebel victory would lead to a pro-Communist government. Bennett said he thought it would. He went on to mention reports that the extremists might well name Juan Bosch as President, for appearance's sake, but that they would dominate him and "probably discard him quickly." The officials in Washington asked whether Dominican army troops could prevent a rebel victory. Bennett pointed out the inefficiency and indecisiveness of the military leaders. General Wessin, for example, had "done little or nothing for the last three days." Those with the weapons and equipment to deal with the rebels were disorganized; those who wanted to fight lacked the necessary weapons.

Bennett was asked what he recommended we do in the next six to twelve hours. He said the most important action that could be taken was "to commit sufficient troops to do the job here rapidly and effectively." He urged that we act immediately to overcome critical shortages of food, medicines, and other supplies in Santo Domingo. He suggested interposing our forces between the rebels and those of the junta, thereby effecting a ceasefire. We could then ask the OAS to negotiate a political settlement between the opposing factions, he said.

This was the background against which we met that night, Thursday, April 29, from 7:30 to 9:10 P.M. in the Cabinet Room. There was complete agreement that we must prevent a Communist takeover and act on a scale that would guarantee the earliest possible end to the fighting, destruction, and killing.

A number of people, then and later, thought the Communist threat in the Dominican Republic was overestimated. I did not and do not think it was. Nor do I believe that the majority of involved governments and competent analysts believe, in retrospect, that the danger was not desperately serious. Unless one understands how a few purposeful men can seize power in the midst of chaos, it may be difficult to accept the idea that 4,000 members of three Communist factions in the Dominican Republic could have been victorious before the end of April. But the fact is that as the situation disintegrated after April 24, the Communists moved quickly to associate themselves with the revolt. They gathered arms and mobilized additional recruits to fight with them. By April 28 they controlled much of the military strength in the rebel movement. Most important, no leaders in either the rebel or the antirebel camp were capable of organizing effective resistance to them. Power is relative. A small group, however disciplined and determined, is not likely to prevail against a larger group under effective leadership. But a small group *can* prevail when it faces no effective opposition.

Between 4,000 and 5,000 armed civilians were involved in the early stage of the revolt. Of these, at least 1,500 were believed by the U.S. Embassy and by our best intelligence analysts to be members of one of the three Communist parties, or sympathizers under the direct command of trained Communist leaders. Concrete information confirmed this figure. The remaining armed civilians included youngsters out for a thrill—some of them no more than twelve years old. There were also the Tigres and other hoodlums responsible for the murders of many policemen and for much of the looting. Finally, there were the patriotic Dominicans who wanted to restore the 1963 constitution. Many of these non-Communist civilians may never have come under Communist discipline, but they did become dependent on the Communists for arms and ammunition and for leadership in "commando" units. As of April 29, 1965, with most of the moderate leaders in hiding or asylum, the Communist leadership had the keys to what Lenin once called "the commanding heights" of power in the Dominican Republic. Of that there is no doubt in my mind.

Advance elements of the 82nd Airborne Division were then en route from Fort Bragg, North Carolina, to Ramey Air Force Base in Puerto Rico. As a first step toward preventing a Communist takeover, I ordered them to go directly to the air base at San Isidro in Santo Domingo.

I met with my advisers again later Thursday night to work out details of the operation. Following this session, the Joint Chiefs instructed Admiral H. Page Smith, the Commander in Chief, Atlantic Fleet, to plan an international security zone, but we ordered him not to set it up until we knew what action the OAS Council, then in session, would take. During the night, the OAS approved a resolution asking both factions to accept a ceasefire and permit immediate establishment of an international security zone. At the same time, the State Department announced that I had ordered additional landings.

The decisions I made on April 29 were as follows: first, that the danger of a Communist takeover in the Dominican Republic was a real and present one; second, that a Communist regime in the Dominican Republic would be dangerous to the peace and safety of the hemisphere and the United States; third, that danger still existed, in the disintegrating situation, for both American and foreign civilians in Santo Domingo; fourth, that the United States would put in sufficient force to achieve two purposes: to create the international security zone recommended by the OAS and to separate the rebels in the downtown area from the regular military forces; fifth, that we would seek a ceasefire, some kind of interim government, and the scheduling of orderly free elections in which all Dominican citizens, not just a minority with guns in their hands, would decide their political destiny.

The recommendations made to me by my senior civilian and military advisers on April 28 and April 29 were unanimous. In the Dominican crisis of 1965 those who recommended the course of U.S. policy were not divided into "hawks" and "doves." They were a group of informed and dedicated Americans who on April 28 were united in their belief that action was necessary if American and other foreign civilian lives were to be saved. They were united on April 29 in deciding that action was required if the citizens of the Dominican Republic were not to fall under the control of a small Communist minority and lose control over their own political destiny.

Very much in my mind at the time—and, I am sure, in the minds of all my principal advisers—was the formal determination reached by all members of the OAS at the Ministers of Foreign Affairs meeting in Punta del Este in January 1962: "The principles of communism are incompatible with the principles of the inter-American system." We were also thinking of the resolution approved at that same conference: "To urge the member states to take those steps that they may consider appropriate for their individual and collective self-defense, and to cooperate, as may be necessary or desirable, to strengthen their capacity to counteract threats or acts of aggression, subversion, or other dangers to peace and security resulting from the continued intervention in this hemisphere of Sino-Soviet powers. . . ." Clear in my memory were the words of President Kennedy less than a week before his death: "We in this hemisphere must also use every resource at our command to prevent the establishment of another Cuba in this hemisphere."

Decisions of the kind we made regarding the Dominican Republic in 1965 are the beginning of a road, not the end. We were not using force to impose a political solution. Our troops did not clear out the center of Santo Domingo, as they easily could have done. They moved between the rebel and the antirebel camps to bring about a de facto ceasefire. Under the leadership of the Papal Nuncio, and with our full support, a ceasefire was signed by the military junta and representatives of the rebels at 5:30 P.M. on Friday, April 30.

The OAS Council had no contingency plans to meet a crisis of this kind. The Council moved too slowly to permit a collective decision in the time available. But once the shooting stopped, we hoped the OAS would take the lead in finding an interim government acceptable to both sides and in arranging free and peaceful elections. That process began on April 30, when Secretary General José A. Mora went to Santo Domingo to establish an initial OAS presence.

We wanted other members of the OAS to share responsibility for creating the conditions necessary for free elections in the Dominican Republic. We were gratified that Brazil, Honduras, Paraguay, Nicaragua, and Costa Rica did send forces for this purpose, and that El Salvador sent officers. On May 29 a Brazilian general, Hugo Panasco Alvim, took command of this temporary peacekeeping force, the first ever established by the inter-American system. Our own forces had increased to about 22,000 men but were being scaled down.

Meanwhile, we used every available diplomatic resource to bring the two sides together in agreement on an interim government. Throughout these days and weeks many of our top officials were going and coming from the Caribbean, trying to encourage Dominicans to find the men and the formula to lead them from stalemate to an interim government and elections.

We took three separate initiatives to accomplish this end. The first, taken by former Ambassador John Bartlow Martin, began on April 30, when he arrived in Santo Domingo. The second began on May 15, when McGeorge Bundy, Tom Mann, Cy Vance, and Jack Vaughn * went to Santo Domingo. The third was in progress from the first meeting of the Foreign Ministers of the Organization of American States on May 1.

Repeated attempts were made to persuade Bosch to cooperate in a settlement. Every attempt failed. The combined efforts of the Papal Nuncio, Ambassador Martin, Governor Muñoz Marín of Puerto Rico, and a team of personal representatives failed to change his mind. One of the

* Vaughn replaced Tom Mann as Assistant Secretary of State for Inter-American Affairs on February 12, 1965.

many who tried to reason with advisers and colleagues of Bosch was my good friend, lawyer Abe Fortas, who was familiar with the Caribbean area and understood the importance of finding at least an interim settlement acceptable to the major factions.

Martin tried to work with the non-Communist left. Because of his excellent reputation, his previous experience, and his many contacts, he was able, after long talks and much persuasion, to convince the Dominicans that they should build a regime around Antonio Imbert Barreras, a general who had helped overthrow Trujillo. Under other circumstances, this plan might have succeeded, since Imbert was identified with neither the military junta nor the Communists. However, Imbert's "Government of National Reconstruction," sworn in on May 7, was strongly resisted by the followers of Bosch among the rebel military officers. It was, nonetheless, a useful interim step.

In mid-May I sent the Bundy-Mann-Vance-Vaughn team to have a try. The timing was not favorable. The rebels obviously felt themselves sufficiently strong to resist efforts at conciliation or negotiation at that time.

The third initiative finally succeeded. A special committee of the OAS, made up of Ambassadors Ilmar Penna Marinho of Brazil, Ramon de Clairmont Duenas of El Salvador, and Ellsworth Bunker of the United States, arrived in Santo Domingo on June 3, 1965. On June 18 the special committee issued a Declaration to the Dominican Republic. This document urged popular support for its proposal: peaceful free elections, a general amnesty, and a provisional government. On August 9 the committee suggested a provisional government under García Godoy, a widely respected civilian who had been Foreign Minister under Bosch. Elections were to be held within nine months. This proposal, called the Act of Dominican Reconciliation, was finally accepted and the García Godoy government was installed on September 3.

Bosch at first took the view that impartial elections would be impossible by June 1966. But in April 1966 he decided to run for President. The other principal candidate was Joaquin Balaguer, a moderate who had been serving as President when Trujillo was assassinated. Balaguer was living in exile in New York when the 1965 revolution broke out. In a record turnout on June 1, 1966, more than 1.3 million Dominican voters chose Balaguer as their President by a decisive margin over Bosch and the third candidate, Dr. Rafael Bonnelly, a conservative and also a former President. Balaguer received 57 per cent of the vote and a sizable majority in both houses of Congress.

The election of June 1966 in the Dominican Republic was one of the most closely watched elections ever held in the Western Hemisphere. OAS observers from eighteen countries in the hemisphere described the election as "an outstanding act of democratic purity." Among the closest observers were skeptical reporters from the American press corps. Yet there was no serious doubt that the results reflected the will of the people at that time.

In April 1965 it took an act of faith to believe that from the wild turmoil on an island whose people had known so little democracy an election of the kind that occurred on June 1, 1966, would be possible. The Dominican people, and all their neighbors, owe a debt to the Provisional President, García Godoy, to the highly professional team under Ambassador Bennett, to the special three-man OAS committee, and especially to that remarkable, compassionate, tough, and indefatigable diplomat Ellsworth Bunker. But the real heroes were the people of the Dominican Republic. They demonstrated what I hope and believe the people of South Vietnam, and other beleaguered countries, will increasingly demonstrate: that men and women in every part of the world will carry out their responsibilities as democratic citizens wisely, with pride, and with conviction—if they are given half a chance.

I knew debate would be heated and intense after we sent troops to the Dominican Republic. I also knew, however, that the debate would have been more severe and more legitimate if I had failed to act. I did not base my decisions on what I thought the public reaction or press reaction would be. I based them on what I knew had to be done: first, to protect American lives and, second, to protect the security of the United States and its neighbors.

Criticism from Latin America troubled me most in those early months after our troops landed in Santo Domingo. I was concerned that the argument over the Dominican Republic might disrupt or slow our cooperation in the Alliance for Progress. That did not happen. Indeed, as political events unfolded in the Dominican Republic, Latin Americans—including some of our most severe critics—came to realize that our emergency actions were for the best. I have a clipping in my files from *The New York Times* of March 7, 1966, reporting this change in view among Latin American leaders. One of those mentioned in the story was Antonio Mayobre, a Venezuelan. At the time of the Dominican crisis he was Executive Secretary of the United Nations Economic Commission for Latin America. He was sent to Santo Domingo by UN Secretary General U Thant. There he was active and vocal against U.S. policy. Months later, however, he told one of my aides he had concluded that our action and the negotiations and reconciliation that followed had advanced the course of constitutional government in the Dominican Republic by fifteen years.

I hope Mayobre's assessment will stand the test of history. I would like to believe that in all three of the major Latin American crises we faced—in Panama, Guantanamo, and the Dominican Republic—we not only successfully met the challenges but took steps to prevent a recurrence of the trouble.

No President seeks crises. They come to him unbidden, and in legions. But we faced these three challenges in Latin America confidently and, I think, successfully. We met them in ways that left each situation somewhat better than it had been when word of trouble first reached my desk.

9

Breakthroughs in Schoolroom and Sickroom

THERE WAS AN OLD SAYING, "The kids is where the money ain't," which summed up one of the major problems confronting the American educational system when I became President. Educators and national leaders had for years been watching our great public school system become overwhelmed by the country's growing requirements. By the 1960s the public schools were in a state of crisis, beset by problems that had been multiplying since World War II. School enrollment had increased 43 per cent in one decade. Classrooms were overcrowded. Teaching staffs were undermanned and underpaid. The quality of instruction had declined.

Of course, the impact was heaviest in the neighborhoods of the poor, where the need was greatest. A study made the year I entered the Presidency showed that tens of thousands of schoolchildren in the nation's fifteen largest school systems needed help in reading, writing, spelling, and arithmetic. Six out of every ten students who reached the tenth grade in those areas could be expected to drop out of high school. The consequences for the country were frightening, but states and communities, suffering from strained fiscal resources, could not meet the challenge of expanding population. It was obvious that federal aid was urgently needed to avert disaster.

Other Presidents and advocates had been trying to provide federal aid to the schools since the days of Andrew Jackson. None had succeeded. Three formidable barriers had blocked every effort. One stumbling block had been the issue of granting federal aid to segregated school systems. But the Civil Rights Act of 1964, which prohibited grants of federal funds to any segregated institution or activity, now minimized this problem. The other two objections—fear of government control of the schools and the issue of church and state—were still strongly entrenched.

The dispute over federal assistance to parochial schools had wrecked President Kennedy's education plan. As a Catholic, he was sensitive to the opposition to federal aid for parochial schools. The bill he proposed in 1961 requested money only to help pay teachers' salaries and to build classrooms in public schools. But in considering the views of one group of Americans, he irritated another group. The Catholics opposed legislation which ignored their needs. An alliance of Catholic Congressmen and the traditional foes of federal aid, many of them Republicans and Southerners, defeated that measure and two succeeding education bills.

With the passage of time it is easy to forget how desperate the education problem the nation faced really was, but when the Kennedy bill was defeated *The New York Times* of July 19, 1961, asserted that the bitterness aroused by the controversy "can only weaken our country in a way familiar to many European lands but up to now virtually unknown to the United States." The issue went beyond that. One commentator observed: "Among politicians of all points of view a consensus has been reached that the religious and philosophical antagonisms engendered by school questions are so bitter that a solution through normal political methods is no longer possible." This gloomy attitude was shared by many, who believed that we faced a crisis of congressional government. Confronted with a critical need, the Congress had shown that it would not, and apparently could not, act.

When the responsibility became mine, I saw three paths I might take. First, I could forget the whole thing. I had plenty of advice to ignore the education issue. A number of people, both in Congress and on my staff, warned me to avoid the subject. But I thought it was possible that as a Protestant I might have more flexibility than President Kennedy had had. Moreover, I felt intense concern. As a young schoolteacher more than three decades before, I had represented the teachers before the Texas Legislature, urging that cigarette tax revenues be used for raising the income level of teachers to that of skilled workmen. I knew what "school" meant for hundreds of thousands of boys and girls: crowded facilities, double shifts, overworked and often undertrained instructors. I knew that unless the federal government could step in and render necessary assistance, many American children would be doomed to inferior education, which presaged an empty future. Not only would those children suffer but so would their country.

Because of these convictions, I made a personal decision during the 1964 Presidential campaign to make education a fundamental issue and to put it high on the nation's agenda. I proposed to act on my belief that regardless of a family's financial condition, education should be available to every child in the United States—as much education as he could absorb. I had no intention of walking away from this fight.

The second choice open to me was to present school legislation that might reopen the emotional wounds which had caused so much antagonism and pain in the past. This route promised to be self-defeating.

Third, I could try to blunt the controversy and obtain the legislation simultaneously. Clearly this approach was preferable. Throughout the government we began to search for the formula that would both override the church-state issue and minimize the fear of federal control. We found it in a simple equation: $\frac{A}{2} \times B = P$. In that formula A represented a state's average expenditure per pupil, B the number of poor schoolchildren in a local school district, and P the payment to that district. The formula was based on an old concept familiar to the Congress: aid to impacted areas. The decision to apply that equation to the school bill was the result of months of effort by many good men, all of whom had been working hard throughout 1964 to draw up an education bill that could find its way through the congressional thickets that had trapped so many previous bills.

Early in 1964 I had asked John Gardner, a Republican and president of the Carnegie Corporation, to head a task force that would take a searching look at the problem of education and make recommendations for action. The report of Gardner's task force confirmed the crisis in American education and stressed the urgent need for taking action. "Every society," it stated, "gets the schools it deserves." The task force declared: "We favor federal aid to education." But it warned the nation not to "go through one more agonizing tug of war over the church-state issue." The report did not offer a specific solution for avoiding that issue, but it threw the spotlight of public attention on one of education's special needs, assistance to disadvantaged areas. It pointed to the possibility of sending federal funds to elementary and secondary schools not on a general aid basis, as earlier plans had specified, but on a selective formula related to the poverty of an area.

In the meantime, other concerned people were working on similar solutions—Anthony Celebrezze, Secretary of Health, Education, and Welfare; Wilbur Cohen, then Assistant Secretary of HEW; Senator Wayne Morse; Francis Keppel, Commissioner of Education; members of the White House staff; and staff men from the Bureau of the Budget. They met regularly during this period—probing, searching, and testing ideas. The result of this activity was the proposal that federal grants to the states be allotted on the basis of two considerations: the number of poor children served by individual school districts and half the state's average expenditure per schoolchild. (Thus $\frac{A}{2} \times B = P$.)

We coupled this plan with a requirement on each school district to make special services—such as educational television, mobile educational equipment, and "shared time" classes—available to children in private as well as public schools.

Another element in our legislation suggested by the Gardner task force provided for a number of innovations to upgrade the quality of education in elementary and high schools. It called for the establishment of community-wide organizations to offer services that individual schools could not provide—such as special courses in foreign languages, music, and art, science laboratories, and programs for the physically and mentally handicapped. Private as well as public school students would be able to take advantage of these programs.

Making the educational grants directly to the states would, we hoped, reassure doubters that the federal government would not endeavor to take over local school boards. The Catholics seemed likely to be satisfied, because children in parochial schools would also benefit.

As we were hammering out the program, we were also developing a strategy to overcome congressional obstacles. The bill was placed in the highest-priority category. I resolved to put the entire power and prestige of the Presidency behind it. All the centers of power and control within the Congress were consulted. These included the key members of the House Education and Labor Committee, whose chairman, Adam Clayton Powell of New York, was both a Negro leader and a Protestant minister. They included the courtly, unrelenting Chairman of the House Rules Committee, Judge Howard W. Smith of Virginia, who had blocked the passage of so many previous education bills that a slogan had been coined for him: "No rules for schools." They also included the members of the Senate Committee on Labor and Public Welfare.

In addition, a coalition of support was carefully built up among educational institutions and other interested groups, including several former opponents of school aid programs who had recently been converted to our cause. Various members of the administration met with Catholic groups. Education Commissioner Francis Keppel met with high-ranking prelates of the church, who assured him that they were not eager for a court test over any program that would give direct aid to parochial schools. Jack Valenti served as our liaison with the Vatican's Apostolic Delegate to the United States, Archbishop Egidio Vagnozzi. After the bill was completed, the delegate advised Valenti that he was in favor of it, and that the majority of the Catholic hierarchy shared his opinion. "Archbishop McIntyre of Los Angeles," Valenti reported to me, "may possibly be the only prelate who might oppose the bill."

Similarly, Lee White of the White House staff dealt with the Jewish organizations; Henry Hall Wilson worked with the Southern leaders; Douglass Cater and Commissioner Keppel remained in close touch with the powerful education lobbies. Our strategy was to line up all available support in advance so that the bill would move speedily through the deliberative process and not be killed or crippled by amendments.

The bill went to the Congress on January 12, 1965. The House Education and Labor Committee opened hearings on January 22, and—despite all efforts to prevent it—the church-state issue erupted in the committee soon afterward. Objection was raised to a provision that would provide schoolbooks to students in parochial schools. I told Larry O'Brien, Cater, and Cohen to get together with Hugh Carey, a Catholic Congressman from New York who was on the committee, and work out a solution.

They met late into the night in Larry O'Brien's office, above mine, and the next morning O'Brien called me and said he thought they had found the answer. The Supreme Court in 1947 had decided that busing of parochial school students was aid to the pupil and not to the Catholic schools. We sought a way to make this "child benefit" theory apply to this case. Why not, Carey asked, give ownership of the books to the public school boards and let them *lend* them to the pupils? The bill was amended to include this provision and one more hurdle was cleared.

But there were others. Opposition had been too strong to vanish overnight. The Catholics were maintaining a wary stance, backing the bill quietly but threatening to oppose it openly if a provision was added permitting a constitutional test of aid to private schools. A convention of B'nai B'rith voiced concern a few days after I had addressed it. Southerners were afraid their poor rural districts would not fare as well as Northern urban ghettos.

But slowly, in curious ways, opposition melted. Billy Graham came to see me one day while the issue was still before the Congress, and we went for a swim in the White House pool. A call came in from a prominent— and irate—Baptist leader who wanted to complain about what he considered the unfair advantage we were giving the Catholics in the legislation. Bill Moyers, a former Baptist preacher, who had worked long and effectively on the bill, took the call. After listening to the man's objections, he explained that I was in the swimming pool, but that he could have the call transferred.

"Is he really swimming at this time of day?" came the indignant response.

Bill explained that I was swimming with Dr. Graham.

There was a pause on the other end of the wire. "Is that with *our* Billy?"

Moyers said that it was, but that he was sure I would not mind being interrupted to take the phone call.

"Oh, no, no," the caller replied. "Just give the President my very warm regards."

One unforeseen obstacle was Chairman Adam Clayton Powell of the House Education and Labor Committee. Powell usually voted with the progressive forces in Congress, but he could be unpredictable. Because we hoped to get the bill through quickly, before lobbyists in the special groups could congeal the opposition, Powell made a firm commitment to take it up in full committee on Monday, February 8, just after it had been marked up in subcommittee.

Instead Powell held the bill hostage to force the funds he had requested for his staff expenses. He canceled the February 8 meeting and rescheduled it for February 17, the day after the House was slated to consider his expenses. Then he left for Puerto Rico. The House approved Powell's expense funds, but the Congressman did not return for the February 17 meeting, or give any indication of when he would be back.

Because delay was dangerous to the education bill, the leadership now had to consider ways of freeing the committee from Powell's control, if that became necessary. They decided to produce a workable majority and a physical quorum at the next regular meeting of the full committee. They would then adopt a resolution to keep the committee in session from day to day until the education bill was reported out.

The next regular meeting day was Thursday, February 25. Chairman Powell, of course, recognized what was happening. He was present at the meeting on February 25, and the hearings on the education bill went forward. When the bill reached the House floor, I asked for frequent reports and received them hour by hour.

On March 24 Secretary Celebrezze's head count showed 248 votes for the bill and Valenti told me that "Celebrezze's people were working feverishly." The White House estimate that day was 229 votes in favor, but twenty members of the House had not expressed themselves one way or another. Our special task force was busy on the Hill, concentrating on 148 wavering Democrats. Valenti reported that a frantic struggle was in progress: "Carl Albert is staying on the floor supporting Carl Perkins. It's been hell today. . . ." Finally, on March 26, by a roll call vote of 263 to 153, the House passed the education bill and sent it to the Senate.

The danger lay now with Senate amendments, which could upset the delicate balance of the bill's various provisions. I talked with Wayne Morse, the floor manager, and with other Senate leaders of both parties. They agreed that no matter how much they might like to change some aspects of the House bill, the dangers of scuttling it in conference were too great to risk. As Morse said on the Senate floor: "The stakes are too high for the children of America for us to run the risk of jeopardizing this legislation in conference." After eleven amendments were beaten down, the measure moved through the Senate with no changes. The vote was 73 to 18.

Passage came on Friday night, April 9, at 7:43 P.M. Normally, ten days are required to process a bill physically, have the papers printed, and accomplish the formalities necessary to send it to the President's desk for signature. During this time the bill is engraved and signed by the Vice

President and the Speaker of the House. The agencies comment on it and the package as a whole is presented to the President. In this case I did not want to wait ten days. After almost one hundred years of waiting, I felt there should not be a single day's delay in putting this bill to work to improve the education of American children. That Friday night at 8 P.M. I told my staff I wanted the education bill engraved and ready for my signature within twenty-four hours. On Sunday, April 11, I signed the Elementary and Secondary Education Act into law.

I signed it in the one-room schoolhouse near Stonewall, Texas, where my own education had begun. I asked my first teacher, Mrs. Kathryn Deadrich Loney—"Miss Kate"—to come back from California to sit by my side as I signed the bill. Present too were other students of hers, and mine, and men and women who were once my classmates and now my neighbors. For me, a pattern had come full circle in the course of fifty years. My education had begun with what I learned in that schoolroom. Now what I had learned and experienced since that time had brought me back to fulfill a dream.

"As President of the United States," I said on that occasion, "I believe deeply that no law I have signed or will ever sign means more to the future of America."

Since I spoke those words and signed that law, thousands of local school districts in every part of the United States have been able to develop special programs to improve the educational opportunities and experience of millions of boys and girls from poor families. By the end of the first year, I received a report from Education Commissioner Harold Howe * telling me where the funds were going. They were being used for language training and remedial reading, for audio-visual equipment, and for specialists to work with preschoolers. The report described the work of nurses' aides, counselors, and bilingual teachers, and the support of evening classes for high school dropouts. But perhaps the bill's impact was summed up best in the words of a boy from a poor family in Iowa. "Happiness," he said, "is two teachers so you can be helped when you need it."

On December 27, 1964, I received a letter from a lady in Auburn, Washington, which read:

> I have never done anything as daring as writing to the top man of our wonderful nation. But things are getting awfully rough at our house, so I thought I would start at the top, as we are already at the bottom. I am hoping you can get Medicare real soon. You see, my husband for almost 46 years has had several strokes. . . . We had both worked and bought bonds and were doing okay, when my husband became ill. Now the bonds

---

* Howe replaced Francis Keppel as Commissioner of Education on December 18, 1965.

are gone. I can't borrow, because we have no way to repay a loan. . . . We have two very fine children, but both have families and homes to keep up too, so can't expect any financial aid from them.

From Orange Cove, California, another woman wrote:

Please remember us old people that look to the ones that rule over our country to help us when we are no longer able to help ourselves. We pray for you daily. We wish the Medicare pass and become law.

"Please try to pass Medicare for us old folks," wrote a lady in Brownstown, Illinois. "I just don't want to be a burden to anyone."

These were typical of many letters that poured into the White House in 1964 and 1965. They described in terms of human suffering the serious need for a bill to assure medical care for the elderly. The volume of that mail made it clear that Medicare's day, at long last, had dawned.

President Harry Truman had tried as hard as any man could to inaugurate a health insurance plan for the American people. He did not succeed, partly because the medical lobby spent millions of dollars in an all-out effort to defeat the plan. Early in 1965 this powerful lobby was still pouring millions into its campaign of opposition. But by 1965, fifteen years after President Truman's courageous fight, the times had caught up with the idea. The cost of illness in old age had become a matter of national concern. Spiraling medical costs struck fear not only in the senior citizens themselves but also in their sons and daughters, who often had to pay staggering hospital bills for elderly relatives while they were struggling to rear their own families.

Throughout the 1964 Presidential campaign I repeatedly promised that medical care for the elderly would be "at the top of my list" of proposals to the new Congress. The election that year brought seventy-one new Democratic members to the House of Representatives. Not all of those young and progressive new members of the Eighty-ninth Congress would survive the next election, but they had their hour in the sun, and a fine hour it was. I will always remember them with affection and gratitude, and America will be long in their debt. Most of these newly elected Congressmen supported Medicare, so it can be correctly stated that the voters of America passed the law. That, I think, is an essential point in Medicare's history.

Soon after the 1964 election my legislative office sent me a memorandum at the Ranch. I read it and returned it with a note saying "be sure to bring this to my attention as soon as I get back." The memo read:

The Democratic share of the House will now be close to 68%. The translation of this into committee ratios will be settled by informal conversation between the Speaker and the Minority Leader. . . . One exception to the usual ratio arrangement is the Ways and Means Committee.

Traditionally, regardless of the party breakdown, 15 of the 25 seats go to the majority party, and there has been no change in the overall figure, with one exception. In 1936 the Ways and Means Committee went 18–7 Democratic.

If the ratio on the Ways and Means Committee were to be made on the same basis at this time, the memo pointed out, the ratio would have to be 17 to 8 in favor of the Democrats. That, along with the fact that three Republican diehard opponents on the committee had just been defeated, provided reasonable assurance that Medicare would be reported out. Clearly a readjustment on the committee was called for. The memo noted that the attitude of Speaker McCormack, who was a former member of the Ways and Means Committee, would be a major factor in this effort. Speaker McCormack's attitude was, for that matter, a key to the enactment of our entire program. He had been a force for progressive legislation in Congress for more than thirty-five years. No man understood better how to convert dreams into programs and no man cared more about accomplishing such goals.

We consulted with the Speaker. He understood the problem and recognized the issue at stake. After consultation with the remainder of the House leadership, the ratio on the Ways and Means Committee was revised. Later two new Congressmen, both friendly to Medicare, were elected to committee membership by the Democratic caucus.

The Ways and Means Committee had been the graveyard for Medicare as long as its chairman, Wilbur Mills, did not actively support the measure. A bill requested by President Kennedy had died in the Ways and Means Committee in 1962. In 1964 a measure originating in the Senate as an amendment had made its way through that body but failed when it met Mills in conference. Chairman Mills was a man who stood on principle— and on principle he was worried about the "actuarial soundness" of the administration's plan to finance Medicare under Social Security. But he was also a man who knew how to count votes. He never liked to be overrun or defeated or outdistanced, and he rarely was. Until the 1964 election, I believe he did not think there were enough votes to propel the bill through the House. When the election changed the head count in Congress, his mind changed as well. A few days after the election, on November 11, he announced publicly that he was willing to bring the measure up in his committee.

In my State of the Union message on January 4, I asked the Eighty-ninth Congress to make Medicare its first order of business. The next day Mills promised me that he would guarantee prompt consideration by his committee. Medicare was the first measure introduced in the new Congress. To dramatize the importance we attached to it, we asked the leadership to designate it "S-1" in the Senate, where it was sponsored by Clinton Anderson of New Mexico, and "HR-1" * in the House, where it was sponsored by Cecil King of California. In the last few days of January the Ways and Means Committee began meeting to consider the bill. Mills set March 15 as the target date for sending the bill to the floor of the House.

With public sentiment now against it, the medical lobby changed tactics but did not diminish its campaign of opposition. The administration bill was basically a hospital insurance plan that omitted coverage of doctors' costs, principally to prevent an American Medical Association charge of "socialized medicine." Trimming their attack to the prevailing winds, the medical lobbyists began criticizing the measure as inadequate, because it did *not* cover doctor bills. I doubt they ever expected to see the Congress seriously consider such a bill.

The ranking Republican on the Ways and Means Committee, John Byrnes of Wisconsin, introduced an alternative bill tailored to the medical lobby's "objections." Byrnes's bill called for a voluntary program covering both doctors' charges and hospital costs. As a voluntary plan, such a measure would not have provided universal protection. Many of those who needed it most would not, through ignorance, have taken it. There were a number of other aspects, I thought, that rendered the plan inferior to our bill, but the political problems were obvious and considerable. If we opposed it, the AMA and the Republicans could turn the whole issue against us, after we had worked so hard and so long to build public support for this much-needed legislation.

Wilbur Cohen, who had helped write the Social Security Act in President Roosevelt's time, was the administration's expert on Medicare. He was empowered to present our point of view and work out whatever solutions had to be arranged on the spot. At Mills's invitation, he sat in on all the Ways and Means Committee's sessions and kept me closely informed of developments.

On the evening of March 2 Cohen came to my office in a state of high excitement. The committee, he told me, had spent the day reviewing all the health bills pending before it. When the review was finished, Mills dropped a bombshell. He suggested putting together a bill that would combine three features—our universal hospital care measure, a supplemental and expanded program to provide for the health needs of the indigent, and a voluntary supplemental program based on Byrnes's proposal to take care of doctor bills and other related services. It was, Cohen said, a "three-layer cake," with Wilbur Mills the chef. "Mills did it so fast," he said, "the Republicans were dumbstruck."

Chairman Mills asked Cohen if he could draft the new bill during the night. "I said that's awfully fast," Cohen reported. "How about twenty-

---

* Indicating that it was the first bill to be introduced in each house of Congress that session.

four hours?" He said no—tomorrow morning. "I could see that he wanted to push it. The tempo was with him."

Cohen called the plan "ingenious." It was almost certain, he said, that a majority would not dare to vote against the bill on the floor of the House. According to the plan, the government would subsidize a substantial portion of the cost of the voluntary supplemental program out of general revenues. I asked how much that would cost.

"About $500 million a year," Wilbur answered. Then he put the essential question to me: "What do you want to do about it, Mr. President?"

I told him about the test that had been given to a man in Texas who wanted to become a railroad switchman. One of the questions he was asked was: "What would you do if a train from the east was coming at sixty miles an hour, and a train from the west was coming at sixty miles an hour on the same track, and they were just a mile apart, headed for each other?"

The prospective switchman replied: "I'd run get my brother."

"Now why," he was asked, "would you run get your brother?"

"Because," the fellow answered, "my brother has never seen a train wreck."

I told Wilbur I thought I would run and get *my* brother if the Ways and Means Committee reported out this extended Medicare bill he had described to me. I approved the proposal at once. I thought that $500 million would be cheap if we could pass the bill into law. I sent Cohen away with instructions to "call them and raise them if necessary, but get this bill now."

The Ways and Means Committee reported out this broadened bill late in March. Chairman Wilbur Mills, so long the villain of the act, was now a hero to the old folks. A delegation of senior citizens threw a victory celebration lunch in the Ways and Means Committee room, rewarding Mills with two standing ovations. "We've seen the promised land," the delegation chairman said.

Mills himself introduced the new bill into the House. The next day I called the leaders of the House and Senate to the White House to review the status of the measure. After our session we went into the Cabinet Room, where television cameras had been set up. For the benefit of the television audience, I described the bill and then introduced the legislators, first the members of the House and then the members of the Senate.

With us was Senator Harry Byrd, Sr., Chairman of the Finance Committee, where Senate hearings would begin. Harry Byrd was a great patrician, a landed gentleman from the Virginia aristocracy, and one of the most powerful men in the Senate. He was also dead set against Medicare and eventually voted against it. He had not expected to be called on in this television interview, but I felt I should not neglect to take note of him and I introduced him last.

"Senator Byrd," I said, "I know you will take an interest in the orderly scheduling of this matter and in giving it a thorough hearing. Would you care to make an observation?"

"There is no observation I can make now," the Senator answered, "because the bill hasn't come before the Senate. Naturally, I'm not familiar with it. All I can say is . . . that I will see that adequate and thorough hearings are held on the bill."

"And you have nothing that you know of that would prevent that coming about in a reasonable time?" I asked. "There is nothing ahead of it in the committee?"

"Nothing in the committee now," Senator Byrd said.

"So," I continued, "when the House acts and it is referred to the Senate Finance Committee, you will arrange for prompt hearings and thorough hearings?"

"Yes," he answered.

Later, as a White House aide was seeing him to his car, Senator Byrd drily remarked that if he had known he was to appear on television, he would have dressed more formally. But true to his word, and having committed himself on national television, Senator Byrd directed his Finance Committee to open hearings in April, after the bill went through the House. On July 9, a day I described as a "great day for America," the Medicare bill passed the Senate.

When the conference report was adopted, Wilbur Mills called it "one of the most significant and far-reaching measures which has ever been before this or any recent Congress." But it was Republican John Byrnes who spoke the most hopeful and promising words of the day. Byrnes had led the fight against Medicare, but he said that "the job now before us is to try to make the system that is established under this bill work as best it can. . . . I would therefore at this point urge all who have anything to do with the administration of the program or with the health needs of our people, if they have any hatchets to bury them, and if they have any disagreements or animosities from the past that they bury them, and that all do their utmost to make the program work as well as possible."

I read that statement to a group of leaders from the AMA, with whom I met two days later. That organization's opposition to Medicare had been bitter and intense to the end. But the medical profession's cooperation was absolutely crucial to Medicare's success. The law, hard as it was to put on the statutes, was only the first step. The hardest job lay ahead. There was wide speculation that doctors, with the support of the AMA, would boycott Medicare.

If any of the AMA leaders came to the meeting that day primed to be difficult, I did not give them the opportunity. I thanked them for coming. I expressed my deep respect for their profession. Then, drawing on my own experience, I talked about how much the devotion of our family doctor had meant during my father's final illness. I think that is a common experience of Americans—their respect for and gratitude toward their doctors. I spoke of the unique strength and influence that doctors possess. Now, I told them, Medicare was going to be an inevitable part of their lives. A program the people wanted, which had been worked out in the most painstaking way in accordance with the exacting rules of our democracy, would need their cooperation if it was to work. I said I hoped they would give that cooperation, and I indicated that I was sure they would.

I cannot say that I changed any minds at that meeting, but I left it believing that some of the antagonism had been removed. And I was right. A few weeks later the AMA announced that it would not endorse any boycott of Medicare.

Forecasts of disaster continued right up to the day Medicare went into effect. There were predictions that hospitals, clinics, and doctors' offices would be flooded with hordes of elderly patients, that the system would collapse under its own weight, and that many poor patients would die on the steps of overcrowded hospitals without necessary medical attention. The Commissioner of Social Security, the Secretary of HEW, and I personally tried to reassure the public that such ominous predictions would not materialize.

After one such reassuring statement had been issued, I said to John Gardner: * "John, if you're wrong in your calculations, we're both going to look like the worst kind of damned fools."

"I hope you're not worried," he said.

"No," I said. "If a man can't take that kind of chance, he doesn't belong in public life."

As time passed, 95 per cent of all the doctors in the country became participants in Medicare. Most of the doubts and distrusts disappeared, but a few scars remained. Typical of such situations, the residue of bitterness was both unreasonable and unfortunate. Early in 1968, when John Gardner left the government to return to private life, there were accurate predictions about whom I would nominate to succeed him as Secretary of HEW. To most knowledgeable people, I think the selection of Wilbur Cohen was natural and right. He had been a valiant and loyal fighter of administration battles. More important, over the span of a generation he had worked hard to advance the health and well-being of the American people. Yet many people remained bitter about the Medicare struggle. More than 1,000 telegrams were sent to the White House, all worded exactly the same. "Please do not appoint Wilbur J. Cohen Secretary of HEW," they read. "It is my opinion that he is an enemy of American medicine." Stacks of these telegrams notwithstanding, I named Cohen to my Cabinet.

* Gardner replaced Anthony Celebrezze on July 27, 1965, as Secretary of HEW.

Wilbur Cohen went on to make his mark as an excellent Cabinet officer. That last campaign against him is the kind of unpleasant thing a dedicated man has to expect if he devotes part of his life to public service.

I had a special reason for wanting to sign Medicare into law before the end of July. It would mean an extra $30 million in benefits to the aged. I had a particular place in mind for the signing. On July 27 I called President Truman and told him that I wanted to come out and have a special visit with him. On July 30 I traveled to Independence, Missouri, to sign the bill in Mr. Truman's presence in the library that bears his name. He had started it all, so many years before. I wanted him to know that America remembered. It was a proud day for all of us, and President Truman said that no single honor ever paid him had touched him more deeply.

The letters expressing public interest in Medicare, which had flooded the White House in 1964 and 1965, did not stop once the law was in effect. They continued to come in, and they still do, describing the impact that measure has had on the lives of the American people. Almost a year after I left office I received a letter from a man in San Diego which sums up the need and the fulfillment:

> Last month I had to take my 86 year old mother to the hospital. I shudder, as a teacher, to think what I would have had to pay if she had not been on Medicare. This is why I am writing to you to thank you for what you did to bring this service to the aged. I am a Republican, but that doesn't matter. I am grateful.

To my mind, the outstanding significance of the Elementary and Secondary Education Act was that it established a foundation on which the country could work toward educational achievement, with equal quality and opportunity for the future. Old fears of federal encroachment were disappearing and that law hastened the process. We were in a position to get on with work too long delayed.

Altogether, we passed sixty education bills.* All of them contributed to advances across the whole spectrum of our society. When I left office, millions of young boys and girls were receiving better grade school educations than they once could have acquired. A million and a half students were in college who otherwise could not have afforded it. Thousands of adult men and women were enrolled in classes of their choice, available to them for the first time. I remember seeing, in the folder of reading material I took to my bedroom one night, the account of a sixty-two-year-old man who learned how to write his name after years of making an *X* for a sig-

* My determined efforts on behalf of education bills were stimulated and inspired by Mrs. Agnes E. Meyer, an old friend who, I believe, did more to influence me on federal education measures than any other person.

nature. He was so excited that he sat for a whole hour just writing his name over and over again. Reading about this man, whose life had been singularly enriched, I was almost as excited as the man himself. In his story our striving for increased opportunity in education took shape and became real and valid.

I had the same sentiments about Medicare, whose overriding importance, to me, was that it foreshadowed a revolutionary change in our thinking about health care. We had begun, at long last, to recognize that good medical care is a right, not just a privilege. During my administration, forty national health measures were presented to the Congress and passed by the Congress—more than in all the preceding 175 years of the Republic's history.* Federal expenditures for health programs increased from $4 billion to $14 billion. The fruits of medical research began to reach all the people. Progress was made in fighting the old killers—heart disease, cancer, stroke, and the tragedy of mental retardation. The death rate from tuberculosis and pneumonia and other traditional scourges declined. Measles was eliminated as a cause of serious concern. New hospitals and nursing homes were built. Thousands of new doctors and nurses were trained who could not have pursued medical careers without assistance. This is not just a tribute to my administration's concern for the people's health but a tribute to the people themselves—a salute to what they demand of their government and to the system that makes it possible to meet the demand.

But I was haunted to the last days of my Presidency by the work still undone in both health and education, and I continue to be concerned. I am deeply troubled that we, the richest nation on earth, are still fifteenth in infant mortality. I am distressed and horrified that every year 750,000 poverty-stricken women do not receive adequate medical care during pregnancy. Think of the burdens life imposes on their babies just to survive. Think of the physical handicaps imposed for a lifetime on those who do survive. And I am aware of the distance we have yet to travel to achieve universal, satisfactory education. We learned a great deal about education during my administration. We learned that education is more than a twelve- or sixteen-year allotment of formal instruction. Education goes on continually, from the first days of life to the last.

Experts tell us that most of a child's full potential is achieved before he reaches school age. Half his eventual capacity has been established by the age of four. By the time he is six, two-thirds of his adult intelligence has been formed. How do such findings square with the notion that the "education" of a child does not begin until he is six? The Head Start

* In the great strides we have made in tackling our health problems, no one is more deserving of tribute than Mrs. Mary Lasker, with whom I have worked closely since my days in the Senate. For years she has been a driving force in making the nation aware of the job to be done, in encouraging the Congress to appropriate the funds, and in mobilizing public opinion.

program we inaugurated led the way in the application of these discoveries to the classroom. Focused on culturally deprived children, Head Start was responsible for calling attention to several incredible facts. Almost half the children we reached with this program the first year came from homes that had no toys, books, magazines, crayons, paints, or even paper. Some of those children, particularly those from city slums, could not recognize pictures of animals from the zoo. The only animal they all knew immediately was a rat. One little black girl literally did not know what the word "beautiful" meant and she was overjoyed to discover its meaning as she watched herself in a mirror, trying on her teacher's hat.

The progress of these children under our Head Start program astounded and gratified us all. I urged that Head Start and its companion programs be made available to all 8 million poverty-level youngsters in this country below the age of ten, and not just to the million who currently are benefiting.* This investment in human life would pay us the highest interest rate of any investment we could make.

I want to see the Head Start experience and lesson applied to *all* children. There are 12 million three-to-five-year-olds in the United States. Only 30 per cent of them are in school. We know this is a tragic waste of human resources, resources our country will sorely need before the turn of the century, when this generation of preschoolers will be leading the nation.

I want a meaningful vocational education for every student who prefers it. Above all, I want all the education of every kind that every boy and girl in the United States can absorb. Until we reach the point where all American youngsters, particularly those from deprived backgrounds, have access to a good education, we are courting a national calamity.

When we squander millions of lives and ignore the potential of millions of minds, the scope is national and the result is a calamity. This calamity accounts for the loss of untold productivity, creates inequality of opportunity, and breeds discord throughout society.

There are many things that remain to be done, but looking back on those years of feverish activity between 1963 and 1969, I find deep satisfaction in recalling what was done and what was initiated. I take pride and comfort in the thought that thousands of children got a head start because of our combined efforts, that many older people learned to read and write for the first time, that our senior citizens are enjoying medical care that would otherwise not have been available to them. And I am convinced that those years were good for most Americans, now and in the future.

---

* As I write this, I have just organized a Head Start program in our neighboring community that will include more than twenty children of Latin American descent, black children, and children of German and Czechoslovakian ancestry—all in one room.

IO

Feeding the Hungry: India's Food Crisis

O N MY TOUR OF ASIA for President Kennedy in May 1961, I saw several countries for the first time, none more important than India. We arrived in the Indian capital on a hot, muggy day. Prime Minister Jawaharlal Nehru was at the airport to welcome us, and as we drove into the city over New Delhi's dusty, crowded streets, I saw for the first time in my life what writers have so often described as the "teeming masses of Asia." One look at those rows of packed humanity told me better than any elaborate technical report what India's "population problem" meant. The worn and shabby clothing of many of the people made me aware of their abject poverty. I saw children with fat stomachs, bloated not from eating too much but from eating too little.

That afternoon I had a long discussion with Nehru and his ministers. The Prime Minister described in detail his government's hopes for development under the new Five Year Plan, including ambitious schemes for better education and for village improvement. That evening after dinner I had another long and more informal talk with Nehru, one that continued until 11 P.M. Ambassador Kenneth Galbraith told me he had never known the Prime Minister to stay up so late.

The next morning I saw portions of the Indian countryside when we traveled to Agra to view the Taj Mahal. As we passed through the surrounding country, it was depressing to observe that primitive plows hitched to water buffalo were still being used to till the soil, as they had been when the Taj Mahal was built during the seventeenth century. I saw little or no irrigation and I wondered how India could ever feed its growing population under these circumstances. If the rains are good, I thought, they can probably get along, but one real dry spell and they are in trouble.

I returned home from Asia with one particularly strong conclusion: The United States alone could not make the dreams of Asians come true. They would have to do much for themselves, and others would have to lend a hand. As I reported to President Kennedy:

> Any help—economic as well as military—we give less developed nations to secure and maintain their freedom must be a part of a mutual effort. These nations cannot be saved by United States help alone.

I suggested linking our aid to the efforts of Asians themselves in order to make our help effective.

"It would be useful," I suggested, "to enunciate more clearly than we have . . . what we expect or require of them."

I remembered that advice four years later when I was called on to help India meet its worst threat of starvation in a hundred years. It was up to me to put my own advice into practice. India's severe food shortage of 1965–1967 was only one of hundreds of foreign problems we faced and dealt with over those years. I describe it here because it illustrates two essential elements of the foreign policy of my administration. The first was to help our friends keep their freedom and overcome their internal problems, but to help most those who helped themselves. The second was to emphasize our realization that world problems had grown far too large, too numerous, and too complicated for the United States to deal with alone. The time had come for other prosperous and advanced nations to take on an increasing share of responsibility for the world's stability and progress.

I understood and appreciated the reactions of my fellow Americans, including many Congressmen, who were tired of Uncle Sam carrying the main load almost everywhere by himself. I was irritated at seeing countries we had helped to regain strength and prosperity after World War II look the other way when another nation was in trouble. I decided to reshape our policy to meet the changed situation in the world. We would insist that our friends make a concerted effort to help themselves before we rushed in with food, money, and sympathy. As for other prosperous nations, we would insist on partnership and fair shares. The world needed a community chest effort, not just the charity of one rich uncle. These thoughts were in my mind in the autumn of 1965 when reports of the great drought in India reached my desk.

I knew how much was at stake. I knew that millions of people might starve unless we acted. Millions of children might be stunted permanently in their mental and physical development if they suffered from malnutrition. I knew what hunger meant. I had seen its effects early in my life—on the faces of children, pupils who came to my school day after day without enough food in their stomachs.

But I had to think of more than the humanitarian side of this matter. We could rush in impulsively and try to solve the immediate problem of 10 or 20 million hungry people simply by pouring food into their markets. By doing that, however, we might contribute to a much more serious problem of starvation in later years when nothing we and all the rest of the world together could do would be enough to stave off a disastrous famine.

Against our advice over the years, the Indian government had systematically neglected agriculture. The Indians had become accustomed to receiving several million tons of grain a year under our 1954 Public Law 480 program, although they had imported less than a million tons annually a decade earlier. Suddenly, in 1965, we faced a request for 7 million tons of grain.

The Indians had been pouring most of their energy and resources into a strenuous campaign to develop a major industrial base. For them, steel mills and the other features of a modern economy were what mattered most, as visible evidence of the "progress" they so desperately wanted. But it was folly, as many countries had learned, to build an industrial nation on the foundation of a weak agriculture—particularly in India, where four out of every five persons still lived in the countryside. Poor farmers make poor customers. If India wanted an efficient modern industry, it first had to have a vital agriculture to feed its own people and to serve as a base for industry itself.

India was not alone in its predicament or in its policy. While a few developing countries like Taiwan, Mexico, and Thailand had made remarkable progress in agriculture and had experienced success in curbing their population increases, others were nearly as bad off as India, even without a drought. What India did for itself, and what more prosperous nations did for it, was bound to have far-reaching effects elsewhere.

There was another problem involved in this crisis. American grain for our Public Law 480 program was no longer coming from the huge surpluses accumulated in the 1940s and 1950s. Those surpluses had been largely depleted. To meet growing needs abroad, we had to expand acreage beyond our own commercial requirements. Increasingly, food for foreign assistance was costing hard-earned taxpayers' dollars, like any other form of aid.

Because of this and various other factors, the Congress was regarding foreign aid with increasingly critical eyes. I talked almost daily with Senators and Representatives and I was aware of their mood on the subject. Every morning I read about the previous day's happenings on the Hill in the Congressional Record. Members of Congress were complaining that American aid encouraged some underdeveloped countries to delay helping themselves. In other cases, they claimed, our contribution was not solving basic problems for the recipients but just making it possible for them to survive or "stay even."

Deeper disillusionment set in when Indians and Pakistanis started fighting over Kashmir in August and September of 1965, using weapons we had provided them to defend themselves against outside attack. This conflict raised grave doubts about military assistance as well as economic aid. Finally, there was the problem of persuading other prosperous nations to assume more of the burden in creating a healthier world. The United States was not the only country that produced grain. And many countries were in a position to supply shipping, fertilizers, and pesticides, or the money to buy them, even if they could not provide food. But most of these countries had fallen into the habit of considering food aid as the special province of the United States. We had begun to move toward a fairer sharing with other prosperous nations of the burdens of economic and technical assistance to developing nations. The time had come, I felt, to extend this trend to the supplying of food aid.

My first action, in the fall of 1965, was to put food aid to India on a short-term basis instead of the long-term commitments of earlier years. I advised my aides that I wanted to judge requirements month by month. I did not want to haggle about sending food to starving people, but I was convinced that unless India changed its farm policy, it risked far greater difficulties for its population in the years to come. The world had little more than a decade, I believed, to bring food supply and population growth into balance. If we failed on that front, the whole world might drown in a tidal wave of hunger and despair. In any event, I was determined to work toward that balance. I knew too that continuing long-term commitments could threaten the foundation of congressional support for maintaining aid in any of its forms.

What we called the "short tether" policy was profoundly unpopular among India's leaders, especially the staunch advocates of industrialization. It was hardly more popular with those in our own government who considered aid to India essential to the survival of that country and to its continued existence as a democracy. I stood almost alone, with only a few concurring advisers, in this fight to slow the pace of U.S. assistance, to persuade the Indians to do more for themselves, and to induce other nations to lend a helping hand. This was one of the most difficult and lonely struggles of my Presidency.*

---

* I read recently in my files a memo prepared in January 1969 by a U.S. government expert on India. Analyzing the food crisis of 1965–1967, he wrote of our lines of action: "That policy was probably as uniquely the President's personal achievement as any that emerged during his administration. For weeks, he held out almost alone against the urgings of all his advisers and, later, against a shrill press."

Those who say a President is the "captive" of his advisers, or vice versa, please note.

Throughout this period I made sure that the grain that was absolutely essential was shipped and arrived on time. But for every shipment we pressed our demands on the Indians and on prosperous countries who could help—Japan, West Germany, and many others. I became an authority on the climate of India. I knew exactly where the rain fell and where it failed to fall in India. I became an expert in the ton-by-ton movement of grain from the wheat fields of Kansas to ports like Calcutta—how many ships were required to move how many tons and how long the operation took. I described myself as "a kind of county agriculture agent with intercontinental clients." One high-ranking State Department official called me "the first Populist ever to arrive on the international scene."

Fortunately, a handful of officials in New Delhi were pressing, in the long-range interests of the Indian people, for exactly the kind of changes I felt were necessary. One was the capable Indian Minister of Food and Agriculture, Chidambara Subramaniam. In November 1965 he and Secretary of Agriculture Orville Freeman met in Rome and worked out a new understanding on Indian agriculture. Freeman made clear our position; Subramaniam saw the problem in similar terms. The agreement, signed on November 25, meant a radical shift in the Indian government's policy, with much greater emphasis on agriculture in India's new Five Year Plan. The Indian government accepted the Rome agreement and announced its new farm program on December 7, 1965. This was the first important direct result of our new policy.

With that strong Indian commitment in hand, I gave Secretary Freeman instructions in a telephone call on the morning of December 11. Move the wheat, I told him. Consider yourself the expediter and throw your weight around as much as necessary to get the job done. I told him to be "the kind of person who would cry when he saw people starving" but who would also find practical ways to "eliminate the causes of hunger and helplessness."

Freeman did a magnificent job. More than any other man, he was responsible for turning my policy into actions that worked. He helped keep millions of Indians alive and helped give them a better future. Like most members of my administration, he disagreed occasionally with my decisions, but once they were made he carried them out with energy and loyalty.

In India the tide began to turn. Some of the ablest young men in the government in New Delhi took jobs in agriculture. Price incentives stirred the farmers to action. The number and scope of irrigation projects and the production of pesticides and farm equipment began to rise, slowly at first, but steadily.

As the principles underlying our future food aid plans took shape, I decided to incorporate them in a special message to Congress. The law permitted me to act on Executive authority. But as a matter of principle, based on long experience, I wanted Congress with me. I wanted it to share an understanding of the problem, to approve the principles of the new policy, and to accept responsibility in its execution. On February 10, 1966, I sent the message with a recommendation that Congress pass a new Food for Freedom program. I suggested increases in our food production, but I also emphasized the principles of self-help and of sharing the burden with other nations.

I said that increasing our aid without regard to what the recipients did for themselves would lead to disaster. Such a program would hurt most those we were trying to help. I proposed that we not take that course. Then I added:

> But candor requires that I warn you the time is not far off when all the combined production, on all of the acres, of all of the agriculturally productive nations, will not meet the food needs of the developing nations —unless present trends are changed.

The Congress discussed and debated my suggestions. Eventually, it adopted most of my principal proposals. The Food for Peace Act of 1966 reached me for signature on November 12. At the signing ceremony at the Ranch in Texas that day, I said that the bill marked "the beginning of one of the most important tasks of our time."

With all its other problems, India faced an important governmental crisis early in 1966. Lal Bahadur Shastri, who became Prime Minister following Nehru's death in 1964, had died suddenly of a heart attack at the Soviet-sponsored peace meeting with the Pakistanis in Tashkent. As his successor the Congress party selected Mrs. Indira Gandhi, daughter of Jawaharlal Nehru, the chief architect of India's independence. I knew something of the problems and pressures this sensitive woman faced as she took the reins of power in her great country. I invited her to Washington and she came late in March. During her visit we had several long, private talks. I sympathized with the new Prime Minister in the heavy burdens she had assumed, and I tried to reinforce her considerable courage.

In our talks on March 28 and 29 I discussed with Prime Minister Gandhi in detail her country's food problem and our considered judgment of the best ways to meet it. She expressed full understanding and support for the principles of self-help and international sharing on which our policy was based. I told her about the special message I was about to send to Congress on emergency food aid for India. I think she particularly appreciated that part of the message which said:

> India is a good and deserving friend. Let it never be said that "bread should be so dear and flesh and blood so cheap" that we turned in indifference from her bitter need.

Congress, thankfully, agreed. A joint resolution supporting U.S. participation in food relief for India came to me for approval on April 19.

But India's torment was far from ended. In 1966 monsoon rains once again were much lighter than usual. The drought persisted, cutting deeply into food production. Stockpiles had been drained the previous year. India's government was placing higher priority on agriculture, as promised, but results that first year came only in areas where the rains were normal. They did not compensate for losses to drought elsewhere.

The new crisis created problems but also, I believed, opportunities. If we went about it in the right way, I thought we could encourage increasingly far-reaching changes in India's farm policy and in the supporting actions of other nations. I knew that our problems with Congress over foreign aid, severe in 1966, would be even more difficult in 1967.

The most critical time for India would be the spring and summer months of 1967, when the poor harvest of 1966 had been used up and the new crop was not yet in. I wanted to use the intervening time to win the necessary support from Congress for what we were trying to accomplish. We held up grain shipments from August to December 1966. In November Secretary Freeman sent several experts from the Department of Agriculture to India to make an independent estimate of the harvest. We also asked them to investigate the possibility of supplementing our wheat shipments with sorghum, which we had in more plentiful supply. Indian authorities resisted this suggestion at first, but in time they found sorghum an important and acceptable addition to wheat.

During this period our policy was the target of a heavy propaganda barrage. Through official and unofficial channels, the Indians pressed us to change our position. Americans who considered themselves India's best friends eagerly joined this effort. In the press and at Washington cocktail parties I was pictured as a heartless man willing to let innocent people starve. *The New York Times* declared in an editorial that our approach was "a serious error." *The Washington Post* ran a five-column criticism of our program, written by an Indian correspondent. His critique suggested that I was doing everything from discouraging Indian democracy to forcing New Delhi to make its own nuclear bombs. Senator George McGovern of South Dakota commented that I had a "negative attitude" and was requiring India to go "begging" for food in a time of drought.

I recognized the emotionalism behind these various allegations and complaints. I realized that only a handful of specialists in the United States and India understood what we were trying to accomplish. But I could not help wishing that those so ready with their opinions would probe a little deeper into the problem, think a little harder, and try to understand that we faced not just a short-range crisis but a possible long-range catastrophe. In any case, I decided I would have to live with the noisy but superficial criticism and do what I believed was right.

In a conversation with Secretary Freeman on November 10, I told him that I was not going to move further unless Congress agreed. The Presidential "giveaway days" are over, I said. We had less food in storage than ever before. I told Freeman that India could get more wheat from Canada and Australia and other producers. I also instructed him to arrange for a group of Congressmen to go to India for an independent survey of the situation. I felt this would result in expert advice and, equally important, would develop additional congressional involvement.

In December Senator Jack Miller of Iowa and Representatives Bob Dole of Kansas and Bob Poage of Texas went to India. Senator Gale McGee of Wyoming was already in India and agreed to join in the fact-finding effort. McGee made a jeep trip through Bihar, one of the most hard-hit areas, and sent in a graphic account. It said in part:

> Barren fields provided mute counterpoint to statistics regarding drought. I am satisfied that it would be difficult to exaggerate [the] magnitude of [the] crisis. For example, CARE estimates [the] minimum emergency feeding requirement [is] three million five hundred thousand meals a day for children and for pregnant and nursing mothers over [an] eight month period.

Just before Christmas I received the recommendations of the congressional group. They suggested that we provide 1.8 million tons of grain on an interim basis to meet demands for February, March, and April. Any additional supplies, they agreed, should be backed by congressional action. I told Freeman, who relayed the recommendation to me at the Ranch, that I would approve half the amount—450,000 tons of wheat and 450,000 tons of other grains, a total of 900,000 tons. I would act on the remaining requirements later. I kept the "short tether" on. No one would starve because of our policies. India would receive the grain needed, but on a month-to-month basis rather than a year-to-year basis.

What happened in the next months, I told Freeman, would depend on two things: what Congress would do and what other nations would do. We would enter a consortium arrangement with other countries, I said, and I suggested that we arrange it through the World Bank or some other multinational agency. I also confided to the Agriculture Secretary that I was losing patience with the extensive pressure campaign being waged in the press.

Meanwhile, we insisted that the Indian government begin an intensive effort to interest other grain producers in its problems. The Indians had achieved a certain amount of success and we heartily encouraged them to continue the effort. Australia announced in mid-December that it was providing 150,000 tons of wheat as a grant to India. The Canadians were loading 100,000 tons and planned to send another 50,000 tons in January. But other nations were turning a deaf ear to India's appeals. The Indians told us that France had informed them that it would gladly sell them 200,000 tons of wheat "on the usual commercial terms."

We clearly needed a system to bring others into the effort. Such cooperation among nations would build habits of cooperation that the world needed in many other fields. On Christmas Eve, 1966, I asked George Woods, President of the World Bank, to take the lead in persuading as many nations as possible to share responsibility for meeting India's critical need for food. Woods quickly agreed.

On January 15, 1967, I sent Eugene Rostow, Under Secretary of State for Political Affairs, on a special round-the-world mission to generate support from other countries. His itinerary began in Japan and ended in Europe. I asked him to make it clear that the United States would do its part but that we expected others to share what constituted a problem for the entire human community. It was no easy job for Woods, Rostow, and others to get cooperation from nations that had never cooperated in special-assistance programs before. But in one way or another, many governments did act with us.

This effort did not involve trivial sums. In 1967 India needed 10 million tons of food grains, which cost roughly $725 million. I was able to report to Congress early in February 1967 that Canada, Australia, and the Soviet Union, as well as the United States, were supplying grain on special terms. India had purchased 200,000 tons with its own scarce foreign exchange. Britain, France, Germany, Japan, and the Scandinavian countries made special contributions in a cooperative plan, for which Rostow won final approval in meetings sponsored by the World Bank in Paris during the month of April. All the nations involved in this joint effort agreed that bolstering India's immediate food needs should not reduce the aid they had agreed earlier to provide to India's program of economic development. With other nations beginning to commit themselves, and with India moving firmly ahead to boost its own farm output, Congress approved our part of the program late in March, and on April 1 I signed the joint resolution on emergency food aid for India.

Our efforts and those of the Indian government ultimately generated assistance from other nations of about $200 million. First, there were the food contributions of the four big grain producers. In addition, Austria, Belgium, France, West Germany, Italy, the Scandinavian countries, the United Kingdom, and Japan joined the enterprise. The effort to educate and persuade other nations that they shared responsibility for food aid succeeded. This experiment led directly to incorporation of the principle in the Food Aid Convention of the International Wheat Agreement—a major step in man's cooperation with his fellow man in meeting and overcoming the hunger in our world.

India's immediate crisis ended in the summer of 1967. There were adequate monsoon rains. India's supply of fertilizer had increased by almost 80 per cent in 1966–1967 over the previous year. Indian farmers were using more fertilizer and pesticides than ever before. They were also beginning to use new high-yield seeds. The result was a bumper crop, the largest in India's history.

The effort had been demanding and strenuous. An average of two ships loaded with grain was required to arrive in India every day for a year. One-fifth of the wheat raised by American farmers was shipped halfway around the world. We sent more than 8 million tons of grain to India in the first year of crisis, and more than 6 million tons in the second year. These quantities were enough to feed 50 million people in the 1965–1966 crisis and 40 million the next year.

As I flew over India on the way from Australia to Rome in December 1967, I thought of all we had been through in this great struggle to make India stronger. From *Air Force One* I sent the following message to Prime Minister Gandhi:

> As I passed over India, my thoughts were much with you. I deeply regret that I was so close and still unable to confer with you. As I looked down at the vast and varied land, I thought of the millions who are struggling to break out of the bonds of poverty, the difficulty of the task, and the courage and spirit of enterprise being brought to it.
>
> I suspect I follow almost as closely as you the course of the rains, the Indian harvest, and new seeds, and the figures on fertilizer application. After the travail of the past two years, I hope and pray your nation will now move firmly forward.

II

Defeating Aggression and Searching for Peace

[*VIETNAM 1965–1967*]

IN THE SUMMER of 1965 I came to the painful conclusion that an independent South Vietnam could survive only if the United States and other nations went to its aid with their own fighting forces. From then until I left the Presidency, we had three principal goals: to insure that aggression did not succeed; to make it possible for the South Vietnamese to build their country and their future in their own way; and to convince Hanoi that working out a peaceful settlement was to the advantage of all concerned. Those three main strands of action—defeating aggression, building a nation, and searching for peace—were tightly braided together in all that we, the other allies, and the Vietnamese tried to accomplish over the next three and a half years.

By the end of 1965 the worst crisis had ended; the downward slide had been stopped. Serious political and economic problems remained in the South, but on the military front things were looking up. There was strong evidence that the strategists in Hanoi hoped to cut South Vietnam in half along a line roughly from Pleiku, in the Central Highlands, eastward to the coast. General Vo Nguyen Giap * had sent in the first regiments of the regular North Vietnamese army into this area late in 1964. Viet Cong units had become increasingly active in the eastern region, and the main east-west highway, Route 19, was unusable because of ambushes and mines.

In August and September South Vietnamese forces and men of the 1st Brigade of our 101st Airborne Division moved into the heart of the threatened area and began to make it secure. In the battle of the Ia Drang Valley in November, the 1st Cavalry Division defeated the cream of the North Vietnamese army. Meanwhile, General Westmoreland was rapidly building

---

*Defense Minister of North Vietnam and his country's best known military figure.

the logistic bases that would support our men in the field. American fighting men had proved that they could operate successfully against guerrilla
forces and regular units of the enemy in the jungle-covered mountains and
swampy lowlands. The confidence of the South Vietnamese was growing.
U.S. forces, which had numbered 75,000 in July, increased to about 184,000
by the end of the year. We felt certain that the South Vietnamese forces,
with our cooperation, could begin to take the offensive in 1966. Clearly,
however, the Communist forces were far from defeated. An estimated 35,000
of their men had been killed and more than 6,000 had been captured during
the year; but heavy infiltration from the North, plus recruitment in the
South, had made up for those losses and had raised the Communist combat
strength to an estimated 221,000. The North Vietnamese were determined to
continue the war.

We had to do what was necessary to resist them. In the meantime, my advisers and I kept searching for some way to bring the war to an end by diplomatic means rather than on the battlefield. Few Americans realize how
intensive—and extensive—that effort was over the years. Only a handful
of my closest advisers knew of all the many attempts we made to get into a
dialogue with Hanoi. The fact is that from 1965 until January 1969 we were
in virtually continuous contact, either directly or through intermediaries,
with leaders in Hanoi or their representatives. Hardly a month passed
throughout that period in which we did not make some effort to open the
gateway to peace. Until March 31, 1968, every attempt we made was ignored
or rejected by the North Vietnamese.

The bombing pause in May 1965 had been a total failure. It produced
nothing, and as usual, the critics shifted ground. The trouble, they insisted,
was that the pause had been too short. If we had just held off a little longer,
we might have obtained results. Over the next few months, we began to hear
the same refrain from Communist governments. Some of them, we knew,
had access to Hanoi's thinking. They assured us that if we stopped the
bombing temporarily, it would "ease the atmosphere" and might lead to a
solution.

In July Secretary McNamara suggested that, once the troop deployments
he was recommending had been completed, we consider making another intensive effort to find a way to peace negotiations. He thought that our effort
should include a bombing pause of considerable length, perhaps six to eight
weeks. By November 1965 McNamara decided that we had reached the
point he had anticipated. He wrote me a long and detailed memo on November 7 setting forth his views. He described the situation in Vietnam as he saw
it and listed the various options open to us. He pointed out that the large
U.S. troop deployments of the previous months had prevented the Com-

munists from inflicting the "serious military defeat" that had been threatened. McNamara was convinced, however, that we would never achieve our desired goals in Vietnam with the force we had there at that time (160,000 Americans in Vietnam and about 50,000 more scheduled to go), and that more men would be needed. He believed that we would also have to step up the campaign of military pressures against the North.

McNamara felt strongly that before we took either of these actions—sending more men and exerting more pressure on the North—we should try to find a way to peace, using a bombing halt to reinforce our diplomacy. He was persuaded that a bombing pause would give Ho Chi Minh a chance to move toward a solution if he wished to do so. If the pause failed to achieve that goal, McNamara argued, it would at least demonstrate our genuine desire for a peaceful settlement and thereby temper the criticism we were getting at home and abroad. He also thought that it would be easier for us to carry out necessary additional military measures in the future if we first made a serious peace move.

My first reaction to McNamara's memo was one of deep skepticism. The May pause had failed, and I thought that Hanoi would probably view a new cessation in the bombing as a sign of weakness. My skepticism was shared by McGeorge Bundy and even more by Secretary of State Dean Rusk. Rusk pointed out that Hanoi had given no sign of interest in a reasonable settlement, and he was convinced that a bombing pause would have no positive result at that time. Rusk also believed that leaders in Hanoi might try to make it hard for us to resume bombing by dangling the possibility of talks before us, talks they had no intention of making into serious negotiations. He felt that a bombing halt would have a bad effect if it led only to prolonged talks while the enemy continued the war full force. Rusk felt strongly, however, that we should continue to try to probe Hanoi's outlook through diplomatic contacts. If the North Vietnamese gave some firm sign that they would lower the level of fighting or enter into serious negotiations, he said, we then should end the bombing.

By coincidence, the same day that Secretary McNamara was writing his memo on a bombing halt Ambassador Lodge in Saigon was preparing his personal assessment of the Vietnam situation. In his report to me Lodge wrote:

> An end of bombing of the North with no other *quid pro quo* than the opening of negotiations would load the dice in favor of the communists and demoralize the GVN. It would in effect leave the communists free to devastate the South with impunity while we tie our hands in the North.

General Westmoreland, our Pacific commander Admiral Sharp, and the Joint Chiefs of Staff all went on record in opposition to a halt in the bombing on military grounds.

The remainder of November and the first weeks of December were a period of widespread diplomatic probing and of comprehensive debate and discussion at the highest levels of the administration. Increasingly, diplomats whose governments were in contact with Hanoi were making optimistic forecasts as to the outcome of a bombing pause. At lunch one day late in November, Soviet Ambassador Anatoly Dobrynin told McGeorge Bundy that if there could be a pause of "twelve to twenty days," we could be assured that there would be "intense diplomatic activity." A Hungarian diplomat advised Secretary Rusk that, in his opinion, "a few weeks would be enough." No one was offering any ironclad guarantees, but their overall tone was hopeful.

Inside our government, the weight of opinion increased gradually in favor of a pause. McNamara was a strong advocate. Mac Bundy moved to uphold his position. George Ball was an outspoken supporter of the idea. Secretary Rusk finally decided that, all things considered, it might be worth the risk. The top civilian echelons of the State and Defense departments were solidly in favor of the proposal. Resistance centered mainly in the military services and in our Embassy in Saigon. I had grave doubts about a pause, but I was reluctantly moving toward acceptance of the risks I believed were involved.

Rusk, McNamara, and Bundy came to my ranch in Texas on December 7, 1965, to argue their case. I listened carefully to all the evidence they had assembled and to the arguments they made. I finally pointed out to them one thing that was troubling me deeply. If we should stop for a while and Hanoi did nothing in return, I said, would we not have trouble resuming the bombing? All three men assured me that if Hanoi made no move in response, the whole world would understand our decision to renew the bombing campaign. Later in our discussion I raised the question again. Are you sure it will be that easy? I asked. Again they argued that they did not see this as a serious problem. As it turned out, of course, we received little credit for stopping the bombing and heavy criticism for renewing it.

On December 18 I met in the Cabinet Room with some of my chief advisers.* I had asked two old and trusted friends from outside the Executive branch to join us for discussion. They were Clark Clifford and Associate Justice Abe Fortas, men whose experience and intelligence I valued highly. I wanted to review all the arguments, all the pros and cons. I began the discussion by saying: "The military says a month's pause would undo all we've done." McNamara reacted quickly: "That's baloney."

"I don't think so," I said. "I disagree. I think it contains serious military risks. It is inaccurate to say suspension of bombing carries no military risks." McNamara and Bundy both pointed out that "we can resume bombing at any time."

* Present at the meeting were Rusk, McNamara, Mac Bundy, Ball, and Alex Johnson.

"If we're confronted with 60,000 or 100,000 more men, and we didn't anticipate it, that's an error," I said. Secretary Rusk said he doubted that the pause would last a month, "unless we are well on the way toward peace."

"I agree," I said. "It could be of very short duration." I asked the Secretary of State to tell me what he thought would be accomplished by a pause in the bombing. His first concern, Rusk said, was American opinion. He was convinced that our people would do what had to be done in a war situation if they felt that there was no alternative. We had to be able to demonstrate to them that we had done everything we could to find the way to a peaceful settlement.

"Haven't we done this?" I asked. "To my satisfaction," Rusk answered, "but perhaps not to that of the American people.

"Second," Rusk continued, "it is our deepest national purpose to achieve our goals by peace, not war. If there is one chance in ten, or twenty, that a step of this sort could lead to a settement on [the basis of] the Geneva agreements and the 17th parallel, I would take it." Finally, the Secretary of State said that he thought a bombing pause would place the responsibility for continuing the war where it rightly belonged, on Hanoi and on those who were saying that only our bombing of the North stood in the way of peace.

McNamara agreed with Rusk's arguments. In addition, he felt that there was no assurance of military success in Vietnam and that we had to find a diplomatic solution. I asked him whether he meant that there was no guarantee of success no matter what we did militarily. "That's right," he answered. "We have been too optimistic. One chance in three, or two in three, is my estimate."

After all the main arguments, for and against, had been placed on the table, I turned to Justice Fortas and asked him to summarize the views presented and to give me an evaluation of them. Fortas said that he thought the key to the matter was whether other governments with influence in Hanoi would use a bombing pause to encourage the North Vietnamese to respond with deeds to our initiative. He said that he had heard no evidence that they would and, therefore, the net result would be negative, he thought. We would receive little credit for trying to find peace and failing. We would also face renewed pressure for drastic action if the peace move failed. On balance, then, Fortas believed that the arguments that had been made were not sufficient to justify a pause at that time.

I turned to Clark Clifford. He had been through the Korean War years with President Truman and the Bay of Pigs with President Kennedy, as well as many other periods of crisis in government, and I valued his opinions. Clifford said that he had tried to figure out the circumstances under which North Vietnam would talk peace. He thought that would happen only when the leaders in Hanoi believed that they were not going to win the war in South Vietnam.

"I don't believe they are at that stage now," he said. "I think they believe they are not losing. They are sending large numbers of men down. They have the example of the French before them. They believe that ultimately the United States will tire of this and go home, and North Vietnam will prevail. Until they know they are not going to win, they will not talk."

Clifford also said he felt the President and the government had talked enough about peace. "Any objective citizen knows the government's position. Talk of peace is interpreted as a sign of weakness." He said that he thought North Vietnam would view any pause in the bombing as our response to the protest demonstrators in our country and around the world. Clifford suggested that the chances of success were too slim and that failure would make the bombing halt look like a "gimmick." The time might come, he said, when a pause would be valuable. That would be when we had reason to think it would succeed in moving toward peace. "Then, and only then, would I do it," he said.

The arguments of two of our country's best legal minds were cogent, clear, and effective. Their opinions carried weight with me, and I was reluctant to overrule the judgment of these old friends and intelligent observers. But the opposing arguments were equally persuasive. This was another of those 51–49 decisions that regularly reach the President's desk and keep him awake late at night.

I left that four-and-a-half-hour meeting still weighing the advantages and disadvantages, but I was inclined to try a pause, at least a short one. If there was a chance, however remote, that stopping the bombing might open a road to peace, I was prepared to take a few risks. I knew too that I faced a serious decision regarding sending more men to Vietnam. I wanted to explore every possible avenue of settlement before we undertook additional military measures.

We had already agreed with our South Vietnamese allies on a thirty-hour truce, including a halt in the bombing of the North, beginning on Christmas Eve, 1965. We decided to extend that suspension several days, and Ambassador Lodge won the Saigon government's agreement. Two days after Christmas I asked Secretary Rusk to tell our Embassy in Saigon that I had decided to extend the bombing pause "for several more days, possibly into the middle of next week." The South Vietnamese government again agreed. We informed our other allies in the Pacific and several additional governments, including the Russians. We also advised UN Secretary General U Thant. I wanted to be sure that Hanoi knew what was happening and understood that we were hoping for some sign of reciprocal restraint in lowering the level of hostilities.

I wrote personal letters to many heads of state and government leaders describing our position and underlining our desire for peace. Vice President Humphrey, who attended the inauguration of the new President of the

Philippines and later went to the funeral of India's Prime Minister Shastri, conveyed our stand to a number of government leaders, including Soviet Chairman Kosygin, who also attended Shastri's funeral. Secretary Rusk talked with numerous Ambassadors and foreign ministers, both in Washington and in foreign capitals. Ambassador Averell Harriman visited Warsaw, Belgrade, and many other capitals to describe our views. Ambassador Goldberg did the same in Rome, Paris, and London, as well as at the United Nations. G. Mennen Williams, Assistant Secretary of State for African Affairs, discussed the matter with African leaders. Tom Mann, then our top man on Latin American affairs, conveyed our position to governments to the south. Our basic message, transmitted through these various channels, was to call attention to the halt in the bombing of the North and to make clear that similar restraint by Hanoi would be welcome and would influence our future actions.

This was one of the most widespread diplomatic campaigns of my Presidency, and it was criticized for that very reason—because it was so extensive and so well publicized. But we wanted to overlook no opportunity for peace, and we wanted the world to be informed. The Communists were using every possible channel of communication—propaganda, diplomacy, gossip, interviews, and conversations—as well as every forum from the United Nations to the world's teahouses to spread their line. But it seemed that in the eyes of American and foreign critics the United States could only do either too much or too little.

During this period of intense and open diplomatic activity, we did not abandon the channels of "quiet diplomacy." On December 28 we sent a message to our Ambassador in Burma, Henry A. Byroade, instructing him to contact the North Vietnamese Ambassador in Rangoon immediately and, through him, to inform the North Vietnamese directly of the bombing halt. He was also directed to say: "If your government will now reciprocate by making a serious contribution toward peace, it would obviously have a favorable effect on the possibility of further extending the suspension." In the absence of Hanoi's Ambassador, Byroade delivered our message to the North Vietnamese Consul General, who said that he would send it to Hanoi immediately.

In the middle of January we delivered the same message to the North Vietnamese Embassy in Moscow. We also urged Hanoi to enter into private and direct talks with us so that together we could find a way to work out a peaceful settlement. Hanoi's only immediate answer was to say that we had no right to bomb North Vietnam in the first place. Once again, the North Vietnamese insisted that we accept their four-point plan—including withdrawal of all American forces—as the only basis for peace. One week later the same message came back to us through the North Vietnamese Embassy in Burma. North Vietnam's envoy told us that there could be a settlement in Vietnam "only when the United States government has accepted the four-point stand of the government of the Democratic Republic of Vietnam" and had "proved this by actual deeds." In other words, Hanoi was not interested in negotiating; it was demanding a settlement on its own terms.

In my State of the Union message on January 12, 1966, I devoted a great deal of time to the problem of Vietnam. I explained why we were there, and why we were determined to find a reasonable settlement that would let the South Vietnamese decide their own future and govern themselves in freedom. Concerning our search for peace, I said:

> Since Christmas your government has labored again, with imagination and endurance, to remove any barrier to peaceful settlement. For twenty days now we and our Vietnamese allies have dropped no bombs in North Vietnam.
>
> Able and experienced spokesmen have visited, in behalf of America, more than forty countries. We have talked to more than a hundred governments, all one hundred thirteen that we have relations with, and some that we don't. We have talked to the United Nations and we have called upon all of its members to make any contribution that they can toward helping obtain peace. . . .
>
> We have also made it clear—from Hanoi to New York—that there are no arbitrary limits to our search for peace. We stand by the Geneva agreements of 1954 and 1962. We will meet at any conference table, we will discuss any proposals—four points or fourteen or forty—and we will consider the views of any group. We will work for a ceasefire now or once discussions have begun. We will respond if others reduce their use of force, and we will withdraw our soldiers once South Vietnam is securely guaranteed the right to shape its own future.
>
> We have said all this, and we have asked—and hoped—and we have waited for a response.
>
> So far, we have received no response to prove either success or failure. . . .

On January 28 Radio Hanoi broadcast the text of a letter that Ho Chi Minh had sent to a number of heads of government and others "interested in the Vietnam situation." In it, the North Vietnamese leader denounced our "so-called search for peace." He accused us of being "deceitful" and "hypocritical." He insisted that we pull all our troops out of Vietnam and that we accept the Communist-run National Liberation Front as "the sole genuine representative of the people of South Vietnam." The choice was either peace on North Vietnam's terms or no peace at all.

Throughout the pause in the bombing, Hanoi continued to rush men and supplies toward the demilitarized zone and into the supply lines through Laos, which were known as the Ho Chi Minh Trail. North Vietnam's actions, and its words, once again said "no" to peace. It was obvious that nothing "good" had happened, as diplomats friendly to Hanoi had forecast;

nor was anything good going to happen. After consulting with leaders of Congress and with the National Security Council, I decided to resume bombing on January 31. On that same day Hanoi's final answer to our diplomatic moves came through the Rangoon channel. It repeated almost word for word what Ho Chi Minh had said in his much-publicized letter.

A word about the bombing is in order here. First, in spite of reports that gave the opposite impression, the vast majority of our airmen made strenuous efforts to avoid civilian casualties. They were not totally successful, it is true, and that was a constant source of sorrow to me. But they tried, and their orders were clear. Our attacks were made against military and industrial targets which increased the enemy's ability to carry the war south. Second, I was always convinced that bombing was less important to a successful outcome in Vietnam than what was done militarily on the ground in the South. As Mac Bundy * wrote me two years after he left the White House:

> The bombing has never been the most important element in our military effort in Vietnam, and the administration has never accepted the view of some military men that the bombing campaign could be decisive.

However, I was convinced that our air strikes reduced considerably both the amount of steel that the enemy had to throw at our men and the number of troops and weapons the enemy could make available to do the throwing.

Among bombing critics, one line of argument claimed that Hanoi had decided precisely the number of men and the quantity of war matériel the regime planned to put into the South. If we cut that down by 20 per cent through our bombing, the North Vietnamese would simply pour 20 per cent more into the top of the funnel. I do not believe wars are fought in so mechanical a way, by the North Vietnamese or anybody else. Down to their maximum effort at Tet in 1968, the North Vietnamese were trying to put every man and every ton of supplies they could spare into the South, consistent of course with their own requirements for defense against air attacks, for repairs of roads and bridges, and for the basic needs of their economy. Every man and every ton of supplies we stopped, or caused North Vietnam to divert to air defense, was to the good.

Naturally, we were hit by a steady barrage of demands, from Hanoi and

---

* Bundy resigned on February 28, 1966, to assume the presidency of the Ford Foundation. He was replaced on April 1, 1966, by Walt W. Rostow, who had served since 1962 as Counselor of the Department of State and Chairman of the State Department's Policy Planning Council.

the whole propaganda apparatus of the Communist world, to stop the bombing altogether. The cry was picked up by some of our friends abroad and, with increasing intensity, by a few of our own citizens. These demands were generally accompanied by the warning that only a total and permanent bombing halt offered any chance for starting serious talks. Most people forgot, or ignored, this central fact: We had stopped the bombing, not once or twice, but eight different times from 1965 to the beginning of 1968. Five other times we had ruled out attacks on military targets in or around Hanoi and Haiphong for extended periods.* The net result of all these bombing pauses was zero. Indeed, it was less than zero for us, because the enemy used every pause to strengthen its position, hastily pushing men and supplies and equipment down the roads of North Vietnam for massive infiltration into the South.

The conflict in Vietnam has been very different from any other war. It included elements of the Korean War, of the Huk Rebellion in the Philippines, of the Greek civil war, yet it was unlike any of them. Our goal was not to destroy the enemy's army on its home ground, nor did we try to eliminate the enemy's dictatorial regime. This was a war of no fixed front. The "enemy" might be two or three divisions at one time, as at Khe Sanh, or two or three armed men sneaking into a village at night to murder the village chief. It was a war of subversion, terror, and assassination, of propaganda, economic disruption, and sabotage. It was a political war, an economic war, and a fighting war—all at the same time.

In spite of the fact that television screens, for the first time in history, brought all the horrors of war into the living rooms of America, I think that the American people never had a real chance to understand the Vietnam conflict in all its dimensions. There were many reasons for this failure in communications. Complex problems always have trouble competing with oversimplifications. Economic development and the building of political institutions rarely get the same attention in the press or on television as the violence of war. Nor is the average American reporter or reader nearly as interested in what the Vietnamese are doing as in what Americans are doing.

But the Vietnamese themselves, in Saigon and in Hanoi, knew very well the kind of war it was. The Communists recognized that cutting off the rice supply to a district town could be as disruptive as an attack by three battalions. They knew that killing one able village chief could do as much damage as wiping out a squad of soldiers. They were aware that effective propaganda could have more impact than a division of troops. Throughout

---

* For a list of the bombing pauses, see Appendix, p. 578.

the war, and especially after the fall of the Diem government, the Viet Cong and North Vietnamese were not satisfied with trying to destroy the military forces that opposed them in the South. They attempted in every way possible to disrupt the economic life of the country. Through propaganda and terror, they worked daily at keeping the political life of the South in turmoil. Until the introduction of American combat forces into Vietnam in the summer of 1965, the downward slide was not restricted to the military arena. The South Vietnamese economy was increasingly disrupted, and the political front came close to chaos.

Putting American fighting men into the battle turned the military tide and led to a strong improvement in South Vietnamese morale. With that came a measure of political stability that the battle-weary country had not known for two years. The military government under General Thieu and Prime Minister Ky reacted as few observers thought it would, or could. The South Vietnamese leaders began to work for the economic improvement of their country. They also developed a blueprint for political development. Meanwhile, they continued to lead their armed forces in the fight against Communist aggression. Prime Minister Ky sounded the theme of their struggle in a "state of the nation" report to the Armed Forces Congress on January 15, 1966. He set three primary goals for his country and for the government: to defeat the enemy and to pacify and rebuild the countryside; to stabilize the economy; and to build a democracy. He advanced specific programs to help achieve each objective. In the political field he pledged to develop a constitution for popular approval in the fall and to hold elections for a new national government in 1967.

As I read the Prime Minister's report, I felt encouraged. I wondered, of course, whether the South Vietnamese were not trying to do too much in a short time. We Americans had required a good many years *after* our revolution to build the institutions of government. This young Asian country was trying to develop democratic forms, to build an economy, and to fight a war for survival all at the same time. I did not know whether the South Vietnamese could do it. I knew they could never do it to the satisfaction of those who were always ready to criticize the Vietnamese people for almost everything they did or did not do. But they were trying—that was the important thing. I was determined to help them in any way possible.

On January 31, 1966, the day we decided to resume bombing of the North, a member of my staff sent me a memo suggesting that a meeting be held in Honolulu with the South Vietnamese leaders, with special emphasis given to the political and economic future of their country. I had been heartened by the South Vietnamese government's new action program, and I thought that the idea of a Honolulu conference had merit. I asked McGeorge Bundy to consult with Secretary Rusk and to make the necessary arrangements if all concerned thought it would be constructive. They agreed, and we invited the South Vietnamese leaders to a conference in Hawaii on February 7–8.

The two Vietnamese leaders and their principal aides arrived in Honolulu on the afternoon of February 6. I went to the airport to welcome them to the United States. Our first formal meeting took place the next morning at Pacific Command Headquarters.* I was impressed, as I think every American at the long conference table in Admiral Sharp's headquarters was, as I listened to the Vietnamese describing their hopes for their country and their countrymen's hopes for themselves. Ky spoke candidly of their problems, their mistakes, their setbacks. But he spoke confidently of their plans, their goals, and their determination to go ahead with political development in spite of the risks.

"We were deluding ourselves," Ky said, "with the idea that our weakness could not be remedied while we were fighting a war. We said that once the aggressors were driven from our land we would turn to our political and social defects. It has taken a long time to realize that we will not completely drive out the aggressor until we make a start at eliminating these political and social defects. We must be indestructible, not vulnerable."

Later he said: "A program for a better society can be established and launched by any type of government, Communist or non-Communist, dictatorial or democratic. But such a program cannot be carried forward for long if it is not administered by a really democratic government, one which is put into office by the people themselves and which has the confidence of the people."

After the opening session, the principal advisers from both delegations divided into smaller specialized groups, some to discuss ways to find a path to negotiations, others to consider how to make pacification and rural development more effective. Some American and Vietnamese specialists studied ways to stabilize and strengthen the economy, and others discussed steps to improve health and education in Vietnam. At our final meeting on the morning of February 8, the principal conferees reported on plans for their respective sectors. I believe everyone at that meeting felt that we all had a better understanding of the problems we faced and of what needed to be done to make progress. I remember Ambassador Lodge saying: "We have moved ahead here today in the fight to improve the lot of the little man at the grassroots. That is what this is all about."

I told my colleagues that I thought we should get together again in four to six months to review what had been accomplished. I made it clear to my Cabinet officers that I wanted to see progress, not just reports. "We don't

---

* Attending with me were Rusk, McNamara, Secretary of Agriculture Freeman, Secretary of Health, Education, and Welfare Gardner, Mac Bundy, AID Director Bell, and several members of my staff and technical experts. Also present at the meeting were Ambassador Lodge, General Westmoreland, and members of our Mission in Saigon.

want to talk about it," I said. "We want to do something about it." I read a sentence from a draft of the planned communiqué: "The President pledges he will dispatch teams of experts."

"Well," I said, "we better do something besides dispatching. They should get out there. We are going to train health personnel. How many health personnel? You don't want to be like the fellow who was playing poker. When he made a big bet they called him and said: 'What have you got?' He said: 'Aces,' and they asked: 'How many?' He said: 'One aces.'

"We have talked about training personnel—for health, for education, for other things. When we come back and check and I ask how many we have trained, I don't want you to say: 'One personnel.' "

After our meeting, we issued a joint statement called the Declaration of Honolulu. In the first part of the declaration, the government of Vietnam stated its principal goals:

1. We must defeat the Viet Cong and those illegally fighting with them on our soil. . . .
2. We are dedicated to the eradication of social injustice among our people. . . .
3. We must establish and maintain a stable, viable economy and build a better material life for our people. . . .
4. We must build true democracy for our land and for our people. . . .

Under the last point, the Vietnamese leaders pledged to have a constitution written "in the months ahead"; to present it to the people for discussion and suggested changes; to submit the final constitution to the people in a referendum; and to elect a new government under the constitution.

At the end of their portion of the declaration, the Vietnamese leaders opened the way for reconciliation with those then fighting under Hanoi's direction. They said:

> To those future citizens of a free, democratic South Vietnam now fighting with the Viet Cong, we take this occasion to say come and join in this national revolutionary adventure:
>
> come safely to join us through the Open Arms program *;
>
> stop killing your brothers, sisters, their elders, their children;
>
> come and work through constitutional democracy to build together that life of dignity, freedom and peace those in the North would deny the people of Vietnam.

In our portion of the declaration, we promised to support the goals and programs the Vietnamese had advanced.

---

* The Open Arms (Chieu Hoi) program offered amnesty, job training, and other incentives to Communist soldiers and political agents who surrendered to the South Vietnamese authorities.

As a result of the Honolulu conference, the government of Vietnam under Thieu and Ky was pledged to an all-out effort to win "the other war" in their country. We were equally pledged to help them in that struggle. I ordered a reorganization of our Mission in Saigon to reflect this new emphasis on nonmilitary programs. At the meeting in Hawaii, I selected our Deputy Ambassador to Vietnam, William J. Porter,* to take charge of this drive. During the next month I established a special office in the White House headed by Robert W. Komer of the National Security Council staff. As my special assistant, he coordinated and supervised Washington support for pacification and other nonmilitary campaigns.

From the Honolulu meeting I flew to Los Angeles, where I met Vice President Humphrey. I had wanted him to attend the Honolulu conference but had decided we should not both be away from the mainland at the same time. I had asked him to meet me in California so that we could discuss the conference results. At Los Angeles I asked him to go to Honolulu to join our Vietnamese allies and fly with them to Saigon for a firsthand look at the situation there. From Vietnam the Vice President went at my request to a number of other Asian capitals. I wanted him to explain to these other free nations what had been done at Honolulu and what these measures meant, and to ask for their continued support.

I returned from the Hawaii meeting refreshed and confident. "The road ahead may be long and may be difficult," I told the reporters, but "we shall fight the battle against aggression in Vietnam . . . we shall fight the battle for peace . . . we shall prevail."

After the thirty-seven-day bombing pause, my principal advisers unanimously agreed that only one development would end the war—Hanoi's conviction that North Vietnam could not win militarily. Clearly the North Vietnamese leaders had not yet reached that conclusion. Their forces had suffered heavy losses in 1965, yet their total strength had grown as a result of increased infiltration and intensive recruitment. Our reports showed that infiltration was continuing at a high level in the first months of 1966.

Under the military rule of thumb—that in a guerrilla war the defending forces need ten men for every guerrilla—more than 2 million men would be needed to cope with the Viet Cong–North Vietnamese forces then in the South. My military advisers and I were certain that we had lowered that commonly accepted ratio—through heavier firepower, increased mobility, the use of airpower both as a weapon and for transport, and other factors. But we knew that the defense still needed considerably more manpower than the offense in this kind of fighting. The South Vietnamese had about 600,000

* Porter had replaced U. Alexis Johnson in 1965.

men under arms, half in their regular armed forces and half in regional forces, popular forces, combat police, and other units. U.S. strength had grown to about 184,000 at the end of 1965. South Korea had sent its crack Capital Division and a marine brigade, a total of about 21,000. The Australians had assigned a combat battalion, which along with support forces, an air unit, and military advisers brought their total commitment to about 1,500 men. A New Zealand artillery battery was operating with the Australians. Thus the total allied force numbered slightly more than 800,000— a ratio of less than 4 to 1.

In July 1965, when we decided to send the first large body of American combat forces into Vietnam, military planners in the Pentagon and on the staff of the Joint Chiefs were thinking in terms of assigning approximately 175,000 men in 1965 and an additional 100,000 in 1966. By the end of the year they were urging that the total be 400,000 rather than 275,000. I held off any decision on sending additional troops until we had tried the long bombing pause, but after January 31, 1966, the need for action was apparent. Throughout February and March we discussed the need, and our capability, for additional troop deployments. Secretary McNamara had gone over the matter with great care with General Westmoreland and Admiral Sharp, as well as with the Joint Chiefs. By early April they were prepared to make a firm recommendation to me.

Meanwhile, Vice President Humphrey had returned from his Asian tour with good news. The South Koreans were thinking of sending an additional army division plus a regiment of marines to Vietnam. That would boost their total strength to about 45,000 men. The Australians were planning to triple the size of their commitment, raising their force to 4,500 men. The Philippine government was preparing to send an engineer battalion with its own security force attached, numbering about 2,000 men in all.

Against the background of this increased effort by the allies and the South Vietnamese—as well as the expanded activities of the North Vietnamese and Viet Cong—I approved an increase in the American effort. The plan worked out by McNamara, the Joint Chiefs, and General Westmoreland called for raising the total level of our forces in all services to about 383,500 by the end of 1966 and to 425,000 by the middle of 1967. With that force, General Westmoreland was confident that the allies could not only meet the increasing threat from the North Vietnamese and Viet Cong; they could also increasingly move to the offensive.

Our deepest worry at that time was not the military threat of the Communists, but the prospect of another major political crisis in South Vietnam. This crucial period began on March 10, with the decision of the military directorate to remove General Nguyen Chanh Thi, the independent-minded commander of I Corps. Prime Minister Ky and his fellow generals regarded Thi as insubordinate, but Thi was a popular officer, especially in central Vietnam, where he had been born. Many military and civilian officials in that region owed him their appointments. He was also a minor hero to some Vietnamese because of his role in the unsuccessful coup against the Diem government in 1960.

Meanwhile, the so-called militant Buddhists and their spiritual leader and main tactician, a monk named Tri Quang, were spoiling for a new confrontation with the government. They had been a key factor in the toppling of Diem and of several succeeding governments, and they were eager to do the same to the Thieu-Ky administration. I always believed that if Tri Quang and some of his principal followers were not actually pro-Communist, at least their movement had been deeply penetrated by Hanoi's agents.

The day after Thi's removal an estimated 1,500 people demonstrated in his support in Danang. Similar protests were carried out the following day in Hué and other cities. In Saigon Chairman Tam Chau of the Buddhist Institute held a press conference. He made many demands on the government, including the restoration of General Thi. Within a few days the Buddhists had expanded their demands, calling for the removal of several generals, then the end of the entire military government, and finally immediate elections. Ambassador Lodge, reporting on the Buddhists' call for prompt elections, was conscious of the dangers. He wrote:

> The Ky Government is moving toward constitutional democracy just as fast as the traffic will bear. To hold elections without a constitution, without electoral laws, with the inescapable minimum amount of public information is to court a wildly irresponsible mess.

After trying for two months to work out some solution, including major concessions to the protesters, the South Vietnamese authorities decided that the situation was too serious to be allowed to continue. On May 14, without informing the U.S. Embassy, the government sent its forces into Danang to restore control. A month later government authority was restored in Hué with a minimum of force. The "struggle movement" against the government was largely ended.

Despite the disruption and confusion caused by the Buddhists' protests, the South Vietnamese government stuck to its promises and moved forward on the political track it had promised to follow. The Election Law Drafting Committee met in May, and by June 7 submitted to the government proposed rules for electing a constituent assembly. The national election was held on September 11 to select the 117 members of the assembly who would write the new constitution. Though the Viet Cong tried to disrupt the election, more than 80 per cent of the registered voters went to the polls. As Ambassador Lodge reported:

> For the Vietnamese to have voted in such large numbers in the face of

terrorism shows their willingness to defy the Viet Cong in order to take a step which they believe is a step forward for their country. . . .

In October I flew across the Pacific once more for a meeting with the South Vietnamese leaders. President Ferdinand Marcos of the Philippines had invited them and the heads of governments whose troops were fighting in Vietnam to meet in Manila for a review of the war and of nonmilitary programs of development, and for a broader purpose—to consider the future of Asia. General Thieu and Prime Minister Ky represented the Republic of Vietnam at the conference. President Chung Hee Park came from Korea, and Prime Ministers Harold Holt from Australia, Keith Holyoake from New Zealand, and Thanom Kittikachorn from Thailand. After two days of intensive meetings and consultations, we issued three statements. One, called Goals of Freedom, stated:

> We, the seven nations gathered in Manila, declare our unity, our resolve, and our purpose in seeking together the goals of freedom in Vietnam and in the Asian and Pacific areas. They are:
>
> 1. To be free from aggression.
> 2. To conquer hunger, illiteracy, and disease.
> 3. To build a region of security, order, and progress.
> 4. To seek reconciliation and peace throughout Asia and the Pacific.

The second Manila document was a communiqué. The portion of it that received the most attention was a declaration by the South Vietnamese government that it would ask its allies to withdraw their forces as soon as peace was restored. In response, the United States and the other nations which had troops in Vietnam declared that "allied forces are in the Republic of Vietnam because that country is the object of aggression." We added:

> They shall be withdrawn, after close consultation, as the other side withdraws its forces to the North, ceases infiltration, and the level of violence thus subsides. Those forces will be withdrawn as soon as possible and not later than six months after the above conditions have been fulfilled.

The decision to make this specific statement on troop withdrawals stemmed mainly from a talk I had had with Soviet Foreign Minister Andrei Gromyko two weeks earlier. He had called on me at the White House on October 10, and we had discussed a number of problems, including Vietnam. During that talk Gromyko noted that our previous statements had been "very general" on the matter of withdrawals, and he thought a more specific statement would be useful. I told the Soviet diplomat that we meant what we had said about not wanting to retain bases in Vietnam or to keep our men there any longer than was absolutely necessary. I said I would consider his suggestion and would take steps to make our position unmistakably clear. This was in mind when I suggested strongly to my colleagues at Manila that we make our stand on troop withdrawals as specific as possible. The South Vietnamese leaders and the other allies agreed, and we worked out the phrasing that went into our communiqué.

One purpose of the Manila conference was to give the South Vietnamese an opportunity to describe directly to us what they saw as their main problems and what their plans were for meeting them. The allies also had to consider ways by which they could help the South Vietnamese more effectively on every front—militarily, economically, socially, politically. But it was also important, I believed, for these seven members of the Asian and Pacific family to look ahead to the future of the region as a whole and to what it could become if we all worked together. This was the reason for the third statement of the Manila conference, the Declaration of Peace and Progress in Asia and the Pacific. I mention this statement because it contained the principal elements of the foreign policy of my administration. If there was a Johnson Doctrine, these were its cornerstones: opposition to aggression; war against poverty, illiteracy, and disease; economic, social, and cultural cooperation on a regional basis; searching for reconciliation and peace.* The concluding paragraph of the declaration ended with this statement:

> We do not threaten the sovereignty or territorial integrity of our neighbors, whatever their ideological alignment. We ask only that this be reciprocated. The quarrels and ambitions of ideology and the painful frictions arising from national fears and grievances should belong to the past. Aggression rooted in them must not succeed. We shall play our full part in creating an environment in which reconciliation becomes possible, for in the modern world men and nations have no choice but to learn to live together as brothers.

That is what we wanted in Vietnam, and it summed up what I wanted to see take shape in Asia. These were goals I wanted to help achieve in every region and on every continent. But I knew that we would never see that day if Vietnam and other small countries fell one by one to aggressors; if we turned our back on trouble every time it arose; if we thought only of our own comfort and prosperity; if we concentrated solely on our own domestic problems, however urgent or acute.

From the very beginning of my Presidency I did everything I could to make one fact clear: that the United States sought only a peaceful settlement

---

* For fuller discussion of this policy see Chapters 10, 14, 16, and 20.

to the turmoil that had raged in Vietnam for so many years. Until January 20, 1969, the search for a settlement continued. We did everything we could to inform Hanoi that we were ready to pull our forces out as soon as an honorable and lasting arrangement for peace could be reached. We explored every avenue that offered the faintest hope of leading to useful talks with the enemy.*

At times we were in direct contact with Hanoi's representatives. At other times we reached them through a third government. In some cases, private citizens were encouraged to pursue contacts that we thought might lead to serious talks. We were in touch regularly with Hanoi either directly or indirectly from early 1965 to the opening of the Paris peace talks in May 1968.†

Then too there was never any shortage of self-appointed "mediators" who, without our encouragement and often even our knowledge, tried to make their own contacts. I did not question the good intentions and sincerity of many of these free-lance "peacemakers," but I do think many of their spontaneous efforts may have harmed more than they helped. I know they often did more to confuse issues than to clarify them. We could never be certain whether we were hearing accurate reports of what Hanoi had said—or what Hanoi wanted us to hear—or whether we were hearing wishful thinking about what Hanoi might be willing to do under various circumstances.

As I look back, I think that we perhaps tried too hard to spell out our honest desire for peace. At one time or another we were in touch with virtually every government or other diplomatic source that might have been able to make contact with the North Vietnamese. Time and time again we passed along our views: We are ready to talk in private or in public; we will meet quietly in any capital; we will stop the bombing if you will do something on your part to lower the level of fighting. These numerous appeals through so many channels may well have convinced the North Vietnamese that we wanted peace at any price.

Never once was there a clear sign that Ho Chi Minh had a genuine interest in bargaining for peace. Never, through any channel or from any serious contact, did we receive any message that differed significantly from the tough line that Hanoi repeated over and over again: Stop all the bombing, get out of Vietnam, and accept our terms for peace. The North Vietnamese never gave the slightest sign that they were ready to consider reducing the Communists' half of the war or to negotiate seriously the terms of a fair peace settlement.

* There is space here for only a brief description of the activities, diplomatic and other, that engaged us so unprofitably for so long. For a list of the major peace efforts by the United States and others, see Appendix, pp. 579–89.

† A chart showing the number and duration of contacts with the North Vietnamese is in Appendix, pp. 590–91.

In the summer of 1966 Ambassador Lodge was approached in Saigon by Janusz Lewandowski, the Polish member of the International Control Commission, who had just visited Hanoi. Talks began. Those exchanges, reported in secret cables under the code name Marigold, continued for six months. In the course of these talks Lodge gave Lewandowski a full description of our position regarding a peaceful settlement. After still another trip to Hanoi, the Polish diplomat gave our Ambassador a draft of ten points which he said covered his understanding of the U.S. position. He said that a representative of the North Vietnamese would meet with a U.S. official in Warsaw, where we could "confirm" the ten points.

We asked Ambassador Lodge whether he had covered with Lewandowski our willingness to halt all bombing *after* we had come to an agreement with Hanoi on the steps each side then would take to deescalate the fighting. After receiving assurance from Lodge on this point, we authorized him to tell the Polish representative on December 3 that we were ready to meet with the North Vietnamese in Warsaw on December 6, using the Lewandowski draft as the basis for discussion. We pointed out, however, that the Polish formulation of our position was subject to "important differences of interpretation." We began to have serious hopes that the Marigold exchanges might lead to private meetings with the North Vietnamese, but this prospect soon evaporated. The Poles told us finally that the North Vietnamese wanted no meetings with us, secret or otherwise.

The day-to-day dialogue and maneuvering in the Marigold channel will probably interest diplomatic historians. They reveal more confusion than intrigue, but they do contain some interesting ingredients of secret diplomacy. I must record, however, that we never received through the Marigold exchanges anything that could be considered an authoritative statement direct from the North Vietnamese. We finally came to the conclusion that the North Vietnamese and the Poles were not nearly so close as Lewandowski and some of his colleagues in Warsaw had indicated. I realized this channel was a dry creek when the North Vietnamese failed to show up for the critical meeting the Poles had promised to arrange in Warsaw on December 6, 1966.

The Poles claimed that the North Vietnamese had failed to appear because we had bombed targets near Hanoi two days before the suggested meeting date. That made little sense, for Lewandowski and Lodge had agreed that one of the items to be discussed in the proposed secret talks was a mutual deescalation formula, including a bombing halt. This was what we called the Phase A–Phase B plan. We would agree to a bombing halt (Phase A), but only after there was full agreement on steps that both sides then would take to reduce the level of fighting (Phase B). If Lewandowski had reported accurately to Hanoi, the North Vietnamese knew perfectly well that the bombing would not end before the talks began. Knowing that, they could hardly give our bombing as the excuse for not entering negotiations. Nevertheless, when the Poles advanced this argument we stopped all bombing in the vicinity of Hanoi. But North Vietnam's position did not change. The simple truth, I was convinced, was that the North Vietnamese were not ready to talk with us. The Poles had not only put the cart before the horse, when the time of reckoning came, they had no horse.

Our estimate of Marigold was confirmed two years later by Wilfred Burchett, a reporter from the Communist side who was familiar with Hanoi's thinking. In an interview reported in *The Washington Post* in December 1968, Burchett said that "the idea [Marigold] had been concocted by 'well-meaning friends' of North Vietnam as an effort to draw up what might be acceptable to the United States and then sell it to Hanoi." He made it clear that the sale had not been successful.

Early in 1967 I decided that perhaps the only way to find a path to peace was through direct contact with Ho Chi Minh. I wrote to him in February, suggesting that our representatives meet in secret to try to find a peaceful solution acceptable to both sides. I noted his repeated insistence on a unilateral and unconditional cessation of the bombing, but I told the North Vietnamese President I was concerned that his army might use a bombing halt to improve its military position. I said I was ready to stop all the bombing and would go further and freeze the level of American forces in Vietnam as soon as I was assured, secretly or in the open, that he had stopped sending troops and supplies into the South. I noted that we had tried for several years, and through many channels, to make clear our desire for a peaceful settlement. It could be, I wrote, that his thoughts and ours, his attitudes and ours, had been distorted or misinterpreted as they went through those various channels.

"There is one good way to overcome this problem and to move forward in the search for a peaceful settlement," I wrote. "That is for us to arrange for direct talks between trusted representatives in a secure setting and away from the glare of publicity. Such talks . . . should be a serious effort to find a workable and mutually acceptable solution."

My letter to Ho Chi Minh * was delivered to the North Vietnamese Embassy in Moscow on February 8, 1967. That same day, I again ordered a halt to all bombing of North Vietnam as part of a general truce surrounding the Tet holiday. We did not have to wait long for Hanoi's reaction. In the first thirty hours our aerial and naval reconnaissance spotted nearly one thousand sampans and other vessels moving southward along the coast, carrying enough supplies and equipment to support large-scale military operations for a long period. Roads in the panhandle of

---

* For the texts of my first letter to Ho Chi Minh and his reply, see Appendix, pp. 592–95.

North Vietnam were crowded with trucks dashing southward. One of our pilots reported that the roads, jammed with southbound traffic, looked "like the New Jersey Turnpike."

In the meantime, Pope Paul VI had written to Ho Chi Minh and to me urging us both to increase our efforts to find a peaceful solution. I replied immediately that we were prepared "at any time and place" to talk with North Vietnam about "reduction in military activity, the cessation of hostilities or any practical arrangements which could lead to these results."

During this same period, early in February, Soviet Chairman Kosygin was visiting Prime Minister Wilson in London. Vietnam was one of the many matters they discussed. Wilson seemed to feel that he and the Soviet leader could serve as mediators and bring about a settlement of the war. I doubted this strongly. I believed that if the Soviets thought they had a peace formula Hanoi would accept, they would deal directly with us rather than through a fourth party. But I was willing for our British friends to try.

At the outset of the London talks, it became clear to me why the Soviets were willing to discuss Vietnam. Kosygin was pressing Wilson hard to use his influence to persuade us to accept Hanoi's vague offer of possible talks in exchange for a bombing halt. When the Prime Minister asked for our reaction to this proposal, I replied: "If we are asked to take military action on our side, we need to know what the military consequences will be—that is, what military action will be taken by the other side." I concluded my message to Wilson by saying: "I would strongly urge that the two co-chairmen [of the Geneva Conference] not suggest a stoppage of the bombing in exchange merely for talks, but instead appeal to Hanoi to consider seriously the reasonable proposals we are putting before them, which would take us not merely into negotiation but a long step towards peace itself."

We had informed the British that I was going to tell Ho Chi Minh that if he agreed to "an assured stoppage of infiltration into South Vietnam," we would end the bombing and also stop increasing our troop strength in the South. I told Wilson that he could talk with Kosygin on the same basis if he wished, in full confidence that this represented our official position. We thought that the sequence was clear: Hanoi would first stop infiltration; we would then stop the bombing and, in addition, we would agree not to increase our troop strength in Vietnam. That is what I told Ho Chi Minh in my letter. I recognized, of course, that the new proposal altered the Phase A–Phase B plan we had discussed earlier with the British and had offered to Hanoi. Instead of asking the North Vietnamese to promise to take steps to reduce the fighting after the bombing ended, I wanted them to begin cutting down their actions against the South before we stopped the bombing. I felt strongly that this change was justified by the hard fact that during the bombing pause then underway very large southward movements of men and supplies were taking place in the area above the demilitarized zone. I refused to risk the safety of our men in I Corps by stopping air strikes before Ho Chi Minh had acted. On the other hand, I went further than ever before by proposing to freeze U.S. troop levels in the South.

The British read our message differently. They considered it a restatement of the Phase A–Phase B plan, with which they were familiar—that Hanoi would have to agree to halt infiltration but would not actually stop until after the bombing was suspended. When Wilson discussed this with Kosygin, the Soviet leader asked for the proposal in writing. The British gave a document to him without specific approval from Washington, which was an error, though I am confident that they acted in good faith. The result was a diplomatic mix-up for which we shared a certain amount of the responsibility. The British, with some embarrassment, had to go back to Kosygin with the revised, and correct, version of our proposal. That was the evening of February 10.

Meanwhile, the Tet truce period was running out. It ended on February 11, but with Kosygin still in the United Kingdom, we agreed to extend the bombing stand-down until he returned to Moscow on the 13th. At their final meeting with Kosygin on February 12, the British made a new proposal: If the Soviets could obtain North Vietnam's assurance that infiltration into the South would end the next day, the British would get U.S. assurance that the bombing, which then had been stopped for five days, would not be resumed and, further, that the build-up of American forces would end. We had agreed to this British approach before it was put to Kosygin. The Soviets in turn passed the offer on to Hanoi. By the time Kosygin left London the following day, there was still no word from Hanoi. Nor was an answer waiting when Kosygin got back to Moscow.

Prime Minister Wilson felt that we had given him and the Russians too little time to get an answer, but Hanoi had had several months to study and consider the Phase A–Phase B plan—and the proposal Wilson made to Kosygin was but a variation of that idea. It does not take all that long to cable "yes" or "no" or "we are giving it serious study," even from as far away as Hanoi. As a matter of fact, Hanoi did not have to send a cable at all. We had already carried out Phase A; the bombing had been stopped. If the leaders in Hanoi wanted to move toward peace, they knew that all they had to do was to take some visible step to cut back their half of the war. That step could have taken many forms—stopping infiltration or sharply reducing it, pulling back some of their units from advanced positions, cutting down the number of attacks, almost anything significant that would have reflected an honest desire on their part to reduce hostilities. We would have quickly recognized such an action and would have responded to it—as we had said time and time again. The hard but unfortunate truth was that the leaders in Hanoi had snubbed the two-phase approach before the Wilson-Kosygin sessions, and they turned it down again late in 1967. So I could not share the Prime Minister's feeling, which he expressed in the House of Commons, that "a solution could now be reached."

Wilson's sentiment was understandable but far from unique. During the many years we spent searching for a peace formula, I learned that everyone who engaged in such efforts came to think that his own particular approach was the one that would, or should, succeed. Whether they were Poles or Italians, Swedes or Indians, the Secretary General of the United Nations, or journalists, or merely self-appointed peacemakers, they were all convinced that their moves were the only ones that promised success, that their route was the one to take. If only we would follow their plan— and as time passed that usually meant giving Hanoi more and more— peace could be achieved. In many cases, they did not realize that the proposals they advocated so strongly had already been tried and had been rejected by Hanoi.

Most of those working so hard to find a peace formula carried no major day-to-day responsibilities in Vietnam or Southeast Asia. This lack enabled them to take a detached, above-the-battle stance. I have no doubt, for example, that the British government's general approach to the war and to finding a peaceful solution would have been considerably different if a brigade of Her Majesty's forces had been stationed just south of the demilitarized zone in Vietnam.

The morning Kosygin returned to Moscow, Radio Hanoi broadcast Ho Chi Minh's harsh and uncompromising answer to Pope Paul's appeal for peace. This ultimatum was written and released while the Tet truce was still in effect and while no bombs were falling on targets in North Vietnam. Ho demanded, among other things, that all bombing and other military action against North Vietnam be stopped unconditionally, that all American and other allied troops withdraw from South Vietnam, and that South Vietnam's future be settled in accordance with the political program of the Communist Liberation Front. In short, his answer prescribed the surrender of the South.

Again Hanoi had closed the door. We extended the bombing pause until Kosygin was safely back in Moscow, but on the afternoon of February 13, we resumed bombing targets in North Vietnam. Two days later I received Ho's answer to my letter. As we had assumed, his reply was almost identical to the one he had sent to the Pope. Not only would the North Vietnamese leader do nothing himself to reduce the war; he would not even talk about peace until all bombing ended unconditionally.

In spite of the unyielding tone of this reply, I knew that if there was going to be any shift in Hanoi's position, Ho Chi Minh was the only person with the power to make it. So on April 6, 1967, I wrote to him again. I expressed my disappointment with his earlier negative response. I said that I was writing in the spirit reflected by a statement Abraham Lincoln had made in 1861 in a speech to the American people:

> Suppose you go to war, you cannot fight always; and when, after much loss on both sides, and no gain on either, you cease fighting, the identical old questions as to terms of intercourse are again upon you.

I reaffirmed our earlier offers—to talk first about a settlement and then stop fighting, or to undertake steps of mutual deescalation that might make negotiation of a settlement easier. We were ready for either approach, and the talks could take place in Moscow, Rangoon, or elsewhere. Surely, I wrote, one day we must agree to reestablish the Geneva Accords of 1954 (on peace in Vietnam) and of 1962 (on Laos); to let the people of South Vietnam determine peacefully the kind of government they prefer; to let the people of the North and the South decide in peace if they wish to reunite and, if so, how; and finally to arrange for overall peace in Southeast Asia. I reminded him that history would judge us by whether we worked to bring about those results "sooner rather than later."

We delivered the letter * to the North Vietnamese Embassy in Moscow. Later the same day, the North Vietnamese returned it to our Embassy. The letter had been opened, and we learned later through intelligence channels that Hanoi had the text. But it was never acknowledged and never answered. Once more Hanoi had slammed the door on peace.

When I met with Chairman Kosygin in the small town of Glassboro, New Jersey, on June 23, 1967, the Soviet leader told me that just an hour earlier he had received a message from the authorities in Hanoi stating that if the bombing of the North were stopped, Hanoi's representatives would talk with us. Kosygin said it was his understanding that those talks could start a day or two after the bombing ended. They could take place in Hanoi or New York, in Moscow, Paris, Geneva, or elsewhere. Kosygin's words made it clear that he was simply passing Hanoi's message on, nothing more. The Russians were giving no guarantee of their own. It was also clear that Hanoi was making no promises concerning its own actions, or its share of the war. Ho Chi Minh was offering only talk in return for real military restraint on our part, but Kosygin urged me to take the action Hanoi requested.

I told the Chairman that I regarded the matter with the utmost seriousness and that I would give it my most careful attention. I advised him, however, that there were five enemy divisions in and near the demilitarized

---

* For the text of my second letter to Ho Chi Minh, see Appendix, p. 596.

zone at that moment. They were poised to attack our troops in northern I Corps as well as South Vietnamese cities and army units in that area. The only thing holding them in check was our air strikes, which kept them off balance and interfered with their supply lines. I had been advised that a suspension of bombing could prove disastrous to our men and to the South Vietnamese if Ho Chi Minh took advantage of it for a quick and massive assault.

I studied Hanoi's message carefully. I discussed it at length with Secretaries Rusk and McNamara. When I met Kosygin again on Sunday, June 25, my answer was ready. Tell Hanoi, I said, that the United States is ready to stop the bombing of North Vietnam. I told him we assumed that following the cessation of bombing there would be immediate discussions between our representatives and those of Hanoi. I said that those private talks could take place "in Geneva, Moscow, Vientiane, or any other suitable location."

I also asked the Chairman to inform Hanoi that American and allied forces in the northern provinces of South Vietnam would not advance to the north. We would expect that Hanoi's forces in and near the demilitarized zone would not advance southward. This was an effort to establish a stabilized front around the 17th parallel, and to provide reasonable protection for our troops in the northern part of South Vietnam if the bombing of the North ended. As for the proposed talks, I said we would assume that "all questions which either side might wish to raise could be raised."

I asked Chairman Kosygin if he had any comments. He said that although the proposal contained "certain qualifications," it looked all right to him "on the whole." He agreed to send it immediately to Hanoi, and I am sure that he did. I then told the Soviet leader privately that I wanted him to know that we were prepared to stop the bombing "as a step toward peace." We were not ready to stop the bombing "merely to remove one-half of the war while the other half of the war proceeds without limit." I said that I was accepting large risks in taking the course I had just offered. If the proposed talks did not lead to peace or if they were used by Hanoi to achieve "one-sided military advantage," we would have to "resume full freedom of action." I said that I was not asking him to agree but merely asking him to "understand what is in my mind."

No response to our proposal ever came back, either directly or through Moscow. Despite many subsequent exchanges with the Soviets on Vietnam, they never gave us an answer. Nor did anything ever come from Hanoi. The door to peace was still tightly barred.

By early 1967 most of my advisers and I felt confident that the tide of war was moving strongly in favor of the South Vietnamese and their allies, and against the Communists. In 1965 the South Vietnamese forces had lost 10,000 weapons to the enemy. In 1966 the number had been cut in half. During that same period weapons lost by the Communist enemy jumped from about 4,500 to more than 9,000. In 1967 the trend accelerated, with South Vietnamese weapons losses going down 20 per cent, while the enemy gave up 50 per cent more weapons.

Other indicators reflected the same unfavorable trend for the aggressors. At the beginning of 1965 the ratio of enemy-to-allied casualties was estimated at 2.2 to 1. The next year this ratio was 3.3 to 1, and in 1967 it was 3.9 to 1. The number of Viet Cong who went over to the South Vietnamese government's side increased from 11,000 in 1965 to just over 20,000 in 1966 and more than 27,000 in 1967. Early in 1967 our forces captured a document written by a Viet Cong official in which the enemy admitted that it had lost control over more than a million people in South Vietnam in the last half of 1966. This gave strong confirmation to our estimate that the number of people controlled by the Communists had dropped from 3.2 million in June 1966 to 2.4 million in January 1967.

This is not to say that we were satisfied with everything that was happening in South Vietnam. The pace of pacification in the countryside was still slower than we had hoped it would be. Many of us felt that improvement of the South Vietnamese armed forces was not nearly as rapid as it might have been. Still, compared with previous years, there were many heartening signs of progress. The capital city of Saigon and the heavily populated area along the northeast coast were increasingly secure. American forces together with South Vietnamese and other allied units were increasingly taking the fight to the enemy. One of the most striking examples of this came in January 1967, when a combined force, spearheaded by the U.S. 1st Infantry Division, moved into the so-called Iron Triangle northwest of Saigon. This forbidding piece of real estate was a hilly, jungle-covered area which the Communists had long ago developed into a major base. For years it had been considered impregnable and had served as the headquarters sanctuary of the Viet Cong's Military Region IV, which controlled Communist armed activities in the area around Saigon.

In this operation, code-named Cedar Falls, the allied troops smashed the base area. They discovered what was described as an "underground city" composed of tunnels four levels deep. Our forces captured enough stored rice in the operation to feed an estimated 13,000 soldiers for one year. They also uncovered an invaluable source of intelligence, nearly half a million pages of enemy documents. Almost a thousand Communist troops were killed or captured and more than five hundred took advantage of the confusion of battle to surrender to the South Vietnamese government. This once "safe" area would never be safe again for the Viet Cong.

Even though the North Vietnamese and their Viet Cong followers were suffering one defeat after another, they showed no evidence that they were ready to pull back. I discussed this with General Westmoreland in the spring of 1967. I asked him whether total enemy forces had been reduced as a result of the heavy losses they were suffering. "No, sir, not yet," he answered. He pointed out that heavy infiltration and continuing recruitment in the South were making up for battle casualties, but he was hopeful that the "crossover point"—when losses exceeded the ability to replace those losses—might be reached reasonably soon. He was not making optimistic predictions, however.

In March I decided that the time had come for another thorough review of Vietnam developments similar to the discussions we had held the previous year in Honolulu and Manila. I invited the South Vietnamese leaders to join me, members of my staff, and members of our Mission in Saigon at Guam. I felt that we could meet in security at that island base, which was situated close enough to South Vietnam so that the Vietnamese leaders and our own field personnel would not have to be away from their action posts too long. I had several purposes in mind for the meeting. I wanted especially to learn in detail what was happening on the pacification front and what plans had been developed for expanding that vital part of our over-all program. I knew the South Vietnamese government had been moving ahead quickly on its plan for democratic political development, and I wanted to hear what the Vietnamese leaders saw in the future. Finally, there was going to be a major turnover in the leadership of our Mission in Saigon and I wished personally to introduce the members of our "new team" to the Vietnamese leaders. It was critically important for us both that our Mission and the Vietnamese leadership work closely together.

Ellsworth Bunker, a man with a long and successful career in business and diplomacy, had agreed to take over leadership of the Mission from Ambassador Henry Cabot Lodge, who was retiring. I had developed a deep respect for Bunker's skill, judgment, and coolness under fire during the Dominican crisis.* As Bunker's deputy in the Saigon Mission, I had selected Eugene M. Locke, an experienced lawyer with an understanding of politics. I had also decided that our Embassy's Office of Civil Operations and the military's Revolutionary Development Support Directorate were interdependent and should be a single operation. To head the new unit I had selected Robert Komer to be General Westmoreland's Deputy for Civil Operations and Revolutionary Development Support.

One of the high points of the Guam conference came at the outset. On March 20, at our first meeting, General Thieu and Prime Minister Ky presented me with a copy of the new Vietnamese constitution, which had been approved only hours before, following a night-long session of debate and compromise between government leaders and members of the Constitu-

* See Chapter 8, pp. 198, 203–04.

ent Assembly. The Vietnamese spoke proudly of this new charter for their nation. One year before, at Honolulu, they had pledged to arrange for the drafting of a democratic constitution. Their proud looks at Guam said: We have done what we said we would, even though many people thought it was impossible.

At our formal meeting, Prime Minister Ky said:

> Very soon this Constitution will be promulgated. Four to five months after that, we will hold national elections for a President and a Senate. One month after the Presidential and senatorial elections, we will hold an election for a House of Representatives. Vietnam will then have a freely elected, popularly chosen government.

I congratulated the Vietnamese on their constitution. I confessed that one year before, when they had outlined their political plans, I had doubted their chances for success. I knew of no nation in history trying, to say nothing of succeeding in, what they had set out to do—to develop a constitutional system in the midst of a savage war. But they had done it, even though the roots of democracy remained fairly shallow and stern tests of survival lay ahead.

At the Guam meeting our talk centered mainly on nonmilitary problems. I think that both we and the South Vietnamese considered that military problems were being handled satisfactorily. The principal military matter we discussed concerned increasing the use of regular South Vietnamese units to provide security for the hamlets and villages and for the revolutionary development teams that were working in growing numbers in the countryside. Those fifty-nine-man teams were becoming more and more the prime targets for Viet Cong terrorists and guerrilla units.

Most of the time at Guam was spent discussing such things as inflation control, blackmarketeering and corruption, land reform, and food supplies. For the first time in any of our bilateral meetings, we discussed at some length the problems of long-range economic development in Vietnam. I had asked former TVA chief David E. Lilienthal and a team of experts to work with the Vietnamese economists and planners on this matter. I wanted the South Vietnamese to know that not only were we at their side in war but we would also be there in peacetime as they forged ahead, using their resources and energy and talents to build a prosperous Vietnam.

One month after the Guam meeting I chose a fourth member of the new "team" in Saigon. He was General Creighton Abrams, a dedicated soldier with a brilliant combat and command record. He became General Westmoreland's deputy commander. General Westmoreland and I agreed that the new deputy commander in Vietnam would spend much of his time working with the South Vietnamese military to improve the effectiveness of their forces. General Westmoreland told me that in his view an important part of the next phase of the conflict would be to turn over a growing share of the war effort to the South Vietnamese forces we were helping to strengthen, a process later called "Vietnamization." He said this would be one of his principal goals in 1968, unless the Communists did something radical to change the military trend that was under way.

The American effort to strengthen the South Vietnamese armed forces took many forms. We helped them improve military leadership, one of their main weaknesses, by developing modern military schools. We encouraged the idea of battlefield promotions, one of the best ways of giving recognition to outstanding combat leaders. We took additional steps to provide more modern weapons and equipment to the South Vietnamese troops. We advised them and helped them improve their logistics and supply systems. All these programs, and many more, were designed to achieve one of our main policy goals: to expand the role of the Vietnamese military in every possible way. Our efforts were succeeding. By the end of 1967, for example, the Vietnamese military forces had full responsibility for the security of their capital city and its immediate environs.

In November 1967, when he was in Washington for consultation, General Westmoreland described publicly the numerous measures we and the South Vietnamese had taken to build up the strength and effectiveness of their armed forces. In his talk at the National Press Club, he also put on the record the expectations we had discussed in private. As the South Vietnamese army modernized and developed its fighting capacity, he said, American units could begin to "phase down." During the question period Westmoreland spelled out what we had in mind.

"My statement," he said, "is to the effect that it is conceivable to me that within two years or less it will be possible for us to phase down our level of commitment and turn more of the burden of the war over to the Vietnamese armed forces, who are improving and who, I believe, will be prepared to assume this greater burden. Now, I made the point at the outset this may be token, but hopefully progressive, and certainly we're preparing our plans to make it progressive."

General Westmoreland's forecast proved extremely accurate. Slightly less than two years after he made this statement, the United States was able to begin withdrawing American combat troops as the Vietnamese assumed a larger share of the burden of fighting.

It may be that some military spokesmen in Saigon and Washington were too enthusiastic in their descriptions of improvements in the Vietnamese army at that time. But many reports published in that period picturing the Vietnamese as inept, cowardly, and lazy were even more misleading. The truth, we believed, lay somewhere in between. Some South Vietnamese units were excellent, some were bad; but most were good—and getting better, which was the important thing.

In July 1967 Secretary McNamara, Under Secretary of State Katzenbach,* and General Wheeler went to Vietnam for another of the frequent surveys our top officials carried out. All three came back heartened by the progress that was being made but deeply conscious of the outstanding problems we continued to face. The biggest worry was on the political front. The election process was moving ahead, but our inspection team reported that there was friction between Generals Thieu and Ky. If rivalry broke out between the two leaders, no one could forecast what might happen. A split in the military forces caused by conflicting loyalties to the two men could have disastrous consequences.

I was less worried than some of my advisers about this possibility. At Guam, Thieu and Ky had given me their personal promises, in private, that they would not let competition between them endanger either progress toward democracy in their country or improvements that had been made at great sacrifice on the battlefield. I was confident that they would live up to that pledge—at least during the critical time of transition in 1967. Our role was not to support either of them in whatever political ambitions they had; they never asked for, or received, our backing in any personal way. We took a strictly-hands-off attitude toward the election campaign, but I did not want to see either of them do anything that would endanger their own people and the large effort we had made to help them stay free.

Reports on the military front from McNamara and General Wheeler were encouraging. They both felt that the situation on the ground looked very different from the impression our people were receiving from many newspapers. I asked McNamara about reports that the military situation was really a "stalemate," as some observers claimed. "There is not a military stalemate," he answered. He said that "for the first time" since we committed troops to combat in 1965, he was convinced we could achieve our goals and end the fighting if we followed the course we had set.

Wheeler supported this view. He said that the Vietnamese and American and allied forces had had "an unbroken series of military successes." The enemy was still aggressive, but it had been thrown off balance. Recruiting in the countryside was becoming increasingly difficult, and thirteen- and fourteen-year-old boys were showing up in Viet Cong ranks. Hanoi was making up the deficit in the only way it could, by increased infiltration of forces from the North Vietnamese army. With all that, the North Vietnamese remained tough, determined, and crafty, and they were far from beaten. McNamara and Wheeler agreed it was important that the pressure be maintained and increased. At the end of our meeting Under Secretary Katzenbach said that "if the American people give us a chance here at home" he had every reason to believe we could succeed in Vietnam.

---

* Katzenbach, an able lawyer and specialist in international law, had agreed to leave his post as Attorney General to become Under Secretary of State on October 3, 1966.

For planning purposes, General Westmoreland had suggested that we consider a force increase of 100,000 men above those already authorized. As had always been the case, this was a contingency figure. The Secretary of Defense, General Wheeler, and General Westmoreland had already begun to work over the proposal, cutting it here and there, looking for alternatives and for ways to make the forces already in Vietnam more effective. When they came back to me the next day, July 13, McNamara reported that there was "complete accord" on how to proceed. They had agreed that nineteen or twenty combat battalions would be required and that a force increase of about 50,000 men in all categories was needed. That would raise our authorized total strength in Vietnam to 525,000 men at the end of June 1968.

As we studied this proposal and went over it in detail, we were assured of help from our allies. Before the end of July Prime Minister Ky announced that Vietnamese forces would be increased by 65,000 men. In addition, the South Vietnamese were considering lowering their draft age to eighteen. Meanwhile, the Thai Volunteer Regiment had begun to arrive in Vietnam and was scheduled to be in position in September. After careful study, I accepted the recommendation of my military advisers. At a news conference, on August 3, I announced that I had approved the deployment of an additional 45,000 to 50,000 men and that the new ceiling would be 525,000 men in all services for the year ahead.

While the war continued, and even increased in ferocity, the South Vietnamese government and political groups went ahead with their plans to hold national elections under the constitution. The Constituent Assembly, the only popularly elected group with a national mandate, took responsibility for writing an election law. The most frustrating problem during the early electoral preparations was the continuing rivalry between Thieu and Ky. They both wanted to run for President, but in the end, both men lived up to the pledge they had made at Guam—that neither would do anything to endanger the unity of their country's armed forces. At the end of June they took their differences to the Armed Forces Council for resolution. After long debate, Prime Minister Ky said that he would withdraw from the Presidential race and run with Thieu as candidate for Vice President. This was an act of statesmanship for which Ky never received the credit I thought he deserved. For two years he had been the leader of the government, and our reports showed that he commanded considerable support in the military forces, especially among the younger officers. Yet he stepped down and accepted the idea of becoming number-two man because he knew that his action would benefit his country.

In the end, there were eleven slates of candidates for the two top offices. The campaign was hard-fought but clean. The government, acting under the electoral law and its own policy, provided all candidates with election posters and free travel to all parts of the country. Some intellectuals, some politicians, and some newspapers—in our country and elsewhere— were ready to write off this experiment in democracy well in advance as a farce or a fraud. But it was neither of these to the Vietnamese people. And by the time the actual election took place, I do not think it could have been so considered by any fair-minded person willing to examine the facts.

The South Vietnamese government had invited official foreign observers to visit the country and inspect the electoral process in action. In addition, political officers in all the foreign embassies in Saigon were following the election closely, and a huge and eager press corps was searching for any sign of irregularities, such as vote buying or coercion. In answer to Saigon's request, I invited a group of twenty-two distinguished Americans to go to Vietnam to witness the election, which was held on September 3, 1967. These observers were a cross-section of our national leadership, both Democratic and Republican—including three Senators; leaders of state, county, and city governments; business, labor, and religious leaders; executives of civic organizations; and representatives of the press, radio, and television.* Former Ambassador Henry Cabot Lodge accompanied the delegation members at my request to help them in every way possible and to insure that they could travel where they wanted and see what they wanted to see.

When the observers returned to Washington on September 6, I met with them in the Cabinet Room to hear their reports. The trip had been a long

---

* The American observers to the Vietnamese elections held September 3, 1967, included Senators Bourke B. Hickenlooper (Rep. of Iowa), George L. Murphy (Rep. of Calif.), and Edmund S. Muskie (Dem. of Maine); Governors William L. Guy (Dem. of N.D.), Richard J. Hughes (Dem. of N.J.), and Thomas L. McCall (Rep. of Ore.); Ed Munro, president of the National Association of Counties; and Mayors Joseph M. Barr (Dem. of Pittsburgh) and Theodore R. McKeldin (Rep. of Baltimore). Representing the news media were John S. Knight, president of Knight Newspapers; Donald H. McGannon, president of Westinghouse Broadcasting Company; Eugene C. Patterson, editor of the *Atlanta Constitution;* and Stanford Smith, general manager of the American Newspaper Publishers Association. The three clergymen who participated were Dr. Edward L. R. Elson, pastor of the National Presbyterian Church in Washington, D.C.; Archbishop Robert E. Lucey of the Diocese of San Antonio; and Rabbi Jacob P. Rudin, president of the Synagogue Council of America. Also present as observers were Eldon James, former national commander of the American Legion; Joseph Scerra, incoming commander of the Veterans of Foreign Wars; James B. Antell, president of the U.S. Junior Chamber of Commerce; Werner P. Gullander, president of the National Association of Manufacturers; David Sullivan, vice president of the AFL-CIO; and Whitney M. Young, Jr., president of the Urban League.

The following electoral specialists accompanied the observers as special advisers: Richard M. Scammon, director of the Elections Research Center and editor of *America Votes;* Prof. Howard R. Penniman of Georgetown University, author of *The American Political Process;* and Prof. Donald G. Herzberg, director of the Eagleton Institute of Politics at Rutgers University and author of *The Right To Vote.*

and tiring experience for these men, but they were unanimously enthusiastic. One observer after another described his personal experiences and observations. All were deeply impressed by what they had seen—a young country undergoing its most crucial experience with the democratic process.

Governor Richard Hughes of New Jersey was the first to speak after I had welcomed them and thanked them. "These were clean elections," Hughes said. He had talked with about two hundred election officials, peasants, village chiefs, and other Vietnamese citizens. He had found great enthusiasm among them, more, he said, than in his own state at election time.

"I agree completely with Governor Hughes," said Senator Bourke Hickenlooper of Iowa. "All of us observed the preparations for the elections, and we observed the voting and the counting of the ballots. I must echo what Governor Hughes said, that the elections were fair. I was very impressed with the effort they put into making this an open and fair election. We have never been that careful."

Mayor Joe Barr of Pittsburgh said he had "learned a lot about elections from these people."

"Too much attention has been placed on the possibility of irregularities, and not enough on the other aspects," Governor William Guy of North Dakota said. "These people with great courage came out with a moving and profound example of desire for self-determination—as much as I have seen anywhere. We visited a precinct at which a bomb went off and killed three and wounded six during the voting. They closed it for forty-five minutes and then reopened it for more voting. I was very impressed."

Reverend Edward L. R. Elson of Washington, D.C., called the election "a noble political exercise for self-enhancement and self-determination."

Whitney Young of the Urban League said that he had gone to Vietnam "with some cynicism and skepticism based on newspaper accounts which I read." "However, I returned completely satisfied that these were free elections—as good as could be expected under the conditions," he said. He thought that "we could put some of the lessons of the Vietnam elections to use in our own country."

And so it went, as one after another of the observers expressed his views and reported on the things he had seen and learned. Mayor Theodore McKeldin of Baltimore concluded the session by saying: "And no one tried to brainwash us." With that, we laughed and adjourned for lunch together.

Before and during the South Vietnamese elections the Viet Cong tried, through harassment, terror, and threats of vengeance, to discourage the people from taking part. Yet more than 70 per cent of all eligible South Vietnamese citizens registered for the election, and four of every five of those voted.

In June 1967 a new possibility for contact with the regime in Hanoi developed, and we decided to follow it up in stubborn hope that it would produce results. A group of scientists and intellectuals from France, the Soviet Union, Great Britain, and the United States met in Paris that month. Among other subjects, they discussed the problem of Vietnam. A group of the participants decided that Herbert Marcovich, a French scientist taking part in the talks, should go to Hanoi to sound out North Vietnamese attitudes toward negotiations. It was suggested and agreed that a second Frenchman, Raymond Aubrac, a friend of Marcovich and a man who had known Ho Chi Minh for many years, should accompany him.

The two set off in July. In Hanoi they met twice with Prime Minister Pham Van Dong, and Aubrac talked once with the aging Ho Chi Minh. On their return to Paris at the end of July, they met promptly with an American who had taken part in the June discussions. He was Dr. Henry A. Kissinger, a professor of government at Harvard and now President Nixon's Assistant for National Security Affairs. The Frenchmen told Kissinger they thought Hanoi would negotiate as soon as the bombing of the North ended. They had the impression that the bombing halt need not be "permanent" or at least that the United States would not have to describe it as being permanent. A de facto stoppage would be sufficient, without public announcements.

Fuzzy as the "impressions" seemed to be, we decided to follow up the matter. After careful study, we authorized Kissinger to inform the North Vietnamese, through the French intermediaries, that the United States was willing to stop bombing the North if a halt would lead "promptly" to "productive discussions" between us. We were prepared to assume that while discussions were going on, either in secret or in public, North Vietnam would not "take advantage" of the bombing cessation. We were ready to discuss this approach, or any other that Hanoi might suggest, in private talks.

In mid-August Dr. Kissinger relayed our position to the Frenchmen, who found it a promising response. They immediately applied for visas to go to Hanoi. Two days later Kissinger told the Frenchmen that they could inform the leaders in Hanoi that beginning August 24 there would be a "noticeable change in the bombing pattern" in the vicinity of their capital. This, we felt, would provide strong proof of our seriousness and would erase any doubts Hanoi might entertain regarding the authenticity of the channel we were using.

But in a few days the North Vietnamese representative in Paris told the Frenchmen they were not going to receive visas. They appealed but obtained no satisfaction. When Hanoi's official in Paris argued that it was "too dangerous" for them to visit Hanoi, they told him that they had assurances on that and were not concerned. Finally, on August 25, when it was obvious that no visas would be forthcoming, the Frenchmen passed along to the North Vietnamese in the French capital the essence of our position as well as the notification of a bombing cessation around Hanoi. It took Hanoi more than two weeks to answer our message. When that delayed reply arrived, it was harsh and totally negative. "The Government of the Democratic Republic of Vietnam energetically rejects the American propositions," it said. Hanoi demanded once again that we stop all bombing, withdraw our forces from the South, and recognize the Liberation Front. In answer, we proposed a direct meeting between Hanoi's representative and Dr. Kissinger. Hanoi replied that such a meeting "cannot take place." The only reason Mai Van Bo, Hanoi's representative, could give was the "threat" of renewed bombing of Hanoi. It was clear that Bo was on a tight leash. Though he said he wanted to "keep the channel open," he could give no cogent explanation. In our opinion, the absence of air strikes on targets near Hanoi during the period of contacts in Paris constituted reason enough from the North Vietnamese viewpoint to keep the talks going. Certainly it was obvious that they were not using the channel for serious discussion.

In a speech before the National Legislative Conference in San Antonio on September 29, 1967, I decided to state publicly the offer we had proposed through the Paris channel and other avenues of contact:

> The United States is willing to stop all aerial and naval bombardment of North Vietnam when this will lead promptly to productive discussions. We, of course, assume that while discussions proceed, North Vietnam would not take advantage of the bombing cessation or limitation.

From that date on the offer came to be known as "the San Antonio formula." It relaxed somewhat the proposal we had made to Ho Chi Minh in February. We were not asking him to restrict his military actions before a bombing halt, and once the bombing ended we were not insisting that he immediately end his military effort, only that he not increase it. Since the leaders in Hanoi seemed to be having difficulty with the idea of making any military commitments prior to a bombing halt, we made it clear that we were prepared to "assume" they would not take advantage of the cessation. All we asked was that a cessation of bombing would lead promptly to peace talks and that those talks would be "productive."

Despite continued lack of movement in the Paris channel, we kept it open and exchanges continued well into October through the French go-betweens. Finally, on October 17, we received the following message from Mai Van Bo:

> At the present time, the United States is continuing the escalation of the war in an extremely grave manner. In these conditions, words of peace are only trickery. At a time when the United States continues the escalation we can neither receive Mr. Kissinger nor comment on the American views transmitted through this channel. . . .

The North Vietnamese representative said that discussions could take place only when bombing of the North had ended "without condition." With this statement, I became convinced again that Hanoi had no interest in serious talk about peace except, as always, on its own stiff terms. But we wanted to leave no stone unturned. On October 18 I met in the Cabinet Room with Secretaries Rusk and McNamara, Walt Rostow, and Dr. Kissinger. We reviewed the entire record of the talks in Paris, and on the strong recommendation of my advisers, I agreed that Kissinger should return to France and make one more attempt to get into serious discussions. He flew to Paris and passed along to the French intermediaries our views and our sense of strong disappointment that nothing meaningful had happened. The Frenchmen immediately called Bo and asked to see him. They reported that the North Vietnamese representative's response was icy.

"There is nothing new to say," he told them. "The situation is worsening. There is no reason to talk again." They pleaded with him. He repeated that "there is nothing new to say." Four times in all he said the same thing; Hanoi's answer was "no." The channel was dead. The door was closed and locked. On October 23, for the first time in two months, our planes hit a military target within ten miles of Hanoi.

We did not know then, but we soon learned, that Hanoi was already feverishly preparing its largest and most ambitious military campaign of the war. Reinforcements were crowding the infiltration trails and many had already arrived in South Vietnam.

As the year 1967 drew to a close, one additional possible line of contact with Hanoi developed. In November Ambassador Averell Harriman had visited Bucharest and had explained to high officials in the Romanian government our position as expressed in the San Antonio formula. On the question of "no advantage," he explained that we did not suggest that Hanoi would have to stop sending supplies to its forces in the South. What we required was that Hanoi guarantee not to use a bombing pause to increase its infiltration effort.

In December a high Romanian official visited Hanoi and talked with leaders there, describing our position and listening to theirs. Early in January he came to Washington to convey directly the message he had received from the North Vietnamese. We could discover nothing new in Hanoi's stand, nothing different from what they had often said before, but the Romanian's report was balanced and, we felt, accurate. There were enough unanswered questions about the precise meaning of Hanoi's position for us to seek further clarification. The Romanian official returned to Hanoi during the third week of January, and he left only one day before the Communist forces launched their massive Tet offensive in South Vietnam.

Early in February, through diplomatic channels, the Romanians sent us Hanoi's answer. Like all the others, the reply was a flat rejection of the idea of making contact with us without a complete and unconditional cessation of the bombing. Hanoi would commit itself to nothing concerned with lowering the level of violence in South Vietnam, across or in the demilitarized zone, or anywhere else.

I could not in conscience order a bombing halt that would subject our troops to greater dangers unless I had reason to hope that such a halt would be effective in leading to peace negotiations. On the other side of the coin, the record was clear that we *would* halt bombing whenever we had any basis for believing a cessation would be worth the risk.

Throughout the fall of 1967 my advisers and I discussed a bombing halt many times. We were all in favor of trying again as soon as we had some reasonable indication that such a move offered a shred of hope. Whether another halt actually produced talks or not, it would at least show—as I said at one of these meetings—that we were ready to "go the last mile" to find peace. But over these same months we were also watching a mammoth build-up of enemy troops and supplies. Our intelligence apparatus informed us conclusively that the Communists were preparing for an all-out assault. In that atmosphere, I remained convinced that any new effort to approach Hanoi and try to start peace discussions would be futile. The North Vietnamese were in the midst of planning a sledge-hammer blow to the South, one that they hoped would shatter the South Vietnamese army, topple the government, and lead the people to rally to the Communist side. They also hoped that a massive military offensive, whether or not it achieved its other goals immediately, would undermine American morale and increase the clamor for U.S. withdrawal. As this strategy became increasingly apparent, I felt we would have to ride out the storm, and then try for peace when Hanoi had learned it could not win by the use of force.

12

Space

JANUARY 27, 1967, WAS a memorable day in the history of America's activities in the new world of space. An hour of great achievement was followed by a tragedy that saddened the nation. Late in the afternoon of the 27th in the East Room of the White House a notable group was gathered, including high U.S. officials, the Ambassadors of Great Britain and the Soviet Union, and representatives from fifty-seven other nations. The occasion was the signing of a treaty to prohibit weapons of war in outer space. It was an assembly of hope. In my remarks that afternoon I said: "This is an inspiring moment in the history of the human race."

A little more than two hours later I was upstairs, in the family quarters of the Executive Mansion, where Mrs. Johnson and I were giving a reception in honor of retiring Secretary of Commerce John T. Connor and his wife. While John was proposing a toast, I was handed a folded note. It was from Jim Jones, my appointments secretary, and it read:

> Mr. President: James Webb just reported that the first Apollo crew was under test at Cape Kennedy and a fire broke out in the capsule and all three were killed. He does not know whether it was the primary or backup crew, but believes it was the primary crew of Grissom, White and Chaffee.

The shock hit me like a physical blow. I heard the applause for Connor's toast die down, and a silence began to settle over the room. Our guests were all looking at me. "I have a sad announcement to make," I said, and read the note aloud. There was a stir in the stillness of the room and the happy atmosphere changed to one of stunned grief. I managed a brief farewell to the Connors and left for the Oval Office.

We had known from the beginning that there would be setbacks, and perhaps even tragedy, involved in the space program. But no amount of planning could have adequately prepared us for the horror of that moment. The news reports confirmed that the astronauts were Virgil I. Grissom, Edward H. White, and Roger B. Chaffee. All through that night I thought in anguish of those brave young men and of their bereaved families.

Taps sounded for all three on January 31. Gus Grissom and Roger Chaffee were buried in Arlington National Cemetery—Colonel Grissom in the morning, Commander Chaffee in the afternoon. I crossed the Potomac twice that day to bid farewell to both men. Lady Bird flew to West Point to attend the funeral of Colonel Ed White. The tragic loss of these astronauts brought an outpouring of sympathy from all over the world. Great leaders and humble citizens alike shared our grief.

Demanding questions followed in the wake of tragedy: What had happened? Could the fire have been prevented? Were we going ahead too fast? Were we pushing too hard? Beyond these questions, I wondered how the nation would regard its space adventure now that disaster had fallen. We had come a long way before this catastrophe—not in time, but in accomplishment. I knew every mile of the road we had traveled.

Security and defense were our primary concerns when we first turned our attention to space hardware in the years after World War II. A good many Americans—and I was among them—feared then that the United States was moving too slowly into the new technology of ballistic missiles, and that we were lagging dangerously behind the Russians. In 1950, soon after I became Chairman of the Senate Preparedness Subcommittee, which kept a congressional watch on our military strength, I annoyed several officials in the Pentagon by pointing out that they were paying too little attention to guided missiles. Later that year, in an article in *Preview* magazine, I urged that we "pool our best scientific brains on guided missile research, just as we pooled our best brains to develop the atomic bomb."

Our missile program did begin to accelerate in the 1950s, as the military services intensified their work with ICBMs and IRBMs. The three high-priority missiles—the Atlas, Thor, and Jupiter—failed eight times on the launching pad in the first eleven tries, but at least we were giving serious attention to these projects and providing funds for their development. We even began talking about a missile launch for experimental scientific research. The International Geophysical Year, a worldwide undertaking composed of many different scientific adventures, was scheduled to open in mid-1957 and was to last for eighteen months. The Eisenhower administration announced that the United States would contribute to the IGY by propelling a small twenty-pound sphere into orbit around the earth.

This plan, known as Project Vanguard, seemed an appropriate American assignment. The United States, we all comfortably believed, was the world's most advanced nation in science and technology.

On October 4, 1957, the Soviet Union launched a 184-pound satellite into orbit around the earth, and simultaneously a new era of history dawned over the world. I was at my ranch in Texas when the news of Sputnik flashed across the globe. After dinner Mrs. Johnson and I and our guests took a walk, as had been our custom since my heart attack two years earlier. No one said very much. We all walked with eyes lifted skyward, straining to catch a glimpse of that alien object which had been thrust into the outer reaches of our world.

As we stood on the lonely country road that runs between our house and the Pedernales River, I felt uneasy and apprehensive. In the open West, you learn to live closely with the sky. It is a part of your life. But now, somehow, in some new way, the sky seemed almost alien. I also remember the profound shock of realizing that it might be possible for another nation to achieve technological superiority over this great country of ours.

Most Americans shared my sense of shock that October night, which now seems so far back in our history. Today people have become accustomed to American superiority in space. Thrilling and dramatic as the first voyage to the moon was, the feat did not stun the nation with surprise. We expected it. There was even some question as to whether the trip was worth it. Whenever I heard such doubts expressed, I recalled that time in October when Sputnik had plunged the America of 1957 into spiritual depression. I wondered what the reaction would have been in the America of 1969 if Soviet cosmonauts had planted their red flag on the moon.

I went into the house that awesome night when Sputnik first orbited over our heads and began calling members of my subcommittee and staff. I returned to Washington soon after, and we assembled what information we had in those first bewildering hours and days. Senator Richard Russell, Chairman of our parent Armed Services Committee, asked my Preparedness Subcommittee to hold hearings as soon as possible. We proposed to make a complete inquiry into the state of our defenses and to determine what steps would now have to be taken. We opened hearings on November 25, 1957.*

By that time, a second Soviet Sputnik had been boosted into earth orbit. This one, weighing more than half a ton, carried a live dog. A feeling of

---

* Other members of the Senate Preparedness Subcommittee included the ranking Republican Styles Bridges of New Hampshire, Estes Kefauver of Tennessee, John Stennis of Mississippi, Stuart Symington of Missouri, Leverett Saltonstall of Massachusetts, and Ralph Flanders of Vermont. As committee counsel I chose an old trusted friend, and one of the wisest, bravest lawyers I know, Edwin L. Weisl. Cy Vance and Ed Weisl, Jr., associates of the senior Weisl's law firm, were chosen associate counsels.

frustration, bordering on desperation, gripped most of the United States. That feeling prevailed for months. Our sole hope was the Vanguard rocket, which was to carry our own four-pound satellite into orbit. Then came the final blow. On December 6, 1957, the Vanguard rocket blew up on its launching pad.

The Soviet success and the Vanguard failure depreciated our prestige. Russia's image as a technological leader suddenly increased to alarming proportions and our own image diminished, especially among the people of the developing nations, many of whom were beginning to believe that the Soviet Union was the real wave of the future. What disturbed us even more was the realization that this second-best position was the possible result of our own shortsightedness and complacency. As the hearings subsequently revealed, Project Vanguard, which had been placed under the management of the Naval Research Laboratory, had suffered grievously from a shortage of funds and resources during the Eisenhower years. The Vanguard director testified that if his project had been given the priority it deserved, "we certainly would have been ahead of the Russians."

Beyond the damage to our pride and prestige was a far more menacing danger. The Russians had announced a few months earlier, in August 1957, that they could fire a ballistic missile from one continent to another. Their satellites in orbit around the earth seemed to confirm this boast. But the sense of urgency that many of us experienced in the autumn of 1957 did not seem to penetrate the White House. Sherman Adams, President Eisenhower's chief of staff, dismissed the Soviet achievement by disclaiming interest in an "outer space basketball game." Secretary of Defense Charles Wilson tried to calm the nation with soothing words: "Nobody is going to drop anything down on you from a satellite while you are sleeping, so don't start to worry about it." President Eisenhower's special adviser on foreign economic policy, Clarence Randall, called Sputnik a "silly bauble." The President himself intimated that the Russian satellite did not raise his apprehensions about our security. On October 16 *The New York Times,* reporting a speech made by Richard M. Nixon, pointed out that "although the Vice President sounded a note of military urgency, he was the second high-administration figure in two days to discount, from a local platform, public apprehension aroused by the Soviet's success in launching October 4 a man-made earth satellite."

In that situation it would have been easy enough to create a partisan issue. I tried to make it clear that the purpose of our subcommittee hearings was not to fix blame on anybody. The hearings were being held to "determine what steps can be taken to strengthen our position and restore the leadership we should have in technology." I was now convinced that the country was in trouble, and that we could find our way out of it not as Democrats or Republicans but only as a people determined to master our problems together. I knew one thing beyond doubt—we had to catch up.

Speaking at a dinner in Austin, Texas, on October 19, 1957, I said: "There is no reason why we cannot catch up and outstrip anyone else— providing we unite and decide to do so. . . . We have plant capacity that is superior in every respect. We can outproduce the Soviet Union in steel, electric power, alloys, aluminum, magnesium—everything that could go into a satellite. . . ."

Less than two months later, on December 10, in a speech in Dallas I said: "If heads must be knocked together, let's do it. If more money is needed, let's spend it. If more resources are needed, let's use them. If more hours are needed, let's work them. Let us do whatever it takes. . . ."

For the next two months, into January 1958, our subcommittee heard testimony from experts across the full spectrum of America's scientific, technological, industrial, and military life. With Ed Weisl, Cy Vance, and Ed Weisl, Jr., acting as my counselors, we probed every pertinent aspect of the nation's defense posture. Our first witness on November 25, 1957, was Dr. Edward Teller, the father of the hydrogen bomb. In his testimony on military preparedness, he discussed man's eventual trip to the moon. "I am certain that people will go to the moon and will get to the planets," he told us. "There is no question about that in my mind." It was the first time I had ever heard that journey discussed in serious practical terms. Before that, it had been more in the realm of science fiction than a serious consideration. No one could say precisely what the results of so vast an undertaking would be, Teller said. But one thing was certain—it would have consequences extending into almost every facet of man's existence.

That was the pattern over the weeks that followed. Amid all the discussion of weaponry and defenses, we heard a great deal about space flight. We were all discovering how thin the line was that separated the two areas. In the course of our hearings, as I explained on the Senate floor, "it became apparent that the new weapons were an offshoot of the tre- mendous scientific advances of the past two decades, which had brought us to the threshold of exploring outer space. The compelling facts of the international scene require that we pursue the development of those new weapons. But it seems to me even more compelling that we not allow the development of the new weapons to blind us to the existence of the mainstream itself."

We discovered some disturbing truths from those three months of hear- ings. Among them were the facts that the Soviet Union led the United States in the development of ballistic missiles, that its research-and- development system enabled it to develop new weapons in less time than the United States, and that it was producing scientists and technicians substantially faster than we were. When the inquiry was finished, our subcommittee wrote a report—approved by all Senators, Republican and Democrat—containing a number of recommendations to strengthen the country's defenses.

In immediate response to that report, the Eisenhower administration asked for an additional $1.4 billion for the defense budget and stepped up missile production. A delayed but even more far-reaching reaction was the National Defense Education Act, the first legislation providing substantial federal aid to education. This law, passed within the year to assure the nation a steady supply of scientists, was a direct answer to our discovery that the Soviet Union was outpacing us in education. We were finally coming to see that our defenses did extend even to the classroom. In our subcommittee's report, filed on January 23, 1958, we observed: "We have reached a stage of history where defense involves the total effort of a nation." As Vannevar Bush, America's wartime head of scientific research, told our subcommittee on November 25, 1957: "The Sputnik was one of the finest things that Russia ever did for us. It has waked this country up."

Our subcommittee's primary concern was defense, but before the hearings were over America had been led—imperceptibly at first, but with dogged inevitability—into the age of space. Suddenly the entire country had become space conscious. As Dr. Wernher von Braun, then in charge of the Army's Ballistic Missile Agency, had told our preparedness hearings: "Space is a very fashionable word today, although it was almost taboo in the Pentagon six months ago."

Science was also upgraded in the White House. President Eisenhower appointed Dr. James P. Killian, president of the Massachusetts Institute of Technology, as his first full-time science adviser. His job was to keep the President informed of the new developments that were so swiftly changing the old order of things.

For a nation entering the new space age, one urgent need was a national policy. I thought the Congress had an obligation and an unparalleled opportunity to help forge that policy. I told the Senate Democrats this at the Democratic conference on January 7, 1958, just before Congress convened.

In a column the next day in the *New York Herald Tribune* Walter Lippmann commented on what I had said:

> It is unusual for the leader of the opposition to make a statement like Senator Johnson's on Tuesday, just two days before the President delivers his message on the State of the Union. . . . The State of the Union message is almost certain to make or break the President's power of leadership in the Congress. Does the President realize the problem? If not, he had a timely warning from Senator Johnson. . . .
>
> Senator Johnson . . . puts this point of principle as follows: "We have,

for many years, been preoccupied with weapons. We are, even now, concerned with what some currently regard as the ultimate weapon. But when we perfect such a weapon for ourselves, we may still be far behind. The urgent race we are now in—or which we must enter—is not the race to perfect long-range ballistic missiles, important as that is. There is something more important than any ultimate weapon. That is the ultimate position— the position of total control over earth that lies somewhere out in space."

The basic truth in this statement lies in the idea that the race of armaments is now an incidental by-product of a much greater thing—the scientific exploration of the nature of the universe through man's ability to project his scientific instruments into outer space.

In February 1958 a special committee was created in the Senate to develop legislation that would speed the country's space efforts. I was named chairman of that committee. The House set up a similar committee, headed by John McCormack, then the House Democratic leader. The administration announced that it was drafting legislation for a space program. Our committees were in operation and waiting to receive it. At the administration's request, Senator Styles Bridges of New Hampshire and I introduced the bill in the Senate. We began hearings on May 6, 1958.

One issue of paramount importance was whether America's space effort was to be run by civilians or by the military. I had put that question to Nelson Rockefeller when he testified before our Preparedness Subcommittee the previous January. Rockefeller was then chairman of the Rockefeller Brothers Fund, which was making a study of our international security. I asked: "Should the organization for future development of outer space, in your opinion, be located in the Pentagon or be established in some civilian agency?" He replied: "Well, because of its intimate relation to the military aspects of our national security, it would seem to me that the Secretary of Defense should have prime responsibility in making the decision where it should be placed. . . ."

Two months later, on March 5, 1958, he changed his mind and recommended to President Eisenhower the establishment of a civilian space agency. The President endorsed his recommendation. The legislation submitted to the Congress called for an independent civilian agency. There were deep misgivings about this move both in our special committee and in the country at large. Space and defense were closely linked, and the military services had the missiles and the experts. Senator Bridges expressed fear that "we have fallen over backward" in the matter of civilian control, and he spoke for many. On the other hand, sentiment for civilian control was growing.

In the beginning, I expressed no firm conviction either way. But by the time the hearings were over, I had made up my mind. All that I learned during those first few months of the space age persuaded me that our best

THE 1964 CAMPAIGN
*I had decidedly mixed feelings about
whether I wanted to seek a four-year term....*
Lady Bird encouraged him

A political campaign is a blur, a whirlwind, an excitement . . .

Barry Goldwater at Republican
National Convention.
BOTTOM: Campaigning
for senatorial candidate
Bobby Kennedy in New York.

LEFT: Chief Justice Warren administers oath of office, January 20, 1965. Reporting to Congress on the state of the union, flanked by Vice President Hubert Humphrey and Speaker McCormack.

CHALLENGE AND RESPONSE: Vietnam 1964–1965. What we face in Southeast Asia today we have faced with courage and have met with strength in Greece, Turkey, Berlin, Korea, Lebanon, and Cuba.

August 10, 1964: Signing Southeast Asia Resolution (L.). BELOW:
Secretary Rusk; General Earle Wheeler, Chairman, Joint Chiefs of Staff.
Johns Hopkins University, April 7, 1965: Urging Hanoi to join in
unconditional negotiations (with college President Milton Eisenhower,
daughter Lynda Bird, and Mrs. Johnson).

Consulting key Democrats and Republicans during summer of 1965.
With Senator J. William Fulbright, Chairman, Foreign Relations Committee,
in small study beside Oval Office; BOTTOM: former President Eisenhower.

TOP, L.: Sen. Thomas Kuchel; R., Rep. Hale Boggs; CENTER, L., Sen. Dirksen; R., Armed Services Committee Chairman Sen. Richard Russell; BOTTOM, L., with Sen. Mansfield; Sen. Wayne Morse and UN Ambassador Arthur Goldberg.

*CRISES IN THE CARIBBEAN. No President seeks crises. They come
to him unbidden, and in legions. But we faced these challenges
in Latin America confidently and, I think, successfully.*

January 10, 1964: Johnson speaks by phone with Panama's President,
Roberto Chiari, after diplomatic relations are broken with U.S.

April 1965: Airlifting Americans during Dominican crisis, BOTTOM, LEFT.
Discussing situation with Governor Muñoz Marin of Puerto Rico.
U.S. asked OAS to help promote free elections in Dominican Republic.

Hands Across the Border. Johnsons meet Mexican President Diaz Ordaz and wife at Ciudad Acuña, December 1966. BOTTOM: Meeting of OAS Presidents at Punta del Este, April 1967.

hope for the peaceful development of outer space rested with a civilian agency. I was impressed by what I had been hearing about the nonmilitary applications of space hardware—how it could eventually be used to forecast weather and to speed communications. I concluded that the military organization should control space activities necessary for the nation's defense, but that all nonmilitary space efforts should be handled by an independent civilian agency.

My report on June 11, 1958, which accompanied the bill out of committee, stated flatly: "The essentiality of civilian control is so clear as to be no longer a point of discussion." This became the conviction of the entire Congress as well, and the bill we finally passed established the National Aeronautics and Space Administration (NASA). It has always been a source of gratification to me that the Space Act, signed on July 29, 1958, bears this opening statement: "The Congress hereby declares that it is the policy of the United States that activities in space should be devoted to peaceful purposes for the benefit of all mankind."

One other major issue had to be resolved before the Act was passed: How should a national space program be planned and coordinated? The draft legislation proposed by the administration called for a space board to advise the administrator of NASA on space matters. I believed that a board, as it was conceived in the administration draft, would be weak and ineffective. We wrote into the bill a provision for a greatly strengthened National Aeronautics and Space Council, which would report directly to the President.

Our bill passed the Senate, but ran into resistance from the White House. The President objected to the powerful Space Council we had proposed. Since the House of Representatives had already passed its version of the bill, the measure went to conference committee. I called the White House and received an appointment with the President on the evening of July 7, 1958. I knew the substance of President Eisenhower's objections, but when I went to see him he restated them for me. The Space Council would have too much power, he thought. He was afraid that in its advisory capacity to the President the Council might make too many demands upon the President and even try to dictate policy to him.

I proposed a solution: What if the President himself were Chairman of the Space Council? President Eisenhower mulled that over. Yes, that might do it. He would have no objection to that. I went back to the Hill, and that afternoon in conference we made the change. The President of the United States became Chairman of the National Aeronautics and Space Council. The Space Act was signed into law on July 29, 1958.

Although I persuaded President Eisenhower to accept the compromise on the Space Council, he never met formally with the Council; nor did he avail himself of its advice regularly, as far as I could learn. However, the new space agency was active during the final years of the Eisenhower administration, developing Project Mercury, which aimed at putting a man into orbit around the earth. President Eisenhower approved the Mercury plans, but nothing beyond them. In his final budget message to the Congress, he said only that further testing would be necessary to determine whether this country should attempt manned space activities after Mercury. Both the use of the Space Council and the development of a program to reach the moon had to wait for the next administration.

Before Christmas of 1960, John Kennedy was relaxing in Palm Beach, Florida, from the rigors of our campaign, and he asked me to come to Palm Beach to meet with him. At that session Kennedy told me that he wanted me to take over an assignment of the previous Vice President— namely, the program to end discrimination against Negroes and other minority groups in industries doing business with the government. He asked me what other responsibilities I would like to assume. I told him that I would like very much to continue my contact with space activities. Without hesitation, he agreed. He announced to the press the same day that he would rely on me heavily for space leadership. I think he was relieved to have me take it on. Every President brings to the office his own special concerns, which are the result of his interests and experience. Space was not one of President Kennedy's primary concerns at that time.

President Kennedy told me he wanted the Space Council to function as actively as the law intended. If I was willing to accept the responsibility, he said, he would ask Congress to amend the Space Act to make the Vice President Chairman of the Space Council instead of the President. I assured him that I was quite willing. In the meantime, he asked me to start meeting with the Council as soon as the administration took over.

My first space assignment after January 20, 1961, was to find an administrator for NASA. President Kennedy had thought about offering the job to a friend of his, General James M. Gavin. When he asked my opinion, I told him that I believed it would be a serious mistake to appoint any military man to head the organization. I reminded him of the great debate and searching inquiry we had gone through at the time the Space Act was passed, before we finally resolved that the space program should be civilian controlled. To put a military man in charge at this juncture, I feared, would make other nations uneasy, would dim the image of peaceful development we had carefully created, and would in the long run be a serious disservice to the entire program. President Kennedy said, in effect: "All right, find another administrator."

After interviewing about twenty outstanding men, I concluded that James Webb was the best possible man for the job. A former Director of the Bureau of the Budget and Under Secretary of State during the Truman administration, and later a distinguished businessman, he had a suitable combination of government experience, executive ability, and the respect of Congress. I had to urge and persuade Webb to take the job. He was engaged in private business at the time and was involved in public activities in Oklahoma. He agreed to return to government only when he became convinced that the country needed his help to achieve leadership in space. The choice of Webb as administrator of NASA was one of the best selections I ever made. Under his forceful administration for eight years, America's space program progressed steadily from dream to fulfillment.

In April 1961 President Kennedy asked Congress to amend the Space Act to establish the Vice President as Chairman of the Space Council, replacing the President. In the course of that action, an interesting document on the role of the Vice President in the activities of the government became part of the historical record. The House Science and Astronautics Committee asked the opinion of the Attorney General as to whether any constitutional bar would prohibit the Vice President from serving as council chairman. The opinion was set forth in a memorandum to me from Nicholas Katzenbach, who was then Assistant Attorney General and legal counsel to the Department of Justice. It is, I have been told, one of the few official reports ever prepared dealing authoritatively with the Vice President's functions and the delegation of responsibility to him by the President. The opinion concluded that the President cannot cede any of his Executive power, but short of that he can assign the Vice President whatever duties he wishes.

By 1961 the United States had begun to achieve a modicum of success in space, particularly with communications and weather satellites, but the gap separating us from the Soviet Union was still growing. In the first few months I was in office the Russians sent several more heavy satellites into orbit with animals aboard.

Toward the end of March President Kennedy called a meeting to discuss space matters. His Budget Director, David Bell, was present, as well as his science adviser, Jerome B. Wiesner. The President was seeking to determine how much additional money for space, above the Eisenhower request, he should ask from Congress in the fiscal year 1962. But at the root of his questioning was one overriding concern: He wanted to know what needed to be done, what should be done, what could be done, and what had to be done to get our space program moving. The immediate technical requirement, which we went over in detail, was the development of more powerful rocket engines. Propulsion represented the most important advantage the Soviets had.

I felt we needed a longer-range answer. Bigger boosters and greater propulsion, vital though they were, are not the stuff that national goals are made of. America, I thought, needed a bold and understandable challenge if it was going to move forward. I discussed this concept with the President at some length over the next few weeks. As persuasively as I could, I suggested that he give the Space Council an assignment that would, in effect, be a charter to determine what the country's capabilities were in space. Then, from the Space Council's findings, the President could announce a concrete national program.

President Kennedy agreed. By now the need for forceful action was more urgent than ever. On April 12 a Soviet spacecraft carrying a Russian cosmonaut had orbited the earth. Major Yuri Gagarin of the Soviet air force became the first human being to depart this planet, enter the void of space, and return. Should anyone doubt the significance of this accomplishment, Nikita Khrushchev told Gagarin, in a telephone conversation which was broadcast around the globe: "Let the capitalist countries catch up with our country!"

On April 20, 1961, the day Congress approved the amendment making the Vice President Chairman of the Space Council, President Kennedy sent me a memorandum. "In accordance with our conversation," it read, "I would like for you as chairman of the Space Council to be in charge of making an overall survey of where we stand in space." The President posed a series of specific questions that he wanted my study to answer:

> Do we have a chance of beating the Soviets by putting a laboratory in space, or by a trip around the moon, or by a rocket to land on the moon, or by a rocket to go to the moon and back with a man? Is there any other space program which promises dramatic results in which we could win?

The President's memorandum came to me three days after the disastrous failure at the Bay of Pigs. I am aware of the allegation that President Kennedy tried to divert attention from that embarrassment by focusing public interest on space and announcing a moon objective. I will simply say that he never gave the least indication in any of our discussions that he thought there was any relationship. The discussions he and I had about space began long before the abortive Bay of Pigs episode, although the decision was reached soon after.

Immediately after receiving the President's questions, I consulted the Space Council, which included Secretary of State Rusk, Secretary of Defense McNamara, NASA administrator Jim Webb, and the Chairman of the Atomic Energy Commission, Dr. Glenn Seaborg. I also asked three distinguished Americans from the private sector to meet with us—Frank Stanton, president of the Columbia Broadcasting System; George R. Brown, chief executive of the construction firm of Brown & Root; and

Donald C. Cook, executive vice president of the American Electric Power Company. We worked almost round the clock with the nation's leading scientists and engineers.

Throughout our discussions and searching inquiries one object figured ever more prominently—the moon. We learned that it was technologically possible to develop a program to reach the moon, and we came to realize that since the Russians did not then have the ability to reach the moon any more than we did, we had at least a fifty-fifty chance of beating them there. Moreover, a moon-landing goal would give a dramatic focus to a space program designed to develop our skills and capacities on a broad technological front.

Eight days after receiving the President's request, we had completed our survey. On April 28 I sent an interim report to the President. I concluded the report with this statement: "The U.S. can, if it will, firm up its objectives and employ its resources with a reasonable chance of attaining world leadership in space during this decade."

In the report I gave this answer to the specific question the President had raised: "As for a manned trip around the moon or a safe landing and return by a man to the moon, neither the United States nor the USSR has such a capability at this time, so far as we know. The Russians have had more experience with large boosters and with flights of dogs and man. Hence they might be conceded a time advantage in circumnavigation of the moon and also in a manned trip to the moon. However, with a strong effort the United States could conceivably be first in those accomplishments by 1966 or 1967."

The President studied the report carefully, and on May 25, 1961, less than a month after the Space Council's recommendations and detailed plans were presented to him, John Kennedy went before the Congress to utter the words that set in motion a program of U.S. scientific and industrial activity without equal in history. For the benefit of the Congress and the nation, he reviewed the searching inquiry that had been taking place.

"With the advice of the Vice President, who is Chairman of the National Space Council," he said, "we have examined where we are strong and where we are not, where we may succeed and where we may not. Now it is time to take longer strides—time for a great new American enterprise— time for this nation to take a clearly leading role in space achievement, which in many ways may hold the key to our future on earth." He then presented his sweeping recommendation: "I believe that this nation should commit itself to achieving the goal, before the decade is out, of landing a man on the moon and returning him safely to earth."

This was a courageous decision for President Kennedy to make, and I know that if the program had gone wrong life would not have been pleasant for the Vice President, who had been the first to urge it upon the

President. The President did find the going rough a little later, when the dramatic novelty of the idea had worn off and critics felt freer to make their attacks. By 1963 those attacks were aired with increasing frequency. On January 29 of that year *The New York Times* questioned whether the moon program was justified on scientific, military, or political grounds. The August 3 issue of the liberal publication *The New Republic* complained that the space program was costing too much. At the opposite end of the spectrum, the conservative *Reader's Digest* that same week charged that the program was not sufficiently oriented to military defense.

Stung by these assaults, Kennedy sought justification for our expenditures. He sent me the following memorandum, in which he referred to the *Reader's Digest* article and appended the editorial from *The New Republic:*

Memorandum for the Vice President

July 29, 1963

The attack on the moon program continues and seems to be intensifying. Note *Reader's Digest* lead article this month. I would be interested in your analyzing the following points and giving me information on them:

1. Did the previous administration have a moon program? What was its time schedule? How much were they going to spend on it?
2. How much of our present peaceful space program can be militarily useful? How much of our capability for our moon program is also necessary for military control in space?

I would be interested in any other thoughts you may have on the large amounts of money we are spending on this program and how it can be justified.

JFK

I replied as follows:

July 31, 1963

Dear Mr. President:

This is in response to your memorandum of July 29, 1963, in which you asked two questions regarding the moon program and our military space requirements.

There was no Administration moon program until your message to Congress in May 1961. The previous Administration undertook studies on this question, but no commitment for hardware, facilities, or schedule was made.

It is not possible to ascribe a quantitative measure to the military spin-offs from the non-military portion of the space program. However, all of the scientific and engineering ability and experience in space has direct or indirect value, no matter whether it is now being applied to military or non-military missions.

NASA's manned space flight program will contribute competence in rendezvous technique, in control and guidance systems, in life protection measures, and in improvement in propulsion. All of these have military significance and can materially contribute to military control in space.

The space program is expensive, but it can be justified as a solid investment which will give ample returns in security, prestige, knowledge and material benefits.

This reply has been concurred in by all members of the Space Council.

Sincerely,
Lyndon B. Johnson

The rest of the story of America in space is familiar to most of us who have lived through these exciting years. When Alan B. Shepard, Jr., made the first American flight out of the earth's atmosphere on May 5, 1961, television cameras and reporters by the hundreds converged on Cape Canaveral. There was an understandable tenseness in the nation. Fear of failure led a few doubters to suggest postponing the flight. Several members of Congress urged President Kennedy to bar press coverage. I recommended the opposite. I believed that we should keep our window open to the rest of the world, whatever happened. President Kennedy came around to this view. From that time on little has happened in our space program in secret. The whole program has operated almost totally in the open.

Early in my Presidency I reaffirmed the national policy that I had helped to forge. "Our plan to place a man on the moon in a decade remains unchanged," I said in my first budget message. I restated that plan often enough to insure that there was no mistaking our purpose. When I accepted the Robert H. Goddard Trophy from the National Space Club on March 16, 1966, I said: "We intend to land the first man on the surface of the moon and we intend to do this in the decade of the sixties." Throughout my time in office I supported the program to the limit of my ability.

People frequently refer to our program to reach the moon during the 1960s as a national commitment. It was not. There was no commitment on succeeding Congresses to supply funds on a continuing basis. The program had to be justified, and money appropriated year after year. This support was not always easy to obtain.

Those were exciting years, as our astronauts climbed step by step to the moon. We were united in a great national adventure as we watched Gus Grissom and John W. Young take off on America's first two-man flight, and Ed White walk in space while James A. McDivitt tried to coax him back into their spacecraft. In August 1965 L. Gordon Cooper and Charles Conrad, Jr., made the longest manned flight on record, 190 hours.

Less than four months later Frank Borman and James A. Lovell, Jr., broke that record with a flight of 330 hours. In the final twenty-five hours of that flight Walter M. Schirra, Jr., and Thomas P. Stafford went into orbit in another vehicle and rendezvoused within a foot of the first ship. The next step came when Neil A. Armstrong and David R. Scott docked with a target rocket in orbit. Then there was more walking and working in space, more docking, and more rendezvousing by Tom Stafford and Eugene A. Cernan, John Young and Michael Collins, Pete Conrad and Richard F. Gordon, Jr., Jim Lovell and Edwin E. Aldrin, Jr.

The fire that killed Grissom, White, and Chaffee on January 27, 1967, threatened for a time to replace our excitement with national despondency, but this did not happen. On the night of the fire I talked for a long time with Jim Webb. He felt the agony of that accident as much as any man, but even in his grief he was courageous. He knew what the nation's reaction would be, but he said, in effect: Mr. President, all we can do is what's right, and we know what we're doing is right. We can't be discouraged and depressed to the point that we throw up our hands. We're going to find out what went wrong, and we're going to correct it. But we're going to continue.

We did learn what went wrong on the launching pad that tragic day, and we did correct it. The country was willing to accept failure and still press on. The American people are slow to start, but hard to stop. Twenty-one months after that tragedy Wally Schirra, Donn F. Eisele, and R. Walter Cunningham went into space on the first three-man Apollo mission. At Christmas in 1968, during my final weeks in the White House, Frank Borman, Jim Lovell, and William A. Anders tendered us an experience no human beings had ever known. They flew in orbit around the moon and sent back photographs not only of that celestial body but of our own earth beyond, shining and luminous in the dark void of space.

The target we had set was within our reach.

In years to come history may record that one of the greatest triumphs of the space program of the 1960s was the basis it provided for reaching accommodations with old adversaries. In 1958, while I was Senate Majority Leader, President Eisenhower invited me to address the United Nations on the subject of space. In that speech I proposed that space-probing nations make the exploration of outer space "a joint adventure." I believe this still may happen. At the least, we are moving toward assuring the peaceful development of space. During my Presidency we signed two space treaties with the Soviet Union and many other countries. One treaty provided for the safe return of any nation's astronauts and space equipment landing within the jurisdiction of another nation. The other banned weapons of mass destruction from outer space. These two treaties can help remove causes of future conflict from the realm of outer space.

I have always felt especially close to the astronauts, those brave pioneers who have blazed new trails across the untraveled wilderness of space and captured the imagination of people around the world. I have flown with them mentally on every flight they have made, anxious and prayerful until the final splashdown. I always enjoyed being in their company, at the Ranch, the White House, and at the NASA Manned Spacecraft Center in Houston. They represent the best this nation can produce; they are the folk heroes of our time.

On the morning of July 16, 1969, at President Nixon's request, I stood under the Florida sun at Cape Kennedy and witnessed the launching of Apollo 11, carrying the voyagers who would first set foot on the moon. As I watched that vehicle rise on its pillar of flame, seeing sky and earth and rocket all tied together in one majestic and unforgettable panorama, I could not help remembering that earlier vigil, twelve years before, when we strained to see the Soviet Sputnik orbiting overhead. In the short span of time between those two events, we wrote a story that will be told for centuries to come. We developed the ability to operate in space with both men and machines. From outside the earth's environment we studied the sun and the planets. We used space machines to forecast weather and to improve communications a hundredfold. But there is even more to the story than that, I believe.

Space was the platform from which the social revolution of the 1960s was launched. We broke out of far more than the atmosphere with our space program. We escaped from the bonds of inattention and inaction that had gripped the 1950s. New ideas took shape. If we could send a man to the moon, we knew we should be able to send a poor boy to school and to provide decent medical care for the aged. In hundreds of other forms, the space program had an impact on our lives. Across the entire range of our technology we are beginning to reap benefits from the investment we have made in space—from the Pacemaker, which can add years to the life of a heart patient, to intercontinental television; from new lightweight electronics equipment to improved navigation techniques for ships and planes.

Within another decade the spinoffs from space will be improving life in ever-increasing ways, from medicine to urban planning. We will use the vantage point of space to locate new supplies of food and new resources on earth. Weather control will save lives and crops and cattle. New concepts of communication will help to banish ignorance. Cameras in space will warn us of crop plagues before they have time to spread across half a nation. We can build laboratories in space that will enable us to learn more about our own earth as well as the planets. We can build natural-resources satellites at relatively little cost that can tell us about mineral and oil deposits, water and fish supplies, and dangers from flood and fire. We can build an Antarctica-type station on the moon. We can marry aeronautics and astronautics to develop a spacecraft that can be reused, and thus lower the cost of space travel.

And we can go on from there. I hope we will move out to other planets. I hope we will pursue new dreams. We must not be content to relegate this great adventure to a business-as-usual status. We should never permit the plaudits that President Nixon and our other leaders have given our spacemen in this noble effort to be silenced by the pleaders for economy. I am concerned and disappointed that as I write this some of our previous plans are being abandoned and our vision appears to be in the process of being replaced by that of thinkers of another day who compared this magnificent thrust to an "outer space basketball game."

The new adventures in space that lie ahead will bring with them excitement and accomplishment as great as anything we have witnessed in the epic period just past, when we proved ourselves once more to be the sons of pioneers who tamed a broad continent and built the mightiest nation in the history of the world.

13

The Six Day War

JUST BEFORE EIGHT O'CLOCK on the morning of June 5, 1967, the telephone rang in my bedroom at the White House. Bob McNamara was calling with a message never heard before by an American President. "Mr. President," he said, "the hot line is up."

The hot line is a special teletype circuit linking Moscow and Washington. The technicians call it Molink. Its purpose is to provide instant communication between the Soviet leaders and the American President in times of grave crises in order to minimize the dangers of delay and misunderstanding. The hot line was installed on August 30, 1963, but had been operated only to test its effectiveness and to exchange New Year's greetings. It had never been used for its intended purpose until now.

McNamara's words were ominous, given the background against which they were spoken. Three and one-half hours before, at 4:35 A.M., Walt Rostow had awakened me with the news that war had erupted in the Middle East. I had been fearing a Middle East conflict and working as hard as I could to forestall it. Trouble in that area was, in my judgment, potentially far more dangerous than the war in Southeast Asia.

The Vietnam conflict, tragic and perilous as it was, was contained, and we were reasonably sure we could keep it from spreading. Conflict in the Middle East was something else. From the founding of Israel in 1948 we had supported the territorial integrity of all the states in that region. Our commitment was not inscribed in any treaty, but it was strong nonetheless. It was rooted in the Tripartite Declaration of 1950, in which the United States, Great Britain, and France promised to oppose any effort to alter by force the national borders in the Middle East. Four Presidents— Truman, Eisenhower, Kennedy, and myself—had publicly reaffirmed this pledge. Congress had supported it in the Middle East Resolution at Eisenhower's request in 1957, and again in 1961 at Kennedy's request.

I believe we had been fair over the years in Middle East matters. We acted in 1958 to preserve the territorial integrity of Jordan and Lebanon. Other Arab nations benefited from our protective influence throughout this period. But in the 1960s it was Israel whose territory was threatened by hostile neighbors.

In an effort to gain influence in the radical Arab states, the Soviet Union shifted in the mid-1950s from its original support of Israel to an attempt to push moderate Arab states toward a more radical course and to provide a Middle East base for expanding its role in the Mediterranean, in Africa, and in the areas bordering on the Indian Ocean. The Soviets used Arab hostility toward Israel to inflame Arab politics to the boiling point. Country after country had shifted to the Russian view. The expanding Soviet presence in this strategic region threatened our position in Europe. Soviet leaders called publicly for the withdrawal of our Sixth Fleet from the Mediterranean, as well as for the liquidation of NATO. If they gained control of the seas, the oil, and the air space of the vast arc between Morocco and Iran, all that had been done since President Truman's time to achieve stability and balance in world politics would have been endangered.

I had watched this process with growing concern. In the fall of 1966 I asked for a special study of Soviet penetration in the Middle East. The work, directed by former Ambassador Julius C. Holmes, revealed a pattern of serious Soviet advances, sparked in large part by emotions generated in the Arab-Israeli confrontation and including the active expansion of Soviet sea power and missile capability.

The danger implicit in every border incident in the Middle East was not merely war between Israelis and Arabs but an ultimate confrontation between the Soviet Union and the United States and its NATO allies. This was the danger that concerned me, as well as the tragedy of war itself, in those hours before dawn on June 5, 1967.

The backdrop to the war that began that day was crowded with the diplomatic maneuvering, pent-up tensions, and explosions of the past twenty years. The most important events, stripped to bare essentials, were these: War had erupted between Israel and the Arabs twice before, in 1948 and 1956. Both times Israeli military forces showed remarkable strength and ability. Both times hostilities ended because of pressures brought to bear in the United Nations, but there was no permanent settlement. In the 1956 war Israeli troops overran the Sinai peninsula. They agreed to withdraw from the area for two reasons: first, a UN decision to put in a peacekeeping force to patrol the borders between Israel and Egypt and, second, President Eisenhower's assurance that the Gulf of Aqaba,

Israel's only outlet to the Indian Ocean, would remain open as an international waterway. To symbolize this assurance, the United Nations sent forces to Sharm el Sheikh. These understandings were contained in public statements at the time as well as in diplomatic exchanges. They were handled this way to satisfy Nasser's sensitivity to the appearance of making peace, or even negotiating, with Israel.

An uneasy truce between the warring states prevailed until 1965. The next year a new radical government in Syria increased terrorist raids against Israel, sending Arab guerrillas across the borders of Syria, Jordan and Lebanon. Such acts are in flagrant violation of international law. Every state is as responsible legally for irregular forces or armed bands attacking a neighbor as it is for attacks made by its own army. Syria's goal was twofold—to force Israeli reprisals against Jordan and Lebanon, thereby helping to weaken or destroy the moderate, pro-Western governments of those countries, and to bring on war.

A most painful and revealing moment in the entire cycle occurred when the issue of Syrian raids was referred to the UN Security Council. Though Syria had boasted of its responsibility for the raids, the Soviet Union vetoed a mild and ambiguous resolution condemning such action. As the raids increased in intensity, Israeli forces retaliated. In November 1966 they struck the Jordanian town of Es Samu, which they believed had been used as a base by Syrian terrorists.

Retaliation had little effect. Syria and Egypt concluded a mutual defense agreement. Terrorist raids continued and tension increased into the spring of 1967. On May 12 of that year Israeli Prime Minister Levi Eshkol warned that more terrorism would bring further retaliatory action. Reports spread in Damascus that the Israelis were mobilizing major forces on the Syrian frontier for full-scale action. We investigated, found the reports to be untrue, and informed the Russians and the nations bordering on Israel of this fact. UN Secretary General U Thant spoke publicly to the same effect.

At the same time, we received reports that Moscow had promised unlimited support to the Syrians. In Washington the State Department took this up with the Soviet Embassy. The Russians denied all knowledge of such a promise and said that Soviet policy was simply to keep the area "calm." Nevertheless, the Russians were helping to spread the rumor that the Israelis were mobilizing with the intention of striking Syria in a few days. In mid-May a theme of Soviet propaganda was that Israel was about to attack Syria, "incited by American imperialist circles and foreign monopolies." Our reports indicated that the purpose of these rumors was to pressure Egypt into military support of Syria. The reports were confirmed later in statements made by President Gamal Abdel Nasser.

Egypt had been trying to dominate the Arab world since Nasser came to leadership in 1954. For a time, in the early 1960s, we hoped that he was beginning to concentrate instead on improving the lot of his own people. On this assumption, we gave substantial aid to Egypt, mainly wheat to feed the people in its teeming cities. In the end, Nasser persisted in his imperial dream. While his strained economy slowed down, he sent troops into Yemen to support revolutionaries trying to take over that country. To support his ambitions, he became increasingly dependent on Soviet arms. Nasser's attitude toward the United States grew more and more hostile and his speeches more inflammatory. It became impossible to maintain congressional support for even token assistance to Egypt.

Through it all Nasser's prestige in the Arab world declined. So even though initial reports indicated that he preferred not to fight, he was susceptible to taunts that he was failing to protect Syria in the face of an alleged Israeli threat to Egypt's ally. And once he moved, events had a tragic inevitability of their own. It was not clear in mid-May of 1967 that any government actually wanted war, but after May 14 the Arab states began to act in ways inconsistent with preserving peace.

On that date, May 14, 1967, Nasser mobilized his armed forces. Two days later Egypt asked the United Nations to withdraw its peacekeeping force in the Sinai. In an action that shocked me then, and that still puzzles me, Secretary General U Thant announced that UN forces could not remain in the Sinai without Egyptian approval. Even the Egyptians were surprised. Nasser's Ambassador in Washington, Dr. Mostafa Kamel, told us that his government thought and hoped that U Thant would play for time. But he did not, and tension increased.

We threw the full weight of U.S. diplomacy into an effort to forestall war. The first necessity was to persuade the Israelis not to act hastily. I knew they would feel anxious about the withdrawal of UN forces, but I also knew that if open conflict was to be avoided, the Israelis would have to remain cool. On May 17, 1967, I cabled Prime Minister Eshkol, spelling out our deep concern over the situation and urging restraint. "I am sure you will understand," I wrote, "that I cannot accept any responsibilities on behalf of the United States for situations which arise as the result of actions on which we are not consulted."

On May 18 UN forces withdrew. Egyptian troops entered the Sinai peninsula and took up positions on Israel's borders. Despite his ill-conceived first maneuver, U Thant then announced that he was going to Cairo to try to preserve peace. We fully supported his effort. As far as possible, I wanted the main thrust of our diplomacy to be through the United Nations. At the same time, I was prepared to use American influence in any way that might be effective and helpful. On May 22 I sent a message to Soviet Chairman Kosygin suggesting a joint effort to calm the situation. I wrote:

The increasing harassment of Israel by elements based in Syria, with attendant reactions within Israel and within the Arab world, has brought the area close to major violence. Your and our ties to nations of the area could bring us into difficulties which I am confident neither of us seeks. It would appear a time for each of us to use our influence to the full in the cause of moderation, including our influence over action by the United Nations.

On the 22nd, I also sent a letter to Nasser assuring him of America's basic friendship for Egypt and my own understanding of "the pride and aspirations of your people." I urged him to avoid war as his first duty and expressed the hope that "if we come through these days without hostilities," I could send Vice President Humphrey to talk to him and other Middle East leaders in a new attempt to find a solution to the old problems there.

That same day, after I sent my letter to Nasser but before it was actually delivered and while U Thant was flying to Cairo, the Egyptian government made its fateful announcement: Egypt was closing the Gulf of Aqaba to Israeli shipping. Although we cannot be sure, it seems likely that Nasser took this mortally dangerous action independently of the Soviet Union.

With UN troops withdrawn from the Egyptian-Israeli border, the settlement of 1957 was undone. On March 1, 1957, in a speech at the United Nations, Ambassador Lodge had affirmed a U.S.-Israeli understanding that Israeli withdrawal from the Sinai was linked to free passage through Aqaba, and that any armed interference would entitle Israel to rights of self-defense under the UN Charter. I knew that on February 26, 1957, Secretary of State Dulles had informed President Eisenhower in a memorandum "that Israel has been assured that a purpose of the United Nations Emergency Force would be to restrain the exercise of belligerent rights which would prevent passage through the Strait of Tiran." I wanted to know precisely how Eisenhower had viewed the matter at that time, so I sought his views and invited any statement he might care to make. General Eisenhower sent me a message stating his view that the Israelis' right of access to the Gulf of Aqaba was definitely part of the "commitment" we had made to them.

There was no doubt that Israel regarded it as such. I believed we had an obligation to state clearly the continuity of our position on Aqaba and to give as much assurance to the Israelis as we legitimately could. In a statement on May 23 I charged that Nasser's blockade was "illegal" and "potentially disastrous to the cause of peace." I also reaffirmed our support of the political independence and territorial integrity of all nations of the area.

Secretary of State Rusk briefed the Senate Foreign Relations Committee that day. He told me later that he believed there was general agreement in Congress that the Arabs should not be permitted to drive the Israelis into the sea. He thought it was generally recognized that we could not stay aloof from the problems of the Middle East. However, the Senators told the Secretary that they were against unilateral action by the United States. The problem, they thought, called for a multilateral solution, hopefully through the United Nations. We had been searching for a multilateral solution since the crisis began. My first hope was the United Nations. But I felt no great optimism.

"I want to play every card in the UN," I told my advisers, "but I've never relied on it to save me when I'm going down for the third time. I want to see Wilson * and De Gaulle out there with their ships all lined up too."

When the UN forces withdrew from the Sinai, I instructed Rusk to find out how France and Great Britain viewed the pledge they had made under the 1950 Tripartite Declaration. He assured me the next day: "We are pressing both the French and the British for a firm answer reaffirming the principles of the declaration of policy."

Our Ambassador to France, Charles ("Chip") Bohlen, talked with officials in Paris and reported that the French believed it would be a mistake to invoke the Tripartite Declaration. The French were even wary of taking any moderating steps on their own. Bohlen concluded that they attached considerable importance to Soviet attitudes and were "playing a careful game."

The British, on the other hand, were actively seeking a way out of the crisis in full cooperation with us. On May 24 their Minister of State for Foreign Affairs, George Thomson, met with Rusk and other State Department officials in Washington to discuss a proposal based on the commitments of the international community made in 1957 at the United Nations. The British proposed two steps. First, there would be a public declaration, signed by as many nations as possible, reasserting the right of free passage through the Gulf of Aqaba. There was hope that the declaration might even be endorsed by the United Nations. Second, a naval task force would be set up, composed of as many nations as possible, to break Nasser's blockade and open the Strait of Tiran. During the next few days we explored the British proposal fully with key Congressmen and with other interested governments.

I was scheduled to go to Canada on May 25 for United States Day at Expo '67. I held off the decision to go until the morning of the 25th, when intelligence reports indicated that I could be reasonably sure the Middle East would not explode while I was gone. As a result of the delay, the only explosion was in the White House press corps. The reporters resented being called on short notice early in the morning to go on a trip they insisted we had known about for two days. They did not realize that we

---

* British Prime Minister Harold Wilson.

were in the middle of a fast-moving crisis and that it was impossible to have firm plans. Nor could we tell them.

On the evening of May 26 I met with Israel's Foreign Minister Abba Eban, who had just flown to Washington. Our conversation was direct and frank. Eban said that according to Israeli intelligence, the United Arab Republic (UAR) was preparing an all-out attack. I asked Secretary McNamara, who was present, to give Mr. Eban a summary of our findings. Three separate intelligence groups had looked carefully into the matter, McNamara said, and it was our best judgment that a UAR attack was not imminent. "All of our intelligence people are unanimous," I added, "that if the UAR attacks, you will whip hell out of them."

Eban asked what the United States was willing to do to keep the Gulf of Aqaba open. I reminded him that I had defined our position on May 23. We were hard at work on what to do to assure free access, and when to do it. "You can assure the Israeli Cabinet," I said, "we will pursue vigorously any and all possible measures to keep the strait open."

I pointed out that we had to try to work through the United Nations first. "If it should become apparent that the UN is ineffective," I said, "then Israel and her friends, including the United States, who are willing to stand up and be counted can give specific indication of what they can do."

I told him that I saw some hope in the plan for an international naval force in the strait area, but that before such a proposal could be effective I had to be sure Congress was on board. "I am fully aware of what three past Presidents have said," I told Eban, "but that is not worth five cents if the people and the Congress do not support the President." I knew from bitter experience that the situation would be worse if the Congress started out supporting Israel and then found excuses to turn tail and run if the going got rough. Some Senators who had been in the vanguard with me on Southeast Asia were already looking for a storm cellar, and I did not want a repetition of this faintheartedness in the Middle East.

State Department officials were working hard to win support for the British plan from other governments. I urged Israel to concentrate its efforts on that diplomatic task.

Abba Eban is an intelligent and sensitive man. I wanted him to understand the U.S. position fully and clearly, and to communicate what I said to his government. "The central point, Mr. Minister," I told him, "is that your nation not be the one to bear the responsibility for any outbreak of war." Then I said very slowly and very positively: "Israel will not be alone unless it decides to go alone."

He was quiet, and I repeated the statement once more. Toward the end of the session, choosing his words carefully, Eban asked: "I would not be wrong if I told the Prime Minister that your disposition is to make every possible effort to assure that the Strait and the Gulf will remain open to free and innocent passage?" I assured him he would not be wrong.

At the end of our talk I believed we had a clear understanding: In the days ahead both governments would concentrate on finding a way to open the Gulf of Aqaba; he could report back to Prime Minister Eshkol that I would, within the limits of my constitutional position, be making a maximum effort to that end. Eban returned to Israel. On May 28 the Israeli Cabinet decided to postpone military action.

On May 30 Prime Minister Eshkol sent me a message confirming that there had been a meeting of the minds on May 26. Eshkol's cable assured me that Eban's conversation with me had had "an important influence on our decision to await developments for a further limited period." He went on to say: "It is crucial that the international naval escort should move through the Strait within a week or two."

As my advisers and I interpreted it, the phrase "within a week or two" meant that we had about two weeks to make diplomacy succeed before Israel took independent military action. This judgment was strengthened by information from other diplomatic sources.

Early in June we sensed that the Israelis might be moving toward a decision to reopen Aqaba on their own, but we still believed that we had time to reach a settlement through diplomacy. On the morning of June 2 a high-ranking Israeli diplomat called on Walt Rostow. He sent me a report immediately afterward containing the following information:

> I then asked . . . how much time did they think they had? He replied that they had made a commitment to hold steady for about two weeks. He would measure that from the Cabinet meeting last Sunday. Therefore, he was talking about things that might happen in the week after next; that is, the week beginning Sunday, June 11—although he indicated that there was nothing ironclad about the time period being exactly two weeks.

On the same day, before leaving for Israel, Ambassador Avraham Harman told Rusk that the test in the Gulf of Aqaba should be made in the course of "the next week." In the meantime, Robert Anderson * was in Egypt on business. He met with Nasser on May 31. Their conversation produced an arrangement for UAR Vice President Zakaria Mohieddin to confer with us in Washington on Wednesday, June 7. His visit would have provided another opportunity for personal diplomacy, but it never took place. His trip was canceled by the outbreak of war. We would never know what purpose, if any, that meeting might have served.

During those trying days I used all the energy and experience I could muster to prevent war. But I was not too hopeful. I sensed that Nasser believed he had achieved an easy reversal of the humiliation of 1956–1957 at the expense of Israel and the United Nations. He was again in the role

* Secretary of the Treasury under President Eisenhower.

he most cherished, hero of the Arab world. I knew that persuading him to reverse himself and reopen Aqaba would not be easy. As I read the reports from Israel, I felt the tensions growing there. If it came to a crunch, I believed the American flag would have to sail the waters of Aqaba alongside Israel's and, we hoped, many other flags as well. We had to prepare for that possibility, and prepare urgently.

Before U.S. military forces could be involved in any way, I was determined to ask Congress for a resolution supporting such a move. I was convinced that Congress would approve the resolution if there seemed to be no alternative, but such a vote of confidence would not be easy to obtain. There were those on Capitol Hill who would willingly exploit the situation for political advantage. In a joint memorandum to me Rusk and McNamara observed: "While it is true that many Congressional Vietnam doves may be in the process of conversion to [Israeli] hawks . . . an effort to get a meaningful resolution from the Congress runs the risk of becoming bogged down in acrimonious dispute."

At the very least, I knew that the Congress would not move until we had exhausted all other diplomatic remedies, through the United Nations and outside it. This was also true of the White House. I was opposed to using force until I was persuaded that every other avenue was blocked. And we were moving rapidly to explore every possibility. The week of June 5, 1967, would have been one of intensive diplomacy and congressional consultation, if we had had our way.

Besides Great Britain and the United States, two other nations had agreed to take part in a naval task force—known informally as the Red Sea regatta—if events proved this necessary. The Dutch had expressed their intention to us in writing. Harold Holt, Prime Minister of Australia, assured me personally in a visit to Washington on June 1 that his country would assign two of its fastest cruisers to the joint task force. We will never know how successful that "regatta" might have been. But I am convinced that Congress as well as the President would have honored President Eisenhower's 1957 commitment on Aqaba when it was clear that every alternative had been exhausted, and that other nations, even a few others, would have gone with us. The reopening of Aqaba was important for several reasons—because hostilities were certain to erupt if it were not reopened; because of President Eisenhower's solemn promise; and because Israel had a right to that access to the sea.

With the deadline nearing, we pressed the search for a peaceful solution with all our energy. We asked the UN Security Council to endorse the appeal U Thant had made, after his return from Cairo, calling on all countries involved to avoid violence and provide time for further diplomatic and UN efforts. Because France abstained, we were unable to get nine votes in the Security Council to force the issue—a dismal comment on the ineffectiveness of that body. With the British, we sought widespread support for a declaration affirming the right of innocent passage through the Gulf of Aqaba. This was slow work. By June 4 only eight countries had agreed, and they included the United States, Great Britain, and Israel. The others were the Netherlands, Australia, Iceland, Belgium, and New Zealand. Five other nations—West Germany, Argentina, Portugal, Canada, and Panama—were still studying the proposition, but we felt they were nearing agreement.

During that final weekend of uneasy quiet Rusk sent cables to all our Ambassadors in Arab capitals urging them to "put your minds to possible solutions which can prevent war." He informed the Ambassadors that we had thus far been able to convince the Israelis to hold back, but that they might be nearing a decision to use force. "It will do no good," his message said, "to ask Israel simply to accept the present status quo in the Strait, because Israel will fight and we could not restrain her. We cannot throw up our hands and say, in that event, let them fight while we try to remain neutral." The central point involving the United States, the message said, was this: "We cannot abandon, in principle, the right of Israeli flagships to transit the Strait."

That same weekend, Saturday, June 3, I went to New York to speak at a dinner given by the New York State Democratic party. I spoke briefly of the subject that was on everybody's mind:

> I know that you share my deep concern tonight about the situation in the Middle East. We have been working on this problem day and night. . . .
>
> We are keeping in very close contact with all of the leaders of both of the parties in the Congress. . . . We are doing everything we can to assist the United Nations Security Council. And you may be sure, also, that we are keeping in very close touch with all the capitals concerned.
>
> To go beyond this tonight would not serve the cause of peace or would not be helpful, but you may be assured that this matter is foremost in our thoughts at all times—even at this hour.

That was the weekend the Israeli Cabinet decided to move. Only the Israelis themselves can describe and assess the reasons for their decision. Perhaps even they cannot sort out all the factors that motivated them. They may have feared that the week ahead would bring about a significant relative weakening in their military position, since Iraqi forces were moving into Jordan, a UAR commander took over the combined Arab forces, and Arab commandos threatened Israeli airfields. Our military men did not share this fear, and their judgment of relative Israeli-Arab strength proved amazingly accurate as the battle turned out.

The economic strains of Israeli mobilization were, we knew, severe; but I did not believe it was wise to seek relief from them in war. The Israelis may also have been afraid that further diplomatic moves would erode their position on Aqaba. I did not share that judgment, because I was determined to honor President Eisenhower's 1957 pledge on Aqaba. Finally, the Israelis may have concluded that it was necessary for Israel to solve the crisis on its own rather than rely on the United States and the international community.

I have always had a deep feeling of sympathy for Israel and its people, gallantly building and defending a modern nation against great odds and against the tragic background of Jewish experience. I can understand that men might decide to act on their own when hostile forces gather on their frontiers and cut off a major port, and when antagonistic political leaders fill the air with threats to destroy their nation. Nonetheless, I have never concealed my regret that Israel decided to move when it did. I always made it equally clear, however, to the Russians and to every other nation, that I did not accept the oversimplified charge of Israeli aggression. Arab actions in the weeks before the war started—forcing UN troops out, closing the port of Aqaba, and assembling forces on the Israeli border—made that charge ridiculous.

When I was first called early on the morning of June 5 with news that war had broken out, the available information was sketchy. The only clear fact was that Israeli and Egyptian forces were fighting. Each side had accused the other of aggression. Whatever the truth proved to be, I knew that tragic consequences could follow.

I decided first to get in touch with the leaders of the Soviet Union. I talked to Rusk at 5:09 A.M. and approved a message to Soviet Foreign Minister Andrei Gromyko. It expressed our dismay and surprise at the reports of conflict and concluded: "We feel it is very important that the United Nations Security Council succeed in bringing this fighting to an end as quickly as possible and are ready to cooperate with all members of the Council to that end."

The activity log for those early morning hours reflects the character of that day:

4:30 A.M. telephone call from Rostow
5:09 A.M. telephone call from Rusk
6:15 A.M. telephone call from Rostow
6:35 A.M. telephone call from Christian
6:40 A.M. breakfast in bedroom (George Christian in and out)
6:49 A.M. telephone call to Rostow
6:55 A.M. telephone call to Rostow

By 7 A.M. the facts were beginning to come into focus. The Israelis had attacked Egypt's major airfields, and with measurable effect.

7:50 A.M. telephone call to Ambassador Goldberg in New York
7:57 A.M. telephone call from McNamara

McNamara's call brought the news that the hot line was activated. I later learned that when McNamara heard Moscow was calling on the hot line, he instructed his communications people to pipe it into the White House. To his amazement, they advised him that it could not be done— that the hot line ended at the Pentagon. McNamara said sharply that with all the money we had invested in military communications there must be some way to send Moscow's message directly to the White House Situation Room, and they had better figure it out. They quickly found a way.

I was informed that Chairman Kosygin was at the Kremlin end. He had agreed to wait until I was on hand before sending his message. I went quickly to the Situation Room, joining Rusk, McNamara, and Rostow. Kosygin's message began to arrive in a matter of minutes.

It expressed Soviet concern over the fighting. Kosygin said that the Russians intended to work for a ceasefire and that they hoped we would exert influence on Israel. I replied, in part, that we would use all our influence to bring hostilities to an end, and that we were pleased the Soviets planned to do the same.

We set about immediately to find a way to resolve the explosive issue in the United Nations. The details of diplomacy were complex, as they always are. But the heart of the matter was simple: We were prepared to support an immediate ceasefire, and we made certain that all UN delegates understood that. We were also prepared to support Moscow's proposition that Israeli troops withdraw to the 1956 armistice lines, but we insisted that such a withdrawal be accompanied by a commitment of all parties to refrain from "acts of force regardless of their nature." Ambassador Goldberg made clear that our resolution had two objectives: lifting the blockade of the Gulf of Aqaba by the UAR and compelling the withdrawal of all military forces, both Egyptian and Israeli, from the Sinai.

At the suggestion of Soviet UN Ambassador Nikolai Fedorenko, Goldberg met with the UAR representative, El Kony. He urged the Egyptians to move quickly. He stressed that this might be the last chance for a quick settlement and mutual withdrawal from the Sinai. But Cairo was not prepared to make commitments on June 5. The Arabs hoped to obtain a ceasefire and withdrawal of Israeli forces only. They pushed Moscow hard to work for that, and that alone. So there was no action in the United Nations on the first day of war. But there was plenty of action in the war zone. Israeli forces pushed forward hour by hour.

Our problems that day were complicated by an error made by a briefing officer in the State Department. Pressed for a statement of American policy, he began well: "I am in no position to speak specifically beyond the President's statement of May 23." But as he continued, speaking in the context of anti-American riots in Arab countries and of danger to American citizens there, he said: "Our position is neutral in thought, word, and deed." Perhaps the remark was designed to reassure the Arabs that we were not engaged in the hostilities, but within minutes those words were carried in radio news bulletins to an unbelieving nation. The statement was an oversimplified approach to a complicated situation. We were certainly not belligerents, but our successive guarantees since 1950 to the independence and territorial integrity of all the states in the area made "neutral" the wrong word. This remark stirred unnecessary resentment among many Americans. Later in the day, in the White House Fish Room,* Secretary Rusk put the matter straight by recounting the history of our Middle East commitments and our active role in searching for peace through the United Nations at that very moment.

The next day, June 6, also began with activation of the hot line. I went to the Situation Room at 6:40 A.M. Already assembled there were the Vice President, Secretaries Rusk and McNamara, Nicholas Katzenbach, Walt Rostow, McGeorge Bundy,† Clark Clifford (then Chairman of the President's Foreign Intelligence Advisory Board), and Ambassador Llewellyn Thompson, who had come from Moscow for consultation.

I spent many hours in the Situation Room throughout the Middle East crisis. During some very trying days the room served as headquarters for the U.S. government. On this particular occasion, as we sat around the conference table at dawn, Lady Bird brought breakfast to us. She had followed me from the Executive Mansion, helped prepare the food for us in the White House staff mess, and aided the stewards in serving it. Over scrambled eggs, in the crisis center of America, we reviewed the message from Moscow. The Soviets felt the Security Council should press for a ceasefire.

Meanwhile, Cairo had falsely charged that U.S. carrier-based planes had taken part in attacks on Egypt. On the basis of this accusation, Egypt, Algeria, Syria, Iraq, the Sudan, and Yemen broke diplomatic relations with the United States. Rusk left the Situation Room and went to the West Lobby of the White House, where the reporters were assembled, to label the charge a lie. I mentioned the false Arab allegation in my answer to Kosygin over the hot line. I told him that since his intelligence knew where our carriers and planes were, I hoped he would emphasize the facts to Cairo.

As Israeli forces moved forward steadily into Jordan and the Sinai desert, the Russian delegation in the United Nations decided to accept a simple ceasefire resolution. As the "first step" toward peace the Security Council adopted that resolution, and an appeal to stop the fighting went to Israel and the Arab states. In a brief television statement I welcomed the

---

* So called because Franklin Roosevelt kept an aquarium there.
† I had called Bundy back from his post at the Ford Foundation to sit in with us.

resolution. I said that it "opens a hopeful path away from danger in the Middle East. . . . We hope the parties directly concerned will promptly act upon it."

June 7, the third day of the war, began with the Israelis announcing that they were willing to accept a ceasefire, provided the Arabs agreed. But the Arab states did not respond. They apparently could not accept the reality of their situation in the field. The Arabs were unwilling to reverse the two steps that had done so much to cause the fighting—the closing of Aqaba and the moving of Egyptian forces into the Sinai. They still believed they could achieve more through diplomacy than a simple ceasefire.

In the absence of an Arab response, the Israelis kept moving forward. They slashed their way across the Sinai. They opened the Gulf of Aqaba. To suppress Jordanian artillery fire into the Israeli sector of Jerusalem, they captured the Old City of Jerusalem from Jordan. Israeli soldiers in battle dress prayed at the Wailing Wall, the first Jews to do so in nineteen years.

At a National Security Council meeting that day, it was generally felt that Nasser had suffered a "stunning loss," both militarily and psychologically. There was a belief that the Russians too had suffered a loss in prestige, for they had badly miscalculated Arab ability and strength. I warned the NSC that I was not at all sure we were out of the woods. I was convinced that the problems of that region would plague us for a long time. "One thing we should do now," I said, "is to develop as few heroes and as few heels as we can."

I told the NSC that our goal should be to find an acceptable long-range solution to the Middle East's problems. I asked McGeorge Bundy to serve as executive secretary of a special group that would not only deal with the current crisis but work at building a lasting settlement. In this effort, his group at the White House would complement the work Eugene Rostow had been doing for months, and continued to do, as chairman of an inter-departmental control group we had organized to prepare policy proposals and direct their execution.

Before the day ended, the good news arrived that a ceasefire was in effect between the armies of Jordan and Israel.

Thursday, June 8, began on a note of tragedy. A morning news bulletin reported that a U.S. Navy communications ship, the *Liberty,* had been torpedoed in international waters off the Sinai coast. For seventy tense minutes we had no idea who was responsible, but at eleven o'clock we learned that the ship had been attacked in error by Israeli gunboats and planes. Ten men of the *Liberty* crew were killed and a hundred were wounded. This heartbreaking episode grieved the Israelis deeply, as it did us. There was a possibility that the incident might lead to even greater misfortune, and it was precisely to avoid further confusion and tragedy that I sent a message to Chairman Kosygin on the hot line. I told him exactly what had happened and advised him that carrier aircraft were on their way to the scene to investigate. I wanted him to know, I said, that investigation was the sole purpose of these flights, and I hoped he would inform the proper parties. Kosygin replied that our message had been received and the information had been relayed immediately to the Egyptians.

Ambassador Llewellyn Thompson reported, after his return to Moscow, that this particular exchange had made a deep impression on the Russians. Use of the hot line for this purpose, to prevent misunderstanding, was exactly what both parties had envisioned.

On the afternoon of June 8, the UN Secretary General announced, at last, that the UAR had accepted the ceasefire. But the Soviet Union then muddied the waters by introducing a new resolution condemning Israel's "aggressive activities" and its "violations" of the ceasefire resolutions of June 6 and 7. This was the beginning of a long campaign, still not ended as these words are written, to force Israel to withdraw from the positions it occupies without a peaceful settlement. As far as the ceasefire was concerned, only the question of Syria remained, but that proved difficult and even dangerous. The Soviet Union was obviously extremely sensitive about Syria, which it appeared to regard as a rather special protégé. We suspected that in addition to large shipments of Soviet military equipment being sent to Syria, substantial numbers of Soviet advisers were present in the country. We did know Israel's military intentions toward Syria, and the situation remained tense on June 9. A ceasefire had been announced, but each side accused the other of violations. Fighting erupted in Syria, where Israeli forces proceeded to clear the Golan Heights. There were rumors of Israeli raids on Damascus.

We used every diplomatic resource to convince Israel to work out an effective ceasefire with Syria. Finally, at 3 A.M. on June 10, we received assurance that the Israelis would implement the ceasefire resolution. They informed the UN Security Council that arrangements were being made in the field. We received more reports throughout the morning. Some information was premature, and there was confusion about timing, but we were reasonably confident that a ceasefire was being arranged.

On the morning of June 10 we thought we could see the end of the road. But new word from Moscow brought a sudden chill to the situation. I was told that the hot line was active again, and that "Mr. Kosygin wants the President to come to the equipment as soon as possible." I hurried to the Situation Room. Already there were McNamara, Rostow, Clifford,

Bundy, Katzenbach, Thompson, and CIA Director Helms. At 9:05 A.M. I received the first rough translation of the Kosygin message.

The Soviets accused Israel of ignoring all Security Council resolutions for a ceasefire. Kosygin said a "very crucial moment" had now arrived. He spoke of the possibility of "independent decision" by Moscow. He foresaw the risk of a "grave catastrophe" and stated that unless Israel unconditionally halted operations within the next few hours, the Soviet Union would take "necessary actions, including military." Thompson, at Rusk's request, read the original Russian text to make certain that the word "military" was indeed the correct translation. Thompson said it was. In an exchange between heads of government, these were serious words: "very crucial moment," "catastrophe," "independent decision," "military actions."

The room was deathly still as we carefully studied this grave communication. I turned to McNamara. "Where is the Sixth Fleet now?" I asked him. I knew our ships were circling somewhere in the Mediterranean but I wanted to know the exact location.

McNamara picked up the phone and spoke into it. Then, cradling the phone, he said to me: "It is approximately three hundred miles west of the Syrian coast."

"How fast do these carriers normally travel?" I asked.

"About twenty-five knots. Traveling normally, they are some ten to twelve hours away from the Syrian coast," McNamara said.

We knew that Soviet intelligence ships were electronically monitoring the fleet's every movement. Any change in course or speed would be signaled instantly to Moscow. There are times when the wisdom and rightness of a President's judgment are critically important. We were at such a moment. The Soviets had made a decision. I had to respond.

The fleet was under orders to stay at least one hundred miles from the Syrian coast in its cruising pattern. I told McNamara to issue orders at once to change the course and cut the restriction to fifty miles. The Secretary of Defense gave the orders over the phone. No one else said a word.

Some of the men in the Situation Room later recorded their memories of that morning. Thompson recalled it as a "time of great concern and utmost gravity." Helms remembered that "the atmosphere was tense" and that conversation was conducted "in the lowest voices I had ever heard in a meeting of that kind."

We all knew the Russians would get the message as soon as their monitors observed the change in the fleet's pattern. That message, which no translator would need to interpret to the Kremlin leadership, was that the United States was prepared to resist Soviet intrusion in the Middle East. But I had to reply directly to Chairman Kosygin. I knew my message must be temperate and factual. As we understood the situation, the Norwegian UN negotiator, General Odd Bull, was very close to completing a ceasefire agreement between Syria and Israel. I told Kosygin this was where we thought things stood and that we had been pressing Israel to make the ceasefire completely effective and had received assurances that this would be done.

Throughout the morning I had additional exchanges with the Chairman over the hot line. Kosygin's messages later in the morning became more temperate. Israel and Syria moved to a ceasefire. The tension in the Situation Room subsided. My last message to Chairman Kosygin went over the hot line just before noon. I pointed out that military action in the Middle East was apparently ending. I expressed my hope that the efforts of both our countries in the time ahead would be devoted to achieving lasting peace throughout the world.

The hot line proved a powerful tool not merely, or even mainly, because communications were so rapid. The overriding importance of the hot line was that it engaged immediately the heads of government and their top advisers, forcing prompt attention and decisions. There was unusual value in this, but also danger. We had to weigh carefully every word and phrase. I took special pains not only to handle this crisis deliberately but to set a quiet, unhurried tone for all our discussions.

As for the substance of what happened during the Six Day War, I regretted that the Israelis had chosen to strike at the Arab forces assembled on their frontier, just as I regretted Nasser's refusal to accept promptly our proposal for a ceasefire accompanied by the reopening of Aqaba and mutual withdrawal from the Sinai. It is much easier to start a war than to make a peace. If Nasser had accepted our proposal, the complex factors that led to the Israeli attack could have been quickly unraveled. The Sinai would have been cleared, and we could have moved promptly toward developing a peaceful settlement in the Middle East, with some hope of early success. Arab delay resulted in the war, ending with Israeli forces still occupying parts of Syria, Jordan, and the UAR.

We achieved a ceasefire, but it was clear that the road to peace would be long and hard. Nevertheless, a true peace in the Middle East was the only appropriate objective for us to pursue. Twenty years of fragile truce, of hatred and anxiety, had yielded three dangerous armed conflicts. This time, I was convinced, we could not afford to repeat the temporary and hasty arrangements of 1957. As we worked for a ceasefire, we began to frame principles of a settlement on which the United States could stand. Framing those principles meant facing some hard, basic truths about the Middle East.

I was aware of the deep resentment Arab leaders felt over Israel's emergence as a nation-state. I knew that many Arab refugees in the area still had not been absorbed into community life. But I also knew that various

Arab leaders had used the issue of Israel and the tragic plight of the refugees to advance personal ambitions and to achieve the dominance of Arab radicals over Arab moderates. I knew that resentment and bitter memories, handed down from generation to generation, could only endanger all those who lived in the Middle East. I was convinced that there could be no satisfactory future for the Middle East until the leaders and the peoples of the area turned away from the past, accepted Israel as a reality, and began working together to build modern societies, unhampered by old quarrels, bitterness, and enmity.

While I understood the special problems of the people of Israel, living in a harassed and beleaguered fortress, I believed the Israelis would have to reach out and help provide a basis of dignity for their neighbors. The Arab nations were humiliated by their defeat in the war of June 1967, and that is a poor psychological foundation for building a solid peace. An Israel overconfident in victory would only weaken that basis further. These were the stubborn facts from which we determined principles that we thought could shape a peaceful Middle East. I stated those principles— the Five Great Principles of Peace in the Middle East—to the National Foreign Policy Conference for Educators on June 19, 1967. They were:

First, the recognized right of national life;
Second, justice for the refugees;
Third, innocent maritime passage;
Fourth, limits on the wasteful and destructive arms race; and
Fifth, political independence and territorial integrity for all.

I asked a question: "Who will make this peace where all others have failed for twenty years or more?"
The answer, I said, was this:

Clearly the parties to the conflict must be the parties to the peace. Sooner or later it is they who must make a settlement in the area. It is hard to see how it is possible for nations to live together in peace if they cannot learn to reason together.

Aside from the tragic accident involving the *Liberty,* no American died in the Middle East war in 1967. But the peace of the world walked a tightrope between June 5 and June 10, 1967, as it does today. Through all the months from June 1967 to January 1969 we never diminished our efforts to bring stability to the region where our civilization began. We did not succeed completely, but I hope that history will assess our efforts as a long step toward that goal. I am confident that the lessons we drew from the crisis of June 1967, and the principles we set forth when the shooting stopped, will stand the test of time.

14

Strengthening the Atlantic Community

O N FEBRUARY 21, 1966, PRESIDENT DE GAULLE told a press conference that although he was not pulling out of NATO, he was going to end French participation in the military aspects of the alliance. This meant that all French ground, air, and naval forces would be withdrawn from the NATO command. It also meant that NATO military headquarters, which had been in Paris for almost twenty years, would have to be moved, as would American bases in France.

Many people expected me to denounce the French leader's move and to resist his disruptive tactics, but I had long since decided that the only way to deal with De Gaulle's fervent nationalism was by restraint and patience. He would not remain in power forever, and I felt sure that the fundamental common interests and friendship of our two nations would survive. To have attacked De Gaulle would only have further enflamed French nationalism and offended French pride. It also would have created strains among the nations of the European Common Market and complicated their domestic politics.

As I told Bob McNamara, when a man asks you to leave his house, you don't argue; you get your hat and go. McNamara and our military leaders moved U.S. bases out of France with magnificent efficiency. While NATO headquarters was being shifted to Brussels, our other allies carried on their responsibilities to the alliance with quiet determination.

What concerned me most about De Gaulle's decision was that it threatened the unity of NATO, which had been so carefully developed over two decades. NATO was essential to the security of Europe and the United States. I was convinced that the stronger and more unified we were, the more incentive the Soviets and their Warsaw Pact allies would have to work with us in solving outstanding problems and differences. If the Communists believed the Atlantic alliance was beginning to fragment, they were likely to hold back to see what would happen. Agreements would be deferred. That was why I viewed De Gaulle's action as ill-considered and dangerous.

But De Gaulle was not the only problem within the Atlantic community. Whenever tensions eased a little between East and West, there were always politicians on Capitol Hill who would say: "Well, it's time to start bringing our boys home from Europe; the danger is over." A few members of Parliament or officials in the Exchequer in London would start talking about recalling the British army on the Rhine. Politicians in Bonn would ask: "Why do we have to pay so much to have American and British forces here? They are defending themselves as much as protecting us." When talk spread in 1966 about cutting America's commitment to Europe, men around De Gaulle began whispering on the diplomatic cocktail circuit: "You see, you can't really depend on the Americans for your security."

I was determined to leave office with NATO stronger than when I entered the Presidency, stronger not only as a military shield but as a forum for allied consultation and a tool for action in nonmilitary affairs. I was also determined to leave my successor a solid transatlantic foundation for a healthy world economy. This effort to strengthen security and economic health in the Atlantic community absorbed the time, energy, and talent of some of the best men in government and private life during my five years in the White House. It also absorbed much more of my time and attention than most people realized. The four crises described below illustrate the kind of problems we had and the ways we met them.

In the summer of 1966 we faced a possible breakdown in the financial foundations of NATO. The crisis arose because of the heavy cost in American dollars and British pounds required to station American and British forces in Germany. This meant a heavy drain of foreign exchange for Washington and London, since the troops stationed in Germany converted their currencies into German marks for local expenses. If an American officer rented a house, if a British soldier took a girl to dinner, if a family went to the Bavarian Alps for skiing, they paid in marks, but in effect they were spending dollars and pounds. This spending produced a huge windfall in foreign exchange earnings for the German economy, the equivalent of thousands of tourists pouring into West Germany each month, spending foreign currency as they went. We estimated that the West Germans were accumulating about $800 million in foreign exchange annually as a result of our troops' presence in their country. The smaller British force was spending more than $200 million.

Since the early 1960s, the West Germans had generally offset this windfall in foreign exchange by making large purchases of American military equipment for their expanding forces. But in 1966 West German Chancellor Ludwig Erhard found himself in budget trouble. His government had increased spending for numerous welfare programs, and as a result of heavy political pressure military spending had leveled off. There was no money for increased purchases of U.S. military equipment. The problem was further complicated because the German authorities had done an unsatisfactory job of explaining to their people that this foreign exchange windfall resulted from our common commitment to NATO, and that they had an obvious obligation to help offset it. Many Germans believed that they were actually paying for the presence of foreign troops, rather than simply offsetting abnormal foreign exchange earnings, by buying goods and services from the United States and the United Kingdom.

On July 5, 1966, Chancellor Erhard sent me a letter outlining his views on these matters. He said that he thought consideration should be given to payments and services other than purchase of military equipment. But it was clear that Bonn had no firm plan for meeting this responsibility to the alliance. We knew too that Erhard was facing serious political problems within his own party. The situation was particularly dangerous because sentiment was rising on Capitol Hill in favor of beginning the withdrawal of our forces from Europe. That sentiment found its clearest expression in a resolution introduced in the Senate on August 31, 1966, by Majority Leader Mike Mansfield. The key section of the resolution stated that "a substantial reduction of U.S. forces permanently stationed in Europe can be made without adversely affecting either our resolve or ability to meet our commitment under the North Atlantic Treaty. . . ."

The problem was compounded by the situation in Britain, for Prime Minister Harold Wilson was in far deeper economic trouble than Erhard. West Germany was enjoying a high level of prosperity and the mark was solid, but Britain faced a continuing foreign exchange crisis which threatened the value of the pound. Wilson's Cabinet insisted that British troops be brought home if no prompt and satisfactory offset arrangement were made with the Germans.

I knew that if the British pulled their forces back from Germany, the pressure would increase in the Senate for a similar U.S. withdrawal. Britain's relations with Germany and the European continent would be strained. I felt certain that the virus would be catching; other allied forces might soon pull out of the integrated NATO command.

I was determined to resist the unraveling of North Atlantic defenses and the collapse of our postwar efforts to build a healthy Atlantic political community. A new test of wills between East and West was certainly not what we needed if the business of building a reasonable and safe world was to go forward. It was crucial that we solve the foreign exchange offset problem and keep NATO strong.

Three basic questions had to be answered: Should we and the British deal separately with the Germans, as Bonn and some of my advisers had proposed, or should we all work together on the problem? What should be the controlling consideration—the financial arrangements or the security of the NATO region? Finally, how could we close the gap between the German position on the one hand and the British and U.S. positions on the other?

After talking these questions over with my advisers, I decided in August that we should make the talks multilateral. Working together would strengthen the alliance; working separately would be divisive. I also thought that a voice speaking on behalf of NATO and its security requirements should be heard in these negotiations. I proposed that we invite the experienced Italian diplomat Manlio Brosio, then Secretary General of NATO, to join the talks. When I made these suggestions to British Prime Minister Wilson, he agreed immediately. The answer from Bonn was noncommittal. Evidently the Chancellor hoped he could postpone facing this difficult matter. But after candidly exchanging views with me during his visit to Washington late in September, Chancellor Erhard agreed to the talks.

This was the job—hammering out an offset agreement—that I asked John McCloy, former U.S. High Commissioner in Germany, to undertake when I saw him in New York City early in October, while I was there to discuss European policy.* McCloy had had long experience working with the Germans and the British, both in government and outside.

The negotiations had scarcely begun when they received a serious setback. Late in October an internal political crisis toppled the Erhard government from power. The new government, a coalition of Christian Democrats and Social Democrats headed by Kurt Kiesinger, did not take office until December 1, and not until January 26, 1967, did the new German Cabinet decide that the Bonn government would continue to take part in the talks.

The delay raised real difficulties for Wilson. He was under strong domestic pressure to proceed with troop cuts if he did not win German agreement immediately to a satisfactory offset arrangement. We lent the British a hand to meet this emergency by offering to purchase $35 million in military equipment in Britain. In return, Wilson agreed to keep British troops on the Rhine through June 1967.

To reduce the size of the problem, my advisers had developed a troop rotation technique called "dual-basing." Under this plan, two of the three

---

* See Chapter 20, pp. 474–75.

brigades in a division would be moved back to the United States, while the third brigade remained at its German base. From time to time, the German-based brigade would return home and be replaced by one of the other brigades. The entire division would remain ready for combat and committed to NATO. The same dual-basing technique was proposed for our air wings in Europe. Defense experts were confident that we could move the U.S.-based planes and troops back to the central front in Germany on short notice. In the meantime, dual-basing would materially reduce the dollars flowing into West Germany's foreign exchange account. The troops involved would be spending most of their dollars at home.

I met with my advisers to discuss this rotation plan on February 24.* Rusk said that he favored using the dual-basing technique with one of our divisions in Germany and with three of our nine air wings. McNamara wanted to go further, applying it to two divisions and six air wings. The Joint Chiefs of Staff were opposed to any redeployment of forces. In a memo sent to me from abroad on February 23, McCloy said that he was prepared to apply dual-basing to only one division and three air wings, but that his agreement was conditional. Before going ahead, he thought it vital that we consult closely with the Germans and get agreement with the other allies; that we demonstrate effectively our capacity to reinforce the NATO forces as promised; and that we pledge to make no additional withdrawals unless there was a reciprocal reduction of forces by the Soviets "or other major changes in the security situation."

After long discussion, I told my advisers that I wanted to move slowly. I was concerned, I said, that a large cutback in our forces might tempt the Soviets to start trouble in Central Europe, especially in Berlin. I insisted that we continue to work closely with the British and the Germans, because I viewed any serious disruption in our relations with those countries, or in their relations with each other, as a blow to European security and to our own safety.

On February 27 I discussed our NATO and offset problems with key congressional leaders over breakfast at the White House.† I explained my reluctance to make any cuts in our forces in Europe since I frankly regarded any reduction as dangerous. However, I said, because there was pressure in Congress for cuts, we were studying ways to accommodate them through the dual-basing system.

Speaker McCormack argued strongly against any cuts, and his House

* Those taking part were Secretaries Rusk and McNamara, Under Secretary of the Treasury Frederick L. Deming, Under Secretary of State for Political Affairs Eugene Rostow, Assistant Secretary of Defense John McNaughton, and Deputy Special Assistant to the President Francis Bator.

† Those attending the breakfast meeting, in addition to some of my principal advisers, were Senators Mansfield, Dirksen, Long, Robert Byrd of West Virginia, and Kuchel, House Speaker McCormack, and Representatives Albert, Arends, Boggs, and Ford.

colleagues supported that stand. Senator Mansfield, author of the resolution favoring troop withdrawals from Europe, said there was strong sentiment in our country for a reduction in forces. Senators Long and Byrd supported him. Senator Dirksen dissented. He was fearful that Moscow would misinterpret any withdrawal. He did not oppose the rotation plan, however, provided our allies agreed.

After further discussion and study, I gave McCloy a letter of instruction on March 1. It set guidelines for renewed negotiations with the British and the Germans. Our general approach, I wrote, involved three interrelated factors. First, NATO allies should determine force levels "on the basis only of security considerations, broadly construed." Second, the Germans should determine how much military equipment they wished to buy in the United Kingdom and the United States. Third, the remaining balance-of-payments effects of allied troops being stationed in Germany should be dealt with by cooperation among the allies "in the management of monetary reserves or by other agreed means."

The third principle was a departure from traditional policy. We were ready to break the link between German military purchases and the offset arrangement and were open to suggestions of other ways to handle the problem. In this new atmosphere, negotiations went well. The Germans agreed to offset the major part of our annual foreign exchange costs for maintaining forces in their country by buying $500 million worth of medium-term U.S. government bonds. This added to the plus side of our balance of payments as much as Germany's purchase of military supplies would have, at least in the short run. In similar ways, the Germans offset the British foreign exchange burden, with a certain amount of help from us in the form of purchases in the United Kingdom. The Germans also promised not to convert their large dollar holdings into gold.

The final hurdle to be cleared was the limited rotation plan. A joint U.S.-German group began intensive study of the proposal late in March. By the third week in April full agreement was reached on all but one factor, the number of U.S. planes to be removed. We suggested bringing 144 aircraft home, but the Germans argued that moving more than 72 would seriously weaken NATO air defenses. McCloy recommended a compromise of 96 planes. I had great confidence in McCloy's judgment, and I accepted his recommendation. We sent a cable that night to London, where the talks were then being held. The next day a message arrived from our negotiator:

> Following morning and afternoon sessions on April 28, trilateral talks concluded at 5:40 P.M. with signature by McCloy, Duckwitz and Thomson of final report to their respective governments. . . .*

* Ambassador Georg F. Duckwitz and Minister of State George Thomson represented West Germany and the United Kingdom respectively in these negotiations.

NATO was still in business. We had proved once again that if there is a will to do so allies can work out their most difficult problems, in spite of divisive domestic political pressures.

I immediately sent a message to McCloy, who had played a crucial role in hammering out the agreement, commending his efforts: "Good work and congratulations. A very important job very well done."

The three-power negotiations of 1966–1967 did not permanently fix the level of American and British forces to be stationed in Europe; nor did it settle the problem of offsetting the related foreign exchange burdens. The Germans agreed that purchases of medium-term U.S. bonds was not a satisfactory long-range solution. From then until the end of my term we continued to explore with the Germans ways to give the alliance a stronger financial base. What we did achieve was an understanding that military cooperation in NATO could not be separated from financial cooperation. If we were to maintain a sound military alliance, intimate partnership in finance was as necessary as close military coordination.

The same kind of partnership was necessary in trade matters. I had inherited authority that gave me more flexibility in this field than any previous President. One legislative achievement of the Kennedy administration had been the Trade Expansion Act of 1962, which authorized the President to cut tariffs up to 50 per cent if our trading partners would give us equal benefits.

Unfortunately, John Kennedy was never able to use the authority that Congress had granted. Serious talks first began in Geneva in 1964, when I instructed our chief negotiator, Christian A. Herter,* to proceed with discussions aimed at achieving a general reduction of tariffs while taking into account exceptions by all the trading nations when they felt their "overriding national interest" was involved.

The trade talks progressed erratically. They were at a standstill during much of 1965, mainly because of problems in the European Common Market. This put us under considerable pressure, since the Presidential discretion authorized under the 1962 law lasted only until July 1, 1967.

I knew that if we could demonstrate our ability to move ahead in economic partnership, especially with the Common Market, we would greatly improve the chances for a healthy NATO and for increased international monetary cooperation. If we failed, Europe might become more insular and more anti-American. Strong protectionist and isolationist groups in the United States might react in the same way.

---

* Herter, who was Secretary of State during the last twenty months of the Eisenhower administration, was selected by President Kennedy and retained by me as Presidential representative for trade negotiations.

Under the Trade Expansion Act, the United States launched major trade talks, and the negotiations came to be called the Kennedy Round. In these discussions with the world's major trading nations,* the goals of the United States were:

major tariff reductions for both industrial and agricultural products, evenly balanced;

a world grain arrangement providing for guaranteed minimum prices and incorporating the principle that food aid to less developed countries would be shared fairly with the United States;

recognition of the sensitive problems we face regarding excessive imports in areas like steel and textiles.

Every trading government wants the lowest possible tariff levels for the goods it sells abroad and high tariffs for its industries and farm products that are particularly vulnerable to international competition. Special-interest groups in each country exert pressures on legislators. The legislators then make demands of their own governments and trade negotiators. The negotiators in turn oppose anything that smacks of "discrimination" against their country's products.

In the spring of 1967 a sense of urgency developed as we approached the July deadline. Ambassador William Roth, who had succeeded Herter as Presidential representative for trade negotiations, moved to Geneva to direct our negotiations. He was assisted by his deputy, Michael Blumenthal, and a group of competent specialists backstopped by a special coordinating team in Washington.†

On May 11, 1967, the outline of a compromise agreement and last-minute instructions for our men in Geneva came to me for approval. Because of the powerful agricultural protectionism in the Common Market, it was obvious that we would not get all the concessions we wanted for American agriculture. The question was whether we should accept what we could get, plus a major liberalization of trade in industrial products, or abandon the effort.

---

* The countries taking part in the full talks, in addition to the United States, were the members of the Common Market (Belgium, France, West Germany, Italy, Luxembourg, and the Netherlands), the United Kingdom, Austria, Denmark, Finland, Norway, Sweden, Switzerland, and Japan. In a special category were Australia, Canada, New Zealand, and South Africa. In addition, at least two dozen other countries contributed to the discussions in Geneva, reflecting the interests of the less developed parts of the world.

† Members of this coordinating group were Under Secretary of State for Political Affairs Eugene Rostow, Assistant Secretary of State for Economic Affairs Anthony Solomon, Acting Secretary of Commerce Alexander Trowbridge, Under Secretary of Agriculture John Schnittker, Ambassador Roth's general counsel, John Rehm, and Francis Bator of the White House staff. Assistant Secretary of State for European Affairs John Leddy frequently took part.

I asked the Vice President and other principal advisers to join me in the Cabinet Room to review the package item by item.* After we had studied the proposals, I instructed them to explain fully what we were considering and why to leaders of business, labor, and farm groups who might be hurt or who feared they might be hurt. The same was done for interested members of Congress.

Although I had pretty well concluded that we should accept the package, I made no decision at that session. I wanted to consider it further and to have my advisers weigh the program carefully as a whole. I asked Francis Bator of the White House staff to contact each of the advisers who had taken part in the discussion and to ask them individually how they would vote on the proposed agreement. In twenty-four hours I received his report. My advisers supported the proposal unanimously. Bator concluded his memo by reporting that Vice President Humphrey and Secretary Rusk had both asked that I be told their vote was "a very strong 'yes.' "

This was not a voting procedure in the usual sense. I wanted to know if there were serious problems or reservations that I had not detected as these men assessed the package as a whole. Now we were ready to go. I instructed Bator to contact Ambassador Roth in Geneva and instruct him to proceed. We wanted Roth to continue to negotiate hard down to the deadline, but once he had won every concession he could, he was authorized to sign the agreement. We had worked out a code in advance, and the instruction to our negotiator was contained in one cryptic sentence: "The man is wearing a white hat." That meant "go."

On May 16 I met with the congressional leadership at breakfast to talk over the Kennedy Round problems. Later that morning the Vice President met in his Senate office with about forty key members of Congress. Rusk and Freeman and other specialists took part in the briefing. The questioning was keen and specific, but the general results were favorable. As expected, members of Congress paid closest attention to trade items of concern to their own states and districts. Speaker McCormack, whose home state of Massachusetts manufactures shoes, asked about increased shoe imports under the new agreement. Senator Robert Byrd of West Virginia asked about glass imports. Senator Herman Talmadge of Georgia was worried about textiles and farm products. Senator George Aiken of Vermont wondered whether maple sugar sales to Canada would be affected. One sweeping question was in many minds, and it was eventually asked by Senator John Pastore of Rhode Island: Had we lost our shirt in our eagerness to make the Kennedy Round a success?

---

* Those taking part were Secretary Rusk, Under Secretary Katzenbach, Under Secretary for Political Affairs Eugene Rostow, and Assistant Secretary Solomon from the State Department; Acting Secretary of Commerce Trowbridge; Agriculture Secretary Freeman; Under Secretary of Labor James J. Reynolds; and members of the White House staff.

We demonstrated that we had bargained hard and patiently. The specialists answered questions to the general satisfaction of the Congressmen. But the Senators and Representatives clearly were reserving final judgment until they could study the details of the package. They knew they would soon hear complaints from nervous special-interest groups back home, though they probably would hear little from the vast majority of constituents who would benefit from the trade agreement.

Later that day I made the following announcement to the White House press corps:

> General agreement has been reached on all the major issues in the trade negotiations. The way is now clear for the conclusion of a final agreement covering billions of dollars' worth of trade among more than fifty countries.

There were tense moments in those final weeks as each nation held out on some matters right down to the finish line. One cable reported that "things look extremely dark" following a stiffening in the British position on chemicals, steel, and grains. Japan's role in food aid to poor countries was not resolved until late in the talks. The Common Market countries resisted opening up their markets to grain imports.

At last, late in June, final agreements were hammered out, *i*'s dotted, and *t*'s crossed. On June 30, only a few hours before the President's power under the Trade Expansion Act was to expire, Ambassador Blumenthal signed the agreements for the United States. We received and made concessions on about $8 billion worth of industrial and agricultural exports and imports. The Geneva talks demonstrated that despite powerful isolationist pressures in all nations, the world community still had the vision to move together as partners, on the principle of fair shares for all.

A few months after the successful negotiation of the Kennedy Round agreements, another dangerous crisis broke. The roots of this problem were deep and varied. The United States had for many years been spending more than it had been earning abroad. We had a balance-of-payments deficit. Our gold stock had increased abnormally during the war years. For some time after the war we were agreeable to having our gold supply reduced, knowing that such a decrease would strengthen the Free World's monetary system and speed European recovery. But after the late 1950s that cushion no longer existed. Whenever confidence in the dollar dropped, foreign holders were likely to convert their dollars into gold at the official rate of $35 an ounce. As a result, our gold supply had decreased past the point of comfort, and when this happened anxiety about the underlying strength of the dollar increased.

A related problem was that not enough gold was being produced and put into monetary reserves to keep pace with the rapid growth of world trade. Expanded dollar holdings had become a supplement to gold as a form of international reserve. There were special-interest groups who wanted to go back to a gold reserve system by raising the price of gold. These groups speculated in the markets in the hope that we would raise the price we paid for gold above $35 an ounce. But I had decided to take another road.

We had been working intensively with other countries since 1965 to develop a new international reserve asset to supplement gold and dollars. On June 16, 1965, I had instructed Treasury Secretary Fowler to set up a special group to consider ways to strengthen the international monetary and payments system.* The new approach developed by that group was called a "special drawing rights" system and was designed to operate through the International Monetary Fund (IMF). The system was a revolutionary development, for it would create, in effect, a truly international currency. By supplementing gold and dollars, the "special drawing rights" system would relieve pressure on both. The new approach had been approved in principle by the members of the IMF in September 1967, but the details of the system had not been fully worked out. When the long-expected sterling crisis broke in November, we had to deal with it by using the tools at hand.

The British were in far deeper economic trouble than we were. An upward spiral of prices and wages had made it increasingly difficult for the British to sell their goods on the world market. This along with resistance to modernization of industry had weakened Britain's competitive position. The crisis finally reached the point where the British could see no solution except to devalue their currency, a move that would lower the price of British goods in foreign markets and raise the price of imports into the United Kingdom. Whether devaluation of the pound would weaken the dollar would depend on how other nations reacted.

On November 17, 1967, British Ambassador Patrick Dean asked to see me on instructions from his Prime Minister. I will never forget Sir Patrick's dejected face as he came into my office that afternoon. We shook hands, and he said he was sorry to bring me bad news. Prime Minister Wilson had asked him to inform me that the British government had decided to devalue the pound from $2.80 to $2.40. We had been forewarned, of course, but it was still like hearing that an old friend who has been ill has to undergo a serious operation. However much you expect it, the news is still a heavy blow.

Dean knew as well as I did that we were moving into a time of peril.

* The text of my June 16 memorandum to Secretary Fowler is in the appendix, pp. 597–98.

If the monetary crisis was not handled with skill by all concerned, it could easily throw the world economy into the kind of vicious cycle that had been so disastrous between 1929 and 1933. We were dealing not simply with money and exchange rates but with trade and jobs and the livelihood of millions of families.

I realized that Sir Patrick was depressed and worried, and I wanted to cheer him up as much as I could. I reminded him that the American people, and all who cherished freedom, owed an incalculable debt to the British for the time when they stood steadfast and virtually alone against the scourge of Hitler. I promised him that we would do all in our power to help Britain through the crisis.

I walked directly from my meeting with Ambassador Dean into the Cabinet Room, where my principal economic advisers and a few key Congressmen were waiting.* We knew that we faced two principal dangers. The first was that other nations might follow the British lead and devalue their own currencies. If that happened, most of the effects of the British action would be nullified. In addition, severe pressure would be placed on the dollar and in turn on the whole international monetary system.

The second danger was that speculators would move in and gamble that the United States would have to abandon its commitment to buy and sell gold at $35 an ounce. Thus if a speculator bought $100,000 worth of gold at the official rate and the price then rose to $40 an ounce, he would make a cool profit of more than $14,000. We wanted to discourage such speculation and persuade our other financial partners to hold fast. That was why I made the following declaration on November 18, the day after the British informed us of devaluation: "I reaffirm unequivocally the commitment of the United States to buy and sell gold at the existing price of thirty-five dollars an ounce."

Nevertheless, there were speculators willing to gamble that under growing pressure we would have to raise the official price of gold. The first week after devaluation, sales from the gold pool were $580 million. The French attitude did not improve matters. Britain's announcement was made on a Saturday. The De Gaulle government chose the following Monday to announce that it had withdrawn from the gold pool. Actually, France had withdrawn several months earlier, but the unfortunate timing of the French announcement complicated an already difficult situation. France had been building its gold reserves and was doing everything possible to force an increase in the official price. This was one of several times when I was

---

* Those present at the meeting were Treasury Secretary Fowler, Budget Bureau Director Charles Schultze, Federal Reserve Board Chairman William McChesney Martin, and Walt Rostow. Speaker McCormack and Representatives Carl Albert, Hale Boggs, Wilbur Mills, and George Mahon also attended. When I noted their absence, I asked Arthur M. Okun, Chairman of the Council of Economic Advisers, and Treasury Under Secretary Joseph W. Barr to join us.

tempted to abandon my policy of polite restraint toward De Gaulle, but I forced myself to be patient once again.

With "special drawing rights" not yet in effect, gold still played a central role in the monetary system. We had agreed to accept the gold pool losses, if necessary, as long as our partners stayed with us and we were not fighting the battle alone. Fortunately, the gold pool did hold together. At a meeting in Frankfurt on the weekend of November 25, the governors of seven central banks (excluding the French, of course) pledged to continue working closely together.* On November 26 the central bankers announced that they would support existing exchange rates based on the fixed price of $35 an ounce. The meeting in Frankfurt and the bankers' statement affected the market dramatically. Demand for gold fell off sharply. Nevertheless, total gold pool losses in the month following devaluation reached $1.5 billion. We were far from being out of the woods.

The problem was further complicated by an increase in our own balance-of-payments deficit. Our payments losses had been running at the rate of about $2.3 billion a year, but in the last three months of 1967 they jumped to an annual rate of about $7 billion. In other words, as many dollars flowed abroad in the last three months of the year as in the first nine months. A special team headed by Secretary Fowler worked night and day through the last half of December to find short-term answers without taking protectionist steps that would generate retaliation and damage the structure of world trade. By the end of the year our program was ready.

At a New Year's Day press conference at my ranch, I spelled out a five-point program to reduce our balance-of-payments deficit by $3 billion in 1968: new and tighter regulation of American investment abroad; restrictions on overseas loans; cutbacks in military and economic assistance to other countries; an urgent request that Americans cut down their travel and spending outside the Western Hemisphere; and an effort to expand U.S. commercial sales in foreign markets.

The program had an immediate stabilizing effect. During the first three months of 1968 our payments deficit fell back from the $7 billion rate of October–December 1967 to an annual rate of $2.7 billion. But congressional action was needed to reinforce the steps we were taking. The most critical need was for passage of the kind of tax bill I had been urging on Congress for almost two years. Congress had delayed action throughout 1966 and 1967, and I realized that in 1968, an election year, it would be even more difficult to convince Congress to act. But the tax bill was vitally needed—to brake inflation and to strengthen the dollar and the international monetary system, which depended on the dollar.

The speculators had been restrained by our actions late in 1967 and

---

* The countries represented at Frankfurt were Belgium, West Germany, Italy, the Netherlands, Switzerland, the United Kingdom, and the United States.

in 1968, but they had not given up. In March 1968 there was another serious outbreak of speculative fever, heightened by rumors that were inspired in large part by those who would gain most if we raised the price of gold. The problem was compounded by a few members of Congress who urged that the United States stop supporting the existing dollar rate. In the first week of March the gold pool had to sell another $300 million in gold. In the second week the fever went out of control. The central banks had to put about $1 billion into the market to meet speculative demand.

Most of the possible cures we studied were difficult, even dangerous. The side effects might be worse than the disease. We finally decided to take the following steps:

close the London gold market;

reaffirm strongly the $35 rate;

try to persuade gold pool countries to agree not to increase their gold reserves and to activate the new IMF reserve currency and rely on it instead;

secure the pledge of gold pool members not to buy gold on the private market and try to convince other countries to join in this pledge;

end the gold pool operation and let the commercial price of gold find its natural level;

arrange new sterling credits and work out methods to offset disorderly money flows through cooperative financial actions.

These decisions were reached early in the afternoon of March 14, a Thursday. The only point of disagreement among my advisers was whether we should close the London gold market on Friday or wait until after the weekend. We had lost $372 million to the speculators on March 14, and I decided that we should move immediately. If the market remained open on Friday, we might well lose another billion dollars in gold, and I had had enough of the speculators.

Our first step was to secure the agreement of the other gold pool countries. Secretary Fowler, Federal Reserve Chairman William McChesney Martin, and other financial specialists telephoned their ministerial and central bank colleagues in Europe. They all agreed to close the gold market the following day and to come to Washington to work out the other matters on March 16–17.

I sent personal messages immediately to British Prime Minister Wilson, Prime Minister Aldo Moro of Italy, and West German Chancellor Kiesinger. It was imperative, I told them, that we cooperate in order to avoid financial disorders that could "profoundly damage the political relations between Europe and America and set in motion forces like those which disintegrated the Western world in 1929 and 1933." I also told them: "The speculators are banking on an increase in the official price of gold. They are wrong."

Over the weekend Fowler and our other specialists won concurrence from the European finance ministers and bankers. We agreed to continue to sell gold at $35 an ounce to other central banks, but henceforth neither we nor they would buy gold in the free market. Gold for industrial or technical purposes, or for speculation, would have to be bought in a separate commodity market. This plan was called the "two-tier system." The experts were confident that once official sales were separated from the private gold market, the price of gold in the latter would drop.

At the end of their weekend sessions in Washington, the central bankers issued an important statement:

> As the existing stock of monetary gold is sufficient in view of the prospective establishment of the facility for Special Drawing Rights, they [the central banks] no longer feel it necessary to buy gold from the market.

We had reached an historic turning point. The world's leading bankers were telling the speculators that henceforth the banks would be looking to the new international currency, not to gold, to enlarge monetary reserves. They were committed to building the international economy on the basis of intensive partnership.

The two-tier system worked well throughout 1968. Speculators did not give up all hope immediately, but the demand dropped and hoarded gold began to return to the market. For the rest of the year the price of gold on the private market averaged less than $40 an ounce.

We faced one more major monetary crisis during my administration, but we dealt with it this time from a position of relative strength. Congress passed the tax bill and I signed it on June 28, 1968. During the March gold crisis Congress lifted the requirement that gold cover 25 per cent of our domestic circulation. Our balance-of-payments figures had moved from deficit to surplus.

The new crisis arose as a result of the French general strike and student riots in May 1968. Those events caused a deterioration in France's trade balance and a flight from the franc. De Gaulle and his government had been most uncooperative in the previous monetary difficulties. Nonetheless, in July we led the way with other nations in arranging a $1.3 billion stand-by credit for France. The international monetary system is not a field for pettiness or retribution. France, whatever its policies, is an important member of the Western world. Instability in France can only be a source of general concern.

France's difficulties in 1968 were compounded by Germany's economic success. The Germans had maintained a high order of discipline in wage and price policies. They remembered from their interwar experience and immediate postwar years the damage inflation can cause. The Germans also had important advantages. Their military and foreign aid expenditures were relatively small compared with those of Great Britain, France, and the United States. In addition, Germany gained foreign exchange from NATO forces, despite the offset arrangements. These two factors combined produced a remarkable increase in German exports relative to imports and a piling up of large reserves.

As talk circulated in November about a possible upward revaluation of the mark, large speculative funds moved out of France into Germany. The critical questions were: Should France take austerity measures to strengthen the franc or should it devalue the franc? Should Germany revalue the mark upward or take other measures appropriate for a country whose surplus was unsettling the international monetary system?

In the fall of 1968 Secretary Fowler was in Europe on a series of farewell consultations. He went to Bonn to take the lead in finding a solution consistent with continued stability of the international monetary system. As it turned out, the German government decided not to revalue the mark but to achieve the same effect to a limited extent by adjusting border taxes so as to reduce exports and increase imports. In this way the Germans recognized their responsibility to the international community.

An agreement was also reached in Bonn on the maximum French devaluation that could be made without disrupting the stability of the international community; but De Gaulle decided that he would not take this route. He imposed austerity measures within the French economy and took steps to increase French exports and reduce imports. I received word of De Gaulle's decision not to devalue the franc on November 23, while Fowler was reporting the outcome of the intense day-and-night negotiations in Bonn.

The next day, when De Gaulle announced what he proposed to do, I thought long and hard about the situation he faced. He had proudly led France for ten years. He had pursued a highly nationalistic policy which disrupted the Atlantic community in many ways. He had not made things easy for the United States or for its President. But he had given France an important interval of stability and, we hoped, a time for healing and for gathering strength after all that country had experienced in the past half-century.

The spring riots had set back much that De Gaulle had sought to accomplish. His monetary schemes and ideas had failed. France had lost much of the reserve it had painstakingly built up. Now, faced with possible devaluation, De Gaulle chose a harder course, but one consistent with his public commitments against devaluation.

I knew how lonely responsibility is at such a moment. On the evening of November 23 I called Walt Rostow and said that I wanted to send a message to De Gaulle expressing our hope that his course would succeed and assuring him that the United States was ready to cooperate in any way possible. There was silence for a moment at the other end of the line. I asked Rostow if he thought it was a bad idea. He said: "No, I'm only sorry I didn't suggest it." Then I told him that I wanted the message sent unless Fowler or Rusk had some overriding objection. The two Secretaries had none. I was pleased that the message, when published at De Gaulle's request, made a small contribution toward stabilizing the situation in Paris.

Monetary strength now is spread more widely over the world than in the early postwar years, when the dollar dominated affairs. That is healthy. But the world does not work well if there is uncertainty about the stability of the dollar. Although many tasks remain ahead in the field of international monetary reform, one of my comforts as I left the White House was that the dollar was once again strong.

15

Quality of Life

THE MEMBERS OF MY CABINET were already assembled when I joined them for the twentieth Cabinet meeting of my administration. The day was Tuesday, July 27, 1965. I sat down at the massive table in the Cabinet Room and quickly plunged into several pieces of business at hand. We were saying good-by to Anthony Celebrezze, who was retiring after a distinguished tour of duty as Secretary of Health, Education, and Welfare, and we were welcoming his successor, John W. Gardner, formerly president of the Carnegie Foundation. This was our first meeting after the death of Adlai Stevenson, and I observed that "all of us in this room feel personally and keenly the loss to our nation and to the world." I introduced the new Ambassador to the United Nations, Arthur Goldberg, who had given up his seat on the Supreme Court to fill the empty place Stevenson's death had left.

We discussed the end-of-the-fiscal-year spending of the various departments and agencies and a few other routine issues of government operations. Then I reviewed the legislative situation. I did so with great pride. I told the members of my official family that the past week had been "the most productive and most historic legislative week in Washington during this century." Medicare had made its way successfully through the House-Senate conference. Final passage of this bill was only hours away. The voting rights bill was in conference. Agreement on it was expected within the week.

Thus the books were closing on our campaign to take action against the most pressing problems inherited from the past—the "old agenda." The War on Poverty was more than a year old. The landmark Elementary and Secondary Education Act had become law in April, at long last bringing the resources of the federal government to bear on the problems of our schools. Now Medicare would bring improved health care for the nation's elderly. The second major civil rights bill in a little more than a year was about to be enacted, and we were finally beginning to redress the long-standing wrongs against our black citizens. In all, thirty-six major pieces of legislation had been signed into law, twenty-six others were moving through the House or Senate, and eleven more awaiting scheduling.

For twenty months action had been the keynote on Capitol Hill. As Tom Wicker wrote in his column in *The New York Times* on August 10, 1965: "They are rolling the bills out of Congress these days the way Detroit turns super-sleek, souped-up autos off the assembly line." Could that pace be sustained? I urgently wanted it to continue, but I sensed two formidable barriers. One was the mood of Congress.

As early as February 1965, immediately after the new Eighty-ninth Congress convened, I had asked all the legislative liaison officers from the departments and agencies to meet with me in the White House. I reviewed for them the troubles other Presidents had encountered with Congress, and the speed with which their popularity had diminished—Wilson, Truman, Eisenhower, even Franklin Roosevelt, whose experience offered the most striking precedent of all. Roosevelt had been reelected in 1936 with the largest margin in history up to that time, sweeping in with him a Congress whose mandate was as clear as any that had ever been written. But by the time that Congress convened in 1937 the mood had changed. The hurrahs had faded away, and from Capitol Hill the distinctive sound was the shuffle of reluctant, dragging feet. I told the assembled congressional liaison aides that the time directly ahead would be crucial for us. We would have to use our strength while it still existed. We had just won a resounding victory at the polls, I said, but "it might be more of a loophole than a mandate."

As summer ebbed, I began to sense a shift in the winds.* I knew intuitively that there would be growing resistance to further legislative action. Moreover, history had afforded me an honorable stopping place if I chose to take advantage of it. The nation, I believed, was impressed and gratified by the season of accomplishments it had experienced. In the same column in which he had commented on our assembly-line speed in turning out laws, Tom Wicker went on to observe: "The list of achievements is so long that it reads better than the legislative achievements of most two-term Presidents, and some of the bills—on medical care, education, voting rights, and Presidential disability, to pick a handful—are of such weight as to cause

---

* That shift was easily detectable in September 1965, when the Congress gave us our first defeat by voting down home rule for the District of Columbia. This defeat was a clear sign that the winds of reform would not blow again as hard as they had through the remarkable first session of the Eighty-ninth Congress.

one to go all the way back to Woodrow Wilson's first year to find a congressional session of equal importance." Visitor after visitor, friend after friend, aide after aide spoke to me in those months with the same message. It was this: "Mr. President, if you stop now and do nothing more, your place in history is secure." Though personally gratifying, these sentiments worried me, for they signaled satisfaction with the new status quo at a time when so much more still needed to be done. This mood was further reflected early in November 1965, when the caucus of Democratic Senators met, and Majority Leader Mike Mansfield began talking about the need to go slow on new legislation. Throughout the fall, congressional leaders, on both sides of the aisle, were saying that the nation needed time to catch its breath; that we needed to consolidate and digest the laws we had already passed.

The second obstacle to further legislative action, as I perceived it, was the lowering cloud of Vietnam. Even as I spoke to my Cabinet officers on July 27 of the triumphs of the legislative record behind us, I had on my desk the list of alternatives from which I had to choose the course we would pursue in that difficult and painful war. Later that day, in fact, I reviewed those alternatives with the National Security Council and made my decision: We would send additional combat troops to Vietnam to meet our commitments and keep hope alive for that struggling nation.*

The demanding decisions of those trying days relating to Vietnam were decisions involving our nation's integrity and its security. But they also involved what I considered to be the promise of the American future. In a wondrous time of hope and optimism we had begun the building of a better society for our people. The danger that we might have to slow that building, in order to take care of our obligations abroad, brought added anguish. So on that July 27, 1965, two great streams in our national life converged—the dream of a Great Society at home and the inescapable demands of our obligations halfway around the world. They were to run in confluence until the end of my administration.

Balancing the arguments against further legislative action was one compelling fact of life: the urgent and unavoidable need to begin work on a new agenda. True, the old reforms, which had been crying for action since Franklin Roosevelt's time, were finally on the books, but in the meantime other needs, just as critical to life in the 1960s and beyond, were accumulating. The powerful technology that we had so proudly built had created its own enormous and complex by-products. Our growth in population, the massive decay of our cities, the steady separation of man from nature, the depersonalization of life in the postindustrial age—these were not as obvious or as familiar as poverty and the need for schools and the black man's right to vote, but they were the overwhelming problems of the future, demanding immediate action. They could not be ignored.

* See Chapter 6, pp. 148–51.

Chief among them were the problems of the cities. Walter Reuther, the volatile and brilliant leader of the United Auto Workers, had given me a memorandum in May 1965 that warned of the "erosion of life in urban centers." That warning was steadily repeated in almost every report that came to me. The cities were on the brink of crisis. Their physical decay was accelerating. The slums were crowded with people untrained for jobs, many of whom were lost even to the census count. The tax base of cities was shrinking as a result of the persistent flight of industry and middle class families to the suburbs. The cities were being choked by the congestion of their own traffic arteries. People were unable to walk the streets at night, because of the rising rate of crime. Across the entire country the problems of urban America were spilling beyond the borders of the cities into the fast-growing suburbs, and beyond them into the rural heartland.

Consumers were being systematically deceived and bilked by unscrupulous elements in the marketplace. Air and water were being steadily poisoned by the uncontrolled wastes of our wealth. New housing was not being constructed rapidly enough to cope with our population growth. The landscape of our beautiful continent was being marred by junk heaps and litter and scarred by the bulldozer.

These were the perplexing problems that could not be put off. In considering what legislative proposals I would make to the new Congress, I asked my staff to develop a program that would deal with the country's highest-priority needs.

At the same time, I turned my attention to the baffling issue of the costs of war. By the end of December 1965 Charles Schultze, Director of the Bureau of the Budget, was warning that the pressures of Vietnam might well drive prices up in the following year. "In practical terms," Schultze said, "this means tax increases"—eventually. He indicated that he did not think it wise to propose a general tax increase at that time. Neither did Treasury Secretary Fowler. While I was at the Ranch over the 1965 Christmas holidays, Fowler cabled me a report of a meeting he had had with Wilbur Mills, Chairman of the House Ways and Means Committee. Secretary Fowler had asked Mills's opinion on a tax increase, he said, and "Mr. Mills responded that he wouldn't do it in 1966. . . . He clearly showed that he had no appetite for a tax increase bill in 1966." *

No estimate relating to war costs can ever be considered firm or precise, but all the indicators suggested strongly that in terms of its effect on the American economy the cost of a limited war in Vietnam could, for the time being, be kept manageable. Those indicators led us to hope and believe late

---

* How futile any effort would have been to get higher taxes at that time was, in retrospect, demonstrated conclusively by our painful struggle to get a 10 per cent surcharge, a struggle that began in 1967 and ended in a photo finish with disaster in 1968. See Chapter 19.

in 1965 that through a combination of restraint, reason, and responsibility, as well as our ability to use the tools of fiscal and monetary management, we could meet our commitments without seeking a tax increase that we had no chance of winning and without denying our cities, our poor, our aged, our sick, our children, and our minorities the assistance they sorely needed. I pointed out on several occasions, however—to the Congress and the nation—that we did not know how long the war would last, that we had no accurate predictions on how much it would cost, and that I would not hesitate to ask Congress for additional taxes if the facts warranted.

On January 12, 1966, I went before the Congress to lay down the framework for the legislative year ahead. "I believe," I said to the assembled legislators, "that we can continue the Great Society while we fight in Vietnam." In that sentence, to which the Congress responded with heartening applause, the turmoil of months was resolved, and the Great Society moved through midpassage into its final years of creative activity and accomplishment.

In the fall of 1965 I had directed my staff to perform the spadework on a full-scale domestic program. Joe Califano and his deputy, Larry Levinson, immersed in that operation, reported that ten task forces were at work, each studying a critical area of need.* Task forces were an important part of the Great Society. They were born in the same speech that had launched the Great Society programs. When I spoke to the graduating class of the University of Michigan at Ann Arbor on May 22, 1964, I said that in order to move forward on the Great Society I would "assemble the best thought and the broadest knowledge" and "establish working groups to prepare a series of White House conferences and meetings."

Previously, the standard method of developing legislative programs had consisted of adopting proposals suggested by the departments and agencies of the government. The Bureau of the Budget and to a lesser degree the White House staff would analyze the suggested measures and submit them to the President. From this process derived the programs that an administration presented to the Congress. I had watched this process for years, and I was convinced that it did not encourage enough fresh or creative ideas. The bureaucracy of the government is too preoccupied with day-to-day operations, and there is strong bureaucratic inertia dedicated to preserving the status quo. As a result, only the most powerful ideas can

---

* In reviewing the papers of that period, I noted that I had penciled the word "Good" on Califano's memorandum. It was a somewhat restrained comment, in light of the fervor with which we were all proceeding. On another staff paper, written about the same time, indicating some progress at last on a transportation and highway safety program that I had been trying to get started, I had written: "Hooray!"

survive. Moreover, the cumbersome organization of government is simply not equipped to solve complex problems that cut across departmental jurisdictions.

I had my first experience with a task force when I worked with a group set up by President Roosevelt in the 1930s to study economic conditions in the South. Throughout my Senate career, and as Vice President, I relied extensively on advice gathered by independent groups of experts. I always remembered my father's advice: "A man's judgment on any subject is only as good as his information."

Hoping for an across-the-board Democratic victory in November 1964, I wanted, if elected, to be able early in 1965 to recommend programs that would deal with the critical problems facing the country. But those programs depended on a tremendous infusion of objective thinking and new and original ideas. For this reason, we established fourteen task forces in 1964 to study critical areas of our national life, including education, transportation, health, natural resources, government organization, urban development, and agriculture. We granted each task force a broad charter to explore its area widely, searching for ideas, proposals, and possibilities. We asked them not to concern themselves with either political or budgetary considerations. Their suggestions would be screened later by a separate set of experts to determine whether they were too costly or impractical.

In July 1964 I described to the Cabinet my plan of putting the task forces to work. I said that I expected them to be "imaginative and not bound by timid, preconceived notions." " You and I," I told the members of the Cabinet, "will have to exercise judgments later about what is feasible." But I made it clear that I preferred having sights set too high rather than too low, at least at first. We did lay down certain guidelines. I wanted to avoid some of the difficulties that John Kennedy had experienced with similar groups he had organized during the 1960 campaign. Those groups had been overweighted with scholars, and very few suggestions had emerged that were practical enough to exploit. I insisted that our task forces have a broad balance of thinkers and doers, both the John Gardners and the Edgar Kaisers of our society. I wanted representative groups that would be familiar with all the elements of the special areas assigned to them, so that we could look at our problems whole. For instance, I felt that a task force investigating juvenile delinquency should have the insight of a nutritionist as well as a psychologist, a priest as well as a parole officer.

I insisted that the task forces operate on an off-the-record basis, making it clear to them that their reports would be available only to the President. This policy came under considerable fire, but contrary to legend, the arrangement did not reflect a passionate desire on my part to operate in secrecy. I was prompted by a wish to obtain the most candid, objective advice possible. When a man is preparing a document for public consumption he is far more cautious and concerned about public image, and far more reluctant to be critical, than when he is advising on a confidential basis.

There were other reasons why it was preferable for the task forces to work off the record. President Kennedy had learned to his regret in 1960 that when the findings of his task forces were prematurely disclosed opposition had plenty of time to form. As details of his programs were leaked to the press, he was subjected to a barrage of criticism before he had had time to read, much less assess, the reports.

I used task forces throughout my administration. Approximately three hundred businessmen, labor leaders, and teachers became, in effect, my Brain Trust, operating almost as a separate arm of the government. On any given day, one or another of these groups of men and women might be flying in to Washington to advise and often to dissent. Some of the finest minds and talents in America worked in these groups. Their ideas stimulated much bold legislation.

More than once at a bill-signing ceremony, while standing at the head of a reception line shaking hands with well-wishers, with men and women especially interested in the new law on the books, I had the experience of greeting a professor from one of the universities or an executive of labor or industry who had served on the task force that had been instrumental in initiating the legislation. In that brief moment while our hands clasped, my task force colleague would tell me how proud he was to be there— to see an idea once debated with such intensity and excitement around a littered conference table become the law of the land.

Out of the work of the task forces, out of endless conferences with officers of government and with members of my staff, out of long discussions with leaders from every facet of our national life, out of consultations and conversations with old friends and family members, out of the conscience and concern of the President, the programs of the Great Society emerged. Toward the close of my administration the members of my Cabinet presented me with a silver desk set I will always treasure. On the pad are inscribed the titles of the laws which those men, who stood at my side so long, considered the landmark achievements of my Presidency. They number 207.

Those laws kept coming right to the end. The congressional resistance we detected in 1965 deepened with the passing months, but it never developed into the impasse I had feared. I remember all 207 of those laws and the work and the worry that went into them, but above all I cherish the satisfaction they brought and the progress they represented. They were the tools with which we cleared up the old agenda and began work on the agenda of the future. I regarded those laws not as ends in themselves but as the building blocks of a better America.

I will not trace here the progression of programs that composed the new agenda as they came out of the Congress year by year. A better and more realistic way to assess them is to consider them as a whole. From that perspective, I believe, they can be viewed as the components of an urban strategy for modern America.

Before we could deal with the problems of the cities, we needed to develop the organizational machinery. Three-quarters of a century after the farmers had been given a voice at the Cabinet table, the cities still had none. Our urban programs had grown into a network of separate fiefdoms. We pulled them all together by establishing a new Department of Housing and Urban Development, headed by the first Negro to serve in a President's Cabinet, Secretary Robert C. Weaver. Transportation was serviced by a hodgepodge of agencies and activities. To bring order out of that chaos we created another Cabinet department—headed by Alan S. Boyd—the Department of Transportation, whose primary assignment was to develop the first coordinated national transportation program. Within the framework of this new institutional machinery, we created numerous specific programs to meet what we saw as the most critical needs of our growing nation.

The sense of home runs strong and deep in me, and better housing would automatically appear on any list of my priorities. I believe that the American home is the bedrock of our national strength and that the physical home is like an umbilical cord that sustains a family. Every family in America deserves a decent home, whether a farmhouse or a city apartment, rented or owned, modest or splendid. What matters is that the home be a place for a family to live in health and grow in dignity. I have been criticized for such statements by people who think I raised hopes that can never be fulfilled, but I believe in the wisdom of the Bible—"Where there is no vision, the people perish." Unless these hopes are held out and unless they are eventually realized, our system of government will undergo a drastic change, and the change may not necessarily be concerned with the Constitution. Men will not support indefinitely a system which denies them a roof over their heads and shelter and warmth for their children. If all our people were properly housed, most of the problems that now threaten our society would be less critical, and we would be an immeasurably stronger nation.

A generation ago the Democratic Eighty-first Congress, under the leadership of President Harry Truman, set the goal of "a decent home and a suitable living environment for every family" when it passed the National Housing Act of 1949. Over the years, in spite of strenuous efforts, the goal had remained beyond our reach. I knew something had to be done, and soon. The first challenge, as my advisers and I saw it, was to attack the problem of rebuilding the slums. In 1965 I set up a task force to study the situation and to recommend ways to solve it. Business, labor, the construction industry, and the Congress were represented on that committee. The academic world was also represented—by Robert C. Wood from MIT and Charles M. Haar from Harvard. As a result of that task force's recommendations, I sent to the Congress early in 1966 a program for an entirely new way of approaching the problems of the slums. This new approach was based on the proposition that a slum is not merely decaying brick and mortar but also a breeding ground of human failure and despair, where hope is as alien as sunlight and green grass. Along with new buildings to replace the crumbling hovels where slum dwellers wore out their deprived existences, we needed to offer those slum dwellers a genuine opportunity to change their lives—programs to train them for jobs, the means of giving their children a better chance to finish school, a method for putting medical clinics and legal services within their reach. The proposal was an approach to the rebuilding of city neighborhoods in a total way, bringing to bear on a blighted community all the programs that could help in that task.

After a stormy debate, the Congress passed the Model Cities Act in September 1966. I believe this law will be regarded as one of the major breakthroughs of the 1960s. It posed two basic challenges to our ability to handle urban problems. First, it forced the cities, through the community action approach, to plan their own reconstruction, with financial assistance from the federal government in the form of block grants. The cities were required to develop the actual renewal plans and to devise their own visions for the future. Second, this legislation provided a graphic test of the federal government's ability to work in harmony with other levels of government.

I asked Bob Wood and Charlie Haar, two members of the task force that had made the original investigation, to stay on to administer the new program. "I'm going to convert you," I told them, "from armchair generals to front-line commanders." I appointed Wood Under Secretary and Haar Assistant Secretary of the new Department of Housing and Urban Development. After the Model Cities Act was signed into law, we set out to tackle the nation's overall housing shortage.

Whenever I asked my key advisers to tell me the number of housing units needed in America, I received varying answers. Secretary Weaver quoted one figure, the Director of the Budget another. Still other figures were reported by my staff. I was convinced that a nation that could be so precise in its analysis of the mix of its strategic defense weapons ought to be able to pinpoint the number of decent homes it needed, and to figure out how to get them.

I turned to a group of experts headed by industrialist Edgar Kaiser to chart the course. This group included businessmen, labor leaders, and scholars. They concluded that in order to solve our housing problem we would have to build federally subsidized housing ten times faster than we had ever built it before. They found that two distinct but interrelated housing problems existed. One was the urgent need for housing for low-income families; the other was a growing shortage of housing for the entire population.

To solve these problems simultaneously, the experts agreed, America would have to undertake a massive ten-year program to construct 26 million housing units, including 6 million for poor families. In the Kaiser experts' view, the necessity for such a program was urgent, and they concluded that the cost was "not unreasonable"—an average of 5 per cent of the gross national product for housing.

The Kaiser group's interim report was submitted to me late in 1967. Based on the committee's findings, I urged the Congress to adopt what became the National Housing Act of 1968. I discussed the bill at length with Congressman Wright Patman of Texas and Senator John Sparkman of Alabama, both tireless workers in the vineyards of housing. No better men ever served the interest of the American people. The act established the blueprint for the construction of 26 million homes by 1978, providing a complex network of fiscal tools to accomplish the job—including direct subsidies, loan guarantees, and below-market interest rates.

Thousands of people stood in the courtyard of the new headquarters of the Department of Housing and Urban Development when I signed the housing bill into law that August day of 1968. All the housing giants of a generation were present. We had high hopes for the new law, but the Kaiser experts had warned us about what could conceivably happen. "Among the most important factors, in addition to congressional appropriations of the necessary long-term level of housing subsidies," they said, "are responsible fiscal and monetary policies. Without the proper mixture of these two key forces, the realization of a goal of 26 million housing units is doubtful."

Today, only a short time later, much of the powerful machinery of that legislation lies idle. The moneychangers have priced housing out of the market. High interest rates and a high-handed fiscal policy have again closed the doors on the American family home. But in a final report that arrived shortly before I left the White House, the Kaiser commission warned that the goal would *have* to be met, in one way or another, because the importance of housing to the future of our country was too demanding to be ignored. If efforts to reach the goal through the full participation of private industry should fail, this commission of practical and experienced men concluded, "we would then foresee the necessity for massive federal intervention, with the federal government becoming the nation's houser of last resort." I agreed and I continue to agree. If all else fails, I believe that the federal government will have to make good on the long-delayed promise that every family in America must have a decent place to live.

The history of March 1968, as it will be remembered by many, was shaped by two decisions I made public on the final day of that month —that bombing would end over most of North Vietnam and that I would not be a candidate for reelection. I made another statement in March, which was less publicized but which may be remembered as long as the other two. At a meeting with a group of businessmen in the Sheraton Park Hotel in Washington, I asked the photographers to get a picture of the entire assembly, because, I said, "I think that every person in this meeting will someday want to point to his children—and if he is fortunate enough, his grandchildren—and say to them: 'I was there when this all began. . . .' "

The men in the Sheraton Park ballroom were organizing a group called the National Alliance of Businessmen and launching a revolutionary program to provide jobs for the hard-core unemployed in the ghettos and slums of America's fifty largest cities. The hard work of two task forces and many dedicated men in the ranks of business, labor, and government had combined to bring us to this noteworthy occasion. Their searching inquiries had exposed two glaring facts. One was that although the continuing health of our economy was steadily creating new jobs and reducing the ranks of the unemployed, and although federal manpower programs were continually decreasing those jobless lists, there were still at least half a million men and women in America identifiable as hard-core unemployed. The names of these people did not appear on the regular unemployed lists; many of them did not appear in the census counts. They were the anonymous human failures of our society, men and women with no skills to offer and no hope of acquiring them. Many had never been gainfully employed in their lives. The second outstanding fact was that the most effective kind of training is on-the-job training, conducted right at the workbench or on the site by private industry.

Those two facts may appear incompatible, but it was out of their marriage that the pioneering program to provide jobs for the unskilled men and women who comprised the hard-core unemployed was born.

One of the groups I had asked to investigate this perplexing problem was a task force on urban employment opportunities chaired by George

Shultz.* In its report the Shultz committee concluded that "the major objective of national manpower programs and policies must be to provide the urban disadvantaged with meaningful job opportunities in the private sector." I had the benefit of that report before me when I received, on September 12, 1967, a proposal from Secretary of Labor Willard Wirtz that we launch a public works program to produce new jobs.

I was far more attracted to the idea of accomplishing the objective through private industry, since six out of every seven jobs in our economy were in the private sector. Moreover, private enterprise had been demonstrating responsiveness to the needs of the times, as evidenced by a billion dollar insurance fund for housing and the so-called turnkey approach to public housing—a method that accelerated construction by cutting government red tape and placing increased responsibility on private industry.

Accordingly, three days after receiving the public works proposal I directed my staff to begin at once to develop a program to increase the involvement of private industry in job training. With the assistance of Secretaries McNamara, Wirtz, and Trowbridge of Commerce, and working virtually around the clock, they hammered out a program the following week. We refined it and launched it on a test basis in five cities on October 2. Essentially the plan was this: The government would undertake to locate the jobless in the test cities, and selected industries would hire them and train them for jobs. The old method had been to train a man and then try to find a job for him. Now industry proposed reversing that procedure under the slogan "Hire—Train—Retain."

The training of these people was expensive. They were men and women who were not only unskilled but often unmotivated. They had to be located, and they had to be enticed to work. A good many had to be taught to read so that they could follow instructions. Some needed medical treatment before they could put in a full day's work on the job. They knew nothing about time clocks, or the reasons for punctuality, or any of the other hundreds of bits of information that regular workers automatically accumulate. All that motivation and knowledge had to be provided. In addition, the attitudes of supervisors and stewards and co-workers had to be reshaped, so that they would accept in a spirit of understanding these new people who required so much special attention. It was unfair to expect industry to pay the bill for all this. The government's share of the bargain would be to underwrite the expenses of the training operation.

These were the essentials of the plan we launched. It was undeniably risky, and there was certain to be criticism over appropriating money to spend on people who would not make any personal effort, who would not

* Shultz was then dean of the University of Chicago Business School. President Nixon made him his first Secretary of Labor, and later Director of the new Office of Management and Budget.

answer want ads or apply at the factory gate in the usual way. The work incentive is a strong part of our heritage and I believe in it deeply, yet I knew that the hard-core unemployed were people who had not shared that heritage. But I believed that in them, as in all of us, there was a potential for pride—the kind of pride a man feels when he is doing useful work and knows he is a contributing member of society. I felt that we could appeal to that pride. On balance, I believed that the risks were well worth taking.

The results of the test program, which were carefully monitored by the White House, were so successful that in my January 1968 manpower message I asked Congress to approve the program for fifty of our major cities. That was the program we were launching when I met at the Sheraton Park Hotel on March 16 with the men who were to form the National Alliance of Businessmen. This group included several of the nation's leading industrialists, headed by the public-service-minded Henry Ford II and Ford Vice President Leo Beebe,* who had agreed to try to make the program work. At their instigation, we cut government red tape to the bone. We set a goal of putting 100,000 hard-core unemployed in the work force the first year. By January 1969 it was clear that our goal would be exceeded.

Since then I have found special satisfaction in newspaper stories attesting to the success of the program, and there have been many. Industry has continued to carry out effectively the obligations it assumed. For their part, the long-term jobless, disheartened by years of idleness and despair, have proved themselves a worthy investment. They buckled down to work, and the rates of turnover and absenteeism among them are about the same as for other workers. There is criticism that the average cost per trainee is too high, but in my view those costs must be balanced against the savings in tax dollars to be gained when a man spends his time at the workbench instead of on the welfare rolls.

I think this program—improved, I hope, with time and experience—should become a continuing government-industry effort. If this joint effort persists, we will have given a new definition to hard-core unemployed. The term will encompass those who cannot work or will not, but never again will it include men and women who were not given the fullest opportunity.

Crime was emerging as one of America's most pressing problems in the 1960s. Prior to that time there had never been a probing examination of the problem of crime in America in all its aspects, including the broader

* Ford reached into his organization and selected Beebe to act as executive director of the National Alliance of Businessmen.

subject of our system of criminal justice. In 1965 I assembled a blue ribbon panel to make such a study—a tough, hard-headed group made up of police chiefs, judges, and lawyers, as well as a few knowledgeable professors. Attorney General Nicholas Katzenbach was placed in charge.

The crime commission studied the complex subject for a year and a half, and when I received its detailed report early in 1967, the effect was like a light cutting through the darkness. Reading the report, I felt for the first time that I could grasp the full dimensions of the problem. It was a more massive and profound problem than any of us had visualized.

Basically, the commission made three vital points. First, most of the police organizations in our country were outmoded and inefficient. They urgently required new equipment and better training for their members. Second, the delay in meting out justice, because of overburdened and clogged court schedules, was assuming the proportions of a national scandal. The whole court system needed to be renovated and strengthened. Finally, most criminals were repeaters, which suggested that there was something drastically wrong with our system of corrections.

The role of the federal government was distinctly limited. Our earliest traditions had regarded the majority of crimes as local problems to be handled at the local level. The solution now was not to abolish those traditions and delegate responsibility for controlling crime to the federal government. The police states we had watched come to power in the twentieth century showed the danger of that approach. The solution, as the crime commission viewed it, was a program in which the federal government was authorized to contribute financial assistance and research techniques to stimulate reforms in areas where the need was outstanding. That principle became the heart of the Safe Streets Act, which I subsequently asked the Congress to enact.

The act had a rough passage through Congress, a circumstance not entirely unexpected, since it was the first major anticrime legislation of its kind. When it was finally passed, the act contained one major disappointment—a provision for wiretapping, which I considered a grave danger to our constitutional rights. Privacy is among the most basic rights of the individual and is too precious to be violated by electronic snooping. The case for wiretapping has never been adequately established in my judgment. It has rarely proven effective and often has just offered a lazy substitute for sound police work.

Some of my advisers were so concerned about the wiretapping provision that they urged me to veto the Safe Streets Act, but I did not accept this counsel. We desperately needed immediate assistance for our local police forces, for our courts, and for our correctional system. I signed the bill, confident that we had finally launched an intelligent national attack on the problem of crime. But for the duration of my administration we did not take advantage of the wiretapping authority. I wanted to make our streets safe, but I also wanted to leave our Constitution as I had found it.

If there had been no education crisis when I became President, if the health needs of our people had been fully met, if justice had already been extended to our black citizens, if poverty in our national life had been only a memory, if the challenge of the cities had been a phrase without meaning—in short, if none of the problems had existed that absorbed so much of the time and attention of my administration—I would have been content to be simply a conservation President. My deepest attitudes and beliefs were shaped by a closeness to the land, and it was only natural for me to think of preserving it. I wanted to continue the good work begun by Theodore Roosevelt, who broke through the barrier characterized by Speaker Joe Cannon's immortal words: "Not one cent for scenery." I wanted, as I once expressed it, to leave to future generations "a glimpse of the world as God really made it, not as it looked when we got through with it."

But conservation could no longer be approached in the manner it had been in the time of Teddy Roosevelt. In the 1960s I had to be concerned not only with the preservation of land but also with the people who lived in the crowded cities, and particularly with those who did not have much money—the taxi drivers and schoolteachers, the clerks and construction workers. What could the beauty of our continent mean to them if that beauty was too far away to be enjoyed? I wanted a new kind of conservation that would bring national parks within reach of more people, that would set aside land for enjoyment in the vicinity of congested urban areas. This is what we set out to do, with a program that contributed, in a five-year period, over one-sixth of all the units in our national park system, units located where a man and his family in Detroit or Houston or New York could get to them and use them.

A memorandum I received toward the end of my administration from Secretary of the Interior Stewart Udall stated:

> These have been good years for the cause of conservation. . . . History tells us that two Presidents this century—the Roosevelts—quickened the land conscience of the nation and provided leadership that saved specific resources and established sound policies of stewardship. I believe the Johnson years will undeniably be regarded as a "third wave" of the conservation movement which quantitatively will compare very favorably with those of these two predecessor Presidents, and which qualitatively will be known for the innovations and insights.

I believe that assessment will stand the test of time. So too will the work done by a concerned and compassionate woman. I believe that Lady

Bird Johnson touched a fundamental chord in the American people with her quiet crusade to beautify our country. She enriched the lives of all Americans.

By the 1960s conservation embraced more than the preservation of land and the beautification of the countryside. The cost of our careless technology had caught up with us. I have flown through the layers of filthy air above Los Angeles. I have seen the oily slime of the Hudson and the Potomac rivers. And I found such experiences repugnant, as perhaps only a man who grew up knowing nature at its cleanest could.

Today almost everyone is conscious of the threat of pollution, and I am glad that there is such widespread awareness of the problem. A few years ago the prevailing idea was that pollution, however deplorable, had to be lived with, and that when corrective action was necessary the states and local communities should take action. In 1959, when I was Senate Majority Leader, the Senate passed a bill by a vote of 61 to 27 designed to increase substantially federal grants for the construction of sewage treatment plants. The House followed suit, but President Eisenhower vetoed the bill. "Water pollution," he said, "is a uniquely local blight." One of the real disappointments of my last year as Majority Leader was that President Eisenhower did not see the necessity of taking forceful action at the national level.

One of the important conservation measures I recommended to the Congress was the Water Quality Act, which required all states to set antipollution standards. Congress passed that act in 1965, and when I affixed my signature to it, I said: "Today we begin to be masters of our environment." On that day we empowered the federal government to act as the agent for responsible action. The Congress passed five other major antipollution measures, aimed at cleaning not only the water but the air, in an effort to begin making our environment livable again. The thrust of those laws was to institute regional attacks on the problem of pollution, for poisoned air and contaminated water do not stop at state boundaries.

These measures met with considerable resistance. Powerful special-interest groups, particularly in industry, foresaw that it woud be expensive to change their methods of operation in order to meet strict new federal pollution standards. Often we had to step on some sensitive toes, and on one occasion I stepped on some toes rather unfairly, but quite by accident.

The occasion was the signing ceremony of the 1965 Water Quality Act. I asked Robert L. Hardesty of my staff to draft a signing statement for the occasion and to "make it tough." "Find out which industries are the guiltiest," I said. "I want the stockholders to know what their companies are doing to our environment." Hardesty called the Department of Health,

Education, and Welfare and asked one of the water experts for a list of the most noxious materials being poured into our water and of the industries that were responsible. The list he sent was enough to turn your stomach. Out of it we developed this paragraph in my speech:

> There is no excuse for a river flowing red with blood from slaughterhouses. There is no excuse for papermills pouring tons of sulphuric acid into the lakes and the streams of the people of this country. There is no excuse—and we should call a spade a spade—for chemical companies and oil refineries using our major rivers as pipelines for toxic wastes. There is no excuse for communities to use other people's rivers as a dump for their raw sewage.

That evening, I watched reports of the speech on the television news shows with considerable satisfaction. I thought to myself: "That should make them stop, look, and listen."

A good many of them did "stop, look, and listen." In fact, in a matter of hours a storm of protest broke loose. I received angry telegrams from the presidents of almost every papermill company in the United States, and in some cases from the chairmen of the board as well, denying that one single ounce of sulphuric acid was poured into the water from their plants.

I asked Hardesty for an explanation, and he immediately called HEW. "Well," came the reply, "it's not really sulphuric acid. It's sulphites. But you said that the President wanted a horror list of pollution abuses, and we just thought that sulphuric acid sounded better." They were just trying to help the President, they insisted, but the President had to make numerous apologies as a result. Still, I believed the point was valid.

If we are serious about making our country habitable for the generations that will come after us, we can no longer tolerate the abuse of the air, the water, and the land as places to dump the waste products of our affluence. We must begin to devote a proportionate amount of our resources and our ingenuity to reversing the tide of pollution we have created. We must confront the careless polluters head on. We need a science of "preventive engineering," similar to preventive medicine, and we need experts trained by the thousands to build safeguards into our environment instead of reacting after the damage has been done. We must be prepared to shoulder the enormous costs this will entail, and we will have to demand that industry bear a fair share of the burden as a cost of doing business. We will have to start thinking beyond costs to questions of population movement and industrial location.

As we wrestle to regain control of our environment, there is another challenge we face. We must recognize that in ways both subtle and serious we have disturbed the delicate balance in nature; and, as best we can, we must try to restore that balance.

The first time Lady Bird and I took a vacation together after we left the White House, we went to Mexico. Lady Bird got into a conversation with a young scientist who had been assigned the job of eradicating mosquitoes and flies in a Mexican village. He and his fellow workers sprayed the community liberally with a powerful insecticide. They got rid of the insects, but in the process they also eliminated all the cats. And now the village is overrun with rodents.

That experience reminded me of a story about an atomic scientist who was walking through the woods one day with a friend when he saw a small turtle. He thought that his children would be delighted to have a new pet, so he picked it up and started home with it. Suddenly he stopped, looked at the turtle, and retraced his steps. He put the turtle back on the ground exactly where he had found it. His friend asked him why he had changed his mind. He answered: "It just struck me that perhaps, for one man, I have tampered enough with the universe."

We are all somewhat like that scientist. We cannot hope to put all the turtles back where we found them; nor should we try. We are committed to a technological society that has created imbalances, and these imbalances we must correct, but the lessons of the past should convince us that the turtles of the future should be picked up only with the greatest of care.

Population control is another problem on the agenda for the future. When I pledged in my State of the Union message of January 1965 to "seek new ways to use our knowledge to help deal with the explosion in world population," I was breaking sharply with Presidential tradition. Population control was not considered a fit subject for the federal government, or a President, to approach. I was constantly warned that I was dealing with the delicacies of the home and the dogma of the church. I understood those feelings, but they were outweighed by an overriding awareness of the dangers we faced. The statistics of those dangers are widely recognized by most people now: The prospect of 3.5 billion more human beings—double the present world population—by the year 2000, most of them in already overcrowded regions of the globe, along with the prospect of another billion every five years thereafter, cannot fail to be disturbing. The hope for a stable and peaceful world trembles before that awesome forecast.

Pakistan's forceful and capable President, Ayub Khan, was one concerned leader who convinced me of the need for action. When I visited his country as Vice President, I was deeply impressed by the progress the Pakistanis were making in housing and other areas. President Ayub acknowledged this, but he said to me, in effect: All our progress will be nothing if we cannot solve the population problem. Then he added: We hope you will help us. In the years that followed I heard the same message many times from other world leaders.

We started on a small scale, but we progressed steadily. When I entered office we were investing less than $6 million annually for population control. During my last year in the White House that investment had grown to $115 million. At first there was a timidity about how AID funds could be used. One of the first actions I took was simply a reinterpretation of a regulation. Horace Busby, my staff assistant assigned to work on the population problem, had reported to me that in many countries in which we had AID missions there were local groups equipped to provide instruction in family planning, but these specialists had to move their materials and exhibits from village to village and often had no means of travel. I was advised that our AID staffs in those countries were supplied with jeeps but that AID regulations, as they were being interpreted, prevented the vehicles from being used for that purpose. We made an immediate change in that interpretation. Other changes followed. In 1967 we took the giant step and allotted AID funds to the missions to make contraceptive devices available.

In our own country we initiated programs to provide family services to those who needed and requested them. With these actions, we brought the awesome problem of the population explosion into the center of national concern; but this of course was and is only a beginning. In the developing countries of the world population growth is still outracing food supply, and among the poverty-stricken in the United States family planning services are available to only one woman in five. Of the 3.5 million children born in 1966, the last year for which such figures were available, almost 500,000 were unwanted. These unfortunate children were born into large, underprivileged families, to mothers who would have chosen not to become pregnant had they had access to instruction and guidance.

In the last year of my administration I assembled a committee of men and women who represented a Who's Who in population control. Secretary Wilbur Cohen of HEW and John D. Rockefeller III were co-chairmen. I asked this group to investigate everything in progress on the subject and to recommend any additional federal actions they considered necessary. I received their report shortly before I left office. The Department of Health, Education, and Welfare printed this document and made it generally available. The report urged that the United States enlarge its worldwide assistance in population control and called for an expansion of the federal government's role in family planning in this country, so that information and services would be available by 1973 to all American women who desired but could not afford these services.

If the American citizen in our time has become the victim of technology's conquests, he has also become the victim of the cynicisms and subtleties— and, yes, the greed—of the marketplace. One of my earliest concerns as President was the protection of the consumer. I was determined to protect the housewife against the huckster, the man of the house against the modern-day usurer, and the entire family against the sellers of tainted meat and dangerous merchandise.

To give the consumer a focus and a voice in my administration, I selected a VISTA volunteer—although to the majority of Americans she was better known as the lady in the refrigerator commercials—Betty Furness. When Esther Peterson, who had served as Special Assistant to the President for Consumer Affairs, expressed her desire to return to her post in the Labor Department, I asked John W. Macy, Jr., who served as my talent scout, to find a replacement. I wanted someone who would dramatize our concern for consumer protection not only to the public at large but more pointedly to the committees of the Congress, where the protection of the law would either be given or withheld. Macy sent me a list of four candidates in February 1967. Miss Furness' name was among them. He described her as a "former television personality" who "seems to have been bitten by the 'public service bug.' . . . Miss Furness has been working as a VISTA volunteer, drumming up support for Head Start projects throughout the country. . . ."

Betty became not only the symbol of consumer protection but the target of the lobbies. But she was a plucky lady who stood up when it counted, not only to the lawyers of the trade associations but to the curmudgeons in the Congress as well, who had not often seen her like. Testifying for our Wholesome Meat Act on November 15, 1967, she spoke out in unmistakably clear terms. "I don't want roaches in my meat and I don't suppose you do," she told the startled Senators. "I don't want to eat meat processed in a filthy plant covered with flies. And I don't suppose you do. I don't want to think about these things while I am eating. And I am sure you don't. Thank you very much."

We obtained most of the laws we sought. They are on the books for the protection of the American consumer, and all of us are consumers. Because of those laws, Americans can feel a little safer now in their homes, on the road, at the supermarket, and in the department store. Perhaps most important, with those laws a whole new era of concern was ushered in, and consumerism became a permanent part of the American way of life and the American political scene.

At precisely 10:44 A.M. on January 16, 1969, my last Thursday as President, I walked into the Cabinet Room, where the members, staff, and families of the Council of Economic Advisers joined me in what had become a yearly ritual, the signing of the President's Economic Report. On this occasion the document I was about to endorse was more than the Council's year-end summary and forecast; it represented the final accounting to the Congress and to the people of our economic stewardship over the previous five years. The report was prepared by a team of economists headed by a young and able Yale University professor, Arthur Okun, who had succeeded Gardner Ackley as Chairman of the Council of Economic Advisers several months before.

As the January sunlight filtered into the Cabinet Room, I took my customary place at the center of the table, flanked by members of the Council. It was a moment of quiet reflection for all of us as we looked back on the work of five years—with a few regrets but also with a real sense of excitement and achievement. The statistics of progress were all recorded there. Almost to the day, we had entered the ninety-fifth month of sustained economic growth and prosperity, the longest and strongest period in American history. The previous five years had produced an unparalleled standard of living for most Americans: An estimated 8.5 million additional jobs had been created by the growing economy; only 3.3 per cent of the work force was unemployed, down from 5.7 per cent in 1963; approximately $460 billion had been added to family net assets. There had been a 50 per cent increase in corporate profits and workers' payrolls; a total of about $535 had been added to the average yearly income of Americans, after accounting for taxes and price rises; and federal revenues had increased by $70 billion, helping to send children to Head Start classrooms and men around the moon.

Looking back over those days late in 1965, I thought that if I had it to do over again I would not have changed much. I would have made the same decision to recommend a guns-and-butter budget to the Congress, and I still would have ignored the counsel of those who called for a breathing spell in the enactment of new legislation. Nothing in the intervening years has changed my mind on those two points.*

The guns-and-butter policy created several problems—particularly, a tendency to heat up the economy. Clearly the increase in defense spending for Vietnam subjected the economy to the strains of inflation, and this situation was sharply intensified by the failure of the Congress to move promptly on the tax bill. But against this fact was another important consideration: The percentage of our gross national product devoted to defense spending, including all the costs of Vietnam, ranged from 8 to 10 per cent,

* Some of those who were most vocal in 1965 in calling for a legislative breathing spell were the very ones who were to call for a $100 billion "Marshall Plan" to rebuild our decaying cities several years later. Had we listened to their advice in 1965, we would not even have made a start in such programs as Model Cities, urban housing, the eradication of rats, and mass transportation.

compared with 13 per cent during the Korean War and around 10 per cent during the peacetime years of the mid-1950s.

What was clear above all was that our sustained prosperity did not depend on the continuation of hostilities; the costs of conflict were an additional burden, not a supporting foundation, and in my judgment they were not an inhibiting factor on our domestic programs. I remained convinced that we had the resources to meet our commitments abroad while we continued economic and social reforms at home.

The last budget I submitted to the Congress reflected that conviction. It was a map of continuing progress on both the foreign and domestic fronts, and it was a balanced budget. I was certain that we could continue and expand our fight against poverty, injustice, and inequality while paying the bills for our commitments abroad.

During the five years of my Presidency annual investments in programs for health increased from $4.1 billion to $13.9 billion; for education from $2.3 billion to $10.8 billion; for our older citizens, including social security, from $17.4 billion to $29 billion; and for the poor from $12.5 billion to $24.6 billion. I wanted to devote even more of our resources to these enterprises, yet money alone has its limitations. Some programs could not absorb additional funding; nor could money itself create the trained personnel in state and local governments required to carry the programs to the people. I recall, for example, that more than $10.3 million in federal antipoverty funds was turned back unused by New York City because it lacked the organization to put the money to work. I was never convinced that Congress would have voted appreciably more funds for domestic programs if there had been no struggle in Southeast Asia. If we had succeeded in stilling the guns in Vietnam, as we tried so desperately to do, I believe that many Congressmen would have demanded tax reductions rather than providing increased funds for the beleaguered cities.

As I sent my final Economic Report to Congress, I could say with both hope and satisfaction that the American economy "has bestowed the great blessings of abundance on the vast majority of Americans in all walks of life. . . . We will not retreat. . . . This nation will remain on the march."

But if we are to remain on the march and move forward we will have to modernize the machinery of government. We made a beginning during my administration. We created the new Department of Housing and Urban Development and a new Department of Transportation. We streamlined the government of the District of Columbia, which had been operating in the same archaic way since Reconstruction days. We ushered in the era of New Federalism to encourage cooperation between the states and the federal government. Still, we left much undone in this age of rapid change.

Today we must face the fact that the government is becoming less responsive to the present-day needs of the people. This is true throughout the chain of government, from the communities where people live to the federal bureaucracy in far-off Washington. From my ranch four county seats are within an hour's drive. We pass through a dozen or more municipalities en route. There is no reason why any one of them could not handle the administrative work of all, and administration would be much simpler and cheaper for the citizens in central Texas if they could be combined. The town-county structure is built around archaic horse-and-wagon conditions of 150 years ago.

The same overlapping is true of the federal government, and there are many ways in which the federal machinery could and should be strengthened. One way would be to extend the term of the Presidency from four to six years and make the incumbent ineligible for reelection. This stipulation almost became a provision of our Constitution when it was originally written. The case for it is even stronger in modern times. The growing burdens of the office exact an enormous physical toll on the man himself and place incredible demands on his time. Under these circumstances the old belief that a President can carry out the responsibilities of the office and at the same time undergo the rigors of campaigning is, in my opinion, no longer valid.

I also believe that the time has come to extend the term of office for members of the House of Representatives from two to four years. I recommended that such action be taken by constitutional amendment in my 1966 State of the Union message. Now, more than five years later, I am even more convinced that the present two-year term does not serve the interests of good government. This is not a new idea. At the Constitutional Convention James Madison argued that a three-year term was necessary, "in a government so extensive, for members to form any knowledge of the various interests of the States to which they did not belong," and that without such knowledge "their trust could not be usefully discharged." He was certain that a shorter term would be "almost consumed in preparing for and traveling to and from the seat of National business."

Since Madison's time, the volume of legislation has increased a thousandfold. The complex problems of our society demand a background, understanding, and degree of technical sophistication that would have dazed most of our early legislators. Sessions of Congress, once lasting four or five months a year, now are held year round, severely restricting a Congressman's ability to keep in touch with his constituents as closely as the times demand. Finally, the cost of campaigning has risen so extravagantly that two-year elections place an unfair burden on those who wish to run. I believe that a four-year term would give members of the House time to become steeped in the complex problems of state, would reduce the cost of running for reelection, and would allow a Congressman to devote more of his attention to the congressional workload and less to the task of mending his political fences at home. In short, I think that the four-year term is an overdue reform.

Every American with a sense of history is deeply stirred when he reads the great documents associated with the founding of this nation: the Declaration of Independence, the Preamble to the Constitution, the Federalist Papers, and many other documents that are less well known. In powerful and eloquent language, these documents reject age-old tyrannies and designate a new sovereign power: "We, the people of the United States." But they also reveal that our Founding Fathers held one assumption that we are no longer able to share entirely. They assumed that "the people"—not only men in public life, but lawyers, merchants, farmers, doctors, and frontiersmen—would take a keen and continuing interest in the art of government. This dream did not materialize and we are all the losers for it.

I believe that we must devote more of our educational process to teaching our youth the art of statecraft, a type of instruction that is being provided in the public administration departments of some of our great universities today. We must encourage more of our citizens to spend a few years in public service as part of a normal career. We must inspire leadership and make the tools available. That is why I have such high hopes for the Lyndon B. Johnson School of Public Affairs at the University of Texas. I want this school to train young men and women to make our government function more effectively at every level, from City Hall to the White House. I do not offer these thoughts lightly, for I know that this free society will not survive unless its citizens pay closer and more personal attention to the processes of government. And I mean continuous and serious attention, not the fitful, once-in-four-years wearing of a campaign button.

We ranchers have a saying about absentee ownership: "The footprints of the owner are the best fertilizer any land can have." Well, the people are the owners of this free society, and if they are absentee proprietors the land will not prosper, but deteriorate.

I have never believed that those who are governed least are governed best. We *are* the people, as Franklin Roosevelt said. And the proper function of a government of the people, by the people, and for the people is to make it possible for all citizens to experience a better, more secure, and more rewarding life. That is my philosophy of government, and government has been the study and the focus of my life.

What we achieved in the Great Society will endure. That I deeply believe. Those achievements are a monument not to any one man but to the will of the American people, who can do anything they choose when they are roused by challenge. I am conscious of all the statistics of progress that are part of the mortar of that monument, but I am even more intensely aware of the work left undone.

As I came to the end of my administration, I often thought of and frequently repeated—too often to suit my staff—a remark Winston Churchill was reported to have made that summed up what was on my mind. According to the story, toward the end of World War II Churchill was accosted by a group of temperance ladies who were distressed about reports of his drinking. "Mr. Prime Minister," their spokesman rebuked, "we are advised that if all the brandy you had drunk during the war were poured into this room, it would come up to here—" and she held her hand at a point about halfway to the ceiling.

The Prime Minister looked at her hand, then at the floor, then at the ceiling, and finally at her. "My dear lady," he said, "so little have we done; so much have we yet to do."

That is the way I felt about the Great Society as I left Washington.

16

The New Age of Regionalism

A T THE END OF 1965, as I worked on the 1966 State of the Union message, I reviewed with special interest a proposal submitted by Dean
Rusk. Under the heading "Interdependence," it read:

> We recognize that in every region of the Free World nations and
> peoples are anxious to take a larger hand in shaping their own destiny. This
> is true whether nations are rich or poor, or in the north or south, east or
> west. But old-fashioned nationalism is proving an unsatisfactory basis for
> dealing with the real problems that we all confront. No nation, including
> the United States, can guarantee its security, its prosperity, or its tranquility
> by pursuing narrow policies of nationalism. Our task is to find ways of
> working together which respect the dignity and the abiding national inter-
> ests of each nation, while respecting also the inescapable interdependence
> of us all in a world of modern weapons, communications, and close eco-
> nomic linkages.

That observation matched my own growing judgment about the way the
American people viewed foreign policy. I believed that we had reached a
turning point in our relations with the rest of the world. After twenty years
of sacrifice, generosity, and often lonely responsibility, the American
people felt that other nations should do more for themselves. What worried
me most was that we might be tempted to pull away from the world too
quickly, before solid foundations could be built to support the desire
of other nations for self-reliance. I knew that there was a deep current of
isolationism in our country that two world wars had not eliminated. In
spite of all we had learned over the years, politicians could still get applause
by saying: "Let's mind our own business."

But most Americans had learned that the world *was* our business. Our security depended on collective strength and a reasonably stable world order. Millions of American jobs depended on expanding world trade. If we suddenly pulled away from the world society we had helped to create, we would find ourselves neither safe nor prosperous. It seemed to me there was a sensible middle course: to pull back, but not too far; to reduce our share of the burden, but not too fast; and to urge others to take a larger hand in their own destiny, but not more quickly than they could manage.

The world was not ready for a global solution. The United Nations had proved its worth in many situations, but it did not have the peacekeeping machinery needed for universal order. The Iron Curtain had rusted through in many places, but it was still there, separating men and nations. A veto in the UN Security Council could still frustrate effective action in crucial situations.

At the other end of the spectrum, individual nations could never solve all their problems alone. This was especially true of weaker and less developed states, and only slightly less true of rich nations and even of great powers. The answer was somewhere between a world community and a system based on narrow nationalism. This line of thought led me to declare, in my State of the Union message of 1966, that a major principle of our foreign policy was "to help build those associations of nations which reflect the opportunities and the necessities of the modern world. . . . We will take new steps this year to help strengthen . . . the regional organizations of developing continents. . . ." Thus the concept of regionalism in areas outside Europe emerged as one of my administration's most serious commitments in its efforts to build a stable world order.

Six weeks after my State of the Union message, economic ministers of the Western Hemisphere met in Buenos Aires. At the final session on April 1, 1966, Argentine President Arturo Illia suggested a summit meeting of the Presidents of the American republics to discuss ways to strengthen the Alliance for Progress. I was attracted at once to the idea, for I believed that it could bring a new life to the alliance. It also offered an opportunity to clarify our role in the Western Hemisphere as I conceived it, one of true partnership rather than the big-brother role of "Colossus of the North."

I went to Mexico City on April 15, 1966, to unveil a statue of Abraham Lincoln, who had been a contemporary of Mexican leader Benito Juarez and was revered in Mexico, as in so many other nations. Standing in the tree-lined Parque Polanco alongside Mexican President Gustavo Diaz Ordaz, I endorsed Illia's proposal.

"Such a conference," I said, "should be prepared with the utmost care. We should examine every idea which might advance our common interest,

On the South Lawn of the White House, with West German
Chancellor Kurt Kiesinger, August 1967

FEEDING THE HUNGRY. Conferring with Prime Minister Indira Gandhi at the White House during India's food crisis, March 1966.

Inspecting "miracle rice" at research institute in Philippines, October 1966.
BOTTOM: Agriculture Secretary Freeman briefs congressional leaders
and Cabinet members on India's food crisis.

STRENGTHENING THE ATLANTIC COMMUNITY. Conferring with West German Chancellor Erhard on NATO problem, September 1966. BOTTOM: Prime Minister Harold Wilson warned that British troops might be "brought home if no prompt and satisfactory offset arrangement was made with Germans." RIGHT: John McCloy (*c.*) named to work out offset arrangement.

November 17, 1967: Sir Patrick Dean tells of Britain's decision to devalue pound; key members of Congress and financial advisers meet on devaluation.

Agonizing over another tough decision (with Rusk, *c.*, and Walt Rostow) May 1966. Johnson frequently sought counsel of experienced men outside government. Among these "Wise Men" were (TOP TO BOTTOM) Arthur Dean, John McCloy, General Omar Bradley, Dean Acheson.

Full employment and economic prosperity . . .

BELOW, L.: Labor leaders George Meany (*r.*), Walter Reuther (*c.*), Joseph
Keenan, Joseph Beirne, November 17, 1965; BOTTOM, L., President's Advisory
Committee on Labor-Management Policy; TOP, R., with Henry Ford II, Chairman,
National Alliance of Businessmen; Leo Beebe (BOTTOM, R.), executive director.

Lady Bird "touched
a fundamental chord
in the American people
with her quiet crusade
to beautify the country."

Detroit, July 24–28, 1967; Meeting with advisers during the early hours of the riots (*l. to r.,* Katzenbach, Ramsey Clark, Cyrus Vance, McNamara.)

Appointments. Abe Fortas *(c.)* became Associate Justice Supreme Court, July 1965 (here with Johnson, Clark Clifford). BOTTOM: Robert C. Weaver *(foreground)* is first black to serve in U.S. Cabinet (May 1967).

Thurgood Marshall becomes first black Associate Justice
of the Supreme Court, October 1967.

be it old or new. Careful preparation need not be the enemy, however, of imaginative action and new adventures."

I wanted the meeting to focus hard on the development of a Latin American common market, but I knew that the economic integration of Latin America raised tough domestic political problems for every one of the continent's Presidents. And Latin America needed much more than expanded trade. Road systems within and between countries were totally inadequate. International telecommunications links were needed. Latin America had grown up largely around coastal cities, while the interior had been neglected. The Latin American nations would have to work together if their inner frontiers were to be developed.

There were other major problems. In many countries people were still farming as their ancestors had done centuries earlier. Education was denied to millions of people. There were major health problems to be met: endemic diseases, a shortage of doctors and nurses, inadequate water and sewage systems. Experts estimated, for example, that by the year 2000 Latin America would need 175,000 more doctors. Clearly our work was cut out for us.

Under Rusk's direction, government specialists went to work to develop a program. They consulted Latin American experts throughout the United States, including such experienced old hands as Milton Eisenhower and Adolph A. Berle.* Our Ambassadors to Latin American countries collected opinions and ideas and sent them to Washington for consideration. From these extensive consultations an action program emerged.

We made it clear to our Latin American friends and the congressional leadership that we would take these proposed actions only if the Latin Americans themselves more than matched our efforts with self-help. Rusk nailed down that understanding at a meeting of foreign ministers in Buenos Aires in February 1967.

On March 13, 1967, I sent Congress a special message outlining our plan for helping to improve the lives of our neighbors to the south. In six years the Alliance for Progress had achieved considerable success, and I recalled those achievements to the Congress. But the unresolved problems were vast. I specified four pillars on which the future progress of our hemisphere should rest: elimination of trade barriers and improvements in education, agriculture, and health.

As our contribution to the common effort, I recommended that Congress make a commitment to increase assistance under the Alliance for Progress by up to $1.5 billion over the next five years. Of that, $900 million would go into agriculture, education, and health. I suggested that we guarantee $250 million to $500 million over a period of three to five years, beginning

---

* Assistant Secretary of State for Latin American Affairs under President Roosevelt, and Ambassador to Brazil, 1945–1946.

about 1970, if the Latin Americans decided to move from traditional economic protectionism to a common market. Finally, I recommended that over the next three years we put an additional $150 million into the Inter-American Bank's Fund for Special Operations. This fund would finance multinational roads, modernized communications, bridges, dams, power plants, and other development projects.

We agreed with the other participants to hold the meeting of the Presidents at the coastal resort town of Punta del Este in Uruguay, the birthplace of the Alliance for Progress six years earlier. I had hoped to go there armed with a joint congressional resolution committting Congress to vote the funds I had requested if the Latin Americans made equally definite promises. The congressional leaders were ready to give me a general statement of support, but there was resistance, especially in the Senate, to naming specific sums in a resolution. I was convinced that it was wiser to go to the summit conference with no resolution than with one that had been diluted. I decided to make my specific recommendations to Congress in the normal way and to be guided by the agreements I was able to reach in Uruguay.

We met at Punta del Este for three days, April 12–14, 1967. They were days of work as intensive as any I had experienced, except during a major crisis. There were formal conference meetings at Punta del Este, and between sessions I met for an hour or so with eleven Latin American Presidents, one President-elect, and one Prime Minister. I also had a working dinner with the Central American presidents. This gave us a chance to talk not only about overall hemisphere problems but about important bilateral problems. With President Raúl Leoni of Venezuela, for example, I settled a difference over oil imports. I also agreed to provide special equipment that he urgently needed to cope with Castro-directed guerrilla operations. With President Marco Aurelio Robles of Panama, I agreed to speed negotiation of a Panama Canal treaty. When I checked the list of items for action after the conference, I found that a dozen of the thirty substantial matters had arisen from my bilateral talks.

On April 14 we signed the Declaration of the Presidents of America. The only real disappointment was that a pledge to limit arms expenses was weaker than I had hoped. The most important agreement was the proposed creation of a Latin American common market in the 1970s. That commitment still is unfulfilled. I am conscious of the many difficulties that stand in the way, but I remain convinced of its necessity.

Flying back from Punta del Este, I told some of my advisers that my strongest single impression from the meeting was this: The Latin Americans realized that in working toward an integrated continent the major responsibility would be theirs. Any U.S. help could only be marginal. The old days, when they had looked to the United States to solve their problems, had ended. We would now be a junior partner in Latin American economic and social development.

The new spirit of self-reliance was pointed up by an incident at the conference. Specialists from several nations responsible for developing guidelines under the Alliance for Progress had decided that Ecuador should increase taxes and raise more local currency before being given the large loans it had requested to improve its transportation system. President Otto Arosemena faced political problems in getting a tax increase, and I could understand that. But he decided to use the Punta del Este conference for an old-fashioned attack on the United States, accusing us of being too tight-fisted with our aid.

Two things were notable about Arosemena's outburst. First, it was the only one of its kind during the entire conference. Second, and more important, no other President joined in the old sport of baiting Uncle Sam, and several criticized Arosemena's approach. Among the latter were the Presidents of Colombia, Costa Rica, Mexico, and Venezuela. Chilean President Eduardo Frei urged with eloquence that Ecuador's President settle for "attainable reality" and not try to "reach for the moon." In the face of criticism from his Latin American neighbors, Arosemena abandoned his hard position.

Though we had adopted the role of junior partner in the development of the Americas, we still had much to do. I was pleased that after the conference Congress voted appropriations to back a substantial part of the program I sent up in my special message on March 13. I suspect that we will have to return to the idea of a special fund to ease the pains of transition if Latin America fulfills its commitment and moves toward a common market.

My goal, before and after Punta del Este, was to promote a new sense of regionalism in Latin America. I was less interested in seeing our country extend its role as the partner of individual Latin American neighbors than in seeing them become partners of each other. I felt that we had moved much closer to that goal during my Presidency. As I told the Congress, Latin America will probably have a population of about 650 million within thirty years. Those people will fully command modern technology. As a result, our relations with Latin America will matter greatly over the next decades. They will help determine the kind of life our children and grandchildren will enjoy here at home. We must be careful not to confuse our role as junior partner with neglect or passivity.

In March 1961 President Kennedy asked me to carry out the first overseas mission of his administration. The new West African republic of Senegal was celebrating its independence. The President also wanted

me to represent him at the tenth anniversary of NATO's Supreme Headquarters in Paris. I had not been to Africa since 1945 when I visited several
North African countries as a Congressman on an investigation into base
arrangements and military problems. Much had happened in the intervening
years. Most African nations had won or had been given independence.
New nations had sprung up almost overnight, and traditional ties with the
former colonial powers were gradually weakening. New approaches and
relationships were developing.

Prime Minister Mamadou Dia and other officials of Senegal were at the
airport in Dakar to welcome Lady Bird and me when we arrived on April
2, 1961. The next two days were filled with formal meetings, parades, and
social events. Nevertheless, I managed to see a good deal of Dakar and
surrounding areas. I had several long and serious conversations with
President Leopold Senghor, Prime Minister Dia, and other officials. At
the receptions I talked with representatives from most of the other African
nations. On the morning of April 5, before departing for Europe, I spent
several hours in a farming and fishing village, visiting at length with the
chief and numerous villagers. I began to understand, from descriptions
given by the people themselves, what life in an African village was like
and what its problems were.

There were many similarities between conditions in Senegal and those
in other less developed countries. All these nations were trying to move
ahead against the same obstacles—widespread illiteracy, poor schools or
none, primitive health facilities, bad roads, lack of capital, virtually no
industry, poor communications, rudimentary transportation, and all the
other problems of economic underdevelopment. In spite of the fantastic
odds against which they worked, men of ideals and education and energy
were striving to move their nations forward. They seemed determined
to make their countries jump a chasm of 2,000 years in one generation.
Above all, they wanted to do most of it themselves, although they needed
outside help, including assistance from the United States. But as I reported
to President Kennedy later, President Senghor had told me privately:
"It is not how much money you spend in Africa, but how you spend it."
Prime Minister Dia had stressed that his country wanted "loans not gifts."

Another thing the Africans disliked was feeling that they were the prize
in a giveaway race between Communist and non-Communist nations.
"We are happy to see the change in policy on aid from your country,"
Dia told me. "Until recently it has seemed to us that those who made the
most noise received the most aid. Senegal does not wish to receive aid on
the basis of noise."

There was another important difference between Senegal and its neighbors and the Latin American countries, with which I was much more
familiar. In Latin America, from the days of President Monroe the

greatest source of business, trade, investment, and tourism—as well as bitterness, jealousy, and even fighting—had been the United States. Africa's ties were with Europe, especially with the British, French, Belgians, and Italians.

After I became President, I carried on a fairly steady correspondence with President Senghor and other African leaders, particularly Haile Selassie of Ethiopia, Jomo Kenyatta of Kenya, Modibo Keita of Mali, Sekou Toure of Guinea, Julius Nyerere of Tanzania, and William Tubman of Liberia. I invited numerous African heads of government to visit Washington so that we could share ideas and work out plans for cooperation. The more I exchanged views with these leaders and learned about their problems and hopes, the more I felt that we needed a coherent American policy to deal with the African continent, at least that portion south of the Sahara. Up to this point we had been dealing with Africa on a buckshot basis—a loan here, a dam project there, a technical assistance program somewhere else. I thought that it was time to look at the area as a whole.

On May 26, 1966, the third anniversary of the Organization of African Unity, I invited the Ambassadors of the thirty-six countries of the OAU and about three hundred guests to the White House. In the East Room I made the first address by an American President devoted wholly to Africa. I spoke directly of enforced inequality and racial prejudice and assured everyone present the United States would not "live by a double standard—professing abroad what we do not practice at home, or venerating at home what we ignore abroad." I then turned to the question of regionalism. The cooperative arrangements emerging in Africa were significantly different from those of other areas. Countries outside the African continent were not full members in any regional or subregional grouping.

In Europe, although there were many exclusively continental groupings, the United States was a full partner in NATO and the Organization for Economic Cooperation and Development (OECD). In Latin America we were a key member of the Organization of American States. In Asia we were linked to the security of the area through multilateral groupings such as SEATO and the ANZUS Treaty with Australia and New Zealand and through bilateral arrangements with such countries as Japan, South Korea, and Nationalist China.

The new Africa wanted to handle its problems alone as much as possible. Thus far, security problems had been dealt with by the African nations themselves or through the United Nations. I discussed this unique feature of African regionalism with the OAU representatives:

> You have built new institutions to express a new sense of unity. Even as you grapple with the problems of early nationhood, you have sought out new possibilities of joint action—the OAU itself, the Economic Com-

mission for Africa, the African Development Bank, and subregional groupings such as the Economic Community of Eastern Africa.

Growth in Africa must then follow the inspiration of African peoples. It must stem from the leadership of African governments. . . .

The need for regional cooperation was great. Boundaries inherited from colonial times had produced many small countries that could never become viable economic units if they operated on conventional lines. They would either prosper together or perish separately. But they also had one great opportunity: At this early stage of development, regional cooperation could be built into the very foundation of efforts to modernize the lives of the African peoples. The vested interests that encourage economic nationalism in more developed regions did not exist to nearly the same extent in Africa. Most African leaders understood this and knew that they had a remarkable opportunity to work together. I pledged our full support in that effort. I also offered help in training Africans to develop the modern communications and transportation systems that such cooperation would require.

I announced that I had asked Edward M. Korry, our Ambassador to Ethiopia, to work full time in the weeks ahead to develop an action program to carry out my decisions. I wanted him to discuss the whole range of problems and possibilities with the African governments as well as with any other governments and international bodies that could help. Korry traveled through Africa, talking with politicians, economists, with government leaders, businessmen, and professors. In the United States he visited universities noted for African studies. He consulted businessmen whose companies had long experience with Africa. He spoke with experts at a number of foundations, with missionaries, and with lawyers.

Korry sent his report to me late in July. It was the most comprehensive study of Africa and our role there ever compiled for a President. Summarizing our past efforts to help Africa, Korry said that our policy over the years had led us to become "enmeshed in an unmanageable range of projects." "It has produced too many U.S. government technicians," he wrote, "in too many fields under too many AID missions without yielding the dividend of particular competence in any one sector."

The tools for better coordination existed, and Korry urged that we use them more effectively. He recommended that we concentrate in all but a few major countries on programs of health, education, and agriculture. He suggested that we ask the World Bank to organize a standing committee of major donor nations. This committee, working closely with Africans, would develop a general strategy for African development and generate the resources needed to carry out its plans. A steering committee of this kind was formed in 1967 by the United Kingdom, Italy, Belgium, and Canada, as well as the United States. We also organized our own committee with representatives from the State Department, AID, and the White House to insure that our part in the movement to help African development would be carried out and that Korry's main recommendations would be realized.

Economic and social development is a slow business, especially among nations in a very early stage of modernization. It takes time and patience to build regional and subregional institutions. But I believe that the stock-taking we did in 1966 and 1967 set our policy on the right long-run course with the new African nations.

The day may come when we pick up the daily newspaper and find on page one that five new schools have been built and only on page fifteen that one schoolroom was torn up by vandals. But human nature and editorial judgment being what they are, we are likely to wait a long time for that day to arrive.* Until then, whether we are Presidents or Congressmen, students or hard-working, taxpaying citizens, we will have to continue to make up our own minds about what is good or bad, important or unimportant, necessary or wasteful. Such judgments are seldom if ever easy.

The war in Vietnam is a good example. Newspapers brought that war to our breakfast tables every morning. Television brought the smoke and sounds and terror of combat into our living rooms each evening. But many things, some of vital importance, were rarely reported or at least emphasized. One of these, ignored by all but a handful of experienced correspondents and perceptive columnists, was the relationship between what we were trying to do in Vietnam and other developments in Southeast Asia and the Far East.

Between the end of 1963 and the beginning of 1969 I talked directly with leaders and high officials of every non-Communist nation in Asia except Cambodia, and we had several diplomatic contacts with Prince Sihanouk of that country. Not one of the many Asian statesmen with whom I talked suggested that we accept Hanoi's demands or unilaterally withdraw from Vietnam. Almost all of them urged us to stay the course. They recognized the direct relationship between our actions and the establishment of a peaceful order in their part of the world. Yet this attitude,

---

* As James ("Scotty") Reston of *The New York Times* wrote in an article in *Foreign Affairs* in July 1966:

The press, radio and television help create the atmosphere in which the nation lives. It is not an atmosphere that encourages calm reflection or wide perspectives, and it makes little allowance for the limitations of human frailty. We have transferred into the capitals of the world the American police-blotter definition of the news—which is the news of violence and contention, of the unusual rather than the usual—given it the voice of the radio and the eyes of the television camera, and added the insistent shouts of the advertiser and the singing commercial.

so widely held by leading Asians, was either not understood or ignored by many who wrote and talked about Vietnam.

The whole exciting story of what was happening in Asia behind the shield of our commitment was largely neglected. I was convinced, even before we decided to send combat forces to Vietnam in 1965, that our struggle there would make sense only if it were part of a larger constructive effort in Asia. We had made our basic treaty commitment to Southeast Asia in 1954, when President Eisenhower and the Senate agreed that the region, the independence of its nations, and the freedom of its peoples were vitally important to the future of all Asia and to the security of the United States. Those who subscribed to the SEATO treaty had not only agreed to resist aggression in the treaty area; they had given their word to "cooperate with one another in the further development of economic measures, including technical assistance, designed both to promote economic progress and social well-being and to further the individual and collective efforts of governments toward these ends."

I was also convinced that in the long run the American commitment in Asia, as in other parts of the world, could achieve its goals only if the nations of that region cooperated with one another, and only if they were ready to gradually take on a larger share of responsibility in managing their own affairs and in shaping their own futures. This was much on my mind when I went to Baltimore on April 7, 1965, to speak at Johns Hopkins University. In that address, after detailing the reasons for our actions in South Vietnam, I called upon the nations of Southeast Asia, including North Vietnam, to join in a cooperative effort to fight the old enemies of their peoples—disease and hunger and illiteracy. I pledged the help of the United States in that effort.

I picked a team of outstanding Americans to handle our participation in those programs of development. I chose Eugene R. Black, the capable former President of the World Bank, to head that team. One of the first things I asked Black to do was to push hard to bring the proposed Asian Development Bank to life. Almost all the nations of Asia and other concerned and more prosperous nations joined in this effort, thirty-two countries in all. The charter of the new bank was signed at Manila on December 4, 1965.

The first year and a half was taken up with planning, recruiting able personnel from many countries, and building a headquarters in Manila. By the end of 1967 the Asian Development Bank was in business. The Bank has two main functions: to make loans for worthy projects and to provide technical assistance. In 1968, its first year of operation, the Bank made seven major loans totaling $41.6 million. Twenty additional loans amounting to $98.1 million were approved in 1969. The Bank's directors had decided from the outset that they could put funds to work quickly and effectively by lending to development banks in individual countries. These banks in turn would make low-interest loans to local industries.

The Asian Development Bank also makes direct loans through its special fund. For example, it is financing the foreign exchange costs of the Tadjun Irrigation Project in central Java. This project will irrigate about 9,000 acres of land and boost Indonesia's rice production by an estimated 16,000 tons a year.

In October 1965 a major event in the history of modern Asia took place. For several years Indonesian Communists had been moving into positions of increasing influence. With the approval, if not the active encouragement, of President-for-life Sukarno, they were readying themselves for takeover. On October 1, 1965, they decided that the time was ripe and they made their move. Non-Communist officials were taken into custody. High-ranking officers were ambushed and killed. It appeared at first that the coup had succeeded.

Then the tide turned. Nationalist officers who had escaped the blood bath rallied the military forces, especially the army, to resist. Soon they routed or destroyed the Communist organizers and forces who had tried to capture the world's fifth largest nation.

The United States played no role in the countercoup. Over the years our Embassy staff in Indonesia had dwindled to a relative handful and our relations with the Indonesians, at Sukarno's insistence, had become almost nonexistent. Of course, we welcomed the news that this rich nation of more than 100 million people had been saved at the brink from falling under Communist dictatorship, though we regretted the bloodshed involved.

Later, a number of Asian statesmen who had good reason for their opinions told me that the Indonesian turnaround would probably never have occurred if the situation to the north, in Southeast Asia, had been different—that is, if the United States and others had not taken a stand in Vietnam. How decisive this factor was in the thoughts of the brave men who put their lives on the line and led the countercoup we will probably never know. But they knew that the strategic region to the north remained in non-Communist hands. They could be reasonably confident that the United States would continue its policy of helping those who wished to remain free and who were willing to help themselves.

Early in 1966 I was heartened by the growing evidence that most Asians understood, or were beginning to understand, both major aspects of our policy in Southeast Asia. First, they appreciated the fact that our word to them was as good as our word to Europeans and others. Second, they realized that they would have to take on increasing responsibility for their future through cooperation with each other. They knew that the United

States could not carry on its shoulders indefinitely an Asia of fragmented and self-centered nations.

A high point in the development of a new Asia came in June 1966. The South Koreans had experienced a remarkable surge of economic and social progress over the previous two years. With the confidence that went with this growth, the South Koreans were determined to play a more active role in the life of Asia. They invited representatives of nine other nations * to their capital to join them in creating the Asian and Pacific Council. There was enthusiasm and a spirit of cooperation at the Seoul meeting, and the formation of the ASPAC was announced on June 16. The organization is dedicated to solidarity against external interference and threats and to cooperation in working for the peace, freedom, progress, and prosperity of its members and of the region as a whole.

Another regional grouping, the Association of Southeast Asian Nations,† was formed in Bangkok, Thailand, on August 8, 1967. The principal goal of this organization is regional cooperation, with heavy emphasis on economic development.

Other Asian groups and institutions have developed: Operation Rice Bowl, sponsored by SEATO, was established to raise food production in Southeast Asia; the Southeast Asian Ministers of Education Council was formed late in 1965 to coordinate work on improving education; the Asian Parliamentarians Union was set up as a result of Japanese initiative; the Asian Institute of Technology in Bangkok is training specialists from every Asian nation; the Agricultural Research Center in the Philippines is doing the same in agriculture. There is also an Asian Labor Education Center in the Philippines.

This is only a partial list of the many important things that Asian nations are now doing for and with each other, and it is a heartening development in an area that for centuries has known far more conflict than cooperation. Traditional hatreds and suspicions are being overcome by the desire of Asians to work with their neighbors to improve the lot of all. The American role in these endeavors has been primarily to provide financial help, to advise when asked, and always to encourage. In no case have we assumed leadership, and in many instances we are not even members of the organizations.

The new spirit in Asia was the central theme of the speech I delivered to the American Alumni Council on July 12, 1966. After noting some of the more important developments of the previous few years, I said:

---

* Present at the meeting were representatives from Australia, the Republic of China, Japan, Malaysia, New Zealand, the Philippines, Thailand, and Vietnam, and an observer from Laos.

† The members of ASEAN are Indonesia, Malaysia, the Philippines, Singapore, and Thailand.

Throughout free Asia you can hear the echo of progress. As one Malaysian leader said: "Whatever our ethical, cultural, or religious backgrounds, the nations and peoples of Southeast Asia must pull together in the same broad sweep of history. We must create with our own hands and minds a new perspective and a new framework. And we must do it ourselves."

For this is the new Asia, and this is the new spirit we see taking shape behind our defense of South Vietnam. Because we have been firm—because we have committed ourselves to the defense of one small country—other countries have taken new heart.

Soon after my speech, South Korean President Chung Hee Park suggested a meeting of the leaders of the nations that were most involved in Vietnam's defense. In August Thai leaders called for an all-Asia conference on Vietnam. The Philippines and Malaysia expressed similar interest. I knew how preoccupied many people were with Vietnam. It seemed to me that the kind of gathering the Asian leaders were discussing would help focus much-needed attention on other developments in Asia, including political and economic progress in Vietnam itself.

President and Mrs. Ferdinand Marcos of the Philippines visited Washington in mid-September as state guests, and we explored the idea further. I told the Philippines President that we approved of the all-Asia conference and would take part, but that the United States would not organize it. He or other Asian leaders should take the lead. After consulting other governments, President Marcos issued joint invitations to the conference in his name and in the names of President Park of South Korea and Prime Minister Thanom Kittikachorn of Thailand. Those invited were the leaders of the governments of South Vietnam, Australia, New Zealand, and the United States. The dates finally selected were October 24–25, 1966.

As I read the newspapers and heard the arguments of our critics, I was aware that they focused on Vietnam alone. They had lost sight of the fact that almost two out of every three human beings lived in Asia. Pushed to its logical conclusion, one that few were willing to state in public, their argument seemed to suggest that our country had no abiding interest in the fate of Asia. I knew they were wrong.

Our ties with Asia went back more than a century. I was certain that those ties would become more, not less, important in the future. I wanted the American people and the world to lift their eyes, for a time at least, from concentration on the war in Vietnam to the larger problems and possibilities of the new and vital Asia—the Asia I felt was being born, in part at least, as a result of our commitment to its security. I had decided by then not only to go to Manila for the Asian and Pacific conference but to visit the capitals of several countries in that vital and growing region of the world.

On October 17 I boarded *Air Force One* with Mrs. Johnson and members of my staff for the long trip to the Pacific. Our first stop was Honolulu, where I was to give a speech expressing several thoughts that were uppermost in my mind and heart. During my first two decades in public office I had been one of the majority of Americans who thought of our destiny largely in terms of relations with Europe. Only in the 1950s did I begin to realize how wrong I had been, and I thought I should say so.

I called in an aide who had been working on my speech and told him what was on my mind. Then I called in a secretary and talked while she took down my words in shorthand. These words went into the speech I made the next day. What I said as I walked around the small stateroom during our flight over the Pacific was this:

> My forebears came from Britain, Ireland, and Germany. People in my section of the country regarded Asia as totally alien in spirit as well as nationality. East and west meant to us that Texas was west of where Sam Gilstrap * lived—Oklahoma.
>
> We therefore looked away from the Pacific, away from its hopes as well as away from its great crises. . . .
>
> I remember we felt we would get some planes out here after they had all they needed in Europe in the early forties.
>
> One consequence of that blindness was that Hawaii was denied its rightful part in our union of states for many, many years.
>
> Frankly, for two decades I opposed its admission as a state, until at last the undeniable evidence of history, as well as the irresistible persuasiveness of Jack Burns,† removed the scales from my eyes.
>
> Then I began to work and fight for Hawaiian statehood. And I hold that to be one of the proudest achievements of my twenty-five years in the Congress.
>
> There are still those who cannot understand the Pacific's role in America's future. But their voices, shrill though they may be, are becoming few and tired, and small.
>
> Most of us who were blind two decades ago can now begin to see.

From Honolulu we went to Pago Pago in Samoa. We saw there how an educational revolution could be brought about on a Pacific island by the use of classroom television.‡ From Samoa we flew on for visits to New Zealand and Australia. I remembered both countries well from my tour of duty as a naval officer in the early days of World War II. In Wellington and Canberra I talked with the Prime Ministers and officials of both governments. These meetings provided opportunities to emphasize the central theme of my trip: that the future of Asia depended on Asian cooperation, which we were ready and eager to support.

---

* An old friend from my NYA days in the 1930s and now deputy chancellor of the East-West Center at the University of Hawaii.

† The Governor of Hawaii.

‡ I think it is inexcusable that we and others around the world have been so slow in using this powerful instrument of progress.

It was apparent that both New Zealand and Australia were reappraising their roles in the world community and that a profound, and doubtless painful, readjustment was under way. These offspring of the United Kingdom had long looked to Britain and Europe for their trade, technology, and political affiliation. But increasingly since World War II, and especially after their involvement in Korea and Vietnam, Australians and New Zealanders recognized that their prosperity and their security were intimately tied to the future of their neighbors in Asia. Britain was steadily reducing its commitments east of Suez. Australia and New Zealand were increasing and strengthening their links with Asia and the Pacific. It was an historic shift of policy.

On the morning of October 23 we stopped at Townsville in northern Australia for fuel. Lady Bird and I attended services at the Cathedral Church of St. James. Then we visited with the mayor and the townspeople. Thoughts of bygone days filled my mind as I passed through the streets of Townsville, but the people were as warm and wonderful as they had been during my stay there a quarter of a century before.* I told them that "never in my life have I gone among a people in any land where I have been received with such open arms and with such unfailing courtesy."

When we arrived in Manila, beautiful Filipino women in their colorful national dress were on hand to encircle our necks with leis. President and Mrs. Marcos welcomed us to their country. As we drove into the capital, the road was lined on both sides by large crowds of people who cheered and waved and wished us well. At one point, Filipino policemen shoved back a group of people, including several children. I told one of the Secret Service men to ask them to stop. "I am traveling 26,000 miles to see these people," I said, "and I can't do it if the police push them away."

That evening I met separately with chiefs of the delegations to the conference. President Marcos came to my suite and we had a good talk. Then I walked to South Korean President Park's rooms for a discussion with him. Later Thai Prime Minister Thanom called on me. Then the Vietnamese leaders, Thieu and Ky, came to my suite.

We all agreed that the upcoming conference would not be a "war conference," though we would discuss the war. Nor would it be a "peace con-

* The visit to Townsville was filled with nostalgia for me. I remembered very well staying there on June 8, 1942. I shared a room with a brave and friendly officer, Colonel Francis Stevens. Early the next morning we flew to Port Moresby in New Guinea, and from there we took off in separate planes. Colonel Stevens never returned from that flight; his plane was shot down by a Japanese Zero.

Only a few months before my visit to Australia, I had the pleasure of inviting Colonel Stevens' son, who had never seen his father, to the White House. There I introduced the young West Point instructor to Australian Prime Minister Holt, who was visiting us in Washington.

ference," for we could not discuss peace without the enemy. We would, however, make clear again our hopes for a peaceful settlement and offer suggestions that might move us closer to that goal.

I told each of my colleagues that I thought one of the most useful purposes our meetings could serve would be to put Asia, for a time at least, into the spotlight of world attention. People around the globe should know, I said, that there was much more happening in Asia than the war in Vietnam, that an important new page in history was being written there.

I told Prime Minister Thanom: "It is important that the world know that there is an Asia; there are serious problems in Asia; there are leaders prepared to face up to them; and the United States wishes to help those leaders, not to dominate them. A road of many miles is ahead, but we wish to begin here."

The silver-haired leader of the Thai government sat forward in his chair. "I agree," he said. "That is why I am here."

With the Vietnamese leaders I reminisced about my own decision to leave teaching and go into politics. The real satisfaction of public service, I said, is that it gives a man a better chance to do more good for more people than anything else he can do, and in Asia, there are more people who need more help than anyplace in the world.

"It's here in Asia where the people are," I said, "two-thirds of humanity. It's here that people die under forty. Here illiteracy is high and income low."

We reached agreement easily at Manila, because it was quickly apparent that we shared similar views about the future. We were able to state our objectives briefly and clearly in the Declaration of Goals of Freedom.* The third of these goals was "to build a region of security, order, and progress."

The day after the conference, I saw something I had heard much about but that I wanted to see with my own eyes. It was the International Rice Research Institute at Los Baños. Per man and per dollar, the institute was probably doing more than any other institution to overcome the growing gap between available food and expanding population. Its scientists had developed new strains of rice, including IR-8, the so-called miracle rice that promised to reduce hunger as a threat for millions of people. The institute was a good example of the growing sense of regional cooperation that was so important to our hopes for Asia. The professional staff at the institute included scientists from seven nations, two-thirds of them from Asia. Financing came mostly from the Ford and Rockefeller foundations. The government of the Philippines provided the land.

I was deeply moved by what I saw at Los Baños. There was cooperation; there was skill; there was rich promise for the future. I expressed my

---

* The complete text of the declaration is in the appendix, page 599.

admiration to the institute staff, and I complimented President Marcos for the interest he and his government had shown in the institute. "You are pointing the way for all of Asia to follow," I said, "and I hope they are looking. I hope they are listening. And I hope they are following."

That afternoon I slipped away from Manila to Cam Ranh Bay, one of our major military bases in South Vietnam. I wanted to visit our fighting men. I wanted to tell them how their President and most of their countrymen felt about what they were doing. I have never been more moved by any group I have talked to, never in my life. The competence and the loyalty of our fighting men in Vietnam—men fighting a complicated and difficult war, in a debilitating climate, under strange circumstances, and against the background of a bitter and divisive debate at home—will, I am sure, be looked upon in the future with deep pride by the American people. The courage of our men day in and day out, and the letters they wrote assuring me of their understanding of why they were there and what they had to do were an abiding source of strength throughout the last four years of my Presidency.

I was physically tired and emotionally drained as I flew back to Manila that night. But the visit to Vietnam, the memory of those strong hands shaking mine, the quiet words of courage I heard from the wounded, and the determined words of the others were an inspiration. The memory of that day is still so vivid in my mind that it could have happened yesterday.

From the Philippines we flew to Thailand, then to Malaysia, and finally to South Korea. I was impressed in each country by the extraordinary vitality and eagerness on the faces of the millions who came to greet us. I felt renewed hope as I saw the momentum so clearly visible in their economic and social projects. Everywhere we went I heard words of thanks to the American people—for the help they had given in the building of new nations, for the cooperation they had shown in realizing the new dreams of Asia, and for the commitment to freedom they had made, which had helped to bring about so much of this progress.

The trip through Asia had not been easy. Each day was long and demanding. We spent much time flying from one capital to another and traveling through the cities and countryside. I knew too—from a telephone call I received from the Mayo Clinic doctors just as I was leaving Manila—that I would have to undergo another operation as soon as possible after I arrived home. But as we moved through the skies homeward, first to Alaska and then on to Washington, I felt hopeful. Perhaps, I thought, the chances for a reasonable settlement in Vietnam have been advanced. Certainly the vision of a new Asia was closer to reality.

We flew into Dulles Airport in the rain on the night of November 2, 1966. Many people had braved the weather to welcome us back—the Vice

President, the Chief Justice and his colleagues from the Supreme Court, members of the Cabinet, diplomats, Senators and Representatives, and numerous dear friends. After the greetings, I stood in the mild rain and reported on my trip. I told them what I had seen and what I had felt. At the end of my remarks I recalled the prayer that had been offered at Sunday services ten days before in the church at Townsville:

> O God, Who has bound us together in the bundle of life, give us grace to understand how our lives depend upon the courage, the industry, the honesty, and the integrity of our fellow men, that we may be mindful of their needs and grateful for their faithfulness, and faithful in our responsibilities to them.

17

The Making of a Decision
[*VIETNAM 1967–1968*]

O N MARCH 31, 1968, while sitting at my desk in the White House and facing the shiny eyes of the television cameras, I announced four major decisions. I would not accept my party's nomination as candidate for another term. I was stopping most of the bombing of North Vietnam in the hope that it would lead to peace. I had decided to make the expansion and modernization of South Vietnam's armed forces a goal of even higher priority. Finally, to meet existing needs, I had decided to make a small increase in the size of our own military forces in Vietnam.

Many factors helped to shape those decisions. In describing them, I will also be describing the Presidential decision-making process. Many books and articles have been written over the years about the way a President makes his decisions. Some have been written by intimates of past Presidents, others by historians and scholars, and still others by men who were neither. But little information on the subject has been supplied by the Presidents themselves. They alone know how and why they reached particular decisions and the many considerations that affected them.

A President reaches a major decision through a complicated process. It is often a painful process as well. Many different threads were woven into the final decisions I announced on March 31. The military and political developments in Vietnam were crucial factors in shaping the ultimate result. Another was the condition of enemy forces and the shape of enemy intentions. Still another strand was the diplomatic front, the possibility of getting into meaningful talks with Hanoi. The state of mind and morale on our domestic front was most important. Finally, and underlying much of my thinking on these other matters, was my personal decision to leave the White House the following January.

It is too strong to say that I had made that last decision irrevocably. I have never considered any important decision irrevocable until it has been announced and acted upon. I have lived too long and seen too much not to realize that the firmest decisions can be altered at the last minute by a dramatic change in circumstances or by new, pertinent information. Faced with decisions affecting the lives of others, or our nation's security, or the prospects for our children, I always wanted every fact I could get until the final moment when I said "yes" or "no." I wanted every element explored in depth. I wanted to hear every argument, pro and con. I wanted the benefit of all the wisdom, insight, and experience available. This attitude has been described as "keeping the options open until the moment of decision." I have always thought it simple prudence.

Nonetheless, the decision to finish my term and go back to my ranch in January 1969 was as firmly fixed in my mind as any decision could be, short of its actual announcement. Mrs. Johnson knew my feelings. I had also shared my thoughts with others, such as Secretaries Rusk, McNamara, and Fowler, John Connally, Generals Wheeler and Westmoreland, Congressman J. J. Pickle, George Christian, and Tom Johnson, though I doubt that any of them would have bet his life on the outcome. Nor would I, for if I had come to feel, for example, that my withdrawal would have seriously affected the attitude or morale of our troops fighting in Vietnam, I would have reconsidered. But I had already discussed that question with General Westmoreland the previous November in Washington, and he had said that he believed our fighting men would understand my action.

I describe my personal political decision in detail elsewhere in this book.* I will concentrate here on the other three decisions: the bombing halt, what is now called "Vietnamization," and military deployments.

Through much of 1967 my advisers and I had repeatedly assessed our bombing campaign against North Vietnam, as we consistently had from 1965 on. Was the bombing accomplishing its purpose? Was it being carried out in the most effective way? Should we extend it to targets and purposes not yet covered? Should we cut back or alter the pattern? Should we end it completely?

In response to military advice, I had approved an expansion of the bombing program in mid-April of 1967. A proposal suggesting a change in the pattern of air strikes came to me on May 6 when I was spending the weekend at my ranch. On the teletype from the White House, a message came in from Walt Rostow describing "the alternatives that face us in Vietnam." On the question of bombing, Rostow wrote:

* See Chapter 18, pp. 425–37.

We have never held the view that bombing could stop infiltration. We have never held the view that bombing in the Hanoi-Haiphong area alone would lead them to abandon the effort in the South. We have never held the view that bombing Hanoi-Haiphong would directly cut back infiltration. We have held the view that the degree of military and civilian cost felt in the North and the diversion of resources to deal with our bombing could contribute marginally—and perhaps significantly—to the timing of a decision to end the war. But it was no substitute for making progress in the South.

Rostow listed alternate bombing strategies. The first was "closing the top of the funnel," blocking the supply lines through which war matériel moved into North Vietnam:

> Under this strategy we would mine the major harbors and, perhaps, bomb port facilities and even consider blockade. In addition, we would attack systematically the rail lines between Hanoi and Mainland China.

The second strategy involved attacks against what was "inside the funnel," hitting supply dumps, stockpiles, and fuel storage areas, as well as bridges, railroad yards, and other targets in the Hanoi-Haiphong area. The third strategy would have concentrated our effort on the "bottom of the funnel," the lines of communication and infiltration routes in southern North Vietnam and through Laos. The memo listed the advantages and disadvantages of each strategy. On balance, Rostow favored the third course, concentrating air strikes in southern North Vietnam and Laos. He recommended keeping the second option open, but he thought we should use it "only when the targets make sense."

Three days later a remarkably similar memo arrived from Bob McNamara and his deputy, Cy Vance, which also listed three broad categories of air offensives and analyzed the pros and cons of each course. This memo concluded:

> We, therefore, recommend that all of the sorties allocated to the ROLLING THUNDER program* be concentrated on the lines of communication—the "funnel" through which men and supplies to the South must flow—between 17–20°, reserving the option and intention to strike (in the 20–23° area) as necessary to keep the enemy's investment in defense and in repair crews high throughout the country.

Using the Rostow and McNamara-Vance memos as a basis, the State Department also analyzed our bombing program. A memo prepared in State and dated May 9 reached essentially the same conclusions: We should "cut back in the near future to concentration on supply routes and restrikes north of the 20th parallel limited to those necessary to eliminate targets

---

* The code name for the air campaign against the North.

directly important to infiltration and, as necessary, to keep Hanoi's air defense and repair system in place."

I was receiving quite different views from the Joint Chiefs of Staff, from Admiral U.S.G. Sharp, our commander in chief in the Pacific, and from General Westmoreland and his military staff in Saigon. They favored more intensive and extensive bombing in the North. They emphasized the advantages of destroying enemy supplies and equipment in the Hanoi-Haiphong area before those materials were scattered along the roads and infiltration trails.

Both proposals, and the justifications for them, had merit. A stronger air program might further weaken the North militarily and might help convince Hanoi that a peaceful settlement was to its advantage. Such an air campaign would slow the flow of supplies from Communist China, and would also convince the South Vietnamese and our own fighting men that we were doing everything possible to help protect their lives. On the other hand, cutting back to the 20th parallel would concentrate our attacks on a principal objective: impeding the flow of men and supplies into the South. In addition, we were losing more pilots in the heavily protected Hanoi-Haiphong area than elsewhere, and concentrating our efforts on the southern portion of North Vietnam would cut those losses.

There were other factors as well. The public was very much aware of the critical and well-publicized views of a few Senators and Congressmen regarding Vietnam. It was much less aware of the equally strong feelings of many other members of both Houses who believed that we should be taking stronger actions against the North and generally doing more bombing, not less. Some of these legislators held key positions in Congress, and we needed their backing if we were to continue to give our fighting men the support they deserved. I knew that a unilateral bombing halt would run into fierce opposition from these powerful men on the Hill.

There was one further consideration. I wanted to link any cutback in bombing, or any bombing halt, to a genuine movement toward negotiations, and no negotiating breakthrough was then in sight.

I decided to steer a course midway between the proposal of those who wanted to cut back our air action and the plan advanced by those who believed we should step up strikes in the North. I felt that a cutback to the 20th parallel at that time would have been misunderstood in Hanoi as a sign of weakness. I also believed that strikes in the Hanoi-Haiphong vicinity were costing more than the results justified. Beginning on May 22, I ordered a halt to air attacks on targets within ten miles of the North Vietnamese capital. Except for one attack in mid-June, the ban on air action around Hanoi continued until August 9.

In July 1967 we made another intensive study of our air offensive in the North. I accepted the view of our military leadership that there were a few significant targets that should be hit. These attacks were carried out between August 9 and August 24. However, I rejected the suggestion that we use air power to close the port of Haiphong and knock out part of the dike system in the Red River delta. I felt that there was too grave a risk of Communist Chinese or even Soviet involvement if those measures were carried out, and I wished to avoid the heavy civilian casualties that would accompany destruction of the dikes. I emphasized again to my military advisers that we were going to avoid actions, in the air or on the ground, that might trigger a wider and more destructive war.

On August 24 we again stopped all air activity in the Hanoi area. This halt was carried out in connection with our efforts to enter peace talks in Paris through French intermediaries.* In this instance, the ban remained in effect for two months. In all, in 1967 the Hanoi area was "off limits" to our fighter bombers for six-and-a-half months.

We were considering other military proposals in addition to the question of bombing at that time. In April 1967 General Westmoreland submitted two suggestions for possible troop increases. One called for a "minimum essential force." The other described an "optimum force." The first proposal involved an increase of two and one-third divisions and five air squadrons, about 80,000 men. The second suggested an increase in our forces of four and two-thirds divisions and ten air squadrons, raising our force level in Vietnam by 200,000, to a total of 680,000 men by July 1968. The military planners were also considering a program of increased air strikes against the North and forays against the North Vietnamese and Viet Cong forces that were enjoying almost complete sanctuary in Laos and Cambodia. Possible ground action against the southern part of North Vietnam was also studied on a contingency basis.

On May 19, 1967, McNamara sent me one of the most detailed memos he had ever submitted since I became President. The subject was "Future Actions in Vietnam." The twenty-two page document covered his estimate of the situation and his recommendations for future action. The Secretary set the tone on the first page:

> This memorandum is written at a time when there appears to be no attractive course of action. The probabilities are that Hanoi has decided not to negotiate until the American electorate has been heard in November 1968. Continuation of our present moderate policy, while avoiding a larger war, will not change Hanoi's mind, so it is not enough to satisfy the American people; increased force levels and actions against the North are likewise unlikely to change Hanoi's mind, and are likely to get us in even deeper in Southeast Asia and into a serious confrontation, if not war,

* See Chapter 11, pp. 266–68.

with China and Russia; and we are not willing to yield. So we must choose among imperfect alternatives.

McNamara strongly opposed the proposal for an "optimum force." He thought we should limit the increase to 30,000 men. He advised against ground action in Laos or Cambodia. We were all concerned that entering Laos with ground forces would end all hope of reviving the 1962 Laos agreement, fragile though it was, and would greatly increase the forces needed in Southeast Asia. With an unfriendly Prince Sihanouk still in power in Cambodia, we feared that any action taken there would lead him to ask Peking for help. On bombing, McNamara again proposed concentrating on the area below the 20th parallel. Any ground action against the North, he thought, would bring Communist China into the war with both ground and air forces. He also considered a confrontation with the Soviet Union elsewhere in the world a distinct possibility.

I discussed these various proposals frequently with my senior advisers during the remainder of May and all of June. I listened to numerous discussions of the advantages and disadvantages of each proposal. I consulted members of Congress, private counselors, and others whose opinions I respected. In the meantime, specialists in the Pentagon and on the staff of the Joint Chiefs were reviewing both our requirements and our capabilities.

Early in July I asked McNamara to return to Saigon for a thorough study of the matter with General Westmoreland. He was in the South Vietnamese capital on July 7–8 and reported back to me on July 12. McNamara advised me that Westmoreland had accepted a troop increase somewhat smaller than the "minimum essential force" he had proposed. General Westmoreland had returned to the United States for his mother's funeral, and he and the Secretary planned a final discussion the following morning.

The following day, July 13, I met with McNamara and Generals Wheeler and Westmoreland in the White House family dining room. McNamara told me that he and the military leaders had conferred all morning and had reached "complete accord" on the question of troop levels. The requirement would be in the neighborhood of 45,000 men, he said, and the approved troop strength in South Vietnam should be raised to 525,000 for the fiscal year ending June 30, 1968. After additional study, I approved this proposal.

The first phase of the Communists' winter-spring offensive began in September 1967. North Vietnamese forces first tried to strangle the Marine base at Con Thien, just south of the DMZ, and later launched major attacks against remote positions along the Laotian and Cambodian borders.

They gained no military advantage in these attacks and suffered heavy losses, but our information warned us of heavier battles to come. Infiltration was increasing. Captured North Vietnamese began talking about a "second wave" of attacks. As I read the daily reports and followed developments on the ground, I became increasingly concerned for our military command and its men. Did Westmoreland have all the men and supplies he needed to deal with a massive enemy offensive?

Westmoreland was becoming more concerned as well. On September 28, 1967, he sent a message to Washington asking that actions be taken to improve his situation in the northern part of South Vietnam while he continued to maintain the initiative in other sectors. What he wanted most was acceleration of the arrival of the 101st Airborne Division, which was scheduled to go to Vietnam in February 1968. He also asked for faster deployment of the 11th Infantry Brigade. All my advisers agreed that we should carry out this acceleration.

In October 1967 the Viet Cong began to move main-force units into the more populated areas of South Vietnam. We learned that North Vietnam was again stepping up its infiltration to the South. We had received reports that elements of two divisions of the North Vietnamese army were moving into Laos, heading for the demilitarized zone and the South.

At a breakfast meeting on November 21,* I asked my advisers for a status report on the speed-up of our previously scheduled troop movements. I told them: "The clock is ticking. We need to get all the additional troops moved as fast as we can."

I was increasingly concerned by reports that the Communists were preparing a maximum military effort and were going to try for a significant tactical victory. If they achieved it, they might then be interested in talking peace, but only on their terms. My own feeling was that the only thing that might produce real peace talks would be a conclusion reached by the leaders in Hanoi that they could not win by military means. That made it vitally important that the coming offensive be thrown back and broken. I agreed heartily with one prophetic report from our Embassy in Saigon: "The war is probably nearing a turning point and the outcome of the 1967–1968 winter-spring campaign will in all likelihood determine the future direction of the war."

Meanwhile, our military services had responded impressively to my request for urgent action. Before Christmas of 1967, many of the troops scheduled to arrive in Vietnam early in 1968 had already joined Westmoreland's command.

---

* At the breakfast were Vice President Humphrey, Secretaries Rusk and McNamara, Ambassador Bunker, Generals Wheeler and Westmoreland, Dick Helms of the CIA, and Bob Komer, Westmoreland's deputy for pacification. Members of my staff also attended.

Throughout 1967 Hanoi and the other Communist capitals kept up a steady propaganda barrage against our actions in Vietnam. They demanded an immediate end to our "aggression" and a total and unconditional halt to the bombing of the North. Some well-intentioned people in the United States and elsewhere were also urging a bombing halt, or at least a pause. Some segments of the press had become increasingly critical of our involvement. At the same time, other individuals and groups were urging us to do more. There were demands to "win or get out." The rhetoric at both ends of the spectrum became increasingly shrill.

During this period McNamara made a major proposal for a new course of action. At our lunch meeting on October 31, 1967, he said that he believed continuation of our current course of action in Southeast Asia would be dangerous, costly, and unsatisfactory to our people. At my suggestion, he returned to the Pentagon after the meeting and set down his thoughts in a long memorandum which I received the next day, November 1. He first described the "Outlook If Present Course of Action Is Continued." He foresaw requests for additional ground forces and believed that American and allied casualties would increase. He expected new proposals from our military leadership to attack targets in Hanoi and Haiphong. It was his opinion that this course would produce "continued but slow progress" but would not be "really visible to the general public either in the United States or abroad.

"There is, in my opinion," he wrote, "a very real question whether under these circumstances it will be possible to maintain our efforts in South Vietnam for the time necessary to accomplish our objectives there." McNamara then explored possible alternatives. He described ways to increase our military actions but opposed these on the grounds that they involved "major risks of widening the war.

"The alternative possibilities," he wrote, "lie in the stabilization of our military operations in the South (possibly with fewer U.S. casualties) and of our air operations in the North, along with a demonstration that our air attacks on the North are not blocking negotiations leading to a peaceful settlement." He recommended stopping all the bombing in the North by the end of the year. "The bombing halt would have dual objectives," he wrote. "We would hope for a response from Hanoi, by some parallel reduction in its offensive activity, by a movement toward talks, or both. At a minimum, the lack of any response from Hanoi would demonstrate that it is North Vietnam and not the United States that is blocking a peaceful settlement."

McNamara concluded his memorandum with three recommendations. First, he suggested we announce that we were stabilizing our efforts and would not expand our air operations in the North or the size of our combat forces beyond those already planned. Second, McNamara proposed a bombing halt before the end of 1967. Finally, he favored a new study of military operations in the South aimed at reducing U.S. casualties and giving the South Vietnamese greater responsibility for their own security.

I studied McNamara's memo carefully. He made a cogent case for the actions he proposed. Though I disagreed with some arguments and questioned some assumptions, I was convinced that his proposal deserved thoughtful attention. I decided to solicit opinions on McNamara's plan from several people whose judgment and knowledge I respected.

I had already received the views of one former staff member. McGeorge Bundy had been in Washington two weeks previously and had talked with McNamara and other officials. On October 17, 1967, Bundy had given me a memo covering the main points in McNamara's plan. Bundy agreed with McNamara in opposing intensification of the bombing of the North, especially in the Hanoi area. He thought that the bombing was "quite intense enough as it stands.

"While I strongly support bombing of communication lines and supply depots—*tactical* bombing," Bundy said, "I see no evidence whatever that North Vietnam is a good object for a major *strategic* campaign." He thought that strategic bombing did not affect "the real contest, which is in the South," and that the political costs of the effort were rising. "We have everything to gain politically and almost nothing to lose militarily if we will firmly hold our bombing to demonstrably useful target areas," he wrote. Bundy also agreed with McNamara's argument that there should be "no large-scale reinforcement beyond totals already agreed." He recommended that we "continue the effort to expand the visibility of Vietnamese participation in all forms."

Bundy's disagreement with McNamara's plan concerned the bombing halt. "The basic objection to an unconditional pause," he wrote, "is simply that the odds are very heavy that you would have to resume, and that if the pause is truly unconditional, the circumstances of any such resumption would be very damaging to us both at home and abroad." He suggested a bombing pause only if, through direct contacts with Hanoi, we received solid grounds for believing that such a move would be productive.

Bundy concluded his memo with a wry warning against advice from outsiders, like himself, whose information was limited: "Finally, I would not listen too closely to anyone who comes from a distance and spends only one day looking at the evidence."

I sent McNamara's memo to Bundy's successor as national security adviser, Walt Rostow, for comment. He too favored holding our forces to already approved levels. Rostow opposed additional actions against the North and expansion of the war into neighboring countries. He believed that we should "gradually transfer the major burden of the fighting to the South Vietnamese forces." But he opposed an unconditional bombing halt.

He thought that it would signify weakness to Hanoi and to our own people. He believed that a bombing halt would lighten Hanoi's burdens and encourage them, if they entered into talks, to protract the negotiations.

I sent the main elements of McNamara's plan, without identifying the author, to General Maxwell Taylor,* whom I deeply respected, for his analysis and comments. On November 3 General Taylor sent me his strongly negative reaction. He described the proposal as one form of "pull-back" strategy. He thought that it would "probably degenerate into an eventual pull-out." General Taylor wrote:

> The curtailment of the bombing under this proposal has all the liabilities which we have noted in previous discussions of this issue. The South Vietnamese would be deeply discouraged by this lifting of the penalty which the bombing imposes on the North. I would suspect that our other allies contributing troops would object strongly to this course of action— they are convinced of the essentiality of the bombing. Our own forces would regard this action as a deliberate decrease in the protection which, they feel, is afforded them by the bombing. The large majority of our citizens who believe in the bombing but who thus far have been silent could be expected to raise violent objections on the home front, probably surpassing in volume the present criticisms of the anti-bombers.

General Taylor added:

> Probably the most serious objection of all to this Pull-Back alternative would be the effect upon the enemy. Any such retreat will be interpreted as weakness and will add to the difficulty of getting any kind of eventual solution compatible with our overall objective of an independent South Vietnam free from the threat of subversive aggression.
>
> I would recommend strongly against adopting any such course of action.

I also sent McNamara's proposals to two long-time friends whose judgment I valued, Abe Fortas and Clark Clifford. I asked them to weigh the arguments pro and con and to give me their opinion on the merits of both. Fortas sent me his reaction on November 5. His reply was strong and persuasive. He had studied the evidence available and thought that it weighed heavily against the suggested bombing pause. "Our duty," he wrote, "is to do what we consider right—not what we consider (on a highly dubious basis with which I do not agree) the 'American people' want. I repeat that I believe they do not want us to achieve less than our objectives—namely to prevent North Vietnamese domination of South Vietnam by military force or subversion; and to continue to exert such influence as we reasonably can in Asia to prevent an ultimate communist take-over."

---

* General Taylor had stepped down as our Ambassador to Saigon in July 1965 and was then serving me as a special consultant.

Two days later Clark Clifford sent me his comments. He felt that Mc-Namara's plan would "retard the possibility of concluding the conflict rather than accelerating it."

"The question is often asked," he wrote, "why does North Vietnam continue to prosecute the war when it appears they have no chance of winning it?" He continued:

> The answer is clear. Hanoi is depending upon a weakening of the will of the United States to carry on the war. Their previous experience with the French has convinced them that the same result will occur again insofar as the United States is concerned.

Clifford then commented on McNamara's argument that Hanoi would be likely to enter into talks with us soon after a bombing halt:

> I am at a loss to understand this logic. Would the unconditional suspension of the bombing, without any effort to extract a quid pro quo persuade Hanoi that we were firm and unyielding in our conviction to force them to desist from their aggressive designs?
>
> The answer is a loud and resounding "no."
>
> It would be interpreted by Hanoi as (a) evidence of our discouragement and frustration, and (b) an admission of the wrongness and immorality of our bombing of the North, and (c) the first step in our ultimate total disengagement from the conflict.

Clifford next discussed the proposition that we announce we were "stabilizing" our effort in Vietnam. "Can there be any doubt as to the North Vietnamese reaction to such an announcement?" he asked. "The chortles of unholy glee issuing from Hanoi would be audible in every capital of the world.

"Is this evidence of our zeal and courage to stay the course? Of course not! It would be interpreted to be exactly what it is. A resigned and discouraged effort to find a way out of a conflict for which we had lost our will and dedication.

"The President and every man around him wants to end the war," he concluded. "But the future of our children and grandchildren requires that it be ended by accomplishing our purpose, i.e., the thwarting of the aggression by North Vietnam, aided by China and Russia.

"Free peoples everywhere, and communists everywhere, in fact the entire world, is watching to see if the United States meant what it said when it announced its intention to help defend South Vienam."

On November 16 Under Secretary of State Katzenbach sent me a long memo on Vietnam giving his personal views. This memo was not a response specifically to McNamara's proposals, but it addressed the same problems. Katzenbach favored what he called a "qualified but indefinite halt in the bombing." By "qualified" he meant that we should have no hesitation about using air power against "visible efforts to expand resupply of the South as well as troop concentrations in and north of the DMZ." He urged that at a minimum we end all air strikes in the Hanoi-Haiphong area. He favored limiting our role in Vietnam to providing "military cover and nonmilitary assistance" and placing greater responsibility on the South Vietnamese themselves.

With all these questions pending, I asked Ambassador Ellsworth Bunker and General Westmoreland to come to Washington in November. We explored their reactions to McNamara's suggestions. Bunker believed that a bombing pause at that time would not lead to serious negotiations. He opposed trading a bombing halt for undefined talks but said that in the reasonable future he would like to see us in a position to be able to test Hanoi with some kind of bombing pause. He favored taking additional steps to bring infiltration under control before we tried a bombing halt.

As for limiting our troop commitment to existing ceilings, Ambassador Bunker was drawn to the proposition, but he thought that we should make this conditional on Hanoi's willingness not to expand its side of the war. The Ambassador strongly opposed sharper actions against the North, such as mining harbors or hitting the dikes. He favored shifting increased responsibility for combat operations to the South Vietnamese, but he felt strongly that transfer should be geared to their capacity to assume the greater responsibility, and that we should avoid giving any impression that we were pulling out and leaving them alone.

General Westmoreland forcefully opposed a bombing halt. He argued that an effective air program required pressure against North Vietnam's entire logistical system, and under any circumstances he considered air strikes up to the 20th parallel "absolutely essential." He was concerned for the safety of American and allied forces near the demilitarized zone.

Westmoreland hoped that the approved level of 525,000 men would be a maximum requirement, but he said it would be "foolish" to announce that it was our limit. As for transferring additional responsibility to the South Vietnamese, Westmoreland said he regarded this as his "central purpose" over the next two years. He was convinced that within that time—that is, by the end of 1969—we could safely begin withdrawing American forces. He also believed that we could methodically and progressively reduce our troop level thereafter. His goal, he said, was to "weaken the enemy and strengthen our friends until we become superfluous." I asked Westmoreland to explain this concept to the Committees on Armed Forces in the Senate and the House, which he did.

On November 20, in answer to my request, Dean Rusk sent me his personal views of McNamara's proposals. On stabilization of our effort, Rusk agreed with McNamara but opposed a public announcement. "To do so," he said, "would give the enemy a firm base upon which to plan and

redispose his manpower and other assets." Rusk agreed fully with Mc-
Namara's proposal to give the South Vietnamese greater responsibility for
their own security. Regarding a bombing halt, the Secretary of State said:

> I am skeptical of an extended pause in the bombing because I don't
> know who would be persuaded. Hanoi would call any pause (i.e., not
> permanent) an ultimatum. We know of their "fight and negotiate"
> strategy discussions. For those in the outside world pressing for a halt in
> the bombing, no pause would be long enough. No one has said to me
> that his view would be changed if we had a prolonged pause in the bomb-
> ing and there were no response from Hanoi.

Rusk did think, however, that we should "take the drama out of our
bombing" by cutting back on operations in the Hanoi-Haiphong area. He
believed we should carry out just enough bombing in the northern sector
to keep North Vietnam's anti-aircraft guns where they were—to prevent
them from being moved farther south—and to keep large numbers of North
Vietnamese busy with repairing damages and maintaining communications
so that they could not move into combat in the South. Finally, he thought
we should not permit "a complete sanctuary in the northern part of North
Vietnam and thereby eliminate this incentive for peace."

In addition to these opinions from well-informed senior officials and
advisers, I was hearing the views of many Senators and Congressmen. My
mail covered the widest possible range of attitudes and ideas. I was reading
the diplomatic cables daily and receiving surveys of foreign opinion. I also
was reading our own press coverage and listening to television reports from
and about Vietnam.

I pondered McNamara's proposals over the next few weeks. During that
period I received many reports pointing to increased offensive action by
the North Vietnamese and the Viet Cong. As I read those reports and
watched the enemy's offensive take shape, I became convinced we would
have to wait until the Communists realized that their military ambitions
were unattainable before we could hope to get peace talks started. For my
own records, I then took a step that I rarely made during my years in
the White House. On December 18, 1967, I wrote a memorandum for the
permanent files giving my personal views of McNamara's proposals.*

I had decided that a one-sided and total bombing halt would be a mistake
at that time, that it would be interpreted in Hanoi and at home as a sign
of weakening will. I thought we should continue to hit significant military
targets but I insisted we weigh heavily in each case whether U.S. losses
might be excessive and whether any strike might increase the risk of Peking
or Moscow becoming more involved. I wanted to remove as much drama
as possible from our bombing effort while doing what had to be done. In

---

* For the full text of my memorandum, see Appendix, pp. 600–01.

my memorandum I said that I had not ruled out calling a bombing halt in the future if there were "reason for confidence that it would move us toward peace."

I also expressed my opposition to announcing a policy of stabilization. I felt that such an announcement would only make things easier for military planners in Hanoi. On the other hand, I saw no basis for increasing the already approved level of U.S. forces. Finally, I accepted McNamara's suggestion that we review our military operations with a view to cutting our casualties and speeding the turnover of responsibility to the South Vietnamese.

The views I put in this memo were much in my mind when I left for Australia the following day, December 19, to attend memorial services for my friend and ally Prime Minister Harold Holt, who had drowned in an accident. I repeated my conclusions in conversations with leaders of other allied governments who were also in Canberra to honor the memory of the late Prime Minister.

Another facet of the Vietnam problem was also on my mind at that time, one that I had not discussed in my memo although it was closely related to the whole process of urging the South Vietnamese to take increasing responsibility for their future. We had been trying for four years to make a meaningful contact with Hanoi that might lead to peace. I had begun to wonder whether a more promising route might not be to encourage direct contact between the legal government in the South and representatives of the Liberation Front, even though the latter was Hanoi's tool.

I mentioned this possibility in an interview with television reporters the day before I left for Australia. I noted that South Vietnamese President Thieu had said that he was prepared for such informal talks and I told the reporters that I hoped the Liberation Front would respond. After the interview was broadcast, some groups in Saigon and a few commentators at home alleged that I was pushing the South Vietnamese into accepting the Liberation Front as a legal entity or political party. That was not what I had said, and when I discussed this approach with President Thieu in Canberra, he agreed there was no difference between our views. He reaffirmed his government's support of a program of national reconciliation to achieve internal peace. One year later representatives of the legal government in South Vietnam and of the Viet Cong were sitting at the same conference table in Paris. I firmly believed then, as I continue to believe now, what I said in that television interview: "The political future of South Vietnam . . . must be worked out in South Vietnam by the people of South Vietnam."

On December 21 I met in Canberra with the Australian Cabinet. It was a sad occasion, and I shared with the Cabinet members my memories of the sense of loss we Americans had experienced four years before with the death of President Kennedy. "I know where you are this morning," I told them. "In adversity, a family gets together. That's why I am here."

They asked me about Vietnam. I said: "The enemy is building his forces in the South. We must try very hard to be ready. We face dark days ahead." I told the Australian ministers I was certain Hanoi was under great pressure to gain some kind of victory and that I foresaw the North Vietnamese using "kamikaze" tactics in the weeks ahead, committing their troops in a wave of suicide attacks. I was convinced Hanoi was in no mood to negotiate, and that such gestures as a bombing halt would produce no results until the planned Communist offensive was launched and blunted. Then, I said, they might be willing to talk. I said it was possible they might hold off until the 1968 elections in the United States, but they could move much earlier.

After leaving Australia, I paid a quick visit to some of our forces in Vietnam, and then our plane headed westward across India. We stopped for fuel in Pakistan, where I had a brief but useful meeting with President Ayub Khan. We then flew over the Middle East and the Mediterranean and finally landed at a remote military airfield in Italy. I first flew by helicopter to a prearranged rendezvous in the country to meet the leaders of the Italian government. Then I reboarded the helicopter and, with a few aides, headed for Vatican City, in the heart of Rome.

The Eternal City is a dazzling sight at night. That evening, just twenty-four hours before Christmas Eve, 1967, we witnessed a spectacular view that we would never forget. Our helicopter circled the Vatican and, after careful maneuvering, put down safely on a small landing pad. We were greeted by Cardinal Cicognani, who escorted us to our meeting with Pope Paul VI. The pontiff was waiting in his private study, a beautiful high-ceilinged room in the Vatican. It was a great pleasure for me to meet His Holiness again. The spiritual leader of the world's Catholics is a quiet, serious, and sensitive man, profoundly dedicated to the cause of world peace. After our meeting had been arranged through diplomatic channels, I had sent the Pope a ten page memorandum of my views, especially on Vietnam and the search for peace. Pope Paul had this document with him and had read it before I arrived.

I told His Holiness of my visit to Australia, and I gave him essentially the same estimate of the Vietnam situation that I had given the Australian Cabinet and the other leaders with whom I had talked in Canberra. I used the same words—"kamikaze" tactics—in describing what I expected the North Vietnamese to do. I explained why I believed a bombing pause was not likely to produce any useful result at that time. However, I told His Holiness: "I would not exclude the possibility that a bombing halt may again appear wise at some point."

I reminded Pope Paul of the many efforts we had made over the years to interest Hanoi in either peace talks or the mutual reduction of hostilities. Hanoi's repeated rejections of these offers, I said, had led me to look increasingly toward what might be achieved toward peace within South Vietnam itself. I told His Holiness that I hoped President Thieu's program of national reconciliation would succeed and that his offer to talk with individuals associated with the Liberation Front would be accepted. I raised this matter at our meeting because the Catholics, though a minority, formed an influential segment of Vietnam's political life. Their support or resistance could be a decisive factor. The Pope agreed to study the matter carefully.

Another reason I had asked to confer with Pope Paul was that I knew his profound concern for the fate of all men, wherever they were and whatever their condition. I had long been gravely troubled about the American military men being held captive in North Vietnam and by the Viet Cong. Hanoi had flatly refused to give us any information on their fate or their condition. They would not even supply us, or the International Red Cross, with a list of their names. I appealed to the Pope to do anything he could for the prisoners, to obtain information about them from the North Vietnamese or to secure their early release on humanitarian grounds. I promised him that we would cooperate with anyone he selected to investigate prisoner conditions in South Vietnam.

I left the Vatican convinced that His Holiness understood our position and my hopes, and that he would do everything in his power to promote the earliest possible just peace. I felt that our long journey halfway around the world to visit the Pope had been well rewarded. As we walked out, one of the Pope's colleagues quoted His Holiness as saying: "What a wonderful talk."

Looking back on early 1968, I am convinced I made a mistake by not saying more about Vietnam in my State of the Union report on January 17, 1968. In that address I underscored how intensely our will was being tested by the struggle in Vietnam, but I did not go into details concerning the build-up of enemy forces or warn of the early major combat I believed was in the offing. I relied instead on the "background" briefings that my advisers and I, as well as the State and Defense departments, had provided members of the press corps for many weeks. In those briefings we had stressed that heavy action could be expected soon. This was one of those delicate situations in which we had to try to inform our own people without alerting the enemy to our knowledge of its plans. In retrospect, I think I was too cautious. If I had forecast the possibilities, the American people would have been better prepared for what was soon to come.

Our intelligence sources indicated the enemy's next attacks in the winter-spring offensive would be launched around the Tet period, the Vietnamese holiday season during the Lunar New Year. General Westmoreland revised his plans to meet this new threat. He canceled planned movements of some units and changed others. Mobile reserves were positioned so they could rush to the places where they were most needed once the offensive started. Just before Tet, the majority of leaves were canceled. Westmoreland urged the South Vietnamese to make similar arrangements, but they were more relaxed about leaves, and as a result many South Vietnamese soldiers were at home with their families when the first blows of the Tet offensive fell.

More than a week before the enemy's offensive began Westmoreland sent us a detailed estimate of enemy intentions. He said the Communists were displaying "a very unusual sense of urgency" in planning what they called "this decisive campaign." Viet Cong headquarters was promising its followers "final victory." Westmoreland reported that the threat in northern I Corps was the most serious of the war. He also noted new intensity in enemy activity in other areas, especially in III Corps, where Saigon is located. He thought that the North Vietnamese saw a similarity between the allied base at Khe Sanh and the base at Dien Bien Phu, where the French had suffered a disastrous defeat in 1954. Westmoreland anticipated that the enemy would make "a major effort for a short period of time in order to gain exploitable victories for political purposes." He had uncovered evidence that the North Vietnamese planned a multibattalion attack on the city of Hué. He also had information that the cities of Quang Tri and Danang were likely targets.

"The two-week general lull in countrywide activity that was interrupted on the 20th indicates preparations for a widespread effort," he reported. "I believe that the enemy will attempt a countrywide show of strength just prior to Tet."

Two days later, on January 24, Ambassador Bunker sent an urgent cable regarding recent military developments. As usual, both the Communists and South Vietnamese had announced plans for a truce during the holiday season. The Communists claimed that they would observe a week-long cessation of hostilities. We planned a forty-eight-hour truce. As the time drew near, Bunker and Westmoreland became increasingly concerned that the enemy would take advantage of our stoppage in action, at least in some areas.

"Our experience with past holiday ceasefires gives us little reason to presume that North Vietnamese forces intend to observe the ceasefire themselves on this occasion when it is not to their advantage," Bunker said. "The present Communist posture along the DMZ and in Quang Tri province removes any doubt as to this.

"Our concern also relates to the cessation of bombing of North Vietnam since the enemy continues to move massive quantities of men and munitions south to support his open invasion of South Vietnam," Bunker added. "If it is not considered politically feasible to maintain bombing throughout North Vietnam during the Tet truce, we consider that it is essential to continue the bombing in the areas through which the main movement is funneling. This would be south of the general area of Vinh, about halfway between the 18th and 19th parallels. . . ."

I promptly approved their recommendation and authorized them to work out a plan with President Thieu. I told one of my assistants that if the decision were solely mine I would cancel any truce because I felt the enemy would use it to our disadvantage. However, I knew that such a move would be widely misinterpreted. I also knew that Tet had a deep significance for the Vietnamese people and that they would be unwilling to cancel completely the celebration of this most important holiday.

The enemy's expected offensive flared up early on January 30 in the northern and central provinces. The main assault in the rest of the country began twenty-four hours later. It took place during the middle of Tet, although the Communists had proclaimed a truce over this period. In all the years of war the Communists had never before so outraged the Vietnamese people by desecrating days that have such special meaning.

North Vietnamese and Viet Cong forces attacked thirty-six of Vietnam's forty-four provincial capitals. They hit five of the six largest cities, and about one-fourth of the 242 district capitals. In Saigon a Viet Cong suicide squad in civilian clothes blasted a hole in the wall surrounding the American Embassy compound and entered the grounds. Army military police and U.S. Marine guards prevented them from entering the Embassy building itself and killed all the attackers.

The enemy's greatest success was achieved in the historic city of Hué where Communist armed forces moved into the Imperial Citadel and held out for twenty-six days. During their occupation, they brutally murdered a great many innocent people. More than 3,000 bodies were later discovered in mass graves. Many victims had been tortured and others had been buried alive.

Because the offensive was aimed at urban areas, allied and Vietnamese forces pulled back from the countryside to defend population centers. This left many regions in rural Vietnam open to the Viet Cong. Actual losses in those areas, however, were more limited than was at first believed. For the most part, regional and popular forces that were operating close to their hometowns and villages stayed in place. Heavy Communist losses prevented the enemy from exploiting the openings that were briefly available. Almost all the urban areas attacked were cleared of enemy forces by February 2, three days after the assault.

Enemy forces paid an extremely high price for this adventure. Of the estimated 84,000 men the Communists sent into the attacks, about 45,000 were killed by the end of February, including some of their most experienced cadre. Thus, in one month, the enemy sustained heavier losses than U.S. forces had suffered in nine years in Vietnam. Thousands more enemy soldiers were wounded or captured. The Tet offensive was, by any standard, a military defeat of massive proportions for the North Vietnamese and the Viet Cong.

Why did the enemy commit so much to this assault? It was clear that the leaders in Hanoi were under strenuous pressure to achieve an impression-making success, however costly. The goals they sought in their Tet offensive were obvious. They hoped to deliver a massive blow that would put the South Vietnamese army out of action. They failed. The South Vietnamese turned back the enemy in every major action and emerged from the experience more confident than ever before. The Communists aimed to topple the South Vietnamese government. They expected their offensive to produce a popular uprising. They failed. In fact, the Saigon government emerged from the experience with greater strength and with more solid backing from the South Vietnamese people than ever before. For the first time the government moved toward full manpower mobilization. Finally, the Communists wanted to erode the resolve of the American people, just as they had brought about the collapse of French will in 1954 by their victory at Dien Bien Phu. This plan had been painfully obvious to us for some time. As I warned a group of Congressmen at a meeting in the Cabinet Room late in the summer of 1967: "Ho Chi Minh thinks he can win in Washington as he did in Paris." I wish I could report that the enemy failed as decisively with that goal as it did with the others.

At a press conference on February 2 I announced that Tet had been a military failure for the enemy. However, I added: "Their second objective, obviously—from what you can see from not only Vietnam but from other Communist capitals, even from some unknowing people here at home—is a psychological victory."

I was asked whether the Tet offensive might lead to the deployment of additional men to Vietnam. I pointed out that we had added the men that General Westmoreland felt were necessary. "We have something under 500,000," I said. "Our objective is 525,000. Most of the combat battalions already have been supplied. There is not anything in any of the developments that would justify the press in leaving the impression that any great new overall moves are going to be made that would involve substantial movements in that direction."

As I look back now, there is no doubt in my mind that the Tet offensive was a military debacle for the North Vietnamese and the Viet Cong. I am convinced that historians and military analysts will come to regard that offensive and its aftermath as the most disastrous Communist defeat of the war in Vietnam. Indeed, some analysts have already reached that conclusion. But the defeat the Communists suffered did not have the telling effect it should have had largely because of what we did to ourselves.

There was a great deal of emotional and exaggerated reporting of the Tet offensive in our press and on television. The media seemed to be in competition as to who could provide the most lurid and depressing accounts. Columnists unsympathetic to American involvement in Southeast Asia jumped on the bandwagon. Some senatorial critics and numerous opponents of America's war effort added their voices to the chorus of defeatism. The American people and even a number of officials in government, subjected to this daily barrage of bleakness and near panic, began to think that we must have suffered a defeat.

This is not to imply that Tet was not a shock, in one degree or another, to all of us. We knew that a show of strength was coming; it was more massive than we had anticipated. We knew that the Communists were aiming at a number of population centers; we did not expect them to attack as many as they did. We knew that the North Vietnamese and the Viet Cong were trying to achieve better coordination of their countrywide moves; we did not believe they would be able to carry out the level of coordination they demonstrated. We expected a large force to attack; it was larger than we had estimated. Finally, it was difficult to believe that the Communists would so profane their own people's sacred holiday.

But there were elements of surprise in the other direction as well. We assumed that any coordinated offensive would include a major effort to overrun Khe Sanh; that effort never materialized because of our bombardment. We assumed Viet Cong intelligence could accurately estimate the reactions of the Vietnamese people; their estimate proved thoroughly wrong. Some officials doubted the ability of the South Vietnamese army to withstand a massive assault by enemy main-force units; in actual fact, on balance the performance of the South Vietnamese troops was excellent. The Communists expected the nationwide blow they were undertaking to shatter confidence and destroy the organizational fabric of the South Vietnamese government; the government's performance improved after Tet.

So there were many unexpected elements in the Tet affair, some positive, some negative. I was prepared for the events of Tet, though the scale of the attacks and the size of the Communist force were greater than I had anticipated. I did not expect the enemy effort to have the impact on American thinking that it achieved. I was not surprised that elements of the press, the academic community, and the Congress reacted as they did. I was surprised and disappointed that the enemy's efforts produced such a dismal effect on various people inside government and others outside whom I had always regarded as staunch and unflappable. Hanoi must have been delighted; it was exactly the reaction they sought.

The two weeks before and two months following Tet represented a period of activity as intense as any of my Presidency. My advisers and I followed developments in Vietnam on a daily, sometimes hourly, basis. Other problems arose in a variety of places. In Korea an assassination squad of North Koreans sneaked into Seoul intending to murder South Korea's President Park. The attempt was broken up only at the last minute. Then the North Koreans seized one of our intelligence ships, the USS *Pueblo,* and imprisoned its crew. Two days later, on January 25, we called up more than 14,000 Navy and Air Force reserves to strengthen our position in Korea without diverting resources from Southeast Asia. Our Korean allies were seriously worried that the Pyongyang regime might launch another invasion of their country. There was a distinct possibility that South Korean forces might be withdrawn from Vietnam.

In addition, we had received intelligence reports that a crisis might develop around West Berlin. We also faced major financial problems. The last three months of 1967 had produced the largest deficit in our balance of payments since 1950. Our proposal for a tax bill was bottled up in Congress. The international monetary system was in danger. At the same time, I was trying to push my domestic program. I submitted my Economic Report to the Congress on February 1 and followed it with a program of major legislation in education, crime prevention, and consumer protection. It was against this background that we had to deal with the Tet offensive and its consequences.

Less than five days after the attacks began General Westmoreland estimated that the enemy had already lost almost 16,000 men and nearly 4,000 weapons, but Communist forces had inflicted considerable damage on the South. Many homes had been destroyed. The flow of food to the cities was interrupted, and public services such as electric power and garbage collection had broken down in Saigon and in other urban centers. The government had to care for thousands of homeless people and refugees who had fled from the fighting. Rather than falling apart under this heavy added burden, as the Communists had hoped, the government of South Vietnam buckled down to solve its problems. In the first days of February a special task force headed by Vice President Ky was organized to carry out "Operation Recovery." Top people from our Embassy and our military staff in Saigon worked closely with the South Vietnamese government in this effort.

On February 12 General Westmoreland sent the Pentagon an assessment of the situation, which General Wheeler forwarded to me. It began as follows:

> Since last October, the enemy has launched a major campaign signaling a change of strategy from one of protracted war to one of quick military/ political victory during the American election year. His first phase, designed to secure the border areas, has failed. The second phase, launched on the occasion of Tet and designed to initiate public uprising, to disrupt

the machinery of government and command and control of the Vietnamese forces, and to isolate the cities, has also failed. Nevertheless, the enemy's third phase, which is designed to seize Quang Tri and Thua Thien provinces has just begun.

Westmoreland thought that the third phase would be a "maximum effort" by the enemy. In attacking the two northern provinces, the North Vietnamese would have the advantages of short lines of communication and the ability to concentrate heavy artillery fire from the demilitarized zone and north of it, and from Laos. In addition to this major effort, Westmoreland expected the Communist forces to try to regain the initiative they had lost in other parts of the country. Our field commander was reinforcing the northern region to meet the expected blow, but that meant having to weaken defensive forces in other areas. To meet these increased needs, Westmoreland wanted to speed up assignment of the remaining forces he had been promised. He then had about 500,000 of the approved 525,000 men. He asked for the earliest possible assignment of six maneuver battalions (about 10,000 men). He saw the situation as one of heightened risk but of great opportunity as well.

"I do not see how the enemy can long sustain the heavy losses which his new strategy is enabling us to inflict on him," he reported. "Therefore, adequate reinforcements should permit me not only to contain his I Corps offensive but also to capitalize on his losses by seizing the initiative in other areas." He believed that exploiting the opportunity "could materially shorten the war."

I met immediately with my advisers on February 12 * to consider Westmoreland's proposal. McNamara recommended that we send the requested troops but that they remain in Vietnam only for "the period of emergency." We had a long discussion about Vietnam and about what might lie ahead. I asked my advisers what the South Vietnamese were doing for themselves. I was advised that the South Vietnamese Cabinet had just voted to begin drafting veterans and to advance the dates for drafting nineteen- and eighteen-year-olds to March 1 and May 1 respectively, as our Mission had recommended earlier. The South Vietnamese were pressing ahead toward their announced goal of an additional 65,000 men for the military forces.

All the participants in this February 12 meeting favored meeting Westmoreland's request for additional troops. "We may waste valuable time and money," I concluded, "but it is better to have them there when they are needed than to need them there and not have them." We reserved judgment on how long they should be assigned. We considered calling up reserves. Wheeler was in favor; McNamara was opposed. I asked them to study the problem further and to agree on a recommendation.

* Attending the meeting were Secretaries Rusk and McNamara, Clark Clifford, Generals Wheeler and Taylor, CIA Director Helms, and Walt Rostow.

The next day, February 13, we met again. Wheeler reported that the troop deployment approved the previous day was being carried out. A Marine regiment and a brigade of the Army's 82nd Airborne Division had been chosen, and advance groups were already on their way. My advisers still disagreed on whether reserves should be called and, if so, how many and in what categories. I told McNamara and Wheeler there were many questions I wanted them to answer. I remembered the complaints about the call-up of reserves during President Kennedy's administration and, more recently, the failure to use effectively those who had been called up during the *Pueblo* crisis.

Why, I asked, is it necessary to call up reserve units at this time? If we decided on a call-up, how large should it be? Could we reduce the numbers by drawing on forces stationed in Europe or South Korea? Could we avoid or at least postpone individual reserve call-ups? If reserves were called, where would they be assigned? How long would they serve? What would be the budgetary implications? Would congressional action be necessary? I said that I would take no action until I received satisfactory answers to these and several other questions.

We then discussed the air offensive in the North. Rusk pointed out that Hanoi had just turned down our latest offer, made through the Romanians, to stop the bombing in return for prompt peace talks. In light of the large-scale and destructive Tet attacks and Hanoi's negative answer to our peace offer, Rusk said he would not object to some added pressure in our air campaign.

McNamara considered the military value of several suggested targets small and the risks high. He opposed hitting new targets in the Hanoi area. Clark Clifford, who was scheduled to replace McNamara on March 1, was disappointed in Hanoi's reply to what he described as "a very just and fair suggestion." Clifford thought their refusal justified stronger action on our part. "I would favor a step-up in the military pressure," he said. But after discussion we decided to hold off taking additional action against the North.

A few days later, on February 17, I visited some of the troops who were leaving for Westmoreland's command. I went first to Fort Bragg, North Carolina, to visit the men of the 82nd Airborne Division. From there I flew to El Toro, California, to call on a detachment of Marines who were leaving for Vietnam. I spent the night on the carrier *Constellation,* which was returning to the South China Sea for another tour of duty off Vietnam.

These visits with brave men were among the most personally painful meetings of my Presidency. The men with whom I talked and shook hands were strong and serious. I told them I regretted more than they would ever know the necessity of ordering them to Vietnam. I spoke personally with as many as I could. I remember vividly my conversation with one soldier. I asked him if he had been in Vietnam before. He said: "Yes, sir, three times." I asked if he was married. He said: "Yes, sir." Did he have any children? "Yes, sir, one." Boy or girl? "A boy, sir." How old is he? "He was born yesterday morning, sir," he said quietly. That was the last question I asked him. It tore my heart out to send back to combat a man whose first son had just been born.

I had decided by this time to send General Wheeler to Saigon for consultations with Bunker and Westmoreland. I thought we would benefit from a full assessment by this level-headed and experienced soldier. I asked him to go over the entire situation with Westmoreland and to form his own judgment of what should be done. I instructed him to find out what Westmoreland felt he had to have to meet present needs, and what he thought future needs would be for troops, equipment, or other support. Finally, I wanted Wheeler to find out how the South Vietnamese army was performing and what additional help we could provide to enable it to fight more effectively and improve more rapidly.

Wheeler left on February 21 for three days of briefings and consultation. He filed a preliminary report from Saigon on February 25. I was at the Ranch, but on February 27 some of my advisers met at lunch in Washington to discuss Vietnam. For several weeks we had been considering a speech I planned to make on Vietnam, and one purpose of their meeting was to review the latest draft. However, the written report I received on this meeting indicated that most of the time had been taken up with discussion of the "tentative proposals of General Westmoreland and General Wheeler for additional troops."

It is necessary to recall the background against which those tentative proposals were made. First, Communist forces in Vietnam were still engaged in their Tet offensive. The main thrust of that assault had been broken, but the Communists still occupied portions of Hué, were dropping mortar shells into other cities, and had regiments on the outskirts of Saigon. Westmoreland knew the North Vietnamese and Viet Cong planned a second wave of attacks that would probably be concentrated on the northern provinces and perhaps Khe Sanh. At that point, we did not know the exact status of the South Vietnamese army, especially of the regional and popular forces. Nor could we be certain how serious the impact of the Tet attacks had been on the people and on the governmental structure of South Vietnam, especially outside the capital.

At the same time, the Korean situation was explosive. The South Koreans were incensed about the attempted assassination of President Park. When the *Pueblo* was seized, our Korean allies urged us to bomb the North Korean port of Wonsan. The South Koreans made clear their determination to retaliate if there was one more major provocation by the North. I sent Cyrus Vance to Seoul to confer with President Park and his colleagues during the second week of February. We knew a major incident could easily erupt into a full-scale war on the Korean peninsula. We were concerned that, in their uneasy mood, the South Koreans might withdraw part of their forces from South Vietnam. Vance managed to reassure the South Koreans, and tempers had cooled measurably by the end of his visit. He reported this on February 15, but added: "In the long run, however, the picture is very dangerous."

While these concerns occupied us, we received warning of a possible Berlin crisis, so there were many sources of anxiety and many unknown factors on February 27. Wheeler and Westmoreland knew we had been considering for a year the possibility of calling up reserves and expanding draft calls in order to build up our strategic reserve in the United States, seriously depleted over the past few years. I had invited General Matthew B. Ridgway, former Army Chief of Staff, to lunch with me on February 1. I wanted the views and advice of this distinguished soldier who had led our combat forces in Korea. The problem of our strategic reserve was uppermost in Ridgway's mind. As an experienced theater commander in both Europe and the Far East, he was gravely concerned that we were in no condition to react to any new crisis that might erupt in another part of the world. He urged me to take steps to remedy this situation.

Various recommendations at that time would have increased our military forces by 400,000 to 500,000 men. I had rejected a similar proposal the previous May, but my military advisers had revived it and the matter was again high on our agenda. Wheeler and Westmoreland undoubtedly presumed that a large build-up of our armed forces was possible, if not likely. They also anticipated a high-level review of our war strategy. This had influenced their suggestions as to what could be done to strengthen our position in Vietnam.

Their preliminary proposal was that we consider assigning about 108,000 men over the next two months, prepare another 42,000 by September, and program a final group of 55,000 by the end of 1968. The total to be readied for possible assignment was slightly more than 205,000. With forces of that size, Westmoreland believed he could not only resist anything the enemy attempted but could move quickly to the offensive and take advantage of heavy Communist losses suffered during the first weeks of the Tet offensive. He also wanted to be prepared in case a change in our strategy permitted operations against enemy sanctuaries in Cambodia and Laos and across the DMZ.

At the February 27 meeting McNamara presented three options for consideration. One was to accept the Wheeler-Westmoreland proposal. This would require an increase in military strength of about 400,000 men, he said, and an expenditure of an additional $10 billion in fiscal 1969. The second option was to combine the military increase with a new peace initiative. At that point Rusk stated that if we made a peace proposal, it should be specific. He suggested that we might stop bombing at the 20th parallel, or stop bombing altogether if Hanoi would withdraw military forces from Quang Tri province, just below the DMZ. McNamara's third option was to maintain the status quo on troop commitments and change our strategy, protecting only "essential" areas and reducing offensive operations in unpopulated regions.

Clark Clifford suggested that there was a fourth alternative. He was not advocating it, he said, but it was possible that we could send in a huge number of men—500,000 to a million more. McNamara said he thought that either doing a great deal more or doing very little more both had the advantage of clarity, but he did not understand the strategy of putting in 205,000 men. He thought that was neither enough to "do the job" nor an indication that our role must change.

Foreign Service Officer Philip Habib, later to serve with our Paris negotiating team, had accompanied Wheeler to Saigon. He reported there were strongly divided opinions in our Mission in Vietnam regarding the wisdom of sending large forces of additional men. Some members favored it, but others felt such an influx might persuade the South Vietnamese to do less for themselves. McNamara argued that our decision must not be made hastily. If we accepted the Wheeler-Westmoreland proposal, many military and economic matters would have to be worked out.

The report of that meeting, sent by teletype to the Ranch on the night of the 27th, pointed out that many key questions raised at the lunch needed careful study: What constituted the military strategy and tactics underlying the troop proposals? What budgetary and balance-of-payments problems would these proposals raise? How could such an increase be justified to the American people? How would Europe and the Communist capitals react? What peace proposals should be included in any Presidential statement? What was the South Vietnamese capacity to carry the load in the days ahead?

Rostow reported to me that the "only firm agreement" among participants at the lunch was this: "The troop issue raised many questions to which you ought to have clear answers before making a final decision." He recommended that after hearing Wheeler's report the next morning I immediately set up a team "to go to work full time to staff out the alternatives and their implications." He suggested Clark Clifford as a good choice to chair this "intensive working group."

I returned to Washington at 2 A.M. on February 28. Wheeler arrived from Saigon four hours later, and we met for breakfast.* General Wheeler

---

* With me at the breakfast table in the Executive Mansion that morning, in addition to Wheeler, were Vice President Humphrey, Secretaries Rusk and McNamara, Secretary of Defense-designate Clifford, General Taylor, Deputy Secretary of Defense Paul Nitze, CIA Director Helms, Walt Rostow, George Christian, and Tom Johnson.

summarized his views on the situation in Vietnam. "There is no doubt," he said, "that the enemy launched a major, powerful nationwide assault against the government of South Vietnam and its armed forces. This offensive has by no means run its course. In fact, we must accept the possibility that he has already deployed additional elements of his home army. . . ."

"Whether he intends to expand himself fully at the current level of intensity or hold out enough to fight next year is not known," he said. "However, the scope and severity of his attacks and the extent of his reinforcements are presenting us with serious and immediate problems."

Wheeler said the South Vietnamese army had "performed remarkably well in most places." He said they had ninety-seven effective battalions and fifty-eight ineffective battalions but that the latter appeared to be "recovering fairly rapidly." The condition of regional and popular forces was "not yet clear," he said. Substantial South Vietnamese forces had withdrawn from the countryside to protect cities and towns. Unless they returned to the rural areas, the Viet Cong might win control there by default.

"It is the consensus of responsible commanders," Wheeler said, "that 1968 will be the pivotal year. The war may go beyond 1968 but it is unlikely that the situation will return to the pre-Tet condition. The forces committed and tactics involved are such that the advantage will probably swing one way or the other during the current year."

It was Wheeler's judgment that Westmoreland needed a reserve force of "about two divisions." He recommended that we seriously consider the three-phase increase he and Westmoreland had worked out. If I approved that preliminary proposal, Wheeler said, he would like to meet in Honolulu with the Joint Chiefs, Westmoreland and his staff, and the Secretaries of the Army, Air Force, and Navy to refine the plan and work out details.

"What are the alternatives?" was my first question. Wheeler said that in his judgment if we did not send troops in the numbers suggested, we might have to give up territory, probably the two northernmost provinces of South Vietnam. I asked about the 65,000 troops the South Vietnamese had pledged they would raise. Wheeler said the troops would be available as promised. President Thieu had told him that he could raise even larger numbers if the necessary equipment and supplies were available.

We finished breakfast and moved into the sitting room to continue our discussion. It was 9:35 A.M. I asked about developments at Khe Sanh, where approximately 5,900 Americans and a South Vietnamese ranger battalion were fighting. They were tying down two enemy divisions. Wheeler said that the enemy would pay a terrible price to take the outpost and that Westmoreland was confident he could hold it.

I asked Secretary McNamara how we could raise the troops to meet the Wheeler-Westmoreland proposal, if we decided to do so. McNamara said that we would have to call up about 250,000 reserves for all services, mostly for the Army. We would have to extend enlistments by six months for men already in service. He estimated that we would have to increase our budget by $10 billion in 1969 and by $15 billion in 1970. I asked him whether he accepted the forecast that we would have to expect to give up territory if we did not send men in the numbers being discussed. McNamara said he disagreed. He thought that adding 200,000 men would not make a major difference, since the North Vietnamese would probably add men to meet our increase. He believed that the key was the South Vietnamese army—how fast it could be expanded and how well it would fight.

McNamara said that one course we could follow would be to accept the preliminary proposal, with all its costs and problems. Another possibility was to send no more reinforcements. The latter would involve a major change in strategy on the ground, having our forces assume a defensive posture and cutting back on offensive actions. The Defense Secretary said he favored a course between these two alternatives. He suggested a small call-up of reserves and a much smaller deployment to Vietnam. He suggested we combine these steps with new efforts to find a negotiating track though he doubted that Hanoi would enter negotiations at that time. In his opinion, the North Vietnamese believed they had lost in their negotiations with the French and would be unwilling to risk a repetition. Rusk disagreed. He said he thought Hanoi might calculate that any peace talks would turn out well for them if they could do what they had done to the French militarily and psychologically. He thought they would use negotiations as a psychological weapon rather than as a serious attempt to reach a peace settlement acceptable to all concerned.

I pointed out that neither McNamara nor Wheeler had made a firm recommendation. McNamara said he would recommend nothing beyond the 15,000 men already programed. He also recommended giving increased responsibility to the South Vietnamese army. He admitted it might have to sacrifice some territory or a few hamlets to the enemy, but pointed out that his course would limit losses in men and dollars and would help ease the growing dissension within our country.

Wheeler said he thought no judgment could be made without an examination of all proposals by staff experts, though he doubted thorough study would produce a result much different from the one he had discussed. He agreed it was impossible to meet the proposal for more than 100,000 men by May 1, but he suggested that we accept the total package he had outlined as a long-range plan.

I told my advisers that I was not prepared to make any judgment at that time. We needed answers to many questions. I asked Clark Clifford to head a group to consider these demanding problems. He had not been living with Vietnam day in and day out as the others had, and I thought that a new pair of eyes and a fresh outlook should guide this study. Also Clifford would be taking McNamara's place in two days, and as Secretary of Defense he would bear heavy responsibility for carrying out any decisions that were made. I suggested that he organize subgroups to deal with such problems as the balance of payments, the complications of a reserve call-up, alternate military strategies, peace moves, and other aspects. The last thing I said was: "Give me the lesser of evils. Give me your recommendations."

After our meeting of February 28, I instructed Rostow to draft a written directive from me to the Clifford group specifying the various problems I wanted examined. Rostow complied and I went over it carefully and approved it. Special couriers delivered this directive immediately to Rusk, McNamara, and Clifford. The directive began:

> As I indicated at breakfast this morning, I wish you to develop by Monday morning, March 4, recommendations in response to the situation presented to us by General Wheeler and his preliminary proposals.
> I wish alternatives examined and, if possible, agreed recommendations to emerge which reconcile the military, diplomatic, economic, Congressional, and public opinion problems involved.

My directive listed the areas I wanted explored, as I had stated at our breakfast meeting:

> What objectives would additional forces achieve?
>
> What dangers would additional forces, if recommended, aim to avoid?
>
> What would our budget problems be and could we meet them?
>
> What problems would be created in our balance of payments, and could they be met?
>
> If we increased forces, what negotiation posture should we take?
>
> What changes would they recommend, if any, in the San Antonio formula?
>
> What other diplomatic problems would we face?
>
> What steps should we take to improve South Vietnamese performance?
>
> What actions would we have to ask Congress to take?
>
> What problems could be expected on the Hill?
>
> Were additional steps needed to expand our production base in support of our total military effort?
>
> What problems would we face with public opinion?

The directive was sent to the principals to guide their work. At McNamara's suggestion, it was made a "draft" so that my top advisers could suggest additions or changes they thought desirable as their study progressed. As it turned out, they proposed only one addition, which I accepted and included in the final draft of the directive. That addition was that the Clifford group consider carefully the question: "What probable Communist reaction could we expect to each of the possible alternative courses of action?" A few days later I signed and sent the final version of the directive to Rusk and Clifford for their permanent record.

Later on the same day that I established the Clifford group, I held a meeting with the Cabinet. I invited General Wheeler to attend and to report on his trip and his findings. The record of that Cabinet meeting reflects my outlook at the time. I said that many people had suggested various peace plans and that I had asked the State and Defense departments to analyze the proposals in detail. "What are all these options?" I asked. "Let's look at all these opinions, all the new, fresh, imaginative proposals and explore them so we know what the options are, and how we can escalate peace."

That afternoon, February 28, the Clifford group held its first meeting. In addition to Clifford, those present included Secretaries Rusk and McNamara, Treasury Secretary Fowler, Under Secretary of State Katzenbach, Deputy Secretary of Defense Paul Nitze, Dick Helms of the CIA, Walt Rostow, General Taylor, and others. An account of the meeting prepared in the Pentagon described it as follows:

> Mr. Clifford outlined the task as he had received it from the President. He indicated to the group that he felt that the real problem to be addressed was not whether we should send 200,000 additional troops to Vietnam. The real questions were: Should we follow the present course in SVN; could it ever prove successful even if vastly more than 200,000 troops were sent? The answers to these questions, the formulation of alternative courses open to the U.S., was to be the initial focus of the review. To that end, general assignments were made concerning papers to be written. These papers were to be prepared for discussion among the group on Saturday, March 2.

In a memo prepared immediately after the meeting Rostow reported that Clifford had given assignments under each heading in the directive. The committee planned to work over the weekend "on a statement of alternatives and on its recommendations."

McNamara and Clifford decided not to circulate the full text of my directive to all those working on the problem. Instead, William Bundy, then Assistant Secretary of State for East Asian and Pacific Affairs, prepared a summary of its esential assignments. The summary went to lower-level officers in State and Defense who were developing staff papers. Bundy's memo listed as the first subject to be considered: "What alternative courses of action are available to the U.S.?"

Thus as February ended an intensive review of our entire position was taking place inside the government. We were at one of those critical junctures where several possible trails lay before us, and I would have to choose which one to follow. I wanted all the expertise, opinions, ideas, and judgments I could possibly get before I made that decision.

One of the most important factors I wanted to consider before making my decision was evidence of Hanoi's possible interest in negotiating a settlement of the war. On February 4, Ambassador Bunker had reported that he thought it likely that the primary purpose of the Tet offensive was psychological, not military. He believed that the campaign might well have been designed to "put Hanoi and the Front in a strong position for negotiations by demonstrating the strength of the Viet Cong while shaking the faith of the people in South Vietnam in the ability of their own government and the U.S. to protect them." President Thieu had expressed a similar view in a talk with Ambassador Bunker that same day. Thieu felt that Hanoi and the Liberation Front were "tired" and "would like to get into negotiations." They could still mount offensive operations and were willing to "take heavy losses in the hope of gaining enough advantage, especially psychological, both here [in Vietnam] and abroad, to put themselves in a strong bargaining position at the table."

On February 21 UN Secretary General U Thant came to the White House. He told me that he had received an indication from unofficial sources that the North Vietnamese would be willing to begin talks with us if we stopped the bombing. If we notified Hanoi officially, the talks could begin "immediately," he said. If not, there would be some delay. He said he also had the impression from one of the North Vietnamese sources that if leaders in Hanoi entered into talks they might be ready to discuss de-escalation of the war in the South. After our conversation, the Secretary General discussed this matter in detail with Rusk and other officials. U Thant's report was interesting but hardly conclusive. We considered it encouraging if in fact Hanoi was ready to talk "immediately" after a bombing halt. We still had no assurances, however, that Hanoi would not take military advantage of a complete pause. I asked Rusk to investigate the matter further and to report back anything he discovered.

A few days later, on February 26, we received an intelligence report quoting a North Vietnamese contact as saying: "President Ho is waiting, but has insisted that the bombing be stopped first." This was only a straw in the wind, but it suggested that the idea of negotiations was alive in Hanoi.

The last day of February brought still another hint of Hanoi's possible desire for talks. An Indian diplomat informed us he had information that Hanoi would enter "prompt" and "substantive" talks with us when all bombing ended. By "prompt" the North Vietnamese meant one to two weeks, according to this source, and by "substantive" they meant anything related to the 1954 and 1962 Geneva agreements on Vietnam and Laos. Hanoi was also reportedly ready to agree not to increase infiltration during a pause. We immediately sought confirmation that the position described came from a responsible level in Hanoi and not from a minor official thinking out loud. We never received that confirmation. Nonetheless, these various indications of Hanoi's possible interest in negotiations played a part in my eventual decision to risk a limited bombing halt.

As we moved into the crucial month of March, the military situation was still serious but improving. I had received intelligence reports that the enemy might be pulling some forces back from the besieged outpost at Khe Sanh. The South Vietnamese were recovering well from the impact of Tet, and we had at least vague hints that Hanoi might be willing to negotiate.

During the first weekend in March specialists in the Defense and State departments and the Joint Chiefs of Staff worked long hours to refine their studies in preparation for the report of the Clifford group. I spent that weekend at Ramey Air Force Base in Puerto Rico with my son-in-law Pat Nugent, who was about to go to Vietnam. On the evening of March 3 I received a heartening report from Westmoreland. He had just visited the Mekong Delta and had conferred with the new South Vietnamese commander of IV Corps, Lieutenant Nguyen Duc Thang, and his staff. Westmoreland had told his own people and our Vietnamese allies:

> We must stop thinking about the next VC attack and start thinking, all of us, of continuing to carry the attack to the enemy. We are fully capable of doing it. It is true that our forces have been operating at a fast pace for thirty days and we have suffered heavy casualties. Some may be tired. However, the main thing now is our state of mind. It will be the side that perseveres and carries the fight to the enemy that wins. And we are going to do it.

"Throughout the country, we are moving to a general offensive," he reported. Westmoreland intended to visit the other three corps areas. He had plans for taking offensive actions in all of them. "I hope that the impact of these simultaneous major operations will convince the people in South Vietnam and in Washington that we are not waiting for either the VC to resume the initiative, or for someone to help us," he reported. "The time is ripe to move out and we will do so."

I was encouraged by Westy's report. I knew there were many worried and disheartened people in Washington, for the Tet offensive had badly shaken their confidence. Obviously, it had not shaken the will or determination of our field commander. He was going forward with what he had and was carrying the fight to what he was sure was a weakened enemy.

I was up early the next morning, March 4, for the flight back to Washington. I arrived at Andrews Air Force Base outside Washington at 12:18 P.M. and flew by helicopter to the White House. At 3:30 P.M. I attended a meeting on the 1970 defense budget. At 4:15 I met with representatives of labor, management, and government in an effort to avert a threatened strike in the copper industry. At 5:30 I went to the Cabinet Room to hear the recommendations of the Clifford group on Vietnam. The Vice President, the Secretaries of State and Defense,* and other advisers were present.

Before the meeting, I read Westmoreland's latest report on military manpower in Vietnam. The net increase in U.S. forces since January 31 was 5,000 men. South Vietnamese popular forces had recovered to 85 per cent of their strength. Regional forces were up to 75 per cent of their pre-Tet levels. Most impressive of all, Westmoreland reported that 118 battalions of the regular South Vietnamese army were combat effective. A week before only 97 had been ready for battle. The curve was clearly upward.

I knew that one of the first things the Clifford group had done was to make a sharp distinction between present needs and capabilities and the longer-run question of strengthening our overall military position during the next year. The full report I received at the meeting of March 4 made that distinction clear. A copy of the group's written report was distributed to everyone at the table. The report first described the Wheeler-Westmoreland proposal for troop increases and Wheeler's suggestions for building up our strategic reserves at home. By calling up reserves, increasing draft calls, and extending terms of service, the total package would have increased our armed forces by 511,000 men by June 30, 1969.

The Clifford group recommended:

> an immediate decision to send approximately 23,000 additional men to Vietnam;
>
> a strong representation to the South Vietnamese urging them to improve their performance;
>
> early approval of a reserve call-up of about 245,000 men;
>
> reserving judgment on the total 205,000 package and examination of requirements "week by week";
>
> an in-depth study of possible new "political and strategic guidance" for our operations in Vietnam and of our overall Vietnam policy;
>
> "no new peace initiative on Vietnam."

On bombing policy, opinions in the Clifford group were divided. Some wanted a "substantial extension of targets and authority" including mining Haiphong harbor; others proposed only a "seasonal step-up through the spring," without new targets.

Attached to the basic report were eight appendices. They discussed several matters—including reasons for increasing our forces in Vietnam and strengthening the strategic reserve; improving South Vietnamese effectiveness; the need to review overall Vietnam policy; possible diplomatic actions; and anticipated congressional, budgetary, and public opinion problems connected with the group's recommendations.

---

* Clifford had succeeded McNamara as Secretary of Defense on March 1.

The report and its attachments addressed the various questions I had raised in my directive of February 28. Some questions were answered in detail; others required additional study and analysis. As I read the Clifford group's report and its attachments and listened to the discussion around the Cabinet table, I detected among a few advisers a sense of pessimism far deeper than I myself felt. I had much greater confidence in Westmoreland and his staff in Vietnam than many people in Washington, especially Pentagon civilians. I also had more confidence in the ability and determination of the South Vietnamese people to defend themselves. On the other hand, I was deeply conscious of the growing criticism we were receiving from the press and from some vocal citizens. In my judgment, our future course of action would be influenced much more by developments on the ground in Vietnam than by staff studies or reviews in Washington.

Clifford declared that he was recommending the limited additional troop deployments "out of caution and for protection," but he thought that we should ponder hard before we did anything additional. I agreed with his thinking. I turned to Rusk and asked him to comment.

"Mr. President," he said, "without a doubt this will be one of the most serious decisions you will have made since becoming President." Rusk said he believed the key to the situation was the ability of the South Vietnamese people to do their full share and to "survive when we leave." I asked Rusk whether a substantial addition to our forces would increase or decrease that ability. He was persuaded that such a course might make the Vietnamese too dependent. He also foresaw a problem of competition for equipment between any new forces we sent out and the South Vietnamese army, which we were trying to strengthen. He believed that providing M-16 rifles and other equipment to the Vietnamese would be a better investment.

The aspect of the Clifford group's report that troubled me most was its totally negative approach to any possible negotiations. On the basis of remarks made earlier by Rusk, McNamara, and others, and knowing the opinions held by various civilians in the Pentagon and the State Department, I had begun to hope that some new approach might emerge from this study. Rusk said that there were indications that Hanoi might make some changes in its position, but he said he had to describe the possibilities of peace talks as "bleak" at that moment. Later in our discussion, we turned again to this subject. Deputy Secretary of Defense Paul Nitze, who had been working with Katzenbach, Rostow, and others in a special Vietnam study group, had concluded with them that a peace initiative might be possible when the worst of the enemy's offensive was over. He said he thought we should make a peace move "no later than May or June."

At that point, Rusk turned to me and suggested that we could stop most of the bombing of the North during the rainy season without too great a military risk. I knew that Rusk never raised this kind of matter without considerable thought. That morning he had sent me a memo prepared by a group of British intellectuals, including economist Barbara Ward, which had been referred to him by British Ambassador Sir Patrick Dean. It was not Rusk's usual practice to forward such items immediately to me, so I realized that he was taking the content seriously. The memo described the general situation in Vietnam, and considered and rejected either withdrawal or a massive invasion of the North. Then, in the key paragraph, the memo stated:

> Is there an alternative? The Communists have invented one which America might adopt. It is called "fighting and negotiating." At some convenient point this spring, America should do two things simultaneously, stop the bombing of the North and mobilize more men for Vietnam. It should announce that it will talk at any time, appoint negotiators, appeal to world opinion, remind Hanoi of its offers to talk and conduct a major peace offensive. At the same time, it would reinforce its armies in the South and continue the talk of "pacification."

I knew that this proposal was on Rusk's mind at our March 4 meeting. So when he suggested the possibility of a bombing halt, I turned to him and said: "Really get on your horses on that." He said he would.

As our meeting drew to an end, I asked General Wheeler whether he had informed Westmoreland that we would send 22,000 combat and support forces by June 1. Wheeler said that he had not—that he had been waiting for my decision. "Tell him to forget the 100,000," I said. "Tell him 22,000 is all we can give at the moment."

The next day, March 5, I met at lunch with my senior advisers.* We resumed the discussion of the previous day and talked about the complications of dealing with a problem such as Vietnam by gradual steps as compared with firm and decisive action early in a crisis. Rusk speculated that if the President's advisers had recommended and President Kennedy had approved sending 100,000 men into Vietnam in 1961, "it might have saved things." I pointed out that Republican candidate Richard Nixon was then criticizing us for not being tougher in our conduct of the war.†

We then discussed the *Pueblo* and its crew. When we concluded this review, I asked Rusk about his suggestion the night before for a bombing

---

* Present at the meeting were Secretaries Rusk and Clifford, Generals Wheeler and Taylor, CIA Director Helms, Rostow, and two members of my staff, George Christian and Tom Johnson.

† For example, see Mr. Nixon's February 5, 1968, speech in Green Bay, Wisconsin (reported in *The New York Times*, on February 6, 1968), in which he opposed our peace offensives and argued that the "only effective way" to bring Hanoi to peace was to "prosecute the war more effectively."

halt. Rusk replied that he had given it considerable thought. He suggested that we include the following paragraph in the speech I was planning to make on Vietnam:

> After consultation with our allies, I have directed that U.S. bombing attacks on North Vietnam be limited to those areas which are integrally related to the battlefield. No reasonable person could expect us to fail to provide maximum support to our men in combat. Whether this step I have taken can be a step toward peace is for Hanoi to determine. We shall watch the situation carefully.

Rusk then read a memorandum he had prepared. He pointed out that for the next month or so northern North Vietnam would be subject to the monsoon season, so we would not make a major military sacrifice if we stopped the bombing. We could resume if the North Vietnamese launched an all-out attack on Khe Sanh or on South Vietnam's major cities. Rusk was opposed to sending official representatives "all over the world" to try to convert the bombing halt into negotiations, as we had during the thirty-seven day pause in December 1965–January 1966. He said that we should simply wait for Hanoi's response. The Secretary of State urged that we avoid "theological debates about words" and put the problem instead on the "de facto level of action." If Hanoi failed to act, we would resume bombing. Rusk emphasized that it was important "not to embroider the statement with all sorts of 'conditions' or 'assumptions.'"

"Just take the action and see whether anybody is able to make anything out of it," he said.

I wanted to give careful thought to Rusk's proposal. I knew from the way he had presented his suggestion, and from the fact that he had prepared a written memo outlining his reasons, that Rusk was not just thinking aloud. Privately, I wondered what the effect would be if we did as Rusk suggested and I also announced my decision not to run for the Presidency in 1968. That day, I gave instructions to my staff not to enter a stand-in candidate to run in my name against Senator McCarthy in the Massachusetts primary.

After considering Rusk's peace proposal, my advisers and I reviewed our long discussion of the previous day. It seemed to me, I said, that we were "about to make a rather basic change in strategy." We were insisting that the South Vietnamese do more of the fighting; we were notifying them that we would send 20,000 men and would do nothing further unless they did more. I wondered aloud how much more the South Vietnamese could do. We explored ways to increase their effectiveness—with more helicopters, additional M-16 rifles, and other equipment. Clifford asked if I was directing him to take "whatever steps are necessary" to boost helicopter and M-16 production. I told him that I was. "Let's give the South Vietnamese the best equipment we can," I said.

At the end of the meeting Rusk gave a written copy of his proposal to Clifford, who in turn sent it to Wheeler and to his own staff for study. On March 6 Rusk instructed an assistant to prepare a cable to Ambassador Bunker describing the bombing cutback and asking for his judgment. However, Rusk and I were both concerned that the peace initiative might become widely known and be destroyed before it received a fair trial, so we decided to withhold the message until the time was right. Rusk knew that I did not plan to make my statement until the end of the month.

During this period additional hints came from diplomatic sources that Hanoi and its friends had not ruled out some form of negotiations. One such indication came on March 7. Rusk sent me a message from an allied diplomat describing the talk he had had a few days before with an Eastern European colleague. The Communist diplomat had told our friend that he could understand U.S. concern about the security of troops at Khe Sanh and near the DMZ, but he thought that our bombing near Hanoi was doing more harm than good. The allied diplomat received the impression that Hanoi could tolerate bombing near the demilitarized zone if it were accompanied by a halt in the air strikes on northern North Vietnam.

The next day, March 8, I received a report quoting a Liberation Front official as saying that his group no longer insisted on full participation in a coalition government in the South. That same day, an Eastern European diplomat in an Asian capital remarked that he thought Hanoi had been bitterly disappointed by the failure of its Tet offensive and no longer hoped to set up any kind of provisional government in the South. I did not consider these reports to be totally reliable, but they showed the way the wind might be blowing in Hanoi.

On March 10 Averell Harriman tried out the key portion of Rusk's bombing pause proposal on an Eastern European Ambassador. After discussing ways of reaching a peaceful settlement, Harriman asked the diplomat whether he thought it would help if we stopped the bombing of North Vietnam except for the area north of the demilitarized zone. The Communist envoy showed some interest but gave no definite reply.

Throughout the weeks of March there was intensive diplomatic activity in many quarters. We were searching for answers, and other governments were doing the same. Our policy was subjected to intense scrutiny and heavy criticism on the Hill, especially in the Senate. Hardly a day passed without one or another Senator speaking out in support of a total and unconditional bombing halt. Rumors of a large-scale increase in our troop commitment spread on the Hill and generated additional criticism. These attacks were directed at a decision that had not been made and that would never be made. I think these critics did more to confuse and upset our people than to inform them.

I met on March 8 with my senior advisers for another review of Vietnam and a discussion of future plans. By that time, Clifford and the Joint Chiefs had determined that instead of the 22,000 additional troops they had suggested earlier, the figure could now be raised to 33,000. This recommendation presupposed the calling up of selected reserves to active duty. I asked the group for further study. Then one of my advisers mentioned the original proposal for a total deployment of 205,000 men.

"I am not going to approve 205,000," I said. I made it clear that I did not favor this proposal, or anything approaching it.

On Sunday, March 10, Rusk came to the White House for lunch. We talked at length about his scheduled appearance in an open hearing before the Senate Foreign Relations Committee the following day. We agreed he should give the Senators as full a picture as possible of our current position and overall policy. We also agreed that certain matters could not properly be discussed for security reasons, but that the Senators should know we were making a thorough review of our position. We spoke briefly about the Secretary's suggestion for a bombing cutback, but that clearly was not a subject Rusk could discuss in the Senate.

That morning, *The New York Times* carried a story under the headline: "Westmoreland Requests 206,000 More Men, Stirring Debate in Administration." This report claimed that the Wheeler-Westmoreland contingency plan had touched off "a divisive internal debate within high levels of the Johnson administration." I suspected where the story had come from after comparing its content and tone with some of the more pessimistic assessments compiled in previous weeks at lower levels in the government, especially by Pentagon civilians.

It was obvious that the sources for the story did not know or understand what was going on in my mind, and they were not party to my dealings with my senior advisers; nor did they understand the decision-making process. A few people with strongly held opinions were trying to put pressure on me through the press to see things their way. I also felt that there was more than a little political motivation behind their action, since the article appeared two days before the New Hampshire primary. I was convinced that this story, and others like it that would inevitably follow, would create controversy and solve nothing. Such reports would further arouse congressional critics and give Hanoi an impression of increased divisiveness in our country. It might help prolong the war. The fact was that I had firmly decided against sending anything approaching 206,000 additional men to Vietnam and already had so informed my senior advisers.

I have always believed that any public official has not only the right but the obligation to support his judgment inside government just as strongly, as eloquently, and as frequently as he can. But once a decision has been made, he has an equal obligation to carry it out with all his energy and wisdom. If he cannot do so in good conscience, he should resign. He has no right to sabotage his President and his own government from within. He has no basis for assuming that he has all, or even most, of the facts. He has no license to make official secrets available to unauthorized persons. Above all, he has no right to leak half-truths or lies or distortions to win backing for his position. This incident raised serious doubts in my mind about the integrity, judgment, and reliability of some lower-level officials in my administration. If I had known who was responsible, I would have fired him, or them, immediately.

The next day, March 11, Rusk went before the Senate Foreign Relations Committee. The proceedings were carried live by television. Rusk remained in the witness chair for a total of six and a half hours that day. On March 12 he went back at 9:30 A.M. and stayed until 2 P.M. This was the most prolonged questioning of a Cabinet officer ever broadcast to the American people. During the hearing Rusk was asked whether Westmoreland had "requested an escalation of the war with an additional 200,000 men." The question showed the impact the news story had had on at least one Senator. Rusk answered:

> Senator, when I saw some newspaper stories yesterday about sweeping reassessment I went by and called on the President yesterday afternoon after he got back from church and talked to him about it. He said that he had come to no fresh conclusions. He had sent General Wheeler out to visit with General Westmoreland, Ambassador Bunker, President Thieu, to look over the situation and come back and inform us of what he found.
>
> Obviously, the so-called Tet offensive calls for an examination of many subjects, including the tactics and strategy of the enemy, the impact on the pacification program and on the military side.
>
> As you know—as you may know—at the end of this month and early next month, certain units will be going out that had previously been scheduled under existing plans—the level of that 525,000 that the President talked about. But he has not made any fresh decisions or come to any new conclusions, and I think it would not be right for me to speculate about numbers or possibilities until the President has had a chance to look at all the information and consult with his advisers and determine how and on what basis he would wish to consult with members of the Congress and the appropriate committees of the Congress if any congressional action should be indicated.

The Secretary was asked if any recommendation was then before the President. He replied correctly that there were then no specific recommendations. "The entire situation is under consideration from A to Z," he said. He added: "The facts and problems and opportunities are being looked at, but I can't speculate about decisions that have not been made or conclusions that have not been reached."

At one point in the hearing Rusk was asked if consideration had been given to a proposal to confine our bombing to the 17th parallel "and the infiltration routes in that area." He answered:

> That proposal has been looked at very closely. Indeed, we do examine all proposals that we can find from any source. Most of the proposals that we get are variations of one sort or another of efforts that have already been made at one time or another. It is quite clear from our recent contacts with Hanoi that they would not accept a partial cessation of the bombing as a step toward peace in any way, shape, or form.

That last sentence was later used by some critics to try to "prove" that we were not then thinking seriously about peace initiatives. In actual fact, Rusk and I and a few others were looking hard indeed. His very next sentence in the hearing was often conveniently ignored:

> That does not mean that, as we move into the future, we won't consider examining that and all other proposals that we can get our hands on or that we can think up ourselves.

Secretary Rusk did a magnificent job under trying circumstances. He remained calm, patient, and clear-headed, even under the provocative questioning of some of the most outspoken critics of our role in Vietnam. I believed that no American who heard the hearings could have failed to understand better why we were engaged in Southeast Asia and what we hoped to see develop there. The mail and telegrams that flowed into the White House following Rusk's hearing were two to one in favor of the Secretary and what he had said.

The same day that Rusk testified on Capitol Hill, we received an interesting new proposal for a peace initiative, presented by a competent neutral diplomat, who had a long talk with Walt Rostow in the White House that afternoon. The idea he suggested was this: A neutral government or other authority would invite North and South Vietnam, the Liberation Front, and the United States to meet on a given date and time. Participants in the war would be asked to reduce all military action one day before the meeting; this would involve ending all major offensive actions, including the bombing of North Vietnam. Representatives of the International Control Commission—composed of India, Canada, and Poland—would also be invited to the meeting. Advance approval would not be sought and the meeting would be held whether or not all those invited agreed to attend.

Rostow listened carefully, agreed to report the proposal to me immediately, and urged the diplomat to get in touch at once with Rusk. One week later, on March 18, presumably after obtaining approval from his government, the diplomat met with the Secretary of State in the latter's office. He described the proposal in detail, even to suggested wording for the invitations. The two men discussed both the advantages and disadvantages of the proposal. Rusk agreed to give the suggestion immediate and careful study.

When he reported to me, I instructed the Secretary to relay the gist of the proposal to Ambassador Bunker. I wanted Bunker's assessment of the plan itself and of its likely reception by the South Vietnamese government. Bunker answered on March 23, expressing "very great interest" in the proposal. He pointed out, however, that timing was crucial to such an approach. The South Vietnamese were just recovering from the Tet offensive. Their army was expanding operations and reasserting authority in the rural areas from which it had withdrawn during the Tet fighting to protect towns and cities. Bunker believed that ending offensive actions before that goal was achieved would work against our allies and give the Viet Cong an advantage. He also pointed out that accepting the Liberation Front as a full participant in the proposed meetings would raise problems for Saigon. We learned how right he was when peace talks began later in Paris.

By this time I had decided in principle to go ahead with the plan first suggested by Rusk for a cutback on bombing to the 20th parallel, but I asked the Secretary to continue study of the neutral diplomat's plan. I wanted to leave no door untried if it might lead to a settlement.

Military reports continued to flow in daily. During the first week in March Westmoreland reported on the improvement in military manpower, especially in South Vietnamese regular forces. On March 9 an intelligence analysis indicated that enemy manpower around Khe Sanh had dropped to about half its earlier level—that is, from 14,000 to between 6,000 and 8,000 men.

Meanwhile, manpower specialists in the Pentagon and on the staff of the Joint Chiefs were refining their estimates of the men and supplies we could send Westmoreland to meet any new North Vietnamese–Viet Cong offensive. By March 11 they had developed several alternate plans. The one that appealed most to Westmoreland was a proposal for sending him seven maneuver battalions. That combat force of over 14,000 men would be supplemented by additional support personnel, tactical air squadrons, and airlift and naval personnel, for a total of 30,000 men.

I discussed this plan in detail with my advisers at a meeting on March 11 but took no final action. That same day, I received a thoughtful cable from Bunker regarding future deployments of American troops to Vietnam. The Ambassador supported the proposal to send seven combat battalions to meet any possible emergency that might lie just ahead, but he had serious reservations about going beyond that. Bunker wanted to keep the emphasis on enlarging and modernizing South Vietnamese forces. U.S. force increases, he wrote, should be limited to "what we consider essential to maintain the offensive and to overcome certain geographic advantages which the enemy has, without unduly widening the war or over-Americanizing it." He hoped that this would be "our basic guideline" in the future.

The Ambassador also reminded us of President Thieu's recent decision to raise an additional 100,000 to 125,000 fighting men over the next six months. If the South Vietnamese met that goal, much new equipment would be needed, especially weapons and vehicles. Rusk had warned us the previous week of possible competing needs for weapons between our forces and the South Vietnamese if we expanded our effort. He favored giving priority to the latter. Secretary Clifford had agreed, and so did I.

On March 12 I met again with my senior advisers at lunch. Rusk was still going through the ordeal of the televised Senate hearings, and we watched part of the proceedings as we ate. Rusk was handling the session with great skill, but I knew he was not enjoying it. Some questioners were using the session less to gain information than to call attention to themselves as champions of peace. I knew that not a man in that hearing room wanted peace more, or even perhaps as much, as Dean Rusk, and I hoped Americans who were watching the hearings understood that.

We had temporarily dropped the idea of a Presidential statement when the Wheeler-Westmoreland report had arrived late in February. But I knew that I would need one by the end of March. At the meeting on March 12, I asked my advisers to consider what should be in such a statement. I also requested a new sounding of opinion from Congress, especially from men on the Armed Services committees. I told them that they had moderated my judgment at our meeting on March 4. At that time I had almost been ready to call up a large number of reserves, not for Vietnam alone but to strengthen our overall military position; to ask Congress for the authority to call additional selected reservists; and to continue to push hard for the tax bill on that basis. My opinion had changed as a result of what I had heard from my advisers and what I saw happening on the ground in Vietnam. "I do think we should evaluate our strategy," I said. I told them to continue the review.

Throughout the fall of 1967 and the spring of 1968 we were struggling with one of the most serious financial crises of recent years.* These monetary and budgetary problems were constantly before us as we considered whether we should or could do more in Vietnam. It was clear that calling up a large number of troops, sending additional men overseas, and increasing military expenditures would complicate our problems and put greater pressure on the dollar. This aspect was on the mind of every man who met with me in the Cabinet Room on March 15 to consider troop call-ups and further deployments. At that meeting Rusk said that his greatest

---

* See Chapter 14, pp. 314–21.

concern regarding new military measures was the effect they would have on our monetary problems. He thought that if we adopted some of the proposals we then were studying without passing a tax bill, the result could be new panic in Europe, heavy inflation at home, and possibly the collapse of the monetary system. "If we do this without a tax bill," he said, "we are dead."

By that time Clifford and his civilian staff, working with the Joint Chiefs, had scaled down their original recommendation for a reserve call-up from 260,000 to 98,000 men. They suggested doing this in two phases: an immediate call for 50,000 and a second call a few months later for the remaining 48,000. That schedule would permit us to provide Westmoreland with the added force of 30,000 we had been discussing.

The 98,000 figure had been worked out only that day by Clifford and Wheeler and their advisers. But even before word of it came to me at our meeting, Press Secretary George Christian had been queried by a newspaperman about "those 98,000 men who are going to Vietnam." This demonstrated again how rapidly even the most closely held matters could leak to the press, though often in distorted fashion. Most of those 98,000 reserves, if called to duty, would have replenished our badly depleted strategic reserve at home, not gone to Vietnam.

Clifford estimated that the cost of the call-up would be an additional $2 billion in 1968 and $5 billion more the next year. With our financial problems in mind, I said I would not make any decisions until we had conferred further with Treasury Secretary Fowler and his staff, with members of key committees on the Hill, and with the congressional leadership.

I had another important reason for delaying a decision at that time. I had just received a message from Westmoreland describing his plan for a major offensive against the North Vietnamese and the Viet Cong in northern I Corps on or about April 1. One of his goals was to open Route 9 and relieve the forces at Khe Sanh. I thought that if Westmoreland had enough confidence to launch an offensive with the forces he had in Vietnam, it would be wise to limit additional commitments. The ground war in Vietnam appeared to be going better than most people realized. Five days later Bunker confirmed this impression. He began his regular weekly report to me as follows: "During the past week, U.S. and Government of Vietnam forces have increasingly assumed the initiative."

Communist mortaring and rocketing of towns and base areas was continuing but on a reduced scale. Sweeping outward from Saigon, South Vietnamese and American troops had encountered no significant opposition. The enemy had split its forces into smaller units to escape and cut losses. We captured many large caches of arms and ammunition in the sweep.

On the evening of March 15, 1968, UN Ambassador Arthur Goldberg sent from New York a detailed memo on Vietnam to Secretary Rusk, who forwarded it to the White House Situation Room the following morning. I was spending a few days at the Ranch and the memorandum was sent to me there. Goldberg knew that our total situation in Vietnam was then under comprehensive review. He urged that in our review we consider a total bombing halt in the North. "It is my considered opinion," he wrote, "that the very best way to prevent further erosion of public support from taking place is to make a new and fresh move toward a political solution at this time." He described his proposal as follows:

> In specific terms, then, my suggestion, based on the San Antonio formula,* means that—without announcing any conditions or time limit —we would "stop" the aerial and naval bombardment of North Vietnam for the limited time necessary to determine whether Hanoi will negotiate in good faith; in my view this can best be determined by what actually happens during the talks rather than by any advance verbal commitments of the kind we have been seeking.

Goldberg thought that our other actions outside North Vietnam should continue. We could resume the bombing, he said, if North Vietnam "were, in bad faith, to take military advantage of the bombing cessation."

I read the memo carefully. Goldberg made a strong case for a total bombing halt, but not strong enough. I could not take the risk of such a move at that time. I continued to believe that the North Vietnamese would interpret it as a clear sign of weakness—an indication that we wanted to stop fighting and come home. If they read our action that way, it would mean prolonged fighting and greater suffering and dying. More important, as Commander in Chief, I could not endanger the safety and lives of our men or our Vietnamese allies. What would happen, I wondered, if we stopped the bombing and the North Vietnamese then launched a major offensive, overran Khe Sanh, and killed thousands of Americans and South Vietnamese? The American people would never forgive me. Nor would I ever forgive myself. I opposed taking that risk with so many uncertainties in the air. But I agreed with Rusk that Goldberg's plan should have a fair hearing. We both wanted Bunker's judgment of this proposal and of the one Rusk himself had advanced earlier, which I was largely persuaded to try. That evening, March 16, Rusk sent an "eyes only" cable to Bunker outlining the two plans without naming their authors. He asked for the Ambassador's private assessment of the effects these two courses would have on the Vietnamese government and on its people.

Two days later Ambassador Chester Bowles in India sent still another proposal for a peace initiative. Like the Goldberg suggestion, it called for a total bombing halt in the North. Bowles proposed, however, that before

* The San Antonio formula is described in Chapter 11, p. 267.

calling a bombing halt we inform key governments and international bodies —for example, India, the United Kingdom, Japan, the Soviet Union, and the UN Secretariat—of our intentions. We would stop the bombing if, and only if, the other nations would "from that moment on take responsibility for bringing about meaningful negotiations." They would also have to promise to cooperate with us and others in a postwar economic development program in Southeast Asia, once a satisfactory settlement was reached.

At our Tuesday lunch meeting on March 19 my advisers and I continued our discussion of Vietnam, the reserve call-up and troop deployment, and related budgetary problems. During this discussion I asked for opinions on the "Goldberg-Bowles proposal." Rusk said he had discussed the plan with Goldberg and a few senior State Department officials. Goldberg felt strongly that we should proceed with a total bombing halt on the basis of the San Antonio formula. This move, he thought, would help unify the country. Rusk doubted that it would have such an effect. He preferred the approach he had repeatedly suggested: to carry out a de facto halt in the bombing above the southern panhandle of North Vietnam and to "see if we get a de facto response from Hanoi."

"I am not impressed by the merits of the Goldberg proposition," Clifford said. "I think it would be fruitless." He then suggested that I consider meeting soon with a group of nongovernmental advisers—popularly known as the Wise Men—with whom I had discussed Vietnam on several previous occasions. The group included former Secretary of State Dean Acheson, former Under Secretary of State George Ball, McGeorge Bundy, former Secretary of the Treasury Douglas Dillon, General Omar Bradley, and others. I decided to do so.

I urged my advisers to continue preparations for my speech on Vietnam, and said that I wanted a draft by Thursday, March 21. I also told them that I was not satisfied with the cost estimates of the troop call-up developed by the Pentagon, and I asked that they be refined and checked out fully with Secretary Fowler.

In the Cabinet Room that evening, I described for Senate and House leaders our thinking on troop call-ups. I pointed out that we needed more men under arms—some to restore our seriously depleted strategic reserve at home and some to reinforce Westmoreland in Vietnam. The call-up would not begin to approach the 400,000 figure rumored on the Hill, and we were not sending 200,000 or more men to Vietnam, as newspapers had reported. But the call-up of approximately 100,000 reserves, which we then were considering, would mean increasing our budget deficit by $8–10 billion over the next year or so. I said that made action on a tax bill all the more urgent. I knew we could not hope for the tax bill unless we cut spending, and we were doing that. I was also ready to accept any sensible cuts that Congress decided to make in appropriations. But the tax bill was a "must."

I gave a good deal of thought that night and the next morning to the speech I intended to make. I planned to describe the situation in Vietnam as we then saw it. I wanted to clarify what the Vietnamese were doing for themselves after Tet, and to note what their goals were for the future. I wanted to explain our plans for a modest reinforcement of our troops in Vietnam and for building up our military forces at home to deal with possible crises elsewhere in the world. I was also determined to make a serious peace proposal. In the final part of my statement I would announce my decision on politics, but I decided to hold that very close until the last minute.

I knew that Rusk had the best understanding of the way I wished to move. He and his closest advisers on Vietnamese affairs were working on raw material for the speechwriters. One of my assistants, Harry McPherson, was the coordinator of the speech. The background material and suggested language that arrived from the State Department that day, March 20, contained the proposal Rusk had made two weeks earlier to offer Hanoi a bombing halt at the 20th parallel.

I considered it important that Secretary Clifford also understand what I wanted the speech to contain. He was handling most of the military and budgetary matters that would be discussed, but he had to know that I wanted to include some sort of peace initiative. He called that morning about another matter, and it gave me an opportunity to discuss the planned speech with him. I told him it would be clear we were going after the enemy with our right hand by offensive action on the battlefront, but with our left hand we had to offer a peace proposal. I urged him to think it over carefully and "come up with something." We again discussed Goldberg's proposal and agreed it was not the answer.

Perhaps we could cut off bombing in the northern part of the country, I suggested. Then, if the North Vietnamese cut back their actions in the DMZ or elsewhere, we could take another step. We had not hit anything in the Hanoi-Haiphong area for some time, but now we could go further. "I think you and Rusk ought to try to explore something we could offer in that way," I said. "My own thought is that we ought to stress peace and we ought to stress the permanence of it. . . . We are willing to have a Geneva conference. . . . We are willing to sit down and pull our troops out of there as soon as the violence subsides."

Clifford was familiar with Rusk's proposal. He had been present when the Secretary of State first suggested it and when he discussed it in detail on March 5. I knew that Clifford had a written copy of the plan. But I also knew that the Secretary of Defense had been working around the clock for two weeks on reserve call-ups, draft problems, combat and combat support ratios, equipment needs, and budget problems. He was also busy learning about the many heavy responsibilities he had accepted when he was sworn in as Secretary on March 1. But now, after concentrating heavily on military considerations for weeks, he turned his attention to the other side of the problem: the search for a settlement. He began looking down the road. If we followed Rusk's proposal and Hanoi reacted by cutting back its own actions, how would we then respond? We needed a plan, Clifford said. He said he would go to work trying to develop one.

That same morning, March 20, Ambassador Bunker answered the questions Rusk had raised concerning a bombing halt. The Ambassador was clearly skeptical about any early move of this kind. He thought that in the wake of Tet many Vietnamese would misunderstand another peace initiative. It was most important, he said, that we consult the South Vietnamese leadership before making a move of this kind. He thought it likely that Hanoi would respond, not by taking a real step toward peace but by trying to give the impression it had taken such a step. Getting down to the specific proposals, Bunker said a total bombing pause "would create the greatest difficulties."

"I recommend strongly that we not pursue this course," he wrote, "since from a Vietnamese viewpoint it would bring out all the disadvantages I have mentioned and it would also mean giving up our principal card without obtaining anything in return." Bunker thought that it would be easier to obtain South Vietnamese agreement on a limited bombing halt. There would be many problems, he said, but he indicated that a limited cessation would be manageable, especially if it followed an announcement of an increase in our military support.

Two drafts of my proposed statement were completed that day. The first draft included the following peace proposal:

> To remove every possible barrier to the encouragement of talks, I have instructed our commanders to refrain from aerial bombardment of Hanoi, Haiphong, and any other targets within a range of _____ miles from those cities, until they are instructed otherwise.

I did not like this formulation. We had never "bombarded" Hanoi or Haiphong; they had never been targets in themselves. I supposed that someone suggesting ideas for the speech had simply been careless. In any case, it was not what I had in mind. The second draft contained no new initiatives. It merely repeated our San Antonio offer to stop the bombing when we had assurances that it would lead promptly to productive talks, and when we could reasonably assume that the enemy would not take advantage of our restraint.

Just after 5 P.M. on March 20, I met in the Cabinet Room with several advisers to discuss the proposed speech. The Vice President was there along with Rusk, Clifford, Goldberg, and others. McGeorge Bundy was in town and I had asked him to join us. I told them I wanted them to help prepare a thoughtful and well-balanced statement, one that would cover our decision to meet emergency military needs and would contain "a reasonable offer on peace." I asked for suggestions. Rusk led off by saying he thought no peace proposal could be promising unless it involved some kind of bombing cessation, although, there were political and military risks involved in a bombing halt. He said we had been exploring the idea of a bombing limitation in the North while continuing bombing in the area north of the demilitarized zone. Rusk then read us his suggested wording for the peace initiative. It was the same proposal he had made on March 5 and later had questioned Bunker about. "Unless we are prepared to do something on bombing," Rusk said, "there is no real proposal for us to make."

Clifford said he thought the speech should contain three elements: what we were going to do militarily and why; what the South Vietnamese were doing for themselves; and some discussion of peace. On the last point, he suggested a program for deescalation of the war. As a first step, we could offer to stop bombing north of the 20th parallel. In turn we would ask the enemy to stop firing artillery and rockets from the DMZ and just north of it. Or, Clifford said, we could stop above the 20th parallel if Hanoi would agree to withdraw its forces from the DMZ.

Mac Bundy favored taking our own action without specifying conditions. Rusk agreed. He said that we should simply stop part of the bombing and then say: "Whether or not this will prove to be a step toward peace is for Hanoi to determine." Clifford considered that approach too "open-ended," pointing out that we would not know whether we could expect anything in return.

Goldberg then repeated his proposal for a total bombing halt. He argued that it offered the only possibility of getting into negotiations. He advised strongly against doing anything less. He also expressed the opinion that support of the war and a peace offer should not be combined in one speech.

Justice Abe Fortas, who had joined us in the Cabinet Room at my invitation, had been listening quietly. I asked him to assess the arguments. He said that in his judgment any bombing pause at that time could be a mistake. It was too one-sided in Hanoi's favor. He found the argument persuasive that I merely emphasize the reasons for our being in Vietnam and the steps the Vietnamese were taking to build their strength and fight their own battles.

Clifford expressed sympathy with Fortas' analysis, but he thought that circumstances had changed. The Vietnam conflict was not the same as earlier wars, when the President needed only to express the will of the American people. The new Defense Secretary said he was coming to the conclusion that the continued application of force did not promise ultimate success. He thought most of the military plans he had heard discussed would widen the war. That was the reason he felt that we had to search for some approach toward peace that the President could advance now and build upon later. He hoped that this approach could eventually lead to adoption of a plan approximating Goldberg's proposal. However, Clifford concluded: "I don't believe that any approach to Hanoi at this time has any chance of success."

I asked Assistant Secretary of State Bill Bundy what he thought. He said he saw the alternatives much as Goldberg had stated them, but he was convinced Hanoi did not want to talk at that time. He felt that some of the proposals then stirring in diplomatic circles might eventually develop into something useful.

I listened as the discussion moved around the table from one man to another. I was sympathetic to the various arguments. But I was deeply concerned that any peace initiative we might take would be misinterpreted both in Hanoi and at home. I therefore suggested that we separate the peace initiative from the rest of the speech. I asked for a study of all the peace proposals then before us—that by Rusk, by Clifford, and the others. I felt certain that I would take the action Rusk had suggested, but I hoped most of my advisers would agree on it before I went forward.

I had another reason for wanting a separate study of peace initiatives. Speech drafts often circulated widely around town. I had just seen how quickly contingency military proposals could get into print, however garbled. I did not want that to happen to any peace proposal we might make, for I felt certain that premature disclosure would weaken and probably destroy any chance for its success. Finally, I wanted to think further about taking a peace initiative at that time. Before making a formal proposal, I wanted to feel that our offer had a reasonable chance of success and that it would not make any serious difference to our military men at the front.

I was weighing one aspect that others around me, except for Rusk, were not. That is, I was judging the possible impact of a peace move linked with an announcement of my decision to withdraw from politics at the end of my term. That consideration put things in another perspective. I knew some of my advisers were thinking of a peace move in terms of public opinion and political consequences. I was wondering whether a new offer might really lead to a settlement. That made a considerable difference.

On March 21, the day after our discussion of my speech, President Thieu made a speech of his own. He delivered a report to his own people and to the world in which he described the situation South Vietnam faced and prescribed certain remedies. Earlier, the South Vietnamese had planned to add 65,000 men to their armed forces. As confidence and need grew simultaneously after Tet, they had raised the figure to 100,000, then to 125,000. In his speech Thieu said he now planned an increase of 135,000 men "in the first phase." That meant calling back veterans thirty-three years old or less who had not served a full five years. It also meant increased drafting of nineteen-year-olds, which had already begun, and of eighteen-year-olds, which was to begin about five weeks later. Thieu pointed out one of the main reasons for his government's increased confidence. In the period after Tet about 22,000 South Vietnamese youths had volunteered for military service and in February alone, while the Tet attacks were continuing, there were five times as many military enlistments as there had been during the previous February. Clearly the South Vietnamese had not broken under the impact of the Communists' attacks. Rather, they were stiffening in their resistance.

Along with building up the military services, the South Vietnamese had begun training civilian self-defense groups. When Thieu spoke they had already issued 10,000 weapons, and almost 70,000 civilians were undergoing training. "Our allies in the Free World will give us military and economic assistance," Thieu said. "But for our part, I think that we must make greater efforts and accept more sacrifices because, as I have said many times, this is our country, the existence of our nation is at stake, and this is mainly a Vietnamese responsibility. We must demonstrate that we deserve their support, and gain the respect of other nations."

Thieu's statement never received the attention it deserved in the American press or elsewhere. More important, the performance of the Vietnamese government and armed forces before and after Thieu's statement was never made clear in most day-to-day reporting. There was continuing gloom and pessimism in the United States because the North Vietnamese and Viet Cong had carried out a nationwide offensive. The fact that the goals of their offensive were never achieved was pushed into the background or ignored. Only now are commentators and analysts beginning to picture the Tet offensive in its true light as a massive defeat for the North Vietnamese and their followers, and as a turning point in the war.

Throughout March I received reports daily on internal developments in Vietnam—military, political, social, and psychological. The net effect was positive and this was one reason for my growing confidence in the situation. These reports help account for the surprise I felt every time I encountered otherwise knowledgeable people who seemed to be sunk in gloom. On March 25 I received a letter from a businessman who had been traveling in and out of Vietnam for ten years. During the last three years he had spent parts of thirty-one months in that country and was just back from Saigon. He wrote:

> On the basis of my observation of the Vietnamese themselves, from throughout the country and from every walk of life, I am convinced that:
>
> 1) the Viet Cong overplayed their hand;
>
> 2) the Tet offensive is providing a great rallying point for the South Vietnamese—a sort of Pearl Harbor experience which unifies them and stiffens their determination;
>
> 3) the violation of Tet (not just the violation of the truce, but the

very spirit of Tet itself) has aroused the Vietnamese. First they were shaken; now they are angry and determined.

Two days later I read a remarkably similar assessment by a leading Vietnamese politician, Dr. Phan Quang Dan. He regarded the Tet offensive as the "worst defeat the Communists have ever experienced." He concluded that "South Vietnam, with all its weaknesses, is emerging from the Lunar New Year storm as a definitely viable state with a basically loyal army and police and a population firmly committed to freedom."

By March 22 we had further refined our estimates of the additional troops needed for Vietnam and to build up our strategic reserve at home. We planned a call-up of about 62,000 reserves and proposed only 13,500 additional troops for Vietnam. These would be mainly support forces to back up the 10,500 combat troops we had sent in the days immediately following Tet.

Four factors led to this further scaling down of our plans. First, and most important, it was our collective judgment that another massive Communist attack was increasingly unlikely. Second, the South Vietnamese were clearly improving militarily and getting in shape to carry a heavier combat load. Third, our financial problems remained serious, despite the solution we had found for the gold crisis. The Congress still had not passed a tax bill and we faced a large budgetary deficit. Finally, domestic public opinion continued to be discouraged as a result of the Tet offensive and the way events in Vietnam had been presented to the American people in newspapers and on television. Critics of our policy became more and more vocal as contention for the Presidential nomination heated up.

I wanted to be certain, however, that in cutting back the level of reinforcement we were not putting our fighting men into serious danger. I also wanted Westmoreland to understand completely the situation we faced at home. I asked General Wheeler to go to the Far East and talk again with Westmoreland. The generals met at Clark Air Force Base in the Philippines on March 24.

If Westmoreland had insisted that only a large number of reinforcements stood between his men and disaster, I would have managed to find them somewhere. But it was obvious that the situation was much more favorable than it had been one month earlier, that it was improving steadily, and that the moment had come to throw more weight behind the Vietnamese with their new spirit of confidence. On his return to Washington on March 24, Wheeler confirmed that judgment. Westmoreland had said that all he required was 13,500 support troops to balance out his forces, and authority to hire more local civilians. With these additions to his command, Wheeler said, Westmoreland felt confident he could carry out his strategy for meeting the enemy and could continue the pacification and battlefield progress that was being made. He was remarkably encouraged by the recent performance and prospects of the Vietnamese armed forces.

General Creighton Abrams, Westmoreland's deputy commander in Vietnam, had returned with Wheeler. The three of us met in the family dining room of the White House on the morning of March 26. Wheeler assured me that Westmoreland understood the situation perfectly and was completely confident. Abrams gave me a full report on the tactical situation and spoke encouragingly of the improvements being made by the Vietnamese military. He also outlined Westmoreland's plan to relieve the garrison at Khe Sanh in an offensive to begin in less than a week.

I had scheduled a meeting that day with a group of outside advisers, the so-called Wise Men.* I asked the generals to join our discussion and to give the advisers a firsthand description of the military situation. "We don't want an inspirational talk or a gloom talk," I said. "Just give them the factual, cold, honest picture as you see it."

I was glad that Wheeler and Abrams were there to report on recent developments. I knew that all the outside advisers had been treated to a heavy diet of pessimistic press reports on Vietnam over the past seven or eight weeks. I knew too that staff officers from the State and Defense departments and the CIA had given them a fairly gloomy assessment the night before. I was bothered because that assessment did not square with the situation as I understood it. Later I called in the briefing officers to find out whether they knew something I did not know, or if they had given the Wise Men information that was not reaching me. They insisted that was not the case. I think the explanation was in part that the briefers, in passing on some judgments about Vietnam, especially concerning the situation in rural areas, had used outdated information. In any case, I decided that the briefings had been much less important in shaping the views of these outside advisers than was the general mood of depression and frustration that had swept over so many people as a result of the Tet offensive.

Wheeler reported on his recent trip and his talk with Westmoreland. He said there had been a sharp turnaround both in the military situation and in the mood in Vietnam since his earlier visit in February. At that time, most military forces had been clustered around urban areas to protect them against a second wave of attacks. Now, he said, Vietnamese and allied forces were moving on the offensive. He spoke of Khe Sanh, which had been

---

* The advisory group was composed of former Secretary of State Dean Acheson, former Under Secretary of State George Ball, General Omar Bradley, McGeorge Bundy, Arthur Dean (who had negotiated the Korean War settlement), former Treasury Secretary Douglas Dillon, Ambassador Henry Cabot Lodge, retired diplomat Robert Murphy, General Matthew Ridgway, General Maxwell Taylor, and former Deputy Secretary of Defense Cyrus Vance. We met in the Executive Mansion for lunch.

pictured as a "sitting duck" and as the scene of a potential military disaster for us. Wheeler explained that the four U.S. and one South Vietnamese battalions at Khe Sanh had kept two enemy divisions tied down and forced another division to stay close by to provide support. That meant three enemy divisions kept away from the population centers. The Communists had been badly battered by our artillery and air power and had suffered huge losses. Wheeler judged that the North Vietnamese had abandoned any idea of taking Khe Sanh by force.

On the Tet offensive, Wheeler stated that he saw no reason for "all the doom and gloom we see in the U.S. press." "Most of the setback was here in the United States," he said, "which was one of their objectives."

Abrams pointed out the ARVN * units had performed well during Tet. "We would have had a catastrophe if they had not fought well," he said. They had been in a weakened position when the offensive began, he explained, because about half their personnel were on holiday leave. But at least three Vietnamese division commanders had canceled all leaves and had placed their men on full alert. Abrams said that of the 149 South Vietnamese maneuver battalions 30 had performed "with distinction;" 8 had performed unsatisfactorily; and the rest had fought well. The 1st Vietnamese Division had cleared out most of Hué after the Communists occupied it. Two-thirds of the men in that division became casualties in the battle, but they freed the citadel. Abrams went on to give a unit-by-unit, corps-by-corps analysis of the ARVN and its performance.

I asked Abrams how he would compare our Vietnamese allies with the South Koreans during the 1950–1953 war. He said that they had the same problems, trying to build an army while fighting a war at the same time. "I would say the Vietnamese are doing as well, if not better, than the Koreans," he said.

One of the Wise Men asked Abrams if the enemy could carry out another series of attacks like that at Tet. "No," he said flatly. Another asked if the South Vietnamese could take on a larger part of the fighting once the build-up of their forces was completed. "Yes," Abrams answered. "I would have to quit if I didn't believe that."

After lunch, we went to the Cabinet Room in the West Wing of the White House to continue our discussion. I asked McGeorge Bundy to summarize the views of the group as he understood them. He said that there had been a shift in attitude since we had met the previous November. At that time, he said, they all had hoped for slow and steady progress. That hope had been shaken by Tet. He said the picture they had formed from their discussions the previous night was "not so hopeful," particularly as concerned the countryside.

---

* Army of the Republic of (South) Vietnam.

Dean Acheson agreed with Bundy. He felt that we could no longer do what we set out to do in the time available; we had to disengage from our involvement. Arthur Dean, Douglas Dillon, and George Ball expressed similar sentiments. Ball urged that we stop bombing "in the next six weeks" as a test of Hanoi's intentions. The best method, he thought, would be to ask a world statesman, such as the Pope, to propose a bombing halt and for the United States to accept it. Cy Vance supported Bundy's assessment and Ball's suggestion.

Some of the Wise Men disagreed strongly. General Bradley concurred with the proposed level of troop reinforcement but argued against giving an indication that our will was weakening. Veteran diplomat Bob Murphy said that he was "shaken" by the position of his colleagues. He described their approach as a "giveaway" policy. General Taylor was dismayed by the Bundy-Acheson-Ball wing of the advisers. He had been reading detailed reports on Vietnam for a long time. He said the picture he had formed was "a very different one" from the gloomy estimate described by the others. All the advisers expressed deep concern about the divisions in our country. Some of them felt that those divisions were growing rapidly and might soon force our withdrawal from Vietnam.

At the end of our discussion, I said it appeared to me that six advisers favored some form of disengagement, one was in between, and four were opposed. Mac Bundy said he thought it was not so clear-cut as that. He advised that we wait and see what a shift of emphasis, transferring more of the burden to the South Vietnamese, would accomplish. We should also see what result might come from a bombing halt. I thanked the advisers for their views and their counsel and asked them to continue to be available to me.

As I walked back to my office with Vice President Humphrey, who had listened to the discussion, I was turning over in my mind the opinions I had just heard and what these reactions meant as a reflection of broader opinion. I knew this group had not been reading the detailed reports on Vietnam each day, as I and my principal advisers had, but they were intelligent, experienced men. I had always regarded the majority of them as very steady and balanced. If they had been so deeply influenced by the reports of the Tet offensive, what must the average citizen in the country be thinking? "Tet really set us back," Humphrey said. I had to agree. But I remained convinced that the blow to morale was more of our own doing than anything the enemy had accomplished with its army. We were defeating ourselves.

Work was proceeding on my planned address. The speech had passed through several drafts. In accordance with my instructions on March 20, mention of peace initiatives or bombing halts was avoided while I weighed the various suggestions that had been made. On March 23 McPherson sent me a memo on the subject. He suggested we announce that we were halting the bombing north of the 20th parallel and were sending representatives to Geneva and Rangoon to await the North Vietnamese. This announcement would, as he saw it, "show the American people that we are willing to do every reasonable thing to bring about talks." Rusk called me shortly after I read McPherson's memo, and I mentioned it to him. I said that it seemed to propose an approach upon which he and I had already largely agreed, but I told Rusk that I would send him the memo immediately and asked him to give me his reaction in writing as soon as possible. He said he would take care of it.

Two days later, on March 25, Rusk sent me his formal comments. The plan to stop the bombing was what he had been advocating privately for a month, but he did not like the idea of sending representatives to other capitals to wait for the North Vietnamese to appear. He would prefer, he said, to ask the two co-chairmen of the Geneva Conference (the United Kingdom and the Soviet Union)—and perhaps the three members of the International Control Commission (India, Canada, and Poland)—to be "available to talk to any interested parties about the possibilities of a peaceful settlement." Rusk maintained his position that we make no conditions or demands on the North Vietnamese, but should simply stop the bombing and see how they reacted. If we did wish to set a condition, then or later, for a full bombing halt, we might consider proposing that the North Vietnamese withdraw their forces from the two northernmost provinces of South Vietnam and restore the DMZ. He reminded me again that we should coordinate our moves with Ambassador Bunker and our Vietnamese allies.

We were moving down to the wire. I had decided that I should announce by the end of March my decision to withdraw from consideration as a candidate for reelection. In the small circle of intimates who knew my intentions, the debate continued. Both those who approved of my withdrawal and those against my action kept giving me their reasons. I believe that those who opposed my withdrawal were confident that I would change my mind —and that those who agreed with me were afraid I would.

The troop proposal had been refined and was almost in final condition. I planned to combine disclosure of those figures with the announcement of a bombing halt at the 20th parallel. On the evening of March 27 I had a long talk with Senate Democratic Majority Leader Mike Mansfield in the White House. In the hours we were together, we discussed many things, including my planned statement. I read to him portions of my address and told him I intended to end all bombing north of the 20th parallel. Senator Mansfield informed the Senate of this discussion in the course of Senate debate on April 2.* I was surprised and amused, as I am sure Senator Mansfield

---

* See Chapter 21, pp. 494–95.

must have been, to read later accounts of my March 1968 decisions which suggested that I had been "forced" to change my mind abruptly on March 28 regarding the bombing halt. But of course those who wrote of this imaginary reversal knew little or nothing of my thinking.

On March 28, the day after my talk with the Majority Leader, Rusk, Clifford, Rostow, Bill Bundy, and McPherson gathered in Rusk's office to work over the latest draft of my statement. Clifford raised the peace question I had discussed with him eight days before in our early morning telephone conversation and had repeated to him several times later—namely, that I wanted him and Rusk to include a peace offer in the speech. During the session in Rusk's office, Clifford argued that the latest draft was unsatisfactory because it offered no deescalation and no mention of negotiations. The speech held out no hope for either military victory or for a negotiated settlement. Rusk agreed with Clifford and promptly dictated a statement to his secretary embodying his original proposal, a de facto bombing halt at the 20th parallel. It was agreed that this proposal would be incorporated in an alternate draft. After the meeting, Rostow called the White House to say that Rusk, Clifford, he, and the others were proceeding on an alternate draft of the speech. They wanted to meet with me later in the day to go over the drafts. We assembled in the Cabinet Room at 6:30 P.M.

I looked over the long earlier draft. Then I went through the seven-page alternate containing the peace offer. I slowly read the key passage:

> Beginning immediately, and without waiting for any signal from Hanoi, we will confine our air and naval attacks in North Vietnam to the military targets south of the 20th parallel. That parallel runs about 75 miles south of the cities of Hanoi and Haiphong. North Vietnam's military reaction to this change in our bombing programs will determine both our willingness to confine it—and the reasonableness of our assumption that they would not take advantage of a complete bombing halt during the course of negotiations.

The statement used the same language Rusk had been using for a month,* and it was what I had decided needed to be done, but I felt I still should not say so flatly for fear of another damaging press leak. I indicated that I did not want to comment further at that time.

I walked from the Cabinet Room into my office with Rusk alone. He said

---

* On March 30 the description of the area where the bombing would end was changed in the draft speech at the suggestion of Acting Secretary of State Katzenbach. We had planned to say that the bombing would end "north of the 20th parallel." Katzenbach suggested that the phrase would have little meaning for most people and proposed that we say the bombing would end in North Vietnam "except in the area north of the demilitarized zone, where the continuing enemy build-up directly threatens allied forward positions. . . ." In describing our proposed action to the South Vietnamese authorities, other interested governments, and congressional leaders, however, we always specified the 20th parallel as the southern limit of the no-bombing area.

we should move at once to obtain South Vietnamese approval of our plans, as Bunker would have his hands full. Rusk showed me the draft of a cable he had prepared instructing Bunker to explain our proposal to the South Vietnamese and to ask for their agreement. The cable described the main elements of the plan, including the increase in troops we had finally agreed upon. I read it carefully and approved it. It went out to Saigon at 8:20 that night. Rusk also told me he would make arrangements for the heads of allied governments to be informed of our planned action before I made my announcement. Those messages went out the night of March 30. Their tone was somewhat more pessimistic than I felt, but I knew that Rusk and his colleagues were skeptical that Hanoi would respond in any favorable way. In any case, the main thing was to let our allies know what was coming; they could judge Hanoi's reaction themselves.

I began to feel the pressure lifting. It had been quite a month, but now the wheels were turning; decisions had been made. Only the announcement of those decisions remained. Work continued on the draft of my speech, but it was largely a matter of refinement of language. George Christian and Tom Johnson were polishing a draft of my personal statement on politics.

On the morning of March 29 I received Bunker's thirty-fourth weekly report. He said the Vietnamese were moving forward with plans to mobilize their resources and manpower for the difficult struggle they still faced. On the military front, he said, "U.S. and government forces increasingly took the initiative last week while the level of enemy activity declined." Pacification, the program to bring security to outlying areas, was reviving. Losses of territory to the enemy had been less than feared. I knew that the northeast monsoon was nearly over and that Westmoreland's long-planned offensive in I Corps was approaching jump-off. Soon the men at Khe Sanh would be relieved. The atmosphere was very different from the worries we had suffered and the doubts we had experienced two months before, when the enemy seemed to be everywhere and hitting everything. Now the tide had turned.

As we moved toward our deadline, the process of consulting with leading members of Congress was proceeding. On the morning of March 29, I had a long talk with Senator Richard Russell of Georgia, a long-time friend and chairman of the Armed Services Committee. I informed Senator Russell of the military moves we were planning and of our intention to halt bombing over most of North Vietnam. I also called Secretary Clifford and urged him to inform other key members of the Armed Services Committee of our intentions. He did so the following day, providing a detailed briefing for Senators John Stennis (Democrat of Mississippi), Margaret Chase Smith (Republican of Maine), Stuart Symington (Democrat of Missouri), and Henry Jackson (Democrat of Washington), among others. All these Senators were told that the bombing halt would be effective north of the 20th parallel.

On the morning of March 30 Bunker reported that he had carried out his instructions. He had just met with President Thieu and Vice President Ky and had given them a detailed explanation of our planned action, including the partial bombing halt. "Both men immediately and without hesitation said it was satisfactory," he reported. The two Vietnamese leaders planned a joint press conference a few days later to underscore their unity and to call on their country to make an all-out effort to meet the enemy threat.

My biggest worry was not Vietnam itself; it was the divisiveness and pessimism at home. I knew the American people were deeply worried. I had seen the effects of Tet on some of the Wise Men. I looked on my approaching speech as an opportunity to help right the balance and provide better perspective. For the collapse of the home front, I knew well, was just what Hanoi was counting on. The enemy had failed in Vietnam; would Hanoi succeed in the United States? I did not think so, but I was deeply concerned.

Every President in this century has had to assume that there would be opposition to any war in which we became involved. That was true not only during the Korean War but also, though to a lesser extent, during World Wars I and II. It is never easy to accept the idea that fighting, with all its horrors and pain and loss, is preferable to the alternatives. I sensed that another idea was now influencing many Americans, including men who had played a major part in our critical decisions since 1965. They seemed to feel that the bitter debate and noisy dissension at home about Vietnam were too high a price to pay for honoring our commitment in Southeast Asia. They deplored the demonstrations and turbulent arguments about Vietnam. So did I. They wanted money poured into the deteriorating cities and into other public programs that would improve the life of our disadvantaged citizens. So did I, though I knew there was no guarantee Congress would vote those additional funds even if the war ended. They seemed to be saying that anything that happened in Asia or the rest of the world was less important than the strains we were suffering at home.

I could never agree with this argument. My own assessment in 1965 and in 1968 (and today) was that abandoning our pledges and our commitment in Vietnam would generate more and worse controversy at home, not less. Such abandonment would bring vastly greater dangers—in Laos, Cambodia, Thailand, and elsewhere, including India and Pakistan—than would a policy of seeing our commitment through in Southeast Asia. In 1947 the British were able to pass on to us their responsibilities in Greece and Turkey. In 1954 the French knew they could transfer the problem of Southeast Asia's security to our shoulders. But if the United States abandoned its responsibilities, who would pick them up? The answer, in the short run, was: No one. As I had said in 1965, we did not ask to be the guardians at the gate, but there was no one else. There was no question in my mind that the vacuum created by our abdication would be filled inevitably by the Communist powers.

As I reflected on the situation in Vietnam and the forces gathering strength in Asia, I felt that there was another answer—*if* this nation of ours had the stubborn patience to see it through. That answer was that we could shift an increasing share of responsibility to the Vietnamese and the other peoples of Asia. It was not inevitable that we would continue carrying the major burden year after year. The South Vietnamese army and populace had withstood the heaviest blows the enemy could launch during Tet, and we had seen them move forward, not fall back. During my trip through Asia in 1966 I had seen one country after another moving forward with great energy in economic and social reform. In addition to that, every national leader with whom I spoke said that in the future Asians would have to work more closely together and take more responsibility for their own security and development.

Looking ahead, I could not see a time when the United States could, with safety, withdraw totally from Asia and the Pacific, for we were a Pacific power with a profound interest in the stability, peace, and progress of that vital part of the world. But I *could* see a time when our share of the burden for that stability, that peace, and that progress would diminish greatly. If we failed to act in that patient, measured way, I believed that we would be risking far greater casualties, far more danger, than we faced in Vietnam. I feared that many Americans did not understand the real choices facing us in Asia. I knew that some people had changed their stand on Vietnam completely because of discouragement, and others for purely political reasons.

At the beginning of March 1968 I was concerned that we might have to contribute considerably more to Vietnam—more men, more equipment, more money. I have described the various influences that eased my concern and shaped my final decision. For me, the key influence was the change in the situation in Vietnam. But other matters, especially our financial problems, played an important part in that final decision.

Early in March I was convinced that I should make some sort of peace offer along the lines Rusk had suggested on February 27. I considered several other proposals during the month, and I considered doing nothing, but the weight of evidence favored a move in this direction and I regarded Rusk's proposal as the best.

I wanted the South Vietnamese to carry a heavier share of the burden of fighting for their country. At the beginning of March I had serious doubts that they could do much more. As each day passed I became increasingly confident that these people whom we had pledged to help were not only willing but able to do more. Their performance represented a remarkable transformation, one that all too few Americans were aware of, then or even now.

Finally, I had decided not to run for another term in the White House. That decision was intimately linked with the others, especially with the plan to stop most of the bombing.

I had made these four decisions, but I could have unmade any one or all of them right down to the time I sat behind my desk and began to speak on television on the night of March 31. If the enemy in Vietnam had suddenly launched a large and devastating new series of attacks, our reaction would have been strong. If I had then become convinced withdrawing from politics would have undermined our men in Vietnam or harmed our country, I would have changed my mind. Hanoi's actions or statements could have caused us to call off or alter the bombing proposal at the last moment. War or a serious incident could have erupted elsewhere in the world. Any one of dozens of things *could* have happened, and in each case I would have reconsidered my decisions and changed my course if necessary. But those things, thank God, did not happen. I went forward with the decisions that had taken shape in my mind years, months, and days earlier.

I repeat: No President, at least not this President, makes a decision until he publicly announces that decision and acts upon it. When did I make the decisions that I announced the evening of March 31, 1968? The answer is: 9:01 P.M. on March 31, 1968, and they are the same decisions I would make in retrospect. Time alone will reveal whether they were wise decisions —but good or bad I made them, and the full responsibility is mine.

18

A Beginning and an End: March 31, 1968

WHEN I TOOK THE OATH as President in January 1965 to begin my first full term in office, I felt that it would be my last, and this feeling grew stronger with every passing week in the White House. I have already described the conviction I had, after the 1964 election, that I would have to get my program through quickly. At the end of the first year of my administration, I was reasonably certain that by the time my term was over I would have gone as far as I could.

Two hospitalizations for surgery while I was in the White House had sharpened my apprehensions about my health. My heart attack of 1955 seemed well behind me, but I was conscious that it was part of the background of my life—just as I was conscious of my family's history of stroke and heart disease. I did not fear death so much as I feared disability. Whenever I walked through the Red Room and saw the portrait of Woodrow Wilson hanging there, I thought of him stretched out upstairs in the White House, powerless to move, with the machinery of the American government in disarray around him. And I remembered Grandmother Johnson, who had had a stroke and stayed in a wheelchair throughout my childhood, unable even to move her hands or to speak so that she could be understood.

I have very strong feelings about work. When it is there to be done, I do it. And the work of the Presidency is demanding and unrelenting. It is always there to be done. Of all the 1,886 nights I was President, there were not many when I got to sleep before 1 or 2 A.M., and there were few mornings when I didn't wake up by 6 or 6:30. It became a question of how much the physical constitution could take. I frankly did not believe in

1968 that I could survive another four years of the long hours and unremitting tensions I had just gone through.

These were considerations I had lived with from the beginning. Others had developed in the course of events. On that last morning in March, as I moved toward one of the most significant hours of my life, several factors relating to the state of the nation fed into the decisions I was preparing to announce. First, we faced the absolute necessity of an increase in taxes.* For two years the Chairman of the Council of Economic Advisers had been stressing the need for a tax increase in the strongest terms. I knew that the stability of the dollar and the economic health of the nation and the world demanded an increase at the earliest possible time. I also knew that the likelihood of obtaining the necessary Republican votes to propel a tax bill through Congress, particularly in an election year, would be close to zero if I were a candidate for reelection. Second, we faced the possibility of new riots and turmoil in the cities in the summer of 1968. We had experienced widespread disturbances the previous summer, many of them exploited, I believe, by men who took advantage of distressed people to advance their own political causes. There were strong indications that rioting might be repeated or increased. FBI Director J. Edgar Hoover had reported to me on May 31:

> The racial violence that has already erupted this spring clearly indicates that the United States faces the probability of riots and disturbances on an even more massive scale in the months ahead. Ever present in every urban area in the land are the sparks of violence which could detonate riots. Although some cities have heretofore enjoyed seemingly harmonious race relations and racial peace, no city is immune from possible violence today.

The principal responsibility for dealing with such disorders rests with the nation's mayors and Governors, but in a few cities in 1967 I had been asked to invoke Presidential authority and send in federal troops. It seemed likely that I might face the same decisions again. I did not want the slightest suspicion to arise—in Congress, the media, or any segment of the public—that I had responded with too little or too much, too soon or too late, with one eye on the safety of our citizens and the other on Election Day.

Finally, there was the question of Vietnam. I had been preparing a speech on this subject to deliver to the American people late in March. In that speech I wanted to restate our position in Vietnam as clearly as possible—why we were there, what we hoped to achieve. I wanted to put the enemy's Tet offensive in proper perspective, and now that the offensive had been blunted and there was a chance that the enemy might respond

* See Chapter 19.

favorably, I wanted to announce our new initiative for peace. If we were going to take the risk of a bombing pause, I felt I should make it clear that my decision had been made without political considerations. I wanted that decision to be understood by the enemy and by everyone everywhere as a serious and sincere effort to find a road to peace. The most persuasive way to get this across, I believed, would be to couple my announcement of a bombing halt with the statement that I would not be a candidate for reelection.

I also hoped that the combined announcement would accomplish something else. The issue of Vietnam had created divisions and hostilities among Americans, as I had feared. I wanted to heal some of those wounds and restore unity to the nation. This speech might help to do that. I deeply hoped so.

For several years Lady Bird and I had spoken many times about our plans to leave the White House at the end of my first full term. Her position had remained perfectly clear and consistent since she had first expressed it to me in the spring of 1964: She did not want me to be a candidate in 1968. We discussed often how to select the proper time and the right occasion to make the announcement.

As the months wore on, we talked it over with our daughters and their husbands. The girls' reactions were divided. Luci did not want me to run. She insisted that she wanted a living father. Lynda's response was more complex. As a daughter, she said, she would prefer that I not run, but as a citizen she hoped I would. Later, when her husband, Marine Captain Charles Robb, was under orders to go to Vietnam, her reaction as a citizen superseded her reaction as a daughter.

Long before I had settled on the proper forum to make my announcement, I told a number of people of my intention not to run again. As far back as the summer of 1965 I had discussed the subject with Willard Deason, whom I had known for many years. Bill was a good executive, and I wanted to assign him to a responsible government post. There were two commission openings for which he was well qualified. One was a post on the Interstate Commerce Commission, for a fixed seven-year term. The other was at the pleasure of the President, for no fixed term. I offered him a choice, but on the basis of our long friendship and association, I told him in confidence that he should know that my plans were not to seek another term. "In that case," Bill said, "I'll take ICC."

A few months afterward, late in the fall of 1965, I confided in Arthur Krim. He and his wife, Mathilde, were loyal and devoted friends, and Arthur was a valued adviser on matters relating to the Democratic party. On this occasion we were discussing ways to reduce the Democratic

National Committee's debt. I said that I regarded the debt as a personal one, to be paid before I left the Presidency. In the course of the conversation Arthur observed that a strong committee would be important to me in 1968. I told him then that I would not be running in 1968. Over the following years I repeated my decision to him many times. I always cautioned him that the Democratic committee should make no organizational or fund-raising plans for 1968 on the assumption that I would head the ticket.

I talked with John Connally early in 1967 at the LBJ Ranch. He was formulating plans of his own at the time. He told me that he had no desire to seek another term as Governor, but that he would run again if I wanted him on the ticket with me in Texas. I told him that I felt certain I would not run and suggested that he base his own decision on that assumption.

In September 1967 I discussed the subject with another friend, George Christian, my press secretary. We were in Texas at the time, and I asked George to get Governor Connally's help in preparing a statement in which I could announce my decision. I thought then that I might find an appropriate occasion to use it later in the year.

I talked privately about the likelihood of my not running in 1968 with both Dean Rusk and Bob McNamara, two of my most trusted advisers. One July evening in 1967, while sitting in the small room adjoining the President's Oval Office, I confided to Secretary McNamara the frank exchanges I had had with Connally. I told Bob I was convinced that once the announcement was made the press would read significance into Connally's decision not to run, as it related to my plans. McNamara assured me many times that he would continue to serve as Secretary of Defense as long as I wanted and needed him, and I know he meant it. As a footnote to history, had I contemplated another four years in the White House, I would not have wanted Bob McNamara to leave the government, any more than I would have wanted Dean Rusk to leave.

At a meeting in the Cabinet Room on October 3, 1967, I again shared my thoughts with Secretaries Rusk and McNamara, and with several other top advisers who were present. They included Walt Rostow, Dick Helms of the CIA, and George Christian. We had had a long session on the Middle East, nuclear planning, anti-ballistic missiles, Vietnam, and other matters. I sat there wondering what the effect on these various pressing considerations would be if I were to announce my intention not to run for another term. Then I confided to the men assembled around the table the gist of my thinking. I told them that if I were announcing a decision at the moment, it would be not to stand for reelection. They all respected my confidence.

In those final months, as the announcement of my decision neared, I believe only one thing could have changed my mind—an indication that the men in Vietnam would regard it as unfair or unwise. I asked General Westmoreland to come home in November 1967, and I put the question directly to him. As we sat in the family living room on the second floor of the White House one evening after dinner, I asked him what the effect on troop morale would be if I announced that I would not run for another term. Would the men think the Commander in Chief who had sent them to the battlefield had let them down?

General Westmoreland looked for a few moments at the windows facing out on the rose garden. Then he turned to me. "Mr. President," he said, "I do not believe so." Measuring his words as he went along, he said that he felt most of the men in Vietnam would completely understand the decision. Westmoreland was a man I could trust, with decisions or anything else, and he never, as far as I know, even told his wife. If he did tell her, she kept the confidence as well as he did.

A few others knew the decision I had made on my political future. One was William S. White, the columnist. I told him as a friend of thirty-six years and not as a newspaperman. He kept my confidence. I also told Marvin Watson, my appointments secretary; Juanita Roberts and Marie Fehmer, my personal secretaries; and one or two others. In the meantime, John Connally had publicly announced in November 1967 that he would not be a candidate for another term as Governor of Texas. I was surprised and relieved, as I told Bob McNamara, that there was so little speculation in the press connecting Connally's political plans with mine.

December came, but a good forum for my announcement failed to materialize, and I put the matter aside for a few weeks. I began to think about including my decision in my State of the Union address to the Congress in January. When I went to Australia to attend the memorial service for Prime Minister Harold Holt late in December 1967, I took Horace Busby with me. A former aide, Busby had worked with me on messages in the past. During the trip I told him what I planned to do and what I wanted to say. I asked him to try his hand at a statement. Busby's draft arrived two days before I reported on the State of the Union and contained the following paragraph:

> I shall not seek—I have no desire to accept—the nomination of my party for another term in this great office of all the people.

I gave it to my wife to read. In all our conversations about declining to run in 1968, Lady Bird had always been most deferential. She never took the lead in these discussions or forced an opinion or a point of view on me. However, I noticed that she made one important change in Busby's draft. Above the phrase "have no desire to accept" Lady Bird penciled in the words we both preferred: "will not accept."

I gave Busby's draft to George Christian. I asked him to compare it with the version he had written earlier and to see whether he could combine the best parts of both statements. John Connally and others had recommended strongly to me that I make the announcement at the end of the State of the Union message, and I wanted as forceful a statement as possible. The draft George returned to me was on four typewritten sheets. It began, "Now I would like to speak to you on a personal matter . . .," and it led to this conclusion: "With the priorities thus divided, and with due concern for the future of my country, I have prayerfully concluded that I will not be a candidate for reelection."

I asked Lady Bird to look this draft over. She too had written one at my request. Hers was shorter than George's and, she thought, not as good. She preferred his version.

When I went to the Capitol that night, I thought I had the statement with me but I discovered that I had failed to bring it. Frankly, I cannot say what I would have done that night if the paper had been in my pocket. But my best guess is that I would not have read it. Although the State of the Union occasion would have provided an excellent forum for my announcement, I sensed that the timing was not the best. I was asking the Congress that night for a heavy and demanding program. To couple such a request with a statement that I was not going to run for President might suggest to various people that I was not willing to fight for what I was asking. After my address, George Christian told me that all through my speech he had waited expectantly for me to pull the paper out of my pocket. I advised him to keep the statement up to date. In the meantime, little attention was paid during this period to the fact that I refused to enter ten primaries in which the choice to enter, before March 31, was mine.*

Once past the State of the Union message, I wanted to put on the books every attainable bill. Another consideration was that my administration was never without at least one crisis. I was concerned that as soon as I made my announcement both my effectiveness in handling crises and my ability to get legislation passed would be impaired. I had to walk that tightrope until the last possible moment.

But I knew that if other Democrats were to have an opportunity to organize and offer their candidacies, they deserved sufficient time to prepare. Harry S. Truman had faced a similar decision on timing in 1952. He had finally made his announcement on March 29. Lady Bird had suggested March as the outside date for announcing my decision not to run. In her memorandum to me of May 1964, recommending that I run for the Presidency that year, she had said: "If you win, let's do the best we can for 3 years and 3 or 4 months—and then, the Lord letting

---

* My name appeared only on the Wisconsin primary ballot. To remove it, I would have had to file an affidavit in February, thus announcing my intentions in an inappropriate way and sooner than I wished.

us live that long, announce in February or March 1968 that you are not a candidate for reelection." She told me that the reason March was in her mind was that she had been influenced by President Truman's timing. I found a certain historical satisfaction in following President Truman's precedent. But March 1968 proved to be exactly the right month for me for another reason: It coincided with the new effort I planned to seek the way to peace in Vietnam. I had found the right forum.

Late in March, while work on my forthcoming speech on Vietnam progressed, I asked Horace Busby to make a new try at drafting the announcement. I told him I wanted a statement that would be as clear and effective as he and I together could make it. Busby sent me his new version on Saturday, March 30. I was in the Cabinet Room going over the final draft of the rest of the address, which was scheduled to be given the following day, March 31. I read what Busby had rewritten and then slid the paper across the table to George Christian. This, I told him, would be the peroration of my speech. George read it in silence, his face betraying no reaction.

Our daughter Lynda had been flying all night from California on the "Red Eye Special." She had just said good-by to her husband, Chuck, who was leaving for duty in Vietnam. Mrs. Johnson and I got up early and were waiting at the south entrance of the White House to welcome her home. When she arrived, a little after 7 A.M. that Sunday morning, we all went up together to the family quarters on the second floor of the Executive Mansion.

Lynda was tired, and she seemed lonely and bewildered. War and separation were cruel intrusions into her young life. The divisions in the country had left their mark on her, as they had on her mother and her sister, Luci. Lynda had been reading about those demonstrators and critics who looked on such sacrifices as hers and Chuck's as meaningless, or worse. The hurt that had been building up inside her was now released in a flood of tears. Why, she asked, was her husband going away to fight, and maybe die, for people who did not even want to be protected? It was a question that might have been asked by any young woman who had just seen her husband off to Vietnam. I wanted to comfort her, and I could not.

That was the way the day started—March 31, 1968—a day that I profoundly hoped would mark the beginning of the end of the war that had brought so much pain and anguish to the people of my country. The day marked as well the beginning of the end of my career, which stretched back over nearly four decades of public service.

After breakfast I went to mass with Luci and her husband, Pat Nugent, at St. Dominic's. This was one of my favorite churches, a somber, gray

Victorian-Gothic structure, with twin spires rising above the modern construction that was going up around it, in a poor section of southwest Washington. Inside St. Dominic's was simple and restful. I had gone there on many Sunday mornings, and on numerous unreported occasions I had dropped in for a few minutes of prayer late at night. I went there with Luci just before midnight in June 1966 when we sent our bombers to hit the fuel dumps in Hanoi and Haiphong.

After mass was over and we were back in the car, I closed the glass partition to the front seat and told Luci and Pat that I had something to read to them and that I wanted them to listen carefully. As we rode through the quiet streets of Washington that Sunday morning, I read to my daughter and her husband the statement destined to change, to some extent at least, the lives of all of us. When I finished, there was silence. I saw tears begin to form in Luci's eyes, and I said to her that I thought this was what she had wanted me to do. Trying to smile, she replied that her reaction was complicated. I understood. No matter how strong and simple the conviction, when you got right to the finish line it *was* complicated.

Looking at both of them, I experienced emotions too overwhelming to express. They were so very young, and they had such promising and happy lives ahead of them, if they were lucky. Pat already had his orders for Vietnam. In a matter of days, by his own insistence, he would be with Chuck Robb in action in Vietnam. The good Lord had blessed us with two brave sons-in-law, and no man could have been prouder of them than I. Now, for a year or more, their wives would wait and pray, as other wives across America would, for their husbands to return to them and their babies.

I was never more certain of the rightness of my decision. I was putting everything I could command and everything I had personally into the search for peace—not a false peace carrying the seeds of a new war, but a true peace forged to endure, with freedom intact. The speech I planned to make that evening would be, more than anything else, my pledge of faith to the Pat Nugents and the Chuck Robbs of our country—and to all the brave young men and women of their generation.

We drove to the apartment of Hubert and Muriel Humphrey. In a separate area of their living room I met alone with the Vice President and told him of my plans. He had already been informed, in effect, more than a year before, when I had urged him to go to every state in the Union and select his best friends, so that they would be ready to rally when he needed them. Now he accepted the news somberly. He planned to go to Mexico City later that day, and as we shook hands and said good-by, he told me that he hoped to God I wouldn't go through with it.

Horace Busby was waiting for me in the Treaty Room on the second floor of the White House when I returned. I worked with him, putting the final touches on the speech—changing a phrase here, a word there, strengthening an idea or a thought. I wanted to say precisely what was in my heart and mind. I believed that because of the "informed guidance" the press had given the people, all the nation—except a dozen or so individuals—would be shocked and surprised. On February 5, for example, the *U.S. News and World Report* had assured its readers:

> At this point, there is just one near certainty about the '68 elections. . . . Lyndon Johnson, health permitting, will be the Democratic nominee for a new term as President.

Carl Rowan, in his February 17 column in the *Chicago Daily News,* declared that the odds of my not running again "can't be better than a million to one." Only a few months before, late in 1967, reporter Tom Wicker had written in *The New York Times:*

> Isn't it possible that Johnson will withdraw? This wistful proposition can be demolished with some confidence. It is as likely that Lyndon Johnson will get out of the White House and go back to Texas as it is that Dean Rusk will turn dove, Dick Nixon will stop running, or J. Edgar Hoover will retire.

These were typical of virtually all the press speculations about my plans. A great misconception had been built up by the press that I was a man who was hungry for power, who would not conceivably give up power willingly. Those who believed this estimate did not understand that power can lose its charm when a man has known it as many years as I had. I was consistently amused at being characterized as avid for power on the one hand and soundly criticized for not using power the way it is used ordinarily—in a political way—on the other. Several columnists commented that I did not take sufficient interest in rewarding party contributors or building strong party machinery, but these observations never detracted from the myth of the power-hungry man.

I used the power of the Presidency proudly, and I used every ounce of it I had. I used it to establish programs that gave thousands of youngsters a head start in school, that enabled thousands of old folks to live in clean nursing homes, that brought justice to the Negro and hope to the poor, that forced the nation to face the growing problems of pollution. In this exercise of power, I knew a satisfaction that only a limited number of men have ever known and that I could have had in no other way. Men, myself included, do not lightly give up the opportunity to achieve so much lasting good, but a man who uses power effectively must also be a realist. He must understand that by spending power he dissipates it. Because I had not hesitated to spend the Presidential power in the pursuit of my beliefs or in the interests of my country, I was under no illusion that I had as much power in 1968 as I had had in 1964.

When we returned to the White House that afternoon, I read the statement aloud to Arthur and Mathilde Krim, who were spending the weekend with us. Previously, when we had discussed my intention not to run again, they had opposed my decision. They purposefully did so again. Arthur argued that the new peace offer we were announcing would strengthen my candidacy. Why go that extra step? he asked. I answered that only by taking that extra step could I assure the effectiveness of the offer. Otherwise, I said, my sincerity would be questioned. The speech would be written off as a political gesture.

Krim continued his opposition through lunch. Luci, Pat, and Mathilde said very little, but they made it clear that Arthur was speaking for them as well. Lady Bird said nothing, but I already knew which side she was on. I listened while Krim outlined the reasons he thought I should abandon my announcement. Essentially, they were based on his belief that of all the likely Presidential prospects, I could best carry forward the important work begun in my administration. I appreciated his confidence, but I was not persuaded by his argument. My own review of the situation, as honest and searching a review as I could make, had convinced me that the course I had chosen was the one that offered the country the best hope of peace and unity.

That afternoon I worked again on the final draft of my speech. I read the text of the speech aloud—without the ending. At 8:10 P.M., less than an hour before I was scheduled to go on the air, I turned the final paragraphs over to Marie Fehmer to be put on the teleprompter. I went into my bedroom and asked Marvin Watson to join me for some last-minute instructions before the speech. I was putting on my jacket when he came in. Arthur Krim was behind him. I looked at the clock. It was 8:40. Arthur waited until I had given my messages to Marvin and then said that I still had time to change my mind and that "everyone outside" hoped I would. I looked with affection and gratitude at my old friend. I did not know who was included in "everyone outside," but it was obvious that Arthur was speaking with great earnestness and deep sincerity. I told him quietly that there would be no change in my decision.

At that moment, two men arrived who had been at my side through the difficult days just past, Clark Clifford and Walt Rostow. I showed them the statement for the first time. Walt read it in silence. Clifford looked at me and said, in effect: "After what you've been through, you are entitled to make this decision. No one would be justified in asking you to go on carrying the burdens of the Presidency."

I left for the Oval Office with Rostow. On the way I told him to ask General Wheeler to telephone General Westmoreland immediately, with the message that I would act shortly on the matter I had informed him of last November. Then I observed to Walt that he had not yet said a word. He answered that as lame ducks it would be hard for us to get all the things done that we would like to do, but that we would give it a good try. He said I could count on his staying with me to the last day. I told him that I knew that.

In the Oval Office the television cameras were waiting. The TV broadcast was being supervised by Deputy Press Secretary Robert H. Fleming, a former television executive. I saw a look of shocked surprise on his face when he read the last portion of the teleprompter tape. George Christian brought a small press pool to the door of the office to watch the proceedings. I thought to myself: "They're in for a surprise too." My wife and daughters and my son-in-law Pat sat to my right, off camera. The technicians made last-minute adjustments.

At 9:01 P.M., on a signal from the network director, I launched into the speech I had been preparing for so long. I described the enemy's Tet offensive, what it had tried to do and what it had failed to do. I announced our plans for strengthening the South Vietnamese armed forces, which had been expanded by the courageous response of the Vietnamese people to the attacks at Tet. I said it was time to begin talking peace anew. I was ready to take the first step to deescalate the war.

"Tonight," I said, "I have ordered our aircraft and our naval vessels to make no attacks on North Vietnam, except in the area north of the demilitarized zone, where the continuing enemy build-up directly threatens allied forward positions and where the movements of their troops and supplies are clearly related to that threat."

I voiced my hope that Hanoi would match our restraint, so that we could halt even limited bombing, and that both sides would sit down together soon to bargain for peace. Finally, I said:

> With America's sons in the fields far away, with America's future under challenge right here at home, with our hopes and the world's hopes for peace in the balance every day, I do not believe that I should devote an hour or a day of my time to any personal partisan causes or to any duties other than the awesome duties of this office—the Presidency of your country.
>
> Accordingly, I shall not seek, and I will not accept, the nomination of my party for another term as your President.
>
> But let men everywhere know, however, that a strong, a confident, and a vigilant America stands ready tonight to seek an honorable peace—and stands ready tonight to defend an honored cause—whatever the price, whatever the burden, whatever the sacrifice that duty may require.
>
> Thank you for listening.
>
> Good night and God bless all of you.

In forty-five minutes I had finished. It was all over and I felt better. The weight of the day and the weeks and the months had lifted. I had done what I knew ought to be done. Now it was history and I could do no more. We walked from the Oval Office back to the Executive Mansion.

The phones started ringing—Hubert Humphrey from Mexico City, John Connally from Austin, and Mayor Dick Daley from Chicago; Abigail McCarthy * and Abe Fortas; Senator Clinton Anderson and actress Tallulah Bankhead; Mariallen Moursund from Round Mountain, Texas, and Dr. Frank Stanton from New York City; Denver publisher Palmer Hoyt and Governor Nelson Rockefeller; members of the Cabinet and staff, friends from every part of my life, and friends from across the nation whose names I had never heard and whose faces I had never seen. The telephone operators reported later that the switchboard was lighted up throughout the night. Basically, all the calls expressed the same sentiments. They were messages wishing me well from people who simply wanted me to know they were thinking of me. I could not take all the calls myself and the callers understood that, but they left their names and something of themselves that I will remember to the end of my life. There was a steady refrain: "Just tell him my prayers are with him."

At eleven o'clock that night I met with the White House regular reporters. I had said all I had to say in my statement, but I spent half an hour or more with them. The first question I was asked was: "How irrevocable is your decision?" I answered: "Completely irrevocable." Another reporter asked: "How do you feel?" I said: "I think I feel pretty good." And I did. When I went back to my guests and friends and staff members, everyone seemed quiet and thoughtful. Most of them appeared to be sad. Someone remarked that I was the only one present who was relaxed. Marie Fehmer jotted down something she heard me say: "I never was surer of any decision I ever made in my life. I have 525,000 men whose very lives depend on what I do, and I must not be worried about primaries. I must be working full time for those men out there. . . ."

At 1 A.M. I went to my bedroom. I was tired. It had been a long day, a day marking an end but also, I earnestly hoped, a beginning. I prayed silently that the action I had taken would bear the fruit I devoutly hoped for. By renouncing my candidacy, I expressed a fervent wish that problems that had resisted solution would now yield to resolution. I wanted Hanoi to know that Lyndon Johnson was not using this new move toward peace as a bid for personal political gain. Maybe now, with this clearest possible evidence of our sincerity thrown into the balance, North Vietnam would come forward and agree to a dialogue—a genuine communication dedicated to peace. Those who doubted me and disliked me, those who had fought my struggle to achieve justice for men and women who had for so long suffered injustice, might now be willing to adjust their rigid views and

---

* Mrs. Eugene McCarthy.

seek to fashion a workable formula for peace in the streets. Members of Congress who had believed that my crusade for the tax bill was linked to personal politics rather than an attempt to defeat inflation might reassess their motives, soften their antagonism, and turn this urgent piece of legislation—so vital to the nation's and the world's needs—into law.

Perhaps now that I was not a candidate commentators in the press and television might regard issues and efforts more objectively, instead of concentrating on criticism and cynical speculation. For a while the nation and the world would reflect on my words.

Just before I drifted off to sleep that night, I prayed that Hanoi had listened and would respond. The chance for peace, the opportunity to stop death and destruction, the opening toward a new decade of hope— all these were enfolded in the words I had spoken. There was nothing more I could do that day. All that I could do I had done.

19

Bite the Bullet

For twenty-nine years Capitol Hill was my home. In all those years I thought I knew Congress fairly well, understood its many moods, grasped its essential nature. But like other Presidents with previous experience on Capitol Hill, I found that once I reached the White House the Congress appeared far less familiar. However close we might remain, I knew that our relationship could never be the same.

The Constitution deliberately makes the President and the Congress competitors as well as partners. The Founding Fathers created an elaborate system of checks and balances to keep each partner self-reliant while still assuring their interdependence. No brief account can fully capture the complexity of this relationship, in which each partner contributes his own share of stubbornness, pride, hostility, warmth, suspicion, skill, and affection. What follows is one scene in a play of many acts. It is the story of my long struggle with the Congress to obtain a tax surcharge, a struggle that reveals the sources of conflict between the President and the Congress.

In the days of the Old Economics federal spending was generally regarded, in congressional rhetoric, as close to sin—unless it was for your own constituency. A budget surplus was the height of virtue, a deficit the symbol of shame. Political figures regularly compared the federal budget to a family budget and warned of disaster if it remained in the red for long. Recessions and depressions were the unavoidable evils of a business cycle in which expansion and decline followed one another as winter follows autumn.

With the triumph of the New Economics in the enactment of the tax cut of 1964, most of these stereotypes seemed to be laid to rest. Many inhibitions against direct governmental intervention to stimulate or brake the economy were apparently lifted. The Legislative and the Executive branches seemed finally to have reached a "meeting of the minds" on taxation. But stimulation proved easier than braking, and the meeting of the minds proved temporary.

True to its sponsors' promise, the tax cut brought our economy close to full employment. It stimulated economic expansion, increased production, and strengthened consumer markets. Unemployment fell to its lowest level in eight years. But this achievement was short-lived. Our sluggish economy had indeed been stimulated, but with the rising cost of the war in Vietnam on top of growing consumer demand, the economy was dangerously close to overheating late in 1965. We tried to cool it down, but with each passing month inflation rose.

The situation reminded me of the day the first train was scheduled to pull out of Fredericksburg, Texas, near where I was born. It was a big occasion for our little town, with a special ceremony, flowery speeches, and a pretty girl ready to cut a bright red ribbon. The excitement grew as the time for departure arrived. The engine sputtered, the ribbon fell to the ground, and a trumpet blared—but the train did not move. An old man sitting in the stands spoke out in a loud voice: "They'll never get it started." The crowd shuffled nervously. Minutes passed. Then the train began to sputter again, and finally it started to move—slowly at first, but picking up speed as it rounded a bend and disappeared from sight. Several spectators turned to the doubting old man. "Well," they demanded, "what do you think now?" He looked down the empty track and growled: "They'll never get it stopped."

The old man's reaction seemed to apply to our economic situation. With the tax cut, our economic train began moving, but once it started down the track it picked up speed and gathered its own momentum. Now the big question was: Could we slow it down without losing the great benefits of prosperity?

The first signs of trouble appeared late in 1965 and early in 1966. Business was spending heavily on new plant and equipment, in response to earlier tax measures that had made investment more profitable and to the rising consumer demand stimulated by the 1964 tax cut. Then came increasing governmental expenditures for critically needed domestic programs in the areas of education, health, manpower, and poverty. Still, we were able to meet all these demands until we ran into the sudden and sharp expansion of our defense requirements. Together, these factors raised total demand faster than production could expand.

As a result, prices increased in 1965. As living costs rose, workers sought higher wages, in excess of productivity increases. As wages raised production costs, producers set higher prices. I saw dangerous inflation creeping in.

In the New Economics the remedy was theoretically clear: immediate government action. Just as the tax cut had stimulated a sluggish economy, so a tax increase was needed to cool an overheated economy. Gardner Ackley, Chairman of the Council of Economic Advisers, sent me a memo in December 1965, stating:

> If the budget is $115 billion, there is little question in my mind that a significant tax increase will be needed to prevent an intolerable degree of inflationary pressure. With a budget of $110 billion the question is more difficult. My tentative view now is that a tax increase would probably still be necessary.*

We soon discovered that the gap between economic theory and political reality was far wider than it had been two years before. The tax cut, despite initial resistance, was popular with the folks back home. As Budget Director Kermit Gordon had pointed out in 1964: "Virtue is so much easier when duty and self-interest coincide." It is not too difficult to convince someone that he will be better off with more take-home pay. But try to convince him that he will be better off tomorrow by losing part of his income today. This obvious difference goes a long way toward explaining the conflict and cooperation between the President and the Congress during the long tax struggle.

One major source of conflict between the Legislative and Executive branches is the difference in constituency. The President is concerned with the economic well-being of the entire nation. Congress, by contrast, is the product of 50 state and 435 local constituencies, each representing only one piece of the national jigsaw puzzle. Many Congressmen and Senators understood my concern for the economy as a whole, but each legislator had one overriding need—to make a record with the people who sent him to office. On the subject of taxes, the people were extremely vocal. Mail on the Hill was running heavily against a tax increase.† On many days in 1966 one or another Congressman would call me to say that he was with me in spirit—he understood my predicament and sympathized with me, but it would be political suicide for him to support a tax increase.

A second area of conflict is the difference in information. On economic questions, I had the opinions of a wide range of experts in the Council

---

* The budget I actually submitted in January 1966 came to $112.8 billion.

† Even as late as January 1968 a Gallup poll showed that 79 per cent of the American people were opposed to raising taxes. (See *The New York Times*, January 24, 1968.)

of Economic Advisers, the Treasury, and the Bureau of the Budget. By 1966 these advisers were united in both their diagnosis of the economic problem and their prescribed remedy. In their judgment, inflation was being created by a high level of income which was forcing prices up because demand was outpacing the capacity to produce. The remedy: a tax increase to hold demand to acceptable levels.

While a President has a large number of experts and statisticians available, the individual Congressman must rely on a personal staff of three or four and a committee staff of half a dozen or less. Consequently, he must either accept our facts, which he often dislikes doing, or find his own sources of information. Those sources were readily available. Though most economists agreed that a tax increase was needed to combat inflation, a significant minority disagreed, and their arguments did not go unheeded.

Throughout most of the struggle a majority of the members of the House Ways and Means Committee, which is responsible for writing tax bills, operated from a different reading of the economy than ours. In their judgment, inflation was caused not by excessive demand but by producers passing on higher costs, especially wages, as higher prices. Other members of Congress believed that the solution was to reduce government spending. There was little agreement on which items of the budget should be cut. In fact, it was difficult to hold back the Appropriations Committee and the Congress as a whole from increasing the amounts in my budget. Senator William Proxmire of Wisconsin, a member of the Joint Economic Committee, held still another view. He agreed that "in a booming, bursting, zooming economy a tax increase is the right medicine to stop inflationary pressure." But he did not believe that our economy was booming. On the contrary, he thought that the principal trouble was excessive cost, not excessive demand, and that demand for most products was actually deficient. If this were true, a tax increase would only make things worse by reducing demand even further.

These were all honest differences of opinion based on conflicting evaluations, varying sources of information, and contradictory diagnoses of the problem. It is no wonder, in such circumstances, that conflict arose over the best remedy.

A third source of traditional Executive-Legislative conflict is the difference in time perspective. The President and the Congress run on separate clocks. The occupant of the White House has a strict tenancy. He has, at most, two terms of four years each to reach his goals. Consequently, the Presidency is geared to force decisions and actions. I knew my responsibility, and I was aware that history's judgment would be based not on the Gallup poll of 1966 or 1967 or 1968 but on what I did to steer the economy between the shoals of recession and the rocks of runaway inflation. In contrast to the President's limited tenancy in the White House, a careful Congressman can make a home for life on Capitol Hill. While the President must live with crises and deadlines, a Congressman can cultivate the art of delay and refrain from commitment—especially if the commitment is to increase everybody's taxes.

As Chairman of the Ways and Means Committee, Representative Wilbur Mills had a different constituency than I. His leadership would be judged by his Arkansas electorate and his colleagues in the House. In building his reputation, Chairman Mills followed a basic principle. He wanted to report a bill to the floor when he felt there was a good chance of passing it. Over the years he developed great skill in estimating votes in the committee and the House. When the votes were lacking, he preferred to wait rather than risk the reputation of his committee and the image of his leadership.

In the tax fight Mills was particularly sensitive about his reputation. On one occasion I remember he suffered a rare defeat. A debt-ceiling bill reported out by his committee was rejected by the House as a whole. Mills did not relish such occasions. He was determined to proceed with maximum caution. By contrast, I felt the need for maximum speed. When the economy shows signs of faltering, prompt countermoves are absolutely essential.

These differences—in constituency, information, and time perspective—are built-in conflicts. They provide tension enough to satisfy the most demanding constitutional system. But in America we are blessed with a watchdog press, often ready to improve on the work of the Founding Fathers as well as the President. The tax issue was an ideal subject. The conflict between Chairman Mills and the President provided headlines. The press enjoys a fight between the White House and Capitol Hill. With each newspaper report, our disagreements escalated. First Mills was reported to be hurt because I had not consulted him on the tax bill. Soon he felt utterly neglected. Before long he was downright angry. In all this, no mention was made either of the many long White House sessions in which Mills participated in the initial drafting of the tax message or of the dozens of hours the Secretary and Under Secretary of the Treasury spent with him throughout the entire legislative struggle.

Actually, Mills was an extremely skillful Congressman and a man of integrity. I liked him, and I enjoyed a close working relationship with him. Yet a myth repeated often enough soon becomes accepted truth. Before long, in some strange way the dignity of our offices became involved, making natural compromise more difficult.

Far more important on most issues are the sources of cooperation that bring the President and Congress together and enable them to work in tandem to advance the public interest. In the politics of taxation, not the least of my troubles in 1967 was that the ordinary forces of cooperation were severely strained.

In many instances, party philosophy serves as a loose cement that binds together the President and many members of Congress, but in the case of the tax bill the Democratic party was split. On the one hand, many conservative Democrats were saying to me: "We'll go with you on the tax increase, but only if you wrap it in the American flag as a wartime measure and use the revenue solely for military expenditures and not for your Great Society programs." On the other hand, several liberals were saying: "We'll go with you, but only if you use all the revenue to build the Great Society programs, not for any of your military efforts." Other liberals insisted on tax reforms as part of any tax bill. And everyone was saying: "We've got elections and we just don't want any new taxes."

I was certain to be criticized whatever direction I moved, and each alternative offered peculiar dangers. To wrap the tax bill in the flag might launch pressures that would widen the war and cut back the reforms our society needed. Nor could I agree that the tax increase should be used solely for domestic purposes and be accompanied by tax reform. The need to support our soldiers in Vietnam was immediate and increasing. Effective tax reform would take months or years. Moreover, I knew that talk of additional outlays for the Great Society programs would give the conservatives the excuse they needed to torpedo the tax bill.

I stuck to the middle ground, for I realized that my Presidency would require dealing simultaneously with major military crises abroad and urgently needed reforms at home. That course was not comfortable. It would have been easier in the short run to break out the flag for an all-out military effort, and perhaps easier still to abandon our commitment in Asia and concentrate on domestic tasks. But I was convinced that the middle ground was the right course for the United States. That was the fundamental approach of my administration, and I was not going to abandon it. Holding to it, however, eroded my popularity from two directions—with those who wanted to do more in the war and with those who wished to do more at home. And Presidential popularity is a major source of strength in gaining cooperation from Congress.

A President must always reckon that his mandate will prove short-lived. Much had happened between my landslide victory of 1964 and the difficult days of the tax struggle in 1966–1968. I had deliberately spent a good deal of my mandate to accomplish many controversial reforms. For me, as for most active Presidents, popularity proved elusive.

A sense of national urgency is perhaps the most important source of cooperation. When the national interest is clear and the need for action compelling, the separate constituencies of the President and the Congress come together. Differences in information are overlooked; contrasting time perspectives disappear; institutional pride gives way to deeper concerns. And that is what eventually happened on the tax bill. Action proved impossible until the spring of 1968, when the international gold market crisis made clear the vital connection between passing the tax bill and avoiding an international monetary catastrophe, and when my withdrawal from politics reduced the political heat surrounding the tax issue.

All these complicated factors taken together spelled one simple message in 1966 and 1967: No go. But we *had* to go. We could not close our eyes and wish inflation away.

Following Gardner Ackley's recommendations in his memo of December 1965, I began to move against inflation early in 1966. My first actions were carefully measured. I knew the obstacles we faced. I had to take one step at a time, hoping to bring the Congress along with me. I began in the State of the Union message delivered on January 12, 1966, with a call for a temporary restoration of automobile and telephone excise taxes and for accelerating collection of corporate and personal tax payments. These measures would add $6 billion in federal revenue, an important start. Two months later Congress responded with the Tax Adjustment Act of 1966.

As soon as the first act was signed, I began exploring the possibilities of a second. In his next memo to me on March 12, 1966, Gardner Ackley pointed out: "We are not facing an explosive situation. A little inflation won't be fatal. But inflationary psychology and inflationary symptoms are taking root. If they do get firmly established, it will be hard to uproot them and hard to resist pressures for overly restrictive action." Early in 1966 I discussed a possible tax increase with my Cabinet officers. I asked for their opinions. Only one Cabinet member, Secretary of Commerce John Connor, spoke in favor of higher taxes. A vote showed the Cabinet to be in overwhelming opposition.

On March 30, 1966, I invited more than 150 leading businessmen to a dinner at the White House. After dinner, I outlined our economic situation and asked them:

> How many of you would recommend tomorrow a tax increase to the Congress for the purpose of restraining our economy? Those of you that would, I wish you would raise your right hand.

Not a single hand went up. Not one of those businessmen supported a tax increase to dampen the rising inflation. A few weeks later I met with a group of labor leaders. I posed a similar question. I got a similar answer. But as the weeks passed, the warning of the Council of Economic Advisers kept haunting me.

I sounded out the congressional leadership on a tax increase, and their answer was painfully clear. The House leadership reported late in the spring of 1966 that of twenty-five members on the Ways and Means Committee, the most support I could then expect was four votes. Chairman

DEFEATING AGGRESSION AND SEARCHING FOR PEACE:
Vietnam 1965–1967. The conditions confronting American troops
were among the most difficult our forces have ever faced. . . .

Reviewing troops at Fort Campbell, Kentucky, July 1966

Far East Trip, October 17–November 2, 1966. Overwhelming crowds welcome American President in Melbourne, Australia.

Visiting wounded at Cam Ranh Bay, with General William Westmoreland;
BOTTOM, with a village elder in South Korea.

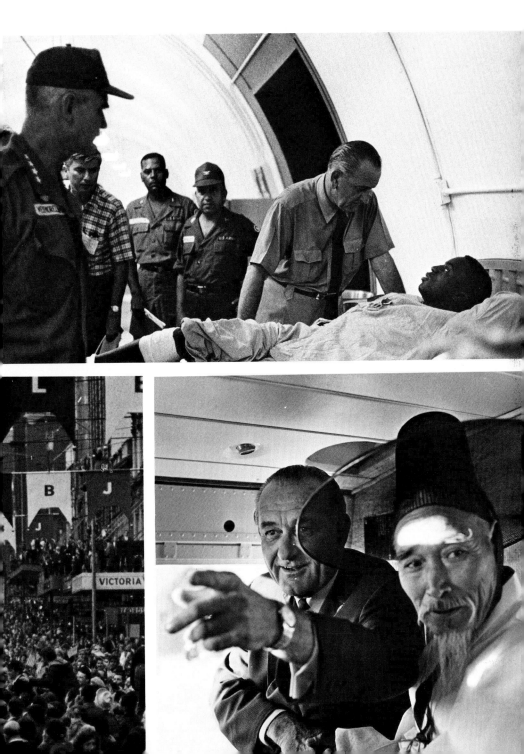

Honolulu, February 7–8, 1966. LEFT: At conference table, with Prime Minister Nguyen Cao Ky and Chief of State Nguyen Van Thieu (*r.*). Manila Conference, October 24–25, 1966. *Left to right,* Ky, Holt (Australia), Park (S. Korea), Marcos (Philippines), Holyoake (N. Zealand), Thieu, Thanom (Thailand). The Vatican: With Pope Paul VI during round-the-world trip, December 1967.

SPACE. LEFT: Inspecting missile assembly plant with NASA director James Webb, December 12, 1967. BELOW: Astronauts Gus Grissom and Ed White, June 1965, with Mrs. Johnson and daughter Luci. Grissom, White, and Roger Chaffee were killed in tragic Apollo fire, January 27, 1967—the same day U.S. signed treaty prohibiting weapons in outer space (BOTTOM).

With principal advisers in Situation Room after Moscow-Washington "hot-line" was used. BOTTOM, L., Israel's Foreign Minister Abba Eban warns U.S. of impending UAR attack. McNamara issues orders for U.S. fleet to change course.

THAWING THE COLD WAR. Summit meeting with Soviet Chairman Kosygin at Glassboro, N.J., June 24–25, 1967, "discussing the state of the world." Foreign Minister Gromyko (TOP, L.) would study nonproliferation treaty with Rusk.

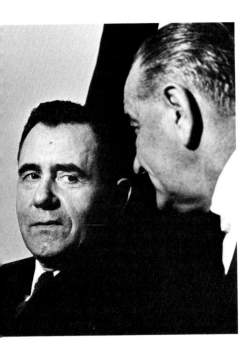

BITE THE BULLET. Meeting with key economic advisers:
Treasury Secretary Henry Fowler, William McChesney Martin,
Gardner Ackley, James Duesenberry. BOTTOM: "chalk talks."

Briefing congressional leaders on 1968 tax bill.
House Ways and Means Chairman Wilbur Mills; Speaker McCormack;
House Minority Leader Gerald Ford, BOTTOM, R.

Mills's vote was not among them. In the highly charged preelection atmosphere, I was advised that I was lucky to be able to count on even four votes.

On August 30, 1966, House Majority Leader Carl Albert told Larry O'Brien bluntly: "The tax bill will be extremely difficult, if not impossible, to pass and certainly will mess up other programs." We were forced to settle for second best: a bits-and-pieces revenue package passed in September that suspended the 7 per cent investment credit, curtailed federal agency borrowing from the private market, and scaled down prospective expenditures. At the same time, we had to try to restrain wage and price increases, using every opportunity to express our concern to leaders of business and labor. In some cases these efforts succeeded; some industries did forego price increases. But our appeal for restraint had only limited success in the absence of a tax increase. Once prices began to rise, it was unrealistic to expect restraint in wage increases. Yet once labor costs rose, management could not easily be persuaded to absorb those increases without boosting prices. The major burden of slowing the inflation was left to monetary policy in the form of higher interest rates, which bore down disproportionately on certain sectors of the economy, such as home building.

Stimulated by a Federal Reserve Board decision in December 1965, this increase in interest rates generated a public "dialogue" between Federal Reserve Chairman William McChesney Martin and myself. My argument with Martin was not over the rate increase but over its timing and the failure to coordinate the action with key fiscal policy decisions just ahead. When he announced the increase, Martin knew that three days later he was scheduled to come to the Ranch with the Director of the Bureau of the Budget, the Secretary of the Treasury, and the Chairman of the Council of Economic Advisers for a comprehensive review of the entire monetary and fiscal situation. I particularly regretted that he had acted before knowing the nature and likely impact of our budget and Vietnam decisions. But the Federal Reserve Board is an independent agency, and I accepted its action.

The fiscal and monetary measures we carried out in 1966 had some effect. Consumer prices had risen about 1.3 per cent annually between 1960 and 1965. But between June 1965 and September 1966 the annual rate of increase rose to 3.4 per cent. As a result of our actions, the rate fell back to 2.3 per cent between September 1966 and June 1967, but that was not good enough. I continued to press for a tax increase. Slowly but surely, more people began to recognize the necessity for an increase in taxes, as it became apparent that the war in Vietnam would continue for some time. In spite of losing forty-seven Democratic seats in the House in the

1966 elections, we seemed to have some chance of success in 1967—compared with almost no chance in 1966.

Early in 1967 we estimated that a 6 per cent tax surcharge, to become effective the following July, would slow inflation without risking a recession. I urged the Congress again to pass a surcharge in my State of the Union message on January 10, 1967. We could not get action on it for the first six months of that year, since the combination of monetary restraints and the repeal of investment credit had produced a serious pile-up of inventories and the temporary threat of recession.

By July 1967, however, the economy was moving up again, and it was clear that even a 6 per cent surcharge would not be enough. But if not 6 per cent, what should the figure be—8 per cent? 9 per cent? 10 per cent? Should corporations pay a higher surcharge than individuals? Should citizens with low incomes be exempted? On these and other details I consulted with the Congress through Wilbur Mills. He was in steady contact with the White House throughout the drafting session late in July.

Long experience—from the National Youth Administration to the U.S. Senate—had taught me the value of such consultation. When Congress helps to shape projects, they are more likely to be successful than those simply handed down from the Executive branch. With Chairman Mills, we worked on the draft of the tax message as if we were marking up a bill in Executive session or in conference. In the process, it became clear that language differences reflected larger policy differences. We had originally written:

> Reduction in spending will not be easy for the budget submitted in January was already lean . . . less essential spending can—and must—be deferred. But the tragic events of recent weeks in Newark, Detroit, and other cities drive home a compelling message: we cannot postpone the urgent work to make the streets of American cities safe from crime or turn our backs on the urgent work that must be pursued to root out the underlying causes of unrest and injustice in our land. To delay now would mean that those pressing problems would have to be attacked later at a much higher cost—human and economic.

Chairman Mills objected strongly to this passage, arguing that it seemed to promise more spending, not less, and that reduced expenditures were essential if our tax bill was to be successful. Our final draft, completed on August 2, reflected this compromise:

> For we cannot turn our backs on the great programs that have been begun, with such promise, in the last 3-½ years. . . . Nevertheless, we must move with determination to assure that those for whom these programs were begun are not robbed by the inflation that would accompany an unacceptable deficit.

Before the message was sent to the Hill, I asked for a survey of the initial reactions of key committee members and interest groups to the proposed bill. This checklist was compiled by members of the White House congressional liaison staff, the appropriate Cabinet members, and agency staff men. On the tax issue, Secretary of the Treasury Fowler and Under Secretary Joe Barr were responsible for checking the House Democrats; Commerce Secretary Alexander Trowbridge * coordinated the check on business and labor; and agency staff men contacted Republican Senators and Congressmen. There is nothing mysterious about this technique. Each man received a list of people to contact and was expected, within one or two days, to describe the attitudes and opinions of those consulted. Taken together, the individual readings gave us a rough estimate of the congressional feeling on the issue at stake.

The key to accurate head counts is personal knowledge or trust and the ability to probe beneath the surface to see what individuals are really thinking and feeling. If a liaison man knew his contacts well—if he knew who was irritated about what, who had a tough election ahead, and who had ambitions for higher office—he could judge their reactions in one conversation or phone call. But if he did not know his men well, he might never be able to interpret tone, nuance, and spirit. Without this kind of preparation, checks on specific legislation are of little use.

In the Ways and Means Committee attitudes were split. Approval was unlikely without the strong support of Chairman Mills. By this time reactions from business and labor were somewhat more favorable, though both groups had qualifications. Business leaders argued that the tax increase should be accompanied by significant spending cuts; labor leaders argued for taxing corporations at twice the rate charged for individuals.

But more than surveys were needed. Throughout my Presidency I insisted that we brief the Congress fully before our messages were sent to the Hill. We made many mistakes, but failure to inform and brief the Congress was not one of them. My insistence on this practice was rooted in an experience I had in the House in 1941, when I witnessed the negative impact of failure to brief congressional leaders. I was standing in the back of the House behind the rail as Speaker Sam Rayburn listened to the House clerk read an important new administration message President Roosevelt had just sent to the Hill. Several dozen Democrats were gathered around him. As he finished, a unanimous chorus of complaints rushed forth: "Why, that message is terrible, Mr. Sam—we can't pass that" . . . "That last suggestion is awful" . . . "Why in the world did you let the President send one up like that?" . . . "Why didn't you warn us?"

Speaker Rayburn listened to all the criticisms and then responded softly: "We'll just have to look at it more carefully. That's all I can say now,

* Trowbridge replaced John Connor as Secretary of Commerce on June 14, 1967.

fellows. We'll have to look at it more carefully." The crowd scattered. Mr. Sam and I were left alone in the back. I could see that something was wrong. "If only," he said, "the President would let me know ahead of time when these controversial messages are coming up. I could pave the way for him. I could create a base of support. I could be better prepared for criticism. I could get much better acceptance in the long run. But I never know when the damned messages are coming. This last one surprised me as much as it did all of them." He shook his head sadly and walked slowly away.

I could see that his pride was hurt. So was the President's prestige and the administration's program. I never forgot that lesson.

I applied it on the morning of August 3, 1967, the day the tax proposal went up. I held a briefing for about seventy Congressmen, including the House leadership, the assistant whips, the House committee chairmen, and the members of the Ways and Means Committee and the Appropriations Committee. I wanted to give them an advance look at the document. Getting a look ahead of others may seem unimportant, but if it helps a Congressman's ego a little bit, it may make all the difference. In dealing with such complex legislation, it was especially important for the President to give Congressmen all the information he had. In the weeks that followed we held a dozen similar briefings, eventually inviting every Democrat and almost half of the Republicans to the White House, where I explained the problem the nation faced and answered all questions. We knew the risks of putting information in the hands of the potential opposition. But I felt that even if some members used our own information against us, at least the debate would be based on fact.

Merely placing a program before Congress is not enough. Without constant attention from the administration, most legislation moves through the congressional process at the speed of a glacier. Every year thousands of bills are introduced in each Chamber.* Moreover, legislative activity is only one part of a Congressman's hectic life. He also has to answer thousands of letters, keep appointments, attend endless meetings, and greet the countless voters who pour in from his state or district to tell him their troubles and to ask him favors.

One of the President's most important jobs is to help the Congress concentrate on the five or six dozen bills that make up his legislative program. For this reason, I insisted that appropriate members of the administration be ready with strong testimony when congressional hearings began on August 14, 1967. Here, as throughout the entire two-year struggle, Secretary Fowler exhibited an extraordinary combination of good judgment, persistence, dedication, and courage. Between August 1967

---

* In 1968 there were 20,587 bills introduced in the House and 4,199 in the Senate.

and January 1968 he took an active part in three full sets of congressional hearings on the tax bill.

From the outset, Chairman Mills insisted on substantial cuts in government spending. We had serious problems with this. The budget submitted in January 1967 was already lean. It represented the considered judgment of my best advisers, and we were deeply concerned that further cuts would endanger critical social programs.

But I sensed the mood of the House, and I recognized that compromise was essential. Late in September 1967 we informed the Ways and Means Committee that we would make significant spending cuts, but only after the regular appropriations bills had passed and we knew what Congress had already cut. We promised to review each appropriation bill once it was enacted. Only then, when we knew what and how much it contained, could we determine further cuts. To specify the cuts first, as the Ways and Means Committee requested, would have been like tailoring a suit before knowing the dimensions of the cloth. We could not cut something out that was not in, and we would not know what was in until the bills were passed.

My problems and preferences were not the only issues. Without the approval of Representative George Mahon, Chairman of the House Appropriations Committee, Mills's formula for reducing spending had little chance of survival. Chairman Mahon was in no mood to weaken the authority of his powerful committee by permitting the Ways and Means Committee to determine expenditures. To accept the latter's demand for an overall spending cut might be interpreted, in effect, as making Mills chairman of both Ways and Means and Appropriations. The argument over who should cut first, Congress or the President, soon began to sound like the chicken-or-egg dilemma. While the Congress stalled, prices continued to rise and the inflationary spiral became an increasingly important factor in wage settlements.

It was late in November before we got a workable compromise approved by both Mills and Mahon. By that time Congress had passed twelve of the fourteen appropriations bills and Director Charles Schultze and his specialists in the Bureau of the Budget were able to work out a plan for the expenditure cuts. Our compromise was embodied in a two-part legislative proposal: the first title incorporated the 10 per cent surtax and the second title spelled out a formula for spending reductions. We were not happy with the size of these cuts; nor was the House Appropriations Committee. But once again the situation demanded compromise.

As autumn turned to winter and the 1967 congressional session drew to a close, the tax bill remained locked up in the Ways and Means Committee. My willingness to compromise had sharpened the appetites of those who saw in this struggle a long-awaited chance to slash the Great Society programs. Every time we neared agreement on spending cuts, the ante was raised—from $2 billion to $4 billion to $6 billion. Something had to be done to break the stalemate, something outside ordinary bargaining channels.

When traditional methods fail, a President must be willing to bypass the Congress and take the issue to the people. By instinct and experience, I preferred to work from within, knowing that good legislation is the product not of public rhetoric but of private negotiations and compromise. But sometimes a President has to put Congress' feet to the fire. The tax surcharge battle was a case in point. For months I had worked through the leaders on the Hill. I had negotiated and compromised as fully and as fairly as I could, but the bill remained firmly locked in the Ways and Means Committee.

I decided to take the issue to the people. I expressed my concern in every appropriate forum, including the 1968 State of the Union address, the budget message, and the consumer message, urging—almost pleading—for a tax bill. The issue was never whether the American people should like the tax or not. Of course they would not like it; I did not like it either. The issue was whether they would dislike it as much as the consequences of *not* enacting the tax. Those consequences would be exorbitant prices, unparalleled interest rates, and dangerous budget and balance-of-payments deficits.

Somehow, I never got those dangers across to the public or the Congress. For one thing, I failed to explain clearly enough that the surcharge was not a 10 per cent increase in the income tax rate but rather a tax on a tax, or ten extra cents on every dollar of taxes—ten cents to buy an insurance policy against damaging inflation. Another thing I failed to get across was my deep concern about the state of the economy and the relation of the dollar to the world economy. At the time I was pleading for the tax bill, several newspapers increased our difficulties by speculating that I did not really want a tax increase, that deep down I hoped it would fail.

Sometimes it seemed that the only way to reach the papers and the people was to pick a fight with the Congress, to say mean words and show my temper. The most widely publicized statement I made in the fall of 1967 was of this character. A reporter at my November 17 press conference remarked that "there are increasing statements from Capitol Hill that say that your tax bill is dead for this session of Congress." In reply I said:

> I think one of the great mistakes that the Congress will make is that Mr. Ford [the House Republican leader] and Mr. Mills have taken this position that they cannot have any tax bill now. They will live to rue the day when they made that decision. Because it is a dangerous decision. It is an unwise decision.

The impact of such a statement is mixed. It may serve to galvanize support in the Congress and the country, but it may also shorten tempers and polarize thought and emotion. Both happened after my "They will live to rue the day" speech. Representative Mills and the Republican leadership were reported to be furious. Predictions came from the Hill that I would "rue the day" that I had made such a statement; that I had killed chances for a tax bill once and for all. At the same time, it seemed that my fighting spirit had aroused many previously apathetic supporters to action.

I sometimes felt that Congress was like a sensitive animal—if pushed gently it would go my way, but if pushed too hard it would balk. I had to be aware constantly of how much Congress would take and of what kind of mood it was in. As winter turned to spring, my worries about how far and how fast to push the Congress were submerged by deepening financial problems in the international market.* British devaluation of the pound in November 1967 had triggered a general deterioration in the gold market and a crisis of confidence in the dollar and in the international monetary system. By mid-March the London gold market was in a panic. Each day brought new losses in gold reserves. Speculation increased that we might have to devalue the dollar. We finally managed to meet the problem with the new two-tier gold system, but the confidence of foreign nations in America's willingness to get its own house in order had been shaken. Our legislative stalemate over taxes was interpreted abroad as a failure of the democratic process and a clear indication that America had neither the will nor the ability to keep its economic affairs under control.

The international crisis had done what we could not do: arouse the American public and many congressional leaders to the need for decisive action. But frequently an aroused public brings on a heightened sense of partisan politics. The nearer we came to the Presidential primaries in the spring of 1968, the more partisanship grew and the more I feared that many Republicans would oppose the tax bill so they could campaign in the midst of galloping inflation and blame it on my "reckless spending and fiscal irresponsibility." This was the situation when I received the Kerner Commission's report on the civil disorders of 1967 and made the difficult decision not to respond directly to the call for major new programs.† With the tax bill hanging by such slender threads, I knew that any call for increased spending would give my opponents the excuse they sought to call me a reckless spender and kill the tax bill. If that happened, it could bring on an uncontrollable world monetary crisis of 1931 proportions and consequences. It was a risk we could not afford.

The whole situation weighed heavily on my mind in the critical weeks of March as I came to my decisions on Vietnam and prepared to deliver my March 31 speech. Next to peace in Southeast Asia and the world, I believed the tax surcharge was the most urgent issue facing the country. I

* See Chapter 14, pp. 314–21.
† See Chapter 7, pp. 172–73.

increasingly felt that on both of these issues my position as standard bearer of the Democratic party would be a serious impediment to further movement. I prayed that my decision to refuse the nomination would turn the tide. On March 31 I expressed these thoughts in the plainest language I knew:

> . . . tonight we face the sharpest financial threat in the postwar era— a threat to the dollar's role as the keystone of international trade and finance in the world.
>
> . . . We must have a responsible fiscal policy in this country. The passage of a tax bill now, together with expenditure control that the Congress may desire and dictate, is absolutely necessary to protect this nation's security, to continue our prosperity, and to meet the needs of our people. . . .
>
> These times call for prudence in this land of plenty. I believe we have the character to provide it, and tonight I plead with the Congress and with the people to act promptly to serve the national interest, and thereby serve all of our people.

The first response to my plea came from an unexpected quarter, the U.S. Senate. Although the Constitution requires that the House initiate tax legislation, the Senate can amend a bill passed by the House. The Senate is very different from the House; it has its own traditions, procedures, precedents, and rules. The Senate's smaller size allows it to operate in a more leisurely fashion, without the strict limitations required in the House. Any subject may be discussed on the floor at any time, simply by moving that an amendment be made to pending business.

On March 22, in the midst of a debate on a bill the House had passed to extend automobile and telephone excise taxes, two Senators decided to take advantage of this flexibility in Senate procedure. George Smathers of Florida, a Democrat, and John Williams of Delaware, a Republican, jointly proposed a package of amendments to the excise bill. Included were two critical additions: our 10 per cent surcharge and a formula for cuts in spending. On April 2, two days after my public plea, the Senate passed the excise bill with the amendments.

We were concerned about the spending formula, which required us to cut outlays by $6 billion. We also anticipated a House claim that this Senate action represented an "invasion of sacred prerogatives." But we had come to believe that positive Senate action was essential to prod the House into movement. We felt that it was the only hope we had for passage.

I greeted with relief the news that the Senate had passed the excise bill, amendments and all. The stage was set for a battle in the conference committee, where the two different bills would somehow have to be meshed into one. The key to compromise was the size of the spending reductions. The Senate was on record for a cut of $6 billion, but the administration, a majority of the liberals in both houses, and most members of the House Appropriations Committee remained firmly committed to a maximum cut of $4 billion. Our only hope was to bring pressure on the Senate from the House conferees and to compromise at $5 billion. Once again, Wilbur Mills held the key to the compromise. On April 11 I had a long talk with him about these matters.

I told Chairman Mills that I had tried every way I knew to find an acceptable compromise and had even forsworn another term, thinking that might help. "But," I said, "I think the situation is as bad now as it was before." I told him that whether he realized it or not, the country's economy was about to go down the drain and we had to write a tax bill that we could both live with. Mills seemed to understand my concern completely. He remarked that although he didn't have the problem in his district, the plight of the cities was critical. He said he knew I could not cut back the budget for urban affairs and that I might even have to ask for more money. Notes I made at the time show that Mills then said he thought he could "get by" with the $5 billion figure as a spending limitation. With those words, our long-sought compromise was finally in sight. We parted in high spirits for the first time in the long surcharge struggle. I began to relax.

In a few days, however, Chairman Mills evidently decided that he would not compromise at $5 billion. Word came from the conference committee that the House conferees, like their Senate counterparts, would insist on a $6 billion reduction. I met with Mills again on April 30 in the Cabinet Room. I had assembled some of the leaders who I thought might help me sway Mills—Speaker McCormack and Representatives Carl Albert, George Mahon, and Hale Boggs. Art Okun, the new Chairman of the Council of Economic Advisers,* was also with us, as was Charles Zwick, the new Director of the Bureau of the Budget,† and J. Barefoot Sanders, Jr., who had replaced Larry O'Brien as chief of my legislative liaison staff.

Mills appeared to be backing away from the $5 billion compromise, and again we tried to reason with him. As I remember, it was Speaker McCormack who asked him pointedly what his actual position was, and faced with such a blunt and direct question, Mills appeared to relent in our favor.

But at any figure—$4 billion, $5 billion, or $6 billion—the conference committee seemed in no hurry to act. In fact, it appeared to some that the Ways and Means Committee was jealously guarding its prerogative of initiating tax measures, but was not initiating any legislation. As the stalemate continued day after day, I decided once again to appeal directly

---

* I had previously nominated Gardner Ackley as Ambassador to Italy.
† Zwick succeeded Charles Schultze on January 8, 1968.

to the people. In a nationally televised press conference on May 3, I stated:

> I want to make it perfectly clear to the American people that I think we are courting danger by this continued procrastination, this continued delay.
>
> . . . I think the time has come for all of the members of Congress to be responsible and, even in an election year, to bite the bullet and stand up and do what ought to be done for their country.

That statement aroused a certain amount of anger on Capitol Hill, but it made headlines all over the country and helped break the logjam. On May 1 the House Appropriations Committee approved a resolution to cut budget expenditures for the fiscal year 1969 by at least $4 billion. Only after this action did the Ways and Means Committee approve a resolution on May 6 recommending a 10 per cent tax surcharge and a cut in spending of at least $4 billion. And on May 9 the Senate-House conferees finally announced their agreement on including the 10 per cent surcharge in the excise tax bill. To our disappointment, they insisted on a reduction of $6 billion in federal spending in fiscal 1969. Apparently, Mills felt that he had left himself an escape hatch when his committee called for "at least" $4 billion in cuts.

The liberals were disappointed with Chairman Mills. So was the House leadership, and so was I. Although he had very strong sentiment that supported him, Mills's insistence on a $6 billion cut had polarized the issue and destroyed all hope of easy compromise. Within hours the $6 billion figure became a rallying cry among liberals to defeat the conference committee's report. The AFL-CIO, the National Education Association, the National Council of Churches, the U.S. Conference of Mayors, the Urban Coalition, and other groups began to lobby against the report.

As lines hardened, tension increased. Barefoot Sanders described the conflict in a memo to me on May 9, 1968:

> If he [Mills] loses the Conference Report his reputation would be severely damaged. . . . Reactions so far indicate that there will be very little support from liberal Democrats. . . . The Speaker is presently opposed to the Conference Report. Albert and Mahon are keeping themselves flexible. But Albert is inclined to oppose the report. Organized labor . . . opposes the report.

Not everyone in the administration shared Sanders' estimate of the importance of passing the conference report. At a meeting on May 14, I reviewed the situation with the Cabinet and asked each of the officers to express his views. "You've all been a good team and a good family," I said. "We are a family, just like men who all have children at home who have to go to college. . . . Sometimes the strongest has to sacrifice more than the others. I want Secretary Fowler to tell us now what he thinks is best for our family."

Secretary Fowler said enactment of the tax bill was "vital" to the solution of the balance-of-payments deficit. Domestically, it was just as important, he said. "I don't want to fuzz it up. I am going to give you the facts of life. . . . If we don't get a tax bill now, we will have to go back for an increase in the debt ceiling. . . ."

Art Okun, Chairman of the Council of Economic Advisers, noted:

> Inflation is a very serious problem. Prices are climbing by 4 per cent a year. . . . We are threatened by a new depression in home building, etc. The international consequences of a tax bill failure would be very great indeed. It could be a calamity. We could have a sharp rise in speculation in the American dollar and another gold run. It could force us to the bitter choice of suspending gold payments or—even worse—increasing the price of gold. . . . We would get a real explosion in the world financial community.

"I agree," Secretary Rusk said. "The international consequences will be very grave if there is no tax bill. It is just absolutely essential."

Defense Secretary Clifford * spoke next: "Whatever has to be done has to be done to get this tax bill. We'll do it."

"What do you think, Ramsey?" I asked the Attorney General.

"All the realities scream for us to continue what we are doing in the cities. . . . I would have to have a much more definite sense of catastrophe from not having a tax bill before I would stop any effort to go on doing what we need to do at the Defense Department, for the cities and all the rest. . . . We must go on. I hope we can find a way to tough it out."

"Yes," I said, "we all want to do well. But can we do more with or without a tax bill? That's the question. . . . Secretary Smith?" †

"I am 100 per cent for the tax bill. I'd rather have $4 billion cut but I would go with $6 billion. Then I would go back up there and ask for more."

"Secretary Weaver?"

"Yes, the tax bill is a must. But . . . I go along with Ramsey. We just cannot in conscience recommend any cuts in our cities program. I'm understanding, but we just can't absorb our cuts without great disservice to our people."

"We all agree on that," I responded. "The question is: Do we do more or less disservice with or without a tax bill at a price of $6 billion?"

Secretary of Labor Wirtz spoke next: "I wouldn't pay one single penny,

* Clifford replaced Robert McNamara as Secretary of Defense on March 1, 1968.

† C. R. Smith, former chairman of the board of American Airlines, became Secretary of Commerce on March 6, 1968. Secretary Trowbridge had resigned because of ill health.

not one single penny. I wouldn't make the $4 billion compromise. I wouldn't get caught in explaining a $2 billion or $4 billion difference. Don't go below your budget, Mr. President. Don't surrender. Take it to the people. . . . The question at this point is whether the government can function or not. When this country hasn't the guts to tax itself, is the New Economics at test? Yes, it is. I'd lay it out on that basis. I'd take it to the country, go to the country, this country can't put up with it. I'd rather see that challenge put to Congress and the people . . . than any cuts in any form. . . . No compromises, no concessions, pay no price in reductions in government expenditures."

Secretary of the Interior Udall picked up the same theme: "I would go most of the way with Secretary Wirtz. I would stand firm on the rule of 'No playing politics now.' They can't accuse us of that, they should never be able to. Maybe Charlie Zwick could spell it out in detail at a press conference. The Senate just doesn't know the consequences now. They need the cold shower treatment. Congress is trying to make us play their game, giving us all the misery. We can't stand there and do it. If they want to play games, let them play it with the facts."

Despite these impassioned pleas to hold our ground, I knew there was no conceivable way I could get a tax increase without accepting some compromise in expenditure reductions. But it was not entirely up to me. The Congress was deadlocked too. The liberals were refusing to go along with spending cuts. We needed a viable strategy to bring them along. We knew one critical element of that strategy. Unless we could get a vote on the $4 billion figure, the liberals would feel they were letting down their constituents, the poor and the blacks, and would probably vote against the conference report. But if a special vote could be taken to register their "conscience" publicly and openly, then perhaps the door to later compromise would remain open.

This was one of many occasions when our Tuesday leadership breakfasts proved invaluable. Those breakfasts gave us the chance to talk frankly with congressional leaders. They provided a forum for debating possible solutions to complicated legislative problems. At a leadership breakfast on May 21, 1968, we agreed to sponsor a motion on the House floor to send the conferees back with instructions to reduce the spending cutbacks from $6 billion to $4 billion. Speaker McCormack and Majority Leader Albert said they would figure out the details with the House parliamentarian and find someone to introduce the motion.

I decided to hold a series of private sessions in the White House for the liberal Democrats to explain our strategy and my position. In the confidence of the Cabinet Room, I told them that I hated the thought of the $6 billion cut and hoped against hope for passage of the $4 billion motion, but that if it failed I did not feel I could let the tax bill die. "It will take a great deal of pulling to squeeze that $6 billion out without hurting key domestic programs," I said. "But if we have to cut that much, I am determined not to let those programs suffer."

On May 29 the motion to reduce the cut to $4 billion was introduced by Democratic Representative James A. Burke of Massachusetts. The votes were tallied, and our fears confirmed. The House rejected the motion overwhelmingly, by a vote of 259 to 137. With this defeat, the unpleasant choice was painfully clear. Either we accepted the $6 billion cut or we would lose the tax bill. I thought about our budget and the difficulty of cutting $6 billion out of it, but I could not let the tax bill fail. Far too much depended on its passage.

One major question remained. Even if we agreed to the $6 billion cut, would a majority of the House accept the conference report? This was where the head count became our most critical tool.

With so many factors at work, we knew that an accurate head count would be very difficult. But my liaison staff had been gathering information on the tax bill for eighteen long months, and the final head count was simply a distillation of that intelligence. In this last survey the members of Congress were asked not simply how they intended to vote but under what conditions they would vote yes or no. And on the basis of their answers—"I'm all for it, but unless the Detroit delegation votes for it as well, I cannot go with you" . . . "I can be swung over but only if I get a chance to see what's going to happen to the programs for the cities" . . . "I am uncommitted and will remain so until the last moment" . . . "I am against it, I've been against it for months, and I don't intend to change my mind" . . . "I will wait in the well and vote yes if, and only if, it's crucial" . . . "I'll go with you but only if the House leadership actively encourages me"—the members were divided into five categories: "with us," "probably with us," "uncommitted," "probably against," and "against."

With the head count as our blueprint, the enormous job of individual persuasion began. We concentrated on the "uncommitteds" and those "probably against," attempting to develop an individual approach to meet the needs of each member. Wild images have been concocted to describe this process of persuasion. A great deal of mystery surrounds the President's role. But the real task of persuasion is far less glamorous than the imagined one. It is tough, demanding work. For despite the stereotyped Presidential image, I could not trade patronage for votes in any direct exchange. If word spread that I was trading, everyone would want to trade and all other efforts at persuasion would automatically fail. To say this is not to say that rewards (such as White House tours, invitations to social functions, birthday greetings, and Presidential photos) do not go to faithful Congressmen. But these are generally delivered by the White

House staff after the fact, and on the basis of a pattern of voting, not by the President personally in exchange for a specific vote.

Nor could I rely on the "big threat" or direct reprisal to produce compliance. It is daydreaming to assume that any experienced Congressman would ignore his basic instincts or his constituents' deepest concerns in quaking fear of the White House. My best hope was to make a good, solid, convincing case for the administration's position.

I tried in every possible way to make a convincing case on the surcharge to the Hill. First, we had to mobilize support in the outside community to ease the path for Congressmen willing to join our effort. In the final days of May, with Secretary Fowler's help, a dozen organizations undertook active support of the surcharge. They included the American Bankers Association, the American Farm Bureau's Federation, the National Association of Manufacturers, and the Chamber of Commerce. In addition, a group of five hundred business leaders, headed by such able men as Henry Ford, was organized specifically to stimulate support for the surcharge. These national leaders in turn contacted their local business representatives, asking each to speak to the Congressman in his own district and let him know that the overwhelming preponderance of responsible businessmen strongly favored the conference report as the only source of sound fiscal policy. These last-minute visits and calls proved especially valuable in helping to sway many Republicans to our side.

Trying to stimulate traditional Democratic support was more difficult. For many months labor leaders had been deeply concerned about the impact of budget cuts on the Great Society programs. It was no surprise when the AFL-CIO spoke out publicly against the conference committee's report. Once again I understood their anger, but I knew that if labor lobbyists were to stalk the Hill, warning Congress that a vote for the tax bill would be a vote against labor, the liberals would have little choice but to vote against the bill. The Burke motion helped a great deal. So did a special meeting with labor leader George Meany. We talked the problem out. Several days later the labor lobbyists quietly lowered their voices.

I knew how hard it was, especially for those heading the domestic agencies, to accept deep budget cuts as the price for the tax bill. Budget Director Zwick and his staff worked day and night to find a way to absorb the $6 billion cut with as little damage as possible to the Great Society programs. At our Cabinet meeting on May 29 I outlined that package and the dimensions of our choice. I described my judgment that in this case we had to take the lesser of two evils and find a way to cut the extra $2 billion. I assured the Cabinet officers that I hated the cut as much as they did, but I added: "It won't be anything like the headache or anything like as bad as saying to the world that we have no fiscal responsibility and we will not pass the tax bill. Therefore I want to ask for something I've never asked a Cabinet to do before. I want to see how much muscle we've got left—if any! I would like you to sit down with these 250 men [Democratic Senators and Congressmen] that you've been associated with, most of them for the last eight years, and see which ones you're willing to sit down and talk with. And say that our country is in trouble and here's why, and you hope they can accept this report, and, if they do, it will not tear their program to pieces."

I knew that in spite of their personal feelings the Cabinet officers would respond to the nation's interests. That same afternoon, they began canvassing the Hill. The following day I made my position public at a press conference:

> So the only choice remaining now is whether the need for a tax increase is so urgent that we must accept a $6 billion reduction. I believe that the need for a tax increase is that urgent. If the Congress will vote for the conference report containing the tax increase and the $6 billion expenditure cut, I shall approve it.

With these words, the struggle entered its final phase. Once again the head count became critical. In such a situation personal contact from the President can be decisive, but generally only with key members whose votes will have a multiplying effect on the votes of many others. So I had my own list of men to contact.

When I made these phone calls, I had no set script. Sometimes I would start with: "What's this I read about your opposing my bill?" Other times I would ask: "What do you think of this bill?" Or: "Say, Congressman, I haven't seen you around in a while, just wondering how you've been." But a common theme ran through these talks—friendship and respect. If I were to name the one factor above all others that helped me in dealing with the Congress, I would say it was the genuine friendship and rapport I had with most Congressmen and Senators. I understood and respected men who dedicated their lives to elective office. Most politicians are men of principle dedicated to the national interest. I believed that I, as President, had the responsibility to appeal to that dedication, to outline what I considered the national interest required, to lay out the alternatives, and to hope that a reasonable man would understand and accept his duty.

Finally, the day of the vote arrived—June 20, 1968. We did not expect the tally to take place until late in the afternoon or early in the evening. In the middle of the day a large number of administration leaders and supporters left the Capitol to attend a luncheon on the other side of town in honor of Representative Albert. About one o'clock H. R. Gross, Iowa's actively partisan Republican, unexpectedly took the House floor. He moved that the House return the conference report to the Senate without action, on the grounds that the bill was unconstitutional because it had originated in the Senate. Gross's proposal was a privileged motion—that is, one allowing time for only an hour's debate. An urgent summons was sent to the congressional luncheon and the members rushed back, worried that they might not reach the House in time. But we were lucky. The tally was still in progress when the luncheon crowd arrived to cast their votes and defeat Gross's motion.

The final roll call on the bill began at 7:05 P.M. At that time, I was attending a reception for foreign educators at the State Department. Several reporters rode back with me to the White House after the reception was over, and we sat in the car talking for twenty minutes or so. Just before 8 P.M. one of my aides came out to the car and handed me a message: "Mr. President: The House has just adopted the conference committee report—with the 10 per cent surcharge." The vote was 268 to 150, reflecting substantial support from all quarters, conservatives and liberals, Republicans and Democrats. The staff had estimated correctly—we'd either win big or not at all. I returned immediately to the Oval Office to make a statement:

> The House of Representatives today declared itself for a responsible fiscal policy. Its voice will be heard around the world. Our democracy has passed a critical test. . . . I am very hopeful and confident that the Senate will promptly complete legislative action on this matter.

The next day, June 21, the Senate adopted the conference report, and the 10 per cent surcharge became the law of the land with my signature on June 28.

Another long struggle had come to an end. The President and the Congress had finally worked out a solution. But such conflict and co-operation will continue. They are part and parcel of politics in Washington.

It has taken me a lifetime to learn the lessons of politics. Many men have been my teachers, but to this day one man stands out above the rest—Alvin Wirtz, a lawyer and a Texas state senator. He taught me the most about the one element in politics that matters the most: the people. I remember one episode in particular. In 1937 Senator Wirtz had arranged a special meeting between a group of private utility company owners and the representatives of the Lower Colorado River Authority in an effort to persuade the big companies to make electric power available to small farmers in rural areas. As I listened to the discussion, I grew more and more impatient with the utility company executives. It seemed to me that they were deliberately holding up progress out of concern for vested interests. I got into an argument about this with one of the company presidents, and in the course of our discussion I told the man that he could "go to hell."

I felt relieved after using that strong language. It had sounded good and tough to the consumer representatives and they loved it. The meeting broke up shortly after that and Senator Wirtz asked me to come into his private office. I expected approval from my mentor, but I got just the opposite.

"Listen, Lyndon," he said, "I've been around this business for a long time. I imagine you felt like some sort of hero talking that way in front of your consumer friends, but let's think it over some. Your speech broke up the meeting. It left us right back where we started, The power companies still own those power lines and the farmers still need electricity. If I have learned anything at all in these years, it is this: You can *tell* a man to go to hell, but you can't *make* him go."

I thought of that story many times during my Presidency. It seemed particularly apt when I found myself in a struggle with the House or the Senate. I would start to speak out, then I would think of Senator Wirtz and remember that no matter how many times I told the Congress to do something, I could never force it to act. In our democratic system only one group has that ultimate power: the people at large. Politics is the art and craft of dealing with people. Politics goes beyond the art of the possible. It is the art of making possible what seems impossible.

20

Thawing the Cold War

I F JULY 1, 1968, figures in the history books of the future, it will be because of what happened that morning in the East Room of the White House. A few minutes after 11:30 A.M., in that gold-draped room, before hundreds of witnesses and in the glare of television floodlights, representatives of the Soviet Union, the United Kingdom, the United States, and more than fifty other nations signed the Treaty on the Nonproliferation of Nuclear Weapons. Under that treaty, nations without nuclear weapons promised not to make them or receive them from others; the treaty assured those nations that they would have access to the full benefits of the peaceful uses of nuclear power. Nations with nuclear weapons pledged to work toward effective arms control and disarmament.

This was the most significant step we had yet taken to reduce the possibility of nuclear war. In my remarks following the signing ceremony, I called the treaty "the most important international agreement since the beginning of the nuclear age." I also said something that I had been hoping to say for more than three years:

> Now, at this moment of achievement and great hope, I am gratified to be able to report and announce to the world a significant agreement— an agreement that we have actively sought and worked for since January 1964: Agreement has been reached between the governments of the Union of Soviet Socialist Republics and the United States to enter in the nearest future into discussions on the limitation and the reduction of both offensive strategic nuclear weapons delivery systems and systems of defense against ballistic missiles.

An historic turning point had been reached. The two great nuclear powers had finally decided to sit down together and work to reduce and control the awful destructive power they had developed, a power that, if misused or used in error, could mean civilization's end.

That night, as I thought about the day just ended, I remembered how much had gone before to bring us to the high point of hope that was July 1. I recalled my talk in 1963 with Deputy Premier Anastas Mikoyan, who had come to attend President Kennedy's funeral. I had told him we were going to stand by our beliefs but that he could be sure no day would go by in which I and my administration would not be working hard to ease world tensions and bring peace closer to us all.

As Congressman, Senator, and Vice President, I had lived through every major Cold War crisis—from the threats to Iran, Greece, and Turkey after World War II to the Cuban missile crisis of October 1962. This long record of tension gave me little reason to feel confident that Moscow would forego the use or threat of force to back its foreign policy if opportunities seemed advantageous. I expected no miracles in terms of U.S.-Soviet relations during my Presidency, but I felt strongly that the two most powerful nations in the world had several things in common—above all, the need to avoid confrontations that could lead to disaster for all mankind as well as for each other.

Rather than try to achieve a single, comprehensive agreement, I thought it more sensible to try to find common ground on lesser problems. If we could sweep away small irritants one by one, perhaps we could then gradually face and solve the greater issues on which a stable peace depends. Under President Kennedy, we had reached agreement to set up the "hot line" and had worked out the Partial Test Ban Treaty, which went into effect on October 10, 1963. This treaty outlawed nuclear testing in the atmosphere, in space, and under water, and placed limitations on underground testing.

One other area of common interest, although never expressed in a formal agreement, developed when Washington and Moscow independently declared that they would put no nuclear weapons into orbit around the earth. The UN General Assembly called on all nations to follow this lead. The resolution was approved in October 1963 with strong support from the American and Soviet delegations.

The first step I took as President in my effort to improve East-West relations was to insist that we avoid wherever possible the harsh name-calling of the Cold War era. Those exchanges of ideological rhetoric accomplished nothing except to stir up angry emotions on both sides. Throughout my administration we avoided personal attacks on Soviet leaders and refrained from using such phrases as "captive nations" and "ruthless totalitarians." This was not a major breakthrough, but I thought that it might calm the waters.

The second step I took was to try to inject new life into talks with the

Russians on several problems on which we had made little or no progress in the past. One was a civil aviation agreement designed to arrange direct flight service between Moscow and New York. We had had exchanges on this matter during President Eisenhower's last year and President Kennedy's first year in the White House, but no final agreement had been reached. I learned that Soviet air officials had invited the head of the Federal Aeronautics Administration, Najeeb Halaby, to visit Moscow. I urged him to go and instructed him to try to solve any remaining technical problems impeding an air agreement. Halaby went to Moscow on December 11 and spent several days with Soviet specialists discussing everything from engine noise to flight menus. But even with this auspicious beginning, it took almost three years to hammer out the final air agreement. The first regular Moscow–New York flight finally took place in July 1968. This was only one of many experiences that proved two of my basic assumptions—that reaching agreement with the Soviets on almost anything would take time, but that agreement could be reached if there were enough patience and understanding on both sides.

On December 17, 1963, I flew to New York to address the United Nations. I wanted to assure its members that though we had lost President Kennedy the United States would continue its wholehearted support of the United Nations as "the best instrument yet devised to promote the peace of the world and to promote the well-being of mankind." I knew that every delegate and every other person present realized that hopes for peace depended heavily on relations between the nuclear powers, so I used the occasion to discuss some specifics in that relationship. One passage that I hoped Moscow would pay particular attention to was this:

> The United States of America wants to see the Cold War end, we want to see it end once and for all;
> The United States wants to prevent the dissemination of nuclear weapons to nations not now possessing them;
> The United States wants to press on with arms control and reduction.

Two weeks later, on the morning of January 2, 1964, Dean Rusk called me at the Ranch to report that Soviet Ambassador Anatoly Dobrynin had just delivered a letter from Chairman Khrushchev to me. The Soviet leader proposed an agreement to settle territorial disputes by peaceful means. He was sending similar messages to many chiefs of governments around the world.

The translation of Khrushchev's letter reached me later that day, and I read it with care and with growing disappointment. It seemed designed for propaganda purposes rather than serious diplomacy. Khrushchev roundly denounced "colonizers" and "imperialism" as the major causes of past wars. Of course, he did not mention the Soviet Union's attack on Finland, the obliteration of the Baltic states, or the "colonization" of Eastern Europe by Moscow after World War II.

There was another notable omission. Khrushchev said nothing about indirect aggression, subversion, or the secret supplying of arms and military supplies across national frontiers. But the biggest disappointment in Khrushchev's letter was its failure to offer any specific proposal for curbing the arms race. The Soviet leader pointed in this direction when he wrote: "An example in the matter of disarmament must be set by the Great Powers." But he did not suggest how that should be done.

I called several advisers, among them Bob McNamara and McGeorge Bundy. I asked them to study the message carefully to see whether we could respond with something positive, constructive, and practical. The day after Khrushchev's letter reached me McNamara sent me a memo recommending one step that we might take—a cutback in U.S. production of fissionable materials for nuclear weapons. I accepted McNamara's suggestion immediately. A few days later, in my State of the Union message on January 8, 1964, I announced our intention to cut back our production of enriched uranium by 25 per cent.

"We are shutting down four plutonium piles," I added. "We are closing many nonessential military installations. And it is in this spirit that we today call on our adversaries to do the same."

When I answered Khrushchev on January 18, I suggested that both our countries present new proposals to the Geneva Disarmament Conference: to prevent the spread of nuclear weapons; to end production of fissionable materials for weapons; to transfer large amounts of fissionable materials to peaceful purposes; to ban all nuclear weapons tests; to place limits on nuclear weapons systems; to reduce the risk of war by accident or design; and to move toward general disarmament.

I concurred wholeheartedly with one statement in Khrushchev's letter—that "the use of force for the solution of territorial disputes is not in the interest of any people or any country." However, I felt that his proposition neglected some dangerous situations and potential developments. I therefore proposed guidelines for an agreement that would be both broader and stronger than the one he had advanced. I suggested that in trying to eliminate territorial disputes we consider not only established borders but such things as internationally agreed demarcation lines and special zones in armistice settlements. I had in mind such precarious areas as the ground and air corridors to Berlin and the demilitarized zones in Korea and Vietnam.

I also pointed out that the "use of force" should cover not merely aggression by regular armies marching across borders but subversion, infiltration of guerrillas, and the covert supplying of weapons across borders.*

One month later—on February 22—I followed up my earlier announcement and informed the Soviet leadership that it would soon be possible to reduce further our output of U 235.† I gave them this advance notice "in the renewed hope that the Soviet government would find it in its interest to take a parallel step." If this were to be done, I suggested that we announce our actions jointly or simultaneously.

On March 2, Khrushchev informed us through Ambassador Dobrynin that the Soviet leadership was ready to explore possibilities of parallel action in this area. For two months the Chairman and I negotiated by letter and through our Ambassadors in Washington and Moscow. But by April 17 no firm agreement had been reached. I decided that the United States would move on its own. Among other things, we faced the problem of setting up an orderly renegotiation of long-term power contracts that would be affected by our cutbacks. I relayed these considerations to Khrushchev and informed him that I planned to make the announcement in three days. Unless I heard from him before then, I would not mention the possibility of parallel Soviet action.

On April 20 I flew to New York City for the annual Associated Press luncheon, where I planned to discuss the basic principles of our foreign policy. The text of my speech also contained the announcement that we were going to reduce further our production of fissionable material. I was disappointed that I could not say the Russians were taking similar action. Then, just before I was due to speak, a courier brought me an urgent message that prompted me to pencil in a new paragraph. I barely finished writing before the presiding officer completed his introduction and made room for me at the rostrum.

Halfway through my speech I came to the key section, announcing the additional cutback in our production of enriched uranium. With the earlier reduction, this meant an overall decrease of 20 per cent in plutonium output and 40 per cent in uranium output. Then I added what I had just written on a sheet of paper:

> Simultaneously with my announcement now, Chairman Khrushchev is releasing a statement in Moscow, at two o'clock our time, in which he makes definite commitments to steps toward a more peaceful world. He agrees to discontinue the construction of two big new atomic reactors for the production of plutonium over the next several years, to reduce substantially the production of U 235 for nuclear weapons, and to allocate more fissionable material for peaceful uses.

* The full text of my letter to Khrushchev containing these proposals is in the Appendix, pp. 602–03.
† Enriched uranium used in the production of hydrogen bombs.

As I flew back to Washington that afternoon, I felt renewed hope for the future of mankind. The world's two greatest adversaries, history's two greatest powers, had taken a step toward disarmament. It was not a big step, but at least it was movement. As I had told the Associated Press executives and publishers in the ballroom of the Waldorf Astoria that afternoon:

> We must remember that peace will not come suddenly. It will not emerge dramatically from a single agreement or a single meeting. It will be advanced by concrete and limited accommodations, by the gradual growth of common interests, by the increased awareness of shifting dangers and alignments, and by the development of trust in a good faith based on a reasoned view of the world.

Cutting production of essential ingredients for nuclear bombs was only one of several areas we explored with the Soviets late in 1963 and in 1964. Since 1956 we had been participating in a program of cultural and technical exchanges with Moscow. Groups like the Philadelphia Orchestra played for Soviet audiences, while the Bolshoi Ballet danced for Americans. Van Cliburn played the piano in Moscow; David Oistrakh played the violin in New York. Each country sent the other exhibits of its goods and its best technology. A relatively small but significant number of Americans and Russians got to know each other and came to realize that men and women on the other side of the Iron Curtain were much like themselves. The exchange agreement expired in 1963, and we worked hard to renew it. We finally signed the 1964–1965 agreement on February 22, 1964.

For thirty years, ever since President Roosevelt first recognized the Soviet government and opened diplomatic relations, there had been sporadic discussion of an agreement between the two countries to cover consular practices and rights. Serious negotiations finally began in September 1963. After seven months of tough bargaining, we reached agreement and on June 1, 1964, the Consular Convention, the first bilateral treaty between the United States and the Soviet Union, was signed in Moscow. We waited almost three more years, however, before the Senate ratified the treaty. Some Senators, still attuned to Cold War ways, felt that no agreement with the Soviets could be good. Others, including the influential Senate Minority Leader, Everett Dirksen, expressed concern that the agreement might lead to the opening of numerous consulates in our country which would be used as espionage centers. Much of this resistance was finally broken down after I asked Dirksen to my office in February 1967 and talked to him for more than an hour about the details of our proposal. I showed him a letter from FBI Director J. Edgar Hoover assuring me that his organization could cope effectively with any increased dangers of espionage. I shared that judgment with other interested Senators, and Hoover himself answered letters from some who had asked about this matter.

The new agreement assured us prompt access to any Americans arrested in the Soviet Union and strengthened our ability to provide reasonable protection for American visitors to the Soviet Union, who were rapidly increasing in number—about 18,000 in 1966. The Senate finally gave its consent to the agreement in March 1967, and the Soviet government ratified the treaty fourteen months later.

Through the first months of 1964 there was much discussion in diplomatic channels of a possible meeting between the Soviet Chairman and me. On more than one occasion Ambassador Dobrynin expressed the view that such a meeting could be useful for both countries. I agreed with this sentiment, but I saw distinct disadvantages to my leaving the country during my first year in office.

There was no Vice President to carry some of the burdens of leadership during the President's absence. I had an ambitious legislative program, and I wanted as much of it approved as possible during the first year of my administration. That meant many hours of work every day. Overseas travel would have interfered with this effort. In addition, toward the end of the year I was involved in an election campaign. Finally, it seemed inevitable that any meeting between the leaders of the two most powerful nations would automatically raise unrealistic expectations of major accomplishments.

I was totally convinced, however, that the more the Soviet leaders and I understood each other's thinking, the better it would be for all concerned. I believed Khrushchev had greatly misjudged President Kennedy, and that was one thing that led him to risk putting nuclear missiles in Cuba. I wanted to make sure he did not similarly misunderstand either me or the will of the American people. One way to build that kind of understanding was to maintain fairly regular contact with him. Through letters, we exchanged views on matters as diverse as the situation in Laos and the possibility of using nuclear power to produce fresh water from salt water. I felt that we were beginning to get our separate viewpoints across as this exchange progressed. Then our correspondence abruptly ended.

On October 15, 1964, I was campaigning in New York State. At 5 P.M. I began a motorcade tour of Brooklyn. Ten minutes later, as I was riding through streets jammed with waving and cheering people, a message reached me over the Secret Service radio in the car. Khrushchev had resigned. Leonid Brezhnev would continue as top man in the Communist party, the report said, and Aleksei Kosygin would head the government as Chairman of the Council of Ministers.

I was certain that the reason for the abrupt change in Soviet leadership was not Khrushchev's health, as the Soviet news agency TASS claimed. There were deeper reasons for the shift. In any case, all the careful work, the exchanges of letters, and the gradual understanding of Khrushchev's thinking and reactions had been undone by the change in leadership. I knew I would have to start all over again and get to know the new man, or men, who decided Kremlin policy.

The next morning at 11:30 Ambassador Dobrynin came to see me at his request. He read me a short statement which repeated almost word for word the announcement TASS had made concerning the change in Soviet leadership. Dobrynin then went on, speaking without notes, to assure me that his government's foreign policy remained the same. The Soviets would continue, he said, to work for "peaceful coexistence and the relaxation of tensions." I thanked him for the report and said that my aim was to work for better understanding with all nations, including his.

There was inevitable concern when governments changed, I said, but I was neither excited nor alarmed by the events in Moscow. We would continue to try to work with him and with his leaders on a basis of candor. I pointed out to the Ambassador that our two countries had begun to make progress on several matters. I hoped that progress would continue. There were many things our people wanted to do more than to make bombs, I said. We needed more schools, hospitals, roads, and houses, and we found no pleasure in spending billions of dollars a year preparing for possible destruction. Dobrynin listened attentively. I thanked him for coming and urged him to report my views in detail to the new leaders in Moscow. He assured me that he would.

One important development earlier that day concerned both the United States and the Soviet Union deeply. I assumed that the leaders in Moscow knew as much or more about it than we did, but they had not instructed Dobrynin to raise the matter. I did not mention it either. That event was the explosion of the first nuclear device by Communist China. Peking's accomplishment came as no great surprise because we had been expecting it for some time. Nonetheless, the fact that a large country with a hostile government had mastered the technology of nuclear explosives was necessarily a source of worry.

I was not concerned for the immediate future. A long and expensive road separated setting off a nuclear blast and developing the powerful and accurate missiles to carry nuclear weapons across seas and continents. But what of my successor? Or his successor? Some future President would have to face the question of how to deal with this situation. The problem was not just a matter of China. It was a question of how to deal with a great many nations, of all sizes and levels of political stability, equipped with nuclear weapons. All I could do was to move as fast and as far as possible during my Presidency to slow the arms race, to achieve international agreements on their control, and to prevent the continuing pro-liferation of weapons that could mean the end of civilization as we knew it.

I knew that we could never break down the distrust between the United States and the Soviet Union if the Iron Curtain survived as an unnatural barrier between East and West. The Soviets had lowered the Iron Curtain against the West, of course. But I felt that we had unwittingly helped strengthen it by some of our policies. In our disapproval of communism we had turned our backs on the peoples of Eastern Europe, who after all had not voted for Communist rule but had had it forced upon them.

As Senate Majority Leader, I had strongly supported President Eisen-hower's call for "open skies" in 1955 as a way to insure effective inspection of disarmament plans—and two years later I had suggested an "open curtain" policy,* in which men and ideas could move freely over the obstacles of suspicion that had been raised against them.

One unfortunate by-product of the "McCarthy era" of the early 1950s was that many Americans continued to see a Communist "conspiracy" in almost every aspect of U.S. policy they opposed, whether in foreign trade, voting rights, or other areas. In the late 1950s and early 1960s "soft on communism" was still a potent accusation in politics. As a result, many political leaders felt it necessary to move with caution in dealings with the Communist world. That was true of my predecessors in the Presidency, though I am sure they wanted to advance faster than they were able to.

When I took office the air was somewhat less charged with blind anti-Communist sentiment. Americans felt a renewed self-confidence, which grew steadily over the years that followed. There were many reasons for that change. Sputnik had given the Communists a tremendous psychological boost, but by 1963 most people realized that the United States was catching up and soon would pass the Soviets in space exploration. Deepening rivalry between Moscow and Peking helped people to realize the Communist world was not a tightly disciplined monolith. Facing down the Soviet missile threat in Cuba removed the immediate danger of nuclear blackmail. Our own economy was growing, and it became obvious that Khrushchev's claim that the Soviets would surpass us in economic output by 1970 was an empty boast. Finally, the Soviet leaders had shown, by their participation in the "hot line" and in the Partial Test Ban Treaty, that they were prepared to consider agreements that involved mutual benefits.

It was increasingly apparent that at least some peoples and governments in Eastern Europe wanted to expand contacts with Western Europe and the United States. I decided that it was time to take the initiative and en-

---

* In an address on June 8, 1957, in New York City at the annual conference of the United Jewish Appeal.

courage these hopes. I was determined to work for that "open curtain" I had urged six years before.

I had agreed to go to Lexington, Virginia, to take part in the dedication of the George C. Marshall Library at Virginia Military Institute. That seemed an appropriate occasion to say some of the things that were on my mind concerning our relations with Europe. On May 23, 1964, I flew to Lexington. With me were several men who had worked closely with General Marshall in both war and peace—Dean Rusk; Dean Acheson, Under Secretary when Marshall was Secretary of State; and W. Averell Harriman, who had helped direct the Marshall Plan in Europe. At VMI we met others who had worked with the great American we were honoring that day—former President Eisenhower, whom Marshall had picked to lead allied forces in Europe; General Omar Bradley, who had directed our ground forces under Eisenhower; and Robert Lovett, Deputy Secretary when Marshall was Secretary of Defense.

In my remarks, I recalled that in proposing the Marshall Plan President Truman had offered friendship and assistance not just to Western Europe but to all of Europe, including the Russians. At first, many Eastern Europeans had hoped to take part in the program, notably the Poles and Czechs. Then Stalin put pressure on them, and the Iron Curtain rang down on our hopes of helping Eastern Europe.

"Today," I said, "we work to carry on the vision of the Marshall Plan." The heart of my message was that the United States would work to "build bridges"—bridges of trade, travel, and humanitarian assistance—across the gulf that divided us from Eastern Europe.

Our move in this direction had been strengthened considerably just a month before, from an unexpected source. At its annual meeting the U.S. Chamber of Commerce called for increased trade between our country and the Soviet Union and other European Communist states. Leaders of the organization pointed out that our restrictions on such trade had not deprived Eastern Europe of goods but had only served to increase the sales of Western European producers. This action by the U.S. Chamber of Commerce helped quiet some of the "thunder on the right" that boomed out whenever an official mentioned increasing trade with Eastern Europe.

Where possible, my administration expanded the list of products and credit arrangements permitted in U.S. trade with Communist nations. However, it soon became obvious that the existing Presidential authority simply did not permit us to go as far as we wanted. In February 1965 I appointed a Special Committee on U.S. Trade Relations with Eastern European Countries and the Soviet Union. This committee was composed of some of the best informed and most able businessmen in our country as well as representatives of the academic world and labor. It was headed by J. Irwin Miller, chairman of the board of the Cummins Engine Company of Columbus, Indiana. I asked the group to explore all aspects of expanding peaceful trade in support of our policy of widening relations with Eastern Europe.

On April 29, 1965, the Miller committee submitted probably the most definitive report on postwar East-West trade relations made up to that time. The committee capsulized its viewpoint in its conclusion:

> . . . trade with the European communist countries is politics in the broadest sense—holding open the possibility of careful negotiation, firm bargaining, and constructive competition. In this intimate engagement men and nations will in time be altered by the engagement itself. We do not fear this. We welcome it. We believe we are more nearly right than they about how to achieve the welfare of nations in this century. If we do our part, time and change will work for us and not against us.

Following the Miller committee's positive report, some of my advisers urged that we move quickly for an East-West trade bill that would allow Eastern European countries to sell goods on the American market at the same tariff rates as other nations. But a careful check showed that there would be strong opposition on the Hill to such a move. Resistance came from several sources. Some members of Congress, as well as others outside government, flatly opposed anything that looked like a "deal" with a Communist nation. A number of Senators and Congressmen had to consider the sentiments of constituents of Eastern European ancestry, who were fiercely critical of any move that might seem to strengthen the Russian economy. Others insisted that if we made trade concessions, the Communists should make political concessions. Still others opposed relaxation of trade barriers with any country giving assistance to North Vietnam.

I understood all these arguments against easing tariffs with Eastern Europe. I sympathized with most of the sentiments behind them. But I could not accept their reasoning. Trade is a two-way street. Moreover, in the words of the Miller committee, trade can be the "means of reducing animosities between ourselves and individual communist countries and can provide a basis for working out mutually acceptable solutions to common problems." I saw increased trade as a way to begin easing some of the worst tensions and suspicions of the Cold War.

Congressmen, friends who came to my office, and citizens writing to their President sometimes asked how we could be fighting Communists in Southeast Asia while negotiating and trading with them in Europe. I explained that these were two aspects of the same policy. We were fighting in Vietnam to demonstrate that aggression should not, must not, succeed. If totalitarian governments felt that they could take what they wanted by force, we would never have the kind of world where differences were settled peacefully. On the other hand, we had to show that there was an alternative to confrontation. We had to work in Europe and elsewhere, as opportunities arose, to erase the worst features of the Cold War. We had to create a climate in which nations of the East and West could begin cooperating to find solutions to their worst problems. Only by chipping away patiently at the Iron Curtain, by trying to get through to the governments and peoples of Eastern Europe, and by developing agreements that served all parties could we achieve a basis for rational international behavior. Thus we were using reason where we could, and force where we must, in both cases working toward the stable and orderly world that was our goal.

The resistance on the Hill—strong enough to spell certain defeat—prompted me to hold off introducing an East-West trade bill for a while, but by the end of 1965 I decided to move ahead. I hoped that once hearings were held and debate was in the open the requirements of national interest would sway opinion in favor of this move. I announced my intentions in my State of the Union message in January 1966, and the following May we asked the Congress for authority to "remove the special tariff restrictions which are a barrier to increasing trade between the East and the West."

We lost. Despite intensive efforts to educate the public and members of Congress on the advantages of the bill, we could not persuade either the Eighty-ninth or the Ninetieth Congress to act on it. Resentment against nations supporting Hanoi politically and materially was too great to be overcome. The East-West trade bill became a victim of the war in Vietnam. I resented as much as anyone what the Russians, Czechs, Poles, and others were doing to help North Vietnam. But it made no sense for the United States, because of that, to tie its own hands in trying to develop a coherent policy toward another important segment of the world.

In spite of the trade bill setback, we continued efforts to build bridges to the East in every practical way. The number of Americans traveling to Eastern Europe increased. Even with existing tariff barriers, trade increased somewhat. Cultural and technical exchanges took place. In January 1967 we raised the level of our diplomatic missions in Bulgaria and Hungary from legations to embassies. We freed additional commodities from the strategic control list. We widened the authority of the Export-Import Bank to help finance export sales to Eastern Europe. I appointed John A. Gronouski as American Ambassador to Poland as a symbol of my desire to strengthen our ties with Eastern Europe. Gronouski, who was Postmaster General at the time, was the first Polish-American ever to sit in the Cabinet. His appointment was greeted with unusual enthusiasm in Poland and he was an enormously popular Ambassador.

In these and countless other ways we were slowly building bridges of contact, commerce, and better understanding to millions of Europeans living under Communist rule. The countries of Western Europe were doing the same, and in many respects they were moving farther and faster than we were. We all had a long way to go, but slowly the Cold War glacier seemed to be melting.

In the summer of 1966 my advisers recommended that I make a detailed public statement of our European policy. We worked on the speech through the summer and early fall. Early in October Rusk told me that he had agreed to address the National Conference of Editorial Writers in New York City on October 7. He thought the time, the place, and the audience were most appropriate for the statement we had been preparing. He suggested that I replace him, and the hosts quickly and graciously accepted the change.

The dining room of the Carnegie Endowment Building, where the editorial writers met that day, was long and narrow and the speaker's dais was at the center of one of the long walls. I found that I had to keep turning right and then left or else seem to be ignoring two-thirds of the audience. The editors laughed when I said: "I am a little baffled by this room. It makes a speaker have to talk out of both sides of his mouth."

That was the only light note in the proceedings. I was in a serious frame of mind, for I was discussing some of the most crucial issues of our time—our country's relations with the most technically advanced segment of the globe, our efforts to heal ancient rivalries and modern antagonisms, and most important our intensified effort to reduce the danger of a major war.

"Europe," I said, "has been at peace since 1945. But it is a restless peace that's shadowed by the threat of violence."

I listed three fronts on which I felt we and our European allies had to move ahead: modernization of NATO, further integration of Western Europe, and more rapid progress in East-West relations. On the third point I said that the goal of our policy, based on the unity of the West, was "to heal the wound in Europe which now cuts East from West and brother from brother."

"That division must be healed peacefully," I said. "It must be healed with the consent of Eastern European countries and consent of the Soviet Union. This will happen only as East and West succeed—succeed in building a surer foundation of mutual trust.

"Nothing is more important than peace. We must improve the East-West environment in order to achieve the unification of Germany in the context of a larger, peaceful, and prosperous Europe. Our task is to achieve a reconciliation with the East—a shift from the narrow concept of coexistence to the broader vision of peaceful engagement."

I spoke of one of the most sensitive issues in European politics—the integrity of borders. One of the bedrocks of our foreign policy, I declared, was opposition to the use of force to change existing frontiers. I had in mind those potentially explosive borders in Europe where NATO and Warsaw Pact forces faced each other. I was thinking of the security of West Berlin and of the land, water, and air corridors linking it with the West. But I was thinking as well of what was probably the most important unresolved border problem in Europe: the frontier between Poland and Germany, along a line marked principally by the Oder and Neisse rivers. The Poles and East Germans considered the Oder-Neisse line as fixed and final. The West Germans insisted that the final determination should be made only when a formal peace settlement was worked out.

Without offending our German allies, I wanted the Poles and Russians to know that we would never resort to force to alter the Oder-Neisse line or any other generally accepted territorial border. That was the meaning of the carefully chosen words I used in New York, and I was sure that every European from the Atlantic to Moscow understood them.*

A central point in my speech was a declaration that the United States urgently wished to avoid the spread of nuclear weapons—in Europe and elsewhere in the world. I wanted to move ahead quickly on a nonproliferation treaty before other nations developed nuclear weapons, thereby further complicating the balance of forces and endangering everyone.

The reactions my speech generated in Europe were encouragingly favorable. Even in Moscow and Eastern Europe the reaction was strangely muted and, in some cases, favorable.

To help carry out an important aspect of our new policy toward Europe, I had talked veteran diplomat Llewellyn Thompson into accepting another tour of duty in Moscow, where he had previously served with distinction. Despite nagging health problems and the exhaustion that sets in after many years of service in difficult and demanding assignments, "Tommy" had agreed to go back to Moscow. On October 7, the same day that I spoke in New York, I sent his nomination as Ambassador to the Senate for approval.

A favorite argument of those who opposed our involvement in Vietnam was that the war prevented us from reaching any agreements with the Soviets or resolving areas of difference between Washington and Moscow. Many critics claimed that I was so preoccupied with Southeast Asia that I was neglecting Europe and passing up opportunities to ease Cold War tensions with Russia and Eastern Europe. The Soviet propaganda machine fed this notion, both openly and through informal contacts with individuals. The argument was not true, but few people took the trouble to compare the allegation with the facts.

---

* I was pleased when the West German government, in December 1970, accepted the Oder-Neisse line as the German-Polish border.

From 1955, when the Austrian State Treaty was signed by the Big Four powers, to 1963, no treaty or major agreement was concluded between the United States and the Soviet Union except on cultural exchanges. In 1963 the "hot line" was set up and the Partial Test Ban Treaty was signed.

During my five years in office we reached agreement with the Soviets on a number of important issues:

> a mutual cutback in production of fissionable materials;

> renewal of the two-year cultural agreement, despite pressures in both countries to let the arrangement lapse;

> the Civil Air Agreement, which opened up the first direct commercial air service between the two countries;

> the Outer Space Treaty, which prohibited the stationing of nuclear bombs on the moon, the planets, or in space;

> the U.S.-Soviet Consular Convention, which improved our ability to protect the interests of Americans traveling in the Soviet Union;

> a treaty guaranteeing the return of astronauts or space vehicles that descended accidentally on the territory of the Soviet Union or that of more than seventy-five other countries;

> a number of special agreements to settle potentially explosive clashes between the fishing interests of the two countries;

> finally, during my last year in office, the nonproliferation treaty, which prevented the spread of nuclear weapons.

The sum of our efforts was the conclusion of more significant agreements with Moscow in the years 1963–1969 than in the thirty years after we established diplomatic relations with the Soviet regime.

Of all the agreements reached with Moscow the most difficult, and the most important, was the Treaty on the Nonproliferation of Nuclear Weapons. I had mentioned the need for such an agreement in my first letter to Khrushchev in January 1964. I reemphasized it in my first formal letter to the new Soviet leaders at the end of December of that same year. I have no doubt that the explosion of a nuclear device by Communist China in mid-October 1964 heavily underlined in the minds of men in the Kremlin the necessity for a treaty limiting the spread of nuclear weapons. But though the need was evident, it took more than four years of painstaking and complicated diplomatic effort before we agreed on a draft of the treaty.

The security interests of many proud nations were involved. Our European allies, for example, wanted some measure of control over nuclear weapons located on their territory. They wanted a voice in whether and when those weapons were to be used. The West Germans, as the strongest and most threatened ally in Central Europe, wanted this kind of sharing most of all.

We had discussed numerous ways in which these sensitive allies could participate in both decision-making and any future use of these powerful weapons. One method suggested as an answer during President Kennedy's administration had been the so-called Multilateral Force (MLF), a proposed allied force of surface vessels with jointly owned nuclear weapons. The ships would have been manned by mixed crews of personnel from all the NATO countries. An alternative suggested by the British was the Atlantic Nuclear Force (ANF), which would have brought together, under unified command, bombers and other possible means of delivering nuclear weapons. In both cases, U.S. agreement would have been required before bombs or missiles were used.

During the nonproliferation negotiations, Moscow tried to rule out allied cooperation of this kind. Indeed, the Soviets wanted to outlaw the existing "two-key system" in NATO, which specified that nuclear weapons could not be fired without positive assent by both the United States and the country on whose soil the weapons were deployed. A Soviet draft in the fall of 1965 proposed that nonnuclear nations be denied "the right to participate in the ownership, control or use of nuclear weapons." There were doubts that, under this Soviet formula, we could have carried out even the kind of intensive consultations on nuclear matters within NATO that we planned to develop.

Meanwhile, a change was occurring on the Atlantic side of the Iron Curtain. Leaders and officials in various nations gradually absorbed the full meaning of the Cuban missile crisis: Nuclear blackmail is not an effective instrument of national policy, at least if the threatened nation is strong and determined. As anxiety lessened, allied diplomats and military leaders concluded that a joint nuclear force was not essential to the vitality of NATO, and that trying to work out details of such a force might be more divisive than unifying. The British came out strongly against a joint force. The Italians were divided. The French denounced it. Even the West Germans, who had supported the idea most enthusiastically, concluded that the political costs exceeded the possible advantages. They insisted, however, and we agreed, that the two-key system and nuclear consultation be protected in any nonproliferation treaty.

In addition, I knew that there was considerable resistance in Congress to nuclear sharing. Any changes in our law required to establish an allied nuclear force would meet stiff opposition on the Hill, even if U.S. control over the firing of weapons was maintained.

A partial break in the logjam came in September 1966. On the 22nd and again on the 24th of that month Rusk and Soviet Foreign Minister Gromyko had long, frank talks in New York. We concluded from these conversations that Moscow might accept a formula allowing the Atlantic allies three things we considered essential: the existing two-key arrangement, intensive consultation on nuclear matters in the NATO alliance, and preservation of the right of a united Western Europe, if it ever developed, legally to succeed the United Kingdom and France as a nuclear power. It was clear, however, that Moscow would oppose any transfer of ownership of nuclear weapons within NATO.

After reading reports of the Rusk-Gromyko talks and discussing the problem with the Secretary of State and others, I invited several senior advisers to Camp David on October 1.* After dinner, we reviewed the progress of discussions on the nonproliferation treaty. The conversation reinforced several things I had believed. One was that although the Soviet Union was seriously interested—as we were—in preventing the spread of nuclear weapons, Moscow would nonetheless try to use negotiations to create trouble among our closest allies. The West Germans were a particular target. Moscow was deeply suspicious of the Germans and wanted to make certain that they had no chance of gaining control over nuclear explosives.

The Russians were used to dealing with allies who, for the most part —with the notable exception of Red China—did as Moscow wished in military matters. The Russians seemed unable to understand the tremendous differences between their relationship with their Eastern European allies and the kind we had with the Germans, the Japanese, and others— nations with the scientific know-how and technical capability to produce nuclear weapons any time they decided to do so. The Germans and our other NATO allies insisted on, and deserved, an important voice in matters affecting their vital security. The Japanese, Indians, and others needed reassurance that their security would not be endangered if they gave up the right to make nuclear weapons or to receive them into their national arsenals.

The next morning, October 2, we continued our talks. Much of the time we wandered over the paths and through the autumn-colored woods at Camp David. I sounded out my advisers on their opinions and recommendations. They gave me not only their own views but those held by others in government who had been working on nonproliferation for a long time. Some of them believed that we had reached a point where agreement with the Soviets was within easy grasp, and that we should move ahead quickly. But others, especially Rusk, believed that we would be taking serious risks if we moved too fast and without thorough consultations with our major allies. I shared this view completely and asked Rusk to inform all concerned of my decision. We could not undertake a treaty

---

* Present at the meeting were Rusk, McNamara, Attorney General Katzenbach, Under Secretary of State for Political Affairs Eugene Rostow, Ambassadors Arthur Goldberg (to the United Nations) and Foy Kohler (to the Soviet Union), and Walt Rostow.

obligation, I said, if it committed us to act as if there were no Atlantic alliance. We could not tell our allies that these matters were none of their business. We should continue to push for a nonproliferation treaty, I told the Secretary, but not at the risk of tearing NATO apart.

During the next six weeks U.S. and Soviet specialists worked overtime to hammer out an understanding. At last, on December 5, the Soviets proposed treaty language we could accept. Rusk informed the NATO ministerial meeting of the Soviet proposal on December 12, 1966.

A full year and a half of intensive and complicated negotiations followed, even though the major hurdle of basic U.S.-Soviet agreement had been cleared. Other nations raised serious questions: What provisions would there be for monitoring and inspecting the terms of the agreements? Would the agreement deprive a nonnuclear power of benefits from the peaceful uses of nuclear energy? How long would the treaty be in force? What arrangements would be made for withdrawal from the treaty if a nation decided that such an agreement was against its vital interests?

During this period I instructed our diplomats to convey our views to all interested governments and to encourage agreement where appropriate. At the same time, I wanted them to avoid taking the lead or exerting pressure. Let our allies and others take the initiative, I told Rusk. This we did, although consultations with Bonn were held up until a new government was formed in December. I knew all too well the problems that some governments faced in explaining to their parliaments and peoples why it was better for their security to accept the agreement rather than keep open the option of making their own nuclear weapons.

Once basic agreement was reached on a nonproliferation treaty at the end of 1966, I decided to push hard for the logical and necessary next step —a way to slow the race in strategic arms and eventually, I hoped, to end it. I considered this the most critical issue in Soviet-American relations.

We had known for some time that the Soviets were installing an antiballistic missile system around Moscow. Pressure rose for us to follow suit to protect our major cities and ICBM emplacements with an ABM system. It was time, if not past time, for mature men to take stock together on how to achieve mutual security without the huge added costs of elaborate protective systems and the expanded offensive systems they would trigger into being. With this in mind, I wrote to Chairman Kosygin on January 21, 1967. I told the Soviet leader:

> I have directed Ambassador Thompson as a matter of first priority to discuss with you and the appropriate members of your Government the possibilities of reaching an understanding between us which would curb the strategic arms race. I think you must realize that following the deploy-

ment by you of an anti-ballistic missile system I face great pressures from the Members of Congress and from public opinion not only to deploy defensive systems in this country, but also to increase greatly our capabilities to penetrate any defensive systems which you might establish.

If we should feel compelled to make such major increases in our strategic weapons capabilities, I have no doubt that you would in turn feel under compulsion to do likewise. We would thus have incurred on both sides colossal costs without substantially enhancing the security of our own peoples or contributing to the prospects for a stable peace in the world.

I suggested that after Thompson made an initial exploration with Soviet officials, "it may prove desirable to have some of our highest authorities meet in Geneva or another mutually agreeable place to carry the matter forward."

Five weeks later, on February 27, 1967, Kosygin replied. He said that he and his colleagues were "prepared to continue the exchange of views on questions relating to strategic rocket-nuclear weapons." He promised that they would send additional thoughts on this matter through Ambassador Thompson. "Nor do we exclude the possibility," Kosygin wrote, "of holding in the future, as you suggest, a special meeting of our appropriate representatives for a more detailed discussion of this entire problem."

In spite of these promising words, the Soviets declined during the next several months to name a time or place for serious talks on curbing the missile race. There was evidence that opinion was then divided in the Soviet government on whether, and how, to proceed with missile talks.

The spring of 1967 was an ominous season. I seemed to wake up almost every morning with a new crisis staring me in the face. Tensions were rising in the Middle East as a result of increased Syrian harassment of Israel. Castro's illegal supply line of men and arms into Venezuela had been exposed to the world. The North Vietnamese were sending larger forces into South Vietnam.

I underlined these "situations" in a letter to Kosygin on May 19, 1967. Each problem was dangerous in itself, I wrote, but taken together they "could seriously impair the interests of our two countries and the attempts which have been made on both sides to improve our relations." I urged that we act, together or separately, "to bring these situations under control." Then I added:

> Beyond these points of danger and conflict, there are two areas of opportunity where I deeply believe it is our common interest and common duty to humanity to achieve constructive results: the achievement of understandings which would limit our respective deployments of ABMs and ICBMs and the negotiation of a non-proliferation treaty. These two enterprises are not explicitly linked; but I am sure you are conscious that our task of persuading the non-nuclear powers to accept a non-proliferation

treaty would be greatly eased if you and we could demonstrate concurrently our will and ability to begin to bring the nuclear arms race under better control. I hope, therefore, your government will find it possible to respond positively to our proposals to enter into serious discussions on the ABM and ICBM problem.

A little more than a month after I sent that letter to Moscow, Chairman Kosygin and I were sitting face to face across a small table in the Early American sitting room of a house in Glassboro, New Jersey.

After the Six Day War between the Arabs and Israelis in June 1967, as the United Nations tried to find a permanent settlement, we learned that a large Soviet delegation headed by Kosygin was coming to New York for the UN meeting. It seemed clear that Kosygin's primary mission was to boost sagging Arab morale and shore up Soviet prestige with its Arab friends. But almost as soon as the trip was known, we began to hear that Kosygin would welcome a visit with me, preferably in New York. After his trip was publicly announced, pressures increased on me, from Senators and others, to work out a meeting.

I shared the belief that a frank exchange of views might help clear the air on several questions and might even pave the way for solution of serious problems. I was particularly interested in discussing the Middle East, Vietnam, the nonproliferation treaty, and prospects for limiting the missile race. I invited Kosygin to the White House, which I felt was the courteous thing to do, though it might pose problems for him. In the charged atmosphere of mid-1967 we recognized that the Soviet leader might prefer not to be an official guest in the U.S. capital. The Arabs, the Chinese Communists, the North Vietnamese, and others might misinterpret it or misunderstand the circumstances. I therefore suggested Camp David as an alternative. Kosygin replied that he did not wish to come to Washington or even the Washington area—what was wrong with meeting in New York?

The United Nations was in an excited, emotional state and hardly provided the setting for quiet, relaxed talks between Soviet and American leaders. There would be problems of security if we met elsewhere in the city of New York. I could visualize a sea of pickets and protesters around any site we picked—people protesting Moscow's support for the Arabs, anti-Communist refugee groups, demonstrators opposing the war in Vietnam, others opposing Soviet assistance to Hanoi—all of them shouting, arguing, and probably fighting with each other.

Rusk was in New York for the UN meeting. I asked him to suggest to Kosygin that we meet at Maguire Air Force Base in New Jersey. Kosygin told Rusk that his going to a U.S. military base would be misunderstood. He argued that people might think we wanted to impress him with our "guns and rockets." Rusk pointed out the air base was not "bristling with guns." We had suggested it, he explained, only because it offered the desirable isolation and security, and because essential communications facilities would be available. Kosygin said he understood, but many people would not. The Soviet leader said that he favored a meeting, and the general area of New Jersey was acceptable, but he could not go to a military establishment. That was June 22.

The day before, my old friend Governor Richard J. Hughes of New Jersey had called the White House and talked to Walt Rostow. Hughes had been reading about the problems of arranging a Johnson-Kosygin meeting. Why not agree on some site in New Jersey? he asked. Then he suggested such possible places as Rutgers and Princeton universities. Rostow promised him we would give his suggestion serious thought and would be back in touch.

Dick Hughes's suggestion was in my mind when I received the report of Rusk's talk with Kosygin on Thursday afternoon. I decided to pursue the New Jersey offer further. I asked Marvin Watson to call Hughes and tell him that we were interested if he could suggest a good site—not a big city, but one close to an airport, and in a quiet setting. Hughes had been thinking hard during the night and had decided that Glassboro would be ideal. It was a small, peaceful college town. It was near the midpoint between New York and Washington. And it was only eighteen miles from Philadelphia International Airport and ten miles from the New Jersey Turnpike.

Colonel James U. Cross, my military aide and chief pilot, was with me in my bedroom along with Rostow. That able pilot and navigator sat on the bed beside me and pored over a New Jersey road map trying to locate Glassboro. Finally, he said: "Here it is." I thought to myself: "That little town doesn't know what it's in for; it will really be on the map in twenty-four hours."

I called Dick Hughes for additional details and authorized him to begin preliminary preparations as he saw fit. I also asked that Rusk be informed in New York so that he could secure clearance from the Russians. Once the Soviet leaders agreed, I called Governor Hughes at his office. He had already left for Glassboro by car, but his office reached him by radio. When he heard I was calling, Hughes stopped at the first pay phone he could find and returned my call. I told him that we were going ahead and would be announcing the meeting immediately. A few minutes later, at 6:35 P.M. on June 22, George Christian informed the White House reporters.

I will always have a warm spot in my heart for Dr. Thomas E. Robinson, the president of Glassboro State College, and for his wife. Few people have the kind of patience and consideration they showed when the "invaders" from Washington descended that evening on their large old stone house called "Hollybush." A massive communications network had to be installed overnight for us and for our guests, as well as for the huge press corps that would invade the tree-lined campus the next day. With so many people likely to be in the house for the meetings, technicians also felt it necessary to install air conditioners. Complicated security arrangements had to be made for both parties. We also had to prepare lunch for the visitors. I was told later that Mrs. Robinson remained stoic throughout all these advance preparations—that is, until she saw all the food being removed from her refrigerator. Then she went upstairs for a good and well-earned cry.

The advance party from Washington arrived at 11 P.M. on Thursday. They worked through the night and into the next day. They received the greatest possible cooperation from Dr. Robinson and the college staff, as well as from Governor Hughes, his wife, Betty, and assistants from the Governor's office. Our helicopters set down on the football field at Glassboro just before eleven o'clock on Friday morning, and when we arrived at Hollybush everything was in order. Preparations that ordinarily would have required twelve days or more had taken just twelve hours.

When word came that the Soviet delegation was delayed by heavy traffic on the turnpike, I visited with the Governor and President Robinson and their wives. Then I walked outside and shook hands with townspeople and students who had gathered for this historic meeting. Finally, at 11:22 A.M., Kosygin's limousine pulled up in front of the house, and I walked down the steps to welcome him. As we walked toward the house, the Chairman and I chatted amiably. He congratulated me on becoming a grandfather two days earlier. "I have been one for eighteen years," he said with a grin, "and I have no regrets."

We went directly into Dr. Robinson's study, just the two of us and our interpreters. We were to spend most of two working days in that quiet room, discussing the state of the world and its major problems, especially those that concerned us both.

For the most part, Kosygin was reserved but friendly during our long talks. We spoke of our grandchildren and of our hopes that they would grow up in a world of peace. He described his experiences in Leningrad through the long German siege of that great city during World War II. The memory of war's horror was always with the Soviet people, he said, and they wanted nothing but peace.

I picked up his point and reviewed all the steps I had taken as President to lessen Cold War tensions. Now, I said, it was time to take new steps. I told him that I had been waiting for three months for his answer on starting talks on ABMs and ICBMs. As soon as I brought up strategic arms talks, he changed the subject to the Middle East. This became a pattern during both days of our talks. Each time I mentioned missiles, Kosygin talked about Arabs and Israelis.

At only one point in our first session did Kosygin seem close to becoming really heated. He said we had talked about territorial integrity before the Middle East war, but we had ended by protecting aggression. He insisted that Israeli troops go back to the original armistice lines, and that the question of opening the Gulf of Aqaba be referred to the International Court of Justice. Then, he said, and the implication was "only then," could we discuss other problems. At that point, he came close to issuing a threat. Unless we agreed to his formula, he declared, there would be a war—"a very great war." He said the Arabs would fight with arms if they had them and, if not, with bare hands.

"All troops must be withdrawn at once," he said.

If they fight with weapons, I replied, we would know where they got them. Then I leaned forward and said slowly and quietly: "Let us understand one another. I hope there will be no war. If there is a war, I hope it will not be a big war. If they fight, I hope they fight with fists and not with guns." I told him that I hoped both our countries could keep out of any Middle East explosion because "if we do get into it, it will be a most serious matter."

With the Middle East, Vietnam, and other problem areas in mind, I suggested at our second meeting that we consider setting aside one week a year during which U.S. and Soviet leaders could meet and review all the major issues dividing us. Kosygin noted that we now had the "hot line" and could use that whenever necessary, as we had to good effect during the recent Six Day War. Kosygin apologized for having wakened me so early in the morning through the "hot line." But, he added, together we had "accomplished more on that one day than others could accomplish in three years."

I tried repeatedly to bring the talks back to limiting the missile race. I invited McNamara to join this discussion. At lunch, he and I made the strongest case we could for opening strategic arms talks immediately, but Kosygin apparently had come to Glassboro with a block against this subject. Time and time again, he implied that we only wanted to talk about limiting ABMs, while the Soviets felt that ABMs and offensive nuclear weapons should be linked. I reassured him repeatedly that we wanted to limit both offensive and defensive weapons, and McNamara said the same. But the point did not get across clearly—or Kosygin chose not to understand.

That Friday, and when we met again on Sunday, I tried several times to persuade Kosygin to agree to a time and a place for missile limitation talks. "Name the place," I said. "Give us a date—next week, next month. We will be there. Secretary McNamara is ready now." But it seemed obvious that Kosygin had come without the authority needed from the Soviet Presidium to make a firm commitment. We did promise to continue our search for agreement through talks between Rusk and Gromyko in New York.

I pointed out that we were in accord on all the essentials of the nonproliferation treaty, except for the controversial safeguards provision. That would be covered in Article III of the treaty. Why not, I asked, put our joint text on the table in Geneva minus Article III? That would give other nations a chance to study all the other provisions and react to them. Kosygin did not answer directly, but we agreed that this was also something Rusk and Gromyko could study.

The two foreign ministers met and talked the following week. Then our chief disarmament negotiator, Ambassador William C. Foster,* followed up the matter and discussed this approach with the Soviets. On August 10, 1967, Foster reported to me that the Russians had agreed at Geneva to table a joint treaty text with a blank Article III. This was done two weeks later.

I left Glassboro on Sunday evening, June 25, with mixed feelings—disappointment that we had not solved any major problem but hope that we had moved to a better understanding of our differences. When I reached the White House grounds that evening, reporters and television crews were waiting. To them and to the American people I voiced my belief that the meetings at Hollybush had made the world a little smaller and also a little less dangerous.

During the first half of 1968 I prodded Kosygin and his colleagues several times on the missile question. I urged them to begin talks. If the world knows we are working toward limiting nuclear weapons, I argued, that will help greatly to win agreement on the nonproliferation treaty. At first, Kosygin could only say that his government was "studying the question."

In June 1968 an agreement finally began to take shape. On June 21 Kosygin wrote that he hoped it would soon be possible "more concretely to exchange views." Then, after one more message from me, and just before the Nuclear Nonproliferation Treaty was opened for signatures, Kosygin advised me that the Soviets were ready to publish in the Soviet press and to broadcast over the Soviet radio on July 1, 1968, the following statement:

> On the forthcoming talks on questions of curbing the strategic arms race:
> An agreement has been reached between the Governments of the USSR and the USA to enter in the nearest future into talks on limitation and reduction of offensive strategic nuclear weapons delivery systems as well as systems of defense against ballistic missiles.

* Director, U.S. Arms Control and Disarmament Agency.

"We have no doubt," he wrote, "that a statement in such a spirit made by our Governments should, undoubtedly, also further the task of inducing the adherence of the greatest number of states to the Nonproliferation Treaty."

At the signing ceremony in Washington on July 1, 1968, I made the same announcement, in the same words. The first step had been taken, agreement to hold strategic arms talks. Now we would have to take the next step, finding an agreed place and time.

It was a moment of hope, but it came just as a new crisis threatened Europe. The people of Czechoslovakia were demanding more freedom. The old Stalinist government under President Antonin Novotny had been overthrown and a more liberal regime under Alexander Dubček took its place. The Dubček government was making concessions in the direction of greater liberty for the people. The Czechs avoided one thing, however, that had caused Moscow to react so violently in Hungary twelve years earlier: They did not threaten to leave the Warsaw Pact.

Nonetheless, the reverberations were felt throughout Eastern Europe. Old-line Communist leaders, such as Walter Ulbricht in East Germany, were dismayed. Conservatives in the Kremlin were no less disturbed. They all seemed to believe, and to fear, that if reforms succeeded in Czechoslovakia demands for the same concessions would quickly spread to the Soviet Union and other Communist countries. If the fire was not stamped out quickly, they might soon face a holocaust.

Leaders in Moscow faced a dilemma. If they used force to crush the peaceful Czech revolt, most of the world would attack the move and Soviet prestige would decline. Soviet leaders remembered well how the sight of Russian tanks roaring through Budapest in 1956 had affected their world position. They remembered too, of course, that no one had moved to stop them except the outnumbered and outgunned Hungarians themselves.

The Soviets began negotiating with the new Czech regime, but they also began moving huge military forces into Central Europe. There was little we could do except watch and worry. Most of my advisers believed the Czechs themselves would tighten the reins on the liberalization program before it reached the runaway point. If that happened, they doubted that the Soviets would risk a military invasion of an allied state. A few advisers, however, believed a military move against Prague was more than likely if the Czechs refused to back down completely.

We considered what we should do if Warsaw Pact forces rolled into Czechoslovakia. We had no treaty commitments, of course. NATO would not support military action. The Czechs themselves had indicated they did not plan to resist with military force, and that they would not welcome any response from the West. We could only try to avoid any action that would further inflame the situation. We hoped that increasing world criticism, combined with the confidence a great power like the Soviet Union should have, would convince Moscow not to crush the modest liberalism among the Czechs.

We had been pressing Moscow throughout the summer for a date and a place to begin strategic weapons talks. If anything drastic happened in Czechoslovakia, I knew it would derail, at least for a time, any chance to start strategic weapons talks. But on August 19, 1968, Ambassador Dobrynin called on Rusk to inform him that the Soviet leaders had accepted our long-standing proposal to discuss peaceful uses of nuclear power. They suggested that these talks begin in Moscow on October 15 "or any other date close to that time."

That evening I flew to Detroit to address the National Convention of the Veterans of Foreign Wars. Just before landing, I received word from the White House that the Soviets had just delivered a message to Rusk, which he was forwarding immediately. I delayed leaving the plane until it came. The message said the Soviet leadership was proposing an early announcement to this effect:

> An agreement has been reached that the President of the United States Lyndon B. Johnson will visit the Soviet Union in the first decade [first ten days] of October 1968 for the exchange of opinions with the leaders of the USSR on questions of mutual interest.

That night, when I got back to Washington, Rusk and Rostow were waiting for me in the White House. We discussed the Soviet messages, agreed to accept the proposals, and planned to release the news on the morning of August 21. The next day the White House press office prepared a news release on my planned trip to the Soviet Union. Tom Johnson alerted the press that afternoon to be on hand the next morning for an announcement they would find of interest.

At our regular Tuesday lunch that day we debated whether the Russians would move against Czechoslovakia, in view of the action they were taking on the talks. Opinions were divided, and I was not completely optimistic. Despite the breakthrough we were preparing to announce, the possibility of an invasion was on my mind.

As it turned out, our press release never reached the hands of the reporters. A story that would have produced banner headlines around the world was never written. At 7:06 P.M. on August 20 the phone on my desk rang. Rostow had just received a call from Ambassador Dobrynin, who had received a message from the highest level in his government with instructions to deliver it personally to the President. He wanted an appointment at eight o'clock that night. I asked what it was about. Walt said that Dobrynin had not told him.

"What's your guess?" I asked. "Is it Czechoslovakia?"

"It could be," Rostow answered.

"Bring him in at eight," I said. "I'll see him."

That evening I walked into the Cabinet Room, where the Ambassador and Rostow were waiting. We shook hands and sat down, I in my regular chair, the Ambassador directly across the table, and Rostow at my left, taking notes.

The Ambassador was obviously tense. I tried to relax him by recalling our meeting at Glassboro. I had seen color movies of that event just the night before, I said. I told him that after watching Kosygin with the friendly crowd at Glassboro "you would have thought he was a county judge in New Jersey or a Senator." Dobrynin smiled and began to look a little more relaxed.

We talked a few minutes more, then the Ambassador's face turned serious once again. "Now, Mr. President," he said, "I have an urgent instruction from my government to tell you about serious business. I will read it."

He then proceeded to read a long statement:

> The Government of the Soviet Union considers it necessary to inform, personally, President Johnson about the following. In connection with the further aggravation of the situation which was created by a conspiracy of the external and internal forces of aggression against the existing social order in Czechoslovakia and against the statehood established by the constitution of that country, the Government of the Czechoslovak Socialist Republic approached the allied states, the Soviet Union among them, with a request of rendering direct assistance, including the assistance by military forces.

He went on reading the message, which tried to justify the Soviet action. It concluded with this statement:

> We proceed from the fact that the current events should not harm Soviet-American relations, to the development of which the Soviet Government as before attaches great importance.

"This," Dobrynin said, "is what I was asked to tell you."

Later that night I sat at the Cabinet table once again with the Vice President, Dean Rusk, Clark Clifford, CIA Director Helms, General Wheeler, and a few others to assess at length this latest development. I concluded there was nothing we could do immediately about the Czech situation, but I instructed Rusk to call in Dobrynin that same night and tell him that there would be no announcements about my visiting the Soviet Union or the technical nuclear talks.

After our meeting, I called the Republican Presidential candidate, Richard Nixon, in New York City. I had promised to keep him informed of all major developments, and since Vice President Humphrey had been in the meeting, I thought Nixon should know what had happened. I explained how near we had come with the Soviets to strategic arms talks and discussions of peaceful uses of nuclear power. And I informed him of the Czech situation and Dobrynin's call. He was grateful for the information, he said, and assured me that he would say nothing that would make my job more difficult.

"You know how I feel," he said. "The hell with the election. We must all stand firm on this."

In the wake of their callous, outrageous assault on Czechoslovakia, the Russians began pressing harder for a summit meeting and nuclear arms talks, probably feeling that these discussions would soften the criticism Moscow was getting around the world. For our part, we waited for withdrawal of Warsaw Pact forces from Czechoslovakia and a quieting of the atmosphere in Central Europe.

In preparation for our meetings and talks with Moscow, we had worked out the following formula. First, there would be an exchange of technical papers in which we and the Soviets would set forth our general positions on limiting strategic arms, offensive and defensive. Second, the Soviet leaders and I would meet at the summit conference and try to reach agreement on broad principles to guide the negotiators on both sides. We would also discuss other world problems at the meeting, especially the Middle East and Southeast Asia. Finally, there would be a continuation of the technical negotiations based on the agreed principles, but under the full control of the new President.

By the summer of 1968, we had developed within the government a solid agreement among the various departments and agencies. Our position was backed by the disarmament specialists and the Joint Chiefs of Staff, and by the Atomic Energy Commission technicians and the political experts in the State Department. We were as well prepared as a government could be for the historic effort ahead.

After the November elections, I understood fully that President-elect Nixon and his advisers would want time to study these complicated plans before committing themselves to a final position. But I was certain that the format we had worked out would protect them. The technical negotiations after the summit meeting would be fully in their hands. I proposed that the President-elect go with me to the summit meeting. Mr. Nixon considered the possibility and finally decided against it. I suggested then that he choose a trusted adviser to go with me as an observer and full participant in the talks. He tentatively selected retired diplomat Robert D. Murphy for this assignment.

The invasion of Czechoslovakia did more than postpone the summit meeting. The Nuclear Nonproliferation Treaty had gone to the Senate, but many Senators were in no mood to approve agreements with Moscow in that charged atmosphere. I considered calling a special session to act on the treaty, but talks with numerous Senators convinced me that this would cause bad feelings and increased resistance. It was clear that leaders in the Republican party wanted to delay approval of the treaty until after the inauguration so the new administration could at least share credit for this historic move. As it turned out, they succeeded. The Senate finally approved the treaty in March 1969, and the Soviet Union acted on it eight months later. The world would have been better off if we both had moved faster.

At the end of November 1968, in a final effort to launch the strategic arms limitation talks, we sent a message to Ambassador Thompson in Moscow authorizing him to suggest a summit meeting in Geneva just before Christmas. He made that suggestion to Gromyko on November 29. The Soviet diplomat said he could not comment at that time, but his reaction indicated that the Soviet leadership still had a possible meeting in mind. In the next ten days, however, Moscow's attitude cooled noticeably. Thompson had difficulty reaching Soviet Ambassador Dobrynin, who had returned to Moscow for consultation. When they finally met, it appeared that Soviet interest in a meeting had almost disappeared.

Dobrynin told Thompson that if I decided not to go ahead with the meeting "that would be understood in Moscow and there would be no hard feelings." When I received the report from Thompson, I wrote in pencil at the bottom: "I'm ready! Are they?" Everything we learned indicated that they were not. I believed the Soviet leaders had been persuaded that it made more sense for them to deal with the incoming administration. I had a strong feeling that they were encouraged in that view by people who were very close to the Nixon camp.

The result was an important loss of time in the effort to curb the missile race. I understood perfectly well that in pressing for a summit meeting so late in my term I would be charged with seeking a dramatic occasion to highlight my departure from office on January 20. My real reason was quite different. I knew how many long and tedious months had been spent in both Washington and Moscow in an effort to work out concrete proposals in this extremely vital area. I knew also that technology was advancing and weapons production was increasing rapidly in both countries. Above all, I knew how long it had taken for the Soviets to come to agreement among themselves on a proposition they could table. I therefore feared the consequences of a delay.

The strategic arms limitation talks did not begin until a year after they might have. I have always felt that year could have been spent in the best interests of the safety of this planet and all the people who inhabit it. The most important thing, certainly, is that the talks did finally begin—in Helsinki in November 1969—and that may have given mankind another reprieve.

As my final months in the nation's highest office dwindled down to a few weeks, then a few days, I spent much time rethinking and reliving the trials and tests of the recent years. I knew I had done my best in those years to move our world toward a more stable and more peaceful order. I recalled the achievements—the problems solved, the agreements reached, the wars avoided. And I recalled some of the setbacks—the failure to find peace in Vietnam and the Middle East, the disappointment of not stopping and reversing the nuclear race.

Through those years in the White House, I had reached two important conclusions concerning our role in the world, and I intended to include them in my final summation to the Congress. The first was that the peoples and nations of Asia, Africa, and Latin America, as well as Europe, were ready to play a larger part than ever before in solving their own problems. That had been a fundamental goal in my foreign policy all along—to encourage this sense of responsibility and regionalism in all continents. The countless talks with world leaders over the years, the flow of reports from every capital—all I had seen and knew—convinced me there was gathering strength and confidence. All these nations wanted a world shaped not merely by conflicts—or agreements—between Washington and Moscow. They were groping toward a future in which their voices would be heard clearly by all. They wanted to deal with Washington and Moscow, and every other capital, from a position of dignity and self-respect.

My second conclusion was worrisome. There was a restlessness in our land among many citizens, and in the Congress, regarding our role in the world. There was growing discontent over the burdens we had carried so long. Why, some people asked, was it necessary to keep U.S. troops in Europe twenty-five years after World War II? Why were we fighting in Vietnam without the help of troops from any of the European countries we had helped to save? Why were we still spending money on aid to nations that seemed to be doing too little to help themselves?

There was, in short, all the raw material for an isolationist reaction. Yet from every political, military, technical, and economic fact available to me, I knew that the world was not one from which the United States could safely withdraw. However much various regions and nations were growing in strength, their future and ours were bound together in a multitude of ways. Our safety and prosperity could never be secure in isolation. As I prepared to leave Washington, this was my greatest single fear. I knew how much we had built, and I knew the many sacrifices that had gone into that effort. Yet it was possible that all this could be destroyed if we turned again to experiments with isolation, whether out of boredom or frustration, out of lack of money, or out of simple foolishness.

But it is a deep article of faith with me that the overwhelming majority of Americans are ready to play their part in the world as long as they are sure others will do the same. It was on this faith that I worked from 1963 to 1969 to face our crises and achieve some of those quiet advances which were so important during those years.

All this and much, much more was on my mind on the night of January 14, 1969, when I threw precedent aside and went to Capitol Hill to address the Congress for the last time as President. I warned the Congressmen and the American people of our need for strength and courage in a world where the weak were still at the mercy of the strong. I recalled our program of more than twenty years of helping the developing nations. I told the Congress we had to continue to support efforts in regional cooperation. Above all, I said, we must continue our search for peace among nations, a search that requires us to seek areas of agreement with the Soviet Union "where the interests of both nations and the interests of world peace are properly served."

Then I said good-by and left the familiar chamber. As I rode back from the Hill that night, I thought of what I had said, and of all that lay behind each paragraph. I thought of all that would be involved in the search for peace I had just talked about.

Five years and more of crises, of meetings and memos, of agonizing decisions and midnight phone calls, had taught me that the work of peace is an endless struggle to tip the balance in the right direction. I had faced so many situations in which the balance between order and disorder, between agreement and chaos, had been a delicate one.

In a few cases, everything we did was not enough to tip that balance toward order or agreement. When we were able to move the balance in the right direction, the satisfaction had been great. I thought of Panama and Guantanamo, of the Dominican Republic and the Six Day War, of Cyprus and Korea, of the Indian drought and of problems across the Atlantic. They all had contained explosive possibilities. But patience and hard work, imagination and good will, had averted tragedies that would have affected the lives of millions of people.

No man should think that peace comes easily. Peace does not come by merely wanting it, or shouting for it, or marching down Main Street for it. Peace is built brick by brick, mortared by the stubborn effort and the total energy and imagination of able and dedicated men. And it is built in the living faith that, in the end, man can and will master his own destiny.

21

"It's the right thing to do"
[VIETNAM 1968–1969]

W EDNESDAY, APRIL 3, 1968, began like most days in the White House. I was up early and read through the morning papers over breakfast. Two assistants, Jim Jones and Larry Temple, joined me to go over the day's schedule. It was fairly full—several private meetings, including one with Senator Robert Kennedy and Ted Sorensen; a session with the Cabinet at noon; a gathering of congressional leaders on tax matters at 6:30 P.M.

I listened to the radio news and glanced again at the front pages of the papers. One item, which I had heard broadcast the previous afternoon, was receiving considerable attention. In a speech to the Senate on Tuesday Senator J. William Fulbright had told the Senate that the partial bombing halt I had ordered three nights before added up to only "a very limited change in existing policy." He forecast that the halt would not move Hanoi in the direction of peace talks. I was surprised by Fulbright's reasoning and by his timing. We had stopped bombing over more than three-fourths of North Vietnam, an area where nine out of every ten North Vietnamese lived. That was much more than a "limited change" in our actions. Moreover, I believed Hanoi was perfectly able to judge the significance of our move without advice from Americans.

I was convinced that this misinterpretation was the result of the last-minute change in the wording of my March 31 speech. My decision had been to stop bombing at the 20th parallel. We had so advised the congressional leaders. We had also informed Hanoi of the limitation through the Soviet government. But on the strong urging of Acting Secretary of State Nicholas Katzenbach, we changed the wording of my speech to read that we would stop bombing "except in the area north of the demilitarized zone where the continuing enemy build-up directly threatens allied forward positions and where the movements of their troops and supplies are clearly related to that threat." Some people wishfully interpreted the sentence to mean a fairly narrow strip of territory just north of the 17th parallel.

On April 1 a few of our planes attacked military targets in and near the town of Thanh Hoa, just south of the 20th parallel. This was a major transfer point for men and supplies moving toward South Vietnam—either due south toward the demilitarized zone or westward into the infiltration routes through Laos. Critics immediately tried to use the air strike as evidence that I had been "misleading" in my description of the no-bombing zone. They ignored the military importance of Thanh Hoa to the enemy's supply system. Nonetheless, when the criticism erupted, I regretted that I had not kept the original wording of my statement.

At a long meeting at the White House on April 2 I discussed this problem with my advisers. As a result of this discussion, I instructed General Wheeler to inform the senior military commanders in the Pacific of the allegations and accusations we faced. They were instructed to use strict judgment in their choice of targets in the days ahead and, specifically, to cancel a second strike on Thanh Hoa, which had been planned for the next day.

On April 3, after we had received Hanoi's response to my speech, I instructed Wheeler to send another message to his commanders in Vietnam and the Pacific advising them that I was particularly anxious to avoid any violation of the bombing restrictions. To insure this, they were ordered to schedule no attacks north of the 19th parallel until directed otherwise by the Joint Chiefs. We planned to make no announcement of this further self-imposed restriction. There were two basic reasons for not making this limitation public. First, we were concerned that Hanoi might take advantage of of our additional restraint. Second, we considered it possible that we would have to go north of the 19th parallel at a later time because of North Vietnam's military activities in that area. In fact, we never again bombed any targets north of the 19th parallel while I remained in the White House.

In the Senate discussion following Senator Fulbright's speech, Majority Leader Mike Mansfield and other Senators spoke up strongly in defense of our action and disputed Fulbright's charges. Senator Mansfield recalled the long talk he and I had had on the evening of March 27 and he disclosed that I had informed him on that occasion that we were going to stop bombing north of the 20th parallel. Mansfield noted that this action meant that more than three-fourths of North Vietnam had been relieved of bombing by my decision. He added that he wanted the record to show that "insofar as the President is concerned—and I can state this on my personal word—he is intent only on trying to stop these men and supplies from going down these trails along the western side of North Vietnam . . . the terminal point of which is the DMZ where they will be used against Americans stationed along that area."

Senator Richard Russell also recalled our conversation the previous week when I informed him of the bombing cessation in the area above the 20th parallel. Similarly, Senator John Stennis noted that he and other members of the Armed Forces Committee had been informed by Secretary Clifford several times that the northern boundary of the area where bombing would continue would be the 20th parallel.

But to my mind, the principal issue was not where the precise line marking the no-bombing area was drawn, but rather how Hanoi would react to our self-imposed restriction. The key question in the Senate discussion, I believed, was raised by Senator Frank Lausche of Ohio: "How can Ho Chi Minh give any affirmative action when the Senator from Arkansas and others attack the government before Ho can respond?"

While Fulbright's allegations dominated the news stories and headlines, Lausche's pertinent question received scant attention. I saw it mentioned only once, in *The New York Times* on April 3, and then only in the thirtieth and last paragraph on page 14. When the North Vietnamese hear what Fulbright said, I thought, they will probably delay their answer—if they intended to react favorably.

These reflections put me in a bad mood as I prepared to leave for the Oval Office, but I cheered up when my grandson Lyn came in. I always felt better when I saw him, and that morning I needed to feel better. He was bouncing on the bed, grabbing the phone and laughing. "Bring him along," I said. Larry Temple picked Lyn up and we walked to the office.

Senator Henry ("Scoop") Jackson of Washington came into my office with his wife and their two children, Anna and Peter. Peter was celebrating his second birthday. I gave the children gifts and the White House photographer took a birthday picture. At that moment, Tom Johnson rushed in from the Press Room with a piece of ticker copy in his hand. He handed it to George Christian, who passed it to me. It was a bulletin from Singapore reporting a Hanoi broadcast. It said, in effect: "Hanoi is ready to talk."

In minutes the Situation Room sent me the full text of Hanoi's statement. After a long preamble criticizing us bitterly, the Hanoi statement said:

> It is clear that the U.S. government had not correctly and fully responded to the just demand of the DRV government, of U.S. progressive opinion, and of world opinion. However, on its part, the DRV government declares its readiness to send its representatives to make contact with U.S. representatives to decide with the U.S. side the unconditional cessation of bombing and all other war acts against the DRV so that talks could begin.

Secretary Rusk was in New Zealand attending a meeting of the Southeast Asia Treaty Organization, so I asked George Christian to call Acting Secretary of State Katzenbach and Defense Secretary Clifford for their reactions. Meantime, Walt Rostow had talked with CIA Director Richard Helms. The three had seen only the brief news bulletin. I asked them to lunch so that we could decide on the best way to respond to this obviously important development.

I showed the news bulletin to Senator Jackson and said: "It looks like it's turning out the way we hoped it would." Then I said good-by to the Jacksons and walked through the outer office and into the Cabinet Room. Bobby Kennedy and Ted Sorensen were waiting. The Senator had asked for an appointment the morning after my March 31 speech. I handed him a copy of the Singapore story. He had not heard of it, and he agreed with me that it sounded encouraging. We did not discuss the matter in detail, but I told him that we would move toward peace if Hanoi would cooperate. We could not be certain, I said, that this was an authentic peace offer, but we would certainly pursue it. Our negotiators were ready if Hanoi was. The Senator offered to help in any way he could.*

Less than an hour later I met with my Cabinet officers. I had not seen most of them since my announcement that I would not seek another term. Several Cabinet members mentioned Hanoi's statement, which they had heard on the radio while driving to the White House. They were intensely interested in this latest development. They hoped, as I did, that it might mean the road to peace was at last open. I asked the Acting Secretary of State to discuss this development.

"The first three-quarters of Hanoi's statement is the standard Communist attack on us," Katzenbach said. "But there is a more interesting and crucial part that follows." He believed that this key passage went "further perhaps than Hanoi has ever gone before."

"It is the first time that they have shown any willingness to have their representatives get in touch with ours," he added. "We still don't know what it means, how it all adds up exactly, but we are studying it and will be following it up very carefully."

Secretary Clifford said Hanoi's message should be "taken in the context of the President's statement of Sunday night."

"The President took the first step so that Hanoi could have an opportunity to take the next step," Clifford said. "Then the President could take a further step. This may be what Hanoi could have in mind. They seem to be responding to the President's initiative." We discussed this possibility for a while, then went on to other Cabinet business.

I had asked my principal foreign policy and military advisers to meet me for lunch after the Cabinet meeting. But several appointments intervened and we could not get together until after three o'clock. Except for Rusk, the

---

* See Chapter 22, pp. 539–42, and Appendix, pp. 576–77, for a more complete account of this meeting.

"regulars" were all present—Clifford, Wheeler, Helms, Rostow, and Katzenbach in place of Rusk. General Maxwell Taylor and Assistant Secretary of State William Bundy were also there, and I had asked Ambassadors Goldberg, Harriman, and Thompson to join us. Our main task was to decide how to reply to Hanoi's statement. Everyone present favored a positive response, but some wanted to go further than others. After hearing various points of view, I asked Katzenbach, Clifford, and Goldberg to go across the hall to the Treaty Room and draft a statement for our consideration.

"We have to prevent everybody from getting their hopes up too high," I warned. "We have to be aware that we're still far from peace." One adviser pointed out that "the debate in the Senate has been washed away by events." Another said: "Apparently it's easier to satisfy Ho Chi Minh than it is Fulbright." One adviser favored delaying any action until we had full agreement with the South Vietnamese and had consulted our other allies. "Let's not rush into this," he urged. "We are not rushing," I said. "But there are two things we have to do: One is to go out to [Ambassador] Bunker to explain what we are thinking; the other is to get out a positive statement now. I want to move, but I don't want to rush."

I approved messages to Saigon and to the capitals of our other allies in Vietnam. We had to work closely with them in any serious negotiations that might develop. Meanwhile, I decided to tell Hanoi that we were ready to meet. My colleagues urged me to release the proposed statement personally, so after we had agreed on the wording, I went out to the West Lobby, where the White House press corps was waiting. As reporters stood taking notes and cameras clicked and whirred, I said:

> Last Sunday night I expressed the position of the United States with respect to peace in Vietnam and Southeast Asia as follows: "Now, as in the past, the United States is ready to send its representatives to any forum, at any time, to discuss the means of bringing this war to an end." Accordingly, we will establish contact with the representatives of North Vietnam. Consultations with the government of South Vietnam and our other allies are now taking place.

I also told the reporters that I planned to leave the next evening for Honolulu for a previously scheduled meeting with General Westmoreland and others from the American Mission in Vietnam. I never made that trip. The following day, Martin Luther King, Jr., was shot and killed in Memphis, and I remained in Washington to deal with the possible violent aftermath of the tragedy. Instead of going to Hawaii, I asked Westmoreland to come to Washington a few days later.

On the evening of April 3 I met in the Cabinet Room with congressional leaders from both parties to discuss the tax bill. During the meeting I received the draft of a message my advisers thought we should send immediately to Hanoi. The message said that we had read the North Vietnamese statement and would accept their proposal. Our representative, Averell Harriman, would be available immediately to meet their representative. We suggested they meet in Geneva on April 8. If that arrangement was not agreeable, we would accept "any reasonable alternative suggestions" by Hanoi regarding time and place. I approved the message and we sent it within the hour to our Embassy in Vientiane. It was delivered to the North Vietnamese in the Laotian capital at noon on April 4 (midnight April 3 Washington time).

Several Americans were in Hanoi at that time, among them William Baggs of the *Miami News,* Harry Ashmore of the Center for the Study of Democratic Institutions, and Charles Collingwood of CBS. Baggs and Ashmore had gone to North Vietnam with our knowledge but with no authority to speak for the U.S. government. They hoped to open a channel of communication that might pave the way for peace talks. Collingwood was in Hanoi gathering news and film for the CBS television network. The day after our acceptance was delivered to the North Vietnamese, these three Americans arrived in Vientiane. Baggs and Ashmore gave William Sullivan, our Ambassador to Laos, a message they had received from the editor of North Vietnam's principal Communist newspaper. They believed that it represented the official position of the Hanoi regime. The message suggested our contact be at the ambassadorial level in Phnom Penh, Cambodia, "or another place to be mutually agreed upon." Collingwood had received the same message during an interview with North Vietnamese Foreign Minister Nguyen Duy Trinh.

I was interested in these messages, for it appeared the logjam might be breaking. I wanted to move ahead, but I felt we had to show reasonable caution. Apparently the North Vietnamese had given their views to the Americans in Hanoi before Ho Chi Minh and his colleagues had received, or had had a chance to study, our proposal. Hanoi was not replying to our offer on either time or place in these messages. Also there is always some doubt that messages passed through private channels are legitimate reflections of official policy. Hanoi could always disavow as a "misunderstanding" anything sent through newsmen or private citizens. We wanted to have this matter in the hands of official representatives as soon as possible.

Meanwhile, Hanoi's suggestion of ambassadorial talks in Cambodia began to leak to the press. To keep the record straight, George Christian told the White House reporters on April 6:

> The U.S. government has not yet received a formal reply from the government of North Vietnam. We have received messages through private individuals recently in Hanoi, but these do not appear to be a reply to our proposal. We hope to receive an official reply from Hanoi soon.

In the meantime, a friendly European government had informed us that one of its diplomats had been told by a North Vietnamese Ambassador that Hanoi would accept Geneva as the site of talks with the United States.

What was Hanoi's official position? We decided the only way to find out was to ask. We also wanted Hanoi to understand our position clearly, so we prepared another message. We pointed out that it would be difficult for us to meet in Phnom Penh because we had no diplomatic relations with Cambodia and no Embassy or staff there. There would be many technical problems with communications and other facilities. We sent the message for delivery to the North Vietnamese in Vientiane. But before it could be delivered, a "flash" message arrived from Ambassador Sullivan in Laos. A North Vietnamese diplomat had come to our Embassy and promised that his government would answer our proposal of April 4 that same afternoon. We stopped delivery of our second message until we learned what Hanoi had to say. Early the next morning, April 8, we had our answer. The North Vietnamese agreed to meetings at the ambassadorial level, but they were sticking to Phnom Penh as the site. They insisted it was an "appropriate" location. They did not mention Geneva or any other place, but their message left the door open for counterproposals.

At noon I met with Rusk, Clifford, and Rostow in the Cabinet Room. We studied Hanoi's reply word by word, line by line. Rusk said he thought the South Vietnamese would strongly prefer New Delhi as the site for contacts, and there was also a good case for Rangoon. We all considered it preferable to hold the talks in Asia, assuming that Hanoi would not accept Geneva. Clifford reminded me that I and others had frequently said we would meet "anywhere, anytime."

"We have to assume that there is drinking water there, don't we?" I said. "You can't hold a formal international conference on a desert or a mountaintop. Both sides need housing and other facilities. The conferees have to be able to communicate quickly and securely with their home governments." I added that if the leaders in Hanoi had suggested quiet talks away from all publicity, I would have sent our representatives any-where. But that clearly was not what they had in mind. The Communists were going to use these talks for every propaganda advantage and we had to protect ourselves. My advisers agreed that they were "trying to test us." We all remembered how the North Koreans had put us at a disadvantage in 1951 when we accepted armistice talks inside Communist-controlled territory. We wanted no repetition of that.

After the meeting, I told the White House reporters:

> I have a message from Hanoi replying to our message of April 3. We have taken steps to notify our allies. We shall be trying to work out promptly a time and a place for talks.

As we awaited word from the South Vietnamese and our other allies,

Ambassador Sullivan reported that the North Vietnamese had asked for another meeting "in order to have further exchanges." They claimed to have new information from Hanoi. Meanwhile, Ambassador Ellsworth Bunker had met with President Thieu. He informed the South Vietnamese leader that he was returning to Washington immediately for discussions with me and other administration officials. On hearing this, the Vietnamese leader said:

> Tell the President that if he has anything to tell me at any time, to do so frankly. He should not hesitate. We are friends. Both of us are trying to do the same job and we have the same responsibilities. If there is anything I can ever do for him, I will try to do it. We are in this thing together and we must do things together. We must help each other.

I was happy to read President Thieu's words. I knew we faced difficult days ahead, and it was important that our governments stay in double harness as we approached negotiations with the enemy. Any divisions between us would only play into Hanoi's hands.

On the evening of April 8 I flew by helicopter to Camp David. It was a relief to get away from the noise and the carbon monoxide of downtown Washington. At the Aspen Lodge I changed into more comfortable clothes and sat in the living room talking with Walt Rostow about the problems we would be discussing the next day. Finally, I dozed off in my chair until dinnertime. The next morning, I drove to the helicopter pad to greet my visitors from Washington. Ambassador Bunker had just arrived from Saigon. Rusk, Clifford, and Wheeler completed the group. We went to the lodge and, over breakfast, talked about Vietnam and discussed the latest exchanges with Hanoi. We later moved outside to enjoy the sunshine and continue our discussion.

I was happy to see Bunker again. He was one of the steadiest and most intelligent men I knew. Now in his seventies, he was running our toughest world outpost. Bunker gave a comprehensive report on Vietnam, the good and the bad, the problems and the accomplishments. We talked at length about steps being taken to strengthen South Vietnamese military forces. Bunker reminded us that President Thieu had announced his intention to increase his forces by 135,000 men, and he reported that Thieu was now thinking of boosting that figure another 25,000.

"What about equipment for them?" I asked. Clifford said that all South Vietnamese combat troops would have M-16 rifles by June 1968, and that regional and popular forces would have them by July or August. Wheeler said he was checking to make certain that all U.S. units had M-16's. If not, he said, "the roof will blow off the Capitol." He promised to see that that did not happen.

Averell Harriman and Bill Bundy joined us shortly after noon and during lunch we discussed the problem of negotiating with Hanoi. I wondered out loud whether Hanoi's move might not be a trap, another Tet truce, another effort to persuade us to drop our guard. Rusk thought Hanoi's principal goal was to "get rid of all the bombing of North Vietnam," though the North Vietnamese seemed determined to continue their part of the war full scale, he said. "The talks are going to be tough," Rusk concluded. "We are going to have to hang in there. We either have to get them to make concessions or make it clear they are responsible for any breaking off of the talks."

Rostow said he thought the Viet Cong recognized they were in a weakened military position, but that they were convinced their political and psychological position, particularly in the United States, was strong. Bunker agreed. "I think they are doing it to exploit our position here," he said. He had in mind the growing clamor in the Senate, in some editorials, and on many campuses in support of ending the war and withdrawing our forces.

Clifford said that "if they play us for fools" and we decided to resume bombing of the North, he and the Joint Chiefs had developed a list of worthwhile military targets. Harriman noted that North Vietnam had broken the 1962 agreement on Laos "before the ink was dry." In the coming talks, he said, we should make sure we get positive results. "The stronger we are on the ground militarily," I said, "the better our position is going to be in negotiations." My advisers agreed.

We turned then to the draft of instructions to guide our negotiators in contacts with the North Vietnamese. The first version was not satisfactory, and we worked it over. Our basic objective, as redefined and approved at Camp David, was: "To make arrangements with the North Vietnamese representatives for prompt and serious substantive talks looking towards peace in Vietnam, in the course of which an understanding may be reached on a cessation of bombing in the North under circumstances which would not be militarily disadvantageous."

Until some control mechanism could be agreed to by both sides, we would have to monitor North Vietnamese performance ourselves. That meant continuing aerial reconnaissance of the North after the bombing ended. As for a ground settlement, we agreed that our first goal should be reestablishment of the demilitarized zone between North and South Vietnam as provided in the 1954 Geneva agreement. We had one other minimum demand: Any talks on the future of South Vietnam had to involve the legal government of the Republic of Vietnam.

During the day we sent another message to Vientiane for delivery to Hanoi. We noted that we had proposed Geneva as a meeting place; Hanoi had suggested Phnom Penh. We pointed out that we had no representation in the Cambodian capital, and therefore were suggesting alternatives convenient to both countries—namely, Vientiane, Rangoon, Djakarta, or New Delhi. We would accept any of these if the host government agreed. We advised them we were ready to meet on April 15 or as soon after as would be convenient to Hanoi. We asked for an early reply. After we had agreed on the instructions to be followed by our negotiators, my guests left by helicopter. I returned to Washington the following day.

The next development concerning a meeting place came on April 11, when TASS, the Soviet news agency, reported that the North Vietnamese preferred to meet in Warsaw. If nothing else, this choice—the capital of a Communist country that strongly backed Hanoi—should have made it clear to everyone that the North Vietnamese were seeking every propaganda and psychological advantage. That was no surprise, of course, but it was ignored by many domestic critics. Even a few people in the State Department who should have known better decided that we should go to Warsaw.

Hanoi's official message arrived from Vientiane in the early morning of April 11. The North Vietnamese suggested April 18 as the date for contacts, proposed Warsaw as the place, and named Ha Van Lau, a veteran of the Laos talks in 1962, as their representative. In a short time news agency bulletins were quoting diplomatic sources as saying the United States would probably give "quick approval" to Warsaw. Once again a handful of people in Washington were ready to read the President's mind, and a few reporters were ready to assume that people who knew very little knew a great deal.

I was opposed to public meetings with the North Vietnamese in an openly pro-Hanoi capital. The deck would be stacked against us, just as it had been in the early peace talks in Korea. The South Vietnamese and our other allies had no relations with Poland, no representation in Warsaw. The Communists would control all facilities and arrangements and would have the local press 100 per cent on their side. Poland was supplying arms and other support to the North Vietnamese and could not pretend to neutrality. In addition, Poland was then conducting an anti-Jewish campaign, and I refused to meet in a place where some members of our delegation or our press corps might be refused entrance or be unwelcome. It surprised me that some members of the press never understood this.

In a matter of hours we answered the North Vietnamese. The words were different but the message was the same as the one George Christian later gave White House reporters at the noon briefing. He said:

> We learned this morning from reading a TASS dispatch that the North Vietnamese government has proposed Warsaw as a possible location for contacts. This was later confirmed by a message received through our Embassy at Vientiane.
>
> The United States government has proposed a number of neutral countries as possible sites for contacts and we have not yet had any response to this proposal.

On serious matters of this kind, it is important to conduct talks in a neutral atmosphere, fair to both sides. The selection of an appropriate site in neutral territory, with adequate communication facilities, should be achieved promptly through mutual agreement.

Those acting in good faith will not seek to make this a matter of propaganda.

By this time Senators and columnists who opposed our involvement in Vietnam were in full cry. They were insisting: "Go to Phnom Penh—go to Warsaw—go anywhere." They were anxious to get peace talks started under any circumstances, but that was not the policy of the United States. I knew that the North Vietnamese were testing us. If we accepted Phnom Penh or Warsaw, they would certainly conclude that we wanted any escape route we could find. I was determined not to send them a fuzzy signal, one they would misread and one that might serve to prolong the conflict. A number of people in our government argued that Hanoi would never accept any other meeting place. I was convinced they were wrong. I knew it was possible to find some place in the world where both sides could expect even-handed treatment—if Hanoi really wanted to talk.

We consulted dozens of governments on this problem. Most of them, I think, understood our position. On April 18 we tried again to solve the problem with Hanoi. We had already offered to meet the North Vietnamese in one European city and four cities in Asia. We asked them now to consider other possible sites. We suggested six in Asia—Colombo, Kabul, Katmandu, Kuala Lumpur, Rawalpindi, and Tokyo, and four in Europe— Brussels, Helsinki, Rome, and Vienna. We informed Ho Chi Minh that our negotiators would meet his at any of these fifteen places "at the earliest date suggested by the Democratic Republic of Vietnam." The next day, Radio Hanoi criticized all our proposals and then, with the twisted logic Communists have mastered, claimed that any delay was our fault.

To break the deadlock, we contacted Hanoi once again. In substance, we said: "Let's consider capitals neither of us has yet mentioned. Our representatives could meet privately in one of them to work out agreement on a place for the contacts. If you nominate three places, we will answer promptly." Hanoi's reply was to suggest again that we meet in Warsaw. Later the Indonesians tried to solve the dilemma by offering an Indonesian ship as a meeting place. There could hardly have been a more neutral site than a neutral ship on international waters. We accepted; Hanoi refused.

I began to wonder whether Hanoi's rigidity was permanent after all. Perhaps the Chinese Communists were exerting such pressure that Hanoi's leaders could not unlock the handcuffs they had put on themselves. We considered whether it would be necessary to resume bombing of the North. We knew Hanoi had used the pause begun on March 31 to improve its military position. Many convoys carrying troops and supplies were pouring through the bomb-free area.

On April 30 I met again with my principal advisers. The Pentagon had selected four targets of military significance between the 19th and 20th parallels that our military men felt were worth hitting. "This is the thirtieth day of the pause," I said. "We are going into our fifth week. We have counseled patience, but you have to look at the calendar. We have to start laying the groundwork for what may come."

I turned to General Wheeler. "Do you think, Bus, that the time is limited when we can continue to keep the area above the 19th 'off limits' without hurt?"

"Yes, sir," he said. "They are moving men and equipment south rapidly." We discussed all the pros and cons of resuming bombing. I decided to hold off a few more days.

The break came three days later. The North Vietnamese called our Embassy in Vientiane on the morning of May 3. They asked Ambassador Sullivan to come to their Embassy at 10 A.M to receive a message from Hanoi. He did so, and his report reached Washington after midnight. Rostow called me immediately.

"Mr. President, Hanoi has suggested we meet in Paris," he said. "They have named a new negotiator, a minister. They also proposed that we meet on May 10 or a few days later." Rostow was calling from home and did not have the full text of the cable. I called the White House Situation Room and the duty officer read the message to me. I liked the way career diplomat Sullivan concluded his "flash" report. He said: "Congratulations to those in Washington whose eyeballs are made of such stern stuff."

I called Dean Rusk, waking him from a sound sleep. We agreed that this move looked like the development we had been hoping for, and Rusk thought we should accept immediately. At 8:30 that morning I met in the White House with Rusk, Clifford, Rostow, and George Ball, who was succeeding Arthur Goldberg at the United Nations. We agreed on our answer to Hanoi. At ten o'clock I went to the East Room for a meeting with the press. I opened the televised news conference by saying:

> I was informed at one o'clock this morning that Hanoi was prepared to meet in Paris on May 10 or several days thereafter.
>
> As you know, we have sought a place for these conversations in which all parties would receive fair and impartial treatment. France is a country where all parties should expect such treatment.
>
> I have sent a message, therefore, informing Hanoi that the date—May 10—and the site—Paris—are acceptable. . . .
>
> We hope that this agreement—on initial contact—will prove a step forward and can represent a mutual and serious movement by all parties toward peace in Southeast Asia.

I would like to sound a cautionary note. This is only the first step and there are many hazards and difficulties ahead. . . .

Our negotiating team was ready to go. On Rusk's recommendation, I had originally selected Averell Harriman and Llewellyn Thompson, our Ambassador in Moscow, as our principal negotiators. However, there were several important arms control matters we hoped to work out with the Soviet Union, so I decided to keep Thompson in his post. To replace him I chose Cyrus Vance, who had handled many difficult diplomatic assignments. He was a tireless worker, and he got along well with people. Harriman had more experience dealing with the Communists than almost any man in government. He had led our delegation at the Laos talks in 1962. He and Vance would be my personal representatives at the Paris talks.

On the military side, I chose one of the ablest officers I knew, Lieutenant General Andrew Goodpaster. He had been Commandant of the National War College and had served President Eisenhower as staff secretary. He was scheduled to become deputy commander of our forces in Vietnam, but I wanted him in on the opening stages of the Paris talks. He would be replaced in a few weeks by Major General George Seignious from the staff of the Joint Chiefs.

The political officer of the delegation was Phil Habib, a tough-minded and hard-working Foreign Service Officer from Brooklyn. He had directed the political section of our Embassy in Saigon and later was the State Department's highest-ranking officer working exclusively on Vietnamese affairs. The other full delegate to the talks was William Jorden, Far East specialist on my National Security Council staff. Jorden, a highly competent foreign affairs expert, whom I fully trusted, and a former newspaperman with long experience in Asia, would act as press spokesman for the delegation.

These men and a small group of specialists and professional staff made up our delegation, one of the smallest that we had sent to a major international meeting in many years. On May 6 I asked the five delegates to join me and my principal foreign policy advisers in the Cabinet Room. I wanted them to know exactly how I felt and what was expected of them in Paris.

"I'm glad we're going to talk," I told them, "but I'm not overly hopeful. I think it is going to be tough going, very tough. . . . Some of you may think that we want a resolution of this because it is an election year. Now be clear, I want it resolved, but not because of this or any election. I don't want any of you to yield anything on the basis of that impression."

"There is just one thing I want you to have in mind," I concluded, "and that is our national interest—now and ten years from now."

We then had a detailed discussion of negotiating problems, our objectives, and the tactics the other side would probably use. There were many opinions, but I am certain no one left that meeting thinking that the Paris talks would be easy or short. I was perhaps the most skeptical person in the room.

Two days later I met the same group of advisers and delegation members in the Cabinet Room. Harriman, Vance, and their colleagues were leaving the next morning for Paris. I looked at the faces around the table—Rusk and Rostow, Katzenbach and Bundy, Clifford, Taylor, and Goodpaster, Harriman and Vance, Habib and Jorden. They had all spent long days and sleepless nights, year after year, dealing with our Southeast Asia commitments and trying to find ways to a just settlement. No group of men in or out of government, in or out of our country, wanted peace more than these men—but not a cheap peace, not a giveaway peace, not a peace at any price.

We went over the issues again—total bombing cessation, no military advantage to be taken, the need for reconnaissance, the participation of the South Vietnamese government in any political settlement, and other matters. We reviewed Harriman's opening statement. Only one change was suggested. In the section where Harriman planned to speak about "international supervision" of a peace settlement, it was suggested that we add:

> We believe the nations of Asia—which have a crucial interest in the peace and stability of the region—should be associated with the monitoring of the agreements at which we may arrive.

I liked the change and approved it. If peace and order were to come to Southeast Asia, they would have to be increasingly the responsibility of those who lived there and their neighbors. We were helping to buy time, but the people of Asia would have to use that time in their own best interests.

I had asked Senate Majority Leader Mansfield and Senate Minority Leader Dirksen to join our discussion, but they were detained on the Hill. They came about half an hour late. I always remembered what Republican Senator Arthur Vandenberg once said to President Truman: "If you want Congress in on the landing, you should have us in on the takeoff." I wanted these key Senators to know why we were going to Paris and what we faced there.

Once again I reminded the negotiating team: "I want you to negotiate with only one point in mind: what is in our national interest—now and in the future."

"There are no Democrats or Republicans on this panel," I said. "This is strictly an American team."

Clark Clifford sounded a note of warning:

> There is only one guarantee, that is that the discussions will be lengthy and difficult. It took a month to get a site. It will take a long time. . . .

I don't know why Hanoi has chosen to negotiate. It's possible they want us to relax our military posture. Hanoi will try to divide the United States during this time. They will attempt to divide the American people.

I asked the Senators for their reactions. Mansfield replied: "I can't find fault with anything said here tonight."

"I haven't let you down yet," added Dirksen.

The American delegation flew to Paris the next morning. On Friday afternoon, May 10, I received word that the first contact had been made with the North Vietnamese. Cy Vance and several colleagues had met for almost two hours with Ha Van Lau and his aides. Their purpose was to arrange for meetings of the full delegations, and they hammered out agreements on most matters during that first session. Vance reported that the atmosphere had been "cordial and businesslike."

The next day, the same group met again and agreed on final arrangements for the formal sessions. Once again Vance reported a "good and businesslike atmosphere." I was encouraged. I remembered the long wrangling in Korea before any agreement was reached on procedures for the armistice talks. I felt that the speed with which these arrangements were worked out in Paris might indicate that Hanoi seriously wanted a settlement. But we would only know that once the full delegations met and got down to the serious business of trying to work out a reasonable agreement. The first full meeting was scheduled for May 13.

Any optimism we felt as a result of the quick settlement of procedural matters in Paris diminished considerably after the full meetings began. The opening statement by the chief North Vietnamese delegate could have been an editorial in Hanoi's Communist party newspaper. We were the "aggressors." All right was on their side, all wrong on ours. Their solution was for us to stop the bombing and pull all our forces out. The Vietnamese —meaning the Communists—would then be able to handle things in their own way. As these denunciations and demands were repeated, meeting after meeting, week after week, our hopes for a fair compromise and an early settlement grew dimmer.

For the North Vietnamese, the dirtiest word in the vocabulary of our Paris delegates was "reciprocity." We assured the North Vietnamese that all bombing would end if this met with reciprocal acts of restraint on their part. Xuan Thuy, their gray-haired, round-faced delegate in Paris, called this "absurd" and "unjustified." Anyone reading his statements could only conclude that Hanoi's position was that it had no role in ending the war in Vietnam. Anything the Vietnamese Communists did was all right; we were the only villains.

It was also clear from their earliest statements that the North Vietnamese planned to use the Paris forum to make a strong appeal to American and world public opinion. They quoted remarks made by Senators Bobby Kennedy and J. William Fulbright against the U.S. position. They repeated statements by French President de Gaulle and Prince Sihanouk of Cambodia. They began to turn the Paris talks into a propaganda sideshow. When Bill Jorden, our spokesman in Paris, was asked whether he saw anything new or interesting in the first North Vietnamese statements, he replied: "I saw nothing I hadn't heard before." I could not have agreed more after reading Xuan Thuy's words.

As usual, the Communists coordinated military strategy with their diplomatic moves in Paris. On May 7, two days before our delegation left for the French capital, Communist forces struck again at Saigon. The attack had no obvious military goal, but the psychological and political aims were apparent. Small squads infiltrated the city and tried to inflict as much damage as possible. Their goal was to instill terror and create as much destruction and as many refugees as possible. Within a week, however, this effort was destroyed and abandoned.

Just before dawn on May 12, the day before the full Paris talks began, a North Vietnamese regiment attacked our troops in northern I Corps, near Laos. Westmoreland reinforced the units under attack, then skillfully pulled them out. Once again the North Vietnamese had been denied a tactical victory, but we knew they would continue to try. They wanted to create the impression that they were stronger than they were and could strike at will. Our intelligence sources reported that large-scale infiltration of men from the North was continuing.

Some of my advisers strongly favored retaliating against the stepped-up military actions of the North Vietnamese and the Viet Cong by moving our armed reconnaissance up to the halfway mark between the 19th and 20th parallels. We discussed this at our Tuesday luncheon meeting on May 14. "I want to hear both sides," I said. "I am sensitive about doing anything that might hinder the negotiations. But I also worry that some of our people might get killed if we hold back to the 19th. Let's study this carefully and talk about it again tomorrow."

We went over the proposal in detail the next day. As I listened to all the arguments, I became aware once again of one of the persistent ironies of the war in Vietnam. Any move we made that we had not made the week before would be regarded by our critics as "escalation." But Hanoi could send men by the thousands down the Ho Chi Minh Trail, could carry out regimental attacks, and could hit Saigon, yet no one would mention "escalation." This double standard was a burden we had borne and would continue to bear.

"We have already made an overly generous concession by taking Hanoi and Haiphong off the list," I said, "but we will wait until next Tuesday."

After the first full week of the Paris talks, I asked Rusk to give me his personal and candid assessment of where we stood. In typical Rusk fashion he got to the heart of the matter:

> The simple truth is that no one in the world can tell us what will happen if we stop all of the bombing of North Vietnam. Hanoi refuses to tell us and therefore no one else is able to tell us. This is not a problem of diplomatic technique; there are many, many ways by which Hanoi could let us know what in fact they would *do* if we stop all the bombing. This could be done without any loss of face on their part. It boils down to a question of will. Of course they would be glad to exchange some sort of [expanded] talks, somewhere, for a full cessation of the bombing while they go ahead with their part of the war full scale.

He added:

> I realize that I am branded as a "hawk" and that this has been an embarrassment to the administration in some quarters. But looking at all of our experiences in the management of crises in the past three decades, I cannot for the life of me see how we can achieve any peace unless some elementary notions of reciprocity, fairness, and equity are maintained.

Rusk's estimate was correct, and his analysis was as valid eight months later as it was in May. From the time the Paris talks started until the day I left the White House, we never received a clear, unequivocal statement from Hanoi's representatives as to what they would do to lower the level of fighting in Vietnam or to bring the war to an end.

We had unilaterally and without fanfare lowered the northern limit of air strikes from the 20th to the 19th parallel within a few days of my March 31 speech. The next time I met with my advisers I raised this matter again. "How long," I asked, "can we go on with the 19th without getting trapped into never being able to do anything above the 19th?"

"I think it was our force that brought them to the table," I said, "and not our eloquence on March 31. All we are doing now is to let them build back up. . . . Their terrorism hasn't blown up the peace conference. Why would our use of force do it? We have a duty to stop all we can from coming down into the South."

I asked my advisers if it was not true that the longer we stayed out of the area between the 19th and 20th parallels, the harder it would be to go back in. Clifford said "no." Rusk thought delay did make it more difficult. After a long discussion, I finally said: "All right, I will put it off again, against my better judgment. Let's wait until Wednesday." So we put it off. Then we put it off again, and again. In fact, we never did strike north of the 19th parallel. I still question whether we made the right decision.

Nonetheless, I think we did gain a significant psychological advantage during those early months of the Paris talks. It became clear to most of the world that Hanoi was merely using the sessions for propaganda purposes. In contrast, we kept trying to get down to serious business, and time and time again we made specific proposals for the North Vietnamese to consider.

Early in June we suddenly saw what looked like a hopeful sign. I received a letter from Soviet Chairman Kosygin on the Vietnam situation. He urged me to halt the remaining bombing of North Vietnam. He and his colleagues thought—and he added that they had "grounds to do so"—that a complete halt would contribute to a breakthrough and produce "prospects" for peace. The action, he said, would not damage either our security or our prestige. On Sunday afternoon, June 9, I met in the Cabinet Room with my principal advisers to discuss Kosygin's message. What did it mean? How should we respond? Was it a "hint" or a "pledge" or a "trap"? Could the Soviets deliver on their promise? What were they really promising?

In one way or another, each of us regarded the note from Moscow as significant, but there were differences of opinion as to what it signified. Rusk thought the message lacked clarity and urged that we go back to Kosygin for more specific answers to our questions. Clifford thought we should just "assume it means what we want it to mean" and proceed on that basis. I still remembered vividly Moscow's assurance late in 1965 that if we stopped bombing the North for twelve to twenty days, "something good will happen." On that basis we stopped bombing, not for twelve or twenty but for thirty-seven days—and nothing happened. As I said to one of my colleagues: "The burned child dreads the fire." What was Moscow saying now that it had not said two and a half years earlier? Could the Soviets back up these vague promises? Just what would Hanoi *do* if the bombing stopped?

Our reply to Moscow included some of our questions. I told Kosygin that we were prepared to stop the bombing but that we needed assurance, which could be entirely private, that our action would result in deescalating the war. We needed that assurance to protect our men in the field and our position at home. We never received an answer to these crucial questions, from Moscow or from the North Vietnamese.

The Paris talks dragged on through the summer. The formal sessions were sterile propaganda exercises. Informal talks during tea breaks and elsewhere were of little more value. We continued to urge the North Vietnamese to give us some idea what they would do once the bombing stopped. Their line was hard and unyielding: Stop the bombing, then we can discuss these other matters.

In mid-July I flew to Honolulu for another meeting with President Thieu and leading members of the South Vietnamese government, my sixth trip to the Pacific during my Presidency. I had not seen Thieu since the previous December in Canberra, where we had attended memorial services for Harold Holt. The Paris talks had been going on for more than two months. I wanted Thieu's personal assessment of developments there and in his country.

I arrived in Honolulu shortly after noon on July 18. The next two days were occupied with an intensive review of Vietnam developments. One matter of utmost interest to me was the progress being made in shifting more of the burden of fighting from our shoulders to those of our Vietnamese allies. During our extensive February-March policy review my advisers and I had decided to do everything possible to increase both the size and quality of the Vietnamese armed forces. This was one of the major decisions I announced on March 31.

The subject of possible American troop withdrawals had come up once again only a week before our Honolulu meeting. President Thieu had visited one of our aircraft carriers in the Gulf of Tonkin and had talked with reporters aboard. He told them that he thought the United States could probably begin to withdraw some forces from Vietnam in 1969.

I had asked Clark Clifford to go to Vietnam in advance of the Honolulu meeting to make his own on-the-spot assessment. I particularly wanted to know what progress was being made in strengthening the South Vietnamese forces. Clifford made his survey and flew to Honolulu on July 18 to report to me and attend the planned conference with the South Vietnamese. Clifford found the overall military situation in Vietnam favorable. Our field commanders and Vietnamese leaders expected another round of enemy attacks similar to the earlier Tet offensive and the May offensive that had followed. They estimated that the blow would fall in August or September. But General Abrams and the Vietnamese were both confident the assaults could be turned back with the forces and supplies then on hand.

Clifford was much less satisfied with the pace of turning a heavier combat burden over to the South Vietnamese. He felt our program for supplying equipment to their forces was inadequate and he told me he was studying ways to expedite the flow of needed war matériel. Clifford was also concerned with the shortage of skilled leadership in the South Vietnamese army, especially of field-grade officers, the majors and colonels who led battalions and regiments. He thought the Vietnamese were too casual about this shortage and that we should press them to do better.

Finally, Clifford said he had been disappointed that the South Vietnamese seemed less interested than we were in an early negotiated settlement. They were concerned that the Paris talks might raise the prestige of the Liberation Front. Some Vietnamese still feared we might reach a secret agreement with Hanoi that would result in rapid withdrawal of U.S. and allied forces before the South Vietnamese had built sufficient strength to defend themselves, especially if troop infiltration continued from North Vietnam. Clifford concluded that the South Vietnamese government simply did not want peace as much as we did.

I knew that our Vietnamese allies were worried about the problems Clifford mentioned. If I had been fighting against Communist conquest for as many years as the South Vietnamese had, I would have been worried too. I did not believe, however, that Thieu and his colleagues did not want a peaceful settlement. Their country and its people had suffered the agonies of war for many years. They wanted peace, I felt sure, but not the kind of peace that would turn their country into another Czechoslovakia. They were worried about what might happen if a highly organized and disciplined Communist minority gained a foothold in their government. They knew what had happened in North Vietnam when the Viet Minh took over. Non-Communist nationalists were tolerated briefly, then forced out or eliminated.

All in all, Clifford's report was optimistic regarding short-run military problems, but pessimistic on other matters. I expected Thieu to reflect this same concern and pessimism at our first working session the morning of July 19. On the contrary, he was more confident than I had ever seen him. He felt that his new government had proved itself during the Tet offensive and its aftermath. The South Vietnamese had stood up well under the shock of the North Vietnamese–Viet Cong attacks.

In our meeting President Thieu said:

> We realize that we Vietnamese are mostly affected by this war, which is waged on our soil, against our own freedom. Therefore, we feel that we are duty bound to shoulder each day an increasing share in this struggle.

Privately, Thieu told me he was confident that we could begin withdrawing American forces by the middle of 1969, perhaps sooner. He urged that we put that announcement in our communiqué. I told him I was happy to hear what he had said and I knew he meant it. I was sure he understood how anxious we were to begin bringing our boys home as soon as we safely could. I realized an announcement of this kind would be well received in the United States, at least for the moment, but I thought it would give Hanoi the wrong signal. We had knocked the Communists back since Tet, but if we indicated we were thinking of withdrawing our forces, we would give them new encouragement. "The thing to do is not to say it, but just to do it when the time comes," I said.

I had taken myself out of politics on March 31. I was interested in long-term results, not short-term popularity. But I was encouraged to know the Vietnamese were thinking, and doing something, about carrying a growing share of the load. The process of putting more responsibility on the shoulders of our Vietnamese allies had begun more than a year before, under Westmoreland, and was stepped up when he assigned Abrams to work almost full time with the South Vietnamese army leadership. They had done a superb job and the effects were beginning to be felt.

August 1968 was convention month, but I deliberately avoided involvement either as antagonist or protagonist. However, with the continuing stalemate in Paris and with the fighting in Vietnam continuing at a reduced but still fairly high level, I felt that I had to speak to my countrymen. I had promised that I would, if at all possible, attend the annual convention of the Veterans of Foreign Wars in Detroit in mid-August. As the time drew near, I decided to go and to talk about Vietnam. With the growing clamor for a full bombing halt in mind, I told the huge crowd of cheering veterans:

> . . . In human affairs there is no more basic lesson than that it takes two to make a bargain and to make a peace. We have made a reasonable offer and we have taken a major first step. That offer has not been accepted. This administration does not intend to move further until it has good reason to believe that the other side intends seriously to join us in deescalating the war and moving seriously toward peace. We are willing to take chances for peace, but we cannot make foolhardy gestures for which our fighting men will pay the price by giving their lives.

An election year is a difficult time to try to carry out an objective and unemotional foreign policy—or a domestic policy, for that matter. I am certain the fact that 1968 was an election year influenced Hanoi and affected the attitude of numerous Americans concerning our dealings with the North Vietnamese and our search for peace. Some people felt the most important political objective was the election of Richard Nixon and anything that helped that cause was good. To those people, movement toward peace in Vietnam before Election Day would not help Nixon and therefore was bad. Others felt the election of Hubert Humphrey was the critical political goal. In their minds, any movement toward peace before Election Day would help his campaign and therefore was good. Some officials in Moscow, and perhaps in Hanoi, may have thought it would be easier to deal with Humphrey than with Nixon. And in Saigon there may have been those who thought it would be easier to deal with Nixon than with Humphrey.

These were a few of the contending forces I had to deal with as I tried to work toward a peaceful settlement. I had deliberately taken myself out of political contention in order to devote all my energy to the urgent tasks that remained. I had done this to remove any doubt about political motivations or ambitions regarding any action I felt had to be taken. I regretted that others had not adopted the same approach, but I could only deal with the consequences of their actions as best I could.

In Paris over the long summer our position had crystallized around three points. If we stopped the remaining bombing, "prompt and serious" talks would have to follow. By "serious" we meant talks involving the legal South Vietnamese government. This was point number one. Hanoi's representatives always referred to leaders of the Republic of Vietnam as "puppets" and "lackeys" with whom they would never sit down and talk. They insisted, however, that the Liberation Front take part in any discussions of the future of South Vietnam.

Our main concern about stopping the bombing was the safety of our fighting men, especially those in northern South Vietnam, who would be attacked first if Hanoi took military advantage of the cessation of air strikes. So our second fundamental point was that Hanoi must not violate the demilitarized zone between North and South Vietnam, not send troops into or through it, and not fire artillery from or across it.

Our third basic point was that we could not sustain a bombing pause if the North Vietnamese and the Viet Cong carried out large-scale attacks, on the ground or by rockets or artillery, against South Vietnam's major cities, such as Saigon, Hué, or Danang.

We made these three points time and time again to the North Vietnamese in Paris. We repeated them to governments friendly with Hanoi so that there would be no misunderstanding. In Paris Hanoi's delegates always reacted by saying we were trying to impose "conditions" on them. They had insisted from the beginning that our bombing halt must be "unconditional."

For our part, I wanted to be absolutely certain that several things were totally clear to everyone concerned with the negotiations. First and most important, I wanted every American involved, whether in Washington, Paris, or Saigon, to understand precisely what we were doing, why we were doing it, and what we expected to happen if we stopped the bombing and the North Vietnamese grossly violated what we regarded as our understanding with them. I talked this over at length in mid-September with our principal negotiator in the Paris talks, Ambassador Harriman. On September 17 he came to Washington and we met in my office. Harriman, who had been dealing with Communist leaders since his days as Ambassador in Moscow during World War II, told me that on balance he thought Hanoi's delegation in Paris was serious about making progress. He was convinced the North Vietnamese knew clearly our position regarding any violation of the demilitarized zone or any significant attacks on South Vietnamese cities during a total bombing halt. But he doubted we would ever get any formal commitment from them on these matters because they wished to claim any bombing halt was "unconditional."

As Harriman was preparing to leave after our review of the Paris talks, I turned to him and said: "I will count on you, Averell, to lead the government in demanding a resumption of bombing if they violate these understandings." He assured me that he would urge a bombing resumption "with enthusiasm" under those circumstances.

A few weeks later our second principal negotiator, Cy Vance, came to Washington. On October 3 he joined me for breakfast in my bedroom and we discussed the latest news from Paris. Vance was basically optimistic that progress could be made. Looking at it from Hanoi's viewpoint, he said, the North Vietnamese might assume that their military situation was likely to deteriorate in the coming months. Meanwhile, the South Vietnamese army was expanding, was receiving better equipment, and growing more confident. Hanoi might wish to settle things sooner rather than later. I told Vance I remained skeptical and reminded him again of our three basic requirements. Vance said our three points had been stated repeatedly, but he and Harriman would continue emphasizing them to make sure there was no misunderstanding.

The break in the stalemate came during the second week of October. In a private meeting with our delegation the North Vietnamese asked if we would stop the rest of the bombing if we had a clear answer concerning South Vietnam's participation in the next stage of talks. Harriman said that he would consult Washington. When the report came from Paris, we felt the ice was beginning to melt. But I wanted some things taken care of before I moved. "First," I said, "get this [Paris message] out to Bunker and Abrams. Tell them we are thinking of going ahead, if we do not take an unwarranted gamble with the safety of our men, and I want their completely frank reactions—with the bark off."

Bunker and Abrams responded promptly and we had their written reaction the next morning. The Ambassador reported that he and our field commander thought the latest exchange with Hanoi in Paris was "a fairly clear indication that Hanoi is ready for a tactical shift from the battlefield to the conference table." They agreed with our proposal to instruct our Paris negotiators to tell the North Vietnamese we were ready to set an early date for total cessation of armed attacks against the North. We planned to suggest that "serious talks" begin the day after the bombing halt and would insist that representatives of the Republic of Vietnam had to take part.

Harriman and Vance would also emphasize that we could not maintain the total bombing halt if North Vietnam used the area in and near the demilitarized zone to attack our forces or otherwise take advantage of our restraint. Nor would we maintain a bombing cessation if the North Vietnamese and Viet Cong continued to strike at the major cities in the South. When we had the Bunker-Abrams answer in hand, I said: "All right, now go back to them and ask them to talk it over with President Thieu. We must be sure he is with us on this."

The next day, Bunker discussed the entire situation with Thieu. He reported that the South Vietnamese leader was ready to go along. "After all," Thieu had told Bunker, "the problem is not to stop the bombing but to stop the war, and we must try this path to see if they are serious."

On October 14 I called my senior advisers to a meeting. We discussed all the possible interpretations of Hanoi's position and the likely outcome if we went ahead. Then I asked each man what he thought. One by one they answered: "I would go ahead." Later that day, I met with the Joint Chiefs of Staff in the Cabinet Room. We went through the same kind of review and discussion. They unanimously favored the halt, provided that we continued aerial reconnaissance over the North and would resume bombing if Hanoi grossly violated the understanding.

At the end of the day I met once again with Rusk, Clifford, Wheeler, and Rostow. We went over final details, including the cables to our Ambassadors in allied countries. We wanted the agreement of our friends before moving ahead in Paris. Once again I asked if we were all agreed. They all answered "yes."

"All right," I said. "I don't want to have it said of me that one man died tomorrow who could have been saved by this plan. I don't think it [peace] will happen, but there is a chance. We'll try it."

We received agreement from all our allies. Then we went ahead with the North Vietnamese in Paris. But the arrangement we had agonized over so long and so patiently began to fall through. The North Vietnamese had said earlier that once the bombing stopped a meeting could be held "the next day." Now when we proposed exactly that, they balked. It was impossible, they said. They would have to consult the Liberation Front. They did not know how long that would take. They charged us with raising new "conditions."

Then the whole arrangement, so painfully developed after so much time, began to unravel not only in Paris but in Saigon and even, in a way, in Washington. There were so many currents and crosscurrents running that it was hard sometimes to know what was happening and why. If this segment of history had been written in a work of fiction about mythical countries, it would have been a comedy. But it was happening before our eyes, and in real life the stakes were too high, the consequences too important, for laughter. We could only try to put the scattered pieces of the puzzle together again.

In Paris we went through two weeks of stalling and haggling and new demands from Hanoi's delegates. They wanted more time. They wanted us to sign a paper stating that the bombing halt was "unconditional." They wanted us to agree to a conference of "four parties" rather than the "two sides" we had consistently demanded.

Finally, step by step, hour by hour, argument after argument, we worked out a new arrangement with the North Vietnamese. They dropped the idea of a written agreement. They shortened the time between the bombing halt and the first meeting from "weeks" to two weeks, to one week, to about three days. They also understood we would regard the meetings as "two-sided" and would not recognize the Liberation Front as an independent entity.

Once all the differences were resolved and Hanoi had met our essential requirements, we felt obliged to go forward on the pledges our negotiators had made. But as we reached accord in Paris, our agreement with President Thieu fell apart. We had planned a joint announcement with the South Vietnamese on the bombing halt. As late as October 28, when Ambassador Bunker and Thieu had gone over the final version that both governments had worked on long and hard, the South Vietnamese President had said: "I don't see how we can ask for anything more." By the next day, however, the South Vietnamese were asking for more—more time and assurances that they could deal with Hanoi, not the Liberation Front. Neither demand was practical. We had narrowed the time between a total bombing halt and the beginning of full-scale talks largely on Saigon's insistence. As for the Liberation Front and Hanoi, we could not force them to act as we desired. The negotiations, however, continued to the last minute. The South Vietnamese knew that we had to make our announcement at 8 P.M. on October 31. Shortly after 7 P.M. we heard from Bunker that Thieu and his colleagues were still asking for two changes in the statement. We had to go alone.

I knew that Thieu had many problems with his compatriots in the government and the National Assembly. When he began trying to win the agreement of his colleagues to move ahead in Paris, he ran into much more apprehension and resistance than he had anticipated. But I believe South Vietnam's failure to move with us on the bombing halt announcement and to send a delegation promptly to Paris had at least as much to do with American domestic politics as with Saigon politics. Thieu and Vice President Ky and their colleagues had become convinced, I believe, on the basis of reports from their Embassy in Washington, that Mr. Nixon would win the Presidential election. Also they had been shaken up by Vice President Humphrey's speech in Salt Lake City on September 30, in which the Democratic candidate had said that he would stop all bombing if he were President. On October 12, McGeorge Bundy made a speech which I believe created further concern in Saigon. Bundy called for the next administration to "steadily, systematically, and substantially" reduce the number of Americans in Vietnam and the cost of the war. Both speeches shook our allies and, I am convinced, created doubts and anxiety in Saigon.

I believe Thieu and his colleagues were eager to get on good terms with what they thought would be the new administration. I had reason to believe they had been urged to delay going to the Paris meetings and promised they would get a better deal from a Nixon administration than from

Humphrey. I had no reason to think that Republican candidate Nixon was himself involved in this maneuvering, but a few individuals active in his campaign were.

In any case, I felt strongly that other governments should not determine American policy. The South Vietnamese had agreed to our position in the middle of October and later. We assumed from what they said that they were with us. When we gave our word in Paris on the basis of that agreement, I felt we had to go ahead with a total bombing cessation under the conditions we had given the North Vietnamese.

I knew I would be criticized if I did, and if I did not. I simply had to do what I believed was right. But I wanted to consult my colleagues again, as I had in mid-October, before finally taking this major step. I found, on doing so, that they all favored going ahead. On the evening of October 27 I had dinner with a group of close friends and advisers. The next morning, among my papers, I found a memo written after midnight by Walt Rostow, who had been at the dinner. I was impressed, since Rostow rarely volunteered a personal opinion unless I asked for it. In his memo he said:

> There were four people in that room at dinner tonight, aside from yourself, who have lived Vietnam, with all its pain, since January 1961: Rusk, Taylor, Wheeler, and myself.
>
> All of us know that, with all its uncertainties, we have the best deal we now can get—vastly better than we thought we could get since 1961.
>
> If we go ahead we know it may be tough. But with military and political determination we believe we can make it stick—not because we are so smart; but because your courage, the quality of our fighting men, and the resilience and simple gallantry of the South Vietnamese people give us the tools to make it stick.

Before I made my decision, I wanted to be absolutely certain that Hanoi understood our position. I asked Secretary Rusk to find out how often and in what detail we had spelled out our view of the restraints Hanoi should display if we ended all bombing of the North. Rusk relayed my questions to Paris. The next day, October 28, Harriman and Vance cabled their reply. By that time the North Vietnamese had accepted participation of the South Vietnamese government in future talks. The other two requirements, restraint in the demilitarized zone and foregoing attacks on major cities, had been spelled out in twelve separate sessions with Hanoi's representatives. Our negotiators reported that the North Vietnamese would give no flat guarantees; that was in keeping with their stand that the bombing had to be ended without conditions. But they had told us that if we stopped the bombing, they would "know what to do." Harriman and Vance were confident Hanoi knew precisely what we meant and would avoid the actions that we had warned them would imperil a bombing halt. They concluded their report by saying: "As we have previously stated on several occasions, the bombing should be resumed if our demands with respect to either the DMZ or the cities are violated."

One other feature of the planned bombing halt deserves mention, and that is aerial reconnaissance. We had decided, even before our delegation went to Paris, that we would have to continue reconnaissance flights after a bombing halt. Until we had some effective system for inspecting and policing our arrangements with North Vietnam, we needed those flights to make sure Hanoi did not take military advantage of our restraint and endanger our men south of the demilitarized zone. The instructions given Harriman and Vance included this sentence: "The U.S. intends to continue certain reconnaissance flights, and the record should not preclude such flights."

At Paris the North Vietnamese demanded from the outset that we stop not only the bombing of the North but "all other acts of war" against their country. They indicated that they regarded reconnaissance as one of those "acts." To meet this point, we proposed a new formulation in July. We told Hanoi's representatives we were prepared to stop all bombardment of the North as well as "all other activities that involve the use of force." Clearly, that would exclude reconnaissance by unarmed or even unmanned flights. We knew, of course, that the North Vietnamese would never formally agree that our reconnaissance could continue with their blessing. We hoped that by making our intentions clear the North Vietnamese would find it possible quietly to accept our actions. We felt reassured on this when, in October, Hanoi's negotiators finally agreed to drop their "acts of war" formula for our "acts involving the use of force."

Once the October decision had been made, we explained to the press in background sessions in Washington and Paris that we would continue aerial reconnaissance. This was mentioned in press stories all over the world, and the North Vietnamese knew precisely what to expect. After the total bombing halt went into effect, however, the North Vietnamese pretended there had been no understanding on this matter. They began shooting occasionally. at unarmed reconnaissance flights. When that happened, we protected the flights by sending armed escorts to accompany them and by retaliating against anti-aircraft sites that were attacking our pilots and planes.

To make doubly sure that there was no misunderstanding of our basic requirements for a bombing halt, either in Hanoi or in other capitals friendly to it, I decided to restate our position to the Soviet Union. On October 27 we called in Soviet Ambassador Dobrynin and gave him a detailed written explanation of our position. We specified that the South Vietnamese would be full participants in the new talks. We also expected, we said, that while the talks continued the demilitarized zone and the cities of South Vietnam would be respected. We urged that the Soviets restate this position to the North Vietnamese "so as to avoid any charge of deception and any risk of misunderstanding." We reminded Moscow of Chairman Kosygin's earlier message that he had "reason to believe" that if the bombing ended productive discussions would follow promptly. We asked for any comments or reactions the Soviet government wished to make.

The following day, we received Moscow's answer. The Soviets welcomed the progress that the Paris talks seemed to be achieving. They said they were convinced the North Vietnamese were "doing everything possible to put an end to the war in Vietnam and to reach a peaceful settlement." Moscow expressed the opinion that any doubts regarding Hanoi's position were "groundless." This exchange gave me additional confidence that Hanoi could not possibly misunderstand our policy or our actions. We would stop all bombing, but the North Vietnamese would have to show restraint as well.

There was one final thing to do before proceeding with a bombing halt. I wanted to look the field commander of our troops in the eye and have him tell me candidly what effect he thought the halt would have on our men. Would we, or would we not, be endangering the lives of our fighting forces? I asked General Abrams to return to Washington. He arrived at Andrews Air Force Base just after midnight the morning of October 29 and came immediately to the White House. I had summoned my top advisers for this unusual middle-of-the-night meeting. At 2:30 A.M., we assembled in the Cabinet Room. Rusk sat at my right and Abrams at my left. Across the table from us were Clifford, Wheeler, CIA Director Helms, Rostow, and General Maxwell Taylor. Several members of my staff were also present.

I opened the meeting with a detailed review of the events of recent months. I explained how we had reached the point at which we then found ourselves. After I summarized the understanding that we believed had been established, I turned to General Abrams and asked: "If the enemy honors our agreement, will this be an advantage militarily?" "Yes, sir," he answered.

Abrams was confident the North Vietnamese would honor the DMZ, especially since their armed strength in that area had been sharply reduced in recent months by our actions on the ground and by our air strikes. He was less sure about rocket attacks on the cities. He pointed out that the Viet Cong and the North Vietnamese still had strong forces in III Corps, where Saigon was located, and along the Cambodian border. An assault on Saigon was always a possibility, Abrams said, though he doubted that it could succeed. He was thinking not of a major ground assault but of the enemy's carrying out rocket attacks on the city or sending in twenty-five or fifty sabotage agents to do as much damage as possible. I asked Abrams if we could resume full-scale bombing if the enemy attacked. "Yes, sir, very easily," he said.

"What will this do to the morale of our men and of the South Vietnamese army?" I asked. "I don't believe it will have a measurable effect on morale," he replied.

We talked of many other things—improvement of the South Vietnamese forces, the supply of arms and equipment, plans for future offensive actions.

I turned again to General Abrams and looked hard at him for a few moments. If I made a mistake, he and his men would suffer the most.

"This is a critical period here," I said. "In the light of what you know, do you have any reluctance or hesitancy about stopping the bombing?"

"No, sir," he said firmly.

"If you were President, would you do it?"

"I have no reservations about doing it," Abrams said. "I know it is stepping into a cesspool of comment. But I do think it's the right thing to do. It is the proper thing to do."

Word arrived during the meeting that Ambassador Bunker was having trouble getting in touch with Thieu to nail down the final agreement. The South Vietnamese insisted they needed more time, that they would be unable to organize their delegation and get it to the French capital in time for the November 2 meeting that we hoped to arrange in Paris.

At 5 A.M. I decided we all needed a break and that Abrams needed some sleep. Rusk returned to the State Department to try to contact Bunker directly. I walked to the Executive Mansion with Abrams. At 6:15 I returned to the Cabinet Room for another urgent meeting with Rusk, Clifford, and the others. We had received information that people who claimed to speak for the Republican candidate were still trying to influence the South Vietnamese to drag their feet on the peace talks. Their argument was: Nixon is going to win; a Nixon administration will be more friendly to Saigon than the Democrats will be; stick with us and we will stick with you. Had this argument strongly influenced the South Vietnamese leaders? Or had Thieu reached agreement with us but failed to obtain the necessary backing among top officials of his government? We never knew for certain. Both were probably true. In any case, we knew that the agreement we thought we had was falling apart.

Clifford argued firmly that we should go ahead with the agreement we had worked out. He found the last-minute South Vietnamese delay "reprehensible and utterly without merit." He said it was clear that Saigon could get a representative to Paris in three days. We should tell President Thieu that we intended to go ahead with the meeting as planned the following Saturday, November 2, that we hoped our South Vietnamese allies would be with us, but that we would be there in any case. My other advisers agreed. I instructed Rusk to pass our views along to Bunker so he could convey them to President Thieu immediately. The sun was just lighting the Washington sky as we walked from the Cabinet Room.

The delay in Saigon was a grave disappointment. I felt that once we had broken through the stubborn resistance of the North Vietnamese in Paris, the peace talks might move forward rather quickly, developing a momentum of their own and moving us toward the final settlement that all Americans wanted, and that the world wanted. A split between us and our Vietnamese allies would only give Hanoi new hope and new opportunities to play additional propaganda games.

The sixty-five-plus hours between that early morning meeting of October 29, when General Abrams came from Saigon, and the evening of October 31, when I announced my decision, were a period of hectic diplomatic and political activity. Those three days were a blur of meetings and phone calls, of cables and conferences. I seemed to be listening, reading, or talking right around the clock. The same was true for all my principal advisers and assistants. In Saigon Bunker and his top aides and Thieu and his lieutenants suffered the same tension and sleepless activity. Similarly, in Paris Harriman and Vance were busy explaining the delay to the North Vietnamese delegates and working out the final details of our agreement.

I met again with my advisers at 1 P.M. on October 29 for our regular Tuesday lunch conference. I had invited General Abrams to join us. I asked Rusk for the latest word from Saigon. He reported that Thieu and his colleagues were meeting at that moment with their National Security Council. It was two o'clock in the morning in the South Vietnamese capital. I asked the Secretary to summarize the situation as he saw it. He recommended we wait until we heard from Bunker but urged that we take a long-range view of the problem.

"President Kennedy said we would make a battle there to save South Vietnam," Rusk said. "That set us on course." Then, he added, we had sent troops in to keep South Vietnam from being overrun. We had lost 29,000 men and invested $75 billion.

"We must be careful not to flush all this down the drain," he said. "But we do have a right to expect cooperation from the South Vietnamese." Rusk said he felt that if the problem in Saigon was only a matter of timing, we should accept it and "set a time convenient to them."

Clifford disagreed. "I thought South Vietnam wanted to be at the talks," he said. "We have now reached an agreement on that." He pointed out that the South Vietnamese had had five months to select their representative for Paris; they were putting Bunker off, making it difficult for him to talk to them; they were letting U.S. domestic political considerations sway them. "I consider this a deep issue of good faith," the Defense Secretary said.

The report we had been waiting for finally arrived from Bunker. I read his account of the National Security Council session in Saigon with deep disappointment. There was still no agreement to move with us. The South Vietnamese had raised several objections to an immediate decision. First, they told Bunker, there was a constitutional question. Under Vietnam's national charter, the President had to have the approval of the National Assembly on major foreign policy questions. That would take time, and perhaps even a plenary session of the assembly.

Second, the South Vietnamese felt they had been given different interpretations of U.S. policy by Bunker in Saigon and Harriman in Paris. This concerned the role of the Liberation Front in the expanded talks. We had said all along that we would regard the coming meetings as "two-sided" and would consider the Liberation Front part of Hanoi's delegation on the "other side." However, we had explained to our Vietnamese allies that we could not control what the Communist side said or claimed on this matter. We knew the Communists would argue that the Liberation Front representatives were a separate delegation.

Third, the South Vietnamese wanted all procedural arrangements for the expanded Paris meetings worked out before they agreed to attend. We knew that was impossible; Hanoi would never accept this condition. Finally, the South Vietnamese told Bunker they could not be ready for a meeting by November 2.

"This may mean that everything we have done is in vain," I said. "There is no basic change—no breakthrough." I asked my advisers to study Bunker's report carefully and consider what we could or should do next. I said we would meet again later in the day.

After the meeting, I talked privately with General Abrams. I told him how proud I was of him and how grateful the American people were for the job he and his men were doing. As a symbol of that gratitude, I gave him the Distinguished Service Medal. Then I told Abrams that I could not adequately put into words what was in my mind. But I had written him a letter expressing what I felt, both about him and about what I wanted him to do in the months ahead. He slipped the letter into his pocket to read on his way back to Vietnam. The letter began:

> One hundred-odd years ago President Lincoln found a general.
> I have been lucky enough to find two field generals. In the last three months you have fully exploited the situation created during the last three years by your predecessor, General Westmoreland.

I said that we had reached the crucial stage of both military and diplomatic operations. We would never achieve the kind of peace we wanted unless the enemy was kept on the run, unless he realized he could never win on the field of battle. I instructed Abrams to use his resources and manpower in a maximum effort to achieve that goal and to inspire the South Vietnamese army to do the same. With that sort of effort, and with luck, we just might be able to achieve peace. I was totally convinced that if we and the South Vietnamese began to ease up, if Hanoi got the impression that it needed only to wait us out, we would never persuade them to talk peace in a serious way. At 3:15 P.M. Abrams left the White House. One hour and fifteen minutes later he was on his way back to the battlefront.

At 6:30 P.M. I met again in the Cabinet Room with my advisers. By then we had received Bunker's recommendation that we hold off any announcement of a bombing halt for twenty-four hours and that we tell the South Vietnamese we were willing to hold the first enlarged Paris meeting on November 4 instead of November 2, which would give them more time to organize their delegation. We discussed this suggestion at length and finally agreed to allow our allies the additional time. "I would be willing to postpone things a day or two before I broke up the alliance," I said.

Meanwhile, our delegates in Paris were in an embarrassing position. The North Vietnamese were pressing for word on what they thought was a firm agreement. Harriman and Vance had to say that they were still waiting for final instructions from Washington.

I did not get to dinner with Mrs. Johnson until 9:30 that night. By ten o'clock I could hardly keep my eyes open. I had been up since 2 A.M., so it had been a twenty-hour day. I fell asleep as soon as my head touched the pillow. Throughout the next day, October 30, I met in lengthy sessions with my advisers, beginning at ten o'clock in the morning and ending at six that evening. We were following developments in Saigon intently, as well as the conversations in Paris. I had sent President Thieu a personal message on October 29 urging him to join us in Paris under the arrangements already worked out. On the 30th, just before noon, I received his answer.

It was friendly and expressed deep appreciation for everything the United States had done to help his country survive, but it was clear that Thieu would not accept our proposal unless certain conditions were met. First, he wanted firm assurance that Hanoi would join in deescalating the war. Second, he wanted Hanoi's pledge to negotiate directly with his government. Finally, he wanted Hanoi to agree that the Liberation Front would not attend the conference as a separate delegation. My advisers and I recognized that these conditions were impossible. Moreover, we had been explaining for months to the South Vietnamese in Saigon and in Paris *why* they could not be met.

I decided then, with genuine regret, that we had to go forward with our plans. Perhaps Bunker could work things out in the next twenty-four hours, but that seemed doubtful. Perhaps our Vietnamese allies would have a change of heart. That seemed equally doubtful. I asked Bunker to do his best, but I knew he was working against long odds.

It was one of the rare occasions, in my years of dealing with them, that I felt Thieu, Ky, and their advisers had let me down. More important, I felt that their action put in peril everything both governments had worked so long and sacrificed so much to achieve. They were, however, Vietnamese and the legally elected authorities of their country. It was their decision to make, right or wrong.

I in turn had to do what I thought was right. If there was a real chance to gain a peaceful settlement in Paris, I could not let that opportunity pass. If I did, I knew I would never be forgiven, nor would I ever forgive myself. All my political advisers urged me to move forward, to halt the remaining bombing and proceed with the peace talks. All my military advisers shared this view and told me we would not be taking serious risks with the lives of our fighting men. Ambassador Bunker and our field commander in Vietnam both supported this move. I knew we would be in a weaker position in Paris without the South Vietnamese at our side, but I felt that it would be far worse to have the Paris talks collapse totally. I prayed that the South Vietnamese would reverse their thinking soon and realize that participation in the Paris negotiations was to their advantage.

I asked Rusk to contact Bunker immediately and relay my decision. I was scheduled to speak to the nation on television at 8 P.M. the next evening, October 31. The bombing halt order would go out at the same time and would become fully effective twelve hours later. The first of the new Paris meetings would be held on November 6 or later. Ambassador Bunker was authorized to inform Thieu of my decision as soon as possible. We instructed him to express again my wish that Thieu join with me in making the announcement. If not, I would make it alone.

The Secretary of State called Cy Vance in Paris, relaying the same information. He authorized Vance to pass along the essentials of my announcement to the North Vietnamese. Six hours later Vance called back to report he had carried out his orders. The North Vietnamese promised to maintain secrecy until the announcement was made. They also agreed to meet Vance on Saturday, November 2, to begin working out procedural arrangements for the new meetings.

From early morning on October 31 to the time I was to make my announcement, we waited anxiously, but with little hope, for word that the South Vietnamese had decided to make a joint statement with us. At mid-afternoon (the middle of the night in Saigon) Bunker reported that he had spent seven hours with President Thieu, Vice President Ky, and Foreign Minister Thanh trying to eliminate the remaining differences. The Vietnamese leaders still wanted to include a statement that North Vietnam intended to deescalate the war. They also wanted to make no statement regarding the first expanded meeting except that the date would be announced after all arrangements had been agreed upon. We knew that the authorities in Saigon hoped to use the procedural talks to get Hanoi to admit that the Liberation Front was not a separate entity and to promise to deal directly with the South Vietnamese government. We knew Hanoi would never accept either proviso and that this tactic could blow the entire peace effort sky high.

I assumed that my announcement would be made at 8 P.M. as planned, and that the South Vietnamese probably would not join us. Meanwhile, there were several things I had to do. I had kept all the Presidential candidates informed of major problems throughout the election campaign. I wanted them to know what I was doing, and why I was doing it, before they heard it on radio or television. At 6:05 P.M. I placed a conference call to Vice President Humphrey in Newark, Richard Nixon in New York City, and George Wallace in Norfolk, Virginia. I explained to them in detail what had happened since the four of us had last talked on October 16. I described the breakthrough in Paris and the problems with Saigon. I listed all the people I had consulted and their individual reactions. Finally, I said:

> I would not want it on my conscience that I had left the Presidential arena and refused to run to try to get peace and then, when they [the North Vietnamese] agreed . . . that I said: "No, I've got to put it off because I'm concerned with an election." I'm *not* concerned with an election. You all *are* concerned with an election. I don't think this concerns an election. I think all of you want the same thing. So I thought if I laid it on the line that way, and presented it to you, you would at least have a complete, full understanding of all the facts. . . .

The candidates asked several questions, which I answered. At the end of our conversation, George Wallace said: "Mr. President, I just pray that everything you do works out fine and I am praying for you."

"Well, I need it," I said. "Any other comments?"

"We'll back you up," said Nixon. "Thank you, Mr. President."

"We'll back you up, Mr. President," said Humphrey.

"We'll back you, Mr. President," said Wallace.

"Thank you very much," I said, putting down the phone.

Five minutes later I picked up the phone again for another conference call. I wanted to inform the leaders of Congress just as I had the candidates. The miracle of modern electronics made it possible for me to talk simultaneously with Senator Mike Mansfield in Marden, Montana, Senator Everett Dirksen in Chicago, Speaker John McCormack at his Boston residence, Senator Tom Kuchel in his Washington home, Representative Hale Boggs in New Orleans, and Representative Leslie Arends in Melvin, Illinois.

I repeated for them what had been happening in Paris. I described the advice I had received from my diplomatic and military advisers. I explained the difficulties in Saigon. I concluded by saying:

> Nearly everybody said if we would stop the bombing, we could really get peace. I am going to see if they knew what they were talking about. Since the North Vietnamese have finally acceded and agreed that they will sit down with these people who they call "puppets," and have acquiesced by their silence that they will not shell the cities or abuse the demilitarized zone, I don't think I could wait another day and have the blood of these boys on my conscience. I hope each of you will support me in that decision so we will have only one voice for the country.

Senator Mansfield said: "I am with you 100 per cent." Senator Kuchel said: "I am with you, Mr. President, all the way." I heard a chorus of voices over the wire and across the miles: "We are with you, Mr. President."

I walked from my office to the Cabinet Room to meet with the National Security Council. At that meeting, Rusk and Under Secretary of State Katzenbach sat at my right; Clifford and Deputy Secretary of Defense Nitze were at my left. Around the table were others whose final judgment I wanted: Secretary of the Treasury Fowler; CIA Director Helms; General Wheeler, Chairman of the Joint Chiefs of Staff; Price Daniel, Director of the Office of Emergency Planning; USIA Director Leonard Marks; and Walt Rostow. I had also invited the civilian secretaries of the military services, the three chiefs of staff of those services, and the Commandant of the Marine Corps.

I had awakened that day with a sore throat. By the time of the NSC meeting my throat was raw and my voice hoarse. The men around the table leaned forward to hear my words. Every person in that room knew we had reached a possible turning point, that the decision I had made was filled with both hope and danger.

"We are ready to announce that we are going to stop bombing North Vietnam," I began. "We have always held that conferences will not be productive unless the government of Vietnam is represented; unless the other side refrains from shelling the cities; unless these is no violation of the demilitarized zone."

"Hanoi has said that it is willing for South Vietnam to sit in on the meetings," I continued. "We have let them know that any violations of the DMZ will trigger an attack from us. We have talked with the Soviet Union and others, and they understand this. We will test their good faith and see."

I went on to discuss the situation as we then saw it, including our differences of opinion with Saigon. I pointed out that all my principal advisers had already given their support to my decision. "If you have any differing opinions," I said, "I would like for you to say so. Do you have any objections?"

I looked, one by one, at the men assembled around the long Cabinet table and asked their judgments on my decision. Were they convinced it was a proper decision? The reactions were quick and unanimous. "Absolutely," said one. "The thing to do," said another. One after another they expressed their support. I had the feeling that I was perhaps the most doubtful man in the room. We would have to wait and see how things came out. It could be the best decision I had made; or it could turn out to be a major mistake. As I stood up to leave, I said: "There will be some hard bargaining ahead." Rusk spoke quickly: "There will be some hard fighting too, Mr. President."

At that point news photographers entered the room to take pictures of the meeting. When they had finished, I walked back to my office. I spoke quietly to Rusk and he went quickly to his car to return to the State Department. We still hoped that Bunker might be able to work out a last-minute agreement in Saigon. I learned shortly after 7 P.M. that that was not to be. Bunker reported that the South Vietnamese were still asking for revisions in our joint statement. We would have to go ahead alone.

At 8 P.M. the order went to our Air Force and Navy to halt all aerial and naval bombardment of North Vietnam as soon as possible, and within twelve hours at the latest. At the same time, I spoke to the American people on television.

"Good evening, my fellow Americans," I began. "I speak to you this evening about very important developments in our search for peace in Vietnam." I discussed what had happened since I announced the partial bombing halt on March 31—developments in Paris and on the diplomatic front.

"Now, as a result of all of these developments," I said, "I have now ordered that all air, naval, and artillery bombardment of North Vietnam cease as of 8 A.M. Washington time, Friday morning."

I announced that a regular session of the Paris talks would be held the following week and that "representatives of the government of South Vietnam are free to participate." I said we had been told by Hanoi that representatives of the Liberation Front would also be present, but I emphasized that their attendance "in no way involves recognition of the National Liberation Front in any form." I hoped that this statement would further reassure the South Vietnamese.

"We have reached the stage," I said, "where productive talks can begin. We have made clear to the other side that such talks cannot continue if they take military advantage of them. We cannot have productive talks in an atmosphere where the cities are being shelled and where the demilitarized zone is being abused."

I warned that the beginning of talks did not mean peace had come to Southeast Asia. "There may well be very hard fighting ahead," I warned. "Certainly, there is going to be some very hard negotiating, because many difficult and critically important issues are still facing these negotiators. But I hope and I believe that with good will we can solve them. We know that negotiations can move swiftly if the common intent of the negotiators is peace in the world."

I added: "What is required of us is a courage and a steadfastness, and a perseverance here at home, that will match that of our men who fight for us tonight in Vietnam."

With less than three months of my Presidency remaining, I concluded my statement by saying: "I do not know who will be inaugurated as the thirty-seventh President of the United States next January. But I do know that I shall do all that I can in the next few months to try to lighten his burdens, as the contributions of the Presidents who preceded me have greatly lightened mine. I shall do everything in my power to move us toward the peace that the new President—as well as this President and, I believe, every other American—so deeply and urgently desires."

It was done. Now we would see whether hope was justified, whether peace could come.

Nearly four weeks went by before the South Vietnamese government decided to send a delegation to Paris. The head of the delegation did not arrive in Paris until December 8. On January 18 agreement was finally reached on all procedures for the new Paris meetings. Only two days before I left office the stage was set for a new round of talks on the substance of peace in Vietnam, and the first of the new meetings was held five days later, on January 25.

I regretted more than anyone could possibly know that I was leaving the White House without having achieved a just, an honorable, and a lasting peace in Vietnam. But during those final days of transition, I felt that I was turning over to my successor a situation more promising and manageable than it had been for years. Almost a year before, in February 1968, we had gone through the Tet offensive. There had been losses in the countryside, but they were far less serious than first estimates suggested. By September 1968 the Tet losses, in terms of the security of the people in the rural areas, were made good and the pacification program had moved forward with remarkable momentum through January 1969.

The South Vietnamese government had not only survived the major Communist effort to overthrow it at Tet, and in the subsequent attacks in May and again in September; it had gained far greater strength and confidence than ever before. The military forces of South Vietnam had grown in size, in quality of equipment, in morale, and in performance. They were fighting and beating the best the North Vietnamese and their Viet Cong followers could put into battle.

And in Paris, through long months of argument and frustration, we had reached an agreement to hold expanded talks at which the South Vietnamese would take part with the North Vietnamese and their followers from the Liberation Front.

I felt I was turning over to President Nixon a foreign policy problem that, although serious, was improving; an ally that was stronger than ever before; an enemy weakened and beaten in every major engagement; and a working forum for peace. These we had achieved through the months and years of pain and sacrifice. But we had accomplished far more than that. We had kept our word to Southeast Asia. We had opposed and defeated aggression, as we promised we would. We had given 17 million South Vietnamese a chance to build their own country and their own institutions. And we had seen them move well down that road.

We had also demonstrated, with our resources and with our blood, that we cared about Asia. I was certain that every man, woman, and child in that vast and important part of the world was, at that moment, more secure and more hopeful because of what we had done—because America had cared enough to stand and to fight, and to keep its promises.

All this we accomplished, but not without great cost at home. The strain of prolonged engagement in a distant war stirred deep controversy among our people. The war created or deepened divisions—between the President and Congress, between "doves" and "hawks," between generations, between those who felt that Asia was deeply important to our future and those who put Europe first, between those who fought and those who objected to fighting.

Much of this I understood perfectly well, for debate and dissension are part of the fabric of a free society, especially in this country of ours. I had not only lived through but had taken an active part in many of the most violent debates of modern times. The New Deal of the 1930s stirred wild enthusiasm among millions of Americans, but it also generated suspicion and even hatred in many hearts. Who now remembers the Pearl Harbor hearings, which a few men tried to use to "prove" that President Roosevelt forced us into World War II? The younger generation knows only from books the divisions that split us as the Korean War dragged on—the conflict that his critics liked to call "Mr. Truman's War."

A certain degree of violent disagreement with our Vietnam effort was inevitable, but I am convinced that it passed the bounds of reasonable debate and fair dissension. It became a self-inflicted wound of critical proportions. There is not the slightest doubt in my mind that this dissension prolonged the war, prevented a peaceful settlement on reasonable terms, encouraged our enemies, disheartened our friends, and weakened us as a nation.

There was no shortage of criticism of those who made and carried out decisions. Those dissents were heard and weighed inside the administration with a seriousness perhaps not generally understood. In addition, the war in Southeast Asia and the political and social currents at work in that region were and are complex; they are difficult to describe in simple formulas. There was certainly justification for debate and for differences in judgment in a free society filled with strong-minded men and women who found themselves dealing with unfamiliar problems on the other side of the world.

But those who created division, who opposed decisions, and who made it more difficult to accomplish the job need to reflect on the consequences of their actions. Those who burned draft cards, waved Viet Cong flags, and shouted obscenities at the police need to think objectively about whether their activities did not make longer and harder and more dangerous the job of the brave men fighting for us all—and the job of Asians fighting for the independence and dignity of their nations. Those who wrote of these events

—whether of war or of protest—should search their consciences to see whether their assessments were accurate, fair, and objective or whether their personal feelings affected their private versions of history and thereby the balance in public opinion.

As I left the Presidency, I was aware that not everything I had done about Vietnam, not every decision I had made, had been correct. Should we have sent as many men to Southeast Asia as we did? Or should we have sent more and sent them sooner? Was I right in refusing to risk expanding the war by using ground forces to attack the enemy's supply lines and sanctuaries in neighboring countries or to mine the port of Haiphong? Did I make a mistake in stopping most of the bombing of the North on March 31? And all the bombing on October 31? Did I do all I could have done to make clear to our people the vital interests that I believed were at stake in our efforts to help protect Southeast Asia?

History will judge these questions and will render its verdict long after current passions have subsided and the noise in the streets has died away. History will judge on the basis of facts we cannot now know, and of events some of which have not yet happened.

Every President I have known has drawn heavily on past history—for lessons, for ideas, and for principles. But none of us can know what future history's conclusions will be regarding our time and our actions. Every President must act on problems as they come to him. He must search out the best information available. He can seek the counsel of men whose wisdom and experience and judgment he values. But in the end the President must decide, and he must do so on the basis of his judgment of what is best—for his nation and for the world. Throughout those years of crucial decisions I was sustained by the memory of my predecessors who had also borne the most painful duty of a President—to lead our country in a time of war. I recalled often the words of one of those men, Woodrow Wilson, who in the dark days of 1917 said: "It is a fearful thing to lead this great peaceful people into war. . . . But the right is more precious than peace."

That belief—that peace is precious but that there are values even more precious to free men—has strengthened us from the earliest days of our nation. It has given us the courage to do what had to be done in times of great danger. We will be a poorer and a weaker people if we ever abandon that belief. And the world will be a much more dangerous place for all mankind.

22

The Last Year: Headlines and History

I T WAS A GLOOMY JANUARY 23, 1968, when I met in the White House
with my top foreign affairs advisers for our regular Tuesday luncheon,
and the gloom was not confined to the weather outside. Seated around the
table to discuss, debate, and evaluate the foreign affairs problems of
the day were the regular Tuesday lunch participants: Secretaries Rusk
and McNamara, CIA Director Helms, Joint Chiefs of Staff Chairman
Wheeler, and White House aides Walt Rostow, George Christian, and
Tom Johnson. In addition, I had invited Clark Clifford to attend his first
Tuesday luncheon in the family dining room as Secretary of Defense-
designate.

Bob McNamara opened the meeting on a note of wry humor, directed
at the man who would succeed him. "This is what it is like on a typical
day," he said to Clifford. "We had an inadvertent intrusion into Cambodia.
We lost a B-52 with four H-bombs aboard. We had an intelligence ship
captured by the North Koreans."

The dapper, confident Clark Clifford smiled a little ruefully, turned to me,
and said: "Mr. President, may I leave now?" I knew how he felt. If I
had to pick a date that symbolized the turmoil we experienced throughout
1968, I think January 23 would be the day—the morning the USS *Pueblo*
was seized. The *Pueblo* incident formed the first link in a chain of events—
of crisis, tragedy, and disappointment—that added up to one of the most
agonizing years any President has ever spent in the White House. As I
look back over the crowded diaries listing the telephone calls and meetings of 1968, as I reread the daily headlines that jumped so steadily and

forebodingly from one trouble spot to another, as I review the memos and the intelligence reports, I recall vividly the frustration and genuine anguish I experienced so often during the final year of my administration. I sometimes felt that I was living in a continuous nightmare.

But the sum total and full meaning of any period of time, be it a week, a year, or a decade, can never be gleaned from the headlines. At any given time there are many forces of history in motion both above and below the surface, and the less obvious currents are occasionally the most instrumental in shaping the future. Recently—after I had gained perspective on that trying year—I began to realize that there were two major and opposing historical forces at work during my last year in office. One was the chain of crises that appeared to be carrying us downhill at an ever-increasing pace. The other, late in beginning and largely obscured by the daily headlines, was a tide of events that was ultimately to sustain us and resolve many of our worst problems before the year had ended.

Unfortunately, I was not aware of this second force of history on that gloomy, gray morning of January 23 as we met to discuss the *Pueblo* crisis. I knew only that we had lived with trouble from the first moment of the year. The government had ended the last three months of 1967 with a balance-of-payments deficit that ran at an annual rate of $7 billion, threatening the stability of the dollar. I had to begin the new year by prescribing strong and unpleasant medicine to stem the flow of dollars abroad. The Viet Cong and North Vietnamese had inaugurated a siege of our Marine base at Khe Sanh on January 21, and we knew that the enemy was preparing to launch a full-scale offensive throughout South Vietnam in a desperate, last-ditch effort to turn the tide of the war. Against this background of financial turmoil, international tension, and an impending major enemy offensive, the *Pueblo* crisis broke.

The crises began, for me, in the darkness of my bedroom at 2:24 A.M. on January 23, when I was awakened by my bedside telephone. The call was from the duty officer in the Situation Room. The first reports were sketchy. The USS *Pueblo,* a highly sophisticated electronics intelligence ship, had been cruising off the coast of North Korea, gathering data from the mainland. Between 10:52 P.M. of January 22 and 12:32 A.M. of the 23rd, Washington time, the *Pueblo* was challenged and then surrounded by a flotilla comprised of a North Korean submarine chaser and three patrol boats, and was finally boarded by an armed party, while Communist jet fighters circled overhead. The *Pueblo* reported that the boarding took place approximately fifteen and a half nautical miles from the nearest land under North Korean jurisdiction, well outside the twelve-mile territorial limit claimed by North Korea. Aboard the ship were six officers, seventy-five enlisted men, and two civilians. Four men were injured, one mortally.

The ship was virtually unarmed and unprotected. This fact prompted former Vice President Richard Nixon to term the *Pueblo* incident a "tactical blunder," but there were good reasons for the lack of cover. The cost of providing military protection for all our sea and air intelligence operations would have been prohibitively expensive, and under any circumstances such armed protection so close to their shores would have been provocative to foreign governments.

I asked the duty officer some demanding questions. I was advised that enemy harassment of our intelligence ships was so commonplace that neither the captain of the *Pueblo* nor the members of the crew had any realization of the danger they were in until it was too late to forestall the action. By the time it became apparent that the North Koreans were serious, the local authorities in the Pacific Command decided that there were not enough daylight hours remaining to get help to the scene. They believed that use of our aircraft, instead of saving our men, would endanger their lives, and they concluded that the pilots of the aircraft would be taking an unacceptable risk, in view of the large number of North Korean jet fighters massed in the area around Wonsan, North Korea. Later a careful review of these circumstances, conducted by the Joint Chiefs of Staff, supported the decision of the local military authorities.

The unanswered question was *why* the North Koreans had seized the *Pueblo*. Piracy on the high seas is a serious matter. Why had North Korea flagrantly risked stirring up an international hornet's nest and perhaps starting a war?

The North Koreans charged that the *Pueblo* had violated their territorial waters. They claimed that they had seized the ship only seven miles offshore. We had proof that this charge was false, not only from the *Pueblo*'s reports but from our own radio "fix" on the ship at the time of the incident. We did not know, of course, whether the ship had inadvertently drifted too close to shore *before* it was challenged, but we considered this possibility unlikely. The *Pueblo* was under strict orders to stay well outside the territorial limits, and given the sensitive mission it was conducting, we doubted that the captain and the crew would be so careless.

Even assuming that the *Pueblo had* veered off course, that would hardly explain North Korea's sudden bellicose action. For years both the United States and the Soviet Union had been employing intelligence-gathering ships, as well as planes, and the ships occasionally wandered off course. In 1965 there were two separate incidents of Soviet vessels entering U.S. waters. We did not make a big issue of the infringements. We merely ordered them to leave.

Communist and non-Communist nations alike naturally resent the intelligence activities of potentially hostile states. But I believe all nations so involved recognize that there are occasions, rare but crucial, when it is of the utmost importance that the opposing side have certain facts verified by its own intelligence efforts. During the Six Day War in 1967, for example, the Arabs accused the United States of supporting Israel with planes from our carriers in the Mediterranean. But a Soviet ship was monitoring some of our fleet's activities and the Russians knew that the Arab charge was false. If the Soviets had not possessed that certain knowledge, the Arab accusation might well have complicated an already dangerous situation.

There was another reason that persuaded us that the seizure was not an impulsive act. As soon as I learned that the *Pueblo* had been seized, I instructed Ambassador Llewellyn Thompson in Moscow to ask Soviet officials for assistance in obtaining the release of the ship and the crew. Ambassador Thompson received the Soviet reply almost immediately, a very negative and chilly response. The Soviets could scarcely have obtained the necessary information regarding the incident from the North Koreans, conferred about it, and taken a position so quickly without prior information.

We believed that the capture of the *Pueblo* was premeditated. But what did the North Koreans hope to accomplish? Were they deliberately trying to force us into a provocative act? Were they preparing for a new invasion of South Korea? Our best estimate then, one that I believe holds up well in the light of subsequent events, is that they were aware of the Tet offensive in Vietnam, which was scheduled to take place eight days later. They were trying to divert U.S. military resources from Vietnam and to pressure the South Koreans into recalling their two divisions from that area, for the seizure of the *Pueblo* was not an isolated incident. The number of border violations and flareups along the 38th parallel in Korea had increased sharply in the previous weeks. Two days before the seizure of the *Pueblo* thirty-one North Korean special agents had infiltrated the northwest section of Seoul, less than half a mile from the Presidential mansion, before they were discovered by military and police sentries and overcome in a heated battle. One of the captured infiltrators disclosed that their mission had been to cut off the head of South Korean President Park and throw it into the street. He also admitted that 2,400 similar terrorist agents were being trained in special camps throughout North Korea.

As a result, South Korea *was* nervous and was seriously considering withdrawing military units from Vietnam to build up defensive strength at home. One of our first actions after the *Pueblo* incident was to dispatch more than 350 aircraft to our air bases in South Korea and to recall to active duty selected units of the Air National Guard and Air Force Reserve to replace our strategic reserve in the United States. We assumed that the South Korean army could look after itself, but the North Koreans had a larger air force and we did not wish them to be tempted by that advantage.

The movement of American air power would inevitably be known at once by the North Koreans. It was an act that would give confidence and strength to the harassed South Koreans.

In response, the North Koreans promptly announced that the crew of the *Pueblo* would be tried and punished as criminals. This announcement pointed up our dilemma. A U.S. ship had been seized on the high seas, one of our men had been killed, and the remaining eighty-two were being held captive and subjected to trial as criminals. But we could not allow our indignation to dictate our response, even though that is the course many Americans would have preferred. Some members of Congress were also demanding strong action, and one of our most vocal Senate doves termed the seizure "an act of war against the United States." But we knew that if we wanted our men to return home alive, we had to use diplomacy. If we resorted to military means, we could expect dead bodies. And we also might start a war.

During the next few days I held dozens of meetings with the National Security Council, with foreign affairs and military advisers, and with congressional leaders. We considered one alternative after another: mining Wonsan harbor; mining other North Korean harbors; interdicting coastal shipping; seizing a North Korean ship; striking selected North Korean targets by air and naval gunfire. In each case we decided that the risk was too great and the possible accomplishment too small. "I do not want to win the argument and lose the sale," I consistently warned my advisers. I wanted the officers and crew of the *Pueblo* home alive, and I was prepared to take considerable political heat to achieve this goal. In taking this position I was fully supported by my advisers, military as well as civilian.

Our diplomatic effort took several forms. First, UN Ambassador Arthur Goldberg brought the matter before the Security Council and urged a resolution condemning North Korea's action and demanding the return of the ship and its crew. Second, we asked the Soviet Union to bring its influence to bear on the North Koreans. In spite of their initial rebuff of Ambassador Thompson's request, the Russians were now urging us to act with restraint, and we believed that they could be helpful. Third, we contacted almost every government in the world and asked them to use their good offices to secure the release of the *Pueblo* crew.

As a precaution, we moved as much military power into South Korea as we could without diverting units from Southeast Asia. We had to be ready in case North Korea started something, and we had to shore up the South Korean defenses.

In spite of every effort we could make, in spite of our patient attempts to balance firmness with reason, and in spite of our innumerable diplomatic moves, eleven miserable months went by before the men of the

Pueblo were given their freedom. Every day that passed during those eleven months, the plight of those men obsessed and haunted me.

On the night of January 31, with Khe Sanh under siege and the *Pueblo* and its crew in captivity, I received a report that two of our airplanes had accidentally violated Communist Chinese air space. In a short covering memorandum, Walt Rostow noted: "Thank God January is ending." The implied optimism was premature, for on that same day the Communists' Tet offensive began, and with it a decline in public confidence.

In March another major crisis confronted us, one that required immediate solution. The run on the gold market during the first two weeks of the month threatened both the stability of the dollar and the foundation of the international monetary system. This crisis emphasized the urgency of enacting our request for a 10 per cent surtax, which was still bottled up in committee. It was obvious that unless we could put our own fiscal house in order, especially by slowing inflation, foreign confidence in the dollar would continue to decline. Unfortunately, we were still unable to overcome congressional opposition to the tax bill or to counteract the fears of many Congressmen of political backlash at home. In another area of the gold crisis we were more successful. As an emergency measure, we persuaded the Congress on March 14 to remove the gold backing for Federal Reserve notes, freeing about $10.4 billion in U.S. gold to meet the international crisis. Two days later, on March 16, the United States and the six other nations of the London gold pool were able to hammer out an agreement that shut off the supply of gold to private buyers and established a two-tier gold system.*

March was a turbulent month for other reasons. We had to make basic decisions regarding our troop levels in Vietnam. In making those decisions, we tried to predict what North Korea's next move, if any, might be, and we scrutinized Berlin and other sensitive areas for possible Communist pressure. March was the month in which we worked out a peace proposal that we hoped Hanoi would accept but that would not endanger the lives of our forces in I Corps, including marines still under siege in Khe Sanh.

And March was a month of profound political frustrations. I was delaying announcement of my decision not to be a Presidential candidate in 1968. That delay resulted in several misunderstandings and disappointments, the most obvious of which was the New Hampshire primary of March 12. I would have preferred to announce my intentions not to run before that primary, since this would have resulted in a clean break and would have been much simpler for me and, I think, much better for the Demo-

* See Chapter 14, pp. 318–19.

cratic party. But all things considered—and these things included the Tet offensive, the bombing halt, and my legislative program—I had concluded that the end of March was the earliest moment I could make my move.

I must admit that the results of the New Hampshire primary surprised me. I was not expecting a landslide. I had not spent a single day campaigning in New Hampshire, and my name was not even on the ballot. And the fact that I received more votes, as a write-in candidate, than Senator McCarthy—49.5 per cent as against 42.4 per cent—seems to have been overlooked or forgotten. Still, I think most people were surprised that Senator McCarthy rolled up the vote he did. I was much less surprised when Bobby Kennedy announced his candidacy four days later. I had been expecting it.

For a few fleeting hours on April 3 I thought that history had turned a corner and that the "bad days" were behind us. Hanoi responded favorably to my March 31 speech and announced that its representatives were ready to meet with us. I felt deep satisfaction in the knowledge that by refusing to be a candidate for the Presidency, I might have hastened the day when peace would come to Vietnam. But satisfaction turned to sorrow in less than twenty-four hours. On April 4 Martin Luther King, Jr., was slain by a sniper,* and it became immediately clear that his assassination had compounded the danger of violence. Stokely Carmichael and other black militant leaders were urging Negroes to arm themselves with guns and take to the streets in retaliation against Dr. King's murder. Sporadic rioting broke out in various parts of the country on the night of April 4, and I postponed my planned Vietnam conference in Hawaii and went on television to appeal to reason.

I remember the sick feeling that came over me the next day as I saw the black smoke from burning buildings fill the sky over Washington, and as I watched armed troops patrolling the streets of the nation's capital for the first time since the Civil War. I wondered, as every American must have wondered, what we were coming to.

But out of the chaos and the guilt and the shame came a renewed sense of urgency in the Congress for action. Within a week of Dr. King's assassination the controversial Open Housing Act became the law of the land. That legislation might have ultimately passed anyway, but it is entirely possible that Martin Luther King bought it with his life.

On June 5, while we were still recovering from the shock of Dr. King's assassination, Senator Robert Kennedy was shot and killed in Los Angeles on the night of his California primary victory over Senator McCarthy.

* See Chapter 7, pp. 174–75.

Another voice that spoke for America's poor and dispossessed was stilled forever.

During the four and a half years of my Presidency I had never been able to establish a close relationship with Bobby Kennedy. It was not so much a question of issues; on most matters of national importance we had similar views, after he became a Senator. We even agreed on Vietnam for a long time. We did not come to any sort of parting of the ways on that question until 1966. Perhaps his political ambitions were part of the problem. Maybe it was just a matter of chemistry. I honestly do not know. I recognized and admired his leadership qualities. He had surrounded himself with loyal and able men and women, and he had organized them effectively.

When tragedy struck him down, I was glad that my last meeting with Bobby Kennedy had been friendly. That meeting had been the result of a public promise I had made, following my announcement that I would not accept the Democratic nomination, to brief all the major Presidential candidates. Senator Kennedy had asked to see me and I immediately arranged a meeting with him in the White House. Shortly after 10 A.M. on April 3 he came into the Cabinet Room with his campaign aide Ted Sorensen and met with Walt Rostow, Charles Murphy, and me for more than an hour. The discussion was an open and frank one. Both Murphy and Rostow took notes.

As I walked into the Cabinet Room, I shook hands with Senator Kennedy and showed him the news bulletin indicating that Hanoi was ready to discuss peace. He had not yet heard the news, and he seemed pleased. He agreed with me that these talks might be the beginning of the road to a peaceful settlement and concurred in the opinion that plenty of hard bargaining remained ahead of us. I pointed out that we could not be certain the press report was authentic, but that we had reason to believe our strenuous efforts were about to be rewarded.

We sat down facing each other across the big Cabinet table. I was in my customary chair, and Senator Kennedy was in the chair usually occupied by the Vice President at Cabinet and NSC meetings. The following notes reflect the tenor of that session:

The President opened the meeting by referring to his speech of March 31st, in which he announced the new initiative with respect to Vietnam and his intention not to run for reelection. He said that he wished and hoped to find areas of agreement because of the critical need to do so in the national interest. He referred to the critical nature of problems facing us and spoke particularly of the explosive situation in the Middle East and of our fiscal and monetary problems. He told Senator Kennedy he had no desire to be a political boss or to determine the Senator's future.

The President said he had only one desire: to do the best he could for the country. He doubted that he and Senator Kennedy would be far apart if they sat at the same table. He had taken himself out of the election to remove any possible suspicion that what he was doing was self-interested. He would try to lead the country in the next nine months. He had great faith and trust in the judgment of the people.

The President said that he would have his own judgments and would exercise them, but except for a few fund-raising dinners, he planned to keep out of campaign politics.

Senator Kennedy: Your speech was magnificent. I regret we have not had closer contact. Will be glad to try to help in minimizing controversy and to keep in touch through anyone you say. Your position is unselfish and courageous and taken in the interest of the United States.

The President: There is a great deal you can contribute. Call up Nick Katzenbach. We both have great respect and confidence in him. He told me he had not been in touch with you, and I told him he ought to talk to you. Secretary Clark Clifford will be glad to come and brief you. If leading spokesmen [of the Democratic party] can be pretty much in agreement on the U.S. course, that will be good for the country.

The President then spoke at some length about the nature and purpose of the current bombing north of the DMZ—generally to the effect that it was to halt traffic which was now flowing heavily to reinforce the enemy in South Vietnam.

The President discussed the current military situation in Vietnam at some length, with particular reference to the specific targets and objectives of the current bombing. He read excerpts from a staff paper or report dealing with this, apparently from the military. He and Rostow supplemented this with reference to a map.

The President again mentioned the facts that the precise language in his speech referring to the limits on bombing was recommended by Nick Katzenbach of the State Department and was then agreed to by Secretary Clifford and Harry McPherson. He said that his purpose in the speech was to go as far as he could at that time in seeking negotiations. He is prepared to go further if, as, and when developments permit. Will go as far as we can without murdering our own boys.

The President then said he would be glad to hear anything Senator Kennedy had on his mind.

Senator Kennedy: That is what I saw in your speech. I didn't understand about how far north of the DMZ the bombing might be, but I've said nothing. I thought there must be something more.

Sorensen: I thought the language of the speech was just right. This session is extremely informative and helpful. If arrangements for continued briefings could be made, that would be helpful.

The President: They can and will be. People try to divide us, and we both suffer from it. I will ask Clifford to brief you. Will make briefings available to McCarthy and Nixon too.

Will be glad for you to make suggestions. I feel no bitterness or vindictiveness. I want everybody to get together to find a way to stop the killing.

1968–1969: *If I had to pick a date that symbolized the turmoil we experienced throughout 1968 it would be January 23, the morning the USS* Pueblo *was seized. . . . It formed the first link in a chain that added up to one of the most agonizing years any President has ever spent in the White House.*

January 23: Top foreign affairs advisers meet for Tuesday luncheon.

The March 31 Decisions: Meeting with General Creighton Abrams a few days before announcement of partial bombing halt. During a later talk with General Westmoreland, grandson Patrick Lyn Nugent arrives.

April 3, BOTTOM, L.: Receiving news bulletin that peace talks are possible (with Sen. Henry Jackson); LEFT: last meeting with Bobby Kennedy. April 5, BELOW, Negro leaders meet in Cabinet Room following King assassination (April 4): viewing Washington damage. April 11, with Clarence Mitchell, a prime mover in the fight for open housing, at signing of bill (BOTTOM, CENTER).

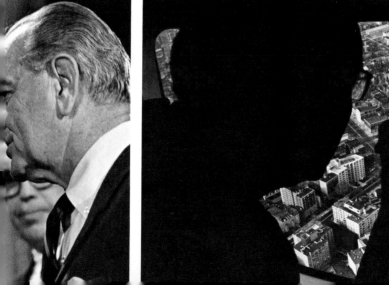

Camp David, April 8–9. Meeting with Ambassador Ellsworth Bunker (*c.*) and senior advisers on coming talks with Hanoi. May 8, Paris delegation meets newsmen in Rose Garden, BOTTOM (*l. to r.,* Philip Habib, Vance, Andrew Goodpaster, Averell Harriman, William Jorden).

Briefing the 1968 candidates: Humphrey, Nelson Rockefeller (CENTER, L.), Eugene McCarthy, Richard Nixon, BOTTOM.

August 20. Soviet Ambassador Anatoly Dobrynin tells Johnson of invasion of Czechoslovakia (with Rostow).

October 29–31. BOTTOM, L.: General Abrams reports total bombing halt
will not endanger men in Vietnam. BELOW: General Wheeler issuing
order to stop bombing; with Secretary Rusk outside Cabinet Room;
viewing address to nation with Mrs. Johnson in Oval Office.

*January 20, 1969—The last morning I would wake up in this room,
the last day I would live in this house . . .*

The President then talked at some length about the program for calling up the Reserves and the need for and extent of the call. He also talked about the progress being made by the Government of South Vietnam, including removal of corrupt officials. He told of the reports on this from Ambassador Bunker, who thinks that progress is being made as fast as it can be made. He told of General Abrams' evaluation of the ARVN and its improvement. He told of plans for increasing the number of ARVN troops.

The President then spoke of international monetary problems and the recent Stockholm meeting. Then the need for a tax bill. He said he "may have goofed" when he got taxes reduced. If the old rates were now restored, that would produce $24 billion more revenue. The surtax he has now asked would only be $9 billion. That perhaps should be a lesson to all of us—never repeal another tax. It's too hard to put it back when you need it.

As to reduced spending, it would be better to reduce NOA [new obligated authority] for 1970 and 1971, but he is willing to agree to cuts for 1969. He will take $10 billion tax increase and $5 billion spending cut. Aid, $600 million; Space, $400 million; Roads, $400 or $500 million; Agriculture, $400 or $500 million; a cut in poverty funds. Will take 2% off in pay rolls and 5% in controllables, to bring the '69 budget down to $181.5 billion. Two and a half billion dollars of this would come off of defense. Doesn't want to abandon or reduce our programs.

Senator Kennedy: This is very helpful.
Rostow: Maybe you should mention operation Pegasus.
The President: Westmoreland is in the middle of an offensive. (This was described in some detail and reference was made to the responsibility of field commanders for certain military decisions.)
The President: Feel free to talk to Murphy, Rostow, or DeVier Pierson. I'll be glad to meet with you at any time.
Senator Kennedy: Thank you very much. Can I ask about the political situation? Where do I stand in the campaign? Are you opposed to my effort and will you marshal forces against me?
The President: I expressed it in my speech. I want to keep the Presidency out of this campaign. I'm not that pure, but I am that scared. The situation of the country is critical. I will try to run this office so as to have as much support and as few problems as possible.

I will tell the Vice President about the same things I'm telling you. I don't know whether he will run or not. If he asks my advice, I won't give it.

If I had thought I could get into the campaign and hold the country together, I would have run myself. If I campaign for someone else, it will defeat what I am trying to do.

My objective is to stay out of pre-convention politics. I have no plans to get into it. That might change at any time. I might have to disagree with you tomorrow. I might say who I'm going to vote for, but I do not plan to do so.

I do not want to mislead you or deceive you, and I must preserve my freedom of action, but I want to follow the course stated in my speech [keeping the Presidency out of the campaign] if I can. But I must be free to react to future developments.

I am no king maker and don't want to be. I did not talk to [Mayor] Daley about this in Chicago.

Sorensen: Will people in your administration be free to take part in pre-convention politics and support candidates?

The President: I will need to think about that.

Senator Kennedy: If you decide later on to take a position, can we talk to you prior to that?

The President: Yes, unless I lose my head and pop off. I will try to honor your request.

Senator Kennedy: I wanted to know, because if I should hear reports that you are doing so and so, I wanted to know whether to believe them.

The President: If I move, you'll know.

The President told Senator Kennedy that he held no enmity for him. He said frankly that he felt much closer to the Vice President, who had been everything the President could ask as Vice President. The President spoke very eloquently and movingly of his reluctance to seek the Democratic nomination in 1960 and his reluctance to become Vice President. He had rather be Majority Leader. That was the best job he ever had. He tried to find some way to avoid running in 1964, but could not. He never wanted to be President and had been counting the days to the end of his term ever since the beginning.

He had never thought of his administration as just the Johnson Administration, but as a continuation of the Kennedy-Johnson Administration. It was carrying on a family matter. He had never fired a Kennedy appointee, and has asked most of them to stay when they wanted to leave. He wanted Sorensen to stay—and the country would be better off if he had.

President Kennedy had always treated him well as Vice President, although he spoke very frankly and sometimes sharply. He had done his best as Vice President to support President Kennedy. (Senator Kennedy agreed.) He had done his best since then to carry on the policies and programs. He thought he had done reasonably well. He thought that as President Kennedy looked down at him every day from then until now, he would agree that he had kept the faith.

Nevertheless, the President said, what he had done had not been good enough. Witness our current difficulties. (The President had spoken earlier of the disaffection of the young people, notwithstanding all that had been done in education; and the disaffection of the Negroes, notwithstanding all that had been done in civil rights.) The next man who sits in this chair will have to do better.

Senator Kennedy responded: You are a brave and dedicated man.

The meeting broke up with a reiteration of the desirability of continued exchange of information and views.

That was the last time I saw Senator Kennedy.

Robert Kennedy's death seemed to symbolize the irrationality that was besieging our nation and the world. The summer months of 1968 brought no easing of disorder and unrest. Our Ambassador to Guatemala, John Gordon Mein, was machine-gunned to death by local guerrillas. Soviet troops marched brutally into Czechoslovakia on August 21 and stamped the heavy boots of oppression on the first serious shoots of freedom that had appeared in Czech soil in twenty years. When the Russians made this move, they slammed the door on the missile talks we had painstakingly worked out and planned to announce the next day, August 22.* That same week, fighting between police and students at the Democratic National Convention in Chicago proved to every television viewer in America how deep the cleavage was in our society, how intense the hatreds, and how wide the gulf between law enforcers and those who had nothing but contempt for the law. These conflicts also exposed the ugly side of the so-called New Politics, in spite of its claims of idealism.

The resignation of Chief Justice Earl Warren in June represented a double blow to me. His departure from the Court deprived the nation of the services of a man whom I considered one of the great Supreme Court justices in our history and resulted in the deliberate and systematic vilification of one of the wisest, ablest, and fairest men I have ever known, Associate Justice Abe Fortas. The irony of that episode, an irony that made the circumstance all the more agonizing for me personally, was that Abe Fortas had never wanted to sit on the Supreme Court in the first place.

The events leading to his appointment began on the afternoon of July 16, 1965, when Ambassador John Kenneth Galbraith and his wife visited me in the Oval Office. During our conversation Galbraith said that he believed Arthur Goldberg, then an Associate Justice on the Court, would step down from his position to take a job that would be more challenging to him. Galbraith speculated that he might accept an appointment either as Secretary of Health, Education, and Welfare (a position soon to be vacated by Tony Celebrezze) or as Ambassador to the United Nations, to replace Adlai Stevenson, who had died three days earlier. Frankly, I was surprised. I was aware that Goldberg, an activist, became restless on the bench from time to time, and I knew that as Secretary of Labor under President Kennedy he had yearned for more freedom and activity. But I could not imagine him giving up his seat on the Supreme Court.

Three days later, on July 19, Justice Goldberg flew to Illinois with me to attend Ambassador Stevenson's funeral. I mentioned that I had heard reports that he might step down from the Court and therefore might be available for another assignment. He told me these reports had substance.

* See Chapter 20, p. 487.

I said that I would like to see him in the Cabinet as Secretary of Health, Education, and Welfare, because that was a department which required imagination and leadership at the top. He replied that the job sounded fascinating but that he had become increasingly interested in foreign affairs.

That was the extent of our conversation that day. I asked Justice Goldberg to "think about it some more" and said that we would discuss it later. The next day he called Jack Valenti and told him that the job he would accept was the UN ambassadorship, if I offered it to him. I appointed him to the United Nations, and I felt he was an excellent choice. He was a skilled arbiter and a fair-minded man, and he had had experience in both domestic and foreign affairs, qualities that I believed would make him an outstanding representative of our nation in that crucial international organization.

Subsequently, I nominated Abe Fortas to fill the vacant seat on the Court. Many people assumed that I was masterminding a great shift at the top echelons of government. The fact is that the Court vacancy presented me with a serious problem. I conferred with many friends and advisers, including Fortas, about a possible successor to Arthur Goldberg. Finally, after studying the list these advisers had compiled, I concluded that there was only one man whose legal qualifications and character I knew well who could take Goldberg's place. I was confident that the man would be a brilliant and able jurist. He had the experience and the liberalism to espouse the causes that both I and Arthur Goldberg believed in. He had the strength of character to stand up for his own convictions, and he was a humanitarian. That man was Abe Fortas, reared in Memphis, Tennessee, with a career as a distinguished lawyer in Washington for over thirty years. But Abe Fortas did not want the job. I urged him to accept the nomination but he declined firmly. He said that he did not want it.

Then, on July 19, he wrote me:

For the President:

Again, my dear friend, I am obligated and honored by your confidence and generosity—to an extent which is beyond my power adequately to acknowledge.

But after painful searching, I've decided to decline—with a heart full of gratitude. Carol thinks I should accept this greatest honor that a lawyer could receive—this highest appointive post in the nation. But I want a few more years of activity. I want a few more years to try to be of service to you and the Johnson family. And I want and feel that in justice I should take a few more years to stabilize this law firm in the interests of the young men who have enlisted here.

This has been a hard decision—but not nearly as hard as another which had the virtue of continuing association with your trials and tribulations and greatness.*

I shall always be grateful.

Abe

We talked about the matter for the next several days, but I could not sway him. Finally, on July 28, I invited Fortas to my office. When he came in, I told him that I was about to go over to the theater in the East Wing of the White House to announce his appointment to the Supreme Court. I said that he could stay in my office or accompany me to the theater, but that since he was the person being appointed, I thought he should go with me. He looked at me in silence for a moment. I waited. Then he said, "I'll accompany you." That was the only way I managed to get him on the Court.

When I nominated Fortas to succeed Chief Justice Warren three years later, I did so for the same reasons I had first appointed him to the Court: because he was the most experienced, compassionate, articulate, and intelligent lawyer I knew, and because I was certain that he would carry on in the Court's liberal tradition. Clark Clifford, a man who had always given me thoughtful advice, told me that he thought Abe Fortas would make a great Chief Justice. To fill Fortas' seat, Clifford urged me to nominate an outstanding constitutional and trial lawyer of unimpeachable and impeccable standing with the American Bar Association. Clifford suggested that the new Associate Justice should be from the Middle West, in order to avoid any charge of favoritism or sectional preference, and that he should probably be a Republican.

At the same time, Ed Weisl, Sr., a friend and an outstanding New York lawyer, reported that Senator Richard Russell had informed him that although he would vote for Fortas for Chief Justice, he would "enthusiastically support" Judge Homer Thornberry if he were nominated to the Court. I thought that Russell's stand would provide strong insurance against a Southern filibuster opposing Justice Fortas. Judge Thornberry, a former Circuit Judge and U.S. Congressman, and then a Federal Judge, had been a close friend of mine for many years. He was one of the most competent, fair-minded, and progressive jurists in the entire South. His was one of three names remaining after we had narrowed the list down to the best possible appointees.

I called Senator Russell to the White House on June 25 and sought his counsel firsthand. He repeated what he had told Ed Weisl: that he thought Homer Thornberry would make an outstanding Associate Justice. When you sit in a duck blind all day with a man, he said, you really get to know him—and he knew Homer Thornberry. He knew him to be a good man, an able man, and a fair man. As I remember our exchange

* I had previously offered Fortas a Cabinet post, which he declined.

in the small room off the Oval Office, Senator Russell said: "I will support the nomination of Mr. Fortas for Chief Justice, but I will enthusiastically support Homer Thornberry."

I picked up the phone and called Judge Thornberry and his wife, and talked to them in Senator Russell's presence. I repeated to Thornberry what Senator Russell had told me and informed him that I had decided to nominate him as Associate Justice of the Supreme Court. I gave Senator Russell the telephone, and he assured Judge Thornberry of his support. On June 26, 1968, I announced my intention to send the nominations of Abe Fortas and Homer Thornberry to the Senate.

In the end, Abe Fortas' chief assets—his progressive philosophy, his love of country, his frank views always spoken from the heart, and his service to his President—brought his downfall. His enemies claimed that they were opposing him because he had violated the principle of the separation of the branches of government by acting as a counselor to the President from time to time while serving on the Court. But that argument was a straw man, pure and simple, and every knowledgeable person in in Washington knew it. Our history is filled with examples of Supreme Court Justices who not only advised Presidents but carried out political chores for them, and those examples go back to Chief Justice John Jay of George Washington's administration.

The truth is that Abe Fortas was too progressive for the Republicans and the Southern conservatives in the Senate, all of whom were horrified at the thought of a continuation of the philosophy of the Warren court. The opposition was strengthened by the fact that the Republicans and the Southerners were convinced that Richard Nixon, if elected, would choose a conservative Chief Justice.

I had my first inkling of trouble after I called Senator James Eastland, Chairman of the Senate Judiciary Committee, in his hometown of Dodds-ville, Mississippi, and asked him to come and see me when he returned to Washington. On June 26 he came. The previous day I had received a memorandum from my Senate liaison man, Mike Manatos, describing "a most discouraging conference" he had just concluded with Senator Eastland. Eastland had told him that Senator Dirksen was opposed to the Fortas nomination, "contrary to the impression he may be giving." Eastland also told Manatos about a conversation he had had with another Southern Senator. That Senator had urged Eastland not to block the Fortas nomination in the Judiciary Committee, because he was looking forward to having "that SOB formally submitted to the Senate" so that he could fight his nomination. Finally, Eastland indicated that there would be a filibuster against Fortas should his nomination come before the Senate, and he concluded that any prolonged debate over the appointment of the Chief Justice of the United States would "tear this country apart."

As soon as Eastland arrived in my office on June 26, I recounted my conversation with Senator Russell, hoping that the judgment of that respected Southerner would moderate Eastland's position. My reference to Senator Russell's statement did not faze him in the slightest. He replied that he had strenuous objections to Fortas and was irritated over a speech the Associate Justice had made in New York earlier in the year. In that speech Fortas had said that the battles of the black man for equality in America were essentially the same as those of the Jew, and that Jews must help in the civil rights struggle. Senator Eastland interpreted that statement as a conspiratorial call for Jews and Negroes to take over America. He said that he was aware of Senator Russell's position but that he did not think that in the end, when all the debate was over, Senator Russell would support Fortas. His prediction proved accurate.

On August 9, while I was vacationing at the LBJ Ranch, Eastland called me from San Antonio. He said that he had several constituents with him and that they would like to stop by the Ranch to pay their respects. I was surprised, but I invited them to come ahead. Later in the day we took a drive around the Ranch and I made one more attempt to bring the Senator to my point of view. He would not give one inch. He told me flatly that Abe Fortas would not be confirmed as Chief Justice and that therefore there would be no vacancy for Judge Thornberry.

I strongly believed that Eastland had received assurances that if he blocked the Fortas nomination and the Republicans captured the White House in November, a Chief Justice more to his liking would be appointed. I had learned over the years that Jim Eastland was one of the best sources of intelligence in the Senate on what the Republicans were doing. He worked closely with them. He bent over backward to support legislation they wanted, and he was often a partner in their maneuvers.

I realized after that August meeting that we probably could not muster the votes to put the Fortas nomination through. Two months later, after the Senate refused by a vote of 45 to 43 to consider his nomination, Justice Fortas bowed to the inevitable and asked that his name be withdrawn. I complied with his request with a heavy heart.

The Fortas incident left me with a sense of deep foreboding. I feared the Congress' action would eventually lead to a conservative Court, a reversal of the philosophy of the Warren court, and a dissipation of the forward legislative momentum we had achieved during the previous eight years. In the end, the result of the 1968 Presidential election foreshadowed such a swing to the right, and it came as the final blow to an unhappy, frustrating year.

I never shared the intense dislike of Richard Nixon felt by many of my fellow Democrats. I had served with him in the House of Representatives and in the Senate, and I was Senate Majority Leader during most of his term as President of the Senate. I considered him a much-maligned and misunderstood man. I looked upon Nixon as a tough, unyielding partisan and a shrewd politician, but always a man trying to do the best for his country as he saw it. I did, however, disagree strongly with his political philosophy. I believed that if he were elected, he would certainly try to undo many of the hard-won achievements of the New Frontier and the Great Society.

It is always difficult to interpret the outcome of an election, but I have several observations to make about the election in 1968. First, I believe that Saigon's misinterpretation of our Vietnam policy, a misinterpretation exploited by some people who claimed to speak for the Nixon camp, damaged Vice President Humphrey's election chances. Politically, I was not overly partisan in the campaign, because I had promised the nation in my speech on March 31 that I would keep the Presidency out of politics, and because that obviously was what the Humphrey organization preferred.

Part of Saigon's foot-dragging about attending the Paris talks,* I believed, stemmed from the Vice President's foreign policy speech in Salt Lake City on September 30, a speech that was widely interpreted as a refutation of the administration's Vietnam policy, particularly with respect to bombing. That interpretation was not discouraged by several Humphrey aides who briefed the press after the speech. The facts are that the Vice President called me from Salt Lake City before he made the speech to tell me about it and to say that it was not intended to be a major departure from our current policies. I believe he meant it.

But what I believed was less important than what the leaders of the government in Saigon construed from the Vice President's statements. They interpreted the speech, and the tone of Vice President Humphrey's subsequent foreign policy statements, as a major departure from our stated policies. We soon learned that the leaders in Saigon suspected the administration of sending up a trial balloon. This suspicion made them extremely nervous and distrustful of the Johnson-Humphrey administration and of the entire Democratic party.

Against this background, people who claimed to speak for the Nixon camp began encouraging Saigon to stay away from Paris and promising that Nixon, if elected, would inaugurate a policy more to Saigon's liking. Those efforts paid off. On November 1, after previously indicating that they would go to the Paris peace talks, the South Vietnamese leaders decided not to participate. That, I am convinced, cost Hubert Humphrey the Presidency, especially since a shift of only a few hundred thousand votes would have made him the winner. I am certain that the outcome

* See Chapter 21, pp. 521–29.

would have been different if the Paris peace talks had been in progress on Election Day.

But that circumstance explains only one aspect of the 1968 election. Another essential aspect of the election was the fact that the Democratic party had pressed too far out in front of the American people. Poll after poll indicated that the average voter thought we had pushed too far and too fast in social reform. There is considerable truth to the statement that in politics, as in physics, for every action there is a reaction. We had had plenty of action during the five years of my Presidency—in the areas of civil rights, health, education, housing, conservation, poverty, hunger, job training, and consumer protection, to name only a few. The nation's reaction to these programs helped to decide the 1968 election.

The blue collar worker felt that the Democratic party had traded his welfare for the welfare of the black man. The middle class suburbanite felt that we were gouging him in order to pay for the antipoverty programs. The black man, having tasted the fruits of equality, began demanding his rightful share of the American promise faster than most of the nation was willing to let him have it.

The disruptive methods of the radicals of the "new left," at the Chicago convention and on university campuses, offended the majority of American citizens and pushed them to the right. The violence in Chicago was one of the greatest political assets Nixon had. The extremists made it impossible for us to carry states like Oklahoma, Kentucky, and Tennessee, which should have been solid Humphrey states.

The average American was concerned about the rising crime rate and failed to understand that under our Constitution the preservation of law and order is basically the responsibility of local government. Somehow, in the minds of most Americans the breakdown of local authority became the fault of the federal government. The votes of all these disenchanted Americans were decisive in the 1968 election.

I would not have abandoned a single major program that we instituted. I would not have postponed a single law that we recommended and passed. We were making up for many years of inaction and lost time. In some cases delay could have meant catastrophe. But I also realize, as I realized at the time, that we were pushing the nation forward at a pace that it was unlikely to sustain. By 1968 it was clear that many people in the nation were tired of being pushed. They wanted time to catch their breath. As the election approached, I felt that I had used up most of my capital as President, and most of the capital of the Democratic party as well.

In spite of this, I am convinced that if I had run again I would have been reelected. The last polls taken in February and March, before I announced I would not run, indicated I could have defeated Richard Nixon, with or without George Wallace in the running. That does not alter the point, but it reflects the fact that the American people do not casually turn an incumbent President out of office.* Hubert Humphrey did not have the prestige and power of the Presidency of the United States going for him, and he had the mounting dissatisfaction toward me and our administration going against him. He became a victim of those hard political facts. This does not mean that when I decided not to seek reelection I was turning over a hopeless cause to my Democratic successor. I was convinced that if we could make a substantial move toward peace in Vietnam, the Democratic nominee could overcome all other obstacles. Achieving such a breakthrough was one of my objectives in stepping out of politics, but for reasons far more profound and far broader in scope than the fate of the Democratic party in an election year.

Sadly, the North Vietnamese decided that 1968 was not to be a year of peace, and given the prevailing mood of frustration and conservatism in the nation, that decision spelled defeat for Hubert Humphrey. Such was the disappointing climax to an unhappy year.

But there were also many positive forces at work throughout 1968. Few of these made banner headlines, and many were not even apparent at the time. But there were forces operating and achievements chalked up that ultimately gave me more satisfaction than I had ever expected or believed possible.

At my last Cabinet meeting on January 17, 1969, some of the Cabinet officers reminisced about the sum total of our more than five years in office. I was particularly moved by an assessment made by UN Ambassador Russ Wiggins: †

> . . . it is seldom that within the electoral span of a single administration do we plant and harvest. Usually the results are deferred until after the administration has been succeeded by others. We are really orchardists and not grain growers. Crop maturity is long deferred. I feel confident, Mr. President, that when the fruits of your policies are gathered in, Americans are going to say, "How great the harvest has been."

Before those remarks had time to sink in fully, Secretary of the Treasury Joe Barr ‡ reminded us that we were turning over to the Nixon administration a balanced budget, a surplus in our balance of payments, and a strong, growing economy. He said:

> . . . I suppose I leave as one of the rare Secretaries of the Treasury who could say the cash register is full. Excuse the expression, sir, but you don't

---

* Whether they would have united behind me once they had returned me to office is another question—one that I had serious reservations about.

† Wiggins became UN Ambassador on October 4, 1968.

‡ Barr replaced Henry Fowler as Secretary of the Treasury on December 23, 1968.

have any options if you don't have any money. You are giving to the next President and to the next administration the options they need.

Yes, I thought, in spite of the unresolved problems the new administration is inheriting from us—including the Middle East, the war in Vietnam, and inflation—we are turning over a much cleaner agenda to the Republicans than the agenda the Republicans presented us in 1961. When John F. Kennedy was inaugurated, we were in a recession. Nearly 5 million workers were unemployed. Our annual growth rate was a dismal 2.5 per cent. Nearly one-fifth of our population was living in poverty, and we didn't even know it. Russia was scoring one spectacular space achievement after another, while we were falling further and further behind. Our balance-of-payments problem was so acute—a $3.9 billion deficit—that President Eisenhower had already taken steps to bring the dependents of American servicemen home from Europe. Southeast Asia was in a state of turmoil and instability. The threat of armed subversion and aggression—masterminded, financed, and equipped by the Communist world—hung over nations of that area like the Sword of Damocles. Our relations with the Soviet Union were about as unpromising as they had ever been, following the U-2 incident and the collapse of the four-power summit conference in Paris in May 1960.

Now in 1968, only eight years later, another administration was preparing to take office, this time with a far larger number of options and opportunities open. Somewhere during the agonizing year of 1968 we had turned a corner.

In spite of a severe gold crisis, we had managed to save and then strengthen the entire international monetary system. In spite of being a "lame duck" administration and suffering a painful defeat on the Fortas nomination, we had enacted more than fifty major items of legislation, a record that honored the Ninetieth Congress. That legislation included:

the 10 per cent tax surcharge;

the Open Housing Act, the third landmark civil rights measure of my administration;

the most far-reaching plan to meet our nation's housing needs ever voted by Congress;

eleven conservation bills, including the capstone bill of the 1960s, Redwood National Park;

six consumer bills, including a truth-in-lending measure that had been bottled up in Congress for nearly a decade;

the strongest federal gun control bill ever enacted.

In spite of setbacks, especially the fatal Apollo fire in 1967, our space program had put the first three human beings into orbit around the moon in December 1968. This feat virtually assured us of meeting our goal of putting an American on the moon and returning him to earth by the end of the decade.

In spite of the international tension related to the war in Vietnam, we reached agreement with the Soviet Union on the nuclear nonproliferation treaty. This accomplishment represented a major breakthrough in the Cold War and set the stage for the strategic arms limitation talks.

In spite of domestic passions and North Korean intransigence, we managed to secure the release of the eighty-two crewmen of the USS *Pueblo* in December 1968.

In spite of the alarming balance-of-payments picture of the previous January, the final quarter of 1968 gave us the first surplus in eleven years.

In spite of foot-dragging in both Hanoi and Saigon, we had resumed the Paris peace talks in January with both the South Vietnamese government and the National Liberation Front taking part.

In spite of the continuing pressures of inflation, we had ended our administration with a balanced budget, with a near-record 75.4 million Americans at work, with unemployment down to 3.3 per cent, with the Dow Jones averages reaching toward the 1000 mark, and with ninety-five months of uninterrupted prosperity behind us.

In spite of the unsettling effects of the Communists' 1968 Tet offensive in Vietnam, the administration ended with an accelerated pacification drive under way. The percentage of Vietnamese living under government administration had risen to nearly 80 per cent, while those under control of the Viet Cong had fallen to about 11 per cent. The remainder were in so-called "contested" areas.* I had no doubt that the military and political defeat of the Communists in the Tet offensive would stand as a major favorable turning point in the war.

So 1968 had really been a year of peaks as well as valleys. Looking back on it during that final Cabinet meeting, I thought with enormous relief that the year had turned out far better than I would have predicted. And one of the most notable achievements of all, to me, was the smoothness with which the transition between administrations of different political parties had been accomplished. In an article in *Newsweek* magazine, just days before President Nixon was inaugurated, columnist Kenneth Crawford expressed it this way:

> Never in living memory has national power passed from one party to the other as amicably and smoothly as it is passing this time from Democrats to Republicans. President-elect Nixon's appointees and agents are finding President Johnson's subordinates graciously helpful; President

* In February 1968, the percentages were estimated as follows: 60 per cent under government administration; 18 per cent under the Viet Cong; 22 per cent in contested areas.

Johnson's associates are finding the Nixonites tactfully appreciative of their help.

The transfer was not easy to accomplish. Transition is never really easy when another political party is about to take over the reins of government. There were occasions when I had to work hard to control my temper, and my tongue, because of some news report I had read or a remark that had been passed on to me deriving from the Nixon camp. I am sure that President-elect Nixon also had to restrain himself on more than one occasion. But there was far too much at stake to let partisan divisions and personal irritations drive a wedge between the outgoing and incoming administrations.

To anyone who had witnessed, as I had, the intense emotional friction that marked the transition from President Hoover to President Roosevelt, the deep personal hurt and resentment that marred the Truman-Eisenhower transition, and the civilized but chilly relations between Eisenhower and Kennedy in 1960, it was obvious that historical precedent left much room for improvement. I believed that the dignity of the Office of the Presidency demanded cooperation and respect between the incumbent and his successor. Even more, I was convinced that at this crucial juncture in our history we could not afford either an abrupt change of administrations or a change filled with rancor and partisan sniping.

In foreign policy a single miscalculation by a President can, in the extreme, bring about the destruction of civilization. The more information and background a new President has, the less likely he is to make such a miscalculation. I was determined that President-elect Nixon, Vice President-elect Agnew, and the entire Nixon Cabinet would be the best briefed and best informed incoming administration in American history. The election was over. It was not the control of the government that was at stake now; it was the future of the country. And for my children's sake, and their children's sake, and the sake of all children, I wanted Mr. Nixon to succeed.

There were deep divisions in the country, perhaps deeper than any we had experienced since the Civil War. They were divisions that could destroy us if they were not attended to and ultimately healed. But they were also divisions I felt powerless to correct. My inability to do so was one of the considerations behind my March 31 decision to withdraw from politics. Having withdrawn, I was determined that my successor would have all the capital I could give him to spend in his efforts to "bring us together again," and Mr. Nixon needed all the help he could get. He was a minority President, faced with a Democratic Congress and elected by only 43.4 per cent of the vote. But if he was a minority President, he was not a President of the minorities. Less than 10 per cent of the black voters and a small percentage of the Spanish-speaking voters cast their ballots for him. Nor was he the President of the so-called doves. This meant that the most vocal and volatile segments of our society were the most alienated from the new President.

Frankly, I thought it was a miracle of our democratic process that there were no major flareups in our ghettos and no major demonstrations on our campuses when Mr. Nixon won the Presidency. The nation accepted the election results tranquilly, and I was not going to do anything to upset that tranquillity. I was determined to do everything in my power to prolong it.

The machinery for accomplishing a smooth transition was set up immediately after my March 31 speech, when I offered to brief all the major candidates on the most sensitive issues facing the government and to keep them briefed throughout the campaign. This meant that the President-elect, whoever he was, would be familiar with all major aspects of government operations and problems as soon as the election returns were in. The briefings reduced the chances of a candidate making statements in the heat of the campaign that would damage our foreign policy efforts, because he was either uninformed or misinformed.

I met with Bobby Kennedy on April 3, with Governor Rockefeller on June 10, with Senator McCarthy on June 11, with Governor Wallace on July 26, and with Mr. Nixon later the same day. I met with Richard Nixon and Spiro Agnew again on August 10 at the LBJ Ranch, immediately after their nomination. Hubert Humphrey was kept fully informed as a matter of course, because of his position as Vice President. These meetings represented much more than superficial briefings. Often Dean Rusk, Clark Clifford, CIA Director Dick Helms, General Wheeler, and Walt Rostow were present to provide in-depth reports on major trouble spots. After a meeting, I frequently conferred alone with the candidate, so that he could feel free to say anything he wanted and to ask the most probing questions that came to his mind. We held nothing back. I was trying desperately to encourage movement toward peace in Vietnam, and I did not want a hasty remark made during the campaign to derail the critical negotiations we were working on. I also made good use of the telephone, especially after the conventions. My logs show that between the end of the Republican convention in August and Election Day in November, I called Mr. Nixon seven times to inform him of fast-breaking developments.

In October I made two conference calls to Vice President Humphrey, Mr. Nixon, and Governor Wallace concerning our negotiations with Hanoi over a complete bombing halt. The first call, on October 16, was made to clarify rumors making headlines across the country that we had reached a breakthrough in our negotiations. The second call, on October 31, was to inform the candidates that we had reached an understanding with Hanoi and that the consensus within the administration was that we should halt the bombing completely to test Hanoi's good faith. In both cases, it was vital that all political parties present a united front in public, and in both cases they concurred. "I hope that you all can give us support," I said, "because I think there's nothing more important to your country than to have an undivided group here at this time, and [to] let one man speak with a single voice to the Communist world and to the rest of the world." Nixon, Humphrey, and Wallace each pledged his support.

As Election Day approached, I felt that we should begin to formalize the transition effort. We would soon need more than briefings; we would need an organization to grapple with the problems of transition. I had already appointed Charles Murphy to handle the transition for me. A former Under Secretary of Agriculture and former Chairman of the Civil Aeronautics Board, Murphy had been through two previous transitions, once in 1953 as a member of President Truman's staff, and again in 1961 as a representative handling some of John Kennedy's transition matters. I concluded that if I did not make an attempt to set up the transition machinery myself, that step would not be taken. It was up to me to make the initial move, but once I invited the candidates to name transition representatives, they complied, and valuable preelection foundations were laid.

Richard Nixon responded to my initiative with seeming gratitude and with some initiatives of his own. On September 13, for example, Billy Graham flew to Washington to meet with me. When he arrived, he told me that what he had to say was of a private nature, so the two of us went into my office. He then told me that he had met with Mr. Nixon just a week before in Pittsburgh and that the Republican candidate had asked him to convey a confidential message to me. The message, in essence, was that while Nixon would naturally be pointing out some of the weaknesses and failures of my administration during the campaign, he would never reflect on me personally. Nixon had also told Graham that if he were elected, he would try to establish a close working relationship with me and keep me fully informed on the crucial affairs of state.

I asked Billy Graham to thank Nixon for his thoughtfulness. "Tell him," I said, "that I intend to loyally support Mr. Humphrey, but if Mr. Nixon becomes President-elect I will do all in my power to cooperate with him." This attitude of cooperation was summed up in a memorandum sent to me by Charlie Murphy on October 10, following a meeting he had had with Mr. Nixon's representative, Franklin B. Lincoln, Jr. "On the whole," Murphy concluded, "I think he [Lincoln] has a definite impression that, while we're not going to help Nixon get elected, if he should be elected, we will do our best to help him get off to a good start."

After the election, there was no reason for restraint on anyone's part and many reasons for establishing a close working relationship. On

November 11, six days after his victory, President-elect and Mrs. Nixon came to the White House for lunch and nearly four hours of conferences and briefings. We listened to briefings from high-ranking members of the administration, and after Mr. Nixon questioned them the two of us went into a private session. We covered Vietnam, the Paris peace talks (I invited the President-elect to send an observer if he wished to do so), the bombing halt, the attitude of the Saigon government, the nuclear non-proliferation treaty, the explosive situation in the Middle East, Czechoslovakia, and NATO. I expressed my willingness to arrange briefings for Mr. Nixon's Cabinet officers as soon as he selected them.

Mrs. Johnson and I took the Nixons on a tour of the second-floor living quarters of the Executive Mansion. I was surprised to learn that it was the first time either of them had seen that part of the White House, in spite of the eight years they had spent in the Eisenhower administration. Following the briefings, we went out to meet the White House press corps, and the President-elect made an extremely gracious and unexpected gesture. He announced:

> . . . if progress is to be made on matters like Vietnam, the current possible crisis in the Mideast, the relations between the United States and the Soviet Union with regard to certain outstanding matters—if progress is to be made in any of these fields, it can be made only if the parties on the other side realize that the current administration is setting forth policies that will be carried forward by the next administration. . . . I gave assurance in each instance to the Secretary of State and, of course, to the President, that they could speak not just for this administration but for the nation, and that meant for the next administration as well.

Later in the week Mr. Nixon apparently had second thoughts about giving me such sweeping support, and he announced that he had made this pledge with the understanding that there would be "prior consultation and prior agreement" between the two of us before I took any major step in foreign policy. I was surprised by that statement. There had been no promise ever requested or given that there would be "prior consultation and prior agreement."

I certainly did not want to destroy all the goodwill we had built up over the past several months by launching into a public debate with Mr. Nixon. But I could not allow the impression to stand that Mr. Nixon had become a kind of co-President. Only one man can make Presidential decisions. The confusion would have been disastrous to public confidence and to our image abroad if people did not know who was making the decisions or if they felt that the President was sharing his responsibility for running the country. As a result, I announced to the press that "the decisions that will be made between now and January 20 will be made by this President and by this Secretary of State and by this Secretary of

Defense." That cleared up the misunderstanding and the President-elect and I remained on cordial terms.

Although I was determined to hold the reins of government firmly while I was still in office, I was just as determined not to take any last-minute action that would tie the hands of the new administration or lock it into a program, unless that action were absolutely necessary. When an administration is leaving office, there is a strong temptation to push through controversial programs that it might not have had the political courage to espouse earlier. I wanted to avoid such action.

On October 23, before the election, I instructed my Budget Director, Charles Zwick, to write all department and agency heads directing them "to be considerate of possible needs of the incoming administration in January, leaving to them decisions on moves, purchases, or other actions that can be delayed, so that such action can be tailored as closely as possible to the new administration's policies and programs." And on December 4 I made the following opening statement at my Cabinet meeting:

> We are now approaching the last month of this administration. We have had five years to initiate and implement new programs and to change existing policy. Every member of the Cabinet may be justly proud of our record.
>
> Of course, the government must go on without interruption until January 20. Each department head will have daily problems to solve, and some program decisions cannot be properly deferred.
>
> However, it is neither desirable nor equitable to bind the hands of the next administration in major program areas unless there is overriding necessity to do so. We should not needlessly foreclose the options of the new administration to initiate their own program changes. It would be particularly unfair to take actions now which must be implemented over a long period of time.
>
> For this reason, I ask each Cabinet officer to review with great care the remaining matters in his department. This is not the appropriate time for fundamental changes in existing programs. It is not the time to revolutionize the government structure with major reorganizations. It is not the time to adopt new policies which would be thus forced on the new administration.
>
> We have had five wonderful and productive years. Let us all take care that in this last month we do not diminish our contribution by rash, eleventh-hour actions carrying consequences which have not been carefully considered at all levels of government, by all affected departments and by the President.
>
> I welcome the opportunity to discuss specific items which might fall in this category with any members of the Cabinet.

But now and then, even when chiefs succeed in establishing a truce, their braves manage to stir things up. This happened more than once, in spite of my efforts to keep Mr. Nixon's options open. My Cabinet officers were idealistic, energetic, and strong-minded people, and on several occasions they tried to lead a raiding party out of the reservation. Secretary of Labor Bill Wirtz nearly submitted his resignation over one incident. Wirtz wanted to reorganize the U.S. Employment Service. There was no doubt that he had the authority to carry out the reorganization under his own signature, and that is what he did. I had previously instructed him through members of my staff not to sign the order for two reasons: because I did not want to force the Nixon administration into a reorganization that might be distasteful to it and because I had promised the nation's Governors that I would not take action of this type without first consulting them, and the Governors were now, with some justification, irate.

I told Secretary Wirtz to rescind the order. He refused and said I could have his resignation instead. I told him that I did not want his resignation, I just wanted the order rescinded, but that if he would not do so I would accept his resignation. This flurry had nothing to do with the merits of the reorganization plan. It was simply in keeping with my order not to lock the new administration into last-minute programs. Finally, after several mutual friends (including our persuasive mutual friend and colleague Secretary of Defense Clifford) talked with Wirtz, he agreed to withdraw the reorganization order—not, I think, so much for my sake as to avoid a public fight that might endanger Vice President Humphrey's election chances.

For the most part, the transition progressed as smoothly on the Cabinet level as on the Presidential level. Even before the election the Bureau of the Budget began preparing issue papers on programs and problems that would have to be faced immediately by the new administration. These papers covered such subjects as the space program in relation to other national priorities, a Post Office Department reorganization, alternatives for raising the income of the poor and for financing higher education, the alarming rise in medical costs, the balance-of-payments situation, the problems of hunger and nutrition, and water pollution control.

On September 9 Charlie Murphy instructed each department and agency head to designate a senior official to begin developing transition plans and a complete briefing book for incoming Presidential appointees. These briefing books covered everything from the organization of each department and the laws governing the departments to pending legislation and major problems the new administration could expect to inherit. I personally met with each future Cabinet member before leaving office, and most of the incoming and outgoing Cabinet officers were well acquainted by the end of the year.

So smoothly had the personal relations gone that on the evening of December 12 an unprecedented event took place. While the Nixon family met with the Johnson family in the Executive Mansion, my Cabinet held a reception for the Nixon Cabinet at the State Department, and my personal staff held a reception for the Nixon staff in the White House mess.

The White House staff reception, I was told, began rather stiffly and formally, since few of the men knew each other and even fewer had much in common politically. Some of those attending the party were eying each other suspiciously, while others made half-hearted attempts at conversation. Finally, Charlie Murphy, sensing the situation, got up and delivered a humorous little speech. "We want to welcome you here tonight," he said, "and we hope you will feel welcome. You will find that the typical Lyndon Johnson staff member is a peculiar breed of cat. He is very loyal to his boss. And when Lyndon Johnson tells him to do something, he does it, without question. Well, tonight President Johnson has told us to be nice to the Nixon people, and you might just as well make up your minds that we're going to be nice to you." Everyone laughed and the tension evaporated.

The final courtesy we extended to the President-elect and his appointees was to provide the logistic support they needed to function as a team. We immediately made available to Mr. Nixon a Presidential jet for his use. We gave his staff members a suite of rooms in the new Executive Office Building across Pennsylvania Avenue from the White House. We gave them the use of White House cars and the White House switchboard, the most efficient and effective telephone operation in the world.

The telephones provided at least one example of comic relief during the transition period. Late one December evening Bob Hardesty, one of my assistants, picked up his phone and asked: "Operator, would you please ring the National Committee?"

"Certainly, sir," the operator replied. It was a request that she must have heard a thousand times before. Then there was a pause and she finally asked with some hesitation: "Uh, Democratic?"

Hardesty was too surprised to say anything at first, but then, as he saw the humor of it, he began to laugh. The operator laughed too. They both realized that the changing of the guard had already begun.

When the change was completed three or four weeks later, I recalled with satisfaction Charlie Murphy's words, ". . . while we're not going to help Nixon get elected, if he should be elected, we will do our best to help him get off to a good start." Looking back, I knew we had done our best, our level best. We had briefed every important member of the incoming administration on every important issue that faced the nation. We had put aside partisanship and offered the hand of cooperation. We had left the administration a balanced budget and a balance-of-payments surplus. We had preserved President Nixon's options and in the process had given up some of our own favorite programs.

On the last night of my term of office, January 19, Lady Bird and I held a small, informal party in the second-floor living quarters of the White House for the members of my staff. In many ways it was a moving and emotional occasion, for we had developed a closeness in our time together. When it was over and the last guest had gone, I walked over to the West Wing to do some final work at my desk. I wandered lonely through the empty offices, silent now after so many months of activity, to make sure that everything was in order for the Nixon takeover the next day. When I walked into one office I noticed a sheet of paper on the desk. Thinking that it was a piece of scrap paper, I started to throw it in the wastebasket until I read what was written on it. The message was for the next man who would sit at that desk. It was signed by the aide who had vacated the office, and it read: "Good luck."

23

Home to the Hill Country

I HEARD A TAP ON THE DOOR and Paul Glynn's voice calling: "It's seven o'clock, Mr. President." I told him to come in. Ken Gaddis was with him. They were both Air Force sergeants who had served as aides to the President during my tenure in office and they usually rotated their days on duty. I was surprised to see them together, but then I realized that they had probably decided to make this gesture to mark the special significance of the day.

The day was January 20, 1969—the last morning I would wake up in this room, the last day I would live in this house. It was the day the mantle of the American Presidency would be shifted, in one of the greatest pageants of our democracy, from my shoulders to those of Richard Nixon.

I looked through the reports that had been assembled through the night for my attention. Even in those final hours there could be no departure from the routine. Presidents come and go, but the Presidency goes on without interruption. Lady Bird came in and we had breakfast together, sitting by the window that looks out over the broad south lawn, across the ellipse, to the Jefferson Memorial. The morning was gray and overcast.

Lady Bird told me she had been up for an hour, going through the rooms, taking her last look at the mansion that had been our home through five crowded, turbulent, eventful years. She had made her good-bys. I had been making many of my own over the past few weeks— to the White House secretaries and guards, to the men of the Secret Service, to all those groups who are a continuing part of the White House operation and who help to keep the institution of the Presidency running smoothly. But I was not ready to cast my last look quite yet. I had four and a half hours left in office and there was still work to do.

I picked up the phone and asked the operator to find out whether any of my secretaries were in. I knew that on inauguration morning some of the offices in the Executive Wing of the White House would be idle and silent for the first time in my administration, their papers removed and their desks cleared, waiting for the new occupants to move in; but I also knew that others, even at 7:30 A.M., would be occupied with last-minute business. The room where my secretaries worked, outside the Oval Office, was one of those. The ladies were all at their desks. I spoke to Mary Rather, who had come to work for me almost thirty years before, when I was a Congressman, and who now was returning to Texas with me. I quickly dictated two letters to her. I told her to ask Jim Jones to bring them over to the Executive Mansion later with other documents that required my signature.

Then I asked DeVier Pierson, one of my staff aides, to come to my bedroom so that I could settle another troublesome matter. Interior Secretary Stewart Udall had recommended to me that in the final weeks of the administration I enlarge the national park system by Executive order—under authority of the Antiquities Act—adding 7 million acres. This was a sweeping proposal and it posed a painful dilemma. As deeply devoted as I was to the cause of conservation, I was concerned about taking Executive action that would set aside so much land, as much as all the Presidents before me had set aside together. If I made this decision, it would be in violation of my own order against binding the new administration through eleventh-hour actions. Even more important, such an action would seriously infringe on Congressional authority. I had reserved making the decision until I could review every word of the recommendation that Secretary Udall had sent me. Now I had to act. DeVier had brought with him several drafts of Presidential proclamations prepared by Secretary Udall. There were eight in all. We spread them out on the bed and I looked through them one last time.

"These are just too big," I said to DeVier. "A President shouldn't take this much land without the approval of Congress." The consultations I had carried on with congressional leaders over the past few days had demonstrated that the Congress was almost totally against such Executive action but that it would give consideration to recommendations made to appropriate committees at the appropriate time.

I selected four proclamations, totaling 300,000 acres. They established a new national monument, Marble Canyon in Arizona, and enlarged three existing ones. "We'll settle on these," I told Pierson. There was precedent for a President laying aside that much land in the public interest. I signed each proclamation and asked Pierson to prepare a press release describing the action I had taken. I wanted to include a statement from me outlining my thoughts and conclusions: that the areas being set aside were of major historic and scientific interest; that I had carefully reviewed the additional proposals presented to me; that I believed such broad Executive action would strain the Antiquities Act far beyond its intent and would be poor public policy; and that I had consequently directed the Secretary of the Interior to submit these proposals to the appropriate congressional committees.

"You'd better get that back here as soon as possible," I told Pierson.

The hands of the clock seemed to be moving faster now. There were nearly a dozen vacancies on various national boards, commissions, and councils that I intended to fill. Also in these last hours of my Presidency I wanted to award the Medal of Freedom to a number of citizens who had distinguished themselves in various fields of our national life. Harry Middleton, one of my staff aides, was in his office clearing out his desk. I called him and instructed him to prepare the citations. It was now a few minutes past nine o'clock.

Paul Glynn and Ken Gaddis selected my clothes—oxford gray club coat, striped trousers, four-in-hand tie, as suggested by the incoming President. While I was dressing, Jim Jones brought a folder of papers for me to sign. Included were some of the Medal of Freedom citations and the two letters I had dictated to Mary Rather earlier. I looked over all the papers and gave the letters back to Jim. "Hold these two letters until later," I said. "But make sure you bring them to my attention before we leave for the Capitol." I signed the citations while the White House barber was giving me a quick trim.

Leonard Marks, my representative for inaugural arrangements, was waiting for me in the hall outside the bedroom. At 10:15 he told me that Hubert and Muriel Humphrey were just a few minutes away. The time had come to go downstairs. Lady Bird, Luci, and Lynda joined us. At that moment DeVier Pierson arrived with the conservation documents. On the elevator, as we descended to the ground floor of the Executive Mansion, I signed the statement to accompany the Executive actions enlarging the national park system to 28.5 million acres. I noted with a certain amount of satisfaction that it had totaled 24.5 million acres when I took office. We had added four million acres in just five years.

Soon after the Vice President and his wife arrived, Vice President-elect Agnew came with his family. At 10:30, precisely on schedule, the President-elect and his wife, his daughters, and his son-in-law came through the northwest gate. We met them all, and the members of Congress with them, at the north portico. Those present from the Congress were Speaker John McCormack, Senators Mike Mansfield, Everett Dirksen, and Everett Jordan, and Congressmen Carl Albert and Gerald

Ford. We escorted them into the Red Room, where a good fire was blazing and coffee was being served.

What do two Presidents say to each other as they come together in that hour of transition? I doubt that the actual words ever measure up to the historic spirit of the occasion. The meaningful conversations have all been held by the time the principals meet for the transfer of power. The briefings have been made. The questions have been asked. The demanding answers have been given, as far as possible.

The atmosphere in the Red Room of the White House on that morning of January 20, 1969, was jovial and light-hearted. At one point I told my successor about a fellow in Texas I had once stopped to talk with. "Let me tell you a story," I had said to my Texas friend. And he had answered, "OK, but how long will it take?"

"Well, Dick," I said, "I don't want to be like that fellow, but I'm curious. How long will your inaugural address take?" The President-elect said that the speech ran just over 2,000 words. He estimated that he would need between eighteen and twenty minutes to deliver it. Then Dick Nixon turned to the man who had fought against him so hard and so well. "Hubert," he said with a smile, "why don't you deliver the address for me?"

"Dick, I had planned to do that," the Vice President answered, "but you sort of interfered. Since you're more familiar with the text than I am, I guess you ought to go ahead and deliver it as scheduled."

The President-elect and I talked privately for a few minutes in a corner of the room. He told me then what his staff members and such close friends as Billy Graham had reported to me before, that he had a deep appreciation of the relationship that had existed between President Eisenhower and me during my term. He said that he intended to maintain this kind of relationship with me and to improve it in any way he could.

I took the remaining papers that Jim Jones had waiting for me. When I had signed all the official documents, I asked for the two letters he was carrying. They were to my sons-in-law, Chuck Robb and Pat Nugent, who were both fighting in Vietnam. They were personal notes indicating the pride that Lady Bird and I had in both of them. Those two letters were the last documents I signed as President of the United States.

At 11:05 we departed from the north portico of the White House. Our motorcade crept slowly out of the White House grounds and along Pennsylvania Avenue, which was lined with people. As I rode and waved, I looked out on Washington, as much of it as I could see from the limousine window. I knew that I would be coming back occasionally, but I also knew that no matter how often I returned I was really saying good-by to the city that had been my home for so many years. Washington had a particular place in my affections, but more than any other spot on earth it would remain for me the site of conflicting emotions. I had ridden its streets both in obscurity and in the spotlight of national attention. All the victories won in the course of my administration had been fought here, in those few square miles which house the seat of the most effective government men have ever devised. Yet the first major legislative defeat of my Presidency had come with my effort to get home rule for the national Capital, a city still governed like a colony.

I had proudly seen parks and playgrounds spring to life and color under Lady Bird's patient leadership and encouragement. And in dismay and sorrow I had watched the smoke of ugly rioting curl above the skyline. I had made this same trip a few days before, when I went to Capitol Hill to deliver my last State of the Union address to the Congress. That had been partly a sentimental journey, for I wanted to pay a final tribute to the men and women with whom I had worked so long. But there was more than sentiment involved on that occasion. I also wanted to remind the Congress and the nation of the solemn commitments we had made together, commitments that had to be met if we were to be faithful to our trust. At the end of my address I looked out on that familiar chamber, at all those faces I knew so well, at the men who soon would be helping a new President find the right way for our country. I told them of my great hope—that a hundred years from now it would be said that together we, the Congress and the President, had helped to make our country a place of justice for all its people and had insured the blessings of liberty for all posterity.

"That is what I hope," I said, in my final words to the assembled group of the nation's lawmakers. "But I believe that, at least, it will be said that we tried."

Now, as I rode in my final Presidential procession through Washington, I knew that although I was leaving, this city would be part of me forever. The Marine band saluted me for the last time with "Hail to the Chief" as I took my place in the inaugural stands in front of the Capitol. Then, in a matter of moments, Richard Nixon stood before us all, and before the world, to take the oath of office as the thirty-seventh President of the United States.

As I watched the ceremony, I reflected—as I have done so many times in the last several years—on how inadequate any man is for the office of the American Presidency. The magnitude of the job dwarfs every man who aspires to it. Every man who occupies the position has to strain to the utmost of his ability to fill it. I believe that every man who ever occupied it, within his inner self, was humble enough to realize that no living mortal has ever possessed all the required qualifications. It is not a question of the incumbents' wanting to do the right thing. The American people, in their wisdom, have never yet elected an evil man to lead them.

No man ever runs for the Presidency on a platform of doing wrong. Every President wants earnestly to do what is right. The enormous challenge he faces, as he looks out on his country and the world from the observation post of the White House, is knowing what is the right thing to do, for the complexities of the problems are past description.

Scholars have been defining and refining the role of the President for almost two centuries. At the core of all those definitions one basic tenet remains: The job of the President is to set priorities for the nation, and he must set them according to his own judgment and his own conscience.

The country's new President, in his hour of triumph, was reciting the same thirty-five-word oath that I had taken for the first time five years, one month, and twenty-seven days before, in an hour of indescribable grief and sadness aboard a hushed and sweltering airplane. But the majesty of the democratic system had illuminated both occasions. Between those two events, like a scroll held by two great pillars, lay the story of the Presidency of a man from Johnson City, Texas—the judgments he had made of what was right, and the priorities for the nation as he had viewed them and set them.

The long, hard effort was over now, and I was glad to see it end. I did not believe that I had ever flinched from the responsibilities or the demands of the office. I had used its powers and prerogatives as fully as I could to accomplish what I thought ought to be done. I had lived thoroughly every hour of those five years. I had known sorrow and anger, frustration and disappointment, pain and dismay. But more than anything else, I had experienced a towering pride and pleasure at having had my chance to make my contribution to solving the problems of our times. I had tried to face up to them all, without dodging any of them, and to provide solutions whenever I could. When we made mistakes, I believe we erred because we tried to do too much too soon, and never because we walked away from challenge. If the Presidency can be said to have been employed and to have been enjoyed, I had employed it to the utmost, and I had enjoyed it to the limit. Now I was putting aside the burden that no President can adequately explain or describe and that no citizen can fully understand.

I heard Richard Nixon conclude his oath of office with the words "so help me God." To me, they were welcome words. I remember two thoughts running through my mind: first, that I would not have to face the decision any more of taking any step, in the Middle East or elsewhere, that might lead to world conflagration—the nightmare of my having to be the man who pressed the button to start World War III was passing; and second, that I had fervently sought peace through every available channel and at every opportunity and could have done no more.

Now my service was over, and it had ended without my having had to haul down the flag, compromise my principles, or run out on our obligations, our commitments, and our men who were upholding those obligations and commitments in Vietnam. I repeated these thoughts to Lady Bird as we walked up the steps toward a room inside the Capitol after the inauguration. I repeated them later to President Nixon. I realize that it may be difficult for people to understand how I felt. As discerning and perceptive as the American people are, I believe that very few of them have ever been able to grasp what transpired in the minds and hearts of the thirty-seven men who have served them in the Presidency. The recognition of unrelenting responsibility reminds me of the truth of a statement I heard my father repeat many times: "Son, you will never understand what it is to be a father until you *are* a father."

When the ceremonies were over, I drove with my wife and daughters to the home of Clark and Marny Clifford in Bethesda, Maryland. There were men, women, and children lining both sides of the streets leading to the Cliffords' house, holding cheerful and affectionate signs that we will always remember. The Cliffords were hosting a private luncheon in our honor—a gesture they had suggested they would like to make for us months before. They asked only our very closest associates. Not all our friends, or even all the members of our families, could be present, but we were glad to see all those who were there.

The luncheon was a carefree occasion, but there were unavoidable overtones of nostalgia. This was an assembly of old friends who had traveled roads both rough and smooth together for many years; and together we had helped to write a rather remarkable chapter in American history. These were people who had been with us in sunshine and in sorrow.

Before I left Clark's house I personally awarded five Medal of Freedom citations I had signed earlier that day. I presented the medals to Dean Rusk, Clark Clifford, Averell Harriman, Walt Rostow, and William S. White. For me, the ceremony was one of the most gratifying moments of that eventful day.

From the Clifford residence we drove to Andrews Air Force Base, where we were to board *Air Force One*. President Nixon had graciously made it available for our return trip home. On that cold, windy afternoon a large crowd had gathered at Andrews and was waiting for us when we arrived. There were faces in the crowd that I had known for almost forty years, men and women whose lives and careers spanned Lady Bird's and mine and who were part of the excitement of Washington when we were young. There were staff members who had worked with me throughout my public life, from the early congressional days of 1931 to the last days in the White House. There were the officers of my Cabinet. There were men and women who had operated the machinery of government in all its departments and bureaus and agencies through the years of my Presidency, who had served the country and the President faithfully and well. And lining the fence at Andrews—as at airports beyond recall, along main streets that crowd my memory—were the American people, thousands of anonymous faces, who had come just to smile, to cheer, to say good-by. They carried signs that spoke of their love and gratitude, gifts of the heart which I reciprocated in fullest measure. People like these, first in my own state and then across the land, had provided the support and strength which had enabled me to serve as best I could. Many times before they had gone unmentioned and unnoticed, but their presence was never more strongly felt than on that wintry January day. Here, along the last mile of the long campaign, I reached out to them for the last time, shaking hands along the fence, to say my own good-by.

Four hours later we were in Texas. A crowd that the press estimated at ten thousand awaited us at Bergstrom Air Force Base outside Austin, the community where my public life had begun. I spoke to them briefly, voicing a hope that was much on my mind. I called upon Americans to "present a united front to the world that is indivisible."

"Let us try," I said, "to help our new leader, who after all is the only President we have. I hope that you will be as good to him as you have been to me, understanding in time of crisis, strong in supporting when we needed you, because we have the best system in all the world. But it takes all of us to make it work all the time. We left a lot of unsolved problems on Mr. Nixon's desk, not because we wanted to but because the times in which we live required us to."

After a short flight we arrived home, to the greeting of several hundred more well-wishers—led by our ranch manager, Dale Malechek, his wife, Jewell, and Father Wunibald Schneider and Reverend Norman Truesdell, our local Catholic priest and Lutheran minister. To them I voiced a simpler sentiment that was uppermost in my heart. I told them I was glad to be home. I saw folks in the crowd from towns within a radius of twenty miles —the preachers and the teachers, the farmers and the ranchers, the men and women I had known all my life—from Stonewall, Hye, Johnson City, Albert, and Fredericksburg. They all looked as if they were glad to see us, and God knows we were glad to see them.

The weather was mild and warm at the Ranch. After we changed into comfortable clothes, Lady Bird and I walked around the yard together. In the carport behind the house the luggage was piled in a giant mound. For the first time in five years there were no aides to carry the bags inside. Lady Bird looked at the scene and began to laugh. "The coach has turned back into a pumpkin," she said, "and the mice have all run away."

That warm night, before retiring, I went outside and stood in the yard again, looking up at the moon in the broad, clear Texas sky. My thoughts went back to that October night in 1957 when we had walked along the banks of the Pedernales River and looked for the Soviet Sputnik orbiting in the sky overhead. I thought of all that had happened in the years between. I remembered once again a story I had heard about one of the astronauts from the crew of Apollo 8, which a month ago had circled the moon only a few miles above its surface. Soon after his return to earth the astronaut had stepped into his backyard at home and had looked up at the moon. He had wondered if it really could be true that he had been there. I had recounted this story a few days before to a group of friends. Perhaps, I told them, the time would come when I would look back on the majesty and the power and splendor of the Presidency and find it hard to believe that I had actually been there.

But on this night I knew I had been there. And I knew also that I had given it everything that was in me.

APPENDICES

I. Letter to President Truman

(See Chapter 3, page 48)

June 28, 1950

My Dear Mr. President:

I want to express to you my deep gratitude for and admiration of your courageous response yesterday to the challenge of this grave hour.

Most Americans, I am sure, share my feeling that your inspired act of leadership will be remembered as the finest moment of American maturity. Your action gives a new and noble meaning to freedom, gives purpose to our national resolve and determination, and affirms convincingly America's capacity for world leadership.

Having chosen this course, there is no turning back. Greater tasks and more grave hours await us on the road ahead. As a member of the Armed Services Committee, I shall attempt to make my services contribute to the success of our undertaking. However and whenever I may assist, I shall work to the limit of my capacity and opportunity. Call on me when I can be of assistance.

For the decisions you must face alone, you have my most sincere prayers and my total confidence. Under your leadership, I am sure peace will be restored and justice will assume new meaning for the oppressed and frightened peoples of the world.

With my highest esteem, I am

Sincerely,
Lyndon B. Johnson

II. White House Statement Following the Return of the McNamara-Taylor Mission, October 2, 1963

(See Chapter 3, page 62)

Secretary McNamara and General Taylor reported to the President this morning and to the National Security Council this afternoon. Their report included a number of classified findings and recommendations which will be the subject of further review and action. Their basic presentation was endorsed by all members of the Security Council and the following statement of United States policy was approved by the President on the basis of recommendations received from them and from Ambassador Lodge.

1. The security of South Viet-Nam is a major interest of the United States as other free nations. We will adhere to our policy of working with the people and Government of South Viet-Nam to deny this country to communism and to suppress the externally stimulated and supported insurgency of the Viet Cong as promptly as possible. Effective performance in this undertaking is the central objective of our policy in South Viet-Nam.

2. The military program in South Viet-Nam has made progress and is sound in principle, though improvements are being energetically sought.

3. Major U.S. assistance in support of this military effort is needed only until the insurgency has been suppressed or until the national security forces of the Government of South Viet-Nam are capable of suppressing it.

Secretary McNamara and General Taylor reported their judgment that the major part of the U.S. military task can be completed by the end of 1965, although there may be a continuing requirement for a limited number of U.S. training personnel. They reported that by the end of this year the U.S. program for training Vietnamese should have progressed to the point where 1,000 U.S. military personnel assigned to South Viet-Nam can be withdrawn.

4. The political situation in South Viet-Nam remains deeply serious. The United States has made clear its continuing opposition to any repressive actions in South Viet-Nam. While such actions have not yet significantly affected the military effort, they could do so in the future.

5. It remains the policy of the United States, in South Viet-Nam as in other parts of the world, to support the efforts of the people of that country to defeat aggression and to build a peaceful and free society.

III. Excerpts from Remarks by President Johnson before the American Bar Association, New York City, August 12, 1964

(See Chapter 3, page 68)

For ten years, through the Eisenhower Administration, the Kennedy Administration, and this Administration, we have had one consistent aim—observance of the 1954 agreements which guaranteed the independence of South Viet-Nam.

That independence has been the consistent target of aggression and terror.

For ten years, our response to these attacks has followed a consistent pattern.

First, that the South Vietnamese have the basic responsibility for the defense of their own freedom.

Second, we would engage our strength and our resources to whatever extent needed to help others repel aggression.

Now there are those who would have us depart from these tested principles. They have a variety of viewpoints. All of them, I am sure, you have heard in your local community.

Some say we should withdraw from South Viet-Nam, that we have lost almost 200 lives there in the last four years and we should come home. But the United States cannot and must not and will not turn aside and allow the freedom of a brave people to be handed over to communist tyranny.

This alternative is strategically unwise, we think, and it is morally unthinkable.

Some others are eager to enlarge the conflict. They call upon us to supply American boys to do the job that Asian boys should do. They ask us to take reckless action which might risk the lives of millions and engulf much of Asia and certainly threaten the peace of the entire world. Moreover, such action would offer no solution at all to the real problem of Viet-Nam. America can and America will meet any wider challenge from others, but our aim in Viet-Nam, as in the rest of the world, is to help restore the peace and to reestablish a decent order.

The course we have chosen will require wisdom and endurance. But let no one doubt for a moment that we have the resources and the will to follow this course as long as it may take. No one should think for a moment that we will be worn down, nor will we be driven out, and we will not be provoked into rashness; but we will continue to meet aggression with firmness and unprovoked attack with measured reply. . . .

IV. Memorandum of Remarks Made to Robert Kennedy Regarding the Vice Presidential Candidacy in 1964

(See Chapter 5, page 100)

I have asked you to come over to discuss with me a subject that is an important one to you and me.

As you might suppose, I have been giving a great deal of thought and consideration to the selection of the Democratic candidate for Vice President. This subject has been brought very much into focus by the results of the Republican convention.

I have reached a decision in this regard and I wanted you to learn of my decision directly from me. You have been a member of my Cabinet since I became President, and I felt a definite sense of obligation to discuss this subject with you and give you the reasons for my decision.

I have concluded, for a number of reasons, that it would be inadvisable for you to be the Democratic candidate for Vice President in this year's election.

I have been keeping an open mind on this subject, awaiting the outcome of the Republican choice. The nomination of Senator Goldwater is the decisive factor in reaching the conclusion that I have reached.

Goldwater's strength will be in the South, the Southwest and possibly in the Middle West; also it is my belief that the Border States will be of unusual importance in this particular election. If Goldwater runs a strong race, it is entirely possible that the outcome of the election could rest in the Middle West.

I believe strongly that the Democratic ticket must be constituted so as to have as much appeal as possible in the Middle West and the Border States; also it should be so constituted as to create as little an adverse reaction as possible upon the Southern States.

These are the considerations that have led me to the conclusion that it would be unwise for our party in this election to select you as the vice presidential nominee. I know you have given thought to this subject also and I know you will understand my reasoning processes.

I have weighed all the factors present in this situation and, upon reaching a final conclusion, I wanted you to be the first to know it and I wanted you to hear it from me.

I am sure that you will understand the basis of my decision and the factors that have entered into it, because President Kennedy had to make a similar decision in 1960.

You have a unique and promising future in the Democratic Party. Your own service to your party and to your country has been outstanding. Also, you bear a name that has become famous and is associated with the highest ideals in American public service. I want to be a factor in furthering your career and I think I can be helpful in that regard.

There are two areas in which I would like to use your great talents. I would like to use you from time to time on important governmental assignments and missions. Such assignments can keep you in close touch with governmental matters and continue and increase the value of the service you can render to this country.

On the other hand, if you are going to be in a position to give full time to government, I would like to have you consider the field, and the position in that field, in which you believe you would be the happiest. In this regard, you might want to consider the possibility of an opening occurring in the position of this country's representative to the United Nations. This is a subject I want you to consider at length and talk to me about again when you are ready to discuss it.

Needless to say that, facing an election of the kind that confronts our party, I will appreciate the help you can give me from the present time to the Democratic convention on August 24th; and, further, there will be an important function for you to perform in the campaign leading up to the election on November 3rd. When you consider the importance of the issues involved and what it means to our party and to our country, I believe you will give me that help.

I have attempted to present my views as clearly and as forthrightly as possible for I believe that constitutes a basis upon which you and I can build a lasting relationship that would prove valuable to both of us and to our country.

V. Bombing Pauses over North Vietnam

(See Chapter 11, page 241)

Date	Duration	Type
May 12–18, 1965	5 days, 20 hours	Complete
December 24, 1965– January 31, 1966	36 days, 15 hours	Complete
December 23, 1966– March 1, 1967	78 days	Within 10 NM * of center of Hanoi
December 24–26, 1966	2 days	Complete
December 31, 1966– January 2, 1967	2 days	Complete
February 8–12, 1967	5 days, 18 hours	Complete
May 22–June 9, 1967	18 days	Within 10 NM of center of Hanoi
May 23–24, 1967	24 hours	Complete
June 11–August 9, 1967	59 days	Within 10 NM of center of Hanoi
August 24– October 23, 1967	60 days	Within 10 NM of center of Hanoi
December 24–25, 1967	24 hours	Complete
December 31, 1967– January 2, 1968	36 hours	Complete
January 3–March 31, 1968	88 days	Within 5 NM of center of Hanoi
January 16–March 31, 1968	75 days	Within 5 NM of center of Haiphong
March 31– November 1, 1968	214 days	North of 20th parallel
November 1, 1968	Remainder of administration	Complete

* Nautical miles

VI. Vietnam: Major Peace Initiatives

(See Chapter 11, page 250)

Date	Initiative	Response *
1964		
June 18	The Canadian representative on the International Control Commission in Saigon, Blair Seaborn, visited Hanoi to discover a possible basis for negotiations.	Hanoi showed no interest in discussions. Seaborn found no change in Hanoi's attitude in subsequent trips in 1964 and 1965.
July 8	U Thant recommended reconvening the 1954 Geneva Conference to negotiate peace in South Vietnam.	A State Department spokesman said there was a need not for a new political settlement but for compliance with previous accords on Indochina. This response was influenced in part by belligerent statements by Hanoi and Peking during the preceding week.
August 7	The UN Security Council invited both North and South Vietnam to take part in Security Council discussion of the Vietnam problem.	Hanoi rejected the invitation and declared that any "wrongful decision" by the Security Council would be "null and void."
September	U Thant relayed to Ambassador Adlai Stevenson his belief, based on third party sources, that Hanoi was willing to talk to an American emissary.	The offer was rejected by the United States since the latest report of Blair Seaborn indicated Hanoi was not prepared for serious talks to end its aggression in South Vietnam. Hanoi later denied that it had suggested any negotiations to U Thant.
1965		
February 20	The British government proposed to the Soviet government that they undertake, as Geneva co-chairmen, to seek the views of the other participants on a possible settlement.	The Soviet Union rejected the proposal and Hanoi denounced it. The British Foreign Secretary reported to the House of Commons that the Soviet Union and the DRV "see no need for negotiations or a conference at all."
February 27	The U.S. government wrote to the Security Council declaring its readiness to withdraw military units from Vietnam if there was a prompt and assured cessation of aggression from the North.	None.
March 4–8	Pakistani President Ayub Khan visited Peking and urged Chinese leaders to accept a negotiated settlement.	He made no progress.

* Unless otherwise indicated the United States either accepted each of the initiatives by third parties or expressed its readiness to discuss the details of the proposals seriously and promptly.

Date	Initiative	Response
1965		
March 8	Secretary General U Thant proposed that the United States, the Soviet Union, Great Britain, France, Communist China, and North and South Vietnam participate in a preliminary conference on Vietnam.	The United States said it could not participate in a conference until North Vietnam indicated a willingness to stop aggression against South Vietnam. The National Liberation Front flatly rejected a negotiated settlement as long as U.S. forces remained in Vietnam.
April 1	Seventeen nonaligned nations (including India, Yugoslavia, and others) appealed for peace and called for negotiations without preconditions.	Hanoi found the proposal "inappropriate."
April 7	President Johnson said in his speech at Johns Hopkins University: "We remain ready . . . for unconditional negotiations."	Hanoi said U.S. talk of peace only "conceals its warlike acts." Peking called the offer a "swindle."
April 7	UN Secretary General U Thant proposed to visit Hanoi and other capitals to discuss prospects for peace.	Pham Van Dong, North Vietnamese Prime Minister, said UN intervention was "inappropriate"; Peking said U Thant should "spare himself the trouble."
April 24	Indian President Radhakrishnan suggested an end to the fighting and policing of the arrangement by an Afro-Asian force.	Hanoi said the proposal was "preposterous" and "at complete variance with the spirit and basic principles" of the Geneva Agreements.
April 14– May 4	Former U.K. Foreign Secretary Patrick Gordon-Walker made a fact-finding tour of Southeast Asia to explore the basis for a settlement in Vietnam.	Hanoi and Peking refused to admit him.
May 12–17	A five-day bombing pause was observed during which the United States sent messages to many countries, including North Vietnam, to explain that the purpose of the halt was to help find a way to a peaceful settlement.	Hanoi called the pause a "trick." Just after the pause ended North Vietnamese officials approached the French and discussed Hanoi's position on a peace settlement. French officials later said that these discussions could "not be regarded as a valid offer of negotiations."
June 17	British Commonwealth Prime Ministers proposed a special mission headed by Prime Minister Wilson to visit capitals of all involved in Vietnam to explore chances for a peace conference.	Hanoi announced that it would not receive the Wilson mission.

Date	*Initiative*	*Response*

1965

June 25 — President Johnson called upon members of the United Nations "to bring to the table those who seem determined to make war."

Response: The New China News Agency commented that the United States was trying to use the United Nations as "a tool," and that the Security Council "has absolutely no right to interfere in the affairs of Indochina."

July 9–13 — Harold Davies (a minister of the British government) visited Hanoi to encourage acceptance of the Commonwealth Ministers' proposal.

Response: The British government reported that Davies found the North Vietnamese convinced that their prospects of victory were too imminent to make it worthwhile to forsake the battlefield for the conference table.

July 28 — President Johnson wrote to U Thant asking the Secretary General to continue efforts to promote peace.

Response: Hanoi said that the United Nations had no role in Vietnam.

July 30 — Ambassador Goldberg wrote to the President of the UN Security Council saying that the United States would

continue to help defend South Vietnam;

continue to assist economic and social development in Southeast Asia;

continue to explore all avenues to peace;

work with the UN Security Council and its members in search of a formula for peace in Southeast Asia.

Response: Hanoi again said that the United Nations had no role in Vietnam, and the Soviet Union indicated that it would have no part in any UN effort to seek a settlement.

August 1 — Prime Minister Shastri of India and President Tito of Yugoslavia called for a conference of parties concerned with Vietnam and urged an end to the bombing of North Vietnam.

Response: North Vietnam denounced the proposal and called the two leaders "advertisers and errand boys" for U.S. "maneuvers."

August 12 — U Thant submitted a three-point proposal recommending

private and confidential dialogues as a preliminary to a more formal conference;

cessation of all military hostilities;

discussions involving those who are actually fighting (including the National Liberation Front).

Response: Hanoi ignored the proposal.

Date	Initiative	Response
1965		
August, September, November, and January 1966	A U.S. representative met with the North Vietnamese in Paris to see if there was any flexibility in interpreting Hanoi's four-point program.	Hanoi was unresponsive.
November 11– December 15	Private Italian initiative was undertaken by Giorgio LaPira to explore Hanoi's position, and further efforts were made by Amintore Fanfani, President of the UN General Assembly, to explain Hanoi's position.	Hanoi denied that any "probe about negotiations" had taken place.
December 2	The United Kingdom issued a twelve-nation appeal for an end to the fighting and negotiated peace.	Hanoi said that it "categorically rejects all British plans and proposals made under the pretense of peace."
December 13	Prince Sihanouk asked for expansion of International Control Commission activities in Cambodia, including supervision of the Cambodia-Vietnam border.	No response from the Soviet Union as co-chairman of the Geneva Agreement.
December 19	Pope Paul appealed for a truce and asked all parties to move toward negotiations.	Ho Chi Minh told the Pope that talk about unconditional negotiations was a U.S. "maneuver" to conceal aggression.
December 24– January 30	A thirty-seven day pause in the bombing of North Vietnam was observed, during which the United States sent emissaries to many capitals of the world to discuss the possibilities of negotiations.	Prime Minister Pham Van Dong in Hanoi called our peace effort a "campaign of lies."
1966		
January 3	The State Department issued a detailed fourteen-point statement of the U.S. position for negotiating peace in Vietnam.	Hanoi said that the United States must accept the four-point stand advanced by the DRV.
January 31	A U.S. resolution in the UN Security Council urged arrangement of a conference of "appropriated interested governments" to help insure application of the 1954 and 1962 Geneva agreements and offered full U.S. cooperation.	No UN action because of Hanoi's opposition.
March 8–11 and June 14–18	Canadian diplomat Chester A. Ronning visited Hanoi to discuss possibilities of peace.	Hanoi authorities were totally negative with regard to any response on their part to a halt in the bombing. Hanoi repeated its insistence on its four points.

Date	Initiative	Response
1966		
March 9	U Thant put forward a three-point plan to promote cessation of the bombing of North Vietnam; mutual reduction of hostilities; negotiations.	Hanoi welcomed the first point; found the second "obviously negative" and the third "unsatisfactory."
April	Special Japanese envoy Masaichi Yokoyama visited twenty countries to try to form a committee of nations to discuss a Vietnam settlement.	Ho Chi Minh described his activities as "aimed at giving publicity to this U.S. swindle."
April 19	President Johnson endorsed a proposal by Senator Mansfield for a "direct confrontation across the peace table."	The North Vietnamese Foreign Ministry described the proposals as "hypocritical" and designed to "sidetrack the attention of world opinion."
July 7	Prime Minister Indira Gandhi called for the reconvening of the Geneva Conference.	The North Vietnamese Ambassador in Peking said that the proposals to reconvene the Geneva Conference were "not acceptable."
August 6	Thailand, Malaysia, and the Philippines called for an Asian peace conference.	Hanoi called the idea "a cheap farce" and a "dirty peace fraud."
August 30	French President de Gaulle, in Phnom Penh, called for a U.S. pledge to withdraw its forces within a "fixed and suitable period" to promote a settlement.	Hanoi endorsed the demand for a U.S. withdrawal but ignored the suggestion of the timetable.
August 31	U Thant reiterated his three-point plan of March 9, 1966.	A North Vietnamese spokesman said that his government "rejects all intervention by the United Nations in the Vietnam affair."
September 19	Pope Paul issued an encyclical containing a plea for peace.	Hanoi said that "certain religious circles, which have always chorused the U.S. imperialists' peace song, have recently made pathetic appeals for peace in Vietnam."
September 22	Ambassador Goldberg, at the United Nations, declared that the United States was ready to offer a phased withdrawal of forces if North Vietnam would agree to withdraw simultaneously.	Pham Van Dong repeated that the United Nations had no right to intervene, and the Liberation Front called Goldberg's statement "stupid and irresponsible words."

Date	Initiative	Response
1966		
October 6	British Foreign Secretary George Brown proposed a six-point plan for peace, including a peace conference, an end to bombing of North Vietnam, and an end to the introduction of new forces and supplies by both the United States and North Vietnam.	Hanoi "sternly rebuffed" the Brown proposal and called it a "rehash" of U.S. proposals.
October 24	At a meeting in New Delhi, the United Arab Republic, Yugoslavia, and India issued a communiqué proposing cessation of bombing of North Vietnam without preconditions; implementation of the Geneva Agreements and the withdrawal of all foreign forces to enable the Vietnamese people to decide their own future free of external interference; the participation of the Liberation Front as one of the main parties to a peace settlement.	Peking accused Mrs. Gandhi and Marshal Tito of trying to "peddle the peace fraud . . . concocted by the United States and the Soviet Union" and labeled the proposal a "reproduction of U Thant's three-point 'peace proposal.' "
October 25	The Manila communiqué pledged that allied forces would withdraw from South Vietnam "as the other side withdraws its forces to the North, ceases infiltration, and the level of violence thus subsides." Withdrawal would be within six months.	Hanoi denounced the Manila proposal as "a demand for our people to lay down their arms."
November 9	Canadian Secretary of External Affairs Paul Martin began talks with Soviet leaders in Moscow on steps that could be taken toward a political settlement.	Peking described Martin's visit to the Soviet Union as part of the Soviet plot for "peace talks fraud."
November 16–20	British Foreign Secretary Brown tried to elicit a response in Moscow to the plan to stop the bombing first and then proceed to mutual deescalation.	Moscow showed interest but insisted that Hanoi's four points and the Liberation Front's five points be accepted as the basis for discussions. No Hanoi reaction.
November–December	The United States agreed to US-DRV talks in Warsaw to discuss the "ten points" drafted by Polish ICC representative Janusz Lewandowski.	On December 13 the Poles informed the United States that Hanoi was not willing to have talks, and on December 15 the Poles terminated conversations on the possibility of direct talks, allegedly at Hanoi's insistence.

Date	*Initiative*	*Response*
1966		
December 8	Pope Paul VI, referring to the coming holiday ceasefire, expressed hope that "this truce becomes an armistice and that the armistice be the occasion for sincere negotiations . . . which will lead to peace."	Peking commented that the Pope has "always served U.S. imperialism in its peace talk swindles."
December 19	In a letter to U Thant Ambassador Goldberg asked the UN Secretary General to take steps necessary to bring about discussion which would lead to a cease-fire. On December 31 Mr. Goldberg informed U Thant that the United States was ready "to order a prior end to all bombing of North Vietnam the moment there is an assurance, private or otherwise, of a reciprocal response toward peace from North Vietnam."	Hanoi's representative in Paris reportedly called Goldberg's letter "the same old song."
December 30	The British proposed a three-way meeting of South Vietnam, North Vietnam, and the United States to arrange a halt to the fighting.	Hanoi rejected the proposal.
1967		
January 7	Prime Minister Ky said that he would be willing to meet Ho Chi Minh in a third country.	The offer was rejected.
January 17	South Vietnam offered to discuss an extension of the Tet truce with representatives of North Vietnam.	Hanoi said: "Who would care to negotiate with them?"
January–February	A U.S. representative made contact with the North Vietnamese representative in Moscow. The United States offered to stop the bombing if the DRV would give assurances that this would be followed by a reciprocal reduction of hostilities.	No response until Ho Chi Minh's answer to President Johnson's letter of February 8, 1967 (see below).
January 6–14	Harry S. Ashmore and William C. Baggs, both U.S. journalists, met with Ho Chi Minh on January 12. On February 5 Baggs and Ashmore returned to Hanoi with a message similar to the official messages being exchanged in Moscow.	Ho Chi Minh insisted that there could be no talks unless the United States stopped the bombing and stopped all reinforcements during the talks. He was adamant against any reciprocal military restraint by the DRV.

Date	Initiative	Response
1967		
February 8	President Johnson's first letter to Ho Chi Minh:	Ho Chi Minh's reply called for an end to the bombing "definitively and unconditionally," demanded that the U.S. forces leave South Vietnam, and called for recognition of the Liberation Front. Talks could occur if all attacks against North Vietnam were halted.
	offered to end bombing of North Vietnam and augmentation of U.S. forces in the South if infiltration from North Vietnam ended;	
	proposed extension of the Tet truce through negotiations between North and South Vietnam;	
	suggested diplomatic talks in secret;	
	asked for any North Vietnamese suggestions.	
February 8–13	A six-day pause in the bombing of North Vietnam was observed in conjunction with the President's letter to Ho Chi Minh and the Wilson-Kosygin talks in London.	Hanoi called the pause another "trick."
February 8	Pope Paul expressed hope that the Tet truce might open the way to negotiations and addressed letters to Ho Chi Minh and President Johnson. President Johnson's reply to the Pope declared that the United States was ready to talk unconditionally and to discuss "balanced reduction in military activity."	Ho Chi Minh's reply to the Pope repeated Hanoi's insistence on an unconditional end to the bombing of the North and on its own four-point settlement.
March 14	U Thant proposed a general cease-fire, preliminary talks, and the reconvening of the Geneva Conference.	Hanoi rejected the proposal and said once again that the United Nations had no right to interfere.
April 6	President Johnson sent a second letter to Ho Chi Minh reaffirming earlier offers either to talk about a settlement first and then stop fighting or first to undertake steps of mutual deescalation which might make negotiations of a settlement easier.	The message was delivered to Moscow and opened but was returned later in the day. It was never formally acknowledged.

Date	Initiative	Response
1967		
April 10	Ceylon's Prime Minister Dudley Senanayake called for a meeting between the Saigon government, the Liberation Front, and Hanoi to discuss preconditions for a ceasefire.	Saigon expressed its willingness to meet with representatives from the other side. Hanoi and the Liberation Front did not respond.
April 11	Canadian Secretary Paul Martin called for a progressive four-stage reapplication of the 1954 Geneva ceasefire terms as a preliminary to discussions. Involved would be demilitarization of the DMZ, no increase in military activity or reinforcement, cessation of hostilities, and return to the ceasefire of the Geneva settlement. On April 19 the United States proposed a mutual ten-mile withdrawal from the DMZ.	Hanoi called the proposal a "trick" to partition Vietnam permanently and said that the United States must get out of Vietnam.
May 23–24	Buddha's birthday truce. The United States observed a full bombing pause and ceasefire and hoped for a constructive response. Hanoi and Haiphong remained off limits until June 9, 1967.	Hanoi and the Viet Cong refused to observe the ceasefire and called for a unconditional bombing halt.
June 23–25	At Glassboro Soviet Chairman Kosygin told President Johnson that Hanoi would talk to us if the bombing stopped. President Johnson replied that the bombing would be stopped if the United States knew that there would be prompt talks and if the DRV took no military advantage.	No answer was ever received from Hanoi, either directly or through Moscow.
July-October	Herbert Marcovich and Raymond Aubrac, two Frenchmen who had been in Hanoi, made contact with Henry Kissinger. Under instructions, Kissinger advanced in August 1967 the proposal that the United States would stop bombing when it would lead "promptly" to "productive" discussions. This became known as the San Antonio formula.	Hanoi gave final rejection in mid-October and increased offensive actions in Vietnam.

Date	*Initiative*	*Response*
1967		
September 2	The United States suggested five points as principles of Security Council endorsement: a complete ceasefire and disengagement of forces; withdrawal of all forces and bases not under control of North or South Vietnam; respect for a demarcation line and DMZ between the two; peaceful settlement by the people of North and South Vietnam on the question of reunification without foreign interference; international supervision of these arrangements.	Exploration proved fruitless in the face of categoric Soviet opposition.
September 10	President Nguyen Van Thieu offered a one-week bombing suspension as a goodwill gesture to create a favorable atmosphere for talks.	Pham Van Dong answered: "There will be no reciprocity. There will be no bargaining. There will be no blackmail, and we will not pay ransom to pirates."
September 12	The World Federation of United Nations Associations proposed a five-nation summit of the Prime Ministers of the Soviet Union and Britain (as chairmen of the Geneva Conference) and of the ICC countries of Poland, India, and Canada.	The Liberation Front reiterated that the United Nations was not qualified to discuss the problem, and Kosygin rejected the proposal on October 30.
September 29	President Johnson stated in his speech to the National Legislative Conference in San Antonio: "The United States is willing to stop all aerial and naval bombardment of North Vietnam when this will lead promptly to productive discussions. We, of course, assume that while discussions proceed North Vietnam will not take advantage of the bombing cessation or limitation."	Hanoi rejected the proposal and reiterated its four points.
November 11	President Johnson urged Hanoi to agree to a political settlement of the war in Vietnam and suggested that a peace conference could be held on a neutral ship on a neutral sea.	The offer was rejected by Hanoi.

Date	*Initiative*	*Response*

1967

December 19 — President Johnson in a television interview urged the Liberation Front to open informal talks with the South Vietnamese government for the purpose of finding a peaceful settlement. On December 21 Presidents Thieu and Johnson issued a joint statement in Canberra, Australia, in which Thieu expressed his willingness to "discuss relevant matters with any individuals now associated with the so-called Liberation Front. . . ." — Radio Moscow called the proposals a "smokescreen" for the continuation of the war.

December– January — A Romanian official talked with leaders in Hanoi and then came to Washington. He was asked to return to Hanoi to obtain the reaction to the San Antonio formula. He was in Hanoi in January 1968 but did not return to Bucharest until the Tet offensive had begun. — Hanoi's response was negative.

1968

January 16 — President Johnson said in his State of the Union message that he believed peace talks should be based on the San Antonio formula. — North Vietnam said that the United States had no right to demand reciprocity.

March 31 — President Johnson stopped all bombing over most of North Vietnam and expressed the hope that this would lead to peace talks. — Hanoi agreed to talks but defined their purpose as solely to determine the unconditional cessation of bombing and "all other acts of war" against North Vietnam. Hanoi made no mention of any action on its part to reduce hostilities.

October 31 — President Johnson announced the end of all bombing in North Vietnam. In Paris U.S. representatives repeatedly explained our understanding that the bombing halt could not be sustained if the North Vietnamese violated the DMZ or carried out attacks on South Vietnam's major cities. They also repeated the U.S. intention to continue aerial reconnaissance of the North. — North Vietnam agreed to broaden the peace talks to include the Saigon government and did not reject the "understandings" as set forth by the U.S. representatives.

VII. U.S. Contacts with North Vietnam

(See Chapter 11, page 250)

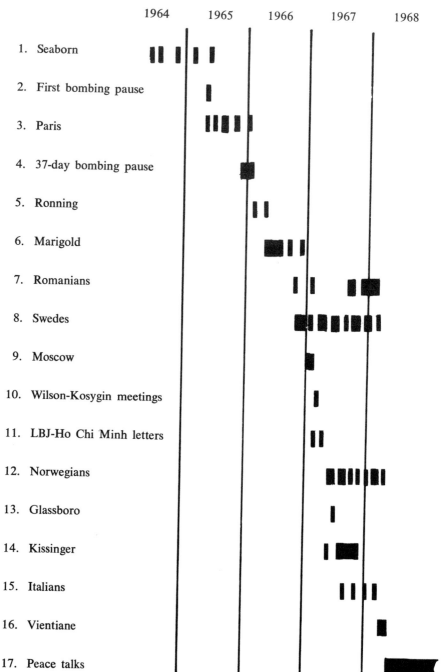

Note: Darkened areas indicate periods of activity.

Peace Channels to North Vietnam (NVN)

1. Canadian ICC delegate—contacts in Hanoi, June 1964–June 1965

2. Five-day pause—contacts in Moscow, May 1965

3. Contacts with NVN delegation in Paris, May 1965–January 1966

4. Contacts with NVN in Moscow and Rangoon, December 1965–January 1966

5. Former Canadian diplomat—contacts in Hanoi, March and June 1966

6. Polish contacts in Saigon, Hanoi, and Warsaw, June 1966–December 1966

7. Romanian initiative—contacts in Hanoi, October 1966–February 1968

8. Swedish contacts in Warsaw and Hanoi, November 1966–February 1968

9. Diplomatic contacts with NVN delegation in Moscow, January 1967

10. Meetings in London, February 1967

11. Delivered to NVN delegation in Moscow, February and April 1967

12. Norwegian contacts in Peking, June 1967–April 1968

13. Johnson-Kosygin meetings, June 23 and 25, 1967

14. Contacts through French intermediaries in Paris, July–October 1967

15. Hanoi initiative—contacts in Rome and Prague, September 1967–March 1968

16. Negotiations on site of peace talks, April–May 1968

17. Peace talks began in Paris, May 1968–

VIII. Letter to Ho Chi Minh

(See Chapter 11, page 252)

February 8, 1967

Dear Mr. President:

I am writing to you in the hope that the conflict in Vietnam can be brought to an end. That conflict has already taken a heavy toll—in the lives lost, in wounds inflicted, in property destroyed, and in simple human misery. If we fail to find a just and peaceful solution, history will judge us harshly.

Therefore, I believe that we both have a heavy obligation to seek earnestly the path to peace. It is in response to that obligation that I am writing directly to you.

We have tried over the past several years, in a variety of ways and through a number of channels, to convey to you and your colleagues our desire to achieve a peaceful settlement. For whatever reasons, these efforts have not achieved any results.

It may be that our thoughts and yours, our attitudes and yours, have been distorted or misinterpreted as they passed through these various channels. Certainly that is always a danger in indirect communication.

There is one good way to overcome this problem and to move forward in the search for a peaceful settlement. That is for us to arrange for direct talks between trusted representatives in a secure setting and away from the glare of publicity. Such talks should not be used as a propaganda exercise but should be a serious effort to find a workable and mutually acceptable solution.

In the past two weeks, I have noted public statements by representatives of your government suggesting that you would be prepared to enter into direct bilateral talks with representatives of the U.S. Government, provided that we ceased "unconditionally" and permanently our bombing operations against your country and all military actions against it. In the last day, serious and responsible parties have assured us indirectly that this is in fact your proposal.

Let me frankly state that I see two great difficulties with this proposal. In view of your public position, such action on our part would inevitably produce worldwide speculation that discussions were under way and would impair the privacy and secrecy of those discussions. Secondly, there would inevitably be grave concern on our part whether your Government would make use of such action by us to improve its military position.

With these problems in mind, I am prepared to move even further towards an ending of hostilities than your Government has proposed in either public statements or through private diplomatic channels. I am prepared to order a cessation of bombing against your country and the stopping of further augmentation of U.S. forces in South Vietnam as soon as I am assured that infiltration into South Vietnam by land and by sea has stopped. These acts of restraint on both sides would, I believe, make it possible for us to conduct serious and private discussions leading toward an early peace.

I make this proposal to you now with a specific sense of urgency arising from the imminent New Year holidays in Vietnam. If you are able to accept this proposal I see no reason why it could not take effect at the end of the New Year, or Tet, holidays. The proposal I have made would be greatly strengthened if your military authorities and those of the Government of South Vietnam could promptly negotiate an extension of the Tet truce.

As to the site of the bilateral discussions I propose, there are several possibilities. We could, for example, have our representatives meet in Moscow where contacts have already occurred. They could meet in some other country such as Burma. You may have other arrangements or sites in mind, and I would try to meet your suggestions.

The important thing is to end a conflict that has brought burdens to both our peoples, and above all to the people of South Vietnam. If you have any thoughts about the actions I propose, it would be most important that I receive them as soon as possible.

Sincerely,
Lyndon B. Johnson

IX. Ho Chi Minh's Reply

(See Chapter 11, page 252)

February 15, 1967

Lyndon B. Johnson
President of the United States

Your Excellency:

On February 10, 1967, I received your message. Here is my reply:

Vietnam is thousands of miles from the United States. The Vietnamese people have never done any harm to the United States, but contrary to the commitments made by its representative at the Geneva Conference of 1954, the United States Government has constantly intervened in Vietnam, has launched and intensified its aggression against South Vietnam for the purpose of prolonging the division of Vietnam and of transforming South Vietnam into an American colony and an American military base. For more than two years now, the American Government, using its military planes and its navy has been waging war against the sovereign and independent Democratic Republic of Vietnam.

The U.S. Government has committed war crimes and crimes against peace and against humanity. In South Vietnam, a half million American soldiers and soldiers from satellite countries have used the most inhuman and barbaric methods of warfare such as napalm, chemicals and toxic gases to massacre our compatriots, destroy their crops and level their villages. In North Vietnam, thousands of American planes have rained down hundreds of thousands of tons of bombs destroying towns, villages, factories, roads, bridges, dikes, dams and even churches, pagodas, hospitals and schools. In your message you seem to deplore the suffering and the destruction in Vietnam. Allow me to ask you: who is perpetrating these awful crimes? It is the American and satellite soldiers. The United States Government is entirely responsible for the critical situation in Vietnam.

American aggression against the Vietnamese people is a challenge to the countries of the Socialist camp, menaces the people's independence movement and gravely endangers peace in Asia and the world.

The Vietnamese people deeply love independence, liberty and peace. But, in the face of American aggression, they stand as one man, unafraid of sacrifices, until they have gained real independence, full liberty and true peace. Our just cause is approved and supported strongly by all the people of the world, including large segments of the American people.

The Government of the United States is aggressing against Vietnam. It must stop this aggression as the only way leading toward the reestablishment of peace. The Government of the United States must stop the bombing, definitively and unconditionally, and all other acts of war against the Democratic Republic of Vietnam, withdraw from South Vietnam all its troops and those of its satellites, recognize the National Liberation Front of South Vietnam and allow the people of Vietnam to settle their problems by themselves. This is the essence of the Four Points of the Government of the Democratic Republic of Vietnam as well as the expression of the principles and essential provisions of the Geneva Accords of 1954 on Vietnam. It is the basis for a just political solution of the Vietnamese problem. In your message, you suggested direct talks between the Democratic Republic of Vietnam and the United States. If the Government of the United States really wants such talks, it must first unconditionally halt the bombing as well as all other acts of war against the Democratic Republic of Vietnam. Only after the unconditional stopping of the bombing and all other American acts of war against the Democratic Republic of Vietnam can the Democratic Republic of Vietnam and the United States enter into conversations and discuss the questions in which both parties are interested.

The Vietnamese people will never yield to force nor agree to talks under the menace of bombs.

Our cause is entirely just. It is our hope that the Government of the United States acts with reason.

Sincerely yours,
Ho Chi Minh

X. Second Letter to Ho Chi Minh

(See Chapter 11, page 256)

April 6, 1967

Dear Mr. President:

I was, of course, disappointed that you did not feel able to respond positively to my letter to you of February 8.

But I would recall to you the words Abraham Lincoln addressed to his fellow Americans in 1861:

> "Suppose you go to war, you cannot fight always; and when, after much loss on both sides, and no gain on either, you cease fighting, the identical old question as to terms of intercourse are again upon you."

In that spirit I wish to reaffirm the offers I made in my earlier letter. We remain prepared to talk quietly with your representatives to establish the terms of a peaceful settlement and then bring the fighting to a stop; or we are prepared to undertake steps of mutual de-escalation which might make it easier for discussions of a peaceful settlement to take place. Talks to either of these ends could take place in Moscow, Rangoon, or elsewhere.

Despite public discussion of our previous exchange of views, our responsibilities to our own peoples and to the world remain; and those responsibilities include bringing the war in Southeast Asia to an end at the earliest possible date.

It is surely clear that one day we must agree to reestablish and make effective the Geneva Accords of 1954 and 1962; let the people of South Vietnam determine in peace the kind of government they want; let the peoples of North and South Vietnam determine peacefully whether and how they should unite; and permit the peoples of Southeast Asia to turn all their energies to their economic and social development.

You and I will be judged in history by whether we worked to bring about this result sooner rather than later.

I venture to address you directly again in the hope that we can find the way to rise above all other considerations and fulfill that common duty. I would be glad to receive your views on these matters.

Sincerely,
Lyndon B. Johnson

XI. Memorandum from the President to the Secretary of the Treasury

(See Chapter 14, page 315)

June 16, 1965

MEMORANDUM TO THE SECRETARY OF THE TREASURY
SUBJECT: *Forward Planning in International Finance*

It has become clear to me that we must develop policies, covering a considerable period in the future, with respect to the development of the international monetary and payments system and the role of the United States in the system. The actions we have taken to bring our payments into balance will, over time, put substantial pressure on reserves abroad and hence on international trade and the growth of the world economy. The Free World will need some way of systematically producing the additional liquidity which has been supplied by the payments deficits of the United States. This will require international agreements among the nations which are the primary sources of liquidity. I recognize that considerable study has been devoted to these issues by the Long-Range International Payments Committee, chaired by the Treasury. However, I believe that it would now be desirable to push forward with more intensive effort, so as to be fully prepared for full-scale negotiations when the time is ripe and right.

In the light of your leading responsibility within the Government for forward planning on international monetary problems, I should like you to organize a small high-level study group to develop and recommend to me—through you, and the other principals directly concerned—a comprehensive U.S. position and negotiating strategy designed to achieve substantial improvement in international monetary arrangements. The Study Group should consist of appropriate senior officials from the Treasury, the State Department, the Council of Economic Advisers, the Board of Governors of the Federal Reserve System, and the White House. I understand that you would have in mind that it would be chaired by the Under Secretary of the Treasury for Monetary Affairs.

Without attempting to lay down rigid terms of reference, the following are some of the questions I have in mind:

1. What are the possible means of reducing the United States' vulnerability to political and economic pressure through the threatened conversion into gold of any overhang of official dollar balances?
2. What are the possible and feasible means of assuring that credit will be available to deficit countries in amounts and on terms—maturity, interest, and automaticity—consistent with the realities of the adjustment process in a world of fixed parities where sharp deflation is not an acceptable alternative?
3. How can we assure that the amount of reserve assets will expand at a rate which will facilitate maintenance of full employment, reasonably stable prices, and expansion of world trade? Any revised or new system

for creating reserves should insure against the instability inherent in a two-reserve-asset or multiple-asset arrangement in which one asset is judged to be absolutely safe in terms of convertibility into the other(s), whereas convertibility the other way is unavoidably judged more uncertain.

The Study Group should explore which of the elements in the various proposed schemes of reform would be acceptable to the United States, which entirely unacceptable, and which might well be appropriate for negotiation.

In considering these questions, I would like the Study Group to take full account of the interrelations between our monetary and economic objectives, and our more general foreign policy objectives. It should explore the entire range of actions open to the United States which would bring to bear our economic strength, and our political strength, to secure reforms which would be desirable in terms of the full range of our objectives. It should take into account a variety of contingencies with regard to the cooperation of other governments and explore what unilateral steps the United States might take to achieve progress. It should spell out alternatives with respect to timing.

In addition to the above general questions, the Study Group should give urgent and thorough consideration to the special situation of the United Kingdom, which is of major foreign policy concern. Specifically, it should consider what steps the United States could take to arrange for a relief of pressure on sterling, so as to give the United Kingdom the four- or five-year breathing space it needs to get its economy into shape, and thereby sharply reduce the danger of sterling devaluation or exchange controls or British military disengagement East of Suez or on the Rhine.

The Study Group should be small and it should work in the strictest secrecy, with knowledge of its existence and access to its work available on a strict need-to-know basis. Its work would not be a substitute for the continuing work, under your chairmanship, of the Cabinet Committee on the Balance of Payments (and the Executive Committee), the National Advisory Council on International and Financial Problems, and the Long-Range International Payments Committee. It is my desire that these committees continue their valuable work.

I believe it would be useful for you also to establish a panel of consultants, consisting of people outside of Government with broad knowledge in this field, who would be available to you for counsel. This consultant group might also be relatively small and include people from the academic, banking, and business communities. It would be appropriate to include people formerly with the Government, such as Douglas Dillon, Robert Roosa, and Kermit Gordon.

I should like to receive a progress report on the work of the Study Group by August 2, 1965, and from time to time as appropriate. In addition, I shall expect periodically to meet with you and the other officials concerned to discuss the problems and prospects.

Lyndon B. Johnson

XII. Declaration of Goals of Freedom

(See Chapter 16, page 362)

Goals of Freedom

We, the seven nations gathered in Manila, declare our unity, our resolve, and our purpose in seeking together the goals of freedom in Viet-Nam and in the Asian and Pacific areas. They are:

1. To be free from aggression.
2. To conquer hunger, illiteracy, and disease.
3. To build a region of security, order, and progress.
4. To seek reconciliation and peace throughout Asia and the Pacific.

Manila, October 25, 1966.

XIII.   Memorandum for the Record

[President Johnson's Reaction to Secretary McNamara's
November 1967 Proposals on Vietnam]

(See Chapter 17, page 377)

The memorandum of Secretary McNamara dated November 1, 1967, attached hereto, raises fundamental questions of policy with reference to the conduct of the war in Vietnam.

I have read it, and studied it, with the utmost care. In addition, I have asked certain advisers to give their written reactions to the memo. These reactions are attached.

I have consulted at length with Ambassador Bunker and General Westmoreland on their recent trip to Washington.

At my suggestion, a group of senior advisers attended a lengthy briefing at the State Department and then met for a full discussion with me.

I have carefully considered the questions presented and the individual views expressed, and I have reached the following conclusions:

With respect to bombing North Vietnam, I would wish for us to

—authorize and strike those remaining targets which, after study, we judge to have significant military content but which would not involve excessive civilian casualties; excessive U.S. losses; or substantial increased risk of engaging the USSR or Communist China in the war;

—maintain on a routine basis a restrike program for major targets through North Vietnam;

—strive to remove the drama and public attention given to our North Vietnamese bombing operations.

I have concluded that, under present circumstances, a unilateral and unrequited bombing stand-down would be read in both Hanoi and the United States as a sign of weakening will. It would encourage the extreme doves; increase the pressure for withdrawal from those who argue "bomb and get out"; decrease support from our most steady friends; and pick up support from only a small group of moderate doves.

I would not, of course, rule out playing our bombing card under circumstances where there is reason for confidence that it would move us toward peace. But with the failure of the Paris track and the opening of Buttercup *—at a time when the North is being bombed—I do not believe we should move from our present policy unless hard evidence suggests such a change would be profitable.

With respect to operations on the ground, I do not believe we should announce a so-called policy of stabilization. An announced change would have, in my judgment, some of the political effects in Hanoi and in the United States of a unilateral bombing stand-down.

On the other hand, at the moment I see no basis for increasing U.S. forces above the current approved level.

As for the movement of U.S. forces across the frontiers of South Vietnam, I am inclined to be extremely reserved unless a powerful case can be made. There

* Another of many unsuccessful efforts to enter into negotiations with Hanoi.

are two reasons: the political risks involved, and the diversion of forces from pressure on the VC and from all the other dimensions of pacification. But I believe it unwise to announce a policy that would deny us these options.

The third recommendation of Secretary McNamara has merit. I agree that we should review the conduct of military operations in South Vietnam with a view to reducing U.S. casualties, accelerating the turnover of responsibility to the GVN, and working toward less destruction and fewer casualties in South Vietnam.

/s/ Lyndon B. Johnson

December 18, 1967
1:40 p.m.

XIV. Letter to Chairman Khrushchev

(See Chapter 20, page 466)

(See Chapter 20, page 466)

January 18, 1964

Dear Mr. Chairman:

I welcome the stated objective of your December 31 letter and agree with much of its contents. It is my hope that we can build on these areas of agreement instead of merely emphasizing our well-known disagreements. This Nation is committed to the peaceful unification of Germany in accordance with the will of the people. This Nation, which has fundamental commitments to the Republic of China, has for many years sought the renunciation of force in the Taiwan Strait. This Nation's forces and bases abroad are for collective defense, and in accordance with treaties and agreements with the countries concerned.

Let us emphasize, instead, our agreement on the importance your letter places on preserving and strengthening peace—and on the need to accompany efforts for disarmament with new efforts to remove the causes of friction and to improve the world's machinery for peacefully settling disputes. In this spirit, let us both present new proposals to the Geneva Disarmament Conference—in pursuit of the objectives we have previously identified:

to prevent the spread of nuclear weapons;

to end the production of fissionable material for weapons;

to transfer large amounts of fissionable materials to peaceful purposes;

to ban all nuclear weapons tests;

to place limitations on nuclear weapons systems;

to reduce the risk of war by accident or design;

to move toward general disarmament.

I am sure you will agree that our task is to work hard and persistently on these and other specific problems and proposals—as you and President Kennedy did on the Test Ban Treaty—instead of confining ourselves to vague declarations of principle that oppose some wars but not all.

Your letter singles out the problem of territorial disputes and concludes that "the use of force for the solution of territorial disputes is not in the interest of any people or any counry." I agree; moreover, the United States proposes guidelines to implement this principle which are even broader and stronger than your own.

First, all governments or regimes shall abstain from the direct or indirect threat or use of force to change

international boundaries;

other territorial or administrative demarcation or dividing lines established or confirmed by international agreement or practice;

the dispositions of truce or military armistice agreements; or arrangements or procedures concerning access to, passage across or the administration of those areas where international agreement or practice has established or confirmed such arrangements or procedures.

Nor shall any government or regime use or threaten force to enlarge the territory under its control or administration by overthrowing or displacing established authorities.

Second, these limitations shall apply regardless of the direct or indirect form which such threat or use of force might take, whether in the form of aggression, subversion, or clandestine supply of arms; regardless of what justification or purpose is advanced; and regardless of any question of recognition, diplomatic relations, or differences of political systems.

Third, the parties to any serious dispute, in adhering to these principles, shall seek a solution by peaceful means—resorting to negotiation, mediation, conciliation, arbitration, judicial settlement, action by a regional or appropriate United Nations agency or other peaceful means of their own choice.

Fourth, these obligations, if they are to continue, would have to be quite generally observed. Any departure would require reappraisal; and the inherent right of self-defense which is recognized in Article 51 of the United Nations Charter would, in any event, remain fully operative.

You will note the basic similarities in our position. Agreement should not be impossible on this or other propositions—and I share your hope that such agreement will stimulate disarmament and peaceful relations.

The prevention of wars over territorial and other disputes requires not only general principles but also the "growth and improvement" to which you refer regarding the machinery and methods for peaceful settlement. The United States believes that the peace-keeping processes of the United Nations—and specifically its Security Council—should be more fully used and strengthened and that the special responsibilities and contributions of the larger countries— particularly the permanent members of the Security Council—deserve greater attention in solving its financial problems.

In consultation with our allies, we shall offer specific proposals along these lines in the weeks ahead. Both the Geneva Disarmament Conference and the United Nations are appropriate places for such discussions.

Mr. Chairman, let me assure you that practical progress toward peace is my most fervent desire. This requires not only agreements in principle but also concrete actions in accord with those principles. I believe this exchange of letters offers real hope for that kind of progress—and that hope is shared by all peace-loving men in every land.

Sincerely,
Lyndon B. Johnson

1. Indochina 1959–1968

In 1959 North Vietnam began infiltrating weapons and men into South Vietnam by land and sea (black arrows). *Most sea infiltration had been blocked by 1966, but supplies to Communist forces continued through Sihanoukville* (dotted arrows). (See Chapters 3, 6, 11)

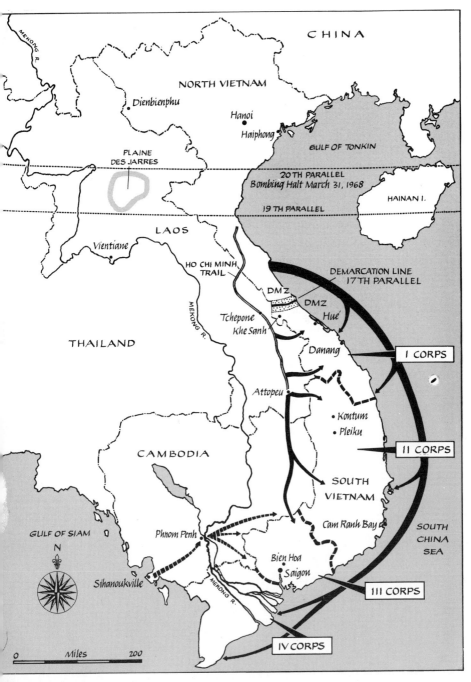

II. Southeast Asia 1965

The Communist pincers—Djakarta-Hanoi-Peking-Pyongyang axis on the move: Hanoi into Laos, Cambodia, and South Vietnam; Djakarta into Malaysia and Borneo; Malaysian Communists and Hanoi-trained guerrillas into Thailand; Peking-trained guerrillas into Thailand and Burma; Pyongyang sends guerrillas into South Korea (black arrows). (See Chapter 6, pp. 134–136)

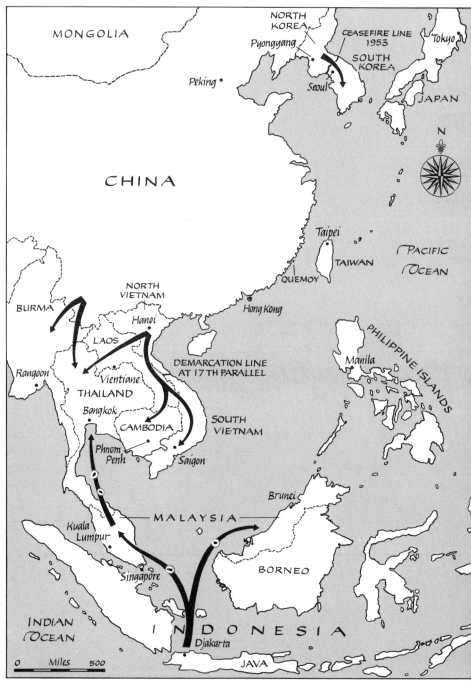

III. The Caribbean 1964–1965

The U.S. faces three crises: Panama breaks relations; Castro shuts off water to Guantanamo; American lives endangered in Dominican uprising. (See Chapter 8)

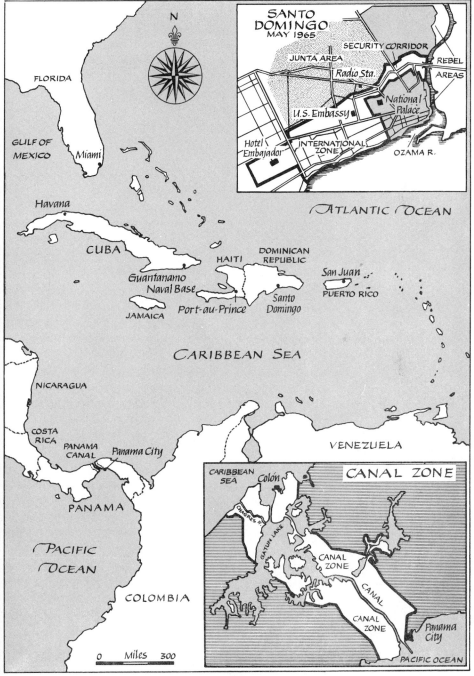

IV. The Middle East 1967

Egypt closes Gulf of Aqaba to Israel. Israel strikes back, driving Egypt out of Sinai (arrows show Israeli offensive). The Six Day War prompts U.S. to redeploy fleet in Mediterranean, resulting in first use of Washington-Moscow "hot line." (See Chapter 13)

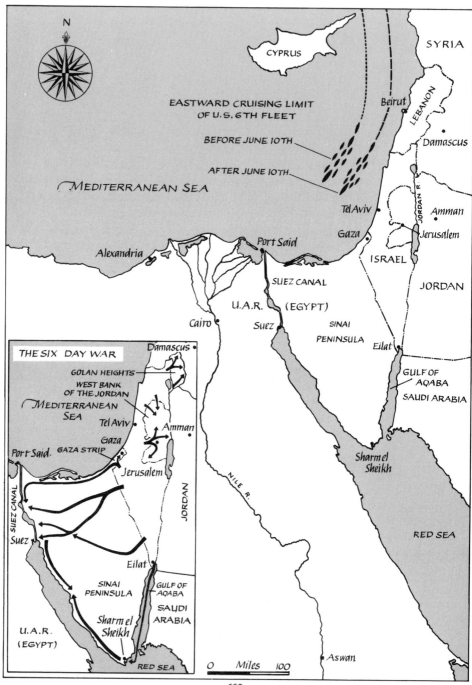

ILLUSTRATIONS

INDEX

ABM (anti-ballistic missile) system, 479-81, 484
Abrams, Gen. Creighton W., 511-13, 515, 541; deputy commander in Vietnam, appointment, 260; Distinguished Service Medal awarded to, 523; and peace talks, 520-23; reports on Vietnam action, 416, 417; and Vietnam bombing halt, 520-21
Acheson, Dean G., 409, 416n., 418, 471
Ackley, Gardner, 342, 440, 444, 453n.
Adams, Sherman, 273
AFL-CIO, 454, 458
Africa, 351-55
  Korry's report on, 354-55
  LBJ in, 351-52
  Organization of African Unity, 353
Agnew, Spiro T., 553, 554, 563
Agra, 222
Aiken, George D., 48, 116n., 313
Air Force One, airplane, 11, 12, 40, 174, 231, 359, 567
Air Force Two, airplane, 2
Alabama: National Guard sent to, 163; violence against civil rights in, 161-63
Albert, Carl B., 40, 81, 116n., 195n., 309n., 316n., 453, 456, 459, 563; and civil rights legislation, 164; and increase of forces in Vietnam, 150; on tax bill, 445
Aldrin, Edwin E., Jr., 284
Alexander, Clifford L., Jr., 179
Alexander, Lucia, sister of LBJ, 1
Alliance for Progress, 22, 204, 348-51
Alsop, Joseph W., 26, 30
American Alumni Council, LBJ's speech to, 358-59
American Bankers Association, 458
American Bar Association, LBJ's speech to, 68n.; excerpts, 575
American Farm Bureau Federation, 458
American Medical Association, Medicare opposed, 215, 217-18
Anders, William A., 284
Anderson, Clinton P., 436, 214-15
Anderson, Robert B., 31, 184, 294
ANF (Atlantic Nuclear Force), 477
Antell, James B., 264n.
Anti-ballistic missile (ABM) system, 479-81, 484
Antiquities Act, 562, 563
ANZUS Treaty, 353
Apollo spacecraft, 284, 285; astronauts killed, 270-71, 284, 551
Appalachia, 79, 102
Aqaba, Gulf of, 288-89, 293, 297, 484; closed to Israeli shipping, 291, 292; reopened, 300; reopening planned, 294-96, 298, 303
Arab-Israeli war, *see* Israeli-Arab war
Arends, Leslie C., 116n., 150, 195n., 309n., 526
Argentina, 296
Armstrong, Neil A., 284
Army: in Panama crisis, 181; in riots, Detroit, 163-64, 168-72; in Vietnam, *see* Vietnam, U.S. forces in

Arosemena Gómez, Otto, 351
Ashmore, Harry S., 498, 585
Asia, 355-64
  LBJ's policy summarized, 249
  regional groups, 358
  Southeast: Communist strategy in, 134-36, 151-52; map, 606; U.S. policy in, 357-58
Asian and Pacific Council (ASPAC), 358
Asian Development Bank, 356-57
Asian Institute of Technology, 358
Asian Labor Education Center, 358
Asian Parliamentarians Union, 358
Associated Press luncheon, LBJ's speech to, 466-67
Association of Southeast Asian Nations (ASEAN), 358
Astronauts, 270-71, 280, 283-85, 569
  see also Space exploration
Atlantic City, N.J., Democratic Convention, 101
Atlantic Nuclear Force (ANF), 477
Atomic weapons, *see* Nuclear weapons
Aubrac, Raymond, 266, 587
Austin, Tex., 4, 7, 110; LBJ's speech in, 1957, 274
Australia, 312n., 353, 358n., 359
  forces in Vietnam, 142, 246
  gunboats in engagement near Singapore, 135
  in Israeli-Arab war, assistance offered, 295, 296
  LBJ visits, 360-61, 378-79, 429
  wheat sent to India, 229, 230
Austria, 312n.
Ayub Khan, Mohammed, 339-40, 379, 579

Baber, George W., Bishop, 175
Baggs, William C., 498, 585
Bailey, Joseph W., 110
Bailey, John M., 107n.
Balaguer, Joaquin, 190, 203
Ball, George W., 43, 148, 409, 416n., 418; in Dominican crisis, 195, 199; at National Security Council meetings, 124, 128, 129, 148n.; in Panama crisis, 181n., 182; and Southeast Asia Resolution, 118; and Tonkin Gulf attack, 113, 114; as UN Ambassador, 504; and Vietnam air strikes, 124; and Vietnam bombing pause, 235; Vietnam policy suggestions, 147
Bangkok, 54, 358
Bankhead, Tallulah, 436
Bao Dai, 50
Barr, Joseph W., 264n., 265, 316n., 447, 550-51
Bator, Francis M., 309n., 312n., 313
Bay of Pigs, 26, 280
Beebe, Leo C., 334
Beirne, Joseph A., 30
Belgium, 296, 312n., 317n., 354
Belgrade conference, Vietnam peace proposal, 133
Bell, David E., 128n., 243n., 279

617

ARCTIC OCEAN

U. S. S. R.

CHINA

Seoul

JAPAN

S. KOREA

Bonn

Rome

TURKEY

IRAN

ALGERIA

EGYPT

SAUDI
ARABIA

Karachi
PAKISTAN

INDIA

U. Tapao

Manila
PHILIPPINE
IS.

Guam

SUDAN

Bangkok
Korat

Cam Ranh
Bay

CONGO

Kuala Lumpur

ATLANTIC
OCEAN

Darwin

Townsvil

SOUTH AFRICA

INDIAN OCEAN

AUSTRALIA

Bris.
Sy
Canber

Melbourne

1. February 1966 – Honolulu, Los Angeles
2. July 1966 – Mexico City
3. October – November 1966 – Far East
4. March 1967 – Guam
5. April 1967 – South America
6. April 1967 – Germany, Adenauer's Funeral